D1217540

PSYCHOLOGY
of CRIME
and
CRIMINAL
JUSTICE

Editor

HANS TOCH
State University of New York at Albany

PSYCHOLOGY of CRIME and CRIMINAL JUSTICE

HOLT, RINEHART AND WINSTON
New York   Chicago   San Francisco   Dallas
Montreal   Toronto   London   Sydney

Contributors

Albert Bandura
John Berberich
Albert Ellis
Gilbert Geis
Charles Hanley
Michael J. Hinderlang
Maxwell Jones
David Lester
Robert F. Meier
Albert I. Rabin
Fritz Redl
Ezra Stotland
Thomas S. Szasz
Hans Toch
Marguerite Q. Warren
William W. Wattenberg
Charles Winick

Material from *Theories of Punishment* edited by Stanley E. Grupp, reprinted by permission of Indiana University Press, copyright 1971.

Material from *The Society of Captives: A Study of a Maximum Security Prison* by Gresham M. Sykes, reprinted with permission from Princeton University Press, copyright 1958.

Excerpts from *Police Chief*, "Recruitment and Retention" by D. Von Blaricom, used with permission from International Association of Chiefs of Police, copyright 1976.

Excerpts from *The Jukes* by R. Dugdale, used with permission by G. P. Putnam's Sons, copyright 1910.

Portions from "Psychiatric Diversion in the Criminal Justice System: A Critique" by T. Szasz, reprinted with permission from *Assessing the Criminal: Restitution, Retribution and the Legal Process*, edited by R. Barnett and J. Hagel, published by Balinger Publishing Company, copyright 1978.

Material from *Wayward Youth* by August Aichorn, copyright 1935, renewed © 1963 by The Viking Press, Inc. Reprinted by permission of The Viking Press and Hogarth Press.

Some portions of this book appeared in a different form in *Legal and Criminal Psychology*, Hans Toch, editor, copyright © 1961 by Holt, Rinehart and Winston, Inc.

Library of Congress Cataloging in Publication Data
Main entry under title:

Psychology of crime and criminal justice.

Bibliographies
Includes index.
1. Criminal psychology—Addresses, essays, lectures. 2. Criminal justice, Administration of—Psychological aspects—Addresses, essays, lectures. I. Toch, Hans.
HV6080.P83   364.3   78-15968
ISBN 0-03-019806-2

PREFACE

Two decades ago, a group of us wrote the first version of this book. Our effort was initially met with what Geis calls "a wave of national indifference." But the book has lived on with remarkable obduracy. Why this strange trend? We know that our interests, at their inception, were not shared by many of our colleagues. Few psychology departments offered courses in criminology or, for that matter, in other "social problems" areas. Advanced criminal justice programs were few and far between. Much later, student pressure for social relevance was responded to with "applied" offerings, and criminal justice programs were upgraded. By then, our book had become faded and dated. Joshua Fishman anticipated this danger when he remarked, in an otherwise flattering comment, that "fortunately or unfortunately, criminology and clinical psychology are so rapidly becoming highly specialized, technical and rigorous professional fields that it is doubtful that introductory reviews on allied topics can long continue to be of value in them."

Another fact of academic life twenty years ago was that of disciplinary parochialism. There was talk then, as there is now, about the desirability of taking interdisciplinary views, of the need to integrate a variety of qualitatively different perspectives to obtain meaningful portraits of reality. Such talk, however, was usually an expression of generic good will and was not matched in avid, or even sympathetic reading of materials produced in one branch of social science among denizens of another.

We tried to facilitate interdisciplinary fertilization in our first venture by indicating that the word "psychology" in the title of our book was not intended to refer, as one might reasonably suppose, to the domain of the professional psychologist. Instead, we wrote, the word was used literally, in its original sense, as "understanding of the human mind." This broad usage, we said, would not exclude academic psychology, but neither would it exclude any academic discipline which could help us to an understanding of people. It also would not rule out practical experience, nor a concern with social problems that impinge on the offender, on his victim, and on the criminal justice system.

In summing up, we characterized the role of academic psychology in our enterprise using the words of Sholom Aleichem, taken from the chatty preamble to his short essay "The Three Widows":

Do you know what psychology is? There is a vegetable called parsley . . . To
look at it's not bad, it smells nice, tastes good when you flavor food with it. But
you try chewing parsley by itself! You don't want to? Then why do you stick
psychology down my throat?

We pointed out that our book carried no such intention. The same point
still holds, but our current view has less of a "no-holds-barred" character.
Twenty years ago, we felt that we might be implicitly shaping a field, a
discipline that had not really been staked out since the publication of Munsterberg's *On the Witness Stand* (1907). But it is probably a fact that fields of
learning cannot be "officially" defined. A discipline is the product of experts
who study similar things and communicate them to each other, and this sort
of product changes (sometimes rapidly) over time.

In our first book, we made an "attempt to challenge thinking and provoke
argument," as we put it. But most "hot issues" or "live issues" are apt to cool
or die, or at least to change complexion, over time. Sometimes the resolution
of controversial issues is heartening, as was the case with the incipient community treatment trends we discussed in 1961, which have become salient
features of today's criminal justice landscape. In other cases, regressive change
has taken some of the excitement out of past ideas and has doused innovative
concepts with the icy waters of disillusionment. Such is the case, for instance,
with the rehabilitation and treatment experiments of two decades ago, and
with the then-spreading "insights" into the etiology of crime.

Our first book was written by a cosmopolitan group, which included
lawyers, correctional experts, and penological practitioners. This choice of
authors was dictated by one of our other aims, which involved the conveying
of some of the realities of the criminal justice enterprise. Though this goal
was a worthy one, we have abandoned it for two reasons: we find that a
literature has arisen in the criminal justice field which describes the criminal
justice system and its operation in some detail. We also know that student
involvement in the "real world," such as through internships and community
activities, has substituted real-life experience for the indirect exposure we
could provide. Though we continue to aim at conveying the "flavor" of institutional practices, our coverage in general will be more conventionally didactic.

I am not suggesting that our authors are a parochial academic group.
Among us are psychiatrists, sociologists, and psychologists of almost every
description. What is probably more important, we have not one author in this
book who has not evolved, perfected, or tested his views in the "real world"
of social action. Among us are persons who have run pioneer institutions for
serious offenders, trained police officers, worked in halfway houses, engaged
in therapy, revolutionized hospital care, originated new treatment enterprises,
and redesigned statewide programs. We have functioned in prisons, retraining
centers, skid rows, family therapy settings, courtrooms, psychiatric hospitals,
drug rehabilitation programs, crisis intervention switchboards, and inner city
schools. We have spent time with offenders and their families, with crime
victims, with prison guards, and with probation officers. The knowledge we

shall attempt to convey is therefore not only shaped by thinking and research, but by extensive and intensive experiences in criminal justice (and related) settings.

This book, like its predecessor, is not primarily a source of facts, but of ideas. Some members of our group (Bandura, Ellis, Jones, Redl, Szasz) are well known as scientific revolutionaries, as men whose contributions have become institutionalized, and who continue to spark new and seminal movements in the field. Others in our group are known for key innovations in such diverse areas as the "psychology of hope," "collective child rearing," and "interpersonal maturity," or as landmark expositors of knowledge whose shaping of criminological categories (alcoholism, drug addiction, white collar crime, juvenile delinquency, violence, crime statistics) is the accepted standard. This book is designed not only to review what has been done, but to inspire us to think in new and different ways about what could, should, or will be done in the future.

Our first book was called *Legal and Criminal Psychology*. We have abandoned this title, not only because it lent itself to unfunny jokes about psychological "Watergates," but because it was too narrow for our revised concerns. We are less interested now than we were twenty years ago with the interface between law and psychology. We are more intent on viewing any and all settings that impact on offenders both in the criminal justice system and in the community. This view is compatible with our interest in seeing the widest range of human services deployed in the treatment of offenders. Parenthetically, we are concerned with the "matching" of resources and clients, and we take pains to present meaningful (and treatment relevant) offender groupings as we review the panorama of crime that we cover.

The word "treatment" in this book is used generously, and we shall attend to the various legal, ethical, and "effectiveness" issues that have been raised by critics of rehabilitation. As a group, we are clearly not ready to throw out the correctional baby (humane and appropriate intervention) with its bath water. We are neither persuaded nor intimidated by the wide support that is currently enjoyed by critics of therapy, who call for sterile storage or systematic nonintervention, on the grounds that we have all tried and failed. Our view is that we have not yet begun to try and that the prevalent cynicism is at best premature. We here assume that "nontreatment" is a fiction, and that it can be a dangerous and destructive fiction. Human warehouses are "treatment" in the sense that they have impact, which as a rule happens to be "antitherapeutic" or personally destructive. In the same sense, a therapy session can be "nontreatment" if the ostensible client takes it nonseriously. The psychological perspective of this book forces us to attend to the impact we have on people and invites us to reappraise what we do to ensure that we reduce suffering and promote personal growth. Where we act on such reappraisals, we "treat" people, whether we recognize it or not. It is in this sense that we shall discuss "treatment" of various kinds of offenders in this book.

We aim this book not only at the expert, but also at the student who wishes to be introduced to its subject. Consequently, we spare no effort to keep the writing as simple, uncluttered, and free of technical language as is humanly possible. We shall be very pleased if both experts and novices learn from this book, but we shall be delighted beyond measure if some persons enjoy reading the book while they learn from it.

H.T.

About the Contributors

ALBERT BANDURA   is David Starr Jordan Professor of Social Science in Psychology, Stanford University, past president of the American Psychological Association, and recipient of scientific awards. He has written books on aggression, social learning, and behavior modification, among other subjects.

JOHN BERBERICH   is Department Psychologist of the Seattle Police Department and Clinical Associate Professor of Psychology at the University of Washington in Seattle.

ALBERT ELLIS   is Executive Director of the Institute for Advanced Study in Rational Psychotherapy and Visiting Professor of Clinical Psychology at Rutgers University. His many books include expositions of a major new approach to counseling and therapy, and pioneer studies of sex behavior, for which he has received national awards.

GILBERT GEIS   is Professor in the Program of Social Ecology at the University of California, Irvine, and past president of the American Society of Criminology. His writings include a popular textbook in criminology and the standard reference work on white collar crime.

CHARLES HANLEY   is Professor of Psychology at Michigan State University and a recognized authority in psychometrics, psychological testing, and child development.

MICHAEL J. HINDELANG   is Professor of Criminal Justice at the State University of New York, Albany. He is an expert on criminal justice statistics and juvenile delinquency, editor of the yearly *Sourcebook of Criminal Justice Statistics*, and author of other books.

MAXWELL JONES   is a psychiatrist best known for pioneering the "therapeutic community" and for prolific writings in social psychiatry. He is the recipient of many honors, including the Issac Ray Award of the American Psychiatric Association.

DAVID LESTER   heads the Psychology Program and the Criminal Justice Program at Stockton State College. He has written books about research, suicide, murder, crisis intervention, and comparative psychology.

ROBERT F. MEIER   teaches in the Department of Sociology at Washington State University in Pullman. He is an authority on drug abuse and has written and edited books about criminology and white collar crime.

ALBERT I. RABIN   is Professor of Psychology at Michigan State University, and consultant to the Veterans Administration and the Michigan Department of Corrections. Among his half dozen books are texts on projective testing and studies of child rearing.

FRITZ REDL   is an internationally famous psychoanalyst known for landmark applications of psychoanalysis to education and delinquency. He is past president of the American Orthopsychiatric Association, and recipient of many honors and awards.

EZRA STOTLAND   is Director of the Society and Justice Program and Professor of Psychology at the University of Washington. He is past president of the Society for the Psychological Study of Social Issues and the author of classic contributions to social psychology.

THOMAS S. SZASZ   is Professor of Psychiatry at the Upstate Medical Center of the State University of New York in Syracuse. He is author of sixteen books about problems of "mental illness," psychiatry, and the law. Among his many awards are the Ralph Kharas Award, the Holmes-Munsterberg Award, the Wisdom Award of Honor, and the Martin Buber Award.

HANS TOCH   is Professor of Psychology, School of Criminal Justice, State University of New York, Albany. He has written about violence, social change, prisons, and the police. One of his books received the Hadley Cantril Memorial Award.

MARGUERITE Q. WARREN   is Professor at the School of Criminal Justice, State University of New York, Albany. She is co-originator of a major diagnostic scheme (the I-Level typology), and has written extensively about classification and treatment of delinquent youths.

WILLIAM W. WATTENBERG   is Professor of Educational and Clinical Psychology at Wayne State University. He is an authority on adolescence and delinquency, and the author of several textbooks.

CHARLES WINICK   is head of the graduate program in criminology and Professor of Sociology at the City University of New York. His books deal with psychoanalysis, crime and criminal justice, and topics in social psychology. He has directed alcohol and drug abuse programs, and appeared as an expert witness on jury selection cases.

CONTENTS

PART ONE

Psychology and the Criminal Justice System

chapter 1

Psychology and Criminal Justice

Hans Toch

The psychological view of social institutions centers on what we might call their "human equation." This means that we are concerned with how people are affected by their settings and how they react to them. Such concern is both short-term and long-term. We may be engrossed in observing how a child does in nursery school, but we also worry about how its early experience carries over into adult personality and behavior.

In viewing people in institutional settings, such as in settings of the criminal justice system, we may be interested in what we might learn from how they behave about human behavior generally, or we may try to use our skill and knowledge to improve a given setting, to make it more humane, responsive, rational, or effective. The first of these interests is "scientific," while the second is "applied," or "professional." The distinction between the two orientations is not water tight, however. Sigmund Freud was a professional therapist who ameliorated the suffering of a great many afflicted persons, from Viennese children and housewives to Russian aristocrats. In the process, Freud combined incisive "clinical" observations and astute inferences into a new portrait of human personality which stands as the single most important scientific contribution to modern psychology.

It also is possible to make use of science to promote constructive change. Kurt Lewin, one of the giants of social psychology, coined the phrase "action research" (1946) to describe the change-relevant uses of science. Lewin saw future scientists working shoulder-to-shoulder with administrators and other change agents, helping them to gauge and understand the impact of progres-

sive reforms. Good research, said Lewin, should occur as part of social programs, and should "show us whether we move in the right direction and with
what speed we move" (p. 206). Lewin envisioned "the training of large
numbers of social scientists who can handle scientific problems but are also
equipped for the delicate task of building productive, hard-hitting teams with
practitioners" (p. 211).

The teaming of scientists and practitioners Kurt Lewin describes can take
many forms, which can include teaming scientists with low-ranking staff in
organizations, or with clients. One can work with police patrolmen, for
example, in teams that explore ways to reduce police-citizen conflict (Toch,
Grant, & Galvin, 1975); one can work with prison inmates to try to understand problems of violence in prisons (Toch, 1969). Unlike "pure" science,
such activity requires the closest possible contact and familiarity with the
settings in which we work. Applied science also often poses serious value
questions. We may have to decide, for example, whether to help administrators whose goals we may question, as opposed to waiting for them to get
into trouble. Frequently, if we do not help, organizational clients may needlessly suffer, but if we do help, long-term reforms may be delayed.

In the next chapters we shall examine some settings of the criminal justice system as they appear, viewed from a psychological perspective. The portraits we shall trace will give us an opportunity to see what researchers have
done as well as what they can and should do to help the staff and clients
of these settings. We must first consider, however, the legal framework in
which criminal justice institutions operate. The law itself is a problem for
psychology; we cannot view the law as "given" and go on to consider more
interesting questions. Whatever else criminal justice agents are, they are
appliers of laws. In this chapter, we shall explore what this fact means.

THE LEGAL FRAMEWORK OF CRIMINAL JUSTICE

Laws are not the embodiments of "objective" human needs, but are reflections of expressed human concerns. Some of the concerns embodied in law
are shared by people in virtually all parts of the world (Newman, 1976).
The same strong reservation about murderers and rapists, for instance, is
voiced by "men in the street" in Karachi, Belgrade, London, and Detroit. In
other respects, our legal systems may vary their emphases from country to
country. The Soviet Union, for instance, takes commercial fraud more seriously than we do, and may execute small-time profiteers. European countries
currently assign high priority to politically motivated violence, while our
legislators worry about youthful muggers and their depredations. People
sometimes back laws which reflect very temporary concerns, as they do when
feelings run high because of a crisis that unsettles them or an episode that
shocks them.

Antisubversion legislation and witch-hunting laws are examples of crisis legislation. An example of legislation inspired by a shocking incident is the "sexual psychopathic law" typified by Michigan's Goodrich Act. The Goodrich Act was passed in reaction to a particularly gruesome and repelling sex crime involving a child. It extended, however, to a variety of sexual offenses and created inequities and enforcement problems (Hartwell, 1950). This was noted by the sociologist Sutherland who studied sexual psychopathic laws in twenty-nine states where they were passed, and made several interesting discoveries. For one, he saw that sex crime statistics had no bearing on the passage of these laws. The "crime waves" that ostensibly inspired legislation were partly the creation of tabloids, which resuscitated old crimes to fuel current concerns. The fear that was thus fanned was, moreover, usually short-lived. By the time most laws were passed, they were the work of lingering committees chiefly backed by special interest groups, such as psychiatrists (Sutherland, 1950).

Even when laws are not a product of hysteria, they reflect problems which concern people at the time the law is passed. One type of problem which the criminal law may reflect has been discussed very often, almost to the exclusion of all other influences. This is the area of economics, or of social and economic relationships. In ancient Rome, land was a very important commodity because it represented wealth and power. The Romans, therefore, took an extremely dim view of offenses involving land. A person who dug up a boundary stone and transplanted it to a more favorable location could expect to be buried up to his neck and to have his head shaved off with a new plow (Duncan, 1940, p. 77). In England, especially in the days of the Industrial Revolution, property became a dominant concern, and the law dealt severely with offenses against property—however slight by modern standards. Starving children were hanged for stealing a loaf of bread or some exchangeable trifle in an attempt to survive. The law also dealt sternly with workers trying to change jobs and created a crime (vagrancy) which covered an unemployed person in transit. Later, vagrancy and loitering laws were used mainly against prostitutes, but the courts (as of 1971) have been invalidating these laws because the ostensible offense is very vaguely defined.

An interesting example of a law influenced by socioeconomic relationships is a nineteenth-century San Francisco fire prevention ordinance making it illegal to maintain a laundry in a wooden building without a permit. This ordinance was passed at a time of job competition between Chinese immigrants and native labor, and the Supreme Court, in the case of *Yick Wo* v. *Hopkins* (1886), found that economic discrimination was the object of law, since two hundred Chinese applicants had been unable to obtain permission to operate laundries, whereas seventy-nine out of eighty non-Chinese applications for permits had been granted.

Less dramatic but nonetheless convincing statistics have been used to raise the presumption of officially blessed discrimination in more recent years. The best known deployment of this argument occurred with gerrymandered pupil allocation to "neighborhood" schools (*Brown* v. *Board of Education*, 1954); the point was also made relative to statutes governing juror selection (*Jones*

v. *Georgia*, 1967), the assignment of tenants to public housing (*Gautreaux* v. *Chicago Housing Authority*, 1969), and use of the death penalty (*Maxwell* v. *Bishop*, 1968). In each case, the law had been phrased in ostensibly neutral terms, but in its application it systematically favored some "targets" at the expense of others.

The fact that many offenses punished by law (such as robbery and burglary) are practiced almost exclusively by poorer persons has been translated into the premise that laws are primarily (or exclusively) aimed at transgressions of the poor. This point is made forcefully by Marxist sociologists (e.g., Quinney, 1974), but it is an argument that preceded both Marx and sociology. Its most dramatic statement is probably Anatole France's comment about the majestic equity with which law punishes poor and rich who sleep under bridges. William Shakespeare noted in *King Lear*, that

"Robes and furred gowns hide all. Plate sin with gold,
And the strong lance of justice hurtless breaks;
Arm it in rags, a pigmy's straw does pierce it."
[IV, 6.]

The point about law and economics is appealing, but may not be as valid today as it was in Shakespeare's day or during the Industrial Revolution. For one, we now tend to take violence, which is of concern to everyone and victimizes mostly the poor, more seriously than we do property offenses, whose targets may be wealthy. But even this fact is of limited import; while the property offender, on the average, is poor, so is his average victim. And while a wealthy victim of a property offense may lose more money, the poor victim's loss is more apt to break him financially.

None of this proves, of course, that the law is "unbiased." While laws are no longer passed to supply cheap labor to merchant princes, and while we take pains to see that enforcement is not aimed at unrepresentative targets such as Chinese laundryworkers, there is a great deal of hidden flexibility behind the ostensible equity of the criminal law. For example, we know that political power has recently brought men immunity from prosecution for acts that were flagrantly illegal. And we shall see in Chapter 18 that economic power today can still "plate sin with gold."

Agencies such as the police (Chapter 2), with limited manpower, must enforce the law selectively. This means that a wealthy youthful offender may be left in the community when his parents promise to get help for him. It also means that a burglar is more likely to get arrested than a dishonest businessman (who accumulates more "loot" at less risk). This pattern is only broken where police agencies are "service"-oriented (Chapter 2), or where prosecutors respond to consumer issues. Money, moreover, can buy lawyers who can invest more time and energy—and frequently, more expertise—than the average indigent's counsel (Chapter 3). Wealth also can supply bail, and a defendant who is out on bail is less likely to be convicted (Rankin, 1964).

We shall see later that the law *in application* is less formal than the law *as written*. Though this fact need not work to the detriment of poorer offenders, the "play" in the system and the room it provides for manipulation is of more benefit to the person who has resources, and who can exercise disproportionate rights to appeal, buy more time, and argue for more favorable interpretation of applicable statutes.

Equity, moreover, is a different concept in law and in practice. In practice, the concept gets murky. Crimes are differently distributed in the population. Unbiased legislators must discourage such crimes, and police and prosecutors who enforce the law to the letter must center their dispassionate efforts on high crime concentrations in the slums and among minority group youth (Hindelang, 1978). The poor not only sleep in larger numbers under bridges, but also disproportionately kill and rape and steal. The brunt of crime fighting of necessity is experienced by the disadvantaged; by the same token, positive "prevention" programs may disproportionately benefit impoverished inhabitants of inner cities.

MORALITY, IMPULSIVITY, AND LAW

Whereas only a part of the criminal law reflects economic interests, most criminal law embodies moral and ethical norms, and early laws were very explicit in applying moral or absolute standards. Under the reign of Edward III, for instance, there was a strongly worded law against wearing a mustache without a beard (Duncan, 1940). American colonies in the seventeenth century passed "blue laws," which at the time were known as "Lord's Day Statutes." Such laws were aimed at persons who were not suitably ethereal and penitent on Sundays, who did not take religious worship seriously, who spent Sundays going about secular affairs, or who visibly amused themselves. These sorts of people were deemed objectionable because they could weaken the resolves of their more dutiful fellow-citizens. "Profaning the Sabbath" included engaging in routine work, and this provision is inherited by more recent blue laws.

Though parts of the puritan law have survived to this day, the motives or purposes behind the law are now presumably very different. The official aim of modern blue laws, as it has been endorsed by the courts, is to promote public health, welfare, and recreation, and "to provide a uniform day of rest for all citizens" (*McGowan* v. *Maryland*, 1960). The Supreme Court has admitted (with an implied chuckle) that "the statutes still (sometimes) contain references to the Lord's Day and [that] some provisions speak of weekdays as secular days," but the court reasonably concluded "that the objectionable language is merely a relic" (*Gallagher* v. *Crown Kosher Super Market*, 1961).

What the Supreme Court did not note is that, while blue laws may not now be religiously motivated, their *real* purpose has nothing to do with their ostensible aim. Blue laws are generally sponsored by businesses that traditionally close on Sundays, and are aimed at competing stores that remain open. While the avowed concern of the law is the health or welfare of Sunday-workers, its real aim is to keep workers off the job, and (more importantly) to prevent widespread Sunday shopping.

Justice Voelker of the Michigan Supreme Court, in a hilarious dissent to a blue law decision affecting furniture and appliance dealers in Flint, Michigan (*People's Appliance, Inc.* v. *Flint*, 1959), wrote:

> For a court to indulge any lofty assumptions that this ordinance, affecting as it does but a handful of local merchants, bears any remote relation to or was motivated by the slightest concern for individual or public health or morality (while at the same time those swarming eerily-lit human anthills, the huge automobile factories of Flint, continue their relentless night-and-day-seven-days-a-week grind and jolt) is to wrap a rhetorical flag of idealism around a mere cabbage. If we must indulge any assumptions on this score then I venture to uncloak one or two of my own. It is that the sole motivation for this towering example of primitive legislative art, obvious to a moderately sharp newsboy, was not health, not morality, not public welfare, but *money*, the good old American lust for the "fast buck," and that the only people who were ever really interested in this ordinance or its passage were none other than the smarting and envious (and evidently politically influential) business competitors of the victims themselves. So much for lofty assumptions (Michigan Reports, 1959, pp. 54–55).

Blue laws, Voelker tells us, are aimed at curtailing commercial competition. The same laws are also, however, impulse-controlling instruments. As such, they have more in common with the Puritan law (and with other criminal laws) than we at first suspect. The targets of blue laws are men who conduct business seven days a week, and the intended beneficiaries are merchants who close on Sundays. We can assume that spontaneous Sunday-closing represents the restraining of avarice, the self-denying of profit-seeking for "higher" ends, such as charcoaling chickens, playing with children, and mowing lawns. Such governing of profit-seeking impulses is relatively easy, *provided* one's competition restrains its impulses too. If a competitor is self-indulging, however, and shamelessly rakes in the shekels, our barbecuing or lawn mowing may take on a nervous cast, because the rewards we deny ourselves are being enjoyed by others.

The Puritans in 1650 frowned on men who tempted "the Godly welafected among us" by "sin, proudly, presumptuously and with a high hand committed." The blue laws made life easier for the self-controlled person by reducing the payoff obtained by the self-indulgent. Master Godley could feel more at peace listening to three-hour fire-and-brimstone sermons, knowing that no one was getting away with secular fun-and-games. Mr. Jones of Jones Department Store could similarly relax, knowing that a phone call to the prosecutor might curb the lucrative orgies at Smith's Bargain Emporium.

Such aims and benefits are built into the criminal law across the board. We shall see later that people generally harbor primitive urges, which are usually governed and held in check—sometimes more precariously than others—by our more "civilized" selves. The process, as we might suspect, is not foolproof. It is punctuated by minor explosions, unscheduled thoughts, and other cues to untamed feelings and urges. No matter how law-abiding most of us may feel, we all know ourselves to be *potential* offenders, because we harbor urges that—if they were left free reign—could lead us to harm people we seriously resent, to steal commodities we strongly covet, and to unceremoniously solicit persons we find desirable as sex partners. The punishment of offenders who assault, steal, and rape reassures us of the righteousness of our path, and tells us that self-controlling efforts (which are sometimes uncomfortable) are well expended.

Psychoanalysts have speculated that feelings of punitiveness (the urge to punish) may express a hidden desire in the lawmaker to engage in the very practices he proscribes (Weihofen, 1956). In Gilbert and Sullivan's *Trial by Jury*, the members of the jury express this type of feeling when they declare:

"Oh, I was like that when a lad!
A shocking young scamp of a rover.
I behaved like a regular cad;
But that sort of thing is all over.
I am now a respectable chap
And shine with a virtue resplendent,
And therefore I haven't a rap
Of sympathy for the defendant!"

The extreme manifestation of vengefulness is the death penalty, which is currently enjoying increasing support.[1] The death penalty, however, also gives the public a sense that "something is done" about alarming statistics showing that violent crime is running out of control, which can imply that more civilized "controls" are ineffective.

INTERPRETATIONS OF LAW

Feelings shift, whereas laws frequently remain undisturbed. As each wave of public or private pressure washes by, it leaves its deposit of unrealistic or unenforceable laws. Thus many states have laws against gambling, covering church bingo games, bridge parties, and social poker playing. These types of laws tend to be ignored, or are only occasionally invoked for special purposes.

Another way of coping with laws which do not meet contemporary psychological needs is to pretend to act in accord with them while one is actually "getting around" them. These are the types of arrangements lawyers call "legal fictions." They permit the law to be changed but in a slow and indirect fashion. A story which has been cited as a prototype of this process is that of Tom Sawyer digging a hole with a pickax but pretending to use a pocket knife—which "was the right course in such cases" (Pound, cit. Garrison & Hurst, 1956, p. 410). By being "legalistic" one can thus achieve a desired result but keep the old forms intact.

A third way of adjusting the law to human needs is to determine the most sensible outcome for a given case and then to pick the law or precedent that prescribes this outcome. This does not mean that all laws apply equally to any given body of facts. It does mean that there usually is a choice of laws or previous cases which can be plausibly invoked. The United States Supreme Court "selects" out of several competing constitutional provisions the one that will produce a desired outcome, in that

> the Supreme Court knows that if it pushes the "deprivation of property without due process of law" button, the answer will come out—unconstitutional. If it pushes the "state police power" button, the answer will come out—constitutional. But the machine of the law does not tell the Court which button to push (Rodell, 1939, p. 159).

A decision may thus be reached on the basis of consideration of what is "just," and a legal justification may be selected for it later. In this connection, one relationship the psychologist can look for is between the law as a *tool*, and the *purposes* for which the law is used by the agents who apply it. The same law should serve different ends for different users. This process is demonstrated by the fact that flagrantly out-of-date laws have been reinterpreted and applied to situations for which they were not intended. Levi (1949) provides an illustration in the history of the Mann Act. This piece of legislation was passed by Congress on June 25, 1910, and was directed against white-slave traffic, which comprised

> any person who shall knowingly transport, or cause to be transported, or aid or assist in obtaining transportation for, or in transporting, in interstate or foreign commerce or in any territory or in the District of Columbia, any woman or girl for the purpose of prostitution or debauchery, or to engage in any immoral practice.

This problem was perceived to be a very serious one. Congressman Mann, who sponsored the law, declared that "all the horrors which have been urged, either truthfully or fancifully, against the black-slave traffic, pale into insignificance as compared with the horrors of the white-slave traffic" (cit. Levi, p. 25). Organized rings of malevolent individuals of alien origin were reputed to have captured young girls in this country and abroad. These men were assumed to have coerced their victims by unspeakable means into engaging in unspeakable practices. The Mann Act was intended to curb the importation of the helpless girls as well as their introduction into the red-light districts of U.S. cities.

Whether the problem ever existed, except in the minds of some sex-obsessed members of Congress, is a moot point. What matters is that the law, once it had been passed, was invoked in a diversity of contexts against a diversity of persons engaged in a variety of sex-related pursuits. As early as 1913, a Southern theater manager was convicted under the Mann Act for having made advances to a chorus girl whom he had hired in another state; in 1915, a prostitute was indicted when she changed her residence from Illinois to Wisconsin. The Supreme Court upheld both convictions, although in the first case transportation occurred for the purpose of employment, and in the second case the woman was admittedly not an innocent victim. In neither case was white-slave traffic involved. In 1944, the Mann Act was invoked against a family that owned a brothel, who was returning there from a vacation trip on which the couple had been accompanied by two of its employees; in 1945, the Supreme Court reaffirmed a conviction arising from a two-block taxi ride in Washington, D.C.; in 1946, the Mann Act was used against Mormons for practicing polygamy.

To be sure, the history of this piece of legislation is not typical. But it does dramatize the general point: laws are interpreted and reinterpreted in the course of being applied. These interpretations can be cumulative, in the sense that a prosecution or court decision of yesterday can be used today as a basis for a more generous interpretation, with the result that the law has radically changed its meaning by this time. The police officer, prosecutor, or judge who finally uses the law may be singularly unconcerned with the problems that motivated its passage. The law is his tool and acquires (within limits) whatever meanings he may need for his purposes. This creative element in the implementation of law makes the people who apply laws the keys to our understanding of what the law means (Gordon, 1975).

THE ADVENT OF PSYCHOLOGY IN CRIMINAL JUSTICE: EVALUATIONS OF FACTS

In order to apply laws, we must have "proven" facts about a crime that fit legal prohibitions, and we must be assured that these facts have been appropriately gathered. Academic psychology became interested in the criminal justice process by systematically viewing the process (testimony) whereby observations related to crimes are presented in court. With variations (Chapter 2) this problem is still the main concern of "forensic" psychologists today.

The pioneer work in this area was entitled *On the Witness Stand*, and was first published in 1907. Its author was the German psychologist Hugo Munsterberg, who had been brought to Harvard to head the psychological laboratory there. Since Munsterberg was passionately interested in applying psychology to practical problems, his attention soon strayed from the laboratory and centered on the courtroom.

In court Munsterberg noted what to him seemed a very interesting problem: despite the fact that individuals had solemnly sworn to tell "the truth, and nothing but the truth," their version of the truth frequently differed markedly from that of other people who had also sworn to tell the truth.

Such differences in testimony could occur even in simple issues such as the speed of a car, the number of people in a room, the location and distance of a sound, and the physical dimensions of a person.

Munsterberg conducted classroom demonstrations and experiments to show that trained observers with generous advance warning could not agree on matters such as the number of squares on a board, the amount of time between two clicks, the pitch of a sound, and the shape of an inkblot. Their testimony, taken immediately after their exposure to an object, would tend to range widely. Munsterberg concluded that perceptual habits have to be taken into consideration in evaluating testimony. He also showed that a person who flagrantly misperceived one situation was very likely to perform just as badly in another. The demonstration Munsterberg used for this purpose featured two squares—one blue and one gray. He asked his psychology class to judge which square was darker. "The gray was objectively far lighter than the dark blue, and any one with an unbiased mind who looked at those two squares of paper could not have the slightest doubt that the blue was darker. Yet about one fifth of the men wrote that the gray was darker." Having established this, Munsterberg proceeded to the second part of his experiment:

> I stood on the platform behind a low desk and begged the men to watch and to describe everything which I was going to do from one given signal to another. As soon as the signal was given, I lifted with my right hand a little revolving wheel with a color-disk and made it run and change its color, and all the while, while I kept the little instrument at the height of my head, I turned my eyes eagerly toward it. While this was going on, up to the closing signal, I took with my left hand at first, a pencil from my vest-pocket and wrote something at the desk; then I took my watch out and laid it on the table; then I took a silver cigarette-box from my pocket, opened it, took a cigarette out of it, closed it with a loud click, and returned it to my pocket, and then came the ending signal. The results showed that eighteen of the hundred had not noticed anything of all that I was doing with my left hand. Pencil and watch and cigarettes simply had not existed for them (Munsterberg, 1925, pp. 29–30).

In comparing the results of the two demonstrations, Munsterberg discovered that *fourteen of the eighteen men* who had given deficient testimony in the color-disk experiment had judged the light gray square to be darker than the dark blue square:

> That coincidence was, of course, not chance. In the case of the darkness experiment the mere idea of grayness gave the suggestible minds the belief that colorless gray must be darker than any color. They evidently did not judge at all from the optical impression, but entirely from their conception of gray as darkness. The coincidence, therefore, proved clearly how very quickly a little experiment such as this with a piece of blue and gray paper, which can be performed in a few seconds, can pick out for us those minds which are probably unfit to report whether an action has been performed in their presence or not. Whatever they expect to see they do see; and if the attention is turned in one direction, they are blind and deaf and idiotic in the other (p. 31).

Munsterberg advocated that psychologists be permitted to test witnesses and to evaluate testimony. He also pointed out that psychology had acquired much information that could help in sorting reliable from unreliable evidence. According to Munsterberg, "every chapter and subchapter of sense psychology" could clear up testimony problems (p. 33). This contention was amplified by such authors as Burtt (1931). Burtt illustrated his point with facts about sensory defects, distance perception, color vision, adaptation, acuity, auditory space perception, tactual perception, the perception of motion, time perception, and aspects of attention and memory. He attempted to show that in each case, facts known by psychologists could be brought to bear on discrepancies in testimony—discrediting some witnesses, supporting others, or accounting for differences among them.

As we shall see in Chapter 3, psychologists occasionally have been used in the courtroom as experts on testimony. One of the earliest instances occurred in Belgium in 1910. The psychologist involved was Varendonck, who was given the task of evaluating information obtained from two little girls under suggestive questioning in a preliminary examination. To this end, Varendonck devised a series of ingenious experiments incorporating questions similar to those which had been asked of the witnesses. Answers were obtained from children much like the two little girls in age and background. These answers clearly showed that the original testimony could have resulted from the suggestive questions. For instance, eighteen children were asked to name the color of the beard of one of the teachers. Sixteen responded, "Black." The teacher had never worn a beard.

In the crucial experiment,

> written answers were required from 8-year-old pupils. "When you were standing in line in the yard, a man came up to you, didn't he? You surely know who it was. Write his name on your paper." No man had come, but 7 of 22 children gave a man's name. The experimenter continued, "Was it not Mr. M_____?" Seventeen of the 22 answered "yes," and in individual oral examinations gave complete descriptions of the man's appearance and dress (Rouke, 1957, p. 54).

The number of experimental psychologists testifying in the courtroom (in a professional capacity) has not increased greatly since 1910. This fact is hardly surprising, because Munsterberg's enthusiasm was not shared by his successors. Munsterberg had made promises that other experimental psychologists (with fewer applied interests) had neither the inclination nor the temperament to redeem. Dean John Wigmore, one of the greatest legal minds of the century, whose classic treatise on evidence draws heavily on psychological writings, arrived—after thoughtful review—at the conclusion that

> there still remains unexploited by psychometry almost the whole field of possibilities in testimonial evidence. In spite of the Munsterberg trumpet-blast of 1909, announcing that "the time for applied psychology is surely near," and that "the judges can test the individual differences of men by the methods of experimental psychology," and "with the same (quantitative) accuracy (as in food materials)

can transform their common sense into careful measurements," the record of psychometric achievement with testimony is still meager (Wigmore, 1937, p. 792).

ASSESSING THE "MENTAL CONDITION" OF OFFENDERS

While experimental psychologists have not entered the courtroom in large numbers, clinicians, by contrast, have invested increasing time and energy as expert witnesses, this is the case because, before the law feels entitled to punish a person, it not only reassures itself that the person has done what he is accused of doing, but also that he is the sort of person who can be "blamed" for his acts or can be held accountable for them. It is in this area that the law makes its most important psychological assumptions. The phrase that lawyers use is "mens rea," which literally means "guilty mind." The origin of this phrase lies in religious thinking, which distinguished between transgressors who had knowingly sinned and those who almost unwittingly transgressed because they were possessed by devils or otherwise incapacitated.[2]

Among the strangest kinds of cases on record are trials in which animals have served as defendants. Swarms of ants, locusts, and mice have been charged and convicted. Cows and pigs have been sentenced to death. One American trial of the thirties resulted in the execution of several dogs. A Spitz has been placed on four-year probation in New York State. A six-month-old puppy named Idaho, also convicted in New York State, was given probation for two years (Duncan, 1940, p. 41).

Such cases strike us as ludicrous and weird because we make two "common sense" assumptions about human crime which we do not make when dealing with acts committed by animals. The first of these assumptions is that a person acts with *awareness*—that he *knows* what he is doing—whereas an animal does not; the second assumption is that we exercise free will—that we *can help doing* what we do—whereas an animal cannot. These assumptions imply that man may be *held responsible* for his actions, and may be taken to account for them, whereas puppy dogs and cows cannot be blamed for their "crimes": they must be viewed as innocent products of their training and limitations.

In the early days this argument exclusively concentrated on the first of the two presumed human qualities. If a puppy was being defended under this formula his counsel might argue: "Poor Bowser cannot be found guilty of destroying the new table top because he cannot tell that if he stepped on his plate he would cause what we view as a calamity. Since he did not know that the act he was committing would be regarded as wrong, Bowser is clearly not responsible for his crime."

This conforms to the rule of insanity formulated for the British House of Lords in 1843, which is still used widely in the United States.[3] In some states, this definition (the McNaghten Formula) is supplemented by the "Irresistible Impulse Doctrine," which (given the same crime) would argue: "Surely you can't hold Bowser responsible for defacing the table, because he could not help doing what he did. After all, Bowser did not *choose* to spill his milk. He acted on a dumb impulse."[4]

Insanity is a legal term which denotes the presumed absence of mens rea where an offender is emotionally or intellectually impaired. The use of the insanity concept will be discussed in Chapter 5, where we shall have an opportunity to face the conceptual and practical problems of the "expert on mental conditions."

The issue of intent is one of many areas in which the psychology of the offender poses legal questions. The most controversial area is, interestingly enough, that of chronological and psychological maturity. In the common law, children who were seven and under had *by definition* no mens rea; they could be farmed out as problem children, but they could not be punished by the courts.[5] When a child was over seven years old but was under fourteen years of age, the law usually *tended* to assume the absence of maturity, but the courts were willing to listen to arguments to the contrary in the case of particularly precocious offenders. Indeed, the test for determining the capacity of a youth and the responsibility of an adult were almost identical.

Our concept of "juvenile delinquency" is an idea that is partly premised on the common law's perception of the incapacity of children, and partly on the notion that the status of being young is a form of impairment which justifies a therapeutic type of approach. Ostensibly, a juvenile court proceeding is not aimed at assigning guilt to an offender, though a "factual finding" is made to establish a youth's involvement in delinquency. Instead of punishing offenders the court arrives at a "program disposition," which invokes "services" that respond to "the child's needs." A great deal of quasi-mental health expertise is mobilized by juvenile courts to trace the offender's history, to "diagnose" his or her "problem" and to map a "program" responsive to the child's presumed "needs."

The juvenile court has been under severe attack from two groups, which are almost opposed to each other. One group points to the increasingly serious depredations of increasingly younger offenders, and strongly questions the desirability of viewing young muggers as "in need of services" instead of "deserving" long prison terms that could at least curb their depredations. Other critics point to lax procedural safeguards in juvenile courts, which permit the institutionalization of children whose offenses would not constitute lawbreaking in an adult, and that comprise vague "status" offenses such as incorrigibility, in which the crime at issue (the "criminal act" or "actus rea") is hard to find.

In thinking about juvenile justice, the two sets of critics are centering (as critics often do) on very different aspects of the same system. Due process advocates tell us of neglected children who are casually dealt with by unchecked courts. Other critics, including the media, center on ridiculously light punishments for predatory juveniles and on low chances for convicting young toughs. The second view is embodied in a well-known cartoon of two shop-worn offenders in the process of asking a judge, "Your honor, can't you look at us as middle-aged juvenile delinquents?"

The two factions of critics converge in a compromise trend, which pro-poses invoking conventional criminal dispositions for youthful serious offend-ers, particularly for "violent juveniles," and the removal or "diversion" from the court system of minor delinquents and "status offenders." Such modern proposals are not tied to the historical link between psychological maturity and mens rea, because if we were concerned with translating maturity level into criteria of culpability, neither seriousness of offense nor arbitrary age limits could be used to draw the line. As we shall see in Chapter 8, a man of fifty may be psychologically in infancy, while a twelve-year-old may go about his criminal depredations in a cold and businesslike manner.

An odd juncture at which mental condition has always been seen as rele-vant is in the postconviction, presentence stage, where "mitigating" factors may be considered by judges in modulating the severity of sentences. At this decision point, mens rea is no longer an all-or-none concept, but becomes a sum of psychological facts such as the patterning of criminal careers, the relationship between the offender and fellow-offenders, the offender's level of intelligence, and the life problems that have shaped a person's motives for crime. Again, psychologically tinged testimony (presentence reports) is ac-cepted as relevant here by the courts.

Chronologically, sentencing is only one "official" stage in the criminal justice process in which psychological facts are assumed to be relevant. The first assessment is "unofficial" and is the police officer's arrest, which is influenced by the suspect's perceived "attitude" (Chapter 3). An early *formal* determination of an offender's mental state occurs when we decide to try him. Though most defendants have little to say at their own trials, we pre-tend that men conduct their defenses, with their attorneys providing tech-nical assistance confined to finer points of law and procedure. We thus assure ourselves that defendants can understand what goes on in court and can "participate" in the trial process. For most criminal cases, it happens that the trial issue is moot, because most defendants "plea bargain" and then plead guilty. For such persons, the remaining legal–psychological issue is the judge's question "are you aware (of the consequences) of what you are doing?" This question tends to be posed by the judge with a suitably serious demeanor, and with appropriate emphasis for the record.

The defendant's capacity to plea bargain is in fact of crucial import, because his attorney functions as a glorified go-between, and the offender himself decides whether to accept or reject the prosecutor's offer. In making this decision, the suspect must weigh the probability of conviction in the absence of a plea, must consider the relative seriousness of probable sentences, the value of time spent in presentence detention, and must assess his relative bargaining power vis-à-vis the prosecutor's. Though the offender's calculus is more complex than his role while on trial, his "capacity to participate in plea bargaining" is not examined by the courts.

The defendant's mental condition is not discussed with respect to plea bargaining because *in practice* he becomes the *object* rather than a *participant* in this process. As Morris (1974) put it, the defendant "is present only for the formalities, the signing of the treaty, not its negotiations" (p. 53). The psychology of bargaining is of practical and theoretical importance, and deserves more attention than it has received. So does the stress that is created for the offender, who may serve heavy time in pretrial detention while the gambits of gamesmanship are played out elsewhere. Aside from peace negotiations, no other bartering process is similarly fateful and potentially costly, and none relegates to "expert" negotiators (who—as we shall see in Chapter 3—benefit from pleas of guilty) equivalent chances for unconscious collusion.

A third assessment juncture (which we shall discuss in Chapter 5) does not arise unless mens rea becomes an issue. Blatant schizophrenics can remain unassessed if they plead guilty to their offenses or if they sit through their trials (having been found competent for trial) quietly and unobtrusively hallucinating. This fact is particularly significant where a criminal charge is minor, so that an offender's attorney could invite a lifetime commitment for his client if he pleads insanity, in lieu of the relatively modest prison term a man faces if he is convicted.

Presentence assessment can "make the punishment fit the crime" (as in the Mikado's song) or it can "make the punishment fit the criminal."[6] Very often it is not clear which of these two aims is the real one. An arsonist with a long history of setting cats on fire may "deserve" a heavy sentence for being a patterned offender, but may also "need" time for "intensive treatment." A first offender may "deserve a second chance," but may also look "like a good bet." Criteria may vary with the crime: bizarre offenses may invite a "criminal-centered" view, while professionals may invite "crime-centered" perspectives.

A universal problem with assessments or diagnoses lies in the role of "the eye of the beholder." This role is dramatized in trials that involve battles between mental health experts who arrive at opposite conclusions, but who show the same loyalty to the side that pays them. The role of the payoff in clinical assessments is not always explicit, but is nevertheless *on the whole* a force that is at work. Usually, clinicians gain by "overpredicting" (Chapter 10), which means that their bread is buttered when they emphasize the seriousness of problems. Overpredicting reduces the risk of a cleared case returning to haunt you; it also increases the clientele for remunerated work.

This fact holds not only for the assessment of offenders, but also for clinical views of agency staff. A recent example involves a dispatch from Sauselito, a wealthy suburb of San Francisco. The story quotes a local psychiatrist who claimed to have interviewed "6,700 police officers and applicants in 20 California communities" and concluded that 35 percent of the police was "really dangerous." Having made this diagnosis, the psychiatrist (not surprisingly) found his services were not in heavy demand. He then concluded that the officers' "personalities are (not only) not suited to police work, (but) they are unable to learn about themselves or accept treatment that would allow them to function adequately" (Associated Press, San Francisco, July 20, 1977).

Law-relevant assessments, of course, are not limited to clinicians. Lay diagnosis of offenders enters into sentences of judges (Chapter 3), affects arrests by police (Chapter 2), directs the services of prison guards (Chapter 4), and affects the charging habits of prosecutors as well as the decisions of parole board members. In each case the practitioner's behavior can benefit where its premises are coldly reexamined.[7]

CRIMINAL JUSTICE AS A PSYCHOLOGICAL PROBLEM AREA

One problem with the criminal justice enterprise is the ambiguity of its general objectives, as well as the fuzziness of its more specific aims. While some objectives conflict, others can be balanced, but formulas that are individually or collectively used for balancing them can take different shapes. A police officer may be enjoined to be "firm and fair," but he can be very firm and cursorily fair, or scrupulously fair at the expense of accumulating some arrests. A parole officer can be a sensitive counselor, a job-broker, or a specialist in surveillance. A prison can emphasize "reintegration" by offering training, or it can run "treatment" groups around the clock. It can also do neither, or both once-over-lightly. A judge can throw the book at a burglar "to make an example of him," while a fellow judge can spare the man "to keep him with his family." A "serious crime" in Cowville may be "chicken feed" in New York City, and prison sentences may be correspondingly disparate (Hagan, 1974).[8]

Others may describe criminal justice as a "system," but psychologists cannot afford this luxury. They cannot afford it, because psychologically such a view forecloses interesting problems. If we think of a system, we conceive of police working hand-in-glove with prosecutors and courts, we envisage judges acquainted with institutions—such as prisons—to which they relegate offenders. We see programs mandated by the courts, faithfully executed by agencies such as probation, corrections, and parole.

Systems have congenial "interfaces" between subsystems, as do wheels in a watch. Systems also furnish goals, to which subsystems subscribe. A defense attorney whose guilty client has been acquitted because the prosecutor (with a little help from the defense) failed to prove his case would be warmly congratulated by police and prosecutors because overriding system goals— justice—have been served. Parole officers would strive for uniformity in their enforcement of parole rules. All sorts of standards would be promulgated and speedily adopted.

Instead of this ideal, we observe cross-pressures, competing goals, stereotypes, and suspicions; efforts to bypass, manipulate, blame, scapegoat, subvert. Parole boards complain of sentences by judges; police deplore probation, prosecutors deplore police practices, judges deplore jail conditions, prisons deplore overcrowding, which is a function of sentences. Given an embarrassment (e.g., a mentally ill parolee who kills) mutual recriminations by "partners" in the subsystems (psychiatrists, judges, parole agents) are the order of the day.

Psychological problems in criminal justice include those involving staff perceptions by other staff, role-related motives, accommodations of goals, conflict negotiation, pressures, and resistance to change. Such problems have to do with the way a *hypothetical* system—which in reality consists of diverse people in parochial enclaves—manages to operate, both routinely and in crisis situations.

In all of this, the offender serves as a source of continuity. As Packer (1965) observes, offenders move on an "assembly line" from agency to agency, and link police to prosecutors, to courts, to corrections. Packer also adds, however, that the offender travels an "obstacle course" which has powerful checks and safeguards. The view of the process as experienced by its "consumer" is clearly another perspective that is relevant to assessing the "system" (or "nonsystem") attributes of criminal justice.

The criminal law is a civilized substitute for old uncivilized options, such as vendettas and lynchings. It is also a harsh substitute for more informal processes, such as family influence, group pressure, and education. The law addresses crimes with substantial sanctions, but it must make sure at every turn that it avoids capriciousness. The law also husbands limited resources, and it must reserve "big guns" for worthy targets. Only a few viable suspects are arrested; many of these persons must spend months awaiting trial and if they do reach prison they add to serious overcrowding.

Men and women who work in the system know such facts. Staff and clients of criminal justice settings live in a pragmatic world, in which "justice" is an obvious product of cross-pressures, and at best a very human product. In this context, there is nothing strange about someone asking questions about the problems (and motives) of individual practitioners, and the sources (and rationales) of organizational practices. In principle, at least, there is a role for the student of human behavior, and for the engineer of human change.

THE PSYCHOLOGY STUDENT IN CRIMINAL JUSTICE AGENCIES

Courts, prisons, and police departments are rich psychological laboratories, and they are also settings in which psychologists can help to ameliorate client suffering, improve staff performance, and implement needed reforms. In engaging in such work, we must be firmly grounded at least in our specialty and must know a great deal about the settings in which we propose to work.

These two types of knowledge are not independent of each other. What a psychologist must know about police, for example, is different from the "police expertise" of an economist, a sociologist, or an expert in public administration. Being tactful may get one's foot in the door, but continued access hinges on earned respect, and this in turn entails demonstrating a perspective which (1) has obvious validity and potential usefulness, and (2) is not available to the people with whom one deals.

Our Sauselito psychiatrist illustrates the danger of caricatured, runaway perspectives which destroy our usefulness. In entering a prison or a police agency, we must check our hobby horses at the door, and this includes both our ideologies and our specialized theories. The patrolman whom we approach for information is a person we must relate to and a man whose accumulated experience we must seek. We cannot suspect the officer of being the "institutional racist" of Sociology 101, or the "overcompensating latent homosexual" of Psychology 232, and persist in approaching him. The prison superintendent we importune is a high-level executive who has thoughts about his role and can share his thinking with us. He is not likely to do so if we discount his sophistication.

Part of the adventure of building knowledge is the sharing of diverse expertise. This adventure can be lost if we see inmates, guards, judges, detectives, prosecutors, policewomen, and parole officers as "subjects," as sources of raw data or case studies of theories. Criminal justice clients and staff are reflective and truth-seeking, and they can participate as full partners in our search for conceptual sense, or for solutions to practical problems. Where practitioners have a real "head start" is in a reservoir of practical experience that they can bring to their partnership with us. We can best contribute as brokers for combining and systematizing experience, and for supplementing experience with more "rigorous" data. We can also bring information to bear from noncriminal justice realms that may help make sense of criminal justice problems. The results of both procedures are illustrated in the next three chapters of this section.

NOTES

1. In a well-known recent case affirming the constitutionality of capital punishment (*Gregg* v. *Georgia*, 1976) the Supreme Court characterized the "expression of moral outrage" as a possibly "unappealing" but objectively "essential" social function. The court quoted itself from an earlier case (*Furman* v. *Georgia*, 1972) in which the court had argued that:

> The instinct for retribution is part of the nature of man, and channeling that instinct in the administration of criminal justice serves an important purpose in promoting the stability of a society governed by law. When people begin to believe that organized society is unwilling or unable to impose upon criminal offenders the punishment they "deserve," then there are sown the seeds of anarchy—of self-help, vigilante justice, and lynch law.

2. The Anglo-Saxons, who were pagans at heart, did not worry about the offender's mental state because they were not concerned about classifying him as sinful. Primitive law centered on the offender's act, and on the damage it inflicted. The

offender was penalized in proportion to the harm he had done. The Laws of Ethelbert, for instance (c. 560–616), prescribed a "bot" (fine or damages) of three shillings for a pierced ear, six shillings for a mutilated ear, six shillings for a decimated front tooth, one shilling for a rear tooth, twenty shillings for a severed thumb, and the same amount for a pierced belly (Pound & Plucknett, 1927).

3. The exact wording of the recommendation—which comes in the form of pre-scribed instructions to the jury— is that "to establish a defense on the ground of insanity it must be clearly proved that, at the time of committing the act, the party accused was laboring under such a defect of reason, from disease of the mind, as not to know the nature and quality of the act he was doing, or if he did know it, that he did not know he was doing what was wrong" (Weihofen, 1933, p. 28). It must be noted in defense of the English judges and the House of Lords, that they did not have infrahuman defendants in mind. They were restating the law of their time, which was the "Right and Wrong Test," a criterion evolved from an earlier wording (the so-called "Wild Beast Test") which required the defendant to "know more than a wild beast."

4. The irresistible impulse doctrine is intended to cover explosions of psychotic rage, and can also be invoked for neurotic compulsivity. It is covered by phrases such as "deprived of will power," "free agency destroyed," "unable to adhere to the right," and "could not help committing the act."

Where the irresistible impulse doctrine supplements the McNaghten rule, culp-ability presupposes the ability to tell right from wrong (with regard to a spe-cific act), and the ability to exercise free will. In civil law, the equivalent cri-terion (for liability) is the ability to foresee the consequences of one's actions. A person is liable for an act when he has been "negligent," which means that he did not exercise reasonable care to prevent harm to others. In the criminal area, negligence is the criterion of culpability for manslaughter.

5. The common law age limit for criminal responsibility was later (in England) raised to ten years, and children of that age were subjected to criminal proceedings.

6. The Supreme Court has endorsed "crime-centered" and "offender-centered" per-spectives. In relation to the death penalty, the court has thus ruled that death for rape is "disproportionate and excessive." But the Supreme Court has also struck down statutes that make execution mandatory for a given type of offense. In invalidating a North Carolina law, for instance (*Woodson* v. *North Carolina*, 1976), the court observed:

> A process that accords no significance to relevant facets of the character and record of the offender or the circumstances of the particular offense excludes from consideration in fixing the ultimate punishment of death the possibility of compassionate or mitigating factors stemming from the diverse frailties of humankind. It treats all persons convicted of a desig-nated offense not as uniquely individual human beings, but as members of a faceless, undifferentiated mass to be subjected to the blind infliction of the penalty of death.

7. One way to surface the rationale behind personal decisions is to use *simulation* exercises, in which all sorts of case material can be systematically presented to decision makers. Wilkins and his associates (Wilkins et al., 1973) have used this sort of technique to help parole board members and judges study themselves at work. The use of simulation for *training* must be distinguished from laboratory exercises *for research purposes* in which students and other persons play "make-believe" roles. Such simulation is very useful for simple experimental variables (e.g., the impact of order of presentation in testimony), but produces noncom-parability and lack of realism in complex situations (e.g., "the prison") whose sustained Alice-in-Wonderland flavor in the laboratory evokes idiosyncratic, bizarre, or pathological behavior. (For a case in point, see Zimbardo, 1972.)

8. To consider the consequences of such disparity, imagine a conversation between two felons (Lionel LaFleur and Milt Midtown) in the yard of a state prison:

LL: You just got here?
MM: Yea' . . . How long you in for?
LL: One to five years. I'm going out on parole next week. How about you?
MM: Ten to fifteen years. Got a long way to go!
LL: (respectfully) I'll say! What did they get you for?
MM: Me and a buddy broke into a gas station in Cowville one night last November and the cops caught us.
LL: That's strange! We also got nabbed breaking into a gas station at night. Why do you figure you're in ten times as long as me?

Among prison inmates, individual sentences are matters of general knowledge; the prevalence of disparate sentences can therefore decrease confidence in the legitimacy (equity) of criminal justice among imprisoned offenders.

REFERENCES

Burtt, M. E. *Legal psychology.* Englewood Cliffs, N.J.: Prentice-Hall, 1931.

Duncan, Y. A. *The strangest cases on record.* Chicago: Reilly & Lee, 1940.

Garrison, L. K., & Hurst, W. *The legal process.* (rev. ed.) Madison, Wisc.: Capital Press, 1956.

Gordon, R. *Forensic psychology: A guide for lawyers and the mental health professions.* Tucson, Ariz.: Lawyers and Judges, 1975.

Hagan, John. Contra-legal attributes and criminal sentencing: An assessment of a sociological viewpoint. *Law and Society Review,* 1974, *8,* 357.

Hartwell, S. W. *A citizens' handbook of sexual abnormalities.* Lansing, Mich.: Michigan Department of Mental Health, 1950.

Hindelang, M. J. Race and involvement in common law personal crimes. *American Sociological Review,* in press.

Levi, E. M. *An introduction to legal reasoning.* Chicago: University of Chicago Press, 1949.

Lewin, K. Action research and minority problems (1946). In *Resolving social conflicts: Selected papers in group dynamics.* New York: Harper & Row, 1948.

Morris, N. *The future of imprisonment.* Chicago: University of Chicago Press, 1974.

Munsterberg, H. *On the witness stand.* New York: Clark, Boardman, 1925.

Newman, G. *Comparative deviance: Perception and law in six cultures.* New York: Elsevier, 1976.

Packer, H. L. Policing the police. *The New Republic,* September 4, 1965, 17–21.

People's Appliance, Inc. v. Flint. *Michigan Reports,* 1959, 358, 54–55.

Pound, R., & Plucknett, T. F. *Readings on the history and system of common law.* Cambridge: Cambridge University Press, 1927.

Quinney, R. *Critique of legal order: Crime control in a capitalistic society.* Boston: Cole Brown, 1974.

Rankin, A. The effect of pre-trial detention. *New York University Law Review,* 1964, *39,* 641 ff.

Rodell, F. *Woe unto you, lawyers.* New York: Reynal & Hitchcock, 1939.

Rouke, F. L. Psychological research on problems of testimony. *Journal of Social Issues,* 1957, *13,* 50–59.

Sutherland, E. H. The sexual psychopathic laws (1950), In A. Cohen, A. Lindesmith, K. Schuessler (Eds.), *The Sutherland papers.* Bloomington: Indiana University, 1956.

Toch, H. *Violent men: An inquiry into the psychology of violence.* Chicago: Aldine, 1969.

Toch, H., Grant, J. D., & Galvin, R. *Agents of change: A study in police reform.* Cambridge, Mass.: Schenkman (Halsted Press), 1975.

Weihofen, H. *Insanity as a defense in criminal law.* New York: Commonwealth Fund, 1933.

Weihofen, H. *The urge to punish: New approaches to the problem of mental irresponsibility for crime.* New York: Farrar, Straus, 1956.

Wigmore, J. H. *The science of judicial proof.* Boston: Little, Brown, 1937.

Wilkins, L. T., Gottfredson, D. M., Robison, J. P. & Sadorsky, A. *Information selection and use in parole decision making.* Davis, Calif.: National Council on Crime and Delinquency, 1973.

Zimbardo, P. Pathology of punishment. *Trans-Action,* 1972, *9,* 4–8.

chapter 2

The Psychology of the Police

Ezra Stotland
John Berberich

A person whom you ask what the goals of police departments are would probably be startled that someone would even think of asking. His obvious answer to so obvious a question might be, "to catch criminals" or "to enforce the law." However, he might then reflect about what he observed police officers doing the last time he saw them at work: helping an old lady injured in a fall get to a hospital; directing traffic around an accident; getting an unruly drunk off the street. This impression of police as observed in actuality (and not on TV) may provide the clue that the goals and functions of a police department are a bit more complex than just catching offenders. This complex of goals has been sorted out and analyzed by James Q. Wilson (1968) from masses of observational data that Wilson and his students acquired through routine observations of police departments. Wilson divided the goals of police departments into three general classes:

1. *Legal,* which refers to the goal of enforcing the law, arresting violators, and preventing crime.
2. *Maintaining order,* which refers to the goal of minimizing the amount of public disturbance in streets, parks, taverns, and so on; keeping fights, drunks, noise, public disputes, and the like to a minimum, and keeping traffic moving.
3. *Providing service,* which refers to giving directions, giving first aid; taking lost drunks, children, and dogs home; and so on.

Wilson found that police departments differ in the degree of emphasis they place on each of these goals, although they have all three goals to a greater or lesser degree. "How," the reader might ask, "can it be that departments can emphasize different goals? Are not the goals defined by law?" To answer these questions, let us examine an example in which different goals can lead to different actions by police officers:

> Two officers in a patrol car are called to a tavern because a serious brawl is reported. On arrival they find a man with a bad cut in his upper arm, apparently inflicted with a broken beer bottle. The victim and the perpetrator are still in a shouting match, both being slightly inebriated but not drunk. The police get the clear impression that the victim is not very interested in having his assailant arrested and prosecuted for assault. On the other hand, the bartender asks the police to get both combatants out of his tavern as quickly and quietly as possible.

If the police are legalistically oriented, they might try to arrest the apparent assailant, and would get as many statements from witnesses as possible. By doing that, they would reject the bartender's request to have things quiet down quickly; in this way, the officers would downgrade the order maintenance goal of police departments. If they did follow the bartender's request, they would find it hard to enforce the law, since witnesses would not be accessible. If the officers simply took the victim to the hospital, they would be acting entirely in terms of a service goal.

How the officers resolve these dilemmas reflects in part the relative importance to their departments of the three types of goals. Wilson found that some departments are legalistic, emphasizing strict law enforcement; others are service oriented; and still others are order-maintenance oriented.

Even given such goals, individual police officers still have to set priorities and personal goals in concrete and specific situations. (How seriously does the victim have to be bleeding before first aid takes priority over arresting the suspect?) Furthermore, the problems faced by officers in different neighborhoods in a department's jurisdiction may demand different styles of police work. (How much weight should be given to the bartender's request if the tavern and those near it frequently have disturbances of the peace?) The priorities of a police department are rarely so firm, rigid, and readily applicable that they can guide all of the conduct of officers.

MEASURES OF POLICE EFFECTIVENESS

Measures of progress toward the attainment of goals are of practical importance, since officers tend to become less motivated and their official activities decline where there are no indicators of progress. In the face of the availability of such data as crime rates and arrest rates, it may seem that there are ample ways of measuring the progress of a legalistic department toward its goals. But it is known to most police officers that official crime rates do not accurately reflect actual crime rates. Police officers also know that arrest rates may reflect the willingness of police officers to make legally weak arrests to inflate their record of arrests. In any case, overall arrest rates in an officer's department may have little relationship to the arrest rate that an officer achieves in his own work, partly because arrests for felonies are relatively rare events in the lives of most officers.

Other problems of motivation may arise because it is obvious to the officer that the overall crime rate does not appear to be dropping consistently; that whenever he arrests one felon, it is not long before another has taken his place, or the arrested person is back on the streets; that the forms or locales of certain problems may change, but the problems themselves remain. Picking up drunks does not eliminate drunkenness; picking up delinquents does not eliminate juvenile delinquency.

A police officer often feels frustrated by the rest of the criminal justice system, since many of the people who he feels are "bad actors," and whom he has worked hard to arrest are set free through the efforts of defense lawyers. Or they are given light sentences because of plea bargaining or the general "leniency" of the courts. The functioning of the criminal courts is generally the most frustrating aspect of police work (McManus, 1976; Kroes, 1976; Kroes, Margolis and Hurrell, 1974). The police place much more emphasis on the content of criminal law and on justice in the world of the street than on the procedural justice of our courts (Skolnick, 1967).

The officer must also live with changes in the laws and norms of a community. How does one evaluate progress in drug law enforcement when marijuana is about to be decriminalized? (In anticipation of decriminalization, officers may make arrests only in serious cases.) And officers may become skeptical about the next law that might be changed after he's worked hard to enforce it. Even if the laws are not changed, there may be differences over time and across neighborhoods in standards of acceptable behavior or the criteria for involving the public. Davis (1975) found that in some neighborhoods in Chicago officers did not make arrests in cases of nonfatal shootings unless the victim insisted, which was only in a minority of instances.

Departments as well as officers may thus begin to lower their aspirations or narrow their goals. Officers may have the goal of simply forcing crime and criminals out of their sector to a neighboring one, or they may see their goal as that of making arrests, regardless of whether the arrests lead to prosecutions, let alone convictions. They may come to believe, probably not without some validity, that the crime rate would skyrocket if they did not do their work. This belief, however, is not a very strong basis for high motivation, since deterred crime is not visible.

A succinct way of summarizing this discussion is that police officers and whole departments tend to move toward routinization rather than goal orientation; toward short-range, expedient goals, rather than long-range ones; toward protection of worker comfort and job security, rather than toward the attainment of professional ends. Often the goal becomes to avoid censure by superiors and peers; to feel secure about one's job; to protect one's retirement; to get a quieter job; to keep one's paper record of citations and arrests up to snuff; to avoid citizen complaints or even suits; and to find some pleasure by kidding around and joking with peers, prisoners, and superiors.

LEADERSHIP AND SUPERVISION

When full-time police departments were first established in the United States, the selection procedures were lax or nonexistent. The chief's (or mayor's) unemployed friends might be the first hired, regardless of education or character. Training was minimal or nonexistent. A badge, a gun, a uniform, a billy-club, and a book of regulations, and the officer was off to do duty. Obviously such laxness led to a rather casual, inefficient, and quasi-legal style of policing. Early in this century, this casual approach began to be rejected. Training was increased; selection procedures improved, professionalism was emphasized as a way of increasing the legitimacy of the police, of freeing them from political pressures, of enhancing the self-esteem and effectiveness of the police departments. And, most importantly, a quasi-military organization was established. If the officers were not people of the highest caliber, then the way to keep them in line must simply be to keep them under tight control in the tradition of early (classical) management theory (Weber, 1964). Police officers were specifically regarded as the equivalents of enlisted men in the military. This orientation toward the military continues to the present; police departments have in the recent past recruited new officers directly from the military. By so doing, they have assured themselves of at least a minimal level of education, training, and health among their recruits.[1]

Over the past few decades, selection and training of police officers has steadily improved, and perception of the need for military discipline to insure proper police action has correspondingly declined. This assumption is shared by police rank-and-file. Lefkowitz (1977) found that police place considerable value on autonomy and self-assertiveness. Furthermore, the nature of police work itself gives the military form of organization only limited value, at best. In the military, an officer can directly observe the actions of the ordinary enlisted men who function as groups, units, or teams, are ordered about as such, and can be observed in the aggregate. On the other hand it is only on exceptional occasions in police work that the military mode of supervision can be used. (Among these occasions are crowd control, some large stake-outs, riot control, etc.) In ordinary police work, the individual officers or officers in pairs are pretty much on their own. The sergeant may sometimes be out in his own car, but he simply cannot directly observe each of his officers as he drives around to places to which he is called, or patrols his area. The officer is on his own, and must use his own judgment in making decisions.

It might be argued that the officers' reports of incidents, citations, or arrests, and so on serve as a way for the supervisor to keep close track of what each officer is doing. The basic difficulty is that many, if not most, situations which patrol officers encounter are fraught with ambiguities, uncertainties, and conflicts of values. How serious is a husband's threat to shoot his wife? How much of a motion does a possibly armed suspect have to make before the officer can infer that he is reaching for his weapon? How much confidence should be placed in a junkie's offer to turn in a pusher?

A further difficulty stems from the fact that in busy urban areas on busy nights, such as Friday and Saturday, the work load of the police is such that they cannot respond to all possible complaints or violations. The judgment as to which call to respond to first, how much time to spend on it, which observed misdemeanor violations (such as jaywalking or making a rolling stop at a stop sign) to react to, must be employed by the officer with little direction from supervisors who (since they are not present on the scene) cannot assess the appropriateness of assigned priorities. We have already noted in Chapter 1 that all laws are not equally enforced. Officers may not enforce a law against smoking marijuana if the amount is small, and they may not arrest a ten-year-old burglar if they know his parents and believe that the latter will punish the youth when an officer brings him home. In many of these instances, the officer may not make a record of an intervention, or, at most, may record it as a minor incident, not worthy of being reacted to as a criminal matter. The problem of report writing as a form of supervision is compounded by the officers' perception that the reports they write often become evidence in court. Thus they write reports to increase the chance of gaining a conviction. With this goal in mind, an officer might not record the drunkenness of an offender where the man's drunkenness may lead the court to be more lenient; the officer might not report his own oversights, especially those which may cause evidence to be discarded by the court because it was obtained improperly.

Other problems also arise when one tries to rely on reports as a means of supervision. For instance, there is the tendency for one officer in a two-man car to be delegated the responsibility of report writing because of greater literary skill. Finally, the sergeants' screening of the reports often tends to be very informal, especially in large police departments.

Other difficulties in supervision stem from the mutual dependency between the officer and his immediate supervisor. Rubinstein (1973), a reporter who spent a year as an observer of street officers, describes the sergeant's stake in his subordinates' making a reasonable number of arrests of the types the chief is interested in seeing in his statistics. For example, word might come down that the chief is concerned with increasing the number of vice arrests. Since the sergeant cannot say to his officers, "Go out and arrest five prostitutes," he can let it be understood that making such arrests would be appreciated. The officers can then patrol more often in areas frequented by street walkers and try to generate some arrests. If they do not make these arrests, the sergeant may suffer more than the officers as a result of the chief's dissatisfaction. A sergeant in this dependent situation is therefore in a very poor position to order his officers to do things that they reject, or to cease activities which he would not want them to engage in.[2]

Police officers may receive a great deal of credit and even publicity for major felony arrests, shooting in defense of life, and other actions. But in ordinary day-to-day police work, the police tradition is to punish officers for infractions of rules or of policies rather than to praise or reward them. The cat-and-mouse aspect of supervision is reflected in the officers feeling that they tend to not be treated fairly if brought up on charges (Niederhoffer, 1967; MacFarlane and Crosby, 1976).

A sergeant may learn of a violation by a given officer, and if the sergeant and the officer do not have the relationship of mutual dependency mentioned above, the safest way for a police officer to avoid reprimand is simply to do as little as possible (Rubinstein, 1973). If you don't make an arrest, you don't make a poor arrest. If you don't get to a family quarrel on time, a wife can't complain that you have roughed up her husband. The more rules a department has about how police officers should do their jobs, the more likely it is that an officer will incur a reprimand from his supervisor, and thus feel more inhibited in his work. Harrison (1975) has found that departments with more spelled-out rules had officers with less sense of achievement or satisfaction from their work, less sense that they were being given recognition by their supervisor, less sense of contributing to the organization, less sense of responsibility, and so on. Wagoner (1976) found that officers in more formalized departments felt more powerless. Experienced officers in many departments sometimes pull back from many activities, and let the young hard chargers, "hot dogs," go out after the arrests. Reiss (1971) observed that experienced officers spent less time on preventive patrol. Bozza (1973) found that they made fewer arrests. The officers who are hard chargers may continue to charge for a long time and be tolerated, if not encouraged, by their supervisors. But they are likely to overstep the boundaries of acceptable behavior and offend citizens enough to cause them problems in their own departments (Grant, Grant, & Toch, in press). They may then pull back and join what Wambaugh has called "the walking wounded."

PEER RELATIONS IN POLICE WORK: PARTNERS

Police most often ride patrol cars and walk beats in pairs. The same two officers tend to ride together for long periods of time, sometimes for years, most often by choice, since requests for changes of partnerships are usually accepted by supervisors. The bonds between two officers who are partners are frequently strong and intimate.

Partners often divide up the responsibilities of the job, partly on the basis of special abilities. For example, the better driver might do the driving; the better writer or typist might keep the logs; one might do the talking with juveniles, another the observing on the street. This division of responsibilities has a number of values. For one, since the partners know which one of them does what, there is not much need to vacillate or waste time.

Often, partners develop a common outlook on law enforcement, on what sorts of things have priority. They may also communicate very speedily and with minimal effort in emergency situations; each knows more or less what to expect of the other. In dangerous situations, partners know that they can depend on one another for protection. Police officers generally are trained not to take danger alone; it is no humiliation to ask for and expect help from a partner or from back-up cars.

Not least important, partners often become personal friends, discuss their personal lives during hours of boredom, and share jokes and points of view. Their sense of unity is enhanced by the fact that together, they face the outside world—the dispatcher, whose voice directs from one call to another; the citizen whom they confront, or are helped by; the prisoner who sits in the back of the car. The partners generally are two vis-à-vis some third party; they relate to each other rather than to the community (Bard & Shellow, 1976).

If one of the partners has violated some rule or law, the other generally knows it. The former, being heavily dependent on the latter, will feel subtle pressure not to inform on his partner. Sometimes this type of dependency may be mutual. Partners who "coop," that is, sleep during the wee hours of weekday mornings, "share a secret" (Westley, 1970).

Because police officers often have to make very difficult decisions—fast judgments on the basis of imperfect information, with ambiguous or uncertain standards on which to base the decision, they can use the assurance of consensus. Laboratory studies in social psychology have shown that even having only one person agree with one's own choice gives one a great deal of feeling in the rightness of one's choices. Thus partners, by developing a more or less common point of view, provide support for the validity of their individual decisions.

PEER GROUP RELATIONS: THE LOCKER-ROOM CULTURE AND OTHER GROUPS

Many of the psychological and other factors that make for strong bonds between partners also make for close ties among patrol officers in general. Futhermore, the nature of patrol work often brings officers together on the street and in the precinct house. Officers may go to a scene of a crime, even if another car has been so ordered, in order to join in the excitement and to relieve the boredom of random preventative patrol on dull shifts and to socialize with other officers. Officers in different cars can arrange to take their lunch breaks at one of the restaurants and cafes that the police regularly patronize (Rubinstein, 1973).

In addition to the factors we have mentioned, patrol officers as a whole have shared problems which tend to cut them off from persons outside of police work and thereby force them to develop strong ties with one another. The hours of work shifts tend to put obstacles in the way of social interactions with nonpolice. When officers do socialize with nonpolice, their professional role sometimes leads to subtle forms of ostracism, as when they arrive at a party and someone shouts, "There come the fuzz!" The officer's professional role is salient both to him and to others. Other persons may treat him warily, question him, or express resentment at the last traffic ticket they got. These problems are magnified by the fact that police officers always have the power of arrest, whether they are at work or not. They are always "on duty." In most jurisdictions, they are required to carry off-duty handguns; their personal appearance, their personal finances, their personal morals are all subject to departmental review. The role pressures are thus always there to remind officers of the fact that they are officers.[3]

The particular set of values and the outlook that police officers develop has sometimes been called the "locker-room" culture. In this culture, "macho" values receive strong support, since one of the first things that an officer needs to establish in any street situation is the legitimacy of his authority in that situation.

Macho values also receive support from the police emphasis on physical abilities, from the occasional need to use violence and physical force, from the respect that macho conduct receives in the community at large, and especially among some people who live in heavily policed neighborhoods. At least the police perceive that if they are to gain respect in these areas, they need to appear strong, dominant, competent, self-assured. These factors may push police in a macho direction independently of the locker room culture, but there can be little doubt that the locker-room group enhances adherence to these values.

Locker-room culture values are expressed and enforced in a variety of ways. The group may develop a set of expectations about a particular officer, consistent with the values of the culture. For example, a very large and powerfully built officer may be nicknamed "King Kong" and called upon by other officers for help in making what might otherwise be difficult arrests. The fact that the officer may have other skills valuable in police work will be overlooked by his fellow officers, and the individual will find it very difficult to break out of the King Kong mold.

An officer may acquire a reputation in his peer culture because of a single incident early in his career. If he did not react fast or effectively when he received a call of "officer in need of immediate assistance," or if he did not back up his partner in a potentially threatening situation, he may become an isolate among his peers. Likewise, officers who are hard chargers and who make felony arrests may be given a great deal of respect in the locker room. However, the locker-room culture also supports older or more experienced officers who are more interested in their security than in making many arrests.

The culture values silence—not talking about possible violations of the rules by a fellow officer (Westley, 1970). Stoddard (1968), as an example, quotes a policeman's description of a young officer who had problems with the code of silence:

> I can remember one policeman who might have made an issue of another policeman taking something. He had that attitude for the first six months that he was on the force but by that time, he had been browbeaten so bad, he saw the writing on the wall. He knew better than to tell anything. In addition to browbeating, this man in very short order was put in a position where they had him on the information desk, or kicked around from one department to another, 'cause nobody wanted to work with him. This kind of a man they called "wormy" because anything that would happen he'd run to the braid.
>
> This fellow, I knew, wanted to be one of the boys, but he wanted to be honest, too. As it turned out, this guy was finally dismissed from the force for having an affair with a woman in his squad car. Just a couple of years before that he would have had a fit if he thought that somebody was going to take a drink on duty, or fool around with a woman, or steal anything. For this reason this man spent a lot of time on the information desk, working inside, and by himself in the squad car.

New police officers go through a kind of initiation procedure in which they are told by old-timers to forget what they believed before entering police work and what they had been told in the police academy and to learn from them how police work really is done (Westley, 1970; McNamara, 1967; Niederhoffer, 1967). The police academy is often viewed by these veterans as an institution which is necessary to satisfy the public, although the school may teach the rookie *some* valuable things. Old-timers not only see themselves as agents of socialization but also as exercising quality control for the peer group.[4] The new officer is tested by observing how he reacts to work pressure. If the rookie shows signs that he will not accept the locker-room culture, or is not dependable, he may become an outcast. Some officers may be forced by this pressure to leave police work. There are also transfers to quieter sectors, to juvenile work, and so on.

The problem of the rookie officer is magnified if the rookie is also highly educated, a graduate of a four-year college. Some of the values of college-educated officers may make it more difficult for them to accept the locker-room culture. Furthermore, the more experienced officer, as well as the sergeant, may be less educated than the rookie, making it more difficult for the rookie to believe he can "learn" from the veteran, while the veteran may feel that the college-educated rookie's knowledge doesn't really mean much on the street. Thus, it is not surprising that the dropout rate of college-educated officers is higher than that for those without a B.A. degree (Cohen and Chaiken, 1973; Levy, 1967). To be sure, other factors are involved here, such as the type of people who choose to pursue higher education.[5] College-educated officers may also feel that their official duties don't make full use of their education. They may have more opportunities than do others for well-paying jobs outside of police work, and may be more dissatisfied at the slow rate of advancement.

The situation of a college-educated rookie is quite different from that of a police officer who seeks education after having been on the force. Since the officer has by then been established as a member of the peer group, educational advancement is viewed as a way to improve himself and the police in general. Such a person is viewed as a police officer seeking an education, rather than as a college graduate seeking to educate the police. Even if a person's increased education yields a competitive advantage, the officer will probably not be rejected if he or she was accepted prior to gaining the education. In recent years, there has been a great increase in the number of officers seeking college educations, both in two- and four-year institutions. This trend has been supported by grants to officer-students from the Department of Justice.

THE POLICE AND MINORITY GROUPS

The ghetto climate of the sixties increased the antagonism between police officers and the black community, as hatred bred hatred and violence bred violence on both sides. Race riots also ironically and powerfully demonstrated the vastness of the gap between the black community and the police. The first major riot in Watts was precipitated by a police traffic stop.

Partly as a result of ghetto riots, attempts were made to enhance the human relations component of police training programs and to recruit more black and other minority police officers. Most political and legal pressure for recruitment of black officers, however, came from outside the police departments. In recent years, courts have ordered police departments to engage in affirmative action programs to recruit more black officers, and in some cases, the courts have forbidden further recruitment of new white officers until more black officers are recruited.

In attempting to join the in-group, minority officers have often run into the same barriers as have the more highly educated recruits. However, for minorities the problem is compounded, in that time and experience may not eradicate the distinctions between groups. Minority officers continue to have a constituency outside the police department, and are thereby subject to conflicts of loyalties. In some instances, black officers have reacted against what they saw as mistreatment of black civilians by white officers. Sometimes black officers have been sent to patrol some of the more difficult ghetto areas, on the assumption that black officers can relate more effectively to the community. However, black officers in such settings have sometimes perceived that they are being given the "worst" jobs, that they are being turned against their own people, and that they are protecting the police department from a charge of racism if any difficulties arise with a black citizen. Some black officers have reacted to this conflict by attempting to be supercops, to show that their loyalty is really to their professional group. They can also resent more deeply the crimes that blacks commit against other blacks, such as pushing dope on children; they may sometimes feel free of the charge of racism if they become rough; they may feel that they can show their status in the black community by being more strongly macho. Thus, the overlapping group memberships of black officers can have wide-ranging effects.

The fact that the police force has felt legal and political pressure to increase the number of black officers presents a direct threat to the independence and power of the police, quite apart from the fact that racial issues are involved. Sometimes the blacks who are recruited do not meet the same standards as whites, thus flying directly in the face of more traditional efforts to increase the professional status of police officers. Furthermore, in recent years, there has been some court-ordered effort to compensate for the relative absence of promotions of black officers by promoting them even when some whites, perceived to be as well qualified or even better qualified, are passed over.

All of these perceived threats to the white officer in-group have the effect of making them even more cohesive than they otherwise would be, and cause it to be even more difficult for the black officer to gain acceptance. Partly as a result, black officers have formed their own groups locally and nationally.

The very nature of police work compounds the problem. Ghettos are notoriously the area of the highest rate of street crime, both perpetrators and victims most often being black or members of other minority groups. This issue of race is emphasized to the officer listening to the police radio identifying suspects by their race,[6] obviously a necessary procedure if suspects are to be caught. Since it is the job of the police to deal with crime, both black and white officers feel pressures to react to crime in the ghetto. Many ghetto residents would like more effective policing of their neighborhoods, although they demand that this policing be scrupulously fair and free of racism. The police officer may thus be caught in a dilemma. If he works hard to catch offenders or to prevent crime, he runs the risk of being accused of over-aggressive police work. If he does a more passive job of policing, he may be accused of ignoring the need of the community for police protection. The conflict of goals is aggravated by the ghetto residents' frequently vocal expressions of resentment toward the police. When these pressures are added to the prejudice which has been endemic in American society and which has been shared by police as Americans, the outcome can hardly be expected to be very salutary—and the black police officer may receive some of the brunt of the effect.

We have noted that in departments where there are a sufficient number of black officers, they have often formed separate unions or formal groups. These groups can provide psychological support for their members, since the officers can gain acceptance independently of both the civilian community and the white police group. Furthermore, such groups can provide a vehicle for protest against any injustice the officers may perceive.

Black and white police officer groups have sometimes clashed politically, verbally, and even physically in urban police departments, such as in Detroit and New York. This polarization obviously cements further resentments and escalates conflict between the groups. It is interesting that the rise of minority group police organizations has not been restricted to blacks. In New York, separate unions for Italians, Spanish-speaking, and Jewish police officers have been formed.[7]

WOMEN

Like blacks, women have been involved in police work for many years, but their numbers have been small and they have served mainly in nonpatrol jobs, such as juvenile work, vice, dealing with women prisoners, and some detective work. It was originally assumed that women would not be able to work on patrol, either in cars or on foot.

The feminist revolution has begun to change this picture. Court orders and pressures for affirmative action have opened up many police departments to an infusion of women, more of whom are applying for positions as police officers than ever before.

There can be little doubt that the appearance of women in patrol cars has upset some of the patrol officers—particularly older veterans of the street. Part of a solution to this problem emerges in a study done in the Washington, D.C. police force, in which some two hundred women officers were added to the department at the same time as two hundred men. Both groups were sent out to work on patrol, as is usual for rookies, and were rated by their supervisors and by observers, as well as from their performance record. For the most part there was little difference in the ratings of men and women, except that the men made more felony arrests than the women. The arrests of both groups were equally likely to lead to the filing of charges. There were some anectodal charges that the women did not handle violent situations as well as men, either directly or as back-up for their partners or for officers in other cars. On the other hand, the anecdotes indicated that women handled family disputes more effectively. If these anecdotal reports are confirmed, the role of the policewoman might tend somewhat to revert to one more in line with the traditional role of women in society, to the more "feminine" areas mentioned above. Such a reversion probably would make policewomen more acceptable to the in-group of patrol officers, while tending to soften the "macho" norms of the locker room (Toch, 1977).

The role of policewomen as partners for male officers may raise some questions in the minds of some officers and their wives. Partners in patrol cars spend more time together than most husbands and wives; partners are more dependent on one another for physical safety than, say, executives and secretaries; they have to communicate as quickly and accurately as surgeon and nurse; and they have to be able to predict one another's actions as accurately as a male-female figure skating team. A successful police partnership thus entails a very close bond, which is in some ways closer than that between husband and wife. To the extent that such partnerships either involve sexuality, even light flirtation, or are just rumored to do so, they might present a threat to the man's loyalty toward his male officer group, and may threaten the stability of the marriage of both police officers, especially since police marriages tend to be unstable in any case.

Though marriage is one of the closest bonds that can exist between two people, the ideal of closeness is not infrequently threatened by a spouse's membership in other groups. People are not just husbands, nor just wives. In the case of police, the problem is merely more acute, since patrol officers share experiences of stress, humor, and decision making which are unique to their profession and very hard to convey to someone outside. Thus, police officers may be unable to share their experiences fully with their spouses. Sometimes sharing is not just a matter of intellectual understanding. It is also a matter of emotion, of tensions brought on by the difficulties of police work which the police officer brings home. The tensions may make him or her abrupt, impatient, withdrawn, and so on—behaviors which do not lead to stable and close family relationships. The officer's spouse may be unable to appreciate these tensions or their causes, and may feel cut off from important segments of his or her spouse's life.[8] It may be hard for a spouse to understand why he or she may not share certain aspects of an officer's professional life, harder than it is for a doctor's or lawyer's spouse, because there is more common knowledge of the stress and strains of a doctor's or lawyer's life. Furthermore, some of the status and monetary benefits of members of other professions make their problems easier for spouses to bear. In fact, being an officer's wife may place a barrier to social relationships with nonpolice friends, who may be very self-conscious not only in the presence of officers but of their spouses. It is thus no surprise that the divorce rate among police families is very high.

Because of strains placed on police families, wives in some departments are being given a better view of the stresses of police work through recently developed educational procedures. They have been encouraged to ride with their husbands occasionally; they have observed police academy training; they have received direct education about police work. In some instances, they have been given diplomas at the same ceremony in which their husbands graduate from the police academy.

In the Los Angeles County Sheriff's Department, a very elaborate training program for wives has been developed (Stratton, 1976). In this program, the wives learn about all aspects of the functioning, procedures, and organization of police departments; they learn how to handle weapons; they ride with their husbands on patrol, and share other activities. They also directly discuss some of the problems of being police wives with the police psychologist, and with more experienced police wives.

POLICE MANAGEMENT

We have already discussed the difficulties which the supervisors of police officers have in attempting to oversee their subordinates. In addition to the factors we have described which lead to these difficulties, the strength of the in-group of officers increases the resistance to directives from above.

Chiefs have sometimes attempted to overcome the strength of the in-group of patrol officers by the use of internal investigation squads. The internal investigators—the "police of the police"—attempt to monitor the behavior of police officers so as to discover any wrongdoing among them. Obviously, such efforts run headlong into the peer group's code of secrecy. Members of internal investigation units also sometimes share the feeling that unacceptable actions by officers should not be subject to much public scrutiny. If they uncover wrongdoing among officers and report this to supervisors, the latter have to be careful in their reactions to make certain that any discipline they invoke does not lower the morale of the other officers.

Around the time of the investigation of corruption of the New York City Police Department (Knapp Commission Report, 1973), Police Commissioner Patrick Murphy established an agency within the department to spy on other officers. Some investigators worked disguised as civilians and offered bribes to police officers—reporting them if they accepted. These so-called "shoflies" were recruited even before entering the police academy and were so segregated that they were never seen by other trainees. In addition to the obvious purpose of permitting such officers to function later as undercover agents, a major purpose of this segregation has no doubt been to minimize the loyalty that the prospective investigators might feel toward other officers.

Police chiefs encounter great difficulties when they attempt any program that goes against the locker-room culture; and this may be one of the factors which accounts for the short terms of police chiefs. In large cities it has been found that chiefs have an average tenure of only 2.8 years in office (Police Chief Executive Report, 1976).

CIVILIAN COMPLAINTS

When civilians have grievances against police officers, one legal recourse is a complaint directed to the police department. These complaints are typically referred to the internal investigations unit, which usually examines the claim quite conscientiously, coming up with one of three possible conclusions: complaint sustained; complaint groundless; and complaint not sustained, in the sense that not enough evidence has been found to sustain a charge against the officer. Research has indicated that relatively few charges are likely to be sustained to the point of inspiring administrative actions against the officer (Cohen, 1972). Likewise, law suits against police officers rarely are successful.

The inability of civilians to sustain charges against police officers is no doubt one of the factors that led to the pressure to establish civilian review boards during the period of the 1960s and early 1970s. During this period, antagonism between police and subgroups of civilians, such as minorities and antiwar militants, was very high. Very few outside review boards were actually established, partly because of the resistance of the police to outside incursions and partly because the majority of the citizenry tended to support the police. In Philadelphia, a board functioned a few years in a very cautious and limited way until police pressure led to its abolition. In New York City, the question of whether to establish police review boards was put to the voters. The police officers' union campaigned vigorously against the boards, and won a clear-cut victory.

Police hostility may also be focussed on newspaper and television reporters, since the very nature of the latter's work requires that they make an assault on the code of silence regarding actions by police officers. Niederhoffer (1967) reports that New York police officers tend to view the newspapers as being far more negative toward the police than appeared to be warranted by their actual writings (cf Westley, 1970). Resistance to the incursions of out-groups enhances the cohesion of in-groups. The strength of the police in-group is reflected in the recent rise of police unions.

COMMUNITY SERVICE

The picture we have painted of the isolation of the officer group from others has been overdrawn for purposes of exposition and analysis. Like any analysis of a human situation, almost any point that is made needs to be balanced by other statements if reality is to be recognized. We thus need to recognize factors which lead police officers toward greater integration into the community rather than to being estranged from it.

The elements leading toward greater police closeness to the citizenry stem primarily from the service and order-keeping functions of police officers, in contrast to their law enforcement functions. A police officer who helps take someone to the hospital, who directs a citizen to an appropriate agency of the government to solve his problems, or who does any of the other things officers do to help people is thereby establishing links with people in the community. If an officer is assigned to the same sector for long periods of time, he has an opportunity to develop strong ties to the people who live or work in that area. The "Blue Knight," for example (Wambaugh, 1972) was an officer who found his ties with people in his area so strong that he could not leave them by retiring and marrying the woman he loved.

Departments are more likely to become integrated into the community if they try not to emphasize law enforcement goals to the detriment of service goals. An extreme legalistic emphasis inhibits the officer from finding more appropriate remedies for problems than the enforcement of criminal law. An officer who shows a family where to get help in settling its tensions, rather than arresting an assaultive husband, for example, may gain a few friends and benefit the family involved.

Ironically, the better integration resulting from a service orientation probably often leads to greater chance of apprehending felons. After all, the police depend heavily on citizens to inform them of the occurrence of crime, since patroling officers rarely come upon a crime in progress. Furthermore, community members may be more likely to be stand-up witnesses in court.

In addition, contact with citizens in a non-law-enforcement mode helps to compensate for the officer's tendency to become cynical and develop a negative perception of reality. He may derive satisfactions from his work that would be missing if he did nothing but chase criminals.

Of course, integration with the community also has its dangers. If the community is itself corrupt and tolerates a high level of crime, the officer may become even more cynical than he otherwise would be. Integration into such communities may even mean that officers become corrupt themselves (Knapp, 1973). In corrupt order-keeping departments, a legalistically oriented "reform" is an effective antedote to corruption.

POSITIVE PROGRAMS IN POLICE DEPARTMENTS

The basic car plan is one technique for police integration into a community. This plan entails an officer being assigned more or less permanently to a given neighborhood, so that a particular area is his. The officer is encouraged to get out of his car to walk around and meet local residents and businessmen. (This is more practical now than it was years ago because of the radios which officers can take with them on leaving the cars, so that they are not out of communication.) The officers are encouraged to attend citizen meetings, such as those of PTAs, religious groups, and service organizations. In some jurisdictions, meetings have been organized by the police themselves to meet citizens.

Another effort to integrate police officers, called Neighborhood Team Policing, also is aimed at a permanent and close relationship with the community but involves a whole group or team rather than an isolated officer. In NTP a number of officers, ranging from twenty to one hundred or more, are assigned more or less permanently to a given neighborhood. NTP often involves placing the officers of all the watches assigned to a given neighborhood under the same supervision. The supervisor is called the team leader. He has freedom to transfer officers from one watch to another as needed, so that all the watches are not necessarily the same size. He can concentrate his patrol cars in a given part of the total neighborhood; take his men out of cars and put them on foot patrol; have them work plainclothes; have them follow through on investigations rather than turn them over to detectives, and so on. The supervisor can do all of this without checking with his central office. In addition, a team may have officers who do regular patrol work, but when possible concentrate on juvenile work or other specialties. The NTP concept not only helps to integrate the police with the citizenry in their neighborhood, but also builds on the strength of the police officer in-group.

Furthermore, teams can set their own objectives, such as the reduction of certain types of crime. Movement toward such objectives can enhance the self-esteem of police officers.

POLICE CHIEFS

As we mentioned above, police departments are subject to many cross pressures—from various groups within the department, from political officials to whom the department is accountable, from groups in the community who are concerned with the functioning of the police. Many of these pressures focus on one person, the chief. He is the public spokesman for the department on policy matters. He is the person to whom a mayor or city manager turns with requests, mandates, complaints, suggestions about the department. He is the one who has to go to the mayor with requests for funding, for changes in laws or regulations. When community groups are angry at the police, he is the focus of their anger. When police unions attempt to negotiate with the department, the chief is the focus of the negotiations.

Like many persons who have to relate to different groups, chiefs are subject to stress just as the officer on patrol is. Balancing off various group pressures is not only an intellectually difficult matter but is also an emotionally charged activity. In his day-to-day work, the chief is on his own, with no peers to provide support and no group to whom he can express his feelings freely. He may be in touch with other chiefs from time to time, but basically he is alone.

The chief's problems are aggravated by the fact that he is not really a "chief," since he has only limited control over his department, especially over the use of discretion on the streets. Not only can this lack of control frustrate a chief and make him feel ineffectual on occasion, it may undermine his confidence in himself.

As part of the movement toward increased professionalism among police officers, there has been a recent increase in the number of well-educated chiefs. A study by Pursley (1974) has shown that such chiefs are more liberal in political outlook and more interested in centralization of authority. However, what is surprising is that the more educated police chiefs tend to be more authoritarian than the older ones. Their great authoritarianism may reflect the difficulties they have in instituting new programs in their departments, especially since most were appointed from outside their departments.

SELECTION OF POLICE OFFICERS

Typical police recruiting practices begin with public announcements (through posting of notices and newspaper, radio, and TV advertisements) by the Civil Service Examiner, stating the date of the next examination for the position of police officer. Accompanying this announcement one generally finds a list of basic qualifications relating to age, health, and citizenship. Interested candidates are directed to make application at the local personnel office, where the individual generally fills out a form and receives additional information about specific qualifications required by the Police Department and Pension Board. There is also informal recruitment work. A study of the New York City Police Department (Hunt, 1971) indicated that by far the most effective recruiting resource was word-of-mouth, from police officers to family members and friends, that the Police Department was seeking new candidates.

In the typical recruiting process, many applicants drop out before taking the Civil Service examination. The high attrition rate among candidates for police work may be due to the extensive length of time between application and hiring. For example, in the New York study we cited above, the average time that elapsed between candidate application and their hiring was seventeen months. Even if at the beginning of the process a candidate's intentions were to take a police job if it were offered, with the passage of time candidates become involved in other occupations. In addition, other career opportunities offer "a bird in hand," and not the beginning of a probationary status (the police situation), which might terminate at any time.

We have already mentioned that minority group and female applicants have become the focus of very competitive recruiting efforts. The history of minority group members in our society has not encouraged entry into the police occupation. Many minority group members see a career in police work as placing them in the position of "renegade" from their own community, and it may mean running the risk of losing close friends and relationships upon entering a police career. Many young male minority group members see the Police Department as representative of a prejudiced, hostile, and oppressive force.

On the more positive side, qualified minority group members are finding better vocational opportunities that pay more and bring them less "stress" than would a police career.

Some insight into the complications of recruiting and selection can be obtained by looking at a program that was conducted by the City of Bellevue, Washington. Bellevue is a city of approximately 70,000 individuals. The racial composition of this city is approximately 98% white and 2% minority group residents; but Bellevue draws its employees from the Seattle metropolitan area, where the racial percentage is 85% white and 15% minority. The city determined that it would attain a racial distribution within the Police Department commensurate with that of the Seattle metropolitan area. (During its 25-year history, Bellevue had only one minority group officer who remained with the Department a short time.)

The Bellevue Chief of Police issued a strong written statement, affirming the Department's commitment to the hiring of minority group personnel, which was directed to every officer and posted as a general order to be read by all current police staff. A Deputy Chief was placed in charge of the minority hiring program. A psychologist familiar with employee testing was hired as consultant and assigned to work with both the Police Department and the Civil Service Commission.

The first act of the Deputy Chief in charge of the minority hiring program was to establish a committee whose responsibility it was to aid in minority recruitment. Both nationally and locally prominent minority group members were asked to serve on the committee. Other members included the psychologist, the President and Vice President of the Police Officers' Guild (to assure rank-and-file involvement), and a minority group officer from the Seattle Police Department. The Deputy Chief served as chairman of the committee.

The minority group members of the committee recommended that medical examinations be conducted by minority physicians as well as white doctors. They also were instrumental in establishing a practice test format for the written Civil Service examination so that all candidates would have an opportunity to see what the test was like before it was administered. Another of their contributions was to serve as liaison between the black community and with potential student candidates from local colleges and universities. Indeed, the minority group committee members actually recruited many individuals.

The next Civil Service examination was taken by 112 individuals, including 86 white and 26 minority candidates. The minority representation was at least three times larger than for any previous Bellevue Police Civil Service examinations. However, at that point the attrition process began. Seventy-eight persons passed the written examination, of whom 65 were white and 13 were minority group members. That is, only half of the original minority group and three-quarters of the white candidates remained after the first testing phase. One of the remaining minority group members chose to drop out before taking the physical agility examination. Forty-eight persons passed the physical agility test. Thirty-eight of those were white and ten were black and Latin. All minority group members passed the oral board examination and the background evaluation. Then the extensive medical evaluation process began. Two minority group members failed this test due to high blood pressure. However, the group had been warned that high blood pressure was a relatively common condition among young blacks and, after consultation with a black physician specializing in vascular disease, a candidate with high blood pressure was hired along with one other black and one Chicano. The remaining position was filled by a white candidate. By now all the minority candidates on the list had been used up (Van Blaricom, 1976).

An important phase of the selection process is the examination of recruits in order to find who, among a number of applicants, are actually qualified to be police officers. Police applicants are typically lower middle class or upper lower class individuals (Lefkowitz, 1977) who generally have a high school education or above and who have prior employment histories. If we chatted with the applicants as they were filling out their forms, we would find them to be enthusiastic, idealistic, generally lacking in knowledge about what police work is really like (Mills, 1969; Van Maanen, 1975), and strikingly different from the stereotype of the police officer as authoritarian, suspicious, and insensitive.

Police applicants also differ widely along a number of dimensions, especially insofar as past life experiences are concerned. Some come from broken homes, while others have always known the stability of an intact family. Some have excellent educational backgrounds while others have very limited school histories. Some applicants have been very athletic while others have never been very active in sports. Many applicants are married while others are not. Some applicants are unemployed while others hold good jobs. The list of differences goes on and on.

The evaluation process often delves into the motivation of candidates for seeking a career in police work. Not a great deal of research has been done into police candidate motivation. There are some findings that indicate that police candidates are primarily motivated by the need for security (Gorer, 1955, and Niederhoffer, 1967). Hunt (1971) collected data about motives of white, Puerto Rican, and black candidates and found that these groups differed in terms of their motivational priorities for entering police work. For example, white police candidates listed: (1) pay, security, and fringe benefits; (2) opportunity to maintain law and order; and (3) helping people (in that order) as motivations for entering police work. The black and Puerto Rican candidates listed: (1) maintaining law and order; (2) helping people; and (3) pay, security, and fringe benefits as their primary motivators. Lefkowitz (1977), in a review of research relating to motivations of police recruits, concluded that police recruits are lower than average in their desire to do autonomous work. Other studies of police recruits have shown that, on the average, they favor a more directive leadership style. Such a finding is not surprising, since (as we have noted) the typical police organization is paramilitary and candidates for police work might be expected to show that they are prepared to accept the existing structure. In this regard, Smith & Schau (1972) discovered that "the ideal patrolman" in the eye of the policeman (not recruit) is capable of assuming leadership "without being directed by higher authority." This, of course, is precisely autonomy. Perhaps those who indicate a willingness to obey superiors while seeking employment might be the same individuals who later prize the autonomous individual who assumes responsibility without being directed. Perhaps those things that we are willing to do in order to get a job might be very different from those things that we establish as personal goals.

It is also well to note that motivation and other personality variables are extremely complicated, and that the derivation of an "average" type results in a bland porridge. Attempts to describe *the* police recruit personality type have resulted in mixed findings seemingly related to national origin (Wilson, 1963), educational background (Hoover, 1975), race (Hunt, 1971), social class (Van Maanen, 1975), and so on. Matarazzo, Allen, Saslow, & Wiens (1964) found the typical police applicant to be very similar to the average male college student. There is simply no consistent evidence suggesting that the individuals who are attracted to police work fit the stereotypes of harsh, controlling people who wish to "lord it over" others.

Applicant examination methods in police departments often measure general intellectual capacity, or some dimension thereof, and require that an individual demonstrate the ability to read and comprehend written instructions. In fact, it has been shown that measures of general intelligence and reading skills are the best measures for predicting who will do well in the police academy, because the academy heavily depends on written materials in teaching knowledge and skills pertinent to police work. However, it should be noted that findings from studies attempting to establish a relationship between academy performance and job performance have been inconsistent. Findings of a positive relationship include those of Cohen and Chaiken (1973) who report that in general men with high IQs advanced through the police ranks to a greater extent than men with low IQs. Further, high IQ individuals were found to have received more departmental awards. Marsh (1962) discovered that candidates with written test scores above the 97th percentile of the original distribution of candidates were most apt to be successful as deputy sheriffs. McKinney (1973) found that the written examinations used by the city of Phoenix in selecting police officers was a valid predictor of on-the-street job performance but that written scores were much better in predicting academy performance than on-the-job performance. Other failures in the attempt to correlate intelligence test performance with later police job performance include those of Leiren (1973) and Van Maanen (1975).

Of course, there is much more to police work than IQ and reading ability. In order to discover the personal attributes which are related to good police work, we need to involve ourselves in a validation process like the one outlined in the following steps:

1. Preparation of a systematic job description to determine what an incumbent in the job we are selecting for is required to do on that job;
2. the derivation, from the job description, of a set of skills, personal characteristics, and other individual requirements for the performance of that job;
3. the development of candidate evaluation methods (tests, etc.) that reliably sample the skills, characteristics, etc., determined to be necessary for the job;
4. validation by correlating test scores with actual job performance measures.

There is really no other way of showing (and therefore knowing) that examination methods adequately predict job performance. We must get into a police car and see what the officer sees while he works. We would want to spend time in observation of patrol officers at work during each of the three different shifts that comprise the full twenty-four-hour coverage offered by the police department, since police duties and activity levels might vary among different shifts. We would also want to observe officers at work in different sectors and neighborhoods where varying police services might be required.

Among other things, we might observe that the officer works alone and receives calls for service through a two-way radio. After we had spent several hours in observation on each of the shifts, we would likely note that police work is often dull and only occasionally very exciting. We might be somewhat surprised to find that the vast majority of the police officer's work is service rather than crime oriented (Wilson, 1963, Lefkowitz, 1977), and that approximately 80 to 85 percent of police duties are of a minor criminal or service nature (e.g., directing traffic, giving directions to lost motorists, finding lost children, settling neighbor disputes, etc.).

We would also be quite impressed with the power the police officer has. This power becomes especially obvious under conditions where criminal action has taken place. Take the following two situations as examples of what a patrol officer might be called upon to handle at any time. As you read the situations, put yourself into the officers' shoes, as it were, in order to better appreciate the decisions they face and the factors which might influence how they respond.

Situation 1:

It is 11 o'clock on a weekday night. Two patrol officers observe an automobile go through a red light and begin to pursue. Upon turning on siren and lights, they notice the driver of the car look over his shoulder, make an obscene gesture at them, and speed up. The police car is now in pursuit of a car whose driver is breaking many traffic laws, thereby endangering the lives of other motorists (and of the officers). The driver of the police car notices that his partner (a married man, veteran of twelve years in the department, and the father of four children) has become tense. His feet are pressed to the floor;—every time the vehicle being pursued runs another red light he mutters under his breath. The driver of the police car feels himself become angry and frightened. Vehicle speed is around 70 miles an hour now, and the car they are pursuing just barely misses hitting three pedestrians. The nondriving officer is "calmly" informing radio that they are in pursuit and is asking for other units to join in. Now three other police cars respond and join in the pursuit. One of the cars goes out of control and hits a parked car, and still the violator goes on at high speed. But he is now driving up a dead-end street, and there is nowhere he can go. The driver of the first police car has clenched his teeth and is breathing hard. The car that is being pursued stops at the end of the street, and the driver jumps out and begins to run. The officers in the first police car chase the suspect down the street. Suddenly he stops, turns, and says, "I give up. I guess I led you on a merry chase," and laughs.

Situation 2:

It is early Sunday morning. Two officers receive a family dispute call. Upon entering the residence, they encounter a very angry man who, upon seeing them, begins cursing and hollering, "You'll never get me out of here." The man's wife sports a swollen and bloody eye which she has obviously recently received, and is crying. The couple's ten children (one of whom called the police) are watching everything with wide-eyed fear. The man continues yelling, and one officer tries to calm him down. Suddenly the man tears off his shirt and says, "You're going to have to throw me out."

These situations, combined with our other observations, allow us to make some inferences as to the kinds of personal qualities demanded of patrol officers. The following are examples of some of the characteristics we may want to test for:

1. Decision Making

There are several aspects pertinent to the decision-making process. Decision making is essentially based on knowledge and information. The police officer's decisions must be based on a combination of knowledge about the incidents with which he deals and an awareness of the law and proper police procedure.

Aside from knowing what needs to be done and how to do it, the officer must also be willing to accept the responsibility, that is, the consequences of his decisions. For example, decisions to arrest or not arrest, to search a person or his home, to enter a closed or secured area, to physically intervene in a domestic dispute or tavern brawl, to use one's service weapon—these are decisions awesome in their potential consequences. Some of the consequences occur immediately; others much later when the police officer is asked to justify his actions to his supervisor or the courts. Individuals who are unwilling to face the consequences of their actions will not be effective police officers.

It is also not enough to know the options in a given situation and to have a willingness to accept responsibility for one's actions. The police officer must have the ability to act calmly and decisively on the information he has at hand. This requires the ability to think on one's feet and to act rationally.

In terms of the important decision-making requirement of the police officer role, it should be recognized that decisions required in this position are rather unique and are based on a body of knowledge (law and police procedure) not available to the typical candidate at the time of his or her examination for fitness as a police officer. Instead, we will likely have to assess the individual in terms of suitability as a candidate for *training* even while realizing that classroom training and actual practice are not necessarily comparable. Of course, this particular limitation is what has led to establishing tests for reading comprehension, memory, reasoning ability, and judgment early in the police candidate screening process.

2. Human Relations Skills

We have observed that in nearly all the officers' duties they have the potential for contact with other persons, many of whom are upset, excited, or disturbed. In order to be most effective, we might infer that the patrol officer must be able to deal with a wide variety of people under a tremendous range of circumstances. We might infer that successful police work requires that the officer be flexible, forceful but not provoking, efficient but not abrupt, emphatic and sympathetic but not wishy-washy, controlled but not rigid.

The patrol officer is required to size up strangers, sometimes under dangerous circumstances. The officer's decision-making abilities have little value if he or she is not an accurate observer of people. Decisions cannot be effective if the police officer does not have the ability to anticipate and positively influence how a particular person will respond to police actions.

Effective human relations for the police officer seems to depend on several qualities. For example, we infer that police candidates should be *motivated* to provide *service* to others. Further, we assume that the police officer candidate must have the ability to *predict* how others will feel, think, and act. This ability rests on the candidate's *sensitivity* to the most subtle aspects of behavior. It is also important for the police officer to be able to place his *communications* into language easily understood by all sorts of people of varying age, sophistication, and ethnic background. Based on the human relations requirements placed on a police officer, we might assume that the assessment of candidates could wisely include evaluation of their vocabulary and ability to understand and converse with others.

3. Emotional Maturity

Many authors note that police work is stressful (see below), and that police officers must be able to perform under conditions of emotional stress. The officer is required to act with an outward calmness in emergency situations which are characterized by danger, provocative elements, and opportunity for violence. The police officer must have the ability to suppress anger and fear.

Though police officers are not frequently asked to make life-and-death decisions, nor often required to deal with extreme danger in pursuit of their duties, the occasions demanding these abilities can occur at any time. This aspect of suddenness and of never being able to let one's preparedness lag is wearing. It takes its toll over time and is mirrored in the high physical illness and psychiatric casualty rate experienced by police officers. The effective police officer must also deal appropriately with the considerable power of his position. Under certain circumstances, the police officer may use force. At other times, the officer may search an individual or arrest him or enter his home. We see quite easily that individuals who seek and enjoy violent encounters, or who glory in the power their position affords them, may cause escalation in violence by their attitudes and demeanor. Indeed, there is considerable evidence that violent individuals tend to remain consistently violent over time (Toch, 1969).

Sometimes an officer may feel that he has performed a highly competent and effective bit of police work, but may be greeted with criticism rather than praise for these efforts. Under such conditions, which are fairly common in police work, our police candidates must be emotionally capable of stoicism in the face of unfair verbal attack. This stoicism must be effective in not allowing the officer to be negatively influenced in future contacts with citizens. Despite negative feedback, we would hope that our officer candidate would not become defensive but would remain willing to re-evaluate his approach, to second-guess his decisions, to go through the agony of introspection so as not to become distanced from the citizens to whom he is ultimately responsible.

We need to recognize that the ability to deal with stress and stand up under stress is difficult to evaluate. Individuals who are currently emotionally unstable can usually be screened out. However, the long-term effects of the stress of police work can have the impact of undercutting a capacity for the handling of situations as a function of their wearing effects over time. Characteristically, it has been very difficult to predict with great accuracy an individual's level of emotional functioning and maturity several years in the future. However, new evaluation methods (discussed below) appear promising in this regard.

4. Communication Skills

The police officer's accurate observational skills, adequate vocabulary, and writing ability are critical to the process of justice. Much of the content of reports depends on the knowledge of evidence and police procedure which is taught in a police academy and in advanced training courses. However, we might assume that prior to selecting a candidate, his or her basic report-writing skills has been carefully assessed. We might wish then to include evaluation of vocabulary skills, ability to attend to the most salient aspects of situations, ability to organize thoughts and ideas in written form, and level of competence in basic grammatical structure.

Of course, interpersonal communication on a verbal level could be something that we would evaluate in conjunction with human relations skills to check for the candidate's ability to organize thoughts and present information accurately in a manner that can be understood and accepted by those with whom the police officer must deal.

5. Physical Qualifications

The duties of the police officer at times place stringent demands on the incumbent's physical capacity. There are a number of situations in which the officer must take physical action. Examples include the apprehension and arrest of unwilling suspects, breaking up fights, rescuing unconscious victims from burning buildings or automobiles, chasing escaping suspects on foot, scaling walls and fences, and so on. Police officers who cannot perform these kinds of activities will be unable to respond to some critical emergency situations where a citizen's life, or the officer's life, is threatened.

Unfortunately, though many police departments have physical examinations for police candidates, few follow up with physical fitness programs for veteran officers. Among the departments that do provide such follow-up, many do so in conjunction with an incentive program for physical fitness (e.g., Tielsch, 1976), with no real sanctions for failure to maintain physical fitness. It is no wonder that applicants have vigorously attacked entry-level physical agility test criteria which have not been imposed on veteran officers. Where these entry-level criteria have not been validated (at least with current officer staff) they certainly appear unfair. There are also those who argue for even more restrictive entry-level physical fitness standards based, not necessarily on job requirements, but on our current assumptions about what constitutes good health and physical fitness (Woods, 1976; Shanahan, 1976).

One physical characteristic which has received considerable attention is height. Many departments have established minimum height standards which exclude most women and many Latin and Oriental applicants. Because minimum heights had generally not been validated as predictive of job performance, they have been ruled as discriminatory hiring practices and cast aside by the courts. Recent research has attempted to correlate officer height (or lack of it) with frequency of being assaulted on duty. The data here have been contradictory.

DEVELOPING TESTS OF OFFICER CHARACTERISTICS

With our dimensions at hand, we are ready to develop some testing methods for assessing our candidate's level of proficiency in each of these areas. We might proceed in many ways. If we are fortunate, we might find tests that are preconstructed and are known to measure characteristics we feel are needed for successful police work. If there are no such tests, we will have to improvise.

In the past, the kinds of selection techniques that have been used most often are oral and written examinations. In a typical police candidate oral examination, the candidate is interviewed by two to five individuals familiar with police work. The interviewers generally ask standardized questions that are the same for each candidate. The areas typically emphasized in oral board interviews include interpersonal relations skills, poise, ability to communicate, emotional maturity, and motivation for a career in police work.

The following are examples of typical oral interview questions:

Why do you want to be a police officer?
How would you feel if someone called you a dirty name?
Have you ever carried a gun?
How do you feel about women working as police officers?
How do you feel about laws governing the use of marijuana?
If you saw another police officer taking a bribe, what would you do?

Oral interviews may last anywhere from a half hour to two hours. At the close of the interview, each of the oral board members rates the candidate. Ideally, this rating is done independently, though in some cases, the candidate might be discussed by the interviewers for a brief period before the evaluation sheets are completed.

Unfortunately, the oral examination has been shown to be a poor method for selecting individuals for police as well as industrial employment (for example: McKinney, 1973; Landy, 1976; Smith & Stotland, 1973; Ulrich & Trumbo,

1965). Reliability between oral interview raters (the degree to which the raters agree about a candidate's ability) tends to be poor. Because of the lack of reliability, the oral interview must be a poor method for predicting future job performance (see Chapter 10). Despite this fact, the oral examination continues to be an often-used police candidate selection method.

A number of written examination methods have been devised for police candidate evaluation. These include tests assessing aptitudes such as IQ, reading ability, observational skills, report writing ability, and reasoning ability. Because written tests are easily and cheaply administered and scored, they tend to be frequently given by police agencies as the first screening test, especially when there are many candidates to be examined. Unfortunately, Civil Service Boards often have borrowed tests from industry and psychology rather than using or developing police-related tests, and obvious validity problems are encountered under such conditions.

More and more police agencies are interested in relevant personality variables such as emotional maturity, resistance to stress, motivation for police work, interpersonal relationship skills, and so on. Typically, psychologists and psychiatrists attempt to measure these dimensions through interviews and a variety of testing methods. Just as with the oral examination, the ability of psychological interviews to predict future police work performance is questionable (Levy, 1967).

Many psychologists also use projective tests to assess certain personality dimensions. A projective test presents the candidate with a relatively ambiguous stimulus—for example, an ink blot or a picture of individuals engaged in an activity, and asks the candidate to describe these stimuli, or to tell a story about what he sees. Though there is considerable doubt about the reliability and validity of such assessment techniques; many psychologists continue their use. Again it should be pointed out that these tests were not constructed for police candidate evaluation, though specialized projective tests (such as TAT cards) can be devised.

The Minnesota Multiphasic Personality Inventory (see Chapter 10) is a very popular paper-and-pencil test for assessing police candidates. Many psychologists who conduct evaluations of police candidates use a battery of tests, including the MMPI. For example, the junior author, who serves as psychologist for the Seattle Police Department, utilizes the Minnesota Multiphasic Personality Inventory, the California Personality Inventory, a sentence completion test, a measure of current and general levels of tension, a measure of orientation to interpersonal relationships, a vocabulary test, and a test of reading ability. Unfortunately, the state of the art is at the level of screening out unsuitable candidates rather than of identifying superior future police officers.

Validity data relating to the use of written tests in the selection of police candidates is sparse. This is rather surprising, because many thousands of candidates are evaluated each year for police positions, and police departments have been using written examinations for many years in hiring police candidates. In his review, Lefkowitz (1977) found that there had been only eleven predictive validity studies published to date for all methods of evaluating police candidates. Wolfe (1970), Kent and Eisenberg (1972), Smith & Stotland (1973), and Cohen and Chaiken (1973) all indicate that most police selection methods have not been adequately tested because there are no agreed-on criteria or measures of good police performance. Of course, this point relates directly back to the necessity for establishing an adequate job analysis prior to developing testing methods for selecting suitable candidates for police work.

Some predictive studies have resulted in different findings for black and white police candidates. That is, different scores on the same measures were predictive of success for black police candidates than for whites (Baehr, Saunders, Froemel, & Furcon, 1971; Cohen & Chaiken, 1973; Dunnett & Motowidlo, 1976). The fact that different scores on the same measures are predictive of success for black and white officer candidates suggests that future research on police candidate selection should include analysis of other "homogeneous" groups within the heterogeneous sample population of available candidates.

"Situational" Testing

A noteworthy "new" method for both the selection and promotion of police officers is "situational" testing. (Note: Situational testing is actually not new and was used in World War II [see Murray et al., 1949]). One of the major disadvantages of written and oral testing procedures is that they do not, in general, require the candidate to do anything that approximates real police work. However, in situational testing (Mills, McDevitt, Tonkin, 1966; Mills, 1972; Kent, Wall & Bailey, 1974) the evaluator has the tremendous advantage of being able to observe the candidate involved in behavior closely similar to that called for on the job. Cronbach (1949), a noted expert on psychological testing, points out that the primary advantage of situational testing methods is that they allow for observation of characteristics which appear infrequently in normal activities, for example, bravery, reaction to frustration, and dishonesty. Cronbach further notes that the subject's desire to make a good impression does not invalidate the test, since he is asked to demonstrate actual behaviors rather than to talk about them.

In a typical situational test, a group of five or six candidates meet with a group leader and two or more observers who evaluate each candidate's performance. The candidates are informed that this is a competitive situation and that the evaluators will observe their behavior. In order to score well, the candidates are told, they must be active in discussing the problems brought to them and in enacting lifelike situations which will be given them. This sets a tone of stress and competitiveness and encourages each candidate to provide data about his or her beliefs as they relate to law enforcement situations.

The candidates are asked to discuss matters such as attitudes toward minority individuals, what it might be like to work with a female partner, and so on. They are asked to role play (play act as if real) relevant situations that might occur in a police career. One of the situations that lends itself to role play is what Mills (1972) describes as "the loitering scene." Here Mills tells candidates that store owners have been complaining to the police that a gang of juveniles has been making a general nuisance of itself by hanging around, obstructing store entrances, leaning on store windows, and making remarks at passing women. One shop owner believes that these juveniles have been stealing cigarettes and soft drinks but has not been able to identify the thieves. The police officer working that district (role played by a candidate) is to arrive on the scene and make contact with the gang leader (role played by another candidate), with the rest of the gang nearby (roles played by the remaining candidates). The individual playing the police officer is instructed to contact the gang leader, and the rest of the gang is asked to wait and see what will happen. Another complicating circumstance is added when one of the evaluators, who is role playing the irate businessman, contacts the "officer" just as he begins talking with the gang leader and says, "Officer, that is the punk who's been ruining my business. He is the worst one. Here I'm trying to put my son through college, and you let this trash stand around on the sidewalk and cause trouble. Officer, why don't you do your duty and run this riffraff out of here?" Each candidate gets an opportunity to handle this situation in the role of police officer. Votes are then taken from the group as to who was most effective in the role. Finally, the role players are asked to criticize their own performances.

There are some problems in situational testing, and these include its requirements for space and equipment and the lengthy period of time required for the evaluation. Further, specialized personnel trained in evaluating situational testing behavior are required. Recently, Gifford (1974) has presented data on a situational testing method in which films are used to portray situations for recruit officer response. The use of films allows for standardized presentation of situations and cuts down the requirements for space and time in setting up situations for candidates' responses.

Despite such innovations, as Chenoweth (1961) points out, the typical police selection procedure today, using physical and mental tests, an oral interview, background investigation, and personal references, is essentially the same as that used about 150 years ago in London, which resulted in the selection of 2,800 men, of whom more than 80 percent were subsequently dismissed from the force. To achieve progress, we need more validity studies based on systematic job descriptions and objective performance measures, coupled with creative assessment methods.

TRAINING

Training in most police departments is carried out in a two-phase manner, beginning with formal school training at the police academy and culminating in on-the-job training under the supervision of an experienced police officer on the street. The training segment in some ways also represents the department's last opportunity to exclude unfit candidates, since the candidate who has completed his training status is very difficult to discharge later.

The recruit is typically placed in a police academy to learn a body of knowledge in a classroom setting. However, in some municipalities a new recruit might be placed on street duties or may work in the jail or in some other police function for a period sometimes as long as one year before he receives formal police training at an academy. This happens because some police departments do not have their own academies, cannot start another academy class immediately, or have a shortage of manpower which needs to be filled immediately. When an individual spends some length of time in police duties before receiving formal training, the effects of the academy can be undercut. At times these "experienced" academy trainees are refractive to training, feeling they already know how things "really" are.

The recruit is usually issued a special uniform that sets him apart as a neophyte in police work. He will not wear a badge or carry a gun. His training will likely be conducted along one of two general approaches. In the stress approach, academy teaching staff treat the recruit strictly and in a formal fashion. Discipline is meted out for infractions of rules. Frequent inspections of clothing and physical hygiene are conducted. In short, in the stress approach to police recruit training a rigid line of demarcation sets the recruit apart as one who is "low on the totem pole" and relatively powerless. Discipline is exaggerated and threat of failure is ever-present. The goal of the stress academy is to place each candidate into situations which tax his coping ability so as to observe him handling difficult situations. In a nonstress academy, the general atmosphere is more informal and pleasant for the recruit. The line between instructors and students is not so great. Often, in a nonstress academy, informal banter is encouraged. The student is not ruled by discipline and fear. The expectation is that the student does not really need to be pushed, threatened, or prodded into good behavior. The nonstress training approach appears to be most like the job situation in the sense that it provides opportunity for the trainee to be self-motivating and relatively free of supervision, just as his job will require him to be.

Earle (1973) compared stress and nonstress classes at the Los Angeles County Sheriff Department Training Academy and found strong support for the superiority of the nonstress approach. He found that recruits trained in the nonstress method performed at a higher level in the field as measured by supervisory ratings, had a higher level of job satisfaction, and had a higher level of performance acceptability by the public than did stress-trained recruits. Despite such findings, some police academies continue to use the stress method, apparently feeling that this method provides them with a better opportunity for spotting those who are unfit for police duty.

In many ways the stress academy has much the flavor of fraternity initiation rites. Incidentally, it is also similar to the initiation period (usually extending through the first year) that confronts the beginning graduate student.

The goals of police academies in general involve the socialization of the neophyte into the world of police work. This aspect of training has been observed to have a remarkably striking effect on the personality of the recruit. Van Maanen (1975) conducted a longitudinal study of job attitudes beginning when the subjects were police recruits and ending two and a half years later. He noted that the beginning recruit is quite vulnerable to persuasion by experienced officers, for he has very few guidelines for directing his behavior. Van Maanen concluded that the police culture molds the attitudes of virtually all those who enter police work. Among the changes he noted were a rapid decline in motivation and no recovery of that motivation over time. Van Maanen observed that the police officer's commitment to the organization declined over time. Niederhoffer (1967) discovered a comparable increase in cynicism within the first few weeks of police academy experience. Similar to many other studies in both police and business organizations, Van Maanen found almost zero correlation (+.02) between academy rank at graduation (training performance) and ratings of field performance.

The socialization process of the academy is of course designed to encourage behaviors believed to be representative of good police work. Either these behaviors do not match what is required on the street, or what is taught and learned in the academy bears little relationship with on-the-job supervisors' views of adequate police work. It is also possible that certain behaviors instilled in the academy are wiped out by the generalized effect of street experience. Perhaps a combination of these factors is at work.

For balance, it should be noted that some investigators *have* found that training academy performance *is* predictive of later job performance (Cohen & Chaiken, 1973; and McKinney, 1973). It should also not be assumed that the lack of correlation between training performance and on-the-job performance means that training is worthless. Without formal training, the police officer could not function.

Van Maanen describes four stages of recruit socialization. The first is the Pre-entry or Choice stage. This particular stage is marked by whatever motivation the candidate brings to police work. In the first stage the candidate is treated as important, but in stage two (Admittance) he is now a recruit and is seen as the lowest on the totem pole and issued a uniform which "gets everybody in the same boat." The recruit learns survival methods by sitting at the knee, as it were, of experienced officers who tell "war" stories. Van Maanen points out that these stories build a common language and a set of shared interests attaching the recruit to the organization. Punishment within the recruit class during the introductory stages teaches the recruit that he can't trust his supervisors. He learns that rules are applied inconsistently, and, for his organizational survival, he learns to "stay low and avoid trouble," since the Police Department will notice your behavior in order to administer punishment but not to administer rewards. In the next stage (Encounter) the recruit has graduated from the academy and into street work. Quite likely he is told by his senior training officer to "forget everything you learned in the academy." He is treated as an apprentice and begins to learn through imitation. The heaviest emphasis for the veteran officer is on observing how the new recruit handles a "hot" (dangerous) call, because this is the big test for the recruit. If he handles such situations well, he is accepted. If he handles a hot call poorly, he will establish a reputation that is likely to follow him forever. At this stage the young officer learns how to back up other officers. He is reinforced for compliance with the "blue code," which in part means helping cover up for the mistakes and inappropriate behaviors of other officers.

Van Maanen discusses the fourth and final stage of police work as Continuance (the Metamorphic stage). Here the contradictory dullness of routine coupled with sudden change have the greatest impact on the police officer. He is now on his own and learns that the best strategy for dealing with the complexity of the job is to stay out of trouble. This may include the falsification of a report to protect another officer or an introductory comment from an experienced partner to a brand new recruit such as, "Being first don't mean shit here. Take it easy. That's our motto."

Once the officer has left the training academy, he begins his "practical" work on the street. Here he tends to be assigned to a senior officer for a limited period of time in order to continue his role as trainee. The freshly graduated recruit is not considered a finished product and begins a formal field training process that may last three or four months. Michael Roberts, a Police Department psychologist, in conjunction with police officer staff at the city of San Jose, has developed a highly systematic field training program which has served as a model for that of many other departments. Within this highly structured program, recent academy graduates are assigned to specially trained Field Training Officers (FTOs) whose responsibility it is to provide on-the-street training and to evaluate the recruit on a daily basis. In San Jose, the Field Training Officer program works the highest crime areas so as to assure maximum exposure and experience for the new officers and to provide every opportunity for rating by the Field Training Officer of the new officer in the broadest variety of police work situations.

The FTO program in San Jose serves as a final recruit evaluation phase and their experience is that this program fails approximately 25 percent of officers who come as fresh graduates from the academy. Obviously, the Field Training Officer Program in San Jose is a difficult program for the recruit in terms of frequent evaluations and the high risk of "flunking out."

One of the offshoots of the San Jose Field Training Officer Program is that the officers who serve as FTOs subsequently move through the promotional ranks more quickly than officers who have not served in that capacity. This would appear to be due partly to the fact that the FTOs are screened selectively before being selected as trainers, and the FTOs probably also learn a great deal as participants in the program, since they teach department policy and police methods.

We are confronted again with one of the obvious facts of life—that one of the best ways of determining whether an individual can perform appropriately is to actually observe him performing. This luxury of observing actual police work is not available early in the selection process as easily as it is available in the academy and field training stages. On the other hand, once a candidate has made it through the academy and into field training, it represents a loss of a sizable financial investment to terminate him. The expense of the process coupled with the psychological agonies of a supervisor terminating an employee's career make termination a difficult task. Also, termination in the latter stages of training, once the individual is wearing a police uniform, goes against the code of brotherhood in police organizations. San Jose attempted to meet this problem by providing lengthy training for Field Training Officers in the use of their evaluation forms so as to avoid meaningless evaluations. They also conducted feedback sessions between Field Training Officers and administrative and psychological staff on appropriate use of the evaluation instrument. Poor evaluations need not mean that an individual must be fired but could point to a need for training in areas where the recruit is showing poor performance. In this context, the evaluator need not feel that he is terminating the career of a candidate but instead may be opening the door to helping the candidate along by appropriately evaluating his behavior and allowing for training in weak areas. Perhaps the locus of power for determining whether a recruit continues as a police officer or not is the most important feature of the San Jose FTO Program. Unlike most departments, where the power of quality control lies ultimately in the hands of the Chief, who is far removed from actual observation of the recruit's performance, at San Jose the effective decision maker is the closest observer and is a fellow police officer of the same rank. The Code of Brotherhood, which can be so inappropriately applied at times, is broken in a way that promotes professionalism.

The conclusion of the field training program ends formal recruit training for the new officer. The final days of these programs are generally geared to gradually fading out the direction and support of the FTO, so that by the end of field training the FTO may be serving only as an observer, with the recruit performing all police functions as if he were in a one-man car. At the termination of FTO training, the recruit is not yet accepted as a veteran officer by his colleagues, but he is prepared to function in the relatively unsupervised manner expected of a veteran. Many police organizations will continue the recruit on a "probationary" status for several months after the termination of the field training phase, but the nature of police work, once formal training is completed, means that this probation will be relatively unsupervised.

EFFECTS OF POLICE WORK ON THE POLICE OFFICER

Police work has been called the most emotionally dangerous job in the world (Roberts, 1977; Wambaugh, 1975). This impression is based on the observation that police work seems to have the capacity to change the behavior and attitudes of those who practice it. Skolnick (1967) developed the notion of the police "working personality," based on the observation that individuals change as a result of their work in order to be functional on the job. He points out that the police officer must be suspicious or he will be fooled and possibly hurt. Skolnick further notes that the responses of the police officer to his job can come to spill over into his nonworking personality. There has been little dispute with this observation. Reiser (1973) has suggested the development of a personality constellation in some police officers which he has titled the "John Wayne Syndrome." Reiser notes that this syndrome begins early in the career of the officer and lasts three or four years. The John Wayne Syndrome is characterized by cynicism, overseriousness, emotional withdrawal and coldness, authoritarian attitudes, and black and white tunnel vision.

In support of the hypothesis that police work experience changes people, research by Niederhoffer (1967) found an increase in cynicism in police officers, reaching its peak at approximately nine years of service. Hadar (1977), who did a multi-attitude study of 800 police officers in Southern California, found that the years 4, 6, and 7 in an officer's career were the sensitive years when negative attitudes peaked. She found that cynicism was highest during years 6 and 7 and that the most powerful negative influence on attitudes was experience with violent crime. She also found that the most negative attitude-producing assignment was patrol (the first assignment for most police officers).

Balch (1972) reviewed the literature on studies which test for the existence of a fixed "police personality" constellation as differentiated from mere attitudes and other surface representations. He notes that there is not enough good evidence to support or refute the picture of a modal personality among police officers. He points out that the devotion of social scientists to the personality model has resulted in obscuring the important role that organizational and experiential factors play in shaping police behavior. Further, Balch notes, "We began with the assumption that policemen are very unusual people, set apart from the rest of the population by virtue of their authoritarian mentality. Now it looks like policemen may be rather ordinary people, not greatly unlike other middle Americans. We cannot even be sure that there is such a thing as a police personality however loosely we define it" (p. 117).

There is some evidence (Jirsk, 1975) that older officers are more alienated than younger officers and that patrolmen are more alienated than detectives and supervisors. As one looks at these data, the complicated nature of the effects of police work on the attitudes of those who practice this profession should quickly come clear. The changes that are observed appear to be, at least in part, a function of particular job experiences, age of officer at time of hire, type of assignment, and years of experience.

Balch draws attention to the importance of variables such as the nature of the officer's assignment. Other research supports this "multi-variable" relationship between personality and police work. For example, Carlson, Thayer, & Germann (1971) found that members of innovative departments were significantly less authoritarian than those of traditional (less innovative) departments. Tifft (1974), working in a large municipal police department, found that officers' perceptions of people were affected by type of assignment. For example, traffic officers described citizens as "just ordinary people" while patrol officers described them as "inferior, incapable of handling their own problems, and despicable." In the same study, tactical force officers described citizens as "anti-police" while detectives resented citizens for their non-cooperation. Tifft also noted (as did Skolnick) that suspicion, distrust, and cynicism emerged as traits that proved useful in interrogation and investigative work as a police officer. On the whole, however, Tifft found that regardless of assignment, officers generally developed an attitude of friendliness.

Though our attempts to develop an understanding of the effects of police work on the police officer have not yielded consistent findings in the personality area, another major body of research into the effects of police work appears more consistent. Data from medical, sociological, and psychological sources indicate that members of the police profession are subject to higher than average rates of psychosomatic illness including circulatory diseases, arthritis, diabetes, ulcers, and allergies. From these and other observations, a unifying concept, namely that of the *stressful* nature of police work, has emerged.

We must recall that the disproportionate frequency of psychosomatic illnesses and of premature death due to natural causes observed in the police occupation (Richard & Fell, 1975) occurs despite the fact that police officers, at the time they are selected as recruits, are very healthy physical specimens. Indeed, police officers are generally selected *because* they are in good physical and emotional condition.

In order to best understand how stress plays its role in the police occupation, it is necessary to develop a working definition of stress. Selye (1956) described three distinct stages in the stress response, which he also called the *general adaptation syndrome*. The first is the "alarm reaction," consisting of neural activation of the pituitary gland causing secretion of ACTH, a hormone which stimulates the adrenal cortex to release its own corticoid hormones. These hormones, among other things, cause increased muscle tone, increased heart rate, and deepening of breathing. The alarm reaction prepares the organism to deal with whatever changes it faces. The second stage is called "resistance." During this period, further physiochemical processes center on the specific sphere of the body which is under primary stress. At the same time there is a decrement in the body's overall adaptive capacity and flexibility. Under prolonged periods of stress the organism enters the third stage, "exhaustion." At this point either death or marked physiological deterioration occurs.

While the stress response prepares us to better deal with our environment and is, thus, adaptive, Selye notes that no organism can exist in a prolonged state of alarm. Under such conditions, resistance is undercut and disease states, including emotional and physical symptoms, occur.

A number of indicators support the view that stress has debilitating effects on the law enforcement profession. We noted the divorce rate among police officers, which is estimated to be nearly 70 percent within the first three years of employment in the police occupation (Roberts, 1977). Police officers have been found to have the third highest rate of suicide of all occupations

(Richard & Fell, 1975). In fact, suicide among police officers has been observed to occur at a rate six and a half times that for the national average among white males (Friedman, 1968), though this figure may vary across departments.

Researchers and practitioners involved with police organizations have identified many sources of stress in police work. Eisenberg (1975), an industrial psychologist who has worked as a police officer, has listed thirty-three sources of psychological stress, which he grouped within six major categories. The work of others (Kroes, Margolis, & Hurrell, 1974; Reiser, 1974; Caplan, 1975; Sarason, Johnson, & Berberich, in press) lists other occupational stressors for police officers. Among the most frequently cited are the frustrating relationship of the police officer with other elements of the criminal justice system (especially the courts), excessive responsibility for the lives of other human beings, negative public image, job complexity, and fear- and anger-provoking duty situations.

STRESS AND THE EMOTIONS OF FEAR AND ANGER IN POLICE WORK

Stress reactions potentiate "fight-or-flight" responses. That is, the organism in stress is prepared to run away or to enter combat. Because we need the police officer to respond in a controlled fashion, we expect him to control his fighting and running away. Yet sometimes feelings of fear or aggressiveness overcome the officer. The officer who acts afraid by failing to back his partner, by leaving the scene of a confrontation, or by running away in any manner is generally not tolerated within a police organization. The police organization attempts to identify the fearful individual early and weed him out.

On the other hand, the overly aggressive officer is not always so obvious. His activity level, that is, number of citizen contacts and arrests, may be high. He is, indeed, working, and tends to be respected by his colleagues for doing his job and living up to the picture of a capable hard worker.

This area of police aggression deserves special attention. There is some need to focus on why or how officers become aggressive. First, it is useful to note that many of the stressors associated with police work bring on frustration and that frustration may lead to aggression (Berkowitz, 1969). Some support for the accuracy of the frustration-aggression hypothesis within police work is provided by Morrison & Hale (1974) who compared three departments in terms of number of assaults on police officers. He found that the worst rated (most frustrated) department had the highest rate of officers being assaulted, which is a reliable measure of officer aggressivity (Toch, 1969). He also found that assaulted officers have a more negative view of their organization than nonassaulted officers. Black and Reiss (1967) found that violence occurs when the police officer feels his authority is not respected by the citizen, and is more likely to occur against offenders than non-offenders, and when there are no witnesses around rather than when witnesses are present. The research of Westley (1970) supports the notion that threats to the authority of the officer are a primary source of police violence. Westley notes that the officer responds violently to lack of respect of his authority because his frame of reference tells him that he *is* the LAW. Having reached that identification, the officer's ego is threatened when his authority is not respected.

There are correlates of aggression and violence among police officers, other than frustration. Toch (1965) notes that the "machismo" syndrome and lack of social skills can be preludes to violence. Guyot (1977) found another situational determinant of excessive aggressiveness in police officers. She observed that officers working alone are less likely to rough up citizens. Based on this research, self-selection to one-man cars was accepted in the police municipality which Guyot studied.

Skolnick (1967) points out that the more danger is perceived by the police officer, the less rule of law will exist. Skolnick speaks of the "symbolic assailant" and the tendency of the police officer to associate certain gestures, language, and attire as indicative of the possibility that violence will occur. He notes that since police do not want to fight alone and feel a lack of public support, police practitioners tend to feel anger and resentment toward the public. In support of Skolnick, Toch and Schulte (1961) found that after police training there was an increase in perception of violence by trainees. Police training appears to teach individuals to expect violence and, circularly, may, in some instances, bring it about. Toch (1965) indicates that the contradiction between the police view of themselves as "knights" and the public derision they sometimes receive leads to bitterness. This places the police officer in an adversary role which increases the likelihood that violence will occur.

The race riots of the 1960s, and the police violence in Chicago, Los Angeles, and other cities seem to suggest that when police officers are assigned to maintain "public order" among hostile citizens, the risk of inappropriate aggressiveness by the police increases. On a smaller scale, a propensity to violence has been observed to occur in situations where a number of officers are engaged in a lengthy car pursuit of an offender at considerable risk to themselves. The offender is then "punished" when the officers finally catch him and get a chance to vent their emotions upon him. It is very probable that situations that cause fear in police officers, making them do things that jeopardize their lives while apprehending a suspect, potentiate inappropriate aggressiveness.

It should not be assumed that a majority of police officers engage in an excessive use of force. Renner and Gierach (1975) and Toch (1969) found that the same small group of officers consistently from year to year had a higher frequency of arrests in which the subject resisted arrest than did other officers. These are the officers that Roberts (1977) calls "hyperaggressive officers."

Clearly, however, hyperaggressiveness cannot be tolerated. In fact, Toch suggests that *any* sanctioning of violence can lead to separation between the police and the public. He developed a program of peer review of hyperaggressive officers (see Toch, Grant, & Galvin, 1975). The officers were identified via their arrest records, particularly where resisting arrest charges were brought against the citizens whom they arrested. The officers were then referred to a review panel of fellow officers and were encouraged to examine how they handled their street duties in order to surface available alternatives. Within the peer review process, discussions focussed on positive methods for avoiding unnecessary obstructing-and-resisting-arrest charges in the future. Preliminary data on the effectiveness of this program were positive.

Other methods for attacking the stress of police work have been proposed. Reiser (1972) recommends the use of in-house behavioral science consultation to provide counseling, training, and research support. Indeed, more and more police agencies have decided to hire full-time in-house mental health practitioners. Police agencies which have done so include Los Angeles, San Jose, Los Angeles County Sheriff, Seattle, Dallas, New York, Chicago, Boston, and the Washington State Patrol. Many other police departments have hired part-time mental health consultants. By and large these agencies have hired psychologists because the training of psychologists typically includes clinical, educational, and research skills.

Though a variety of approaches are utilized, there are certain similarities between the programs of each of these police agencies. First of all, these programs offer confidential treatment to officers and family members who seek treatment on a voluntary basis. Some of the programs, such as in Los Angeles and Seattle, also provide evaluation or treatment for officers who are referred by superiors for disciplinary or other work-related reasons. Where an officer is referred by a superior for evaluation, confidentiality cannot be offered.

The practitioners in the psychological services programs within police departments have been able to acquire a great deal of clinical experience within police populations in a relatively short period of time. At a recent conference at the FBI Academy (1977), a number of psychologists were invited to discuss their findings with top police administrators of the nation's largest police departments. It appeared that family problems were the most frequently seen cases by each of the practitioners. Police officers were described by the practitioners as good treatment cases since they were highly motivated for change and tended to work hard to improve their situations. Alcoholism (a common reaction to stress) was suspected by all to be a significant problem within police organizations but difficult to identify and therefore difficult to treat. One department, Boston, had developed an alcohol treatment program which has realized considerable success in reaching police alcoholics, encouraging them to identify themselves and seek treatment. Other programs have not been as successful in dealing with police alcoholism.

As another method of dealing with stress, several police departments offer a personal stress management course for academy students. In such a course, Sarason, Johnson, & Berberich (1977) focussed on teaching specific stress management skills. These included skills in monitoring behavior, thoughts, and feelings, methods for giving "positive self-statements" (talk-ing to oneself so as to promote effective rather than ineffective behaviors), and methods of relaxation.[9] This course met with some resistance in the police academy but resulted in superior handling (as rated by academy staff) of certain provocative (anger-producing) situations when trainees in this course were compared with a control group of trainees not given stress management instruction.

Another example of a program that responds to police officers in stress is the Personal Assistance Team concept developed in the Seattle Police Department, where several individuals came to the department psychologist to discuss the psychological trauma they had experienced after being involved in a fatal shooting situation while on duty. They spoke of feelings of sadness and guilt for having had to take the life of another. These feelings existed despite the justified nature of the shooting. Nightmares, family problems, flashbacks of the shooting, and anxieties about being investigated by their own colleagues were openly discussed. Many of the anxieties were traced back to a lack of knowledge of what was to happen in the course of a shoot-ing review board and an inquest. Needs for information are especially high in individuals who are in stress.

In Seattle, the Personal Assistance Team consists of the department psy-chologist, the department legal advisor, administrative and supervisory staff, and volunteer police officers. The team members seek out any officer involved in a shooting situation, to provide support and information designed to help the officer and his family through the difficult time following the shooting.

One of the major obstacles to the implementation of stress amelioration programs is the lack of understanding among police administrators of the sources and effects of stress in their organization. Without the backing of top police administrators, stress alleviation programs (like other programs) face severe problems of implementation. Thus, the most logical first step in developing such programs is to promote stress awareness among police administrators. Once administrators have been sensitized to the negative effects of stress upon police personnel, formal training can be started. For example, first level supervisors can be trained in recognizing and dealing with stress-related responses in their subordinates (Reiser, Sokol, & Sake, 1970). They can be trained in basic interviewing and counseling techniques so they can talk to employees who may have stress-related problems. Also, they can be taught to evaluate the seriousness of stresses and to make referrals as indicated. Thereafter, programs can be designed to help the officer deal with the stress-related problems he encounters in his daily work.

NOTES

1. It is interesting that many police officers are in the military reserves to this day. Police Sgt. Olson may be Col. Olson in the reserves, with his police captain supervisor serving as his military sergeant.
2. Sergeants themselves make no claim that they do a great deal of directing of

their subordinates (Lefkowitz, 1972). In questionnaires, officers revealed that sergeants had little legitimate power based on recognized expertise, on officers' tendencies to identify with sergeants, or on the sergeant's ability to reward officers for good work (Tifft, 1974). Sergeants' attempts to direct are judged as unwanted intrusions (Balzer, 1976).

3. Joseph Wambaugh, in his powerful novel, *The Choir Boys* (1975) describes a group of officers who met often in a park in the early hours of the morning after their shift was over, ventilating their feelings, expressing their anxieties and bitterness, drinking and sharing female companions. Only with other officers could they feel free to express their feelings freely and relax completely.

4. Old-timers have been known to tell rookies, "Your job is not to enforce the law, but to make sure I get home tonight!"

5. Of course, many of these problems may not exist in departments in which there is a predominance of college-educated officers.

6. A black officer and his white partner had been together for a number of years in a ghetto area. They would frequently hear robbery suspects described over the car radio as "black male." One day the black officer exclaimed, as a report of an ongoing robbery came over the radio, "Lord, let it be a white, red-headed son-of-a bitch!"

7. Some departments have trained black and white officers to work together, but such programs have sometimes had negative effects (Teahan, 1975a, 1975b). Part of this negative effect may stem from the fact that the programs are generally imposed on the departments. When all levels of a department and the police union are involved in the search for minority officers and maintain high standards in doing so, the cleavages and the problems may not occur (cf Van Blaricom, 1976).

8. The policeman may sense that his wife is unable to share some of his feelings and thus may simply not talk about them at home. Furthermore, he may want to protect his wife and children from the more gory aspects of his work. He may feel that showing too much emotion at home will undermine his manly image in the eyes of his family. Communication may break down because of the officer's work shift, and because he is frequently late coming home because of a last minute arrest or other disturbance (Stratton, 1976). Parker and Rothe (1973) found that more experienced officers indicated less willingness to disclose feelings about their work and themselves to their wives. In any case, large segments of the officer's life remain unknown or inaccessible by his wife.

9. A similar type of course, offered by Novaco (1977), emphasizes sensitization to anger-producing situations and the management of hostile feelings.

REFERENCES

Baehr, M. E., Saunders, D. R., Froemel, E. C., & Furcon, J. E. The prediction of performance for black and for white police patrolmen. *Professional Psychology*, 1971 2, 46–57.

Balch, R. W. The police personality: Fact or fiction? *Journal of Criminal Law, Criminology and Police Science*, 1972, *63*, 106–119.

Balzer, A. A view of the quota system in the San Francisco Police Department. *Journal of Police Science & Administration*, 1976, *4*, 124–133.

Bard, M., & Shellow, R. *Issues in law enforcement.* Reston, Va.: Reston Publishing, 1976.

Berkowitz, L. Control of aggression. In B. M. Caldwell & H. Ricciuti (Eds.), *Review of child development research*, 1969, 3.

Black, D. J., & Reiss, A. J., Jr. Patterns of behavior in police and citizen transactions.

In *Studies in crime and law enforcement in major metropolitan areas* (Vol. 2, Sec. 1). Washington, D.C.: U.S. Government Printing Office, 1967.

Bozza, C. M. Motivation guiding police in arrest process. *Journal of Police Science & Administration,* 1973, *1,* 468–476.

Caplan, T. Job demands and mental health. *NIOSH,* April 1975, Publication No. 75–160.

Carlson, H., Thayer, R., & Germann, A. C. Social attitudes and personality differences among members of two kinds of police departments (innovative vs. traditional) and students. *Journal of Criminal Law, Criminology and Police Science,* 1971, *62,* 564–567.

Cascio, W. F. Formal education and police officer performance. *Journal of Police Science & Administration,* 1977, *5,* 89–96.

Chenoweth, J. H. Situational tests: A new attempt at assessing police candidates. *Journal of Criminal Law, Criminology and Police Science,* 1961, *52,* 232–238.

Cohen, B. The police internal system of justice in New York City. *Journal of Criminal Law, Criminology and Police Science,* 1972, *63,* 54–67.

Cohen, B., & Chaiken, J. M. *Police background characteristics and performance.* Lexington, Mass.: Lexington Books, 1973.

Cronbach, L. J. *Essentials of psychological testing.* New York: Harper & Row, 1949.

Davis, K. C. *Police discretion.* St. Paul, Minn.: West Publishers, 1975.

Dunnette, M. D., & Motowidlo, S. J. *Police selection and career assessment* (Law Enforcement Assistance Administration, U.S. Department of Justice). Washington, D.C.: U.S. Government Printing Office, 1976.

Earle, H. H. *Police recruit training: Stress vs. non-stress.* Springfield, Ill.: Charles C Thomas, 1973.

Eisenberg, T. Job stress and the police officer: Identifying stress reduction techniques. In W. Kroes, & J. Hurrell (Eds.), *Job stress and the police officer.* U.S. Department of Health, Education, and Welfare (NIOSH) Publication No. 76–187, 1975.

Friedman, P. Suicide among police: A study of ninety-three suicides among New York City policemen (1934–1940). In E. Schneidman (Ed.), *Essays in self-destruction.* New York: Science House, 1968, 414.

Furcon, J. E., Froemel, E. C., & Baehr, M. E. Psychological predictors and patterns of patrolman field performance. In J. R. Snibbe & H. M. Snibbe (Eds.), *The urban policeman in transition.* Springfield, Ill.: Charles C Thomas, 1973.

Gifford, R. Evaluating police recruits in an era of civil service transition. Paper presented at the annual meeting of the American Psychological Association, New Orleans, August 1974.

Gorer, G. Modification of national character: The role of the police in England. *Journal of Social Issues,* 1955, *11*(2), 24–32.

Grant, J., Grant, J., & Toch, H. Police-citizen conflict and the decision to arrest. In V. Konecni & E. Ebbeson (Eds.), *Social psychological analysis of the legal process.* San Francisco: Freeman, in press.

Guyot, D. The organization of police departments: Changing the model from the Army to the hospital. *Criminal Justice Abstracts,* June 1977, *9*(2), 231–256.

Hadar, I. National Conference on Police Stress & Personal Crisis. Federal Bureau of Investigation, 1977.

Harrison, F. Bureaucratization: Perception of role performance and organizational effectiveness. *Journal of Police Science & Administration,* 1975, *3,* 319–328.

Hillgren, J. S., Bond, R., & Jones, S. Primary stressors in police administration and law enforcement. *Journal of Police Science & Administration,* 1976, *4,* 445–449.

Hoover, L. T. *Police educational characteristics and curricula* (Law Enforcement Assistance Administration, U.S. Department of Justice). Washington, D.C.: U.S. Government Printing Office, July 1975.

Hunt, Y. C., Jr. *Minority recruiting in the New York City Police Department: Part I. The attraction of candidates.* New York: New York City-Rand Institute, 1971.

Jirsk, M. Absenteeism among members of the New York City Police Department on Staten Island. *Journal of Police Science & Administration*, 1975, *3*, 149–161.

Kent, D. A., & Eisenberg, T. The selection and promotion of police officers. *Police Chief*, February 1972.

Kent, D., Wall, C., & Bailey, R. A new approach to police personnel decisions. *Police Chief*, June 1974.

Knapp, W. *Knapp Commission report on police corruption.* New York: Braziller, 1973.

Kroes, W. H. *Society's victim—the policeman.* Springfield, Ill.: Charles C Thomas, 1976.

Kroes, W. H., Margolis, B., & Hurrell, J. J. Job stress in policemen. *Journal of Police Science & Administration*, 1974, *2*, 145–155.

Landy F. J. The validity of the interview in police officer selection. *Journal of Applied Psychology*, 1976, *61*, 193–198.

Lefkowitz, J. Evaluation of a supervisory training program for police sergeants. *Personnel Psychology*, 1972, *25*, 95–106.

Lefkowitz, J. Attitudes of police toward their job. In J. R. Snibbe & H. M. Snibbe (Eds.), *The urban policeman in transition.* Springfield, Ill.: Charles C Thomas, 1973.

Lefkowitz, J. Industrial-organizational psychology and the police. *American Psychologist*, May 1977, 346–364.

Leiren, B. D. Validating the selection of deputy marshals. In J. R. Snibbe & H. M. Snibbe (Eds.), *The urban policeman in transition.* Springfield, Ill.: Charles C Thomas, 1973.

Levy, R. J. Predicting police failure. *Journal of Criminal Law, Criminology, and Police Science*, 1967, *58*, 265–276.

MacFarlane, T. N., & Crosby, A. Police officer discipline: A study of experience and attitude. *Journal of Police Science & Administration*, 1976, *4*, 331–340.

Marsh, S. H. Validating the selection of deputy sheriffs. *Public Personnel Review*, 1962, *23*, 41–44.

Matarazzo, J. D., Allen, B. V., Saslow, G., & Wiens, A. N. Characteristics of successful policemen and firemen applicants. *Journal of Applied Psychology*, 1964, *48*, 123–133.

McKinney, T. S. *The criterion-related validity of entry level police officer selection procedures* (TR 1–75). Phoenix, Ariz.: City of Phoenix, Personnel Department, 1973.

McManus, G. P. What does a policeman do? In A. W. Cohen & E. C. Viano (Eds.), *Police community relations.* New York: Lippincott, 1976.

McNamara, J. J. Uncertainties in police work. In D. Bordua (Ed.), *The police: Six sociological essays.* New York: Wiley, 1967.

Mills, R. B. Use of diagnostic small groups in police recruit selection and training. *Journal of Criminal Law, Criminology and Police Science*, 1969, *60*, 238–241.

Mills, R., McDevitt, R., Tonkin S. Situational tests in metropolitan police recruit selection. *Journal of Criminal Law, Criminology and Police Science*, 1966, *57*(1).

Mills, R. New directions in police selection. Presented in a symposium, *Profile of the*

U. S. police officer, at the annual convention of the American Psychological Association, Honolulu, Hawaii, September 1972.

Morrison, P. M., & Hale, C. D. Perceptions of the police. Bureau of Government Research, University of Oklahoma, Norman, Oklahoma, 1974.

Murray, H., et al. *Assessment of men: Selection of personnel for the office of strategic service.* New York: Holt, Rinehart and Winston, 1949.

Niederhoffer, A. *Behind the shield: The police in urban society.* New York: Anchor Books, 1967.

Novaco, R. W. A stress inoculation approach to anger management in the training of law enforcement officers. *American Journal of Community Psychology,* 1977, 5, 327–346.

Parker, L. C. & Rothe, M. C. The relationship between self-disclosure, personality, and a dimension of job performance of policemen. *Journal of Police Science & Administration,* 1973, 2, 282–286.

Police Chief Executive Report. Washington, D.C.: Law Enforcement Assistance Administration, 1976.

Police National Advisory Commission on Criminal Justice Standards and Goals. U.S. Government Printing Office, Washington, D. C.: 1974 (0–557–053).

President's Commission on Law Enforcement and Administration of Justice. *The challenge of crime in a free society.* Washington, D.C.: U.S. Government Printing Office, 1967.

Pursley, R. D. Leadership and community identification attitudes among two categories of police chiefs: An exploratory investigation. *Journal of Police Science & Administration,* 1974, 2, 414–422.

Reiser, M. *The police department psychologist.* New York: Charles C Thomas, 1972.

Reiser, M. *Pratcical psychology for police officers.* New York: Charles C Thomas, 1973.

Reiser, M. Some organizational stresses on policemen. *Journal of Police Science & Administration,* June 1974.

Reiser, M., Sokol, R., & Saxe, S. An early warning mental health training program for police sergeants. *Police Chief,* June 1970.

Reiss, A. J. *The police and the public.* New Haven: Yale, 1971.

Renner, K. E., & Gierach, D. A. An approach to the problem of excessive force by police. *Journal of Police Science & Administration,* 1975, 3, 377–383.

Richard, W., & Fell, R. Health factors in police job stress. In W. Kroes & J. Hurrell (Eds.), *Job stress and the police officer.* U.S. Department of Health, Education, and Welfare (*NIOSH*) Publication No. 76–187, 1975.

Roberts, M. Paper presented to National Conference on Police Stress & Personal Crisis. Federal Bureau of Investigation, 1977.

Rubinstein, J. *City police.* New York: Ballantine, 1973.

Sarason, I., Johnson, J., & Berberich, J. Stress management training for police recruits. Unpublished manuscript, in press.

Selye, H. *The stress of life.* New York: McGraw-Hill, 1956.

Shanahan, M. A factor for survival: Police officer physical efficiency. *Police Chief,* February 1976.

Skolnick, J. *Justice without trial.* New York: Wiley, 1967.

Smith, D. H., & Schau, E. Perceptions of police performance. *Proceedings of the 80th Annual Convention of the American Psychological Association,* 1972, 7, 789–790. (Summary)

Smith, D. H., & Stotland, E. A new look at police officer selection. In J. R. Snibbe &

H. M. Snibbe (Eds.), *The urban policeman in transition.* Springfield, Ill.: Charles C Thomas, 1973.

Stoddard, E. W. The informal "code" of police deviancy: A group approach to "blue coat crime." *Journal of Criminal Law, Criminology and Police Science*, 1968, *59*, 201–213.

Stotland, E. Police feedback cycle. In V. Konecni & E. Ebbeson (Eds.), *Social psychological analysis of the legal process.* San Francisco: Freeman, in press.

Stratton, J. Pressures in law enforcement marriages. *Police Chief*, November 1975, 44–47.

Stratton, J. The law enforcement family. *FBI Law Enforcement Bulletin*, March 1976, 16–22.

Teahan, J. E. Role playing and group experience to facilitate attitude and value changes among black and white police officers. *Journal of Social Issues*, 1975a, *31*, 35–46.

Teahan, J. E. Longitudinal study of attitude shifts among black and white police officers. *Journal of Social Issues*, 1975b, *31*, 47–56.

Tielsch, G. P. Physical fitness incentive program. *FBI Law Enforcement Bulletin*, August 1976.

Tifft, L. The "cop" personality reconsidered. *Journal of Police Science & Administration*, 1974, *2*(3), 266–278.

Toch, H. Psychological consequences of the police role. *Police*, 1965, *10*, 22–65.

Toch, H. *Violent men: An inquiry into the psychology of violence.* Chicago: Aldine, 1969.

Toch, H. *Peacekeeping: Police, prisons, and violence.* Lexington, Mass.: Lexington Books, 1977.

Toch, H., Grant, J. D., & Galvin, R. T. *Agents of change: A study in police reform.* New York: Wiley, 1975.

Toch, H., & Schulte, R. M. Readiness to perceive violence as a result of police training. *British Journal of Psychology*, 1961, *52*, 389–393.

Ulrich, L., & Trumbo, D. A. The selection interview since 1949. *Psychological Bulletin*, 1965, *63*, 100–116.

Van Blaricom, D. Recruitment and retention of minority race persons as police officers. *Police Chief*, September 1976.

Van Maanen, J. Police socialization: A longitudinal examination of job attitudes in an urban police department. *Administrative Science Quarterly*, 1975, *20*, 207–228.

Wagoner, C. P. Police alienation: Some sources and implications. *Journal of Police Science & Administration*, 1976, *4*, 389–403.

Wambaugh, J. *The blue knight.* Walton, Mass.: Little, Brown, 1972.

Wambaugh, J. *The choir boys.* New York: Delacorte Press, 1975.

Weber, M. *The theory of social and economic organization.* New York: Free Press, 1964.

Westley, W. A. *Violence and the police.* Cambridge: MIT Press, 1970.

Wilson, J. Q. *Varieties of police behavior: The management of law and order in eight communities.* Cambridge: Harvard University Press, 1968.

Wolfe, J. B. *Some psychological characteristics of American policemen: A critical review of the literature.* Proceedings, 78th Annual Convention of the American Psychological Association, 1970, 454.

Woods, M. The University of Washington police officer physical efficiency battery. *Police Chief*, February, 1976.

chapter 3

The Psychology of the Courtroom

Charles Winick

The trial is so significant a nexus of the tensions and problems of our society that the courtroom drama is the single most popular format for television plays. In the decades since television became a national phenomenon, there has always been at least one courtroom drama on a network (Winick, 1974), a statement which cannot be made about any other program genre.

The interaction in the courtroom called a trial involves many assumptions about human behavior on the part of judge, attorneys, members of a jury, witnesses, and the law itself. Such subjects are of great interest to the psychologist and although we do not know enough to have a fully valid psychology of the courtroom, we can sketch some of its components.

The ethics of, and restrictions on experimentation with, human subjects make it impossible to conduct actual research on an ongoing trial, manipulating conditions and variables in order to explore the validity of hypotheses. Our knowledge must therefore come from observations of trials, interviews with witnesses and officers of the court, analysis of documents, and experiments involving simulated trials.

SOME PROCEDURES AND ROLES IN THE COURTROOM

After a defendant is arrested and arraigned, the charges against him may go to a grand jury, which can indict him. Once a person is indicted, a trial is the next logical step. The attorney and defendant must decide whether to plead innocent or guilty. Their decision will be based on factors such as the likelihood of conviction or acquittal, the judge's reputation, availability of witnesses, and the possibility of plea bargaining.

Most criminal cases are handled by a filtering process, which may include charges being dropped, defendants agreeing to plead guilty to a lesser offense than the one with which they are charged, applying pretrial time spent in jail toward a sentence or even toward a trial itself, or diversion programs.

In large American cities, over three fourths of all cases and nine tenths of those coming to felony courts are negotiated by plea bargaining, in which there is an informal negotiation over the lowest level of offense to which the defendant will agree to plead guilty, in exchange for avoiding a trial. The plea bargain often includes an understanding between the attorneys on a sentence as well as on an offense to which the defendant will agree to plead guilty.

With plea bargaining, a number of the defendant's rights are bartered away. The presumption of innocence, right to avoid self-incrimination, the right of appeal, right to a trial by jury, and the right to hear and cross-examine witnesses are lost in plea bargaining. If a defendant waives his right to a trial by jury, the waiver must be knowing and intelligent (*Dranow* v. *United States*, 1963).

Why is the filtering process so widespread that in New York City less than one percent of the recent felony arrests eventuate in an actual trial? In recent years we have, for a variety of reasons, witnessed a substantial increase in the number of persons arrested and charged with crimes. The resources of courts and prisons are under enormous strain. There are simply not enough judges and prosecutors to try persons accused of crimes, nor enough prisons to hold those convicted, and funds are not available to expand such functions. In New York State, for example, it costs $625,000 a year to maintain one judge and the personnel and other activities ("retinue") associated with his court. Our prisons are overcrowded and taxpayers are reluctant to give the criminal justice system priority on scarce resources. As a result, a premium is placed on moving defendants forward on a kind of assembly line, with not too much time spent on any one case. "Clearing the calendar" becomes a major priority.

Attorneys for the defense use their knowledge of the filtering process on behalf of their clients, as does the government. There is continual negotiation between the two, with the prosecutor attempting to get as substantial a sentence and the defense as minimal an incarceration as possible. Most public defenders spend a very large proportion of their time engaging in plea bargaining with a prosecutor. As time goes on, the two adversaries can often predict what will emerge from their negotiation over pleas, because they have been doing it so frequently and for such a range of cases. Because these sessions are private and because neither side is enthusiastic about discussing the details of what happens, it is difficult to identify the schematics of the negotiations.

The prosecutor has the most bargaining power, since his recommendation for a sentence carries tremendous weight with a judge. The defense attorney can bluff and pretend that he is willing to go to trial, knowing that the prosecutor does not have the time to try every case. The defense counsel can also bargain by obtaining continuances, so that the defendant is accumulating jail time, which will contribute to his sentence. Plea bargaining may take place in a corridor, in the office of the prosecutor, or in a judge's office, depending on circumstances and local custom. Ironically, the only person who generally is excluded from plea bargaining is its subject, the defendant, who has the greatest stake in the outcome of bargaining.

There is considerable hypocrisy in the conduct of plea bargaining (Newman, 1966). A defendant may say that he is entering his guilty plea voluntarily and intelligently and that no one has promised him anything or threatened him. In fact, his attorney may urge him to plead guilty; he may not be able to follow the legal terminology of the relevant charges; he may have been assured a specific sentence and threatened with a much longer sentence if he goes to trial.

A defendant is usually at the mercy of the plea bargaining system, which is contrary to the adversary procedure which is the official court approach. There is so much pressure to plead guilty in exchange for a definite but lenient sentence that it is a rare defendant who is offered such an arrangement and refuses to participate in it. The accused person's cooperation in plea bargaining may so be viewed as a sign of contrition for his. offense (Rosett & Cressey, 1976).

During the last decade, diversion of defendants outside the criminal justice system has become an increasingly common technique for avoiding the whole criminal justice process. Diversion is most likely to be an option in cases of alcohol or drug dependence, delinquency or youthful offender cases, and those in which an insanity defense is possible. In a diversion, the defendant is removed entirely from the criminal justice system and placed in a new situation, such as a treatment program, a community work program, or a mental hospital. In most cases, the diversion involves a period of supervised work in the community or incarceration in a therapeutic facility of some kind, rather than a correctional facility. There is often a fixed residential period and a term of residence in the community, successful completion of which may lead to clearing the defendant's criminal record.

As court diversion programs have emerged in the last several years, the defense counsel's role has become more complicated and he now has the duty to explore a variety of alternatives. The counsel must advise his client of the considerations involved in accepting a diversion program and the client will usually want to estimate the likelihood of being found guilty if there were to be a trial. In addition, he will attempt to speculate on the length of any sentence. The defendant may opt for a trial with a relatively short sentence if found guilty, rather than submit to an extended period of treatment and later supervision.

SEQUENCE OF EVENTS IN TRIALS

In those cases which are not disposed of by the filtering process, there is a reasonably fixed series of events and activities which constitute a criminal trial. Though the reader is probably familiar with the trial process, we can provide a summary of its highlights.

The trial may be with or without a jury. Assuming that a jury has been chosen, once it has been empaneled, the judge usually gives some guidance ("preliminary instructions") to its members on how the different aspects of the case will be presented, especially in terms of his role, deportment of the jurors, roles of the attorneys, cautions on not discussing the case with persons outside the jury, injunctions not to begin deliberations with other jurors until submission of the evidence has been completed, and the need to avoid mass media presentations of the case.

The prosecutor then makes an opening statement, summarizing what he expects to prove. The defense attorney follows, indicating the highlights of his approach. Both attorneys seek to create a favorable atmosphere in their opening statements.

A defense attorney may not make an opening statement until the prosecution has finished with its case. He might feel it would be more effective to wait until he is ready to present his case, or believe that any statement he makes early in the trial will be nullified by the impact of the prosecution's presentation. He will tend to make an opening statement if he feels that the prosecutor's statement has been effective with the jury.

The prosecution then presents its case by direct testimony from witnesses. After each witness' direct testimony, he or she may be cross-examined by the defense. When the prosecution witnesses have finished, the defense introduces its witnesses. After the defense attorney completes direct testimony of each witness, the prosecutor cross-examines them. After all direct testimony is finished, each side may present additional witnesses for rebuttal. Or, either side can reintroduce a witness for redirect testimony, after which the other side can cross-examine the witness.

If the attorney for either side asks a question of a witness or seeks to introduce evidence which the opposing attorney believes to be hearsay, irrelevant, immaterial, incompetent, or otherwise inappropriate, the latter will rise, call, "Objection, your honor," and explain to the judge why the question should not be answered. Many prosecutors and defense attorneys advise their witnesses, when being cross-examined by the opposing counsel, to delay answering each question until they see that there is no objection to it.

The judge rules, usually immediately, on each objection. Although the attorneys typically accept the judge's ruling, they may try to convince him that he is wrong by citing appropriate decisions, precedents, situations, or legal publications. If an extended wrangle over admissability of evidence takes place, the judge will often ask the jury to retire to the jury room while the matter is being debated.

A lawyer for either side who wishes to lodge a detailed and/or vigorous objection which might prejudice the jury will ask, "Your honor, may we approach the bench?" He will then go, along with the opposing attorney, to the raised platform where the judge sits, and state his objection out of the jury's hearing. The opposing attorney will explain why a line of questioning or evidence is appropriate, and the judge decides whether or not to modify his ruling.

Each item that is introduced into evidence will be given a number by the court clerk, e.g., "people's exhibit number 7," or "defense exhibit number 8." These items of evidence will be retained by the court.

The submission of evidence ultimately is over and the attorneys prepare summations. Each attorney, with the defense first, ranges over what has been presented and attempts the most favorable interpretation of the evidence, from his point of view. The other side's theses are downplayed.

After the closing arguments have been made, the judge instructs the jury, in his charge, on the relevant law and on the options available to jurors. He usually reads such "substantive instructions" in order to be sure of their precision.

The jury then retreats to the jury room and engages in its deliberations, which are secret and may not be recorded by any of its members. The attorneys and defendants wait in the courtroom until the jury announces it has reached a verdict, which is reported by the foreman. If the defendant is acquitted, he is released. If he is found guilty, the judge will often request a probation report before sentencing the defendant. Only a tiny proportion of verdicts in criminal cases is ever appealed, because of the expense and uncertain outcome of appeals.

Trial Tactics

How the prosecutor and defense attorney behave is crucial to their ability to achieve victory in the adversary proceedings of a trial. Jurors may be responding to the tone and manner communicated by the lawyers at least as much as they are relating to the evidence. Even in the process of excusing potential jurors from service, each attorney will be careful to do so in a manner which does not irritate or alienate the other jurors.

Lawyers for each side will make various motions to the judge before the trial begins. A motion may call for dismissal of the charges, argue that the jury panel is unrepresentative, request change of venue, request that the judge disqualify himself, ask that specific kinds of evidence be suppressed, argue that the court has no authority to try the case, claim that the defendant cannot get a speedy trial to which he was entitled, urge that the indictment was defective, or in other ways attempt to get the judge to engage in some action favorable to its side. Most motions are likely to be presented by defense lawyers. In general, the defense will make such motions to the extent that it feels that it will have difficulty in obtaining an acquittal on the basis of the facts to be presented.

Requests for motions are usually made in felony trials rather than those concerned with misdemeanors. In the lower courts, the penalties are less stringent, lawyers are less knowledgeable, and there is more pressure to move matters forward. Perhaps the most frequent motion calls attention to violation of a defendant's rights.

The prosecutor attempts to maintain a sense of seriousness of an offense, the need to enforce the laws, the responsibilities of the jury to carry out its functions, and hazards to the community resulting from consequences of crime going unpunished. He attempts to construct a case.

Prosecutors generally maintain a consistently aggressive attitude toward the defendant because such consistency may reinforce the jurors' feeling that the defendant has done something wrong. The prosecutor wants to avoid communicating any sympathy for the defendant. He will tend to avoid him during recesses and not use his first name. He will refer to the defendant as "Defendant Smith," rather than "Mr. Smith."

The prosecutor must present enough evidence to provide "proof beyond a reasonable doubt" that the accused has committed the crime with which he is charged. By the evidence he introduces, he creates a picture of what the accused did.

Defense attorneys attempt to generate as much positive feeling as possible toward their clients. They may stress sociological circumstances, like poverty, or conditions such as illness, which may seem to be mitigating. Unfriendly witnesses or police procedures or officials are likely to be castigated. The central issues of the case may be confused and the victim or complainant may be denounced.

If the defense attorney can find a way to introduce humor into the situation, it may help in diverting attention from the seriousness of the crime. Injection of humor could turn a jury's attention from a case's substantive aspects. The defense counsel will do everything possible to raise doubts, pick apart, and tear down the prosecution's evidence and approach.

The attorneys' demeanor, clothing, and appearance will have an impact on the jury. One consultant has published guidelines for what attorneys should wear in court (Anonymous, 1974). An attorney arguing a case in a big city, where judges are likely to have worked their way up from lower or middle classes, is advised to wear conservative clothes, avoid boots or soft shoes. In a small town, the South and Midwest, attorneys are urged to dress conservatively but with a touch of flair, like a club tie or silk foulard.

Prosecutors often glower at the defendant and other unfriendly witnesses. Defense counsel may attempt to be patient and understanding to all witnesses. Both attorneys are likely to have particular approaches to where they stand when questioning a witness, how to use sarcasm, walking round the defense table, and other "tricks" of communication and presentation of self.

The attorneys will object to testimony which they feel to be inappropriate. They try, however, to avoid objecting so frequently that members of the jury feel the attorney is trying to prevent significant evidence from emerging. Objections are used during cross-examination in order to ease a friendly witness' composure, or to imply what kind of answer is appropriate. An attorney may also, via an objection, try to bring to the jury material that might be otherwise inadmissable as evidence. The opposing attorney will presumably be alert for such efforts to bring in evidence via the "back door."

Both attorneys must be practical psychologists in terms of continually evaluating how their witnesses are coming across to the jury. Each attorney must estimate when a witness is beginning to bore the jurors, how to interrupt a witness who is rambling or is beginning to make damaging statements, how to prod a witness' memory.

The attorney for the government or for the defense may have the option of deciding whether to put forward the most powerful evidence early or late in the course of the presentation of his case. Presenting the strongest material last was found, at least in a simulated trial, to have more impact on a jury (Walker, Thibaut, & Andreoli, 1972).

This conclusion is particularly relevant for the prosecution's case. It is possible, however, that searching cross-examination may interfere with the effectiveness of the climactic order of presentation. There is also the possibility that witnesses may not be available on the day when they would have maximum effect.

The lawyer for each side always faces the question of confining his evidence to whatever will clearly buttress his case, or introducing evidence which will contradict opposition arguments before they are made. Although no courtroom studies of this option have been made, research conducted for other purposes has concluded that giving both sides of a position is more persuasive than making a one-sided argument (Lumsdaine & Janis, 1953). Dealing with opposing arguments in advance could convey a feeling of being equable and careful, especially to jurors who are hostile.

The attorneys will use their closing arguments as opportunities to deal directly with the members of the jury and to go beyond the direct presentation of evidence. They are likely to give opinions and make inferences as well as engage in hortatory and theatrical techniques of rhetoric and persuasion (Thibaut & Walker, 1975). In a closing statement, the defense attorney will usually remind the jurors of the presumption of innocence and the requirement that a defendant be proven guilty beyond a reasonable doubt.

Before the judge undertakes to change the jury, the attorneys for each side may attempt, via meetings outside the jury's hearing, to persuade the judge to include specific kinds of material in the charge. Each attorney will try to encourage material which will benefit his side of the case.

If a defendant is found to be guilty, the defense lawyer will make some comments to the judge, usually urging leniency. He often will also request that the defendant be free on bail pending the outcome of the presentencing procedures such as probation examinations.

The Defendant

The defense attorney must decide whether or not he will have the defendant appear as a witness. He may feel that the defendant will come across as a psychologically attractive person (for example, married, with a good job, without a police record, with a serious demeanor) and believe that such a person will make a favorable impression on a jury (Kaplan & Kemmerick,

1974). Where the evidence is ambiguous, such an impression may be important.

Physically attractive and well-dressed defendants are probably going to be viewed by the jury more favorably than others (Efran, 1974). They may also be expected to be more credible (Widgery, 1974).

If there are aspects of the defendant's background which might be perceived negatively by a jury, such as a previous conviction, and if the defendant may make damaging admissions on the witness stand, his attorney may decide not to present him as a witness.

Witnesses

The major modality by which evidence is introduced into a trial is via witnesses. They may appear voluntarily or be required to do so as a result of being served a subpoena.

Attorneys will usually tell their witnesses not to volunteer any information. Attorneys will generally rehearse their witnesses and go over the questions to be put to them in direct examination and may also try to anticipate and rehearse the questions that may arise during cross-examination.

A leading question is not permitted on direct examination because the jury should hear what the witness has to say without suggestions from the lawyer. It is permissible in cross-examination, the purpose of which is to demonstrate bias or raise doubts about the witness' accuracy.

Witnesses usually are cautioned by the attorney who is helping them prepare not to make their answer to questions sound too pat and rehearsed. When the attorney and witness role play, they try not to lose a sense of spontaneity for the actual trial.

The way in which witnesses frame their answers to questions is crucial. In one trial, the defense attorney told his client to seek to obtain sympathy from the jury by stressing his poverty. Asked by the attorney how much money he made, the witness said, "I make three dollars an hour." He then, to the dismay of his attorney, volunteered that, "I work seven days a week and, with overtime, make four hundred dollars a week." The additional statement made him much less likely to get jury sympathy.

Witnesses communicate nonverbally as well as verbally. Squirming, looking out the window, undue nervousness, blushing, and related behavior may be perceived by the judge or jurors and interpreted by them.

Buckhout (1974) has established that someone who is emotionally aroused, like a person who is witnessing a crime of violence or is a victim may be fearful and relatively unable to observe and recall what is happening. When a videotaped presentation of an attack on a professor was shown to a large sample of possible witnesses, 60 percent of the latter, including the professor, could not correctly identify the assailant. Eyewitness testimony may thus be very unreliable, even though it is generally welcomed in criminal trials.

The lineup, in which a witness is asked to identify which one of several persons is the culprit, may be a focus of a witness' testimony. Some psychologists have called attention to the need to distinguish between the factors affecting perception and recall of a criminal event and the variables operating during the identification procedures of a lineup, such as expectancy and group pressures (Levine & Tapp, 1973).

The defense may introduce character witnesses who testify to the defendant's sterling reputation for probity, socially constructive activities, general character, and similar qualities. The witness will indicate how long and in what connection he has known the defendant, their social activities together, and other aspects of the defendant's life which will reflect favorably on him as a solid citizen, with roots in the community. The prosecutor, in cross-examination, will try to bring out that the witness would not be in a position to know if the defendant had actually committed the crime with which he is charged, and question the recency of the witness' contact with the defendant.

Attorneys for either side can call expert witnesses, who are hired because they have special knowledge of some aspect of the case. Just as a pathologist may testify how long a person has been dead before the body was found by police, a psychologist could discuss whether a magazine appealed to prurient interest, a sociologist may testify that a specific kind of sexual invitation constituted prostitution, or a psychiatrist may speak as to the sanity of a defendant. In each case, the attorney will permit the expert to set forth his educational, experience, and other qualifications, including honors achieved, publications, and other evidence that his views are authoritative. The attorney will then, after the judge has accepted the witness as an expert, ask him questions that are relevant to the case. The attorney for the other side will attempt to undermine the qualifications and testimony of the expert and frequently will introduce his own expert witness.

The expert witness will usually use a technical vocabulary for the judge, and then translate into common-sense terminology for the jury (Nopto, 1973). He will attempt to strike a happy medium between arrogance and humbleness and avoid expressing contempt for the other side. Ideally, he will not become flustered but will maintain a cool attitude.

With any kind of witness, the judge may interrupt a lawyer's questioning at any time, to put questions directly to the witness. The judge does so if something said by the witness is not clear to him or if he believes it is obscure to the jury.

A lawyer may ask the witness a series of short questions and get relatively precise answers. Or, he may ask a global question ("Would you tell us what happened?") and get a less precise and more rambling answer.

Accuracy of witness' testimony may reflect the wording of questions. Asked, "Did you see the man?" subjects in one study were more likely to answer in the affirmative than if they were asked, "Did you see a man?" (Loftus, 1974). Asked how fast two cars were going when they "smashed into" each other, a higher figure was given than when the subjects were asked how fast the cars were going when they "hit" each other (Loftus & Palmer, 1974).

Judge and Jury

A decision that the attorney must make relatively early in his relationship to the client is whether to try the case with or without a jury. In some kinds of cases, a jury must be used. But in others it is possible to have a judge conduct the trial and waive a jury.

The judge and the jury were never formally created as separate institutions. The jury derived its powers from the judge's willingness to accept its verdict. In theory, the jury is still an instrument used by judges to reach a decision. The jury's verdict has no legal effect until the judge's judgment is entered.

The judge is the umpire in the court room warfare who has a role in jury selection. By his rulings on specific applications of law, the judge contributes toward the record of the trial that will be necessary in any appeal that may be taken. The subpoena powers of the judge enable him to compel the production of records and the appearance and testimony of witnesses. It is the duty of the judge to maintain order and discipline, and control the conduct of attorneys and other participants in a trial. The judge's power to set aside verdicts, to direct verdicts, and to rule on the various motions of counsel, enables him to dominate the course of litigation.

The judge sets the schedule of the trial—when it begins, hours of the lunch break, and how late it will continue each day. He makes the ultimate decision on what evidence will be admitted or excluded.

Most defense attorneys prefer trial by a jury to trial by a judge. A jury may be believed to be a more likely source of acquittal, perhaps because so many criminal court judges at one time were prosecutors. Even if the lawyer thinks conviction is probable, he may prefer a jury because appeals are more likely to be possible than if a judge is trying a case alone. A frequent basis for appeal is the manner in which evidence is accepted or not accepted during a trial. The attorney will make an "offer of proof" for the record to indicate what he would have introduced as evidence and why, if the judge had permitted him to do so. But if a judge is trying a case by himself, he can say that he is permitting the evidence for the time being, but will give it proper weight at the appropriate time. The judge's charge to a jury is another fertile source of errors which might later lead to appellate overturning of a verdict.

An aspect of the jury research done at the University of Chicago was an analysis of differences in verdicts reached by juries compared with a large sample of judges, polled by mail, in 3,576 criminal cases (Kalven & Zeisel, 1966). There was agreement between judges and juries 78 percent of the time. In the cases involving disagreement, the judge was six times more likely to convict than a jury.

In a national survey, where trial judges were asked their opinions of jury performance in criminal cases, 77 percent reported it was thoroughly satis-factory, 20 percent found it satisfactory if some changes were made, and 3 percent said it was unsatisfactory (Kalven, 1964). The judges tended to believe that juries were less likely than themselves to observe the precise letter of the law and more likely to be flexible. The judges surveyed felt that juries' favorable perception of defendant characteristics like widowhood, pregnancy, or crying was related to their leniency, especially if the evidence was ambigu-ous. However, other characteristics like arrogance or multiple divorces may lead to a jury's being harsher on the defendant than a judge would be. A defendant's lawyer is more likely to have an impact on a jury than on a judge.

In the case of victimless crimes such as gambling, juries seem to be more lenient than judges. They are also likely to be more lenient in situations in which the victim may be perceived to be contributing to the crime, as in rape, and in trials in which they believe the punishment is overly severe. In a few kinds of cases, such as sex crimes against juveniles, juries are probably more stringent than judges.

JURIES

Juries may be approached via the panels from which juries are drawn, studies of jurors' backgrounds, voir dire examination, effects of pretrial pub-licity, size of juries, and a review of their deliberations.

A jury involves a situation with group process, leaders and followers, analysis of information, implementation of values, persuasion, conflict, and a decision. Small wonder that psychologists have paid so much attention to the jury in America. The jury's primary role in a criminal trial is to determine the facts and the guilt or innocence of the accused.

In the United States, about 3,000 different courts use some 20,000,000 juror days each year (Bird Engineering, 1975). Chief Justice Warren Burger has estimated that jury costs come to $100 million per year (U.S. News, 1970).

One survey found that 6 percent of the general population had jury service during their lifetime and that 3 percent had their only direct con-tact with the court as a result of jury service (Kalven, 1957). Some 55 per-cent of the public, however, had been in court in some capacity, including 23 percent who had been a party to litigation, and 21 percent who were wit-nesses. Fifty-five percent of the public had known someone who had been a juror.

Of those who did not serve, 36 percent would like to serve, 48 percent would not like to serve, and 16 percent were undecided. But of those who had served in the previous years, 94 percent said they would like to serve again, and only 3 percent said they would dislike it, with 3 percent willing to serve again as a duty. The great majority of the jurors who actually did serve in a case, and did not suffer economic hardships from serving, would like to serve again.

Although there have been considerable changes in criminal codes, there have been practically no changes in the jury system. Its many alleged imperfections have been discussed, but such discussion seems to have had little effect on jury procedure, possibly because of the power of custom or lack of confidence in alternate procedures. Attempts to change the jury system have been attacked as attempts to upset the system of checks and balances which judge and jury present to each other.

The subject has occasioned novels (Postgate, 1940), first-person accounts (Zerman, 1977), best sellers by judges (Bok, 1941; Ulman, 1933) and motion pictures like *Twelve Angry Men*, in addition to extensive scholarly discussion (Busch, 1949; Williams, 1955; Simon, 1974), especially since the growth of the "legal realist" movement of the last half century (Green, 1930; Arnold, 1935; Frank, 1949).

Panels from Which Juries Are Drawn

On federal and local levels, jury selection is covered by the equal protection clause of the Fourteenth Amendment, which entitles all litigants to have prospective jurors selected from a cross-section of the community. This does not mean that a black litigant, for example, must have a black on a jury which is trying his case, but it does mean that the panel of prospective jurors should include blacks on some approximation of their proportion of the total population.

In recent years, defense attorneys have increasingly sought to quash indictments by arguing that the grand jury which handed down the indictment was not representative of all "cognizable groups" in the community. The Supreme Court has ruled that both grand and petit juries must be representative of all such groups (*Taylor* v. *Louisiana*, 1975). Sex and race are cognizable groups, and age has been accepted as such a group in a number of jurisdictions. A challenge of the array is a challenge to the entire jury panel, usually because it is said not to be representative of the cognizable groups in the community.

During the Huey Newton trial in California, several expert witnesses testified that most defendants come from lower socioeconomic classes, but juries tend to be from other groups, so that a trial by a jury of a person's peers is unlikely (Ginger, 1969).

Jurors in federal trials are generally drawn from lists of registered voters and are more broad based than state or local jury panels, which may use automobile registration and property and tax rolls as well as voter lists.

Uniform qualifications for federal jury duty are prescribed by law (United States Code, 1952). Jurors in state and local jurisdictions are usually selected by commissioners charged by law with this responsibility. Some states, such as Nebraska, Tennessee, and Virginia, have many specific requirements. Other states, such as Massachusetts, Ohio, and Delaware, permit jurors to be selected on the basis of relatively few requirements.

Many occupational groups, such a lawyers and other professionals, are often exempt from jury duty. Other prospective jurors may have schedule conflicts, be sick, have business out of town, or are otherwise unable to be present at the specific time that they are called. Groups that are underrepresented in juries include those with very low incomes and very high incomes and the very well educated as well as the very poorly educated. Exemptions and excuses usually eliminate from 60 to 80 percent of the persons on the original list of prospective jurors. The process of being excused from jury duty is conducted in camera. There is no real supervision of how and why decisions to excuse a potential juror are made. Officials tend to accept reasons offered by potential jurors for not serving, on the ground that a juror who is not positive about wishing to appear will probably not be a fully effective juror.

Many citizens refuse to serve on a jury because the pay is so low. Payment schedules vary from state to state, but the 2 cents a mile travel allowance and $5 per diem maximum in New Jersey, one of our wealthiest states, is not atypical. If an employer does not pay the employee serving on jury duty, he or she will probably suffer financially. Daily fees generally do not exceed $30 anywhere in the United States and payment for serving on a federal jury, which is higher than that in most states, is $20 a day.

In a study of three thousand jurors in a metropolitan court system, about half (1,557) appeared for service when originally called (Mahoney, 1976). Of those appearing, 27 percent did not serve. They were likely to be over 60 and to cluster in a few occupations, like small business proprietor, laborer, college professor; or in law-related fields, such as legal secretary. Being called but not actually serving on a panel decreases enthusiasm for subsequent jury duty. Some persons dislike jury duty because they are uneasy about judging others and uncomfortable in a new experience.

Studies of Jurors' Backgrounds

Lawyers have long been aware of the importance of the psychological dimension in jurors' behavior, on an impressionistic basis. They have sought areas within the prospective juror's personality which could be exploited by building bias into the make-up of the jury, arousing its feelings, and influencing the terms of its decision (Goldstein, 1935; Nizer, 1946–1947; Cutler, 1949; Belli, 1956).

The crucial role of juries in criminal trials has led to a variety of efforts to maximize the information available to attorneys on each potential juror. In several states (e.g., California, New York, Pennsylvania, West Virginia), commercial organizations sell "jury book" information to lawyers. These companies take the total list of potential jurors called at a particular time and compile demographic, police, credit, reputational, previous trial experience, and similar information on each potential venireman. The lawyers use this information in deciding whether or not to challenge a juror during voir dire.

In recent years, social scientists have devoted considerable time to helping select juries, usually on behalf of defense attorneys, via a "systematic approach." This type of approach to jury selection involves four steps: (1) a survey of preexisting attitudes and their relationship to demographic variables; (2) investigation of jurors' backgrounds by interviews with a network of friends and analysis of records; (3) ratings of the jurors' appearance and behavior in court; (4) analysis of how the jury that may be chosen will function as a group. Probably the first full use of this approach was in the 1971 Harrisburg, Pennsylvania, conspiracy trial of Father Phillip Berrigan.

In pre-voir dire investigations of a potential juror, the juror himself is never contacted, nor is his immediate family. Friends who are approached are asked not to discuss the matter with the juror, because to do so will be considered jury tampering.

In a number of highly publicized criminal cases, social scientists of the National Jury Project have used the systematic approach in helping to select juries (Schulman, et al., 1973). The Project typically conducts a sample survey of attitudes toward the issues in the case, in the community in which the trial will take place. The survey demonstrates which demographic subgroups in the population are likely to hold views favorable to the defense. The defense attorney, knowing the demographic characteristics of the jurors, can attempt to select jurors who are favorably inclined to his client's situation. Most of the cases on which the Project staff has worked have resulted in acquittal.

The systematic approach to jury selection increases the number of people involved in the assessment process. The more persons who are involved in such assessment, the less likely is any individual idiosyncratic judgment able to influence the decision to keep or challenge a juror.

In a relatively small and homogeneous community, attitudes are so similar that a survey will not be useful, because a survey is primarily relevant when there is significant attitudinal variation among socioeconomic categories. If there are only a few peremptory challenges allowed, the systematic approach is probably useless because the challenges will be used on conspicuously undesirable jurors. The systematic approach is most effective in developing a "good" jury from the middle ground of the jury pool.

In voir dire, lawyers and psychologists helping them attempt to interpret behavioral cues of jurors. Some kinds of juror behavior are easily interpretable by a lawyer, like a white woman who is visibly upset about sitting in the jury box next to a black male or a venireman who is curt with the defense attorney but expansive with the judge or prosecutor. More difficult to analyze systematically are behaviors like how the juror speaks, tone of voice, pauses in speaking, disturbances in speech, anxiety level changes and when they occur, changes in affect, eye movements, and body language.

Attorneys generally try to select a jury that will not have more than one or two leaders, in order to avoid a conflict situation once the jury retires for its deliberations. Attorneys also attempt to avoid zealots, who will be unyielding in deliberations. Peremptory challenges are employed by each side to achieve such exclusions.

Efforts are sometimes made by psychologists helping lawyers in voir dire selection to rate potential jurors as "persuasive" or "persuadable." There are certain kinds of people who have a general susceptibility to persuasion and social influence (Janis, 1954). They are likely to have high social inadequacy, high inhibition of aggression, and feelings of depression. By contrast, persons who are resistant to persuasion are likely to manifest persistent aggressiveness, social withdrawal, and acute neurotic symptoms. A persuasive juror who is favorably disposed toward the attorney's side of the case is, of course, sought. A persuasive juror believed to be unfavorable, or with unknown views, is avoided. A persuadable juror is often acceptable to the attorney even if he is believed unfavorable to his client (Berman & Sales, 1977).

In a study of a mock jury, a questionnaire measuring authoritarian and egalitarian attitudes was administered, after which a criminal case was presented via recordings (Boehm, 1968). The authoritarians tended to be "tough" and the egalitarians tended toward leniency in their deliberations. Lawyers try to assess how a potential juror might rate on such a dimension, with the defense seeking egalitarians and the prosecution favoring the authoritarian.

Voir Dire Examination

Jurors usually wait in a jury assembly room until a group of them is randomly selected and sent to a courtroom where a trial is about to take place, for the screening process called the voir dire examination. If a panel is to consist of twelve jurors, several times that number will be sent to the courtroom where attorneys and judge will examine them in order to determine their suitability for serving in the case.

The voir dire may be either individualized or group. En banc or group voir dire, in which all the potential jurors can observe the questioning of each one, may have the effect of giving panel members training in how to give acceptable but nonresponsive answers to the questions asked. The juror is in an unfamiliar situation, could feel threatened by it, and may conceal his actual attitudes (McGhee & Teevan, 1967). Many lawyers prefer to conduct individualized voir dire, out of the hearing of the other jurors, because there is no group pressure and the juror will have no models for behavior.

En banc voir dire is generally employed in most nonfederal cases. Questioning may deal with potential jurors' attitudes toward race, religion, ethnicity, political parties, women, personal experience with crime, police, youth, occupations and organizations, exposure to pretrial publicity, and a defendant's notoriety. Many lawyers use the group voir dire in order to help create a communal feeling, with the members of the jury serving as an audience for the attorney's theatrics.

The attorney conducting a voir dire examination has the problem of determining which potential jurors will be most sympathetic, while keeping the questioning away from important issues which might give the juror away as being favorable to the attorney's side of the case. By the manner in which the prosecutor and defense attorneys deal with the voir dire, they are already beginning to influence the jurors.

The judge is more likely to be active in the conduct of voir dire in a federal court than in a local or state courtroom. However, there are some reasons for questioning how effective a judge is in the conduct of voir dire. Potential jurors can conceal information because of their regard for the judge's role. The judge may not know as many details of a case as the lawyers who have been preparing to argue it, so that his questions might not be very searching. Voir dire conducted by a judge is usually relatively brief. Lawyers often dislike it because judges may be talking over the jurors' heads and minimize questions on jurors' background or attitudes. The lawyer, in contrast, tries to use the voir dire as a means of educating the jurors and establishing a relationship with them before the opening statement.

A number of studies have raised questions about the accuracy and honesty with which potential jurors answer questions during voir dire questioning. One study of the jury panelists during the trial of the "Camden 28" concluded that a considerable proportion of the jurors gave substantially different answers in private interviews conducted after the trial than they provided to the same questions during the formal voir dire at the trial (Murray & Eckman, 1974).

Investigators from the National Jury Project, who have studied juries in many states, have estimated that 25 percent of potential jurors believe that an accused person is guilty, otherwise he would not be charged (Fahringer, 1977). Thirty-six percent believe that the defendant is responsible for proving his innocence rather than that the state has the duty to prove him guilty.

If the voir dire examination indicates a specific reason for believing that a prospective juror will be prejudiced, his presence on the jury may be challenged by a lawyer for either side. Each lawyer is permitted an unlimited number of such challenges "for cause." Each lawyer is also permitted a fixed number of peremptory challenges, which permit him to disqualify a prospective juror without giving a specific reason for doing so. Lawyers typically engage in many more peremptory challenges than challenges for cause.

Peremptory challenges do not derive from the Constitution but represent rights of the prosecution and defendant. In most state and local courts, prosecution and defense have an equal number of peremptory challenges. A few states, like Florida, New Jersey, and North Carolina, give the defense more peremptory challenges than the prosecution, which is also the case in federal felony trials. In any jurisdiction, the trial judge has the discretion to increase the defense's peremptory challenges. In many states, the first juror chosen acts as the jury foreman. In federal courts and in other states, the foreman is elected as the jury's first act of deliberation. The life of a jury is usually two or three weeks, or until the completion of the case for which it has been assembled and at the conclusion of which it is dissolved.

Effects of Pretrial Publicity

In recent years, the likelihood of mass media publicity in many kinds of criminal trials has been substantially increased because of the increase in investigative reporting and emergence of special prosecutors, organized crime strike forces, extraordinary grand juries, and other activities which generate much publicity. There has always been some conflict between the public's interest in criminal proceedings and the defendant's ability to get a fair trial, but the conflict has been exacerbated because of the growing prominence of the media in crime reporting.

One way of attempting to insulate criminal trials against unfavorable publicity is the gag rule, through which the judge stops reporters and trial participants from discussing what takes place in the courtroom. In spite of the First Amendment, the Supreme Court has declared gag orders constitutional (Nebraska Press Association, 1976). The Reporters Committee for Freedom of the Press has documented 174 gag orders since 1966.

If a defense attorney feels that unfavorable publicity about a trial adversely affects a client's chances for a fair trial, he tries to show that the community has been exposed to such publicity, and that people are very familiar with it and tend to presume the defendant's guilt. The attorney may conduct a survey to demonstrate that prejudice exists and use the survey results to request a change of venue, which may or may not be granted by the judge.

The employment of surveys in order to determine the effect of pretrial publicity on potential jurors is so acceptable that such surveys have been commissioned and paid for by the courts. In the cases of the 164 American Indians tried in the Wounded Knee "rank-and-file" cases in South Dakota (U.S. v. Ackerman et al., 1974) the federal district court judge hearing the case in Lincoln, Nebraska provided funds for a survey of potential jurors. The court was asked to provide the funds under the Criminal Justice Act, which sets forth the conditions under which assistance may be rendered to indigent defendants. In another case, a local court paid for a survey in order to determine if a change of venue would be appropriate (Court of Common Pleas, Berks County, Commonwealth of Pennsylvania v. George Arms, 1975).

In the 1975 Jo Ann Little case (State of North Carolina v. Little), the defendant's attorneys argued that unfavorable publicity precluded her getting a fair trial for killing a jail official who forced sexual activity on her. State law requires that a change of venue take place to an adjacent county, but all twenty-one counties contiguous to Wade County were shown in a survey to have racist attitudes, so the case was transferred from the eastern to the Piedmont part of North Carolina.

In the most substantial experimental study of the subject, 23 juries in New York State were created out of actual jury pools (Padawer-Singer & Barton, 1974). One group of juries was exposed to newspaper clippings on a defendant's prior criminal record and his retracted confession, while control juries read news stories that omitted the presumably prejudicial information. Both sets of juries then heard the audiotape of the trial. A "guilty" verdict was delivered by 78 percent of the exposed jurors but only 55 percent of the control jurors. The experimenters concluded that there was a "definite impact" resulting from the newspaper stories.

There is likely to be considerable opposition to changing the venue of a trial. The District Attorney usually has subpoenas out for his witnesses and the court has cleared its schedule to accommodate the trial. Rather than grant a change of venue, a judge may order other remedies. In the case of *Common-wealth of Massachusetts* v. *Susan Saxe* (1976), in which Saxe, a fugitive, was being tried for bank robbery, the judge held a hearing to determine the amount of prejudice existing in the community. As a result of the hearing, the judge ordered individual voir dire and gave the defense thirty-two peremptory challenges instead of the sixteen provided by statute.

Size of Jury

Beginning in ninth-century France, the jury was originally a group of men compelled by the king to take an oath. The Normans imported this institution to England, where the jury was a body of men used in an inquest and not part of the administration of justice. The oath was a guarantor of veracity, and only the king could compel the taking of the oath. The beginning of the modern use of juries was due to an order by Henry II to the Grand Assize, that a litigant in a dispute about title to land could summon a royal jury. The men on the jury were called because they knew the facts in the disputed case, and were rejected if they did not. A litigant won when he got twelve oaths. This was the origin of the trial, of the requirement of unanimity, and of the use of twelve jurors. Twelve jurors were used because of the traditional English abhorrence of the decimal system and because of the English preference for twelve, as in the twelve pennies in a shilling.

A jury of six persons may, in some states, try misdemeanor and some felony cases, in accordance with a Supreme Court decision (*Williams* v. *Florida*, 1970). The court felt that such a jury was valid because of lack of social-science or other evidence that the size of the jury influenced the outcome of verdicts.

A jury with twelve members is more likely than a six-person jury to include a range of views on the issue of guilt or innocence. If a defendant's case is not strong, the full twelve-person jury is to his advantage because of the greater likelihood that it will be unable to reach a verdict.

In an experimental study of jurors conducted in a courtroom setting, six-person juries tended to have fewer women, blacks, and persons from a broad range of age and educational groups than twelve-member juries (Padawer-Singer, 1977). Such smaller juries would seem to favor the prosecution. The six-person jury also was more polite, examined the evidence less carefully, and was more likely to have secret ballots than the twelve-person jury.

Because of the small number of jurors, six-person groups engage in less deliberation than the larger jury. They are more likely to enter the jury room with their minds made up so that they are, in effect, polling their members rather than deliberating the case.

Jury Deliberations

Just what happens inside a jury room can only be inferred or extrapolated, because it is not possible to monitor a real jury conducting its work. We can, however, individually survey jurors after they have been discharged and we can set up mock juries, either from rosters of real jurors or, more frequently, from panels of students.

Probably the first serious research on juries was conducted by lawyer-psychologist William M. Marston (1924), using simulated juries. He concluded that female were better than male jurors. The juror's previous experience was related, Marston found, to his skill at fact finding. Written evidence was superior to oral evidence, and the self-confidence of a witness might have more effect on a jury than the logic or psychological soundness of other testimony. Direct examination proved to be a more complete and accurate method of presenting testimony than cross-examination.

Two law professors made the first empirical study of what happens in a jury room (Hunter, 1935). After a trial, they questioned jurors on various phases of the litigation on which they had rendered a verdict. They concluded that the typical juror does not understand the rules of law involved in a lawsuit and does not apply them to the relevant issues. Two federal judges later published the results of a questionnaire they had sent to 375 jurors on federal and state courts in three midwestern states (Hervey, 1947). Of the 185 jurors who answered, 73 said that they had not understood the judge's instructions.

The value of discussion among the members of a jury has been documented in two experiments (Dashiell, 1935). An incident occurred in front of a college class, two members of which reported it to seven jurors. Each juror wrote out his individual version of the story and then each jury reported on a version on which all the jurors agreed. The two original witnesses reported sixty-two and fifty-five percepts, respectively, with five and eight errors. The indivdual jurors reported forty-four percepts and averaged ten errors. After discussion, each jury agreed on an average of thirty-two items, but averaged only four errors.

Psychologists have explored the hypothesis that the opinions of a jury vary in the course of a trial (Weld & Roff, 1938). The evidence in a famous bigamy case was read to a group of listeners, who rated the defendant's guilt or innocence after each installment, using a scale of 1 for certainty of innocence to 9 for certainty of guilt. At the beginning of the presentation, the subjects felt strongly that the defendant was guilty and felt so even more strongly after the prosecution presented its case. They were less certain as the defense progressed. When the prosecution spoke again, they again began thinking in terms of guilt. After the next and last defense presentation, the subjects again began thinking in terms of innocence and the average final evaluation was 2, or innocent. In the next version of the experiment, all the defense material was presented first, followed by all the prosecution material—and the subjects voted 4.4. When all the prosecution material was presented first and followed by all the defense material, the voting again yielded 2. The experimenters conclude that the usual order of presentation, with the defense coming last, is favorable to the defense.

Jurors often carry their status and other characteristics into their deliberations. In the 1974 trial of former Attorney General John Mitchell and Maurice Stans for Watergate-related fraud and perjury, juror Andrew Choa, a banker, was the most highly educated member of the panel and had been able to arrange a number of favors and accommodations for the other jurors during their long sequestration. Posttrial interviews disclosed that he had been extremely influential during the actual deliberations which led to the defendants' acquittal.

One study with mock juries examined how the status of panelists affected their work (Strodtbeck, James, & Hawkins, 1957). In over half the cases studied, the foreman was nominated by one member and quickly accepted by the others. When the mock jurors had completed their deliberations, they were asked what kind of person they would like to have on a jury trying a member of their family. Most jurors, irrespective of their occupational groups, said they preferred to have a member of their family tried by a jury which consisted largely of proprietors. In general, jurors of higher status participate more than jurors of lower status, have more influence on other jurors, derive more satisfaction from their service, and are perceived as being more competent by other jurors. Jurors can size up the status of other members of their panel by obvious cues such as dress, speech, and references to previous experience.

One Chicago study continued the examination of the effect of status of jurors (James, 1959). A recorded criminal trial was presented to panels which totaled 204 jurors. In electing a foreman, the jurors usually selected someone of relatively high status. The jurors in this study spent about 50 percent of their time exchanging experiences and opinions, 25 percent of the time on procedure, 15 percent reviewing facts, and 8 percent on court instructions.

Juries sat in mock trials at the Yale Law School (Hoffman & Bradley, 1952). The researchers concluded that juries seem to try the lawyer rather than the litigant whom he represents. Juries often ignore a judge's instructions to disregard a statement previously made. Juries generally tend to disregard the rules of law, and they find the recollection of great masses of testimony extremely difficult.

Jurors seem able to evaluate the testimony of expert witnesses reasonably intelligently. In several cases studied, they appeared to comprehend specialized vocabularies used by experts and integrate such comprehension into their assessment of the facts (Kalven & Zeisel, 1966).

A related study, involving experimental jurors, concluded that over two-thirds had developed some opinion on the case to be decided and the opinion was confirmed by group discussion in the jury room. For 19 percent of the jurors, participating in a group discussion helped to modify the views they had previously developed. Many jurors concurred with the majority, but without being truly convinced.

In the experimental jury situations, there was no evidence that one juror was able to maintain a point of view in opposition to the majority and then convince the majority to shift its verdict. There was also little evidence that a jury could be hung by one juror's insistence on not going along with the others, either in actual jurors' recollections of their experiences in the experimental situation.

A large number of jurors were interviewed after they had served in an actual case (Kalven, 1957). In 71 percent of the cases, there was no unanimity on the first ballot. In 36 percent of the cases the split was at least 8 to 4. In 90 percent of the cases where the majority voted guilty on the first ballot, the verdict was guilty. In 97 percent of the cases where the majority voted not guilty on the first ballot, the verdict was not guilty. Hung juries which could not reach a verdict occurred only when the initial balloting showed a substantial minority. The perennial fear that one "strong man" could lead to a hung jury was not confirmed. A hung jury seems to reflect the closeness of the case and of a juror's feeling that his minority view can get several other supporters.

Almost all jurisdictions require the jury to return a unanimous verdict, but nonunanimous verdicts of guilty, in state courts, are now possible (*Johnson* v. *Louisiana*, 1972; *Apodaca* v. *Oregon*, 1972). If a jury cannot agree on a verdict, a mistrial is declared and the case may be retried.

In general, the individual juror's perception of the case will determine the whole jury's analysis of it (Stone, 1969). There appears to be a tendency for jury deliberations to advance a consensus toward a more lenient verdict (Izzett & Leginski, 1974), perhaps because of general acceptance of the notion that it is better to let a guilty person go free than to convict the innocent.

In some instances, the assumptions of lawyers are valid if viewed in the light of psychoanalysis. Juries, for instance, can clearly be induced to identify with the lawyer's client (Belli, 1956). Another psychoanalytic mechanism which may be helpful in understanding what jurors do is projection. It may be difficult for jurors to avoid injecting themselves into their observations of what the merits and demerits of each litigant's case might be, projecting some of their own needs onto litigants. Some jurors may not project their needs directly onto a litigant but may engage in the related mechanism of displacement. Their behavior as jurors is an expression of feelings which they did not express in other situations, such as at work or in the home. They might not be able to express their feelings about an employer directly to him, but they might transfer such feelings into a courtroom situation in which an employer is a defendant.

The juror's evaluations are likely to involve his self-concept, how he perceives other people, and his expectations of the behavior of people at different age levels who possess different physical and emotional characteristics. What he selects is a reflection of his needs, aspirations, life situation, prejudices, and previous experiences. Juror X will not overnight become a judicious evaluator of evidence merely because he is sworn in.

Studies in set (expectations based on past experience or needs) also are relevant to jurors' performance of their jobs. Cartoons have made us familiar with how the set of jurors can change when a pretty girl trips to the witness stand. The set of jurors may change less dramatically when other witnesses go to the witness stand, but it is certainly subject to change. A special kind of set is that of a juror prejudiced for or against a particular kind of witness. How important this may be can be seen in the derivation of the word "prejudice" from the Latin for prejudgment. Jurors may not wish to admit their prejudice when being qualified in routine pretrial examination, but their prejudice may assert itself during the trial.

Studies with simulated juries have generally found that they often are aware of and sensitive to the outcome of a verdict of guilty, even though they have the responsibility of determining innocence or guilt and are, in theory, not concerned with penalties (Goldman et al., 1975).

In an important and highly publicized case, the jurors may be sequestered for the whole trial. In other cases, juries can be sequestered only during their period of deliberation. Defense attorneys tend to believe that a sequestered jury, even though it takes its work more seriously, favors the prosecution. They feel that jurors will blame the defendant for their removal from family and friends and are concerned about the effects of the jurors being surrounded by sheriffs and other law enforcement officers, whose ideology may be pervasive. If jurors live at home, they may also be exposed to news about government wrongdoing which might have adverse effects on the jurors' view of the prosecution's case.

JUDGES

An understanding of the role of judges is facilitated by an examination of their careers, psychology, some factors in their decisions, and sentencing procedures. Our ability to generalize about judges is severely hampered by a variety of difficulties in access to data, since we cannot simulate the judge's role in the way that we can simulate jury functioning. Information on judges must come from their own decisions, reports, observation of their courtroom behavior, and retrospective analysis.

Judges' Careers

There are approximately 16,700 full-time judges, over 90 percent of whom are trial judges.

The exceptionally high status of judges and their removal from ordinary interpersonal contact is underscored by their robes of office, the judges' sitting above the general room level, and the rather absolute power of judges in their courtrooms. Great respect is generally shown for the office, which is usually designated by very honorific titles. Judges indicate awareness of the reification and depersonalization of their offices by referring to themselves as "the Court" or "the Bench." Many lawyers see a judgeship as a proper climax to a career in the law. Judges tend to come to the bench relatively late in their careers, after they have been doing some other kind of work. There is little formal preparation for the work of the bench.

Fifteen states, mostly in the northern Midwest and Far West, select judges by election in which they are not identified by party. Fifteen states, mostly Southern, select judges by election on the basis of party affiliation. Ten states, primarily Eastern, choose judges by appointment of the governor. Nine states, in the Prairie and Mountain areas, use the merit selection or Missouri Plan.

Federal judges are appointed for life by the President, if confirmed by the Senate. There is a long tradition that the two senators from each state will have significant input into the recommendation of a candidate for the federal bench.

Local judges tend to be appointed by the mayor or other chief executive. In general, local judges tend to be less qualified than state judges, who, in turn, are generally less qualified than federal judges.

In twenty-one states, mostly in the south and west, justices of the peace still handle some criminal matters. Most justices of the peace are not lawyers and many finance their activities on the basis of the fines they levy.

Psychology of the Judge

If we define "personality" as everything about a person which has a bearing on his relations with other people, then many different dimensions of the personal and social background of the judge are relevant. A possible interest in dominance, various personal needs, self-concept, ways of achieving security, and use of defense mechanisms like projection, rationalization, sublimation, repression, and suppression may all be important.

The behavior of the judge represents a kind of natural convergence between decision theory and role theory in social psychology. The judge makes decisions, but under circumstances in which his role is a reflection of other and previous roles and of group memberships. Any kind of multiple group identification creates problems for the individual. Different judges may have different reference groups with which they identify and which provide conflicting standards for decisions. These groups may include the leaders of the judiciary, colleagues on higher courts, the common man seeking justice, the impersonal majesty of justice, friends and interest groups in the community, the established power structure of society, an ideal of social amelioration, the lawyers who appear before them, and others. Conflict between the judge's reference groups must somehow be reconciled in his decisions.

Judges' power over others has been a source of concern to many students of the bench. Some may glory in the power, some may dislike it, and others may be ambivalent about it. It is possible that the power and dominance of the judge's role attracts persons who have an authoritarian inclination. Authoritarian persons are likely to see things in an either-or fashion, rather than in the balanced and democratic manner which is traditionally associated with the judicial temperament (Adorno, 1950). The process of socialization in office may temper the power strivings of judges.

Since our courts are based on the adversary system, in which points of difference and conflict are explicitly the foci of courtroom discussion, it is possible that there is some self-selection of lawyers who seek the bench because of their interest in this kind of expression of disagreement. Many years ago, in *Bleak House*, Charles Dickens expressed the view that there is a specific kind of judge who enjoys the battle of the courts.

The courtroom may provide an outlet for the kind of exhibitionism which has traditionally characterized actors and other near-exhibitionists. The judge has a captive audience, in contrast to the actor whose audience may walk out on him at any time, or not even buy a ticket to the theatre. No matter how egocentric the judge's behavior becomes, the lawyers for either side are hardly likely to complain about it. As is true of most professionals, but perhaps especially because the judge's name is affixed to his opinions, the ego of the judge is likely to be deeply involved in his work.

Judges' perception may be very important because their alertness in a trial is of critical importance to both sides. One example of idiosyncratic perception of judges occurred not long ago when a federal trial judge revealed, after years on the bench, that he always assumed that any witness who rubbed his hands while testifying was a liar (Frank, 1949). It is only possible to speculate on the number of unfair decisions which such a judge gave. One noted student of the law has reported that his task as a young lawyer was to drop books on the floor when a judge began getting drowsy (Gross, 1947).

The well-established difficulties of memory and cognition which plague witnesses are likely to be multiplied in the case of a judge, who is a witness of the witnesses, and thus perceives at two removes from the reality the circumstances which gave rise to a trial.

Some Factors in Judges' Careers and Decisions

When they are handing down decisions and drafting opinions, different judges may be talking to different audiences. Some judges seem to be addressing the general public in comments associated with decisions in sentencing, which may reflect the judge's belief in the power of his observations to deter future criminals, a desire to maintain a particular reputation, a wish to cater to public pressures, or a desire to keep his name before the voters for purposes of election. Those judges who seem to be communicating with their colleagues may be demonstrating their awareness of the human condition, or a flair for fine reasoning, apt citations, or legal scholarship. Or the judge may be giving his opinion in order to avert possible higher judicial reversals or to obtain agreement and support for his opinion at peer levels and from superiors.

The jurisdiction of a court may be related to the kind of decision which its judges typically make. The higher the level of a court, the more scrupulous is the care likely to be shown to procedural matters and the greater the concern for all legal rights and protocol. The area of responsibility of a court may be relevant to how its judges perceive their cases. A lower court, such as a magistrate's court in a large city, can, and almost invariably does, pass a case along to another court if there is any indication that the case is problematical, thus postponing its role in the entire decision-making process. A traffic court or a justice of the peace in a smaller community may dispense rough-and-ready justice which often violates the rights of defendants, but this may seldom be discovered because such cases are only rarely appealed to a higher court. Such a judge is likely to be relatively freewheeling in his decisions.

The judge who sits in the court of original jurisdiction, in his role as trial judge or sentencer is involved in the legal, interpersonal, and emotional dynamics of the small group in the courtroom. Even though together for a short time, the members of the court room group interrelate with each other.

Another variable related to the social structure of the court is the role of the judge's law clerk or legal secretary. He or she is usually a lawyer, and may have political connections or graduated from a law school with distinction. His or her role may range from legal errand-runner and citation-searcher through being a sounding board for the judge and a participant in making decisions in important cases. There is reason to believe that these anonymous law clerks may be important participants in some decisions.

Political pressures may contribute to the context of the judge's decision. Even though there may be no pressures on specific cases, the judge may not wish to offend those who have contributed to his past advancement, or may control his reappointment or renomination. Federal judges and other trial justices appointed for life are presumably above political pressures, yet they may be interested in promotion. Inasmuch as judgeships are often political rewards, there is likely to be an assumption of repayment by the judge, although such assumptions are apt to be tacit on both sides. Appropriate repayment may be in the form of judicial sympathy for the interests of the sponsors or former associates of the judge when prosecution involving such interests comes before him.

The American Bar Association has promulgated its own Canons of Judicial Ethics (Cheatham, 1955). These moral guidelines to judical conduct are based on sources like the Magna Carta (XLV), the Bible (Deuteronomy 16), and Francis Bacon's essay on judicature. There is some question about the extent to which judges are guided by the Canons of Judicial Ethics, but the relationship between the formal ethic and actual practice is a fascinating one for the psychologist to observe. The relationship is also one that concerns judges (Botein, 1952). It is difficult to tell whether judges' conduct is ever evaluated dispassionately by others in terms of how judges face these conflict situations. The fact that so few judges were removed from office by impeachment suggests that either judges' handling of these conflicts is impeccable, or there may be a feeling that judges' behavior is best left unscrutinized.

A number of the judge's personal characteristics may be presumed to enter into his decision-making habits. The age of the judge as well as that of the litigant before him may be relevant. Observers have noted, for example, that younger offenders are likely to get more lenient treatment from some judges than are older offenders.

A career on the bench has its own life cycle, and a judge who has just assumed his robe of office may perceive his duties and responsibilities quite differently from the way an older judge perceives his. In contrast to an older judge, the younger man may be very eager to make his mark. It has been noted that many judges tend to become more cautious or conservative with age. Other judges tend to become more confident and less susceptible to pressures as they grow older. With experience, some judges tend to become more reserved than they originally were in giving the specific rationale behind a decision. Aging is doubtless a factor in aberrant behavior of judges, and is particularly important because judges are generally named to the bench fairly late in life.

Ethnic, nationality, religious, and race factors may help or hinder a judge in being appointed, elected, or promoted. In American political life, judge-ships are often regarded as offices that should be allocated on the basis of these factors. These background factors may also be very relevant to the judge's judicial behavior. It is likely, for example, that a judge from a minority group might be very harsh on litigants of the dominant ethnic group, per-haps as one means of demonstrating some of his feelings about the dominant group. Another judge from such a group might be "soft" on litigants of the dominant ethnic group as one way of expressing his identification with the regnant group. But to avoid any imputation of favoritism, a judge from the minority group might be especially harsh with a litigant from the same group. Still another judge from the same minority group might be an exceptionally hard worker in order to demonstrate that he made his way to the bench on the basis of merit alone. In all these cases, the specific background of the judge would be directly related to his judicial behavior, though the direction of influence is impossible to predict.

The kind of legal practice in which the judge engaged before his appoint-ment undoubtedly has some relationship to the type of decisions he makes. A judge who has been a corporation lawyer is likely to see things differently from a judge who has been a criminal lawyer. Individual differences are im-portant because a person who was a criminal lawyer may become an extremely harsh and tough-minded judge when dealing with the kind of criminals he used to defend, either because he is reacting against his past, or because he believes in severe punishment, or for other reasons. Another judge who was a criminal lawyer may be relatively lenient toward his former clients because he does not believe in severe sentences, or as one means of identification with his past, or because of other reasons.

A number of similar dimensions of a judge's career lines can be distin-guished. They seem to suggest a typology of at least three different kinds of judge. The existence of such types has possible importance, because it is likely that each kind of judge perceives the bench differently, has his own motiva-tions for it, and thus may behave differently as a judge.

What can be called the Lower Level of judicial career development is the course followed by perhaps the great majority of lawyers who become judges. Such a person has usually attended a low-level law school and has joined a political club as well as a variety of fraternal, benevolent, and religious orga-nizations. This kind of lawyer will generally take all kinds of cases, perhaps even including some at the suggestion of political leaders. After years of faithful service to his party, such a lawyer will be given an opportunity to fill a vacancy on the bench. This kind of "ideal type" pattern is likely to be found in many courts of first instance and appearance.

A Middle Level pattern would typically include graduation from a law school which is accredited but below the level of the national law schools. Such a lawyer is likely to have a moderately successful and discriminating practice, but he is not with a first-rate law firm. He is likely to exhibit political leadership substantially above the routine service of the Lower Level judge, and to get a higher level judgeship.

The Upper Level judge is likely to have come from an elite family, to have been graduated from a national law school, and to have been a member of a well-regarded law firm (Miller, 1951; Mills, 1951). He is also likely to have held relatively important political office and to have demonstrated exceptional ability before getting a relatively high-level judgeship.

There are, of course, many judges who do not fit into these ideal types. No typology can adequately capture the range of judicial career patterns. Some lawyers may get to the bench because they are special friends of an unusually well-placed politician. Some lawyers may be wealthy enough to be able to give a large sum to their political party and, all other factors being equal, such a lawyer is more likely to get to the bench than an equally qualified person who has not given any money to the party in power. Some lawyers may be singled out for the judiciary merely because of their brilliance and knowledge.

By the time of Oliver Wendell Holmes' (1881) pioneering studies, it was becoming clear that law was the result of human experience. Up to the early twentieth century, writers on jurisprudence had generally held that judges were able to keep their personalities out of their decisions. Soon after the turn of the century, some students of the courts who were less "tough-minded" than the legal realist school (which held that the law was the decision of judges in particular cases—in contrast to the traditionalist view that the law consists of general rules) were developing the thesis that law is a form of social control. Some of the great exponents of what has been called sociological jurisprudence noted that even distinguished Supreme Court judges like Marshall and Taney differed in their interpretation of the Constitution, and that such differences are partially attributable to the different social, economic, and political backgrounds of the judges (Pound, 1923, 1938).

As long ago as the sixteenth century, Montaigne commented that the judge's mood and humor varied from day to day and were often reflected in his decisions. Legal scholars have occasionally mocked such nonrational aspects in a decision and referred to them as "gastronomical jurisprudence," or an explanation of a judge's decision in terms of factors like gastronomical ailments. Such factors doubtless do enter into some decisions but are hardly likely to be explicitly stated. Chancellor James King said, well over a century ago, in explaining how he reached a decision: "I might once in a while be embarrassed by a technical rule, but I almost always found principles suited to my view of the case. . . ." (Frank, 1930). Even Holmes (1881), perhaps the classic exponent of the modern approach to law, has said that "a decision is the unconscious result of instinctive prejudices and inarticulate connections," and "even the prejudices which judges share with their fellow men have a good deal more to do than the syllogism in determining the rules by which men should be governed." Justice Cardozo (1921) stated that forces which judge "do not recognize and cannot name have been tugging at them . . . and the result is an outlook on life . . ."

One federal judge, after years of service, concluded that he reached his decisions by hunch or feeling: "I . . . give my imagination play, and brooding . . . wait for the feeling, the hunch—that intuitive flash of understanding . . ." (Hutcheson, 1929). Frank (1949) has pointed out that the "sentence" which the judge pronounces comes from the Latin verb *sentire*, which means "to feel," and that the judge experiences his decision on an emotional level. In a decision, he wrote that "much harm is done by the myth that merely by putting on a black robe, and taking the oath of office as a judge, a man ceases to be human. . . . If the judge did not form judgments of the actors in those courthouse dramas called trials, he could never render decisions."

Supreme Court Justice Jackson (1944) frankly stated: "I know that in this great mass of opinions by men of different temperaments and qualifications and viewpoints, writing at different times and under varying local influences, some printed judicial word may be found to support almost any plausible proposition." This supports the proposition we noted in Chapter 1 that the judge first reaches his decision and then may look for a precedent to document it, in contrast to the usual view that the precedent search precedes the decision.

A number of judges have frankly stated that they reach their decisions by an intuitive Gestalt impression of the case and its issues. If there are many judges who do reach their decisions in this way, the implications for juridical science are central: it is like the difference between explaining a particular learning phenomenon in Gestalt principles in contrast to the traditional theory that judges reach their decisions by a logical process akin to learning theory. Among the possible implications for the student of the bench is that the precedents and legal reasoning cited by the judge may not actually be the rationale for some decisions.

One authority who conducted psychological studies of judicial decisions said flatly that every judicial opinion "amounts to a confession" by the judge (Schroeder, 1918). He presented a hypothetical case in which the judge's decision was a direct reflection of "fearful phantasies from his own past," instead of a wise adjudication. An early student of personal factors in decisions examined how different New York magistrates were handling the same offense (Haines, 1923). The proportion of cases dismissed ranged from 6.7 percent for one magistrate to 73.7 percent for another. One magistrate discharged 18 percent of his disorderly conduct cases and another discharged 54 percent. Haines reasoned that personality factors in each judge were probably responsible for the huge spread between the sentencing behavior of one judge and another. The fate of a litigant who appeared in this court was clearly a function of the judge before whom he was fortunate or unfortunate enough to appear. More recently, questions have been raised about the considerable range in sentences given to people committing similar crimes (Korbakes, 1975 a, b). The race and socioeconomic status of defendants have been found to be significantly related to sentences (Thornberry, 1973). Other studies have suggested that some judges have favorite numbers which they use in establishing sentences (Burtt, 1931; Gaudet, Herrick, & St. John, 1934, Winick, 1962). The availability of computers has facilitated the analysis of idiosyncratic, attitudinal, and emotional factors in judges' decisions (Schubert, 1963).

Sentencing Procedures

Once the defendant has been found guilty, the judge must decide if the subject is to be fined, set free on suspended sentence, placed on probation, or sent to prison. Frankel (1973) has pointed out that judges generally receive no instruction in sentencing, observe no guidelines, and do not consult one another. How the judge handles sentencing is central to the defendant's future because appellate review of sentences is possible in only thirteen states, and federal district court sentences are not subject to review.

In the established view, sentencing reflects such purposes as deterrence, incapacitation, retribution, and rehabilitation. The judge's considerations in sentencing a defendant may also involve the degree to which he is dangerous to the community if not incarcerated, the harm caused by his offense, the circumstances and needs of the criminal, and public opinion. The offender's age, previous convictions, whether violence was perpetuated, and the availability of probation are among the factors involved in sentencing. Judges may also be aware of the extent of overcrowding in prisons and take this into account.

Building on a procedure developed by the United States Parole Commission, sentencing guidelines which structure judicial discretion have been developed (Wilkins, 1976). These guidelines assign weights to specific characteristics of the offense on a vertical axis and to characteristics of the criminal on the horizontal axis. A judge who plots the offender score against the offense score finds the cell within the grid which is most relevant to the case and which sets forth the suggested kind and length of sentence. The guidelines derive from actual practice of the courts in a specific jurisdiction but do not prescribe what a sentence must be.

Such an approach seems to be attractive to many courts, which tend to believe that the certainty of a specific sentence may act as a deterrent to future criminal activities (Zimring and Hawkins, 1973). If a criminal knows that he will get a specific sentence if convicted of a particular offense, and that idiosyncratic views of a judge will not significantly affect his incarceration, the criminal will presumably be more uneasy about attempting another crime. Other courts, however, resent such interference with the traditional sentencing prerogatives of the judge, and the resolution of the disagreement over this issue will be a major clue to the future of the criminal court judge.

SUGGESTIONS FOR REFORM

Ever since the jury system began to flourish in America, after complaints by colonists that the king was depriving them of trial by jury, there has been a considerable debate over its relative merit. Opponents of the jury system point out that the two countries which gave rise to the jury, France and England, have been using it less and less.

Ranging from the suggestion that juries be abolished and that cases be tried by a judge, to modifications in jury procedure, the debate over the merits of the jury system has assumed much momentum. The jury has been said to be the epitome of the democratic process, with citizens gathering to evaluate the merits of the contention of another citizen. Others have claimed that the jury is the antithesis of democracy because it is responsible to no one, is completely anonymous, and is not required to give any grounds for whatever verdict it reaches, in contrast to the judge, who gives the reasons for his decision.

The traditional defense of the jury system emphasizes that juries are especially qualified to perform their critical function of fact finding (Bell, 1940). It is contended that the mode of selection of jurors and their representativeness, disinterested approach, and open-minded discussion contribute to jurors being able to weigh the possibilities and to reach a sound decision in a case. Critics have pointed out that lawyers disqualify potential jurors who have special knowledge of the subject matter of the litigation. They also note that the best-qualified potential jurors in the community either are exempt from serving or are likely to avoid jury duty because of the considerable economic loss it may represent to them.

One of the most frequently heard arguments for the jury system is that the jury is a kind of legislature which wisely corrects the law by applying extralegal considerations and popular attitudes to the issue under consideration (Wyzanski, 1952). This has been further expressed as the jury's refusal to apply a particular law if it believes the law to be unjust. Opponents of the jury system believe that it is curious that we should support a jury's nullification of the work of elected legislators, and they believe that such a viewpoint assumes a degree of sophistication which the average jury does not possess. Since the deliberations of the jury are secret, there is no way of knowing why a jury nullifies the law.

Another debate between friends and critics of the jury system is whether jury service is an educational experience which provides participation in a democratic activity and helps to create confidence in government and law (Curtis, 1952). Critics aver that this experience usually lasts for only two weeks, and that the education of the jury occurs at the expense of the litigants. They feel that jury duty may lead to cynicism about the workings of the courts, and that the confidence of the public in the democratic processes by which juries work has been undermined by juries' acquitting notorious criminals who were obviously guilty, or convicting the innocent (Borchard, 1932). The reluctance of many citizens to serve on juries is cited by critics as the best evidence that many citizens are actually not interested in the educational experience of jury duty.

Juries have traditionally been said to be reliable in criminal proceedings because they are sensitive to the special circumstances of the alleged crime.

Opponents of the jury system believe that alleged criminals who are members of certain minority groups may not experience this benevolence of the jury. They also note that the public needs protection against groundless acquittals.

Proponents of the jury have praised the procedure whereby the judge gives instructions on the relevant law to the jury, and the jury interprets those instructions and applies them to the facts at hand (De Sloovere, 1933). Critics of juries feel that it is almost impossible for the judge to present the law in a way which is understandable to the untrained mind (Farley, 1932).

Other critics have observed that many issues of fact have legal status, and any attempt to distinguish law from fact is unreal. Some students of juries have complained that it is naive to have the jury listen to all the evidence before the judge explains the relevant law, because it then must try to recall the evidence retrospectively in terms of the judge's explanation.

One reform which has been urged would begin with the selection of the jury itself (Note, 1956). The proponents of reform in selection have stated that the traits desired in effective jurors are relatively easy to measure objectively. These traits include a fund of general information and of information on legal institutions, personal stability, reasonable critical judgment, and reasonable attitudes. Some jurisdictions use standardized tests of intelligence, memory, and perception in jury selection; such valid psychological tests to screen jurors might be used to serve a number of purposes. The use of standardized tests might mean that less time would be spent in voir dire examinations, and thus decrease court calendar congestion. Another benefit which has been foreseen is that attorneys would tend to stress rational rather than emotional appeals.

The rules which limit the evidence that can be presented in court could be liberalized if relatively alert jurors could be assumed. The prestige of jury duty would increase if jurors were selected more carefully.

The objective psychological tests recommended for jury selection have proved useful in screening personnel in the armed forces and in industry. No new legislation is required and a ruling by a commissioner of jurors or courts is all that would be required to deploy such tests. The courts have held that the Constitution guarantees the jury mode of trial but not its specific features or procedures (Robinson, 1950).

Some reformers of the jury system have felt that even more widespread use of the screening procedures may fall short of the mark. These reformers recommend that there should be regular use of jurors who are specialists in the matter under consideration, who would be able to consider relatively technical or complex matters in a presumably more efficient way than would ordinary juries. These reformers believe that it is foolish to exclude from a jury the very people who know most about a particular problem or area.

A number of judges have urged that adult education groups and students in public schools receive instruction in the nature of jury activity and fact finding. One procedure for improving the performance of juries is the orientation booklet that describes the workings of the court and jury (Miner, 1946). Some judges give orientation talks to groups of prospective jurors. It is certainly possible that the citizenry's increasing awareness of and interest in jury functioning may lead to the dissemination of more accurate information about juries and to more effective juror performance.

Another suggestion for improving the performance of juries would encourage the judge to call in a variety of experts to render expert testimony about testimony (Beuscher, 1941). The judge, in certain circumstances, may refer complex testimony to an expert, who may report on the testimony to the jury.

Another proposed procedure is to give judges the right to comment on the evidence. Also suggested is the wider use by judges of cautionary instructions, in which the judge makes suggestive comments on testimony that may have occasioned an emotional ferment in the jurors. The purpose of doing this would be to bring into the open some of the emotional factors that may be influencing the jurors.

The wisdom of excluding some kinds of evidence which are not permitted under current procedures on narrow legal grounds has been challenged (Morgan, 1936) by some legal scholars, who have suggested that such evidence may help juries. Others have questioned the desirability of forbidding jurors to take notes during a trial (Comment, 1948). Increasing jurors' pay has been urged as one way of getting better juries.

A number of suggestions for improving the performances of juries focus on the procedure by which verdicts are reached. It has been urged that there be a stenographic record of jury deliberations so that the judge can determine how the verdict was reached (Galston, 1943). If it were reached improperly, he could set the verdict aside. Polling the jury on the method by which it reached its verdict is another procedure which has been urged. Such polling would presumably make jurors more likely to behave in a responsible way. A related procedure which has been recommended is the interrogatory, a written statement by the jury about specific questions on specific facts, which is provided by the jury along with a verdict. The interrogatory permits the judge to obtain an insight into the jurors' reasons for the verdict they render.

Some scholars have recommended more use of the special rather than the general verdict (Sunderland, 1919). The general verdict is an either/or decision, and is thus either all right or all wrong. The special verdict requires the jury to determine specific issues of fact. It thus maximizes the separation of the three dimensions of law, facts, and application of law to facts. It enables errors to be localized and may improve the jury's morale by its abandonment of secrecy. The trial judge applies the appropriate law to the facts which are established by the special verdict, and the jury is less able to tell which side will benefit from its finding and is less likely to be swayed by nonrational considerations. The special verdict would require greater singleness of allegation and greater precision of presentation. The special verdict and the interrogatory have been authorized for the federal courts and in some states, but judges have made little use of either procedure.

Another suggested reform has attempted to combine the positive qualities of the group decision with the experience and wisdom of the judge by having several judges deciding each case instead of a jury. This would temper the possibility of a judge's being capricious or arbitrary and at the same time insure that the litigant's case would be discussed by several people.

Another suggestion for improving decisions is to incorporate more behavioral science into court findings, and possibly train judges in the nature of behavioral science. Classical sources like Wigmore on Evidence (Wigmore, 1940), do not take cognizance of what behavioral science currently says on subjects like perception and consciousness. Judges daily deal with subjects on which the behavioral sciences have collected much data, but seldom refer to such data. One reason for this is that judges may be afraid of being considered "unlawyerlike" and possibly overruled. Another reason is the nature of law school training and the history and development of legal institutions, including the common law. The writings of legal philosophers and judges, beginning with Henry De Bracton in the thirteenth century, express yearning for predictability and certainty. The law often appears to be a closed system of great orderliness that manifests a grand design which rules relationships. Judges trained in such a system and accustomed to the doctrine of stare decisis, or the following of precedent, may understandably be reluctant to use social science materials which are seldom precise and definitive.

Recommendations for improving the quality of the work of judges are usually made very cautiously because of the established tradition of reluctance to criticize the judiciary. One recommendation is that trial judges make written findings of fact (Note, 1948). This might help in the review of a case, define the scope of the decision, increase public confidence in the courts, and reassure the litigants that their case had been carefully considered by the judge. Findings of fact will, it has been suggested, act as a partial check on the judge's subjectivity.

Another suggestion made by an imaginative judge was that prospective judges undergo psychoanalytic treatment (Frank, 1949), as one way of recognizing the judge's "personal equation." Frank also questioned the whole system of precedent-following by judges, saying that it has roots in emotional immaturity and a need for certainty. Good judges "will not talk of 'rules' and 'principles' as finalities while unconsciously using them as soporifics to allay the pains of uncertainty" (Frank, 1930).

Federal Judge Julian Mack refused to wear a robe when presiding at a trial, and often conducted trials in his chambers, sitting on the same level with the witnesses and lawyers. Others have pointed out that Thomas Jefferson was opposed to any distinctive costume for judges. Robes have priestly connotations which many observers believe to be irrelevant to modern life. Other students of the courts have suggested that courts abandon the complicated language which they currently use and speak more plainly, so that they can be both understood and criticized more directly.

Applying a "sunshine" approach to the pretrial filtering process is another suggestion, so that the actual discussions which lead to plea bargains and diversion are systematic and recorded, rather than informal and even covert, as they tend to be now. There is no reason why the defendant, his relatives, and social workers as well as others with knowledge of his circumstances should be excluded during the bartering of his future.

A sunshine approach is also reasonable for the process by which potential jurors are excluded from serving. Casting light on the procedures by which so many people evade jury service could help make the system more viable.

Much attention has been given to ways of selecting judges more equitably, so that political loyalty and wealth become less important. If the power to sentence is largely removed from judges, it would be possible to have trial judges who are primarily technical courtroom arbiters. Such judges could be trained for the bench, take civil service tests, and devote their career to it, rather than enter it late in life and without any special training for so important an occupation.

The increase in crime and resultant inability of courts to deal with the rush of defendants have combined to make many citizens question the established procedures of criminal justice, particularly those centered in the courtroom. Understanding the psychology of the courtroom will enable us to determine which of its procedures are fair and just and which deserve serious reconsideration. Better understanding of the intrapersonal and interpersonal dynamics of the courtroom will contribute significantly to the administration of justice.

REFERENCES

Adorno, T. W., et al. *The authoritarian personality*. New York: Harper & Row, 1950.

Anonymous. What to wear in court. *Newsweek*, December 16, 1974, *52*.

Apodaca v. *Oregon*, U.S. 404, 1972.

Arnold, T. W. *The symbols of government*. New Haven: Yale University Press, 1935, 128–138.

Bell, L. Let me find the facts. *Journal of American Bar Association*, 1940, *26*, 552–555.

Belli, M. *Ready for the plaintiff*. New York: Holt, Rinehart and Winston, 1956.

Berman, J., & Sales, B. D. A critical evaluation of the systematic approach to jury selection. *Criminal Justice and Behavior*, 1977, *4*, 219–240.

Beuscher, J. H. Use of experts by the courts. *Harvard Law Review*, 1941, *54*, 1105–1127.

Bird Engineering, Research Associates. *A guide to juror usage*. Washington: U.S. Institute of Law Enforcement and Criminal Justice, 1975.

Boehm, V. R. Mr. Prejudice, Miss Sympathy, and the authoritarian personality. *Wisconsin Law Review*, 1968, 734–750.

Bok, C. *Backbone of the herring*. New York: Knopf, 1941.

Borchard, E. M. *Convicting the innocent*. New Haven: Yale University Press, 1932.

Botein, B. *Trial judge*. New York: Simon and Schuster, 1952.

Buckhout, R. Eyewitness testimony. *Scientific American*, December 1974, *231*, 23–31.

Burtt, H. E. *Legal psychology*. Englewood Cliffs, N.J.: Prentice-Hall, 1931, 263.

Busch, Francis X. *Law and tactics in jury trials.* Indianapolis: Bobbs-Merrill, 1949.

Cardozo, B. N. *The nature of the judicial process.* New Haven: Yale University Press, 1921.

Cheatham, E. *Cases and materials on the legal profession.* Brooklyn, N.Y.: Foundation Press, 1955.

Comment: Should juries be allowed to take notes? *Journal of American Judicature Society,* 1948, *32,* 57–59.

Comment: Psychiatric evaluation of the mentally abnormal witness. *Yale Law Journal,* 1950, *59,* 1324, 1341.

Curtis, C. P. The trial judge and the jury. *Vanderbilt Law Review,* 1952, *5,* 150–166.

Cutler, A. S. *Successful trial tactics.* Englewood Cliffs, N.J.: Prentice-Hall, 1949, 76–81.

Dashiell, J. F. Experimental studies of the influence of social situations. In C. Murchison (Ed.), *Handbook of social psychology.* Worcester, Mass.: Clark University Press, 1935, 1097–1158.

De Sloovere, F. The functions of judge and jury. *Harvard Law Review,* 1933, *46,* 1086–1110.

Dranow v. *United States,* 325F 2nd 481, 8th Cir. 1963.

Efran, M. G. The effect of physical appearance on the judgment of guilt, interpersonal attraction, and severity of recommended punishment in a simulated jury task. *Journal of Research in Personality,* 1974, *8,* 45–54.

Fahringer, H. P. And the right path appeared not anywhere. Unpublished paper, 1977.

Farley, R. J. Instructions to juries—their role in the judicial process. *Yale Law Journal,* 1932, *42,* 194–225.

Frank, J. *Law and the modern mind.* New York: Brentano, 1930, 104, 166.

Frank, J. *Courts on trial.* Princeton: Princeton University Press, 1949, 126–146, 250, 270, 335.

Frankel, M. E. *Criminal sentences.* New York: Hill and Wang, 1973.

Galston, C. G. Civil jury trials and tribulations. *Journal of American Bar Association,* 1943, *29,* 195–198.

Gaudet, G. F., Herrick, G. F., & St. John, G. W. Individual differences in penitentiary sentences given by different judges. *Journal of Applied Psychology,* 1934, *18,* 675–686.

Ginger, A. F. *Minimizing racism in jury trials.* Berkeley: National Lawyers Guild, 1969.

Goldman, J., Maitland, K. A., & Norton, P. L. Psychological aspects of jury performance. *Journal of Psychiatry and Law,* 1975, *3,* 367–379.

Goldstein, I. *Trial techniques.* Chicago: Callaghan, 1935.

Green, L. *Judge and jury.* Kansas City, Mo.: Vernon Law Book, 1930, 153–185, 395–417.

Gross, H. A psychological theory of law. In P. Sayre (Ed.), *Interpretations of modern legal philosophies.* New York: Oxford University Press, 1947, 766–775.

Haines, C. G. General observations on the effect of personal, political and economic influences in the decision of cases. *Illinois Law Review,* 1923, *17,* 96–116.

Hervey, J. G. Jurors look at our judges. *Oklahoma Bar Association Journal,* 1947, *18,* 1508–1513.

Hoffman, H. M., & Bradley, J. Jurors on trial. *Missouri Law Review,* 1952, *17,* 235–251.

Holmes, O. W., Jr. *The common law.* Boston: Little, Brown, 1881, 35.

Hunter, R. M. Law in the jury room. *Ohio State Law Journal,* 1935, *2,* 1–19.

Hutcheson, J. C. The judgment intuitive: The function of the "hunch" in judicial decision. *Cornell Law Quarterly,* 1929, *134,* 274–478.

Izzett, R. R., & Leginski, W. Group discussions and the influence of defendant characteristics in a simulated jury setting. *Journal of Social Psychology,* 1974, *93,* 271–279.

Jackson, R. Decline of stare decisis is due to volume of opinion. *Journal of American Judicature Society,* 1944, *28,* 6–8.

James, R. M. Status and competence of jurors. *American Journal of Sociology,* 1959, *64,* 563–570.

Janis, I. L. Personality correlates of susceptibility to persuasion. *Journal of Personality,* 1954, *22,* 504–518.

Johnson v. Louisiana, 40 USLW 4254, 19722.

Kalven, H., Jr. A report on the jury project of the University of Chicago Law School. *Insurance Counsel Journal,* 1957, *24,* 368–381.

Kalven, H., Jr. The dignity of the civil jury. *Virginia Law Review,* 1964, *50,* 1055–1075.

Kalven, H., Jr., & Zeisel, H. *The American jury.* Boston: Little, Brown, 1966.

Kaplan, M. F., & Kemmerick, G. D. Juror judgment as information integration. *Journal of Personality and Social Psychiatry,* 1974, *30,* 493–499.

Korbakes, C. A. Criminal sentencing: Is the judge's sound discretion subject to review? *Judicature,* 1975a, *59,* 112–119.

Korbakes, C. A. Criminal sentencing: Should the judge's sound discretion be explained? *Judicature,* 1975b, *59,* 184–191.

Levine, F. J., & Tapp, J. L. Psychology of criminal identification: The gap from Wade to Kirby. *University of Pennsylvania Law Review,* 1973, *121,* 1079–1136.

Loftus, E. F. Reconstructing memory: The incredible eyewitness. *Psychology Today,* 1974a, *8,* 111–119.

Loftus, E. F., & Palmer, J. C. Reconstruction of automobile destruction. *Journal of Verbal Learning and Verbal Behavior,* 1974, *13,* 585–598.

Lumsdaine, A. A., & Janis, I. L. Resistance to counterpropaganda produced by one-sided and two-sided propaganda presentations. *Public Opinion Quarterly,* 1953, *17,* 311–318.

Mahoney, A. R. The rejected juror. Paper presented to the American Sociological Association, New York, N.Y., September 3, 1976.

Marston, W. M. Studies in testimony. *Journal of American Institute of Criminal Law and Criminology,* 1924, *15,* 1–31.

McGhee, P. W., & Teevan, R. C. Conformity behavior and need for affiliation. *Journal of Social Psychiatry,* 1967, *72,* 117–121.

Miller, W. American lawyers in business and in politics. *Yale Law Journal,* 1951, *60,* 66–76.

Mills, C. W. *White collar.* New York: Oxford University Press, 1951, 121–128.

Miner, J. H. The jury problem. *Journal of Criminal Law and Criminology,* 1946, *37,* 1–15.

Morgan, E. M. The jury and the exclusionary rules of evidence. *University of Chicago Law Review,* 1936, *4,* 247–258.

Murray, J., & Eckman, J. A follow-up study of jury selection. Paper presented to the Annual meeting of the American Psychological Association, Montreal, 1974.

Nebraska Press Association v. *Stuart*, 96 S. Ct. 2791, 2805, 1976.

Newman, D. J. *Conviction: Determination of guilt without trial.* Boston: Little Brown, 1966.

Nizer, L. The art of the jury trial. *Cornell Law Quarterly*, 1946–1947, *32*, 59–72.

Nopto, D. (pseudonym). How to witness expertly. *SPSSI Newsletter*, November 1973, 3–4.

Note: The law of fact: Findings of fact under the federal rules. *Harvard Law Review*, 1948, *61*, 1434–1444.

Note: Psychological tests and standards of competence for selecting jurors. *Yale Law Journal*, 1956, *65*, 531–542.

Padawer-Singer, A. M. Justice or judgment? Paper presented to the annual Chief Justice Earl Warren Conference on Advocacy in the United States, 1977.

Padawer-Singer, A. M., & Barton, A. The impact of pretrial publicity on jurors' verdicts. In R. J. Simon (Ed.), *The jury system in America: A critical overview.* Beverly Hills: Sage, 1974, 123–139.

Postgate, R. W. *The verdict of twelve.* London: Collins, 1940.

Pound, R. A theory of judicial decision for today. *Harvard Law Review*, 1923, *36*, 940–959.

Pound, R. Fifty years of jurisprudence. *Harvard Law Review*, 1938, *51*, 777–812.

Robinson, W. S. Bias, probability and trial by jury. *American Sociological Review*, 1950, *15*, 73–78.

Rosett, A. & Cressey, D. R. *Justice by consent: Plea bargaining in the American courthouse.* Philadelphia: J. B. Lippincott, 1976.

Schroeder, T. The psychologic study of judicial opinions. *California Law Review*, 1918, *6*, 89–113.

Schubert, G. (Ed.). *Judicial decision making.* New York: Free Press, 1963.

Schulman, J., Shaver, P., Colman, R., Emrich, B., & Christie, R. Recipe for a jury. *Psychology Today*, 1973, *6*, 37–44.

Simon, R. J. (Ed.). *The jury system in America: a critical overview.* Beverly Hills: Sage, 1974.

Stone, V. A. A primacy effect in decision making by jurors. *Journal of Communication*, 1969, *19*, 239–247.

Strodtbeck, F. L., James R. M., & Hawkins, C. Social status in jury deliberations. *American Sociological Review*, 1957, *22*, 713–718.

Sunderland, E. R. Verdicts, general and special. *Yale Law Journal*, 1919, *29*, 253–267.

Taylor v. *Louisiana*, 419 U.S. 522, 1975.

Thibaut, J., & Walker, L. *Procedural justice: A psychological analysis.* Hillside: Lawrence Earlbaum Associates, 1975.

Thornberry, T. P. Race, socioeconomic status, and sentencing in the juvenile justice system. *Journal of Criminal Law and Criminology*, 1973, *64*, 90–98.

Ulman, J. N. *A judge takes the stand.* New York: Knopf, 1933.

United States Code, 28 USC 1P1861, 1952.

U.S. News and World Report, December 14, 1970.

Walker, L., Thibaut, J., & Andreoli, V. Order of presentation at trial. *Yale Law Journal*, 1972, *82*, 216–220.

Weld, H. P., & Danzig, E. R. A study of the way in which a verdict is reached by a jury. *American Journal of Psychology*, 1940, *53*, 518–536.

Weld, H. P., & Roff, M. A study in the formation of opinion based upon legal evidence. *American Journal of Psychology*, 1938, *51*, 609–628.

Widgery, R. M. Sex of receiver and physical attractiveness of source as determinants of initial credibility perception. *Western Speech Communicator*, 1974, *38*, 13–17.

Wigmore, J. H. *Wigmore on evidence* (Vol. II). Boston: Little, Brown, 1940, 41–190, 244–293.

Wilkins, L. T., et al., *Sentencing guidelines*. Albany: Criminal Justice Research Center, 1976.

Williams, G. *The proof of guilt*. London: Stevens & Sons, 1955, 190–272.

Williams v. *Florida*, 90 S. Ct. 1893, 1970.

Winick, C. Preference for individual digits. *Journal of General Psychology*, 1962, *67*, 271–281.

Winick, C., & Winick, M. Courtroom drama on television. *Journal of Communication*, 1974, *24*, 67–73.

Wyzanski, C. E. A trial judge's freedom and responsibility. *Harvard Law Review*, 1952, *65*, 1281–1304.

Zerman, M. B. *Call the final witness*. New York: Harper & Row, 1977.

Zimring, F., & Hawkins, G. J. *Deterrence: The legal threat in crime control*. Chicago: University of Chicago Press, 1973.

chapter 4

The Psychology of Imprisonment

Hans Toch

Most of us are "imprisoned" in some fashion, in the sense of having our activities circumscribed by circumstances, and in the sense that we are not free to go wherever we wish, whenever we want. As we shall see in Chapter 8, it is one of the functions of the ego to keep the rest of the human organism abreast of the constraints under which it must labor, and to help it accept these constraints with grace. The ego also has the task of helping each of us achieve our purposes within the limited opportunity structures of our environments. In the more jaundiced sense of the word, "adjustment" means making the best of what are invariably imperfect conditions.

To pose the issue this way need not blind us to the point that the lives of some of us are more circumscribed than the lives of others, nor to the important fact that any of our lives *at some points in time* are more restricted than at other junctures. Both facts are important in thinking about prisons: In prison, men can compare their fates to the relative freedom of the "outside" world. They must also face their transition from the "free" world to the prison world, and their prospects (if any) of regaining "freedom."

One difference between prisons and other restrictive circumstances is that prisons restrict men as a goal, instead of doing so as a means to others ends. Prisons have a restraining function, which consists of keeping inmates off the streets so that one is protected from their undesirable patterns of conduct. This aim of prisons is much more tangible than their other functions, such as trying to change the offender, or impressing people with the presumed fact that crime doesn't pay.

In this sense, prisons are different from other imprisoning environments, in which restraint is designed to accomplish something beyond imprisonment, such as inculcating knowledge, curing diseases, promoting spirituality, manning trenches, or sailing ships. Prisons are also different because they are directed at acts the person has committed—or is alleged to have committed—in the past. Most of our 250,000 prison and jail inmates are convicted offenders, and many have been arrested, but are still awaiting trial. In either case, the offender stands officially accused of serious misdeeds, and knows that his life is being circumscribed as a result of this accusation.

TOTAL INSTITUTIONS

Though formal imprisonment has *some* unique features, it has a lot in common with membership in other imprisoning environments which separate people from the world, force them into close proximity, and govern a good portion of their lives. Goffman (1961) has coined the term "total institutions" to describe such extreme environments. With this suggestive phrase, Goffman draws our attention to characteristics that very segregated and demanding environments have in common. One such feature is a social division into a world of keepers and a world of kept (an inmate world). The keepers tend to regard the environment as theirs, while the kept are subjected to it. There is also a tendency for keepers and kept to view each other with reserve and ill-disguised hostility. This fact holds even for "benevolent" imprisonment, such as in hospitals and mental hospitals.

Goffman suggests that total institutions tend to create clients who permit themselves to be managed. A dependent frame of mind may be induced in a person by subjecting him to "a series of abasements, degradations, humiliations, and profanations of self" (Goffman, 1961, p. 14). The inmate is stripped of his preprison identity by having to give up his clothes and his possessions, having to be deferential to his keepers, and having his privacy invaded in all sorts of ways. Goffman (1961) adds that for most imprisoned persons "mortification and curtailment of the self is very likely to involve acute psychological stress" (p. 48).

A common feature of the total institution is a system of control which involves a set of "house rules," and which permits keepers to dispense minor privileges and relatively severe punishments. For the inmate, these privileges and punishments are psychologically important. Minor privileges are apt to occupy the inmate's concern and attention, while punishments force him to play a small-child role with which he must psychologically cope.

Different inmates evolve different styles of coping with their dependency. One adjustment mentioned by Goffman is "situational withdrawal," which ranges from reduced interest in other inmates to psychotic shutting off of reality. There is also the "intransigent line," which entails refusing to cooperate with the administration or staff. A third style mentioned by Goffman is "colonization," which involves "building a stable, relatively contented existence . . . out of the maximum satisfactions procurable within the institution" (Goffman, 1961, p. 62).

Goffman also speaks of "conversion" of inmates who think of themselves in staff terms, and "act out the role of the perfect inmate." Such inmates, like the others Goffman describes, are rarely found in pure form. Most inmates follow a combined strategy, which involves "playing it cool" and doing whatever one must do to "stay out of trouble."

An important point made by Goffman about prison inmates is that their scars seem to heal quickly. The resilience of the average person is such that "shortly after release the ex-inmate forgets a great deal of what life was like on the inside and once again begins to take for granted the privileges around which life in the institution was organized" (Goffman, 1961, p. 72).

THE PAINS OF IMPRISONMENT

A number of writers have dealt with the stress-producing aspects of prison. The most famous book on the subject is a delightful small volume by Sykes (1958), who tells us that deprivations suffered by the inmate are always affronts to his or her self-esteem. Prisons cast doubts on the average inmate's worth as an adult human being, and the inmate must deal with these doubts. Prisons clearly produce Deprivation of Liberty, which includes the knowledge that one is officially set aside as untrustworthy. Sykes (1958) maintains that "somehow this rejection or degradation by the free community must be warded off, turned aside, rendered harmless. Somehow the imprisoned criminal must find a device for rejecting his rejectors, if he is to endure psychologically" (p. 67).

The second affront of prison involves the Deprivation of Goods and Services, including whatever a man owns or might accumulate while free. "In modern Western culture," Sykes (1958) writes, "material possessions are so large a part of the individual's conception of himself that to be stripped of them is to be attacked at the deepest layers of personality" (p. 69). Though a man's needs may be satisfied in prison, he does not contribute to his own maintenance; "the failure is *his* failure in a world where control and possession of the material environment are commonly taken as sure indicators of a man's worth" (Sykes, 1958, p. 69).

The Deprivation of Heterosexual Companionship is another critical impact of prison. The most important stress here is not the inmate's physical suffering, but his self-doubt. Relating to persons of the opposite sex provides criteria of manhood or womanhood. The effort to prove that one is still "manly" becomes a dominant issue for male prisoners; sexual concerns also shape the social world of women's prisons.

In prison, Deprivation of Autonomy means the control prison exercises over every aspect of the inmate's life. Being regulated and being ordered about poses "a profound threat to the prisoner's self-image because they reduce the prisoner to the weak, helpless, dependent status of childhood"

(Sykes, 1958, p. 75). The inmate may have to struggle with doubts about his own adulthood, particularly where he has adolescent identity problems that are alive and touchy.

A paradoxical affront of prison is the Deprivation of Security, which derives from one's proximity to other inmates. Males are especially prone to be concerned about how tough they are. They must face "tests" designed to find out whether they are afraid, or whether they can stand up under pressure. They cannot seek protection from staff because this labels them as weak, or as disloyal to the inmate culture.

Like Goffman, Sykes points out that prisoners must deploy resources and energy to defend against the stresses of confinement. He writes that "if the rigors of prison cannot be completely removed, they can at least be mitigated by the patterns of social interaction established among the inmates themselves. In this apparently simple fact lies the key to our understanding of the prisoner's world" (Sykes, 1958, p. 82).

THE "REAL MAN"

The principal adjustment formula among male inmates that neutralizes prison stress is the model of the "real man," the inmate who "does his time" in a tough, inviolable, dignified fashion. Such an inmate stays untouched or cool, thus "denying the custodians' power to strip him of his ability to control himself" (Sykes, 1958, p. 102).

The "real man" has attributes which are partly related to each other. He preserves his equanimity under trying circumstances. He cannot be provoked into unscheduled reactions. He shows no feeling, and stays aloof and emotionally uninvolved. He is, especially, unafraid. On the other hand, he is capable of inspiring fear—or at least, respect—in other persons. The real man handles prison situations in an efficient, detached, self-sufficient fashion. He never asks for help, and never needs help. He is powerful as nails, and his demeanor makes his toughness obvious. He also behaves so as to make it obvious that he keeps distance from lesser mortals. His contacts are formal, self-selected, and pointed.

The real-man model can solve adjustment problems for the person who can play the John Wayne role. It may help where the inmate sees himself as a "real man" and strives to behave like one. The model is not helpful where it cannot be implemented.

Some men can act tough but they are transparently not cool, others can pretend coolness but not toughness, and some have trouble being tough or cool. In trying to adjust to prison a man faces not only the stress of confinement, but also his divergences from the "real man" norm. Sykes' issue of security is a case in point: tough inmates can inspire fear in some of their fellows; fearful inmates have trouble facing their fear (which is a nontough thing to do) and seeking help from staff (which is distinctly noncool). They have options such as affecting a facade of toughness, reacting with violence, retreating into a shell, or using pretexts to approach staff. They can also admit to being scared, which translates into being "weak," and—by implication—"unmanly." There are also extreme options such as panic, paranoid reactions, self-injury attempts, and self-segregation. Such options often mark failures of strained efforts to be "cool" (Toch, 1975).

The ideal of the "real" man implies that departures from the ideal are unmanly, while caricatures of the model are manly. Goffman's intransigent inmate (in Sykes' scheme, the "ball buster") may feel manly because he stages demonstrations of toughness. The man's self-view, however, may not be matched by his reputation. A man's self-defined effort to be proudly militant may be viewed by his peers as an immature explosion, which is distinctly noncool. "The ball buster," says Sykes (1958), "is often regarded as a fool." A fellow-inmate may describe such a man as "the sort of person who'll come up and ask you for a stamp while you're washing your hands" (p. 100).

In inmate relationships, contests of manliness can take their toll in destructiveness to the contestants and to the inmate community. A man's image of manliness may entail proving that he can inspire terror in someone else, whom he can define as "a non-man." This strategy describes the "wolf," "booty bandit" or "jocker" who makes predatory overtures to the inmate who looks "afraid" and is seen as a "punk." The target of such overtures has serious problems not only in feeling unsafe, but also through the discovery that his manliness is questioned. His options may be to "prove" himself through violence or to seek sanctuary. The first option may be threatening, and punishable by staff. The second option confirms and perpetuates the stigma.

The aggressors are suspect as homosexuals. In Sykes' (1958) words, "the wolf—no matter how 'tough' he may be—cannot entirely avoid the attitudes commonly elicited by his perversion" (p. 98). The wolf also faces discontinuity issues when he leaves prison, because his pattern of bullying is ill-adapted to free world socializing.

The "wolf-punk" game is destructive in a variety of ways which are not obvious. The inmate who "wants to do his time" must witness conduct that violates everything he ordinarily stands for. He is forced (in the interest of "coolness") to stand by while principles of fairness are ignored, and while suffering is inflicted in his presence. Prison staff face out-of-control predatory conduct, and the knowledge that if they help the victim they may increase his vulnerability.

The situation is aggravated by the fact that the "real-man" model is endorsed by many staff members (Toch, 1976). An officer may share contempt for the "weak" inmate, who "invites" victimization by "not taking care of himself" through combat. An officer may thus counsel a victim to "stand up and fight," even though the victim is ill-equipped for fighting, and the officer must apply disciplinary sanctions to fight participants.

The "real-man" model is of concern to psychologists because it affects mental health. The "real man" cannot admit to feelings, and must deal with anxiety or despair by trying to suppress them. He must erect elaborate defenses against the discovery of being stressed. Manliness dictates stoicism, which involves outward calm for the man who is anything but calm under the surface. A man in trouble must affect a cool facade, and face paralyzing depression in the privacy of his cell. Unresolved tensions can produce conversion symptoms (physical complaints) which contribute to the popularity of sick call. Issues that could be addressed through counseling early in the game come to attention too late, when they have been compounded and aggravated.

THE "REAL WOMAN"

Woman prisoners face the same deprivations Sykes lists for male inmates, and these deprivations translate into "pains of imprisonment" that are commensurate in quality. But the *meaning* of prison deprivations clearly differs for women, and so do the strategies used by women to cope with their stress.

There are many definitions of stress generally. Typically, these definitions revolve around the experience of abruption or disruption. This means that a new situation is said to become stressful to the degree to which it differs from what we know, expect, and feel entitled to. Unfamiliar situations invariably pose threats because we don't know how to interpret them, and because our usual strategies of adjustment no longer work (Cantril, 1941; McGrath, 1970).

The prison experience differs from the free world experience of women (as opposed to that of many men) in several ways. The most salient difference rests in the prison's disruption of *meaningful, intimate, relationships* that have strongly figured in the preprison lives of female inmates. While a man may be translated into prison from the streets (and in some instances, from work-settings), women are often torn primarily from home, and from valued links with spouses, children, and other closely significant persons. The differences in primary sources of free-world meanings and personal involvements translate into differences in the experience of imprisonment.

Various researchers have studied women's prisons (Giallombardo, 1966; Heffernan, 1972; Ward & Kassebaum, 1965), and their descriptions of what they have observed are very similar. All of the writers describe the importance of relationships that spring up among inmates, which are reminiscent of love relationships in the free world. Where prisons contain inmates of different ages, inmates form make-believe "families"—groups in which they play stereotyped roles such as "mother," "husband," "uncle," and "daughter." In such groups there are norms of conduct reminiscent of the free world (such as "respect" to parents and domesticity for "wives"), and norms insuring material and emotional support.

It is not difficult to see a link between stress experienced by women prisoners and the strategy they adopt for dealing with stress. The fence of the reformatory severs each inmate from ties that have nourished her and have helped to shape her sense of self. There is no longer anyone to feed, protect, love and be loved by, care and be cared for. Such significant others are critical for the self-image of women in Western society, in the same sense in which "real-man" norms may shape the self-conceptions of men.

We note that we may see in sharper relief under stress societal themes that take more quiet and gentle shape in ordinary life. Such is the case with the myth of the macho male in male prisons, and that of the nurturent female for women.

In all prisons there are coping styles that vary from inmate to inmate. As with men, some women are isolates, others are gregarious; some seek privileges, while others do not. There are also prison norms, such as those that call for distance from staff and condemn the inmate who "rats." But male and female prison themes have different nuances. While young males and females both grouse about staff "disrespect," men are less apt than women to accuse staff of being "uncaring," callous, or "cold."

The "real-woman" inmate is a person who expresses emotions and feels entitled to do so (Fox, 1975). In this sense, she stands coolness on its head. She expects her feelings to show, wants them to be considered, and thinks she ought to be responded to. She is noncool, in that she assumes that people naturally need each other and are interdependent. If the "real woman" has problems, she shares them with a few women she trusts. She assumes that unsolved problems cause tension.

The "real man's" illusion of invulnerability is not shared by women. Female inmates may feel misunderstood and rejected, unloved and ignored. Such openness makes it less likely for conflicts to arise which result from emotional overcontrol, or that produce unconvincing efforts to become the paragon of coolness one isn't.

But problems of conflict can come up for women, particularly where adjustment entails shutting off or downgrading one's links to persons one has left behind. Giallombardo (1966) observes that:

> it must be kept in mind that letters often bring unpleasant news. A particularly frustrating aspect of imprisonment for the female inmate is that she is not in a position to control the course of events in the outside world: children may be neglected, for example; husbands may become unfaithful or may obtain a divorce; a loved one may die. To dwell persistently on events in the outside world is to run the risk of doing "hard time." . . . Therefore the prisoner must learn—and here her sister prisoners are helpful—to suspend deep emotional involvement in outside events. She develops an immunity to emotional shock to events both within and without the prison gate for the term of her sentence" (p. 94).

The psychoanalytic term for the deemphasizing of one's personal involvements is "decathexis," which is defined as the withdrawal of love from persons or things one has loved. Decathexes liberate love energy (libido) which must be deployed elsewhere, as it is in the social organization of women's prisons. In prison, the inmate does "easy time" by securing love from her peers with less risk than she would in "keeping her head outside." But substitute love may miss some of the attributes of primary love. A make-believe "husband" who really is a female drug distributor from Detroit strains the reality-mediating functions of the ego (Chapter 8). Such relations have a sandbox-quality that is basically unconvincing, or that requires childlike (regressive) or quasipsychotic self-deception to bring them off. The women's prison has the charged climate of a junior high school with its feverish pre-adolescent "crushes," and this fact is incongruent with psychological attributes of hardened urban offenders in their early thirties.

There are also difficulties in recathexing the outside when the occasion demands it. Offenders who renew ties with their loved ones against the backdrop of homosexual involvements in prison must deceive themselves and others. At minimum, they must "compartmentalize" prison and post-prison personalities at the expense of consistency and continuity.[1]

Women inmates sometimes suffer from emotional "under-control" problems, including occasional tantrums of explosiveness (Fox, 1975). Such inmates may pride themselves in their vulnerability, to the point of self-prescribing "blow-ups" where their tension accumulates. This strategy is a roller-coaster syndrome, in which the person seesaws from tension to catharsis or from despondency to violence. It may entail manic-depressive moodchanges, with no interludes for rational problem solving. The strategy neutralizes stressing agents, who must back off from the "whipped child" who is reactively sullen, pouting, and sometimes explosive. The norm here is advertised "brittleness" not advertised "toughness." Stress is not countered by building immunity to it, but by overreacting to frustrations.

While this strategy discourages some people, it places the inmate at the mercy of others who can annoy her and control her feelings. At some point, the inmate may lose control completely, and break down.

VARIATIONS ON ADJUSTMENT THEMES

The extreme adjustments of male and female inmates are not adjustments of the *average* inmate. They represent coping efforts of the "career" or "institutionalized" inmate. Past experiences that highlight norms similar to those of prison are most apt to inspire prison games. In his book *The Felon*, Irwin (1970) traces the career patterns of inmates who arrive at prison with different backgrounds. He shows that some male offenders are involved to a greater extent in the prison culture than others. Heffernan (1972) documents the same point for women offenders.

Middle-class inmates and others who are unaffiliated in the free world ("Square Johns") are least prone or likely to become enmeshed in the inmate subculture, and they are least ashamed of "relating" to prison staff. Offenders with reformatory experience (State-Raised Youth) are the most callous and experienced practitioners of predatory games. Narcotics offenders ("dope fiends," "heads") are high on coolness; working-class offenders ("lower-class men") are sold on toughness. The professional property offender ("thief") prizes stoicism, while suspiciousness is important for career "hustlers."

Greater pliability may be shown by "disorganized criminals" who are non-specialized—and largely penny ante—offenders.

Irwin (1970) describes three categories or "styles" of adjustment to prison. He sees inmates as either "jailing," "doing time," or "gleaning." Irwin's "jailer" is Goffman's "colonizer"—he is comfortable in prison, and advances immediate ends or interests among inmates and staff; he seeks "cushy" jobs, benefits, sinecures, advantages, and chances for exploiting peers. He manipulates the formal prison, while engaged in its informal economy, which includes gambling, loan-sharking, sexual pursuits, and assorted sub rosa practices. In both systems, "jailers" do their best to seek advantages, and to carve out empires for themselves.

"Time doers" play it cool in Erwin Goffman's sense. This involves promoting a low profile, "doing your time," and keeping out of trouble. The "time doer" aims to get out of prison as early as possible, with the least discomfort possible. He is oriented toward reducing risk and pain; to fill time so that it passes more quickly, to join "respectable" programs and prison activities. In a poker game, "time doing" would describe the player who considers the odds, and who very rarely bluffs. Such a man buys his peace of mind by minimizing risks where he can.

"Gleaners" use prison as an arena for their self-betterment, and seek "to radically change their life styles, and to follow a sometimes carefully devised plan to 'better themselves,' 'improve their mind,' or 'find themselves' while in prison" (Irwin, 1970, pp. 76–77). For the "gleaner," the prison is a learning environment, and other inmates or staff are classified as resources or impediments to learning. Time and activity are rationed or are allocated to maximize the opportunity for profit and for personal growth.

Each coping style has implications for ways of being involved in the prison's social system. The "jailer" joins the subculture of the yard and wheels, deals, or exploits in close concert with other "jailers." "Time doers" are relative isolates and come closest to the cool "real-man" ideal of prison lore. The "gleaning" style has its specialized peer group, which serves to reinforce "gleaning."

Culture intersects with crime in affecting the way inmates react to prison. Urban youths are less likely to find prison difficult than are unsophisticated rural offenders. Younger inmates are more prone to seek friends in prison than are older inmates (Glaser, 1964). The ease of adjustment is strongly affected by inmate mix. A "gleaner" may be tempted and disturbed by "jailers"; "jailers" are frustrated where other men do solitary time. Prison psychological climates are made or unmade by prison population profiles.

An inmate's work or living assignment may prove crucial. Intimate groups with close supervision are less stressful to the average inmate than chaotic large groupings, such as mess hall work (Glaser, 1964). Routines, peers, supervisors define environments as healthy or unhealthy. Environmental presses (Murray, 1938) may be matched or mismatched to the inmate's needs. A man may find solitude as a porter, autonomy as a farmer, distraction in a hobby shop, hope in a law library, faith with a chaplain, or goals in weight lifting.

One man's haven may be another's prison. A cell can mean safety and sanity to one inmate and spell claustrophobia and panic to another.

The pains of prison can have very different import for different inmates. In classifying and assigning an inmate, such differences are important to consider. If a man needs security, he "fits" in a structured prison; but the same institution may grate uncomfortably on an autonomy- or freedom-centered inmate. For a family-oriented inmate, distance from home may be vital or primary. Other persons may need health care, training, or congenial friends (Toch, 1977).

Prisons must prevent violence if they can. This may include avoiding standard "age-grading" so that one can remove victim-prone young inmates from the company of age mates who are predatory (Glaser, 1964). But to protect an inmate may also stigmatize him. A "sissie tier" or "homo company" may yield safety, but do so at the cost of the inmate's social reputation, and—ultimately—of his self-esteem. Assignments must be juggled with sensitive concern for each inmate's mental health, because traumas sustained in prison may affect a person for the rest of his or her life.

STAFF IN PRISONS

Prisons are obsessed with security and custody. Like the military, prisons waste human and social resources to protect society from fear. Inmates are employed in token ways; more often than not, their jobs are part-time and dead-end. Men make license plates and women sew sheets. "Make work" activity of this kind translates poorly into motives, and it does not lead to "free world" careers.

The fate of staff is similarly sterile. Officers man guard towers for hours on end. Others count, sort, escort, and open gates. Other staff fill out forms for folders no one reads. Inmates rarely meet or talk with staff as human beings. The inmate norm says "never talk to screws"; the officer "knows" he musn't "get close to cons."

Such distance, in Goffman's terms, is the cost of total institutions. But "total/nontotal" is not a sharp nor a clean break. Past prison life differs as much from that of today's prisons as modern prisons differ from life in the "streets." Men do not march silently in cadence to their rock piles under hostile eyes of armed guards. They no longer die of exhaustion or succumb in solitude. They read, run teaching machines, play checkers, exercise, write home; get visits, new noses, and root canals. They watch color TV, play instruments, join teams, form clubs, buy snacks, see therapists, and are seen by parole agents.

Staff are selected, upgraded, trained. The "keeper" of yesterday's prison is now a "correctional officer" or "correctional counselor." He is unarmed, literate, and (within limits) courteous. He receives in-service course work in criminology, minority groups, or human relations. He may attend community or junior college.

Wardens have deputies for treatment, programs, training. Correctional staff preach rehabilitation, reform, professionalization, modern management. They seek public support and good community relations.

The main purpose of prisons, though, is still that of *imprisoning*, and this is important. Custody converts wasteful routine into "useful" tasks because ritual spells security. Security tells us where each inmate is, and keeps him from being elsewhere—such as loping through the underbrush on his way to mugging someone's mother. The aim of programs is to keep a man busy where we can watch him. It matters little what he does, as long as he "gives no trouble." We avoid personal intimacy on similar grounds. To be friendly reduces staff control, which is based on rank and authority, and it spells danger through the dilution of discipline.

To worry about custody does not mean that we must be uncivilized. But we can best watch a man if he goes nowhere, receives nothing, sends nothing, owns nothing. Such a man, however, may explode—which is dangerous— or break down—which is messy. He also makes us question ourselves, because we are committed to humanness and decency.

Staff goals are goals that must sit easily on staff's conscience, must leave them peace of mind, and reduce possible conflict and discomfort. Custody makes a *goal* out of the easiest and safest things staff do. Sykes (1958) has noted that inmates really monitor and control themselves. Escape risks are largely mythical. The real gain of custody is ease of processing. Goffman (1961) points out that "as materials upon which to work, people can take on somewhat the same characteristics of inanimate objects" (p. 74). Custody streamlines management. It also protects staff from intimacy, which "brings the staff member into a position to be hurt by what inmates do and what they suffer" (Goffman, 1961, p. 82).

Custody insures that prisons and their staff cannot "fail." Noncustodial goals tend to pose testable criteria of effectiveness. If we "train" a man effectively, he gets a job; if we cure a man, he must leave healthy. We can fail as resocializers if a graduate robs a liquor store two weeks after he is released. But custody claims only to warehouse people. It looks no worse if all inmates recidivate. And given the large number of inmates who in fact are reconvicted, this goal-statement is necessary. Staff can also buttress their stand with the claim that offenders "can't really be changed" because they are hard core and too set in their ways.

Prisons look bad during riots. We assume that riots cannot break out if there is tight security in prisons. This presumption forms part of our illusion that we can control our world (Freud, 1957). It is difficult to think of violence as just happening, particularly when it is very annoying to us (Walster, 1966). We forget that custody does not create security unless it is accepted as legitimate by the inmates, who must obey rules, and must do as they are told. Riots occur *precisely because the legitimacy of authority is questioned.* In a typical riot, staff control is rejected because of rumors of guard brutality or injustice. Such rumors are accepted where complaints and unsatisfied grievances have accumulated (Milgram and Toch, 1969). Beyond these grievances, riots seem to offer few warnings. Once they break out, events unfold fast. The only option is usually to "lock down" the prison and enter a state of siege.

THE OFFICER AS A MENTAL HEALTH AGENT

Custody does not routinely rely on the use of force, but hinges on the purchase of inmate consent (Sykes, 1958). A good custodial officer, like a good police officer, must be seen as fair and square. This means that he must use his discretion broadly, rather than "playing it by the book" and enforcing minor rules. By overlooking illegal hotplates, sandwiches, and after-hours talk the officer buys good will to act effectively where it counts. He also buys cheerfulness (rather than surliness) and critical access to information he needs.

Officers, like inmates, do time, and they must avoid trouble. For the inmate "trouble" spells punishment; for the officer, trouble means more work; conflict for the guard's supervisor also means a perceived failure on the guard's part to exercise custodial control. The guard must live with inmates. To do so, he must relate to inmates with give and take.

Officers vary in the closeness of their links with inmates. While most guards see their job as pure custody, some do not. They take a close interest in inmates, spend time with them, protect them and "go to bat" for them. Guards assigned to settings that contain stressed inmates may spot stress symptoms, and may refer or counsel inmates in crisis. Officers may bend rules or seek help for inmates who are disturbed or upset. In the lives of such officers, acts of crisis intervention are a source of pride and may be warmly recalled by the officer in conversations with outsiders, and in interviews:

This goes back quite a few years, and this fellow had done something like eight years on a fifteen-year sentence, and he had a child that was nine. And whatever the case was, he had never spent Christmas with the child. And he met the board and he got an open date for six months and he did not have an approved program and he had promised the child that he would be spending Christmas together, buying him presents and right on down the line. And he did not get out in time for Christmas and he was really down in the dumps. He was real low, about as low as you can get. And this is right after Christmas and he was bitter about a lot of things and he was very disappointed with everything and he worked for me and I talked with Mr. S. who was in charge of the service unit at that time—and I asked him if he would at least call the guy off the block and let him get it off his chest, and he did. . . . And something occurred to him that had occurred to nobody else and that was that the guy had worked in the plate shop for a good number of years and at that time he had saved half of his money. And so I asked the man how much they had in reserve for him and I said, "Let's take a chance and withdraw it and make a deposit in the bank in New York City and see if we can get you out on a reasonable assurance." And he did and he got it and he was out in ten days. And I think that it made an awful difference in that the man was let out and I think it could have been done before Christmas if someone had done more. If someone had taken the time.

* * *

I went around the system a little bit and I told this inmate, "Explain to [a disturbed Latin inmate] that he has to go on sick call in the morning to see the psychiatrist, and what you do, you put a slip in for sick call in the morning with the man. This way you'll both go to the psychiatrist together, you'll be there to interpret." I said, "You may have a little bit of problems with the sergeant, but explain to the sergeant why you're there. If he has any questions, tell him to come to me because I'm the one that told you to do it." And he came back to me the next day and he thanked me, because they had moved the man out.

* * *

I have my clerk that I work with, he's a man in for murder, which means nothing to me, what he done out there. Now he's my clerk, I know he's a highly nervous person. He can't accept problems; he can't deal with them too fast. And he explodes. He doesn't mean to, but he does. And a lot of times I tell him, "Stay in your house [cell]. Don't even bother coming out, just rest up." . . . Yeah. "Don't do your work today." I can see when he's nervous or upset. I got him now so he'll come and tell me, somebody's bothering him. He wants to stay in for a couple of days. "Go ahead, stay in." We pay him; it don't make no difference. And he'll come back around in a couple of days—he's all right, works good. Actually he's a good inmate, but if you didn't recognize his problems, you would have him in keeplock. The next thing you know he'd be over in idle somewhere, or segregation. He wouldn't want to be, but it would break him right down. He can't adapt to the situation.

* * *

He was pacing around and he didn't know where to turn. And I know more of the problem because when he has no one to turn to he turns to me. . . . I'm his boss and his feeling for me is very close and he tells me almost every problem which he has. And we discuss it. And when he's uptight I talk about my own life and how my wife and I do this and that. And it kind of relaxes him and it's interesting for him. . . . We talk about the family all the time. And he was telling me about a dream the other night that he was on parole and he had married his girlfriend and she had gone to work and he was going to have dinner and while he was out he ran into me and my wife and my aunt and her husband and we went out and he got his wife and the six of us went to Vegas just for the evening having a grand old time. And with a dream like this his feeling for me is more than just—we're very close friends.

These examples (drawn from a study reported in Toch, 1975) are interesting on at least two counts: (1) The incidents defy our stereotypes of the guards, since we mostly assume that officers must be tough and distant, and must be custodially oriented. Like the police, we classify prison guards as law enforcers, who must watch, apprehend, and punish. We forget that the job (in both instances) offers few opportunities for dramatic enforcement. (2) Helping incidents are officially unrecognized, and entail relaxing rules the officer is supposed to enforce. The system doesn't reward mental health-related and human services work by the officer, and the officer stretches things to help inmates.

We have talked of informal pressures, particularly pressures that condemn inmate help-seeking or acceptance. We know that "rats" are frowned upon and "square Johns" are unpopular, and that "real men" must be cool and tough.

In tracing this picture, we forget that prison is stressful, and that even in nonstressful contexts the adjustment modes we have noted are more easily prescribed than lived up to. The manliness of "real men" is mostly nonsubstantial. It is a skin deep defense or facade. Many prison norms invite losing battles or trench warfare. "Jailing" is self-deception in which the outside world must be shut off. But the outside world is real, and it can reassert itself with vigor. "Time doing" is a feverish fight, because time sits heavily when one relaxes.

Subcultural adjustment often hinges on peer conduct. The exploiter needs his victim to convince himself that he is brave. Tough inmates need others to pretend that they are tough. (Tough staff also have their locker room talk, which exaggerates the prevalence and the efficacy of violence.)

Solutions may not "solve" much. They may ameliorate stress at much expense in self-control or reality-mediation or self-esteem. Adjustments are, to varying degrees, unhealthy, and leave inmates in precarious equilibria, producing groups or communities in tension. There is new stress—often substantial stress—built into efforts to cope with the pains of imprisonment or the vicissitudes of life.

This point holds not only for inmates, but for staff, and for the custody orientation of prison. We can think of custody *as an adjustment mode elevated to a goal.* Custody involves self-deception, because it entails exaggerating risks of escape or threats of danger. It means pretending that force works. It means attaching meaning to make-believe jobs (like being a tower guard) or to unnecessary rituals, such as collecting useless information. Custody must disguise the waste and pointlessness of not doing anything for the inmate while he's in prison—particularly for the inmate who appears amenable to assistance or needs help.

Inmates argue that doing time makes sense because staff don't care about inmates. Staff "know" that inmates resist help, and that they cannot be changed. Staff also "know" that superiors "don't give a damn" about prisons.

Most prisons are alienated organizations, in the way that some factories and schools are alienated. This means that a group of people feels that another group belongs to a powerful, pervasive "system" which makes one's activities limited, pointless, or constrained. Each group (management, workers, students, teachers, inmates, officers, prison staff) invariably point to *others* as the sources of their enslavement. Neither tests the validity of their presumption. The status quo always exists because others want it or have "investments" in it.

The assumption may be real, but the facts need not be. "Helping" guards and "helped" inmates are the exceptions that may prove a rule. They may show that *staff and inmates can escape from group norms and from paralyzing premises about the "opposition."* The officers in the incidents we have cited have cared about inmates; their inmates seem responsive and affected. "Good work" obviously is sometimes done, and it is done outside custodial and subculture frames.

The officers we have quoted have mostly acted on their own. Their achievements may be unsung among superiors, and would not fall among macho exploits admired at neighborhood taverns. The officers have acted in defiance of formal and informal incentive systems that place their emphasis elsewhere or nowhere.

But what if incentives rewarded the officer for activities related to inmate mental health? The officers in our incidents would benefit, and other guards might be tempted to try their hand. Glaser (1964) cites experiments involving officer-counselors in federal prisons. Fenton (1958) describes a California program in which officers ran groups. In "therapeutic communities" in prisons, guards show skills and enthusiasm in assuming new roles. Briggs (1973) talks about guard "role blurring" in a program at Chino. According to Briggs, officers at Chino assumed "the roles of the counsellors and the small-group leaders." In later phases of the Chino program,

> the officers became more involved with the administration of the project and acted as "consultants" for the residents, who in turn were performing roles more like those of the counsellors. The officers were supportive of the men's efforts to try new things and were now able to teach them skills which they themselves had recently acquired, such as leading small groups, interviewing, intervening, and using crisis situations, reviewing things they had done, and generally promoting and supporting their ideas . . . The officers moved into new areas of probing into research and evaluation, thinking, understanding, teaching, and supporting what the men were doing (Briggs, 1973, p. 146).

The Briggs program is of interest because it assigned staff roles (including custodial ones) to inmates. We shall return to this point later. Our concern now is *the broadening of the officers' roles* at Chino, which includes the assignment of noncustodial (human services) functions.

Human service functions can be integrated in traditional definitions of officers' roles. A New York program, for example, defines the duties of its officers as follows:

1. Maintain written reports of observed behavior of inmates assigned to him.
2. Follow up and evaluate inmates' participation in different aspects of the program, especially for those he is responsible.
3. Participation in group and community meetings or other activities.
4. Submit opinions and evaluations of inmates' behavior through observation.
5. Involvement in training, education, and self-improvement.
6. Be fully aware of Institution policy changes and the ways to implement them in order to maintain the security of Institution.

7. At all times be responsible for custody, supervision and control of the inmates. (Marshall *et al.*, undated, p. 7.)

This roster contains only two items (6 and 7) which are traditional custodial tasks; one item (1) is traditional, but reinterpreted; the other four functions are new ones.

OTHER PRISON STAFF AS MENTAL HEALTH RESOURCES

Prison staff *other than officers* already have tasks that are often *exempt from custodial norms*, and that permit "working with" inmates, or helping inmates-in-trouble.

Glaser (1964) points out that prison work supervisors can be very significant figures in the lives of their charges. They can motivate prisoners to try to rehabilitate themselves. Work supervisors can take a personal interest in inmate workers, and they become paternal figures for offenders who have had no family experience in the real world. Work also provides a very tangible context for man-to-man (or woman-to-woman) relationships between keepers and kept. Supervisors are "tax exempt" from freedom or autonomy concerns of the inmate, while officers must cope with their uniform in changing roles.

In practice, case workers, service unit staff or prison counselors have the greatest difficulty relating to inmates (Glaser, 1964). As professionals (Rogers, 1961) mental health staff can deploy technology to maintain distance from clients. They can give priority to paper work at the expense of client contacts, and can define such task distributions as "the nature of the job." Mental health staff in prison function as a conduit for privilege requests, and keep records of their contacts. This makes open communication with inmates, free of consequence, very difficult. The chaplain is a unique figure in prison, dating from the first days of imprisonment. Glaser (1964) shows that chaplains play a role in the lives of inmates that is vastly disproportionate to their numbers. Given the confidentiality of religious contacts, and given the chaplain's links to the outside, he is in a key position to deal with inmate problems, particularly problems that relate to significant others in the community. With pastoral counseling, chaplains can acquire training that prepares them to be sensitive and responsive to mental health issues.

Prison staff can also act as referral networks or can form teams that increase the flexibility of their responses. Officers can be the eyes and ears of such teams, and can observe inmates for signs of distress, such as changes in mood or conduct. Officers can interview or informally counsel inmates. If needed, an officer could consult another team member, such as a psychiatrist or case worker. He can refer or pass on the inmate to a fellow team member. He can also recommend interventions, such as assignment changes for the inmate. Professionals could work with the officer on the tier or in the shop, if needed. This arrangement is familiar from family crisis work by police, where psychologists work hand-in-hand with police officers (Bard, 1970).

In mental health settings, the team concept is a standard way of delivering services. Psychiatrists, psychologists, social workers, child-care workers, nurses, and other staff often work in concert in dealing with the same patient. At a given time, the patient deals with whatever team member is best qualified to address his problem, or with the person to whom the patient relates most readily. Jones (1953) has coined the phrase "therapeutic community" to describe institutional staff that is organized democratically, with everyone responsible for the treatment of patients. In Jones' model, fellow-patients are key influences in therapy, which consists of "learning" from "living" experiences with others. We shall explore this paradigm—and its implications for prisons—in Chapter 20.

THE INMATE AS REHABILITATION AGENT

Since peers can influence a man for the worse, it follows that they can also influence him beneficially (Cressey, 1955). This should hold particularly for adolescents, who are peer-oriented and responsive to peer norms. The use of adolescent groups can "turn around" prodelinquent norms, if one can create a culture that prizes cooperation, helping, and positive social contributions (Vorrath & Brendthro, 1974).

There is no reason why personal problems experienced by inmates cannot be ameliorated (or even solved) by other inmates. Younger offenders may accept "advice" from older offenders in areas where older inmates are more experienced (Glaser, 1964), such as in dealing with family problems. Prison inmates often rely spontaneously on "homies"—persons from their community of origin—for advice, protection, or support. Inmates also team with others to engage in studying or other self-betterment pursuits.

The main barrier to nonconvivial inmate relationships is the attraction of the "do your own time" concept, and the low trust or suspicion of many inmates. There is also the importance assigned to expertise. A man may reserve problems of consequence for professionals who "know what to do." He may particularly avoid "an inmate like myself" who has "problems of his own" (Toch, 1975). This stance ignores the dramatic success of "self-help" groups in the community. In such groups, persons who share a problem help each other to solve it.

Self-help groups have found that the act of helping is beneficial to the helper (Riessman, 1965). In listening to others, a person forgets his problem, or places it in perspective. He also finds a rewarding mission, which gives him meaning and raises his self-esteem. The benefits are mutual for helpers and helpees. School drop-outs who are assigned to tutoring can become interested and proficient in learning while they lead to the progress of younger children (Pearl & Riessman, 1965). Alcoholics who reform other alcoholics find that this helps both parties to the transaction (Co-founder, 1957).

One prison (F.C.I. Lompoc) routinely trains inmates as counselors. The coordinator of the program reports that

> Inmates who reach counselor status are rarely involved in behavioral difficulty within the institution. They are relied upon for assistance in their respective living units in maintaining unit stability. Indeed, there have been occasions of peer counselors being asked to remain in their regular units rather than transfer to an honor unit (with more personal freedom) because of such valued service. . . . Peer counselors, in spite of past chronic drug backgrounds on the part of many, project strong anti-drug attitudes. They are rarely seen on sick leave, and, to a man, have never appeared before the disciplinary committee. They appear to have high status among their peers, show few traces of dependency upon others for conducting their institutional and personal affairs, and enjoy mature relationships with their correctional supervisors. . . .
>
> In addition, inmates who have served as peer counselors have taken an increased interest in academic programs, as evidenced by the fact that every inmate on the executive board of the peer counseling program is presently enrolled in the maximum number of college courses possible (two). Very few of these inmates completed college classes prior to their involvement in the program. Peer counselors may be found among the leadership of almost all other institutional programs (Kerish, 1975, pp. 48–49).

Inmate counselors graduated into jobs that capitalized on their training and experience. Kerish (1975) traces individual careers of the first five inmate counselors released from Lompoc:

> The first was a youth counselor for a locally administered urban improvement project and has been thus engaged for the past eight months. The second was a full-time student at the University of Hawaii, trying to decide between staying with his original major in business and his newer interests in psychology and sociology. The third, also a full-time student, had been leading encounter groups at a community college while serving as a consultant to urban improvement groups. He worked with a former graduate student intern who was similarly employed in a neighboring area. The fourth was living with a group of students and looking for work in the construction trades to finance school attendance in the fall. He was a volunteer counselor at a community night counseling service. The fifth worked forty hours a week as a counselor at a drug clinic and was taking fourteen units of junior college work majoring in psychology. These five men, all past chronic offenders, had been diagnosed as antisocial personalities during previous incarceration (p. 50).

The teaming concept can introduce inmates as team members with prison staff. Staff-inmate teams can (1) insure that the technical expertise of staff is available where it is needed; (2) provide subcultural "bridges" that help the professional to communicate; (3) train inmates in mental health concepts or careers; and (4) close the gap that now exists between keepers and the kept. Inmate team members can be invoked individually or in supportive groups. They can be carefully selected, trained, and monitored. If they are powerful or influential inmates, they can become carriers of a helping culture in the yard.

INMATE SELF-GOVERNMENT

One effort to close the gap between keepers and kept in prison is the movement to give inmates a role in governing their institution. This movement dates to the Civil War period, when Zebulon Brockway organized a self-governing system in the Detroit House of Corrections. Similar experiments were organized by Osborne in New York and by Gill at the Norfolk Prison Colony in Massachusetts.

Inmate government today mostly takes the form of elected councils and of staff-inmate grievance machinery. These procedures differ in their scope from early experiments, and are usually more limited. Most "advisory councils" today have restricted jurisdiction, and they deal with recreational schedules and other "pure inmate" issues. But grievance procedures are exceptions to this rule, since they involve complaints against staff or about prison routines.

A model grievance experiment is that of the California Youth Authority, and it was designed by social scientists, inmates, and staff. The system permits inmates to file complaints with a fellow inmate (a grievance clerk), for early hearing by a mixed panel, which

> includes two elected wards (inmates), two staff members and a non-voting chairman who may, if necessary, act as mediator. The grievance clerk also attends meetings. The grievant may represent himself or have another ward or staff member represent him at hearings (Denenberg & Denenberg, 1975, p. 44).

If the inmate is dissatisfied with his panel decision, or if he feels the decision hasn't been pursued, he's entitled to file an appeal. He selects a member of a three-man Review Board, and the superintendent of the institution appoints a second member. The third board member is a professional arbitrator. This procedure is alienation-reducing, because it implies that the inmates are not, in fact, powerless.

Inmate involvement in governance is a plausible gambit for neutralizing antistaff cultures of the yard. Less plausibly, it can also be a means for resocializing offenders, because it provides a laboratory for participation in community life. This aim of governance was first advanced by William George, who founded his "junior republics" in 1895. In George's republics, the United States federal government (with its Cabinet, Supreme Court, and Houses of Congress), was faithfully replicated, as were American economic institutions, in the form of mini-"corporations." In a model that is reminiscent of Kohlberg's view of moral development (Chapter 7), George assumed that delinquent boys in a self-governing setting could move from a pragmatic morality to "doing good for its own sake" (George, 1909).

A much more lifelike model of governance was instituted by Makarenko in Russia, who founded his Gorky Colony for juvenile delinquents in 1920, and a second institution (the Dzerzhinsky Commune) in 1927. Makarenko's settings were fully self-governing, and his delinquents were systematically engaged in productive work. All day-by-day decisions (including admission, custody, and release) were made by the residents themselves. Makarenko's theory was one of normalization, because it assumed that offenders could be institutionally dealt with *as if they were no different from nonoffenders*. In a "normal" environment, wrote Makarenko, resocialization can be a quick, and almost casual process:

> Generally speaking, the distance between moral social standards and moral social distortions is very slight, almost negligible. . . .

> I come to the conclusion that since this distance between anti-social habits, between a kind of experience which is unacceptable to our society, and normal experience is very insignificant, this distance should be spanned as quickly as possible (Makarenko, 1938, p. 242).

Normalization, said Makarenko, promotes "evolution in the ordinary sense in which we understand growth, development." If the offender is dealt with like any other student or worker, "he works at a factory, becomes more proficient, and acquires skills and habits of a social nature. But this is ordinary growth and not readjustment, not some kind of evolution from a spoilt warped character to a normal one" (p. 242).

The key intervention for Makarenko was not the work itself, but the act of showing the offender that he is trusted and valued. Such a demonstration must be explosive—dramatic and sharp:

> By explosion I do not mean a situation in which you put a charge of dynamite under a person, fire it off, and run for safety before that person blows up. What I have in mind is the instantaneous effect of an action which revolutionises all of a person's desires, all his strivings (p. 242).

Such an "explosion" is Goffman's "stripping," "abasement" or "depersonalization" in reverse. It means the shock of discovering that the prison refuses to imprison you, but seeks to enhance your personality:

> These children will never forget the reception given to them at the railway station. They will never forget that bonfire of rags, the new dormitories, the new treatment, the new discipline, and these will remain indelible impressions as long as they live (p. 243).

A former resident of the Gorky Colony (Kalabalin, undated) recalls Makarenko's version of inmate "stripping." He remembers being paroled into Makarenko's care from prison, and being driven directly to a government office building:

Coming into the courtyard of the Department of Education Makarenko placed the Colony's horse and cart at my disposal, and sent me on an errand that startled me.

"Can you read and write, Semyon?"

"Yes."

"Good."

He took a paper from his pocket and handed it to me, saying, "Please get these products for me—bread, fats, and sugar. I have no time to do it, I'll be busy today running around the government offices. As a matter of fact, I hate having to deal with storekeepers, weighers and what not. As a rule they cheat me scandalously—give me short weight and short change. You'll do a better job, I'm sure."

Giving me no time to collect my wits or even make a show of protest he quickly went away. You could have knocked me over with a feather! A fine business this! I scratched the back of my head, that traditional spot where all the answers to life's puzzling questions are born, and continued to ruminate: What do you know? Straight out of jail, and to be trusted with receiving supplies of bread and sugar! Maybe this was a sort of test? Maybe there was a catch in it? I stood there for quite a time thinking it out and finally came to the conclusion that Makarenko was a bit dotty. How, otherwise, could he trust a fellow like me with all this stuff! (p. 71).

The second stage of the intervention occurred as soon as the youth returned (somewhat to his own surprise) with a cart of groceries:

When we were about two hundred metres away from the Educational Department building, Makarenko told me to stop and turned to me with the following words:

"I forgot to tell you. There was a slight misunderstanding about these products. They gave us two extra loaves of bread. Take them back, please, will you, otherwise those storekeepers will kick up a hell of a row. I'll wait for you here."

My ears and face flamed with shame. What could it be? This had never happened to me before. I jumped off the cart, pulled two loaves out from under the hay and walked back to the store. In my mind was the thought: What sort of a man is he? He told me himself he had been cheated, and I thought, what was the best way to take revenge on those storekeepers? Two loaves isn't much, but he says, "Go and take 'em back, please."

"Thank you very, very much, young man," the storekeeper greeted me. "We guessed it was just a mistake and it would be cleared up. Good day to you. Thanks."

I gave him a dirty look and quickly went out.

"Have some roasted sunflower seeds?" Makarenko said, offering me a handful when I got back into the cart. "I like them." (Kalabalin, p. 72).

Beyond demonstrating trust in inmates, Makarenko felt it crucial to surround them *at once* with productive, goal-oriented, responsible groups. Makarenko called such groups "primary collectives," and targeted their membership at seven to fifteen. In such groups, sociability or conviviality was to be avoided ("this is not a group of friends who have come to some arrangement") in favor of shared and sharable aims to which each member could contribute ("a community, a body having certain obligations, a certain duty, a certain responsibility," p. 247).

Makarenko's institutions were governed by a council which was composed of group leaders. The decision of this council could be influenced by staff, but were not subject to staff veto.

Makarenko's was a total institution that was designed to involve the inmates, and to commit them to its goals. The peer culture in such an institution would own its goals, and would enthusiastically participate in programs. In more conventional institutions programs are staff-run, and the inmate culture is *at best* very tenuously committed to them.

MENTAL HEALTH PROGRAMS IN PRISON

Psychological services in prisons have aims which can be separately viewed. One clear treatment problem is that of mental illness—particularly, of psychosis—among persons *who happen to be* in prison, but who are *also* very disturbed. The goal here is no different than the aim of psychotherapy with similar disturbed men outside prisons, in all sorts of settings. In fact, such inmates are frequently transferred to standard mental hospitals.

A second sort of goal is to help inmates who have situational coping problems. The aim of such intervention is to ameliorate stress, and to assist the inmate (sometimes very tangibly) to "solve his problem." Though the stress of inmates is usually related to some aspect of imprisonment, the interviewer's function (crisis intervention) parallels a role played in the free world with people under stress.

A third goal of treatment has to do with remedying personal deficiencies that impede or impair the inmate's adjustment in the free world. This treatment goal is called "rehabilitation," but it has nothing to do with crime or recidivism—at least, not in principle. We see rehabilitation in the free world where a person is handicapped by deficits (such as having a speech defect) or where he suffers from dispositions (such as alcoholism) which interfere with his performance.

If the aims of intervention are logically "pure," the inmate culture offers *least* resistance to psychotherapy for inmates who are *transparently* disturbed. Psychotics who live in prison fall under the inmate rubric of "dings" (or its semantic equivalents), which covers persons who are unpredictable and are difficult to live with. Since prison is an abnormal environment, peer acceptance of idiosyncratic conduct is generous enough to cover a variety of adjustment modes. But it does not cover extreme bizarreness or explosiveness, which produce discomfort and fear of danger. An occasional psychotic may be protected by his inmate-friends, but there is generally no objection to staff removing a sick inmate from the prison yard and transferring him to a mental health setting.

It is clear that one must *never* confuse *real* therapy problems with those of management. A psychotic who "acts out" must be dealt with as a psychotic, and he is *thereby* a candidate for therapy. An inmate who "acts out" but who is free of disturbance is *not* an obvious mental health client. Promiscuous selection of therapy clients invites resistance that covers every other inmate in therapy.

Crisis intervention is a very difficult goal, because it runs into the taboo against inmate "weakness," and into overgenerous definitions of "ratting." A man who is in trouble may be loath to seek help if he must purchase it at the expense of his reputation. He must also feel reluctant to risk treatment if this classes him as unself-sufficient, which may unfavorably impress the parole board. The ultimate "Catch 22" is where the inmate feels anxiety about his parole, and is classified as "psychologically unprepared for release."

Rehabilitation programs are the most difficult to implement, because we *may* be tampering with motives or causes of crime. The fact that a person is in prison does not entitle staff (as some critics see it) to do more than ask him to serve time. This view holds that we can "treat" the inmate *in* prison but that we cannot *use* prisons for treatment purposes. This means that we can raise cognitive or skill levels as a humanitarian move, but not as a resocializing technique. Morris & Hawkins (1977) make this argument as follows:

> The fact is that rehabilitation programs for convicted criminals in prison do not overcome the socially alienative effects and other disadvantages of conviction and imprisonment. The cage is not a sensible place in which to cure the criminal, even when the medical analogy makes sense, which it rarely does. But this does *not* mean that such treatment programs as we now have in prisons should be abandoned; quite the contrary, they urgently need expansion. No one of any sensitivity can visit any of our mega-prisons without recognizing that they contain, as in all countries, populations that are disproportionately illiterate, unemployed, vocationally untrained, undereducated, psychologically disturbed, and socially isolated. It is both in the prisoners' and in the community's best interest to help them to remedy these deficiencies.
>
> Nevertheless, it should be recognized that rehabilitative programs to that end are not *the* purpose or even *one* purpose of imprisonment. "Rehabilitation," whatever it means and whatever the programs that give it meaning, must cease to be the claimed purpose of imprisonment. We should avoid hypocrisy: we send men to prison as punishment for what they have done; sometimes also to deter those who are like-minded, and sometimes because we do not know what else to do with them. We cage them for what they have done; it is an injustice to cage them also for what they *are* in order to change them, to attempt to cure them coercively. There is a sharp distinction between the purposes of imprisonment and the opportunities for the training and assistance of prisoners that may properly be pursued within those purposes (pp. 67–68).

The strongest objection is to our forcing inmates to be treated *involuntarily*. In the words of Morris & Hawkins, "We must stay out of the business of forcibly remaking man" (p. 68). Where resocialization is at issue, inmates often take a passive or resistant role in programs. Even where an individual may seek to participate in treatment, he may have a tough time doing so where other clients mark time or actively resist.

If programs are voluntary, this tends to mean "participate, or else." At worst, parole hinges on "demonstrating the right attitude" by "getting with the program." At best, treatment may offer a change from prison routine, provide fringe benefits or something to do. Given such contexts, we can expect surface compliance or a frantic going-through-motions. Even inmates who are deeply involved with therapy may have to pretend they are "just doing it for the board."

Another problem is the expected goal of reduced crime. Treatment is supposed to change the client, but it cannot affect the environment he returns to. If a program "rehabilitates" a person, it does so up to the termination point of treatment. Treatment work may be promptly undone when the ex-inmate faces lack of support, antisocial peers or unemployment. A man may also commit a crime which bears no relationship to the problems which were linked to his past offenses. And he may be "better adjusted," but criminal.

Moreover, no matter what sort of a person an offender may be, there are probably many other persons like the offender who do not commit crimes. If the person is nonpathological and comparatively content, can we still try to change him? We shall explore this question later, but ultimately have to answer it each for ourselves.

Staff must decide what "treatment" is, and what it isn't. Psychoanalysis (Chapter 8), behavior modification (Chapter 9), and rational emotive therapy (Chapter 17), are formally, treatment. But is a group session run by a case worker treatment? Is the same session treatment if it is led by an officer? Can education be treatment? What about vocational training? Or hobby work? Recreation? Talks with an inmate? Furloughs with one's family?

Ideally, treatment must be as treatment does. Therapy in which inmates filibuster may be a nontreatment experience, since nothing is permitted to happen. But a furlough in which a relationship is cemented, a classroom in which inmates find themselves, or a conversation in which they gain insight may—by the same criterion—be treatment.

PRISON IMPACT: A PSYCHOLOGICAL PERSPECTIVE

If we define "treatment" very broadly, we think of prison as a *psychological environment*, a milieu with *impact* on the inmate. We think of ways to reduce the harm that prisons may do. And we think of ways in which a person may be benefitted in prison.

Though prisons are stressful, they need not be wasteful or destructive. Men acquire knowledge in prisons, make friends, follow meaningful pursuits, reminisce, plan, and (on occasion) find new purpose in life. There are experiences in prison that are pleasurable, constructive, healing, and growth-promoting.

We have shown that it may be difficult, *but not impossible,* to make the prison experience a more fruitful one for many inmates. The "pains of imprisonment" need not translate into adjustment modes that are personally and interpersonally destructive.

If a man *has to be* in prison, we must do our best to see that he learns and grows if he can. To do this across the board may be "treatment." Treatment in this sense requires no assumption about abnormality, about special need for support, or about criminal tendencies. It means examining each prison experience of each inmate for its negative and positive consequences. It means doing what we can to reduce negative consequences of prison and to increase positive ones.

This task can be accomplished by simply doing what we do at present, but doing it more systematically. It means maximizing the impact of staff members as well as that of other inmates. It means classifying people sensitively, and placing them in matched climates and settings. It means invoking programs for their timeliness and impact. It means attending to the subculture and using it as an ally instead of working against it. It means linking the outside with the inside to prepare people for release.

It means, above all, to have an inmate-centered view in which whatever happens to each inmate is assessed in terms of (1) the degree of stress it produces, (2) the relationship of each experience to the inmate's purposes and assumptions, (3) the adjustments the inmate must make to cope with his experience, and (4) the support the inmate needs to benefit (if possible) from his treatment.

The prison must undergo similar review. We must know whether prison twists or regenerates, offends or respects integrity. Our task must be to help staff create institutions which are nondehumanizing. Such institutions must have walls that are permeable. They must have personnel who care and peers who are friends. They must be places where doing time means spending time, and where life has as much decency, normalcy, and meaning as imprisonment allows.

NOTE

1. This fact is dramatized for the inmate who joins her husband bearing self-administered prison love-messages in the form of tattoos (Fox, 1976).

REFERENCES

Bard, M. *Police management of conflicts among people.* Final Report to NILECJ. New York: Psychological Center, CUNY, 1970.

Briggs, D. A transitional therapeutic community in a prison. In S. Whiteley, D. Briggs, & F. Turner, *Dealing with delinquents: The treatment of antisocial behavior.* New York: Schocken, 1973, 117–150.

Cantril, H. *The psychology of social movements.* New York: Wiley, 1941.

Co-founder. *Alcoholics anonymous comes of age.* New York: Harper & Row, 1957.

Cressey, D. R. Changing criminals: The application of the theory of differential association, *American Journal of Sociology,* 1955, *61,* 116–120.

Denenberg, R. V. & Denenberg, T. Prison grievance procedures. *Corrections Magazine,* 1975, *1,* 29 ff.

Fenton, N. *An introduction to group counseling in correctional institutions.* New York: American Correctional Association, 1958.

Fox, J. *Self-imposed stigmata: A study of tattooing among female inmates.* (Unpublished Doctoral Dissertation) Albany: State University of New York, 1976.

Fox, J. Women in crisis. In H. Toch, *Men in crisis: Human breakdowns in prison.* Chicago: Aldine, 1975, 181–204.

Freud, S. *The future of an illusion.* New York: Doubleday, 1957.

George, W. R. *The junior republic.* New York: Appleton, 1909.

Giallombardo, R. *Society of women: A study of a woman's prison.* New York: Wiley, 1966.

Glaser, D. *The effectiveness of a prison and parole system.* Indianapolis: Bobbs-Merrill, 1964.

Goffman, E. *Asylums: Essays on the social situation of mental patients and other inmates.* New York: Doubleday, Anchor, 1961.

Heffernan, E. *Making it in prison: The square, the cool, and the life.* New York: Wiley-Interscience, 1972.

Irwin, J. *The felon.* Englewood-Cliffs, N.J.: Prentice-Hall, 1970.

Jones, M. (and collaborators). *The therapeutic community: A new treatment method in psychiatry.* New York: Basic Books, 1953.

Kalabalin, S. How A. S. Makarenko educated us. In *Makarenko: His life and work.* Moscow: Foreign Languages Publishing House, undated, 69–78.

Kerish, B. R. Peer counseling. In R. E. Hosford, & C. S. Moss, *Crumbling walls: Treatment and counseling of prisoners.* Urbana: University of Illinois, 1975.

Makarenko, A. My experience (1938). In *Makarenko: His life and work.* Moscow: Foreign Languages Publishing House, undated, 240–266.

Marshall, C. D. et al. *Overview of therapeutic program to be housed in diagnostic and treatment unit IV Adirondack Correctional Treatment and Evaluation Center, Dannemora, Clinton County, New York.* Unpublished, undated, mimeographed.

McGrath, J. E. (Ed.). *Social and psychological factors in stress.* New York: Holt, Rinehart and Winston, 1970.

Milgram, S. & Toch, H. Collective behavior: Crowds and social movements. In G. Lindzey & E. Aronson (Eds.), *The handbook of social psychology,* Vol. 4. Reading: Addison-Wesley, 1969, 507–611.

Morris, N., & Hawkins, G. *Letter to the president on crime control.* Chicago: University of Chicago Press, 1977.

Murray, H. A. (and collaborators). *Explorations in personality.* New York: Oxford, 1938.

Pearl, A., & Riessman, F. *New careers for the poor: The nonprofessional in human service.* New York: Free Press, 1965.

Riessman, F. The "helper" therapy principle. *Social Work,* 1965, *10,* 27–32.

Rogers, C. R. *On becoming a person.* Boston: Houghton Mifflin, 1961.

Sykes, G. M. *The society of captives: A study of a maximum security prison.* Princeton: Princeton University Press, 1958.

Toch, H. *Men in crisis: Human breakdowns in prison.* Chicago: Aldine, 1975.

Toch, H. *Peacekeeping: Police, prisons, and violence.* Lexington, Mass.: D. C. Heath, 1976.

Toch, H. *Living in prison: The ecology of survival.* New York: Free Press, 1977.

Vorrath, H. H., & Brendthro, L. K. *Positive peer culture.* Chicago: Aldine, 1974.

Walster, E. Assignment of responsibility for an accident. *Journal of Personality and Social Psychology,* 1966, 3, 73–79.

Ward, D., & Kassebaum, G. *Women's prison: Sex and social structure.* Chicago: Aldine, 1965.

chapter 5

Insanity and Irresponsibility

Psychiatric diversion in the criminal justice system

Thomas S. Szasz

For obvious reasons, there has long been a close relationship between psychiatry and the law, especially between institutional psychiatry and the criminal law.

The criminal law deals with behavior that violates criminal laws, and with the social disposition of persons who are accused or convicted of such violations. Institutional psychiatry deals with behavior that violates the norms of mental health, and with the social disposition of persons "diagnosed" as "suffering" from "mental disorders." Both disciplines are thus concerned with the study of certain kinds of "bad" human behavior, and with the social control of certain kinds of "bad" persons. Since the criteria for intervening in the lives of persons who are said to be criminally guilty or psychiatrically sick overlap, and since the methods of intervention are often similar, it is not surprising that psychiatry and the criminal law should themselves overlap and interlock in their principles and practices. This close connection between them is, however, obscured by certain semantic and social conventions which make it appear as if criminologists dealt with one sub-

---

Some of the material in this chapter was presented in March 1977 at a symposium on "Crime and Punishment" at the Harvard Law School, sponsored by the Liberty Fund. These portions are reprinted with permission from *Assessing the Criminal: Restitution, Retribution and the Legal Process*, edited by R. E. Barnett and J. Hagel, copyright 1978, Ballinger Publishing Company.

ject and psychiatrists another. Actually, they do not deal with different subjects, but apply different strategies to the same subject—deviant acts and actors (Szasz, 1963).

CRIMINAL RESPONSIBILITY

The criminal law draws many common-sense distinctions among various types or degrees of responsibility. For example, when a gangster ambushes and kills a rival, he is considered responsible for criminal intent and first degree murder. Whereas if an intoxicated driver kills a pedestrian he does not know, he is considered responsible (at most) for criminal negligence and manslaughter. In the first instance, the defendant's responsibility is for the murder; in the second, for the negligence. Although both victims are equally dead, the criminal law distinguishes—without recourse to psychiatric examinations, explanations, or experts—between two radically different acts.

There are certain circumstances, however, in which psychiatric consideration are deemed relevant to assessing the defendant's criminal responsibility. In practice these assessments center on, and culminate in, judgments about whether the "patient" has or has not a "mental illness" which impairs or nullifies his "criminal responsibility." If the psychiatric verdict is that the defendant is sane, then he is handled by the criminal justice system. If it is that he is insane, and if that verdict is upheld in court, then he is diverted to the institutional psychiatric system. I need not stress here that, in the latter case, his confinement and punishment may be (and, in cases of serious crime, is nowadays likely to be) more lengthy and severe than they would be if his disposition were purely judicial and penal (Szasz, 1961, 1965, 1977).

Accordingly, there is a vast literature—in criminology, law, and psychiatry—devoted to the problem of so-called criminal responsibility.[1] Through the constant use of this term, many people have come to believe that there is such a thing as "criminal responsibility," and that all that is needed is a psychiatrist to ascertain whether or not an offender "has" it.

But criminal responsibility is not an object, like a table; nor is it a natural phenomenon like a rainbow. Furthermore, the idea is neither synonymous with, nor derivable from, the concepts of physical or mental illness. Pneumonia, hypertension, schizophrenia are terms designating physical and mental diseases, yet none provides a consistent clue to the criminal responsibility of its bearer.

Despite these difficulties, it is possible to provide a more accurate definition of criminal responsibility. Briefly, by criminal responsibility we usually refer to a particular kind of relationship between an offender and the society in which he lives. In other words, "criminal responsibility" is essentially synonymous with "punishability." In short, it is a serious mistake to think that criminal responsibility is a trait or quality which may be detected by accurate observation of the offender. The concept refers not only to the offender but also to society's right to punish him. The meaning of the concept must therefore be sought in the offender's actual situation in society.

THE STRUCTURE OF PSYCHIATRIC DIVERSION

Psychiatrists and lawyers have long maintained that there are two classes of human beings—the sane and the insane—the difference between the two consisting, among other things, of the alleged fact that the former are responsible for their actions, whereas the latter are not. This proposition has slowly infiltrated popular and professional opinion and has increasingly affected the administration of the criminal law in the United States. As a result, psychiatric diversion is now a regular feature of American law enforcement.

By "psychiatric diversion" I refer to any psychiatric intervention in connection with individuals who are charged with or convicted of a crime, as well as with individuals whose "misbehavior" might but need not be construed as constituting lawbreaking. Psychiatric diversion thus includes such diverse sanctions as civil commitment, pretrial examination of persons accused of crime, declaring defendants psychiatrically unfit to stand trial and committing them as criminally insane, the insanity plea and the insanity verdict, and the imposition of coerced psychiatric outpatient treatment in lieu of prosecution or sentencing. Such psychiatric interventions and dispositions are now commonplace in the day-to-day work of the police, the courts, and psychiatrists (Szasz, 1970, 1977).

Types of Psychiatric Diversion

From a practical point of view, the most important psychiatric diversionary tactic is the pretrial psychiatric examination of defendants, ostensibly to determine their fitness to stand trial. The request for such an examination may come from any of the parties concerned with the trial of a criminal defendant—that is, from the defense attorney, the prosecuting attorney, or the judge. In New York State, it seems to have become a matter of routine in recent years to submit virtually every person accused of a major violent crime to such an examination—a symptom of the degree to which crime has become psychiatrized in our age. If such a person is found unfit to stand trial, he is committed to a mental hospital until he is found fit or until the charges against him are dismissed. If he is found fit to stand trial, he is tried (at which time he may still plead that he was insane at the time of the offense).

From a theoretical point of view, the most important tactic of psychiatric diversion is the insanity defense. That maneuver, which is by now centuries old, consists, in effect, of the plea by the defendant that although he committed the act with which he is charged, he is not criminally responsible for it because, at the time of the offense, he was insane and therefore lacked the "criminal intent" (or mens rea) legally necessary for the commission of a crime. The practical consequences of sustaining such a plea depend on whether, in the jurisdiction where the defendant is tried, there is or is not a law mandating the automatic commitment of persons acquitted by reason of insanity; and, further, on the nature of the act with which the accused is charged and on the caprices of the administration of the psychiatric commitment system.

The Dangers of Psychiatric Diversion

One can argue that both our criminal justice system and the social fabric of our society are now being undermined by psychiatric diversion—partly because psychiatric diversion subverts the rule of law, and partly because the rhetoric of diagnosis and therapy diverts attention from the fact of wrongdoing and the moral legitimacy of punishment (Szasz, 1961, 1970, 1977).

The rule of law, the bedrock on which our political freedoms rest, means that the innocent must be left at liberty, and that the guilty must be punished as prescribed by law. The former requirement (with which I shall not be concerned here), often makes people feel frustrated at not being able to control other people who annoy or offend them; the latter (with which I am very much concerned here), often makes people feel guilty for having to punish those guilty of lawbreaking. Psychiatric diversion comes into play because it provides a mechanism that simultaneously allays the citizen's guilt for punishing certain acts and actors, and satisfies their need for security by depriving certain acts of their legitimacy and certain actors of their liberty. It does so by treating certain actors as insane patients and their acts as the symptoms of their "mental illness," for which they are not responsible, but for which society may justly impose compulsory "therapeutic" measures on them.

Examples of Psychiatric Diversion

Although, in principle, psychiatric diversion is a matter of political philosophy, jurisprudence, and forensic psychiatry, and may therefore be appropriately discussed in the abstract vocabularies of those disciplines, it is, in practice, a brutal fact of everyday life and hence must also be discussed in the ordinary language of everyday life. I shall do so, to begin with, mainly by citing and briefly commenting on contemporary American examples of psychiatric diversion.[2]

A recent article, revealingly titled "Presidental Assassination: An American Problem," by Edwin A. Weinstein, a professor at Mount Sinai Medical School and an acknowledged expert on such matters, begins with the following two sentences:

> Assassinations of Heads of State of foreign countries have usually been carried out by organized political groups seeking to overthrow the government or change its policies. In the United States, on the other hand, Presidential assassinations have been the work of mentally disturbed individuals (Weinstein, 1976).

To demonstrate the depravity of this sort of writing, let me rephrase these sentences from the point of view of a hypothetical Soviet mental health expert:

Emigrations from capitalist countries have traditionally been the acts of poor and persecuted people seeking better opportunities for themselves elsewhere. Emigrations, and attempts at emigration, from the Soviet Union, on the other hand, are the acts of mentally disturbed dissidents.

Weinstein's account implies that those persons who have killed foreign heads of state had valid reasons for doing so, whereas those who have killed American heads of state lacked such reasons. My sarcastic Soviet modification of it implies that it is reasonable to leave capitalist countries, but not communist countries. Certain classes of acts and actors are thus diverted, literally with the stroke of a pen, from matters of moral, political, and judicial discourse, into matters of psychiatric diagnosis and disposition.

Ironically, when psychiatric diversion is now practiced in the Soviet Union, it provokes indignant condemnation by Western observers and by Alexander Solzhenitsyn. For example, in his *Warning to West*, Solzhenitsyn writes: "In Odessa, Vyacheslav Grunov has been arrested for possessing illicit literature and put into a lunatic asylum." (Solzhenitsyn, 1967, p. 118).

If we replace illicit books with illicit drugs, and change the scene to the United States, Solzhenitsyn's sentence reads: "In Chicago John Jones has been arrested for possessing illicit drugs and put into a lunatic asylum."

Many thinkers—Ludwig von Mises (1949) among them—have suggested that books can be more dangerous than drugs. Hence, if it makes sense for a government to ban dangerous drugs, it makes sense for it to ban dangerous books—and to question the sanity of persons who disagree with such policies. I do not see how we can have it both ways. That is, how we can support the proposition that the American use of dangerous drugs constitutes a form of mental illness and that those who use such drugs may appropriately be controlled by means of psychiatric sanctions—and oppose the equivalent Russian proposition about dangerous books?

The most famous modern American victim of psychiatric diversion is undoubtedly Ezra Pound. Pound, it may be recalled, lived in Italy during World War II. Allegedly he made some broadcasts over the Italian radio that were treasonous. After the war he was arrested and charged with treason. However, instead of being tried, he was declared to be schizophrenic and hence unfit to stand trial. As a result, he was locked up at St. Elizabeth's Hospital in Washington, D. C., for thirteen and a half years (Szasz, 1963).

The chief characteristic of psychiatric diversion, as of all departures from the rule of law, is capriciousness. Pound was incriminated and punished by means of it. The woman whose brief story I shall next cite was exonerated and allowed to go unpunished by means of it.

On April 11, 1976, Melissa Morris killed her three-month-old son by beating him to death. She claimed she did it to rid him of the devil. On September 15, 1976, she was released from a Maryland mental hospital "after a judge found 'no clear and convincing evidence that she presents a danger to herself or society.' The decision by a Montgomery County Circuit judge, John Mitchell, followed a murder plea of not guilty by reason of insanity by Melissa Morris, 19, of Wheaton" (*International Herald Tribune,* September 17, 1976).

I want to emphasize the capriciousness of the judgments that go into the decision to psychiatrically divert or not divert a case, since, as we have already noted, it is arbitrariness, rather than brutality, that is the hallmark of a totalitarian system of criminal law (Hayek, 1960). Accordingly, I shall next cite the case of a man who acted crazy and committed a crime, but who nevertheless escaped both psychiatric and legal punishment, while his victim, whose freedom he infringed, was punished (through his insurance company). On the night of July 4, 1975, Robert Henry went barhopping with friends on Long Island. Off Montauk Highway, he stripped naked, "finding it [according to the judge] a fine night for a stroll . . ." The police sighted him, started after him, and shouted to him to halt. Instead of obeying that order, Mr. Henry tried to avoid arrest by dashing across the highway. As a result, he was hurt by a truck driven by Richard Rusillo. Henry sued for damages, and a Long Island judge upheld an award of $2,030 to him and $525 to his lawyer, payable by the Great American Insurance Company (*New York Times,* September 24, 1976). In this case, "streaking" (that is, running around naked), crossing a highway illegally, obstructing traffic, and resisting arrest all went unpunished and unpsychiatrized.

The above case stands in sharp contrast to television star Louise Lasser's recent encounter with psychiatric law. Miss Lasser was apprehended for possessing cocaine, a criminal offense. Unlike Mr. Henry, Miss Lasser harmed no one. Her act—that is, possessing cocaine—was quintessentially private. Nevertheless, she could have been legally punished for it. But she was not. In fact, she was not even tried. Instead she was "placed in a drug diversionary program, consisting of seeing her psychiatrist. . . . In ordering the program [explained the newspaper story of the case], which is common for first-time drug offenders instead of trial, Beverly Hills Municipal Court Judge Leonard Wolfe set December 1 for Miss Lasser's return to court. Charges could be dropped at that time" (*Syracuse Herald-Journal,* June 9, 1976). Charges subsequently were dropped.

Here is another case, illustrating the use of psychiatric detention in lieu of incarceration in jail:

JoAnne Brown, who was acquitted last February [1975] in the slaying of Burr C. Hollister, . . . has been ordered confined to the Nassau County Medical Center for further psychiatric examination. Mrs. Brown, who was found not guilty by reason of mental disease or defect, was accused of shooting Mr. Hollister in September, 1974. Last week, the State Department of Mental Hygiene declared that she was now capable of release. However, Judge Bernard Tomson of Nassau County Court said that he would not release Mrs. Brown without another psychiatric opinion being made within the next 60 days. He also said she would not be released unless conditions were established that she have psychiatric therapy or chemotherapy (*New York Times*, July 30, 1976).

This story speaks for itself—imprisonment in a building called a medical center; chemotherapy for murder. The medicalization of mayhem is here complete.

THE FUNCTION OF PSYCHIATRIC DIVERSION

Commitment to the rule of law places a heavy moral burden on the citizens of a free, or would-be free, society. That is so for two reasons, one of which has received much more attention than the other. First, because such a commitment implies that the majority of the citizens, through the government, will eschew infringing on the freedom of those of their fellows who obey the law, even if the latter annoy or offend the sensibilities of their neighbors. That, essentially, is what we have come to mean by the phrase "the rule of law."

The rule of law has, however, another implication as well which constitutes an important additional burden for those who commit themselves to it. That burden has to do with the enforcement of the laws and with the dilemma of the citizen—especially as legislator, judge, district attorney, or juror—faced with laws he regards as stupid, unjust, or evil. I refer here to the obvious, but often neglected, fact that the rule of law requires not only that the innocent be left at liberty, but also that the guilty be punished. Both often make those entrusted with implementing the law feel guilty. Thus arises the question: What can a people, and especially its law enforcement authorities, do when they are confronted with acts or actors whom they do not want to punish as severely as the law prescribes or whom they do not want to punish at all? Actually, they have only a few options. They can look the other way. They can acquit. They can repeal the offensive law. Each of these options is used in the administration of the criminal law. But each suffers from a serious defect—namely, that it impairs the collective sense of security which the impartial administration of the law is supposed to provide. It is precisely at this point that psychiatric diversion comes into play: it provides a mechanism that simultaneously allays the citizens' guilt for punishing certain acts and actors, and satisfies their need for security by depriving certain acts of their legitimacy and certain actors of their liberty. An historical example illustrates this core function of psychiatric diversion.

An Example: Suicide and Madness

To set the matter before us in its historical context, it is necessary to note briefly the history of the legal status of suicide and madness in English law. According to Henry Fedden, the origin of the secular prohibition of suicide in England can be pinpointed, as follows:

Bracton, the legal authority of his time, writing in the thirteenth century, does not rank suicide as a felony. Thus fifty years after the Magna Carta, the suicide was not yet legally a criminal in England. His fate, however, was in the melting-pot. Many of Bracton's contemporaries had not agreed with him, and by the middle of the next century, in spite of Bracton's ruling, the person who intentionally took his life had become guilty of *felo-de-se* (self-murder) (Fedden, 1938).

Suicide, long considered a sin against the Church, now became a crime against the Crown as well, and the penalty for it was accordingly severe: the deceased person's body was buried without Christian rites at the crossroads of a public highway, perhaps with a stake driven through it, and his "movable goods" were confiscated and went to the Crown.

With respect to insanity, our historical starting point is the ancient position which did not regard insanity as having any bearing upon criminal guilt. According to Rollin M. Perkins, "Principles of criminal liability dating prior to the Norman Conquest persisted into the thirteenth century and a 'man who has killed another by misadventure, though he deserves a pardon, [was considered to be] guilty of a crime; and the same rule applies . . . to a lunatic . . .'" (Perkins, 1957, p. 738). In the thirteenth century, the issuance of such a pardon to lunatics who committed homicide came to be granted "as a matter of course" (Perkins, 1957, p. 738). Then, in the time of Edward III (1327–1377), "madness became a complete defense to a criminal charge" (Perkins, 1957, p. 739). Inasmuch as suicide was considered to be a species of murder, lunacy was, after the fourteenth century, a complete defense against it also. It appears, however—although the records concerning this matter are sketchy—that such a verdict was issued quite rarely in cases of suicide before the seventeenth century.

The earliest reliable records concerning deaths by suicide in London go back to 1629. From then on we can trace the incidence of both "suicide (in nonlunatics)" and "suicide in lunatics." They reveal that by the seventeenth century, the traditional penalties against the offense had not been rigidly enforced, the body often being buried privately or at least without indignities. In the early part of the eighteenth century, there was a sharp increase in the incidence of suicide in England, and with it there occurred an important change in the behavior of the persons who sat on coroners' juries.

"The rise in suicide in 1721," according to Sprott, "may have been occasioned by the bursting of the South Sea Bubble in the previous year; in the eighteenth century financial failure probably became one of the common 'entrances' into the deed. . . . At the same time [as suicide increased] . . . coroners' juries brought in more and more verdicts of lunacy" (Sprott, 1961, p. 99). Uncontaminated by modern psychiatric doctrines, Sprott describes the process of "discovering" that the person dead by suicide was insane as a phenomenon that points to what went on in the minds of the jurors rather than in the minds of those destined to be posthumously diagnosed as lunatics:

In the eighteenth century juries increasingly brought in findings of insanity in order to save the family from the consequences of a verdict of felony; the number of deaths recorded as "lunatic" grew startlingly in relation to the number recorded as self-murder, whereas in the previous century, according to a modern legal authority, ninety percent of self-killers sat on by coroners' juries had been returned as having made away with themselves. Devices were employed to bestow the goods of the deceased, and by the 1760's confiscation of goods seems to have become rare. (Sprott, 1961, p. 121)

Fifty years later English sentiment overwhelmingly favored the view that "Every human being must wish to soften the rigour of our laws respecting suicide (Sprott, 1961, p. 158). The more heavily the punishment of suicide weighed on the shoulders of the jurymen who had to bring in the verdict, the more brazenly they discarded the burden by declaring the deceased person a lunatic. Such an evasion of the laws punishing suicide was, of course, too obvious to deceive legal scholars. Thus, Sir William Blackstone (1723–1780), the most important jurist of his age, realized at once that if a finding of lunacy could be contrived to nullify the laws against suicide, it could just as easily be contrived against every other crime. Noting that for suicide to be a crime, the person who commits it must be "in his senses," Blackstone writes:

But this excuse [of lunacy] ought not be strained to that length to which our coroner's juries are apt to carry it, viz., that the very act of suicide is an evidence of insanity; as if every man who acts contrary to reason had no reason at all; for the same argument would prove every other criminal *non compos*, as well as the self-murderer (Blackstone, 1962, p. 212).

Sprott (1961) cites a part of this passage and emphasizes Blackstone's "disgust" with the behavior of jurors who so conduct themselves. What then disgusted Blackstone now delights every intellectual, scientist, and right-thinking person: although suicide is no longer a crime, it is in all "civilized" societies a violation of the mental hygiene laws and, if it is unsuccessful, is punishable by appropriate psychiatric sanctions (Szasz, 1977a). It is clear, I hope, how well this arrangement satisfies simultaneously the need to condemn suicide and to control suicidal persons as well as the need to avoid feeling guilty for doing so.

The same considerations now apply to virtually all prohibitions and punishments. Cut adrift from religion and natural law, modern man floats without a compass on an existential sea of choices, unsure of what he should condemn and how he should punish. The result is the massive escapism into the embrace of what may be called the Therapeutic State (Szasz, 1970, 1977b).

I trust that the example I have cited demonstrates that psychiatric diversion has, in fact, nothing to do with modern psychiatry. It is not the result of, and does not depend on, the modern understanding of the mind or of mental diseases, as its contemporary proponents claim; instead, it is the result of, and depends on, its psychosocial utility, especially in a free and democratic society, for managing the guilty conduct of certain persons and the guilty consciences of those who sit in judgment on them.

UNDOING PSYCHIATRIC DIVERSION

In the eighteenth century, the Age of Enlightenment (see Chapter 6) the main argument of social critics was that traditionally most societies have been tyrannical. Those who wished to secure liberty or to enlarge its scope were thus occupied with efforts to curb the powers of the rulers, whether they be theocratic, aristocratic, or democratic. From Montesquieu and Jefferson to Mises and Hayek, the magic formula has been limited government. That made sense in the context of its underlying premise: the rulers wanted to do too much (especially in the way of coercing others); hence the thing to do was to make it difficult or impossible for them to do certain things (especially coercing others who were not guilty of law-breaking). Thus was constitutional government born.

Today, however, we are confronted with some societies, in particular with American society, in which that classic premise is no longer valid, or rather is not valid in its original form. The American government is now a threat to the freedom of its own people not because it punishes the innocent, nor because its punishments are too harsh, but rather because it does not punish the guilty enough, and because it is loath to punish at all for punishment's sake. One result is an ever-increasing army of thieves and thugs, muggers and murderers abroad in the land, preying on people unprotected by their own police and judiciary. Another result is an ever-increasing tendency not to punish those who commit evil acts but instead to treat them for nonexistent illnesses.

I only state the obvious when I say that our personal liberty is now as much threatened by a desperado as by a despot, by a mugger as by a monarch. Why, then, do we keep asking stupid questions, such as: Why is crime increasing? Why do so many people rob and kill? The answers to these questions are, unfortunately, also obvious.

One answer lies in inverting the patently false adage that "crime does not pay." Crime indeed pays, and it pays not only for the criminals but also for the criminologists (by which term I refer here to all those who make a living confining, diagnosing, treating, rehabilitating, and otherwise managing and studying offenders). And it pays each of them both economically and existentially—that is, by putting money in their pockets and meaning into their lives. We cannot reduce crime until we recognize these facts. And even when we do recognize them, we shall be able to reduce crime only in proportion to the degree to which we either make noncriminal pursuits more attractive for would-be criminals, or make criminal activities less attractive for them, or both. We are not likely to do any of these things so long as we look to professional criminologists to solve a problem of which they themselves are so important a part.

Another answer to the foregoing questions lies in remembering the painfully true adage that "power corrupts." Muggers and thugs now abuse their powers for the same reason that so many priests, kings, businessmen, judges, politicians, and psychiatrists have abused theirs in the past: in a sense, because that is what power is for. This answer, too, is obvious; and perhaps because it is so obvious, it really does not matter. What matters, indeed what alone matters, is how we can curb the powers of malefactors. Putting the problem that way points to a fresh (albeit fundamentally time-honored) solution for it. As the solution for too much power for rulers lay in curtailing their powers, so the solution for too much power for robbers lies likewise in, curtailing theirs. There is, moreover, only one decent and dependable way to achieve these objectives: in the one case by means of checks and balances, or a responsible, limited government, vouchsafed by a citizenry that ranks liberty above security; in the other case, by means of a morally vigorous criminal justice system, vouchsafed by a citizenry that ranks punishing offenders (who injure others) by means of fines, deprivations of liberty, and even life above protecting individuals (who injure themselves) by means of coerced psychiatric treatment.

CONCLUSION: THE PROPER PLACE OF PSYCHIATRY IN THE CRIMINAL JUSTICE SYSTEM

My views on the role of psychiatry in the criminal justice system rest on the same premises that animate my views on its role in society at large: namely, that psychiatry deals not with disease but with deviance; that its interventions are not medical cures but social controls; that, in short, it is a discipline unlike science but like religion.

It follows, then, that in a free society—such as one that guarantees a separation of church and state—psychiatry and the state should also be separate and separated. Lawyers and judges cannot call on priests and rabbis to testify about the spiritual condition of persons accused of crime; nor can judges sentence criminals to imprisonment in institutions run by clergymen. I maintain that, similarly, lawyers and judges should not be able to call on psychiatrists and psychologists to testify about the mental condition of persons accused of crime; and that judges should be unable to sentence criminals to imprisonment in institutions run by clinicians. Nothing short of such a seemingly radical—but actually conservative—policy would suffice to eliminate the now rampant abuses of coercive and deceptive psychiatric and psychological interventions imposed on persons caught up in the criminal justice system.

Only if psychiatry and the state were separate, as church and state are now, could genuinely voluntary psychiatric interventions for the benefit of the criminal-client come into being (Szasz, 1977b). Only in such a legal and human context could the criminal-client regard psychiatry as a potential source of help with his personal deficiencies, and could the psychiatrist regard himself as the agent of his client.

NOTES

1. In this connection, see the text and references of Rubin, 1965; Blumberg, 1967; Goldstein, 1967; and Arens, 1969.
2. Examples from the past and from other countries abound. I will not dwell on them here, as my emphasis in this chapter is on the practices of psychiatric diversion in the present-day administration of American criminal justice.

REFERENCES

Arens, R. *Make mad the guilty.* Springfield, Ill.: Charles C Thomas, 1969.

Blackstone, W. *Commentaries on the laws of England: Of public wrongs* (1755–65). Boston: Beacon, 1962.

Blumberg, A. S. *Criminal justice.* Chicago: Quadrangle, 1967.

Fedden, H. R. *Suicide: A social and historical study.* London: Petter Davies, 1938.

Goldstein, A. *The insanity defense.* New Haven: Yale University Press, 1967.

Hayek, F. A. *The constitution of liberty.* Chicago: University of Chicago Press, 1960.

Perkins, R. M. *Criminal law.* Brooklyn, N.Y.: Foundation Press, 1957.

Rubin, S. *Psychiatry and criminal law.* Dobbs Ferry, N.Y.: Oceana, 1965.

Solzhenitsyn, A. *Warning to the west.* New York: Farrar, Strauss and Giroux, 1976.

Sprott, S. E. *The English debate on suicide: From Donne to Hume.* LaSalle, Ill.: Open Court, 1961.

Szasz, T. S. Criminal responsibility and psychiatry. In Hans Toch (Ed.), *Legal and criminal psychology.* New York: Holt, Rinehart and Winston, 1961a.

Szasz, T. S. *The myth of mental illness.* New York: Harper & Row, 1961b.

Szasz, T. S. *Law, liberty, and psychiatry.* New York: Macmillan, 1963.

Szasz, T. S. *Psychiatric justice.* New York: Macmillan, 1965.

Szasz, T. S. *Ideology and insanity.* Garden City, N.Y.: Doubleday-Anchor, 1970.

Szasz, T. S. *Psychiatric slavery.* New York: Free Press, 1977a.

Szasz, T. S. *The theology of medicine.* New York: Harper & Row, 1977b.

Szasz, T. S. The ethics of suicide. In T. S. Szasz, *The theology of medicine.* New York: Harper & Row, 1977c.

Von Mises, L. *Human action: A treatise on economics.* New Haven: Yale University Press, 1949.

Weinstein, E. A. Presidential assassination: An american problem. *Psychiatry,* August, 1976, *39,* 291–293.

PART TWO

The Psychology of Crime

chapter 6

Perspectives on the Offender

Hans Toch

How we view the offender affects what we do with him, and determines what, precisely, we hope to accomplish. In this connection, it is not really self-evident that rehabilitating offenders is a particularly desirable goal. Nor is it evident that psychological knowledge—as opposed to other sorts of information—is useful.

We have arrived at our present assumptions as part of a historical tradition, which we shall reconstruct in this chapter. The current situation is harder to describe. Most psychologists see rehabilitation as an important objective in dealing with criminals, but most criminal justice experts nowadays tend to describe treatment as wasteful, futile, archaic, inhumane, and as flagrantly unresponsive to public demands. In the eyes of some experts, efforts to rehabilitate individual offenders are unlikely to "pay off," in the sense that they can reduce crime rates (Martinson, 1976). These same experts claim that the graduates of treatment programs, *on the average*, return to crime in the same relative numbers as nontreated offenders. Some critics also maintain that treatment inevitably leads to nightmarish abuses involving clients who have no desire to be treated (Mitford, 1973). Still others tell us that rehabilitation requires unfairly disparate prison terms for persons who have committed equivalent offenses (Von Hirsch, 1976). The public is deemed better served by a system that self-consciously punishes, attempting to punish each offender to the precise degree to which he has harmed others, and taking great care not to be excessively harsh. Besides the proposed equitable use of punishment, experts advocate (1) the use of prison to "incapacitate" criminals so that they cannot (for a while, at least) harm others; (2) efforts to dissuade the criminal from crime through the assured prospect of facing discomfort; and (3) the making of sobering examples of apprehended offenders to make crime unattractive to others. The second of these goals is called "individual deterrence" and the third, "general deterrence." There are persons of stature, widely respected in criminal justice circles (e.g., Van den Haag, 1975; Wilson, 1975), whose arguments for other-than-treatment goals have been extensively disseminated and have won substantial following.

The current situation is not only interesting on its own account, but is a good illustration of the intriguing thesis that history moves through back-and-forth swings of its pendulum. In comparatively recent times, we have seen a progression from the advocacy of punishment and the idea of general deterrence toward the birth of individual deterrence; from the emphasis on deterrence (and particularly, on individual deterrence) toward the ideal of rehabilitation. Each phase not only contributed something new, but represented a rejection of evils or abuses "built into" preceding phases.

Contemporary criminology was born in England and Italy as a reaction against *arbitrariness* and against *unpredictably excessive harshness*. Less than two hundred years ago, the prevalent way of dealing with convicted offenders was corporal punishment. Favorite forms of punishment included flogging, mutilation, branding, and the stocks and pillory (Barnes, 1930). Capital punishment was applied with horrifying frequency. According to one estimate 200,000 witches were executed in Europe in the sixteenth and seventeenth centuries. Henry VIII slaughtered 72,000 of his subjects, and legalized boiling to death as one means of doing so (Lawrence, 1928). Before the revision of the English penal code in the first half of the nineteenth century, 222 types of offenses could result in hanging.

This is not to say that there was anything uniform about the application of punishments. In most instances the offender could expect no due process, and the nature of his offense gave him no information about the severity of the punishment he could anticipate.

Judges were concerned not only about punishing the offender for his misdeeds, but also about deterring others from turning to crime. Hangings were considered to be highly educational, and were widely advertised. Branding and mutilation in part served the same purpose, in that each victim, if he survived, could provide a roadside warning to others. Thus William the Conqueror decreed "that no one shall be killed or hung for any misdeeds, but rather that his eyes be plucked out and his feet, hands and testicles cut off, so that whatever part of his body remains will be a living sign to all of his crime and iniquity" (Barnes, 1930, p. 61).

Both the aim of harsh punishment and that of general deterrence were firmly rooted in a religious conception of human nature, in that Man was viewed as a moral agent, and was seen as being able to freely choose between righteous behavior and evil conduct. A philosophy of deterrence followed from the premise that the potential criminal could choose *not* to commit evil acts. Deterrence also was a sacred obligation from the religious viewpoint, since a crime deterred represented a soul saved.

THE REVOLUTION OF THE ENLIGHTENMENT

The eighteenth century was a period of ferment, which combined residues of the Middle Ages with the most thorough self-analysis to which Western society has ever subjected itself. This movement of self-criticism was centered in France, and it featured writers such as Voltaire, Montesquieu, and Rousseau, who in turn influenced other writers.

Among those who fell under the spell of the Enlightenment were an English eccentric named Jeremy Bentham and a group of Italian aristocrats whose spokesman was Cesare Bonesana, the Marquis of Beccaria. Bentham and Beccaria have become known as the principal spokesmen of the Classical School of Criminology. This school is credited with wholesale criminal law reforms in the early eighteenth century, and we are seeing a resurgence of their views (in modern dress) as the twentieth century draws to a close.

Beccaria's monograph *On Crime and Punishments* was published anonymously in 1764. The first English translation of this small book appeared in 1766. By that time Beccaria's impact had been such that his translator writes that "perhaps no book, on any subject, was ever received with more avidity, more generally read, or more universally applauded" (Cit. Paolucci, 1963, p. x). Beccaria's no-holds-barred critique of contemporary penology was an inspiration to reformers in all parts of the world, but it "aroused the hostility and resistance of those who stood to gain by the perpetuation of the barbaric and archaic penological institutions of the day" (Monachesi, 1960, p. 38). While Voltaire himself described the pamphlet as "the code of humanity," the Vatican placed it on the Index, and prominent judges "accused Beccaria of being the protector of robbers and murderers, because he wanted to abolish the only means of compelling them to a confession, the torture" (Ferri, 1910, p. 19).

Beccaria incisively attacked the unfettered exercise of discretion by various authorities, which allowed for unchecked barbarism and flagrant arbitrariness. He specifically condemned such practices as capital punishment, torture, the debtor's prison, pretrial incarceration, secret accusations, reinterpretation of laws by judges, the use of "scalp-hunting" rewards, and the disproportionate punishment of minor offenders. The central thesis of his treatise, which appears as its Conclusion, is that "in order for punishment not to be, in every instance, an act of violence of one or of many against a private citizen, it must be essentially public, prompt, necessary, the least possible in the given circumstance, proportionate to the crimes, dictated by the laws" (Beccaria, 1963, p. 99).

A central item in this list is that punishment must be "proportionate to the crimes," which means that the individual offender's motives are less relevant than the harm that he has done to others. This is a necessary criterion because punishment is a message to society (it is general deterrence) and must be a justifiable response to a breach of the social contract in which we all share. Individual motives vary greatly from offender to offender "according to the swift succession of ideas, of passions and of circumstances" (Beccaria, 1963, p. 65). But the law must provide a consistent message, by forgetting about motives and centering on the gravity of the offense, which can be fairly equated with punishment. Punishment must "make the strongest and most lasting impression on the minds of men, and inflict the least torment on the body of the criminal" (Beccaria, 1963, p. 42). By linking punishment to crime in an appropriate "impression" we promote *just enough* fear of crime to prevent it. However, Beccaria adds, "the surest but most difficult way to prevent crimes" is not punishment, but the "perfecting (of) education" (p. 98).

Jeremy Bentham wrote much more extensively than Beccaria, but was less widely read. For Bentham, as for Beccaria, "the aims of punishment . . . are to prevent recidivism and to deter others from the commission of similar offenses" (Geis, 1960, p. 61). This theme runs through Bentham's many books on penology including *The Theory of Legislation, An Introduction to the Principles of Morals and Legislation, The Limits of Jurisprudence Defined,* and *Rationale of Punishment.* In these prolific writings Bentham advocated (but did not work out in detail) a meticulously graduated scale of crime-relevant penalties. Bentham was a hedonist thinker. He believed that, "Nature has placed mankind under the government of two sovereign masters, pain and pleasure" (Bentham, 1907, p. 1). Bentham saw crime, like other human conduct, as representing an effort to gain pleasure. The criminal was a special case because he derives pleasure at the expense of the community: his search for happiness provides pain to others. Punishment must be designed to deter this type of effort by making it unprofitable. This could be accomplished by making the punishment "not less in any case than what is sufficient to outweigh [the value] or the profit of the offense" (p. 179). The pain inflicted by punishment must equal the pleasure to be derived from the crime. By the same token, arbitrariness or cruelty would serve no purpose: "The punishment ought in no case to be *more* than what is necessary to bring it into conformity with the rules here given" (p. 182). Bentham lists countless "rules" for making the punishment fit the crime in equitable fashion.

Like Beccaria, Bentham was a reluctant advocate of punishment, and he saw punishment as "an evil" only to be used "to exclude some greater evil" (Bentham, 1963, p. 68). The object of the game, as he saw it, was to deter offenders and "prevent mischief." This meant that "the greater the mischief of the offense, the greater is the expense, which it may be worth while to be at, in the way of punishment" (Bentham, p. 77).

Bentham's punishments are *in part* aimed at influencing the offender who is punished (as well as other offenders) and Bentham makes provision—in principle, at least—for the fact that "a punishment which is the same in name will not always either really produce, in two different persons, the same degree of pain" (Bentham, p. 77). Though this implies individualization of penalties,

Bentham's intent is to *standardize the discomfort* that must be experienced by those who commit similar harm.

While Jeremy Bentham tells us that punishment must not be used where it does not deter, Bentham cannot conceive of undeterrable offenders. He regards all human actions as responding to a "hedonic calculus" in which pleasure is maximized and pain is minimized. In this scheme, there is no room for conduct which is not freely engaged in for psychological profit.

Both Bentham and Beccaria saw man exercising free will in the service of self-interest. This perspective is an uncomplicated and, on the face of it, unflattering view of human nature. But by the same token, the classic criminologist also saw man as intelligent, educable, and as fundamentally civilized.

Both Bentham and Beccaria prescribed punishment as a very last resort, preferring rewards and education as remedies, and relying on man's presumed responsiveness to positive social controls. Deterrence, for the Classical School, had none of the terror-inspiring quality of punishment in the Dark Ages. On the contrary, classical deterrence was an epitome of due process, and projected an image of fairness, restraint, and equity. The message which was communicated to the offender was that, "Crime does not pay, and you are better off joining the rest of us in building a community in which we work for common ends and ultimately strive for enlightment."

THE REVOLUTION OF SCIENCE

The nineteenth century saw the development of early science, which stressed that everything—including crime—had natural causes, which could be understood and could be controlled. This meant that crime (among other things) could be dealt with directly if one could neutralize its causes or manipulate them. Such was the position of the Positive School of Criminology, which flourished in the late half of the century, again principally in Italy.

Enrico Ferri, a prominent positive criminologist, pointed out in a lecture that

> the classic school of criminology, being unable to locate in the course of its scientific and historical mission the natural causes of crimes, . . . was not in a position to deal in a comprehensive and far-seeing manner with this problem of the remedy against criminality. (Ferri, 1901, p. 229).

"It is a noble mission to oppose the ferocious penalties of the middle ages," said Ferri, "But it is still nobler to forestall crime" (Ferri, p. 230). With respect to revised penal codes inspired by the classic school, Ferri argued that

> we have but to look about us on the realities of contemporaneous life in order to see that the criminal code is far from being a remedy against crime, that it remedies nothing, because either premeditation or passion in the person of the criminal deprive the criminal law of all prohibitory power. The deceptive faith in the efficacy of criminal law still lives in the public mind, because every normal

man feels that the thought of imprisonment would stand in his way, if he contemplated tomorrow committing a theft, a rape, or a murder. He feels the bridle of the social sense. And the criminal code lends more strength to it and holds him back from criminal actions. But even if the criminal code did not exist, he would not commit a crime, so long as his physical and social environment would not urge him in that direction. The criminal code serves only to isolate temporarily from social intercourse those who are not considered worthy of it. And this punishment prevents the criminal for a while from repeating his criminal deed. But it is evident that the punishment is not imposed until after the deed has been done. It is a remedy directed against effects, but it does not touch the causes, the roots, of the evil (Ferri, p. 231).

Positive criminologists objected strongly to the classic school's view that punishment could be made to "fit the crime" by fixing sentences that are tied strictly to the nature of the criminal acts. In this connection, Ferri wrote:

Add your sums and subtract your deductions, and the prisoner is sentenced to one year, seven months, and thirteen days. Not one day more or less! But the human spectator asks: "If the criminal should happen to be reformed before the expiration of his term should he be retained in prison?" The judge replies: "I don't care, he stays in one year, seven months, and thirteen days!"

Then the human spectator says: "But suppose the criminal should not yet be fit for human society at the expiration of his term?" The judge replies: "At the expiration of his term he leaves prison, for when he has absolved his last day, he has paid his debt!" (Ferri, 1910, pp. 84–85).

THE INFLUENCE OF LOMBROSO

The Positive School of Criminology was inaugurated in the 1870s by a brilliant Jewish physician and amateur anthropologist named Cesare Lombroso. Lombroso was a strict determinist. He described criminal behavior as a "natural phenomenon" which he felt was "as necessary as birth, death, or conception" (1911b, p. 377). For Lombroso the most prevalent criminal was the born criminal. Such a person, said Lombroso, could be identified by physical characteristics or "stigmata": an asymmetrical face, unusually large or small ears, a low, receding forehead, and prominent eyebrows, jawbones, and cheekbones. The fact that the long list of Lombroso's stigmata calls to mind the image of lower animals is not an accident. Influenced by Darwin, Lombroso regarded these features as "atavistic," which means "inherited from early ancestors." Lombroso conceived of his born criminal as an individual who had retained characteristics of his prehuman ancestors, with utter disregard for evolutionary developments in the interim.

Physiological and psychological stigmata were also listed by Lombroso as "atavistic" characteristics. Among these were insensibility to pain, sharp vision; the ability to recover quickly from wounds; a great resemblance between the sexes; laziness; a complete lack of shame, honor, remorse, and pity;

recklessness, excitability; a passion for gambling and alcoholic drinks; vanity, and a special conception of God. There were also habits, such as tattooing, an excessive use of gestures, and an addiction to picturesque language (Lombroso, 1911a, 1911b). Lombroso saw a substantial area of overlap between the born criminal and the epileptic, and regarded epilepsy as an important cause of crime.

Although Lombroso described criminal types other than his born criminal, and although he discussed (especially in his later writings) many causes of crime, his emphasis always remained on biological causation: "The study of crime does not lessen the fatal influence to be assigned to the organic factor, which certainly amounts to 35 percent and possibly even 40 percent; the so-called causes of crime being often only the last determinants while the great strength of congenital impulses remains the ultimate cause" (1911b, p. 376).

Whichever the combination (it varies markedly among Lombroso's followers), criminal behavior was seen as completely predetermined. This is a general characteristic of the theories of criminal behavior which were current in the late nineteenth century and early twentieth century. It is even shared by investigators who were otherwise completely opposed to each other. Thus Goring (1913), whose sophisticated statistical study of English convicts was intended to demonstrate that Lombroso's "stigmata" were not widely evident in prisons, simultaneously maintained that crime was almost entirely a product of heredity.

In their view of crime, Lombroso and his followers concentrated on the "anthropological factor," which "represents the organic and psychological condition of the criminal" (Ferri, 1910, p. 61). Within the "anthropological factor" the positive criminologists were primarily concerned with anatomical differences.

Lombroso (1911a) ascribes the birth of his system to the following event:

I . . . began to study criminals in the Italian prisons, and, amongst others, I made the acquaintance of the famous brigand Vilella. This man possessed such extraordinary agility, that he had been known to scale steep mountain heights bearing a sheep on his shoulders. His cynical effrontery was such that he openly boasted of his crimes. On his death one cold grey November morning, I was [chosen] to make the post mortem, and on laying open the skull I found on the occipital part, exactly on the spot where a spine is found in the normal skull, a distinct depression which I named *median occipital fossa*, because of its situation precisely in the middle of the occiput as in inferior animals, correlated with the hypertrophy of the *vermis* known in birds as the middle cerebellum.

This was not merely an idea, but a revelation. At the sight of that skull, I seemed to see all of a sudden, lighted up a vast plain under a flaming sky, the problem of the nature of the criminal—an atavistic being who reproduces in his person the ferocious instincts of primitive humanity and the inferior animals. Thus were explained anatomically the enormous jaws, high cheek-bones, prominent superciliary arches, solitary lines on the palms, extreme size of the orbits, handle shaped or sessile ears found in criminals, savages and apes, insensibility to pain, extremely acute sight, tattooing, excessive idleness, love of orgies, and the irresistible craving for evil for its own sake, the desire not only to extinguish life in the victim, but to mutilate the corpse, tear its flesh, and drink its blood (pp. xiv–xv).

In relation to the Vilella type of offender, Lombroso felt that neither individual deterrence nor rehabilitation were possible. In extreme situations of this kind, Lombroso saw the goal of punishment as the criminal's incapacitation. But for all other offenders, Lombroso saw the goal of intervention as that of rehabilitation or reform, which requires that we "make the punishment fit the criminal" rather than the crime. Marvin Wolfgang, in a scholarly review of Lombroso's writings, paraphrases this thinking as follows:

> If the first object of punishment should be the protection of society, the second is the improvement of the criminal. The fundamental principle, he consistently repeats, is that we ought to study and to treat not so much the abstract crime as the criminal. Resulting from this emphasis was his demand for individualisation of treatment, "which consists in applying special methods of repression and occupation adapted to each individual, as a physician does in prescribing dietary rules and special remedies according to the various illnesses" (Wolfgang, 1960, p. 299).

Lombroso was an early advocate of the indeterminate sentence, which is nowadays in considerable disfavor in the U.S. Indeterminacy requires that we *not* fix the time an offender must spend in prison, so that we can release him whenever he is "ready" for freedom. With an indeterminate sentence, the length of a person's stay in prison is at least in part determinated by a parole board. Parole has been defined as "a method of selectively releasing an offender from an institution prior to the completion of his maximum sentence, subject to conditions specified by the paroling authority, a method whereby society can be protected and the offender can be provided with continuing treatment and supervision in the community" (National Conference on Parole, 1957, pp. 65–66).

In theory, parole means that no person need remain in custody if he has been converted into a respectable, law-abiding citizen. On the other hand, dangerous offenders upon whom treatment may not have made sufficient impact can be retained until their correction is accomplished. When a person is released on parole, his treatment need not be abandoned. He remains under the supervision of a parole officer, who not only has the task of watching over him, but also can provide various types of assistance and support. Such assistance could range from personal counseling and therapy to help in locating a job.

Followers of Lombroso were among the first proponents of parole, probation, the juvenile court, experiments with youthful offenders, and other measures of early twentieth-century penology. Lombroso himself firmly supported these ventures, especially in the United States where many of them originated.

Some students of Lombroso's—notably, Ferri—foresaw *prevention* as another goal of crime control. They argued that since causes of crime could be isolated, we could attack them through social reforms. Ferri predicted that "the problem of criminality will thus be solved as far as possible, because the gradual transformation of society will eliminate the swamps in which the miasma of crime may form and breed" (Ferri, 1901, p. 239).

THE CAUSE-AND-EFFECT GAME

The distinguishing feature, the hallmark, of the positive school's approach was its "scientific" orientation. Science, in the nineteenth century, took a mechanistic view, featuring causes and effects. According to this view, effects or consequences were always inescapable. Human behavior, like other natural events, was predetermined. By introducing new causes, however—such as in "treating" criminals—new results could be anticipated. This is a view that differs considerably from the "free will" conception of the middle ages. It is related, nevertheless, to the classic Bentham-Beccaria view, in which free will is "engineered" by changing the incentives and penalties a person faces.

Scientific determinism lends itself to investigations in which the "true cause" of a phenomenon can be distinguished from other causes, or in which responsibility for a phenomenon can be parcelled out among a number of different "causes." Positivism is thus characterized by the advocacy of favorite "causes of crime," each one of which has enjoyed some popularity. Lombroso's championship of biology gives way to the socialist bias of his followers, and in each case the link between cause-of-crime and crime is seen as direct and inescapable.

The singlemindedness of positivism becomes very obvious if we review the work of crime theorists influenced by Mendelian researches on genetics, and of those impressed by early experiments in psychometrics, particularly by the discovery of IQ tests.

The most famous exponent of the view that crime is a result of heredity is probably Robert Dugdale, who in 1877 published his study of the Juke family. In the course of an official inspection tour of county jails in New York State, Dugdale had come upon six members of a unique family:

> These six persons belonged to a long lineage, reaching back to the early colonists, and had intermarried so slightly with the emigrant population of the old world that they may be called a strictly American family. They had lived in the same locality for generations, and were so despised by the reputable community that their family name *had come to be used generically as a term of reproach.*
>
> That this was deserved became manifest on slight inquiry. It was found that out of twenty-nine males, in ages ranging from fifteen to seventy-five, the immediate blood relations of these six persons, seventeen of them were criminals, or fifty-eight percent; while fifteen were convicted of some degree of offense, and received seventy-one years of sentence. . . . The crimes and misdemeanors they committed were assault and battery, assault with intent to kill, murder, attempt

at rape, petit larceny, grand larceny, burglary, forgery, cruelty to animals. With these facts in hand, it was thought wise to extend the investigation to other branches of the family, and explore it more thoroughly (Dugdale, 1910, p. 8).

Dugdale embarked on a careful study of seven generations of Jukes. He found, among the less conventional members of this family, 200 thieves and related criminals, 280 beggars, and 90 prostitutes. In 75 years, the family had cost the state an estimated $1,300,000. Dugdale assumed that the generous prevalence of criminality in the ranks of the Jukes could only be interpreted as a function of heredity. He recognized "environment" grudgingly as a secondary, contributing factor, which works in the same direction as heredity. For instance, he describes the living conditions of the Jukes as a contributing cause of their high illegitimacy rate:

They lived in log or stone houses similar to slave-hovels, all ages, sexes, relations and strangers "bunking" indiscriminately. One form of this bunking has been described to me. During the winter the inmates lie on the floor strewn with straw or rushes like so many radii to the hearth, the embers of the fire forming a center towards which their feet focus for warmth. This proximity, where not producing illicit relations, must often have evolved an atmosphere of suggestiveness fatal to habits of chastity. . . . Sometimes I found an overcrowding so close it suggested that these dwellings were the country equivalents of city tenement houses. Domesticity is impossible. The older girls, finding no privacy within a home overrun with younger brothers and sisters, purchase privacy at the risk of prudence, and their night rambles through woods and tangles end, too often, in illegitimate offspring (Dugdale, 1910, pp. 13–14).

Another line of evidence which was followed by the advocates of hereditary predetermination was the study of twins. These studies were intended to show that if one member of a pair of identical twins embarked on a criminal career, the other member of the pair was *predestined* to do likewise. The best known of these studies—that of the German physiologist Johannes Lange—is revealingly entitled *Crime and Destiny* (1930).

Heredity was also seen as exercising its predestination indirectly. Thus several early studies (e.g., Goddard, 1914) purported to demonstrate that criminality was a result of feeblemindedness.[1] The same claim was made for "imbalance" of the endocrine glands (Schlapp & Smith, 1928). "Moral insanity," the grandparent of the modern concept of antisocial personality (see Chapter 14), was regarded as an inherited deficiency. Alcoholism was similarly cited.

The proponents of constitutional, hereditary, or biological causes of crime did not have a monopoly on the view that crime was an inescapable consequence of powerful forces. The early advocates of environmental or social causation talked of crime in a similar fashion. Quetelet, who is considered to be the first "social criminologist," formulated a "thermic law of delinquency" according to which crimes of blood would result from Southern climes whereas crimes against property would be produced in the North. "Society prepares crime," he stated; "the criminal becomes its executive" (Quiros, 1912, p. 19). Kropotkin, the author of a book on prisons published in 1890, went even further: "Take the average temperature of the month, and multiply it by 7; then, add the average humidity, multiply again by 2, and you will obtain the number of homocides that are to be committed during the month" (Quiros, 1912, p. 34). Economic statistics were repeatedly used to support the argument that crime is a function of deprivation or prosperity. One famous study, that of George von Mayr, found an increase of one theft per 100,000 persons for every half-penny increase in the price of rye in Bavaria (Sellin, 1937).

SOCIOLOGICAL POSITIVISM AND PSYCHOLOGICAL POSITIVISM

The deterministic models of early positivists had one important side effect. In hunting for "causes" of "crime" the positivists never really looked at criminal behavior or at offender perspectives, and were only remotely interested in offender motives.

A positivist model is one in which a measurable condition (independent variable) produces a measureable effect (dependent variable). Where crime is the effect, the question "What goes on in the mind of a criminal?" or "What motivates the offender" becomes an irrelevant black box that lies between correlated statistics that identify the "cause" (low IQ scores, prominent cheekbones, high temperatures) and the "effect" (crime rates). The advocates of feeblemindedness or genetics rested their case once they had demonstrated (or thought they had demonstrated) that many convicts scored low on tests or had disreputable parents. It never occurred to positivists to ask *how* feeblemindedness could affect an individual, causing him to rob a stagecoach or habitually drink to excess. This fact is of practical importance, because it limits the applicability of positivist findings. To preach individualization of sentences is sterile when all you can tell practitioners to guide their treatment efforts is that an offender is dull-normal or poor, is endowed with bad genes or languished in a hot climate. Such facts carry no implications for action, because there is nothing we can do about them.

Early psychiatrists who were positivists contributed to this problem as much as anyone else because they saw "causes" in terms of conditions or syndromes, such as "moral imbecility" or epilepsy. Epilepsy is an example of a double-problem, because it stigmatizes all sorts of epileptics who are not offenders and ignores the question of why and how some epileptics become offenders and others do not.

If psychology is the study of the human mind, no positivist was a real psychologist, though some positivists had ready-made catalogues of "motives" (such as hunger and greed) which were armchair-produced and were invoked as presumed facts. One can draw a conceptual distinction, however, between "psychological" positivists, whose concern was with individuals, and "sociological" positivists, who viewed people *en masse*.

The "causes" invoked by sociological positivists tended to be composite constructs (such as "social disorganization") which summarized cultural forces operating on a large number of people. The impact of such forces showed up in the prevalence of some measurable forms of behavior, such as crime or suicide. The individual was so completely irrelevant to this scheme that he was by definition replaceable; if the conditions were ripe, a given crime level could be safely anticipated. This meant—among other things—that treating offenders must of necessity be a waste of time. If we whisk one delinquent off his street corner, he will be promptly replaced (given the same culture context) by an understudy or proxy.

More psychologically oriented positivists do not allow for such understudies. A person is viewed as a very special product of forces that personally impinge on him, rather than as a random symptom of social malaise. Psychological positivists can accommodate the fact that one person in a given culture turns to crime, while his neighbor is law-abiding. What such experts cannot explain, however, is how one individual high on a criminogenic trait turns to crime, while another who is similarly situated does not. One resolution to this dilemma (which remains in the positivist camp) was the "multiple factor" approach, which added causes of crime together like ingredients in a recipe. The two best known psychological advocates of the multiple-factor approach were Healy (1915) and Burt (1925). Healy enumerated 138 factors, and found that most delinquents could be adequately described by invoking one major and two minor factors. (His most important factor was "mental abnormalities and peculiarities.") Burt enumerated 170 factors, which he classified into nine categories.

SUPPLEMENTING THE POSITIVISTIC PERSPECTIVE

The questions that are left unanswered by early criminologists can be addressed if we go beyond the kind of data the positive school sought, and beyond the inferences the positivists accepted as "solutions." What we must specifically recognize in such supplementary research is that "a factor cannot become a cause before it is a motive" (B. Glueck, cit. Bovet, 1951, p. 20).

The possibility of *supplementing* positivist findings is illustrated in the work of the Chicago School, which did ground-breaking research into antecedents of crime and delinquency. In 1921 a leading member of this school, Clifford Shaw, set about the task of carefully pinpointing the residence of 100,000 Chicago school truants, juvenile delinquents, and adult offenders. He published the results of his labors in a volume entitled *Delinquency Areas* (1929). Shaw found that his offenders were "largely concentrated in certain areas adjacent to the business district and the large industrial centers." He

concluded that "since delinquents are largely concentrated in these characteristic areas, it may be assumed that delinquent behavior is closely related
to certain community situations which arise in the process of city growth"
(p. 204). Specifically, Shaw suggested that the *disintegration* of community
life in the zone of transition creates "criminal patterns" which come to "shape
the attitudes and behavior of persons living in the area. Thus the section
becomes an area of delinquency" (p. 206).

How are delinquent attitudes and behavior shaped? Shaw illustrated the
process in a group of case studies published under the heading *Brothers in
Crime* (1938). The studies center about five brothers who grew into delinquents on the shores of the Chicago River. According to Shaw, delinquency
for these youngsters started as a game played with other children in similar
circumstances. Rather than go to school, the brothers and their friends would
browse through department stores in the Loop, stealing inconsequentials.
Such early experiences were reinforced by the teachings of all manner of
people with whom the boys came into contact later in life. The family influence, which might have counteracted these teachings, was too weak to be
effective. The family was far from close, and no affection or loyalty was lost
in its bosom. The parents had neither the time nor the desire to exercise control. Thus, these five "careers in delinquency, from the first simple acts of
stealing to the more serious crimes which occurred in later years, represent a
gradual process of informal training, education, habituation and sophistication in the process of stealing" (p. 350).

Can we move beyond influences, and take a close look at the reactions
and motives of the offender who is being influenced? The Chicago School
answered "yes," and illustrated its contention with biographies that sensitively relay the thoughts, values and perspectives of individual delinquents.
The best document of this kind was produced by Shaw in 1930, and is entitled
The Jack-Roller: A Delinquent Boy's Own Story.

Shaw's account is a portrait of a young man named Stanley, whose first
brush with the law occurred at age six, and who was very precariously on
parole when Shaw met him at age sixteen. Shaw's relationship with Stanley
extended over six long years, and was interrupted for a whole year while Stanley served a term at the Chicago House of Correction.

Shaw's data were collected through stenographically recorded interviews,
which were supplemented with autobiographical notes written by Stanley
himself. During the last years of the research, Shaw successfully devised and
supervised Stanley's rehabilitation program, which was tied to the insights
Shaw had obtained about Stanley's personality through his interviews.

Shaw saw "the delinquent's own story" as a source of information about:

1. *The delinquent's own unique point of view.* The self-descriptive approach, according to Shaw,

is of primary importance as a device for ascertaining the personal attitudes,
feelings and interests of the child; in other words, it shows how he conceives
his role in relation to other persons and the interpretations which he makes of

the situations in which he lives . . . the child reveals his feelings of inferiority and superiority, his fears and worries, his ideals and philosophy of life, his antagonisms and mental conflicts, his prejudices and rationalizations (Shaw, 1966, pp. 3–4).

Clinical work related to the Chicago School that illustrates Shaw's point was that of James Healy (a psychiatrist who had twice examined Stanley) and Augusta Bronner. Healy and Bronner (1936) had conducted a monumental study in psychiatric clinics of three large cities. In this study, in which delinquents and nondelinquents within the same families were compared, it was found that delinquency resulted whenever a child felt that it could not carry out its purposes and gain satisfactions in the family setting. Delinquency, in other words, was as much a result of the child's view of its parents as of parental actions.

According to Healy and Bronner, as one views a delinquent child one is struck by "the immense amount of discoverable emotional discomfort that clearly has been part of the story of the origins of delinquency" (p. 7). Most of the delinquent youngsters studied by Healy and Bronner differed from their nondelinquent brothers and sisters in that they felt rejected, unloved, thwarted, disturbed, and generally unhappy. Whether in any particular case the parents had actually done anything to provoke this, or whether the feeling was mostly the child's doing, is a question we need not ask if our problem is to locate the motives which give birth to criminal acts, as we must deal with them in practice.

Healy and Bronner also pointed out that delinquents engaged in similar delinquency have different aims, resentments, perspectives and values. In the case of truancy, for example,

> One boy may be avoiding a situation in which he feels inadequate and discouraged; another has developed out of family life antagonism toward all forms of authority—school representing one form; another has such need of recognition that, even though he does not dislike school he truants in order to be a "regular fellow" with his companions; still another is the victim of peculiar anxieties which make the classroom hateful to him (1936, p. 6).

Thus we must ask about each offender in turn, What is he trying to accomplish? What do his offenses mean to him? How does he, personally, view his antisocial acts in the context of his own purposes, attitudes, and values? Such questions require a "first-hand" perspective of the offender, which can only be obtained by interviewing him.

2. *The interpersonal influences and social contexts to which the delinquent responds.* This aspect of the data was an important one to Chicago sociologists, who had pioneered superb *descriptions* of social settings to which delinquents were exposed. The interviews supplied the counterpart of this picture. They showed "the manner in which these cultural factors become incorporated into the behavior trends of the child" (Shaw, 1966, p. 7).

3. *The sequence of formative past experiences in the life of the delinquent.*

Though the Chicago School was not psychoanalytically oriented, it shared Freud's view that "any specific act of the individual becomes comprehensible only in the light of its relation to the sequence of past experiences in the life of the individual" (Shaw, 1966, p. 13). In light of this developmental assumption, Chicago students favored the gathering of case histories, in which "the delinquent behavior of older offenders may be traced back to experiences and influences which have occurred very early in life" (Shaw, 1966, p. 14). Moreover, wrote Shaw, "the 'own story' reveals the essentially human aspects of the problem of delinquency. For in such documents one gains a sympathetic appreciation of the child's own personal problems and the sort of world in which he lives" (Shaw, 1966, p. 17).

THE RELATIONSHIP OF DATA TO PRESCRIPTIONS

Together with the psychiatrist William Healy, the Chicago School pioneered in efforts to link research to treatment in delinquency, and in the drawing of action-relevant inferences from research findings. Both for Healy and Shaw this approach was possible because innumerable clinical interviews yielded rich first-hand portraits of delinquent personalities.

In a statement that is relevant today, Shaw writes that

> the large amount of failure in probation and parole work is not at all surprising, since the worker is forced, under the pressure of a heavy case load, to deal primarily with the more formal and external aspects of his cases. . . . In many cases, (relevant) knowledge is to be secured only after painstaking study and prolonged contact with the delinquent. In the absence of such knowledge, the worker's relation to his case is necessarily more or less formal, and the treatment consists chiefly of attempts to gain control and affect adjustment through threats of arrest and punishment (Shaw, 1966, p. 18).

Shaw's contacts with Stanley yielded (among other things) a personality portrait which fit a type of delinquent which Burgess, a colleague of Shaw's, described as the "Self Defender." The Self-Defender, according to Burgess, is an "individual who is able even under adverse circumstances to maintain his ego against an unfriendly and even hostile social world" (Burgess, in Shaw, 1966, p. 191). Burgess saw the self-defender syndrome as an adaptive reaction to early adversity. He lists Stanley's adaptive "traits" as including:

1. Early rise and persistence of a sense of injustice
2. Self-pity
3. Hypercritical of others
4. Always right; never takes blame but readily blames others
5. Readily makes friends and as easily breaks with them
6. Excessive interest in attention
7. Lacks insight into his own motives and those of others

8. Suspicious toward others without sufficient cause
9. Ideas of persecution
10. Substitutes rationalization for insight
11. Builds up rational system of explanation
12. Absorbed in his own ideas and plans and relatively immune to suggestions from others
13. Resentment of correction and resistance to direction
14. Tendency to escape from unpleasant situations by the method of protest
15. Tendency to moralize
16. Speed of decision and strength of reaction (Shaw, pp. 190–191).

Some of these defensive features made it difficult for Stanley to hold a job in a conventional organization; others militated against his tenure with most available foster parents. Shaw's "treatment program" included the selection of a nonauthoritarian foster mother, and Stanley's placement in a job (as salesman) in which he could select his own tasks, exercise one-way influence, and work independently. These interventions (and the advent of a supportive girlfriend) converted Stanley into a respectable and law-abiding citizen.

"SEARCHING FOR CAUSES" VERSUS "UNDERSTANDING"

Most of the following chapters will remind us of the point made by Healy and Burgess that we need to *subdivide* real groups of offenders into psychological *types* or *subtypes*, of which the individual (such as Stanley) is a reasonable representative. This is a different procedure from the positivist stance, which classified *antecedents* of delinquency, and looks for products of these antecedents.

The second approach makes sense if we are concerned with highlighting particular causes of crime, making a case for their impact. This sort of approach has been used by criminologists to draw attention to a number of social problems (slums, broken homes, malnutrition, etc.) which contribute to delinquency. The practical implication of this strategy involves mobilizing social reform as a means of crime prevention. This approach was deployed recently under Presidents Kennedy and Johnson, who fought a war on poverty, as—among other things—a war on crime.

Positivist approaches to classification help to produce explanatory theories, which in turn help us to "understand crime." These theories, however, do not permit us to "understand criminals," because they are segmental views rather than full-blooded portraits. We can achieve both objectives (as we shall see in Chapter 7), only where we invoke theoretical explanations if and when they seem relevant to the understanding of individual delinquents. This still, however, brings only *partial* understandings, and these must be supplemented with portraits of offender perspectives, and with a review of unique personal histories.

The latter types of data are particularly important if we seek to work with offenders, whose perspectives face us on the firing line, and the impact of whose histories we must seek to undo or neutralize. In this connection, we must have tools that help us to understand the psychological meaning of the offender's acts, and to locate the forces that have shaped the offender, and that can hopefully reshape him.

Such tools will be discussed in Chapters 8 and 9. Chapter 8 deals with the psychoanalytic perspective, which has added significant and unprecedented depth to our comprehension of human behavior. This perspective attends to the person as a social and biological being, who must satisfy his basic needs while he tries to solve the immediate life problems he faces. Psychoanalytic portraits are three-dimensional, in that they accommodate the internal conflicts inherent in our struggle to cope, and attend to nuances and overtones of what we say and do. They are (as we shall see in Chapter 8) ways of sensing the full gamut of meanings that the person wittingly and unwittingly conveys.

Chapter 9 deals with the "social learning" perspective. This perspective draws our attention to the shaping of motives, meanings, and behaviors over time, and to the role that other people play in making us what we are. Chapter 8 views this process from the viewpoint of academic psychology, and Chapter 20 sees it in terms of education and social psychiatry.

The learning area is unique in that representatives of all disciplines that are interested in crime agree on its importance. In sociology, the emphasis on learning dates to the work of the Chicago school, which we have already mentioned. This research is particularly significant, because it documented on street corners and in slum homes the same processes that have been highlighted in the laboratory, in consulting rooms, in hospitals, and in schools. The role of social learning in crime causation is thus one of the few subjects which has been illuminated by diverse research in variegated settings.

KNOWLEDGE AND ITS APPLICATION

In Chapter 11 we shall return to the issue of how we can apply what we know in our dealings with offenders. Chapter 10, however, describes a policy-relevant area (prediction) in which the knowledge we have acquired limits what we can do.

The public's concern about individual offenders revolves around its desire that they not offend again. No matter what we do with apprehended criminals, the public wants assurance that those who return to the community do not return to crime. The public would also like to identify and locate potential offenders before they have embarked on their depredations. On both counts, psychology has tried to accommodate the public, and has failed. At this stage we cannot offer crime prevention programs directed at "high risk" predelinquents and we cannot fix release dates from captivity that promise negligible recidivism.

These facts, combined with the developing state of our knowledge about therapy, and the magnitude of the crime problem we face, underlie the current demand that we ignore what we know about offenders. "There is no point," this view holds, "in capitalizing on knowledge about offenders, if we cannot select 'high risks' for attention, and promise that they are 'low risks' when we are done with them."

If psychological knowledge is of no practical consequence, why not return to classic criminology, and forget about "understanding" and "resocializing" criminals? In the words of James Q. Wilson:

> The only instruments society has by which to alter behavior in the short run require it to assume that people act in response to the costs and benefits of alternate courses of action. The criminologist assumes, probably rightly, that the causes of crime are determined by attitudes that in turn are socially derived, if not determined; the policy analyst is led to assume that the criminal acts *as if* crime were the product of a free choice among competing opportunities and constraints. The radical individualism of Bentham and Beccaria may be scientifically questionable but prudentially necessary (Wilson, 1975, p. 62).

Such a view is inviting because it promises due process, and because it satisfies our desire for equity, which makes us want to respond proportionately to those who have harmed us. But "to alter behavior in the short run" is what we have tried on a very large scale for twelve long decades. If we have failed, it is not because knowledge (in the shape of token "treatment" as window dressing) has proved sterile, but because crime was never "the product of a free choice among competing opportunities and constraints," and has not responded to this assumption.

Neoclassicists forget that crime is the sum total of criminal acts committed by individual offenders, and not a statistical abstraction that we can address with "as if" premises. To solve the crime problem, we must motivate individual offenders not to commit crimes, and this can only be done if we understand the offenders' motives and if we know how to affect them. We shall address both sets of problems in the remainder of this book.

NOTES

1. This discovery of testing led to the secondary "discovery" that large portions of the public (military inductees, students, etc.) were "subnormal" or "feebleminded." Estimates of subnormality among prison inmates routinely ranged as high as 70 percent or more.

REFERENCES

Barnes, M. E. *The story of punishment.* Boston: Stratford Co., 1930.
Beccaria, C. *On crimes and punishments* (1963). Indianapolis: Bobbs-Merrill, 1963.
Beccaria, C. *An essay on crimes and punishment.* Philadelphia: Philip H. Nicklin, 1819.

Bentham, J. *An introduction to the principles of morals and legislation.* Oxford: The Clarendon Press, 1907.

Bentham, J. Punishment and utility (1823). In J. G. Murphy (Ed.), *Punishment and rehabilitation.* Belmont, Calif.: Wordsworth, 1973.

Bovet, L. *Psychiatric aspects of juvenile delinquency.* Geneva: World Health Organization, 1951.

Burt, C. *The young delinquent.* New York: Ronald, 1925.

Dugdale, R. *The Jukes.* New York: Putnam, 1910.

Ferri, E. Lecture III: Remedies (1901). In S. E. Grupp, *Theories of punishment.* Bloomington: Indiana University Press, 1961.

Ferri, E. *The positive school of criminology.* Chicago: Charles H. Kerr, 1910.

Geis, G. Jeremy Bentham (1748–1832). In H. Mannheim (Ed.), *Pioneers in criminology (1960).* Montclair, N. J.: Patterson Smith, 1973, pp. 36–50.

Goddard, H. H. *Feeblemindedness: Its causes and consequences.* New York: Macmillan, 1914.

Goring, C. *The English convict: A statistical study.* London: His Majesty's Stationery Office, 1913.

Healy, W. *The individual delinquent.* Boston: Little, Brown, 1915.

Healy, W., & Bronner, A. *New lights on delinquency and its treatment.* New Haven: Yale University Press, 1936.

Lange, J. *Crime and destiny.* New York: C. Boni, 1930.

Lawrence, J. *A history of capital punishment.* London: Low, Marston, 1928.

Lombroso, C. *Criminal man.* New York: Knickerbocker Press, 1911 (a).

Lombroso, C. *Crime: Its causes and remedies.* Boston: Little, Brown, 1911 (b).

Martinson, R., et al. *Rehabilitation, recidivism and research.* Hackensack, N.J.: National Council on Crime and Delinquency, 1976.

Mitford, J. *Kind and usual punishment: The prison business.* New York: Knopf, 1973.

Monachesi, E. Cesare Beccaria (1738–1794). In H. Mannheim (Ed.), *Pioneers in criminology* (1960). Montclair, N.J.: Patterson Smith, 1973, pp. 36–50.

National Conference on Parole. *Parole in principle and practice.* New York: National Probation and Parole Association, 1957.

Paolucci, H. Translator's introduction to C. Beccaria, *On crimes and punishments.* Indianapolis, Ind.: Bobbs-Merrill, 1963, pp. ix–xxii.

Park, R. E., Burgess, E. W., & McKenzie R. D. *The city, the ecological approach to the study of the human community.* Chicago: University of Chicago Press, 1925.

Quiros, C. B. *Modern theories of criminality.* Boston: Little, Brown, 1912.

Schlapp, M. G., & Smith, E. H. *The new criminology.* New York: Liveright, 1928.

Sellin, T. *Research memorandum on crime in the depression.* Bulletin No. 27. New York: Social Science Research Council, 1937.

Shaw, C. *Brothers in crime.* Chicago: University of Chicago Press, 1938.

Shaw, C. *Delinquency areas.* Chicago: University of Chicago Press, 1929.

Shaw, C. R. *The Jack-Roller: A delinquent boy's own story.* Chicago: University of Chicago Press, 1930. (Phoenix Edition, 1966)

Van den Haag, E. *Punishing criminals.* New York: Basic Books, 1976.

Von Hirsch, A. *Doing justice: The choice of punishments.* New York: Hill and Wang, 1976.

Wilson, J. Q. *Thinking about crime.* New York: Basic Books, 1975.

Wolfgang, M. Cesare Lombroso (1835–1909). In H. Mannheim (Ed.), *Pioneers in criminology* (1960). Montclair, N.J.: Patterson Smith, 1973, pp. 232–291.

chapter 7

Current Explanations of Offender Behavior

Marguerite Q. Warren
Michael J. Hindelang

It should be obvious from the preceding chapter that many theories have been presented to explain crime. Some of these—sociological theories—place all or most of the causal factors in the social environment. Some theories (psychological) place all or most of the criminogenic factors within the individual offender. And a number of theories explain crime by placing part of the cause in the person and part in society. This last position is based on the observation that no social environment leads to crime in all individuals who are exposed to it; and, on the other hand, no individual is criminal all the time in all circumstances.

SOCIOLOGICAL THEORIES

In the United States for the past fifty years, the study of crime and delinquency has been dominated by sociology. Most current theories of the etiology of crime and delinquency have been postulated by sociologists, most criminology textbooks have been written by sociologists, most research on delinquency and crime has been conducted by sociologists, and (until very recently) most courses on crime and delinquency have been taught within departments of sociology. It should not be surprising then that the field is sociologically oriented. We are not suggesting, of course, that a psychological or individually focussed approach has been entirely lacking, but rather that such an approach has not been dominant. Before we turn to some prominent psychological theories, it is necessary to familiarize the reader with some of the major categories of sociological theories; this will facilitate a discusson of some ways in which some psychological and some sociological theories may be compatible.

Sociological theories of crimes have often been categorized into three broad groups: strain theories, subcultural deviance theories, and control theories. Briefly, *strain* theories are characterized by the premise that crime and delinquency result when socially approved ends (e.g., material possessions) cannot be achieved through conventional channels, and illegal activities are chosen as alternative means of obtaining the desired ends. *Subcultural deviance* theories postulate that some subgroups of society hold values that are contrary to the values of the society at large and that some of these subgroups condone and even encourage criminal and delinquent activities. *Control* theories argue that involvement in delinquency and crime results when an individual's bond to conventional society is weakened or destroyed. As will be apparent below, some theories have components, for example, of both strain and subcultural deviance.

Strain Theories

In 1938, Robert Merton published "Social Structure and Anomie" in which he presented a classic strain theory. In this paper, Merton postulated that some combined factors may actually exert pressures upon certain societal members to engage in nonconforming, rather than conforming behavior. His analysis isolates two crucial elements. The first are the culturally defined goals, purposes, and interests; these are desired "ends." The second is the social structure which defines, regulates, and controls the socially acceptable "means" of achieving the "ends."

In some egalitarian societies, the culturally defined "ends" are held out as universally available to all members of society. At the same time, the culturally defined "ends" may be overemphasized to the extent that the stress upon the "ends" may be quite out of proportion to the stress on the socially acceptable means of achieving the valued "ends." Merton argued that societal equilibrium persists as long as satisfactions accrue to those who attempt to achieve the "ends" through the use of socially prescribed means. However, antisocial behavior may be produced if advance toward the "ends" using legitimate channels is difficult or impossible for a substantial portion of those living in the society—namely, those with little formal education and economic resources. That is, if the "ends" are emphasized virtually above all else, and if the social situation restricts access to the legitimate means of achieving these ends, strain is created and those with restricted access to legitimate means may attempt to achieve the "ends" via illegitimate means.

In the United States, for example, material goods are universally valued, and the notion that all Americans can achieve material comfort is often propounded. However, those who are discriminated against, who are very poor, who lack formal education, and so on, are effectively cut off from achieving material goods by means of socially acceptable channels; therefore, as material goods become valued by us above virtually all else, pressure on the poor to use socially unacceptable channels to achieve material goods will be exerted. One such socially unacceptable channel, of course, is delinquent or criminal activity; for those who have no other realistic channel of achievement open, Merton suggests that illegal activity may ensue.

Cloward and Ohlin (1960) have extended this notion by suggesting that just as there is differential access to *legitimate* means of achieving socially acceptable goals—through hard work, ingenuity, a good education, and so on —so too is there differential access to illegitimate means of achieving socially acceptable "ends." For example, where organized crime flourishes, it may be possible to participate in it *only* if one has the right connections; if the individual doesn't know the right people he will probably be forced to explore other illegitimate means of achieving the socially acceptable "ends."

According to the theory of Cloward and Ohlin, there are three primary delinquent adaptations to strain. The first is a *criminal* adaptation in which time is spent thieving and disposing of stolen goods. The second is a *conflict* adaptation in which status in the delinquent group is conferred upon those who are accomplished at gang fighting skills. The third is a *retreatist* adaptation in which activities of the group revolve around the procurement and consumption of drugs.

Since Cloward and Ohlin's adaptations involve groups as well as alienated individuals, their theory has elements of the *subcultural* perspective, which stresses the influence of group norms. The same point can be made about the contribution of Albert Cohen (1955) who further developed and discussed the importance of subcultural influences on delinquent behavior. In *Delinquent Boys: The Culture of the Gang*, Cohen argues that delinquent behavior is a group phenomenon that occurs disproportionately among lower class males. Cohen suggests that American public schools reflect middle-class values and are dominated by middle-class teachers and administrators. The values that are seen by Cohen as emphasized much more heavily in the middle class than in the lower class include ambition, individual responsibility, achievement, deferral of gratification, planning ahead, cultivation of manners, control of aggression, and respect for property. Schools, according to Cohen, use a middle class measuring rod to judge the performance of students, regardless of their social class background. Because of the middle-class orientation of schools, children from the lower class disproportionately fail to measure up to the demands of the school. Thus, the status and recognition that middle class children are able to achieve in school are much less often available to lower class children. The result is that children from lower class backgrounds experience frustration and failure within the school system because they are ill-equipped to compete with middle-class children in this arena.

Boys who experience such failures come together and form subcultural groups in which middle-class standards are not the measuring rods used; in fact, middle-class standards are inverted so that what is right by middle-class standards is necessarily wrong by the standards of the delinquent subculture. In the delinquent subculture, status is conferred upon those who disdain, rather than on those who abide by, conventional values. The subculture thus promulgates a value orientation antithetical to that of the main culture. As a result, much of gang delinquency has certain hallmarks: it is *malicious* in the sense of taking enjoyment in the discomfiture of others; it is *negativistic* in that what is "right" in the delinquent subculture is often determined simply by noting what is wrong by most people's standards; it is *nonutilitarian* in that its law violations may be less important for the material gains produced (e.g., by theft) than for the satisfaction of annoying victims; finally, the delinquent subculture is characterized by *short-run hedonism* in which thoughts about the future and long-range planning simply don't occur. The aspects of the delinquent subculture make it an attractive alternative to the frustrations and the failure which the school represents to the lower class child.

Subcultural Deviance Theories

The roots of modern subcultural delinquency theories can be traced to the intellectual tradition exemplified by the social ecologists at the University of Chicago whose work we have already alluded to (pp. 158, ff.). These researchers—particularly Thrasher (1927) and Shaw and McKay (1942)—used a combination of quantitative and qualitative research techniques to study the nature and distribution of delinquent behavior that came to the attention of police and court officials in Chicago. In his classic work, *The Gang*, Thrasher made detailed studies of more than 1,300 gangs in the Chicago area. His research, which relied primarily on observational methods, indicated to him that the gangs he studied arose out of spontaneous play groups which were solidified as a result of disapproval from conventional adults and confrontations with rival gangs. The gang gives support to the adolescent who may not be deriving any gratification from family, conventional friends, or school. Thus, the gang is not only a source of status for its members, but also is a primary group in which information about techniques of committing crimes can be exchanged.

Although Shaw and McKay also used observational methods to study delinquency, their *Juvenile Delinquency in Urban Areas* used quantitative techniques to map and study the correlates of variations in rates of juvenile delinquency across census tracts. Like Thrasher, Shaw and McKay believed that understanding delinquent groups was fundamental to understanding the delinquent activities of individual adolescents. Shaw and McKay studied the importance of delinquent subcultural support by conducting an interesting study into the court records available in Chicago. Shaw and McKay hypothesized that delinquent "traditions" survive because of the "age-graded" nature of subcultural groups—that is groups in which younger adolescents are recruited by older adolescents into the gang and taught both techniques of committing delinquent acts and values supportive of delinquent conduct. In their studies of court records, Shaw and McKay found that boys arrested together for a delinquent act could be traced back through the records to earlier offenses in which older boys were also arrested. They found that some members of each delinquent group had appeared in court for offenses committed with older boys "backward in time in an unbroken continuity as far as the records were available" (Shaw & McKay, 1942, p. 175).

Another of the most influential figures in twentieth-century criminology was Edwin Sutherland. He is well known both for his classic empirical examination of the professional thief and white collar criminals (1937, 1949), which we shall review in Chapter 18, and for his theoretical contributions.

Sutherland argued that in our society individuals are exposed to a wide spectrum of "models," some of whom define the laws as rules to be observed and others who define them as incumbrances to be violated. These two counteracting sets of models are forces which shape the character of the individual's orientation toward the legal code. The *principle of differential association* argues that an individual becomes delinquent or criminal because he has been subjected to more powerful definitions from significant persons in his life that favor violating the law rather than observing it.

A contemporary theorist who subscribes to the subcultural deviance perspective is Walter Miller. He argues that illegal behavior results when individuals are attuned to subcultural values that are more compatible with criminal activity than the values of the parent culture.

Miller argues that delinquency is disproportionately found among lower class males because they subscribe to "focal concerns," the pursuit of which brings these individuals into conflict with the law. The focal concerns are trouble, toughness, smartness, excitement, fate, and autonomy. Briefly, Miller postulates that the lower class culture places a value on courting *trouble*— flirting with danger. Courting *trouble* not only results in *excitement*, but also provides opportunity to display *toughness*. The lower class extols *smartness*, defined by Miller as the ability to get what one wants with a minimum of physical exertion. Members of the lower class overtly value autonomy (determining their own fates), but often covertly seek out the security of institutions, such as the Army, where autonomy is limited. Ultimately, they believe that their fates are determined by forces beyond their control.

Miller believes that lower class males come to pursue such concerns in order to be accepted by their peer group and as a means of obtaining status within the group. And the pursuing of focal concerns, Miller argues, often leads to crime and delinquency.

Control Theory

Hirschi (1969) has expanded upon the work of earlier theorists (Durkheim, 1961; Matza, 1964) to formulate his social control theory. This theory states that the important question is not, why do some people become delinquent and criminal, but why don't most people become delinquent? After all, he argues, don't we all begin life without moral constraints on our behavior? If so, what stops us from taking the most direct road (which may often be illegal) to satisfying our desires?

Hirschi suggests that the social control mechanism by which the behavior of individual societal members is constrained can be found in the *bond* of the individual to society. That is, if the bond between an individual and society is strong, to that extent the individual will conform to society's norms; to the extent that the bond between the individual and society becomes weakened, the likelihood of norm violation increases. Thus, although Hirschi is a sociologist, it is clear that his emphasis on both the individual and his or her social environment qualifies the perspective as social psychological in nature.

The individual's bond to society has four elements: attachment, commitment, involvement, and belief. From the point of view of control theory, *attachment* to conventional persons is a major deterrent to crime. Attachment is the bond of affection which an individual feels for conventional persons—how much he cares about those persons, how much he values their opinions and expectations of him, and so on. An individual who is attached to others is likely to consider the effects that his behavior may have on others and on how such persons will subsequently view him; an unattached person has only himself to think of.

Commitment to conventional behaviors is another important element in the bond of the individual to society; to the extent that an individual has invested his time, energy, and himself in conventional activities (getting an education, shaping a career, etc.) his bond to society will be strengthened. Individuals who are thus committed have an investment in conformity that is risked when society's norms are violated. Clearly, control theorists argue, those who do not risk a conventional investment are more likely to engage in delinquent or criminal behavior than those who have a substantial stake in conformity.

Involvement in conventional activities is a third element that bonds an individual to society. This element is assumed to be important because, given limited time and energy, a person engrossed in conventional activities has relatively little time for nonconventional concerns.

The final component of the bond is the *belief* that the individual should obey the rules of society. Those individuals who refuse to grant, for whatever reason, society's legitimacy in laying down rules, are more likely to violate those rules.

As might be expected, the four elements of the bond do not operate independently; those who are attached to conventional people also tend to be committed to behaving conventionally; they also generally subscribe to the idea that society has the right to set down rules. In general, as the individual's bond to society becomes weakened, illegal behavior becomes possible, though not necessary.

PSYCHOLOGICAL THEORIES

Psychological theories emphasize the characteristics of the *person* (i.e., the personality or psychological functioning of the individual) as the primary factor in crime causation. Four quite different psychological approaches are briefly described here: psychoanalytic theory, moral development theory, social learning theory, and a biologically rooted conditioning theory. We shall have more to say about two of these approaches in Chapters 8 and 9.

Psychoanalytic Theory

The central argument in psychoanalytic theory is that delinquency and criminal behavior result from a failure of effective personal controls due to faulty early training or parental neglect or, alternately, that crime or delinquency may be symptomatic of problems in coping with a basic issue of adjustment.

Although Freud's contribution to analytic psychology was enormous, he dealt little with the crime problem specifically. As we shall later see, the psychoanalytic approach to crime claims August Aichhorn as a fountainhead. According to Aichhorn (1935), problems experienced in the first few years of life make it impossible for the child to control his impulses. The child lingers on as a sort of aggrandizing infant, living with a pleasure orientation and failing to develop the reality principle of life. Redl (Chapter 8), who is a disciple of Aichhorn, calls attention to the failure of delinquents to develop a management system over their impulsivity; that is, he argues that they fail to develop a well-functioning ego (see pp. 185, ff.).

Kate Friedlander, in *Psychoanalytic Approach to Delinquency* (1947), suggests that faulty development in the first few years of life adds up to an antisocial character structure, which is incapable of handling reality properly. The social environment may precipitate antisocial conduct but only in persons with antisocial characters.

In addition to these early works, a large number and variety of off-shoot theories flowed from Freud's conceptualizations. It is possible that never before has so much constructive work been done in reaction to—or in argument with—the master. From these various psychoanalytic contributions, it appears that five interpretations can be offered for criminal behavior:

(1) Criminal behavior is a form of neurosis which does not differ in any fundamental way from other forms of neurosis (e.g., while some neurotics work too hard, others set fires); (2) the criminal often suffers from a compulsive need for punishment in order to alleviate guilt feelings and anxiety stemming from unconscious strivings; (3) criminal activity may be a means of obtaining substitute gratification of needs and desires not met inside the family; (4) delinquent behavior is often due to traumatic events whose memory has been repressed; and (5) delinquent behavior may be an expression of displaced hostility. All of these interpretations would suggest that,

although an original difficulty arose in the child's early environment, by the time delinquent behavior occurs such causal factors are operating contemporaneously within the offender.

Moral Development Theory

Lawrence Kohlberg is the formulator of a conception of moral development based on movement through six stages of moral judgment. The theory has much in common with development theories generally or perhaps can be considered an ego-development theory (Loevinger, 1976). According to Kohlberg, there are major differences in forms of moral orientation corresponding to developmental stages, and these differences in the shapes of moral judgment are related to moral or immoral behavior. Accordingly, marked differences in the form of moral orientation may exist between serious offenders and nonoffenders.

The six stages of moral judgment are:

Stage 1: Right is obedience to power and avoidance of punishment.
Stage 2: Right means to take responsibility for oneself, to meet one's own needs and leave to others the responsibility for themselves.
Stage 3: Right is being good in the sense of having good motives, having concern for others and "putting yourself in the other person's shoes."
Stage 4: Right means to maintain the rules of a society and to serve the welfare of the group or society.
Stage 5: Right is based on recognized individual rights within a society with agreed-upon rules, a social contract.
Stage 6: Right is an assumed obligation to principles applying to all humankind, principles of respect for human personality and justice and equality (Kohlberg, Kauffman, Scharf, & Hickey, 1973).

Individuals generally would be classified along this growth continuum, with respect to the stage where the person's development has ceased. Like most psychological theories, the concept is relevant to any population, and not simply offenders. But Kohlberg and his associates have attempted to determine where, along their continuum, offenders tend to fall. Studies suggested that criminals are remarkably lower in moral judgment development than nonoffenders of the same social background. In fact, the majority (75 percent) of noncriminal adolescents and young adults were classified at Stage 3 or 4, while the majority of adolescent offenders were positioned at Stage 1 or 2. Some higher stage people have been imprisoned for their moral principles; however, individuals who commit ordinary crimes are usually at the lower stages (Kohlberg & Freundlich, 1973). Kohlberg's theory suggests that growth to higher stages will generally protect a person against becoming delinquent or criminal.

Social Learning Theory

Social learning theorists reject the idea that offense behavior is symptomatic of an underlying condition (such as repressed impulses, defense mechanisms, inadequate ego development). Instead, it is the delinquent behavior itself, not the meaning of the behavior, which is at issue. According to social learning theory, delinquent and criminal behavior is learned via the same psychological processes as any other behavior. Behaviors are learned and repeated through exposure to rewards (reinforcements) that support the behavior. Conversely, behaviors that have either received no support or received negative reactions are not learned—that is, such behavior will not recur. Parents and others "shape" a child's behavior by reinforcing responses that approximate approved conduct and by withdrawing reinforcing responses from behavior that they wish to extinguish.

Some social learning theorists (e.g., B. F. Skinner, 1969, and his students) see no significant role for conscious or ego faculties. Their theories explain behavior entirely with externally controllable variables. Other social learning theorists (e.g., Bandura, Chapter 9) argue against such a formulation as overly simple. Instead, they see learning as a process in which stimuli are selectively perceived by the individual, who codes and organizes stimuli and develops hypotheses concerning the information. As hypotheses are evaluated over a number of experiences, a mediating rule for dealing with the information is created by the individual. These symbolic processes often provide an individual with the ability to judge an act's consequences without performing the act. This extension of the fundamentals of learning theory to include internal processes avoids a view of people as automatons who react uniformly to given external stimuli.

The social learning theorist offers a causal model that sees socially maladaptive behavior, such as delinquency, as resulting from contingencies in the person's environment that make such behavior productive for him or her. Persistent antisocial behaviors are sometimes said to result from intermittent rewards or reinforcement of delinquent behavior. The youth behaving delinquently may receive indications of parental wrath but he may also receive parental attention, a commodity that may be hard to come by in his family. Or the youth's peer group may provide social reinforcers by hanging on his every word as he describes his delinquent adventures.

In addition to stressing the positive reinforcers of delinquent behavior, the social learning perspective also suggests that antisocial behavior may result from failures to enforce appropriate contingencies. In these cases, negative consequences, promised or not, do not follow from negative behaviors. And finally, the social learning perspective suggests that antisocial behavior may result from inappropriate or excessive use of aversive stimuli, or punishments.

A Biologically Rooted Conditioning Theory

In *Crime and Personality* (1964), Eysenck has put forth his rather unique conceptions regarding the etiology of criminal behavior. Eysenck argues that there is biological variation among individuals in the constitution of the brain. Specifically he suggests that there is variation that relates to the properties of the cortex of the brain, namely to the rapidity with which individuals build up cortical inhibition. This is a Pavlovian (1927) notion that can be thought of as cortical fatigue—something which builds up during cortical stimulation and dissipates in the absence of stimulation. When cortical inhibition is built up, the cortex becomes somewhat insensitive to stimulation. When exposed to the same level of continuous sensory stimulation, those who build up cortical inhibition rapidly (CIR's) will experience subjectively less stimulation than those who build up cortical inhibition slowly (CIS's). If there is individual variation in the rapidity of cortical inhibition build-up, then there are several significant consequences.

First, Eysenck postulates, conditioning will be more difficult for CIR's than for CIS's. This is due to the fact that, for the former, cortical inhibition will build up relatively quickly during conditioning trials and thus conditioning will occur more slowly for them as the cortex becomes less sensitive to stimulation. Eysenck further suggests that "conscience," or the internalization of societal norms, occurs as a conditioning process and, since CIR's condition poorly, they will have been inadequately socialized; for these people society will have failed to inculcate its values.

Second, CIR's and CIS's differ in their perception of the intensity of sensory stimulation. For example, if a CIR and a CIS are listening to the same stereo at the same distance, it may seem too soft to the former and too loud to the latter. Thus, some people are relatively "stimulus-seeking," while others are relatively "stimulus-avoiding." Therefore, it would, Eysenck postulates, be expected that the former would eat more, drink more, have sexual intercourse more frequently, enjoy parties more, and so on—all because of the stimulation which these activities offer. Finally, since CIR's have a tendency to view the environment as relatively stimulus-deficient, they will become bored more rapidly and will tend to seek sensory excitement. It is Eysenck's position then that the internalization of norms is a conditioned reflex, and since CIR's condition poorly, they are not adequately socialized. Since they become easily bored, time passes more slowly for them, and their seeking of stimulation often brings them afoul of the law—especially since the bounds of their behavior are not internally constrained by "conscience." These individuals have personality characteristics that we associate with extroversion. Thus, Eysenck believes that those engaging in criminal and delinquent behavior are more extroverted than those not engaging in illegal activity.

APPLYING THEORIES TO CASE HISTORY INFORMATION   Although we have only been able briefly to discuss some examples of theories developed to explain crime and delinquency, it is apparent that a very wide range of such theories has been developed. Why are there so many different theories of crime and delinquency? A rather common-sense view is that there is, in fact, a variety of kinds of offenders. That is, offenders vary, not only in the form of their delinquent and criminal behavior, but also in the reasons for and the meaning of their behavior. For example, some individuals violate the law because the peer group, *upon which they depend for approval,* "prescribes delinquent behavior as the price of acceptance," or because the values, *which they have internalized*, are those of a "deviant subculture." Other individuals break laws because of *insufficient socialization*, which leaves them at the mercy of "all but the most protected environments." Still others delinquently act out *internal conflicts, identity struggles*, or "family crises." Interestingly, each of these illustrations of the meaning of delinquent behavior suggests both a characteristic or a state of the individual offender *and* a condition of the environment which, in interaction, lead to the offense behavior. In the preceding explanation, the sections which refer to person characteristics are italicized, and those which refer to environmental characteristics appear in quotes.

Most delinquency causation theories purport to explain all delinquency or most of it. However, it is difficult to believe that one theory can offer a universal explanation. In fact, most theories seem only to have described one segment of offenders. All perspectives appear to have some validity when applied to some segment of the offender population, but seem to be based on questionable assumptions when applied across the board. No one theory is sufficiently complex to account for the full range of observable factors.

Can we match up the theories with certain categories of offenders? In an attempt to do this, it is useful to have a way of subdividing or categorizing offenders. Two major approaches to this task have been used frequently: theoretical and empirical.

One approach to the categorization of offenders involves the development of a *theoretical* classification system. Ego-development theories represent such an example, and a specific such system is called the development of Interpersonal Maturity (I-level) (Sullivan, Grant, & Grant, 1957).

I-level theory, like other ego-development theories, describes a continuum of human growth, and defines seven steps along this continuum which can be used to identify the stage a particular person has reached at any point in growth process. As individuals proceed through this continuum, the world they perceive becomes increasingly complex; more and more is taken into consideration as the person views the world and tries to make sense of it. For example, individuals further along this continuum consider the *feelings and attitudes* of other people in their interactions with them, while persons less far along the continuum may take only the *behavior* of others into consideration.

When offenders are classified along the I-level continuum, one finds a few individuals categorized at Level 2, quite a few at Level 3, even more at Level 4, and only a few at Level 5. This may be only slightly different from a non-offender population. The reason for this classification is not to differentiate offenders from nonoffenders, but rather to subdivide the heterogeneous offender population in order to better ask whether certain delinquency causation theories fit certain subgroups of the offender population. Research using I-level categories does show that different causal factors are at issue with the various I-level groups (Warren, 1976).

Another example of an approach to the categorization of delinquents, a development by Jenkins and Hewitt, is described in Chapter 12. Still another example is the Behavior Categories developed by psychologist Herbert Quay. Using three measuring instruments—a true/false test taken by the offender, a behavior check list filled out by a correctional worker who has observed the offender, and a rating of items from a case history of the offender—Quay identified four statistical factors: Psychopathic, Neurotic, Immature/Inadequate, and Subcultural. Individuals are classified by identifying the factor on which they have their highest score.

In the next section of this chapter a number of delinquent youths will be described. In order to illustrate the point that individuals are different from each other in ways that are relevant to the meaning of the delinquent behavior, four vignettes are traced out. All are descriptions of actual male adolescents who have been committed to a state correctional agency, and all may be considered serious or habitual delinquents, in that each has five or more prior arrests.

Jason is fourteen, the oldest of three boys of a poverty-level family. Jason is close to his family, although the boy and his mother both seem slightly embarrassed about the father's inability to earn a better income. Mother points her own father out to Jason as a real man he should emulate. Jason does relatively well in school and thinks education is important. He has some friends at school who are not delinquent, although most of his friends "have been in juvenile hall a few times at least." Jason is a clear leader among his friends, presents loyalty to friends as an important value, and takes considerable responsibility for younger and weaker members of his peer group, as well as his younger brothers.

Jason describes himself as mature, adequate, independent, responsible, and enjoying having new adventures. This picture seems consistent with the way others see him.

For a fourteen-year-old, Jason has a long "rap sheet," which shows a five-year record of property thefts. Jason admits to many more than those for which he was caught. He seems to enjoy talking about them. The offense which brought him to the correctional agency involved picking the lock of the front door of a department store and taking lots of clothing. The police said it was a "pro job." When asked why he committed the crime, Jason explained that his parents understand that he likes to dress well. They work hard to get the money to buy him an outfit. But styles change quickly and they can't possibly afford to keep buying him new things. So he steals what he wants. Stores are insured, he says; they don't lose anything. He certainly wouldn't steal from anyone he knows.

As for his future, Jason wants to "make something of himself," although he thinks society isn't too fair and it may be difficult. He admires people who are strong and who mean what they say. That's the way he wants to be. He doesn't know if he'll give up crime or not.

Of the crime causal theories described in this chapter, which fit Jason's case best? Clearly, material gain is an important factor in Jason's stealing. One could say that he agrees with the goals of our materialistic society. He wants things and he wants status. But the means, which society approves of, are unavailable to him or he has a definition of appropriate means—a definition that is at odds with the parent culture. This is a statement of strain theory (e.g., Merton).

Where it is possible to test the theories from the data available, the other theoretical perspectives seem to fit Jason less well. The psychoanalytic assumptions of neurosis, guilt, and/or anxiety do not fit. Jason clearly has both a strong ego and a strong superego. His bonds to family, friends, and school are strong and thus control theory assumptions that delinquents are weakly bonded to society (e.g., Hirschi) are not met. The subcultural deviance perspective does not fit well. Jason is not simply conforming to the standards of a deviant subculture (e.g., Sutherland). He has both deviant and nondeviant values, and behaves both in ways acceptable to a delinquent subculture (stealing) and acceptable to the parent society (school).

Robert is fourteen. He was abandoned shortly after birth and lived in one foster home for his first thirteen years. At the request of the foster parents, Robert was removed from this home when he began getting picked up for delinquent behavior. During the subsequent year, Robert has been moved from one foster home to another, not getting along in any of them and continuing to get into delinquent difficulties. As Robert looks back at his first foster home, he wonders if they would take him back; maybe it wasn't so bad there after all, although he thought they preferred all the other children to him.

The boy is seen as a nuisance in school; he clowns around to entertain the other kids, and asks for lots of attention from the teachers. Truancy is frequent ("They'll call me chicken if I don't cut."). Although Robert says he has many friends, the peer group tends to avoid him. He's a fringe group member at best.

Robert seems to desperately seek the approval of both adults and peers. He wants adults to see him as a good boy, not a delinquent bone in his body. With peers, he is eagerly compliant to any prescription which will lead to social approval. This peer group prescription often involves delinquency.

Robert describes himself as having good intent, as being sorry he got into trouble, and as being convinced that he will never get in trouble again. He says he is a follower and that other kids lead him astray. He doesn't want to be delinquent because he is always scared that he will get caught. He goes along with the other kids though, because he doesn't want them to dislike him.

Almost all of Robert's official delinquency has occurred in the past year. All of the delinquent behavior (purse snatches and petty thefts) took place with peers. The most serious offense, the one leading to commitment to the correctional agency, involved vandalism. According to Robert, they "tore up a house inside." In addition to the group delinquencies Robert was picked up by the police several times as a runaway.

When asked about his future, Robert says that, if his first foster home will take him back, he'll never be in trouble again. When asked how he will manage this, he says that he will just stay at home and never go out. He has no longer range plans than that.

The absence of bonds to society are extreme in this case (Hirschi). Attachments to family and friends are missing, as is the commitment to school and involvement in conventional activities. At this point Robert seems to have little belief system of his own, but rather seeks clues outside himself as to what constitutes appropriate behavior.

None of the strain theory or psychoanalytic themes are present. There is an absence of the subcultural deviance focal concerns (Miller); rather than toughness and excitement, the needs presented are for acceptance and belongingness via compliance.

Tom is fifteen, the third of five boys. The father has been gone from the home for some time. The mother has had a difficult time both financially and emotionally. Tom became a street child very early, his needs being met by brothers and peers. He is not close to any adult. All of Tom's brothers have been in trouble with the police, as have all of his acquaintances. Tom does not have any particularly close friends but runs around with all the kids in the neighborhood. The peer group activities include shooting pool, drinking beer, and speeding in stolen cars. The activity Tom likes best is fighting. He fights every day and says that, in the last six years, he has only lost three fights. Tom indicates no interest in being a leader with his peer group.

Tom always hated school and has dropped out. He couldn't read and didn't get along with the teachers. He describes himself as not being bothered or worried about anything, but as having a temper when anyone calls him names.

The first of Tom's officially recorded delinquencies occurred when he was eleven. The record lists fights and property offenses, with car theft the most frequent. All were group offenses. According to Tom, many were bum raps; he and his friends were framed. When asked why he committed the last car theft, Tom said that they needed transportation.

Tom doesn't think much about his future, and he tells us he might become a mechanic or join the Army (even though he doesn't like to take orders).

The subcultural deviance theory seems to fit Tom's situation reasonably well (Sutherland, Miller). Tom conforms to the norms that surround him. Delinquency is prescribed as appropriate behavior by peers and brothers. His subculture is deviant and he fits in. Lower class focal concerns of toughness, excitement, trouble, smartness, fate, and autonomy clearly characterize Tom and his peers. It is the expression of these concerns which lead to the delinquency.

Psychoanalytic theory would have to be stretched considerably to fit this case. Strain theory (Merton) does not fit as well as in the case of Jason because fun and excitement seem more powerful motivations to Tom and peers than material gain. Control theory (Hirschi) is not a bad fit. The strongest of Tom's bonds are attachment to his brothers and, to some extent, peers.

He has no commitment to school, no involvement in conventional activities, and no protective belief system. Although the fit with control theory is not bad, the case is not as strong as that of Robert because of Tom's attachment bonds to his peers.

John is sixteen, the oldest of three boys of a low income family. The father, who left the family when John was 12, was a brutal man and, according to John, a bum ("He just hung around the house and slept all day."). John felt that his mother asked him to be the man of the house for a while, but subsequently remarried. John expresses great contempt for this interloper: "He is just like another one of the kids. . . . He has to go home whenever *his* mother calls him." John places great demands on his mother to accept his own adult status but she refuses. John feels he is blamed for leading his younger brothers astray.

John is a loner, with no close friends; he has fantasies about a "girlfriend" with whom he has never spoken. He hangs around with older guys sometimes but is not accepted as a group member. A number of older men have been important figures for John. In elementary school John stayed after school every day and helped the janitor clean. He had a close relationship with the owner of a grocery store where he worked. This man helped John save $100 to buy a deer rifle.

In describing himself, John says he is the kind of person who likes to help others. He elaborates on this theme by describing his volunteer work at the Easter Seal center, where he "helps the cripples." He also rescues animals that are being tormented. He "feels very sorry" for the cripples and the injured animals. In criticism of himself, he says that he always lets people down, giving as examples letting his probation officer and his parents down by getting into trouble again.

John has been stealing things since he was twelve. This began, he says, right after his grandmother died. He was very close to her and, for several weeks after her death, couldn't eat or sleep. He steals small items—candy, money from the cigarette machine, vitamin pills. He reports being caught most times. He earns money working at the grocery store and gardening for the neighbors. And he often steals when he has money in his pocket; he doesn't know why.

As for his future, John like Jason wants to "be somebody." He wants to get an education for this reason. Unfortunately, he says, he stays out late at night and can't get up in the morning. So he just "hangs around the house all day" (like his natural father) and misses school.

Psychoanalytic theory best explains John's self-defeating delinquency. His crimes have a private meaning; for example, they do not seem aimed at material gain or peer group approval. There seems to be considerable inner conflict. John is identified with the hurt and the helpless. He is also identified with the natural father—the "bum" he and his mother hate. The fact that John always gets caught assures him of punishment which may reduce his guilt. John is trapped in wanting to do things which he then prevents himself from doing (for example, getting an education), thus playing out what is sometimes called a "negative life script." A case can also be made that John tries to steal love which is not available elsewhere; at least he does get more of mother's time and attention when he is arrested or confined.

Neither strain (Merton) nor subculture deviance (Sutherland, Miller) theory apply very well to John's circumstances. John not only agrees with the goals of the parent society, but with the legitimate means as well. He violates his own principles when he steals. He does not define himself as delinquent nor do his friends see him as delinquent. He has no interest in the focal concerns of toughness, excitement, trouble, and so on. His bonds to family, school, work, and to belief systems are not so much missing as pervaded with ambivalence; there are strong positive ties but strong negative ones as well. Thus, control theory (Hirschi) also does not seem as explanatory in John's case as is psychoanalytic theory.

Although one could continue to describe individual delinquents and they would all be unique in some ways, one would find that a number would be similar to Jason in the meaning of their delinquency: A number would be similar to Robert or Tom or John. And many delinquent girls would also fit into the same categories. We are not suggesting here that there are only four kinds of delinquent patterns. More categories can be and have been identified. Rather, we have used the case material to illustrate the important point that, while one can find individuals who make each crime causal theory seem appropriate, we cannot make any one theory fit all our cases. On the other hand, the sum total of the various theoretical perspectives presented here seem together to explain a large proportion of the meanings found in a serious delinquent population.

It is important to emphasize that most etiological theories of criminal and delinquent behavior are neither "right" nor "wrong." That is, many perspectives seem to explain the origins of illegal activities for some (but not all) offenders. Furthermore, there is nothing inherently incompatible between sociological and psychological theories; theories falling into each group may be useful for explaining the behavior patterns of some individuals. If our understanding of the complex processes which lead to law violation is to progress, it seems critical that we consider the likelihood that a range of theoretical approaches—sociological, psychological, and others—is required to explain the range of law-violating behavior. It seems reasonable, also, that future research on delinquents and criminals proceed, not so much with an eye toward falsifying various perspectives, but more toward ascertaining which perspectives seem best-suited to explain which patterns of illegal activities.

REFERENCES

Aichhorn, A. *Wayward youth.* New York: Viking Press, 1935.

Cloward, R., & Ohlin, L. E. *Delinquency and opportunity: A theory of delinquent gangs,* Glencoe, Ill.: Free Press, 1960.

Cohen, A. *Delinquent boys.* Glencoe, Ill.: Free Press, 1955.

Durkheim, E. *Moral education,* trans. by E. Wilson & H. Schnurer, New York: Free Press, 1961.

Eysenck, H. *Crime and personality.* Boston: Houghton Mifflin, 1964.

Friedlander, K. *The psychoanalytic approach to juvenile delinquency.* New York: International Universities Press, Inc., 1947.

Hirschi, T. *Causes of delinquency.* Berkeley: University of California Press, 1969.

Kohlberg, L., & Freundlich, D. Moral judgment in youthful offenders. In L. Kohlberg, & E. Turiel (Eds.), *Moralization, the cognitive developmental approach,* New York: Holt, Rinehart and Winston, 1973.

Kohlberg, L., Kauffman, K., Scharf, P., & Hickey, J. *The just community approach to corrections: A manual.* Niantic, Conn.: Connecticut Department of Corrections, 1973.

Loevinger, J. *Ego development.* San Francisco: Jossey-Boss, 1976.

Matza, D. *Delinquency and drift.* New York: Wiley, 1964.

Merton, R. Social structure and anomie. *American Sociological Review,* 1938 *3,* 672–682.

Miller, W. Lower class culture as a generating milieu of gang delinquency. *Journal of Social Issues,* 1958, *14,* 5–19.

Pavlov, I. P. *Conditioned reflexes,* trans. by G. Vanup, New York: Oxford University Press, 1927.

Shaw, C. R., & McKay, H. D. *Juvenile delinquency and urban areas.* Chicago: University of Chicago Press, 1942.

Skinner, B. F. *Contingencies of reinforcement.* New York: Appleton-Century-Crofts, 1969.

Sullivan, C., Grant, M., & Grant, J. D. The development of interpersonal maturity: Applications to delinquency. *Psychiatry,* 1957, *20,* 373–385.

Sutherland, E. *The professional thief.* Chicago: University of Chicago Press, 1937.

Sutherland, E. *Principles of criminology,* Philadelphia: J. B. Lippincott, 1947.

Sutherland, E. *White collar crime.* New York: Dryden, 1949.

Thrasher, F. *The gang.* Chicago: University of Chicago Press, 1927.

Warren, M. Q. Intervention with juvenile delinquents. In M. Rosenheim, *Pursuing justice for the child.* Chicago: University of Chicago Press, 1976.

chapter 8

The Psychoanalytic Perspective

Fritz Redl
Hans Toch

It is no coincidence that this chapter is called "the psychoanalytic *perspective*." Like the elephant in the famous story of the blind men, psychoanalysis is many things (trunk, tail, legs) depending on the aspect of psychoanalysis you grab on to. Each aspect of psychoanalysis is also "live," in the sense that it is evolving and changing.

Sigmund Freud coined the term "psycho-analysis" in 1896, when he was forty years old. Freud continued to revise his ideas until he died in 1960 at the age of 84. At the time when he succumbed to cancer, Freud was writing a comprehensive new book setting forth the latest version of his views (Freud, 1940). The last of four wholesale shifts in Freudian theory occurred in 1926, and it centered on the role of anxiety in adult life (Sjöbäck, 1973). As a person Freud was anything but closed-minded. One of his biographers points to a remarkable readiness on Freud's part "to consider any fact, however new and extraordinary, that was presented to him" (Strachey, 1966, p. xvii).

What are some of the "elephant parts" of the psychoanalytic perspective? A key feature, most students of psychoanalysis would agree, is Freud's *theory of neuroses*, which points to the psychological (as opposed to physiological) origins of disturbances that had previously been considered in the medical realm. In this discovery, Freud was preceded by a Viennese physician named Breuer, who recognized that hysterical symptoms in adults could be a sediment of very unpleasant, undigested experiences (traumas) in early childhood. Breuer felt that a person's past can haunt him or her unless it is relived or remembered. Freud complicated Breuer's picture by pointing to psychological processes (repressions or resistances) which prevent us from reaching the experiences that make us suffer. These Freudian concepts led to the discovery of new *treatment methods* which depended on the establishment of an intimate type of relationship of patient to therapist (transference), through which the past could be rehearsed, sorted out, "coped with," and set aside.

Transference is a phenomenon which exists in "real life" as well as in therapy. It consists of an inescapable tendency to replay significant relationships—to apply lessons drawn from prior emotional attachments, usually inappropriately, to current encounters with significant others. This occurs, for example, where we explode in undignified fashion when someone's criticism reminds us (at some level) of our parents' strong interest in our youthful affairs, or where jealousy, upon minor provocation, is aimed at a succession of mates selected for their physical attractiveness.

In therapy, the transference consists of strong feelings directed at the therapist, which evolve when the client feels "threatened" by unwelcome discoveries about himself. As Freud saw it, this transference reaction is a last-ditch defense against self-discovery (Freud, 1924). The advantage of the transference to the analyst is that it creates a "laboratory" for change, in which past problems unwittingly come alive in the "here and now" (the patient's responses to the analyst) and are thus subject to examination. The liability of the process lies in the dependency that it creates, from which the patient must be weaned. The process of weaning includes dramatizing the inappropriateness and immaturity of dependence, and building up the person's resources to stand on his or her own feet (Alexander & Selesnick, 1966).

In recent years, Freud's ideas on therapy for neuroses have been extended to the treatment of so-called "psychotic states," with proper modification of techniques, including the creation of intimate hospital and "treatment home" settings (Bettelheim, 1974).

PSYCHOANALYTIC PERSONALITY THEORY

In trying to help his patients with their neurotic difficulties, Freud evolved or developed a *theory of personality*. This fact was not a coincidence. Freud, like Newton, was scientifically oriented. If a non-scientist is faced with fallen apples, he would probably snack on them, while the apple that hit Newton's head motivated him to look for theoretical assumptions that would explain why bodies fall toward the earth under regular and clearly measurable conditions, increasing their speed with mathematical expectability. Freud's observations of the phenomena of neurotic afflictions, of irrational anxieties in otherwise competent adults (such as a sudden fear of crossing a special place in a road, with no visible "reason" for danger, for instance), raised the question: What would we have to assume about human personality in order to explain what we by now can clearly observe as facts? The main line of these deliberations led Freud to the two most important facets of the psychoanalytic theory of personality (which still remain basic, even in the minds of those who deviate from Freud in other points). One such facet is the *mapping* of the human personality into three major "departments" with a specific function for each. One is the so-called *id*—the sum total of our desires, wishes, urges, drives, including those we are not aware of at the time they hit us. The second is the *superego*, which comprises all values we have incorporated from adults whose influence reached us in our childhood years. The superego includes the "ego ideal," which features behavioral norms, values such as strivings for fame or applause, need for approval by our peers, and the fulfillment of our own vanity goals, such as "being good at" balancing on a fence, diving into water, throwing a ball, or opening other people's safes. The third, but certainly not least, personality component is the so-called *ego*, under which Freud subsumed some very special functions of our personality. This fact is important, for translation can confuse the psychoanalytic meaning of the term ego with popular expressions of daily conversation, where we say that something "hurt" or "flattered" our "ego". The psychoanalytic concept of the ego as a series of jobs or tasks of the human personality, includes the following functions:

1. My ego is tuned to keep me in contact with "reality." Freud had two types of reality in mind: the realities of the physical universe (my ego must tell me that it isn't wise to jump into deep water if I can't swim), and the legal and other social consequences of my behavior (a twelve-year-old ought to know that telling a story his aunt might find "cute" won't make him popular with older and tougher kids; or he ought not to run around with the illusion that he can never be caught no matter what risks he takes in stealing).

2. My ego, however, also has the obligation to *stop* my behavior if it is too far out or too much in contrast with said "reality." Bobby's ego may fulfill the task of "reality testing" quite efficiently and warn him about what he is getting into, but greed for gang approval, or vanity, or the gratification of feelings of rage, triumph, excitement may be too much for the ego to manage, and dysfunctional behavior takes place, even though the insight system functioned quite properly. A frequent type of "ego trouble" of delinquent youngsters is thus a lack of "temptation resistance," and a deafness to what the ego infers from previous experiences, which ought to make one "wiser" next time. Our whole theory of deterrence is somehow tied up with this problem, and we shall return to this point later.

A second key area of theory and exploration of psychoanalysis are the human experiences we usually describe and subsume under the name of *drives*—needs, emotions, impulses, affects, and their close relatives. Among *basic drives*, Freud primarily focused on two—"love" and "aggression."

Here we run into another linguistic problem—one that didn't start with translations from German into English, but with German usage of terms. Freud, instead of separating, in the customary way of his times, "pure love" from "sex," decided to call all positive affect "sex." Then he proceeded to draw distinctions on the basis of differentiations between "objects" and "forms of gratification." Thus, for instance, "loving your country" or "your profession" features a wide variety of behaviors that are "gratified" and demonstrated, which are not meant to have much to do with "sex" in the original meaning of the term. This fact is independent of problems psycho-analysts ran into when they pointed at clearly "bodily" and thus "sexual" components of loving behavior in the very young child, an insight which contemporary societal counterpressures objected to. Things became easier when Freud decided to use the term "libido" for the energy put into love rela-tionships, but trouble of a new sort evolved through problems of translation. As opposed to German usage, the English word "drive" allowed no adjective! There is no such word as "drival" in the English language. This is the reason why translators had to resort to "instinct" instead of drive. They had to talk about drives as "instincts" because two lines later they might want to talk about "instinctual inhibitions." This can obviously be very confusing, and controversy and misunderstanding have been the result of semantic muddles. In face of these, psychoanalysis has persevered in effort to explore the development of drives—basic or secondary—from the earliest years of child-hood, and has put special weight on the concept of "traumatic experiences" —the observation that experiences can be so overwhelming that they arrest emotional development in a given area, with disturbances or neurotic symp-toms as a consequence. Psychoanalysts, however, also learned that this process is not automatic, and what may lead to traumatization in one society or cul-ture may be free of such consequences in another. In the evaluation of which "terrible experiences," a youngster who grew up under "miserable" condi-tions is *causal* to his present delinquent development and which other prob-lems we need to look at for causal links constitutes one of the most complex tasks in our explorations of the behavior of offenders.

Probably one of the most disturbing subjects Freud introduced—worse than his insistence on taking sex seriously—was his development of the con-cept of the *unconscious*. We must again make sure of avoiding linguistic com-plications: the use of the noun is not literal. It would probably be wiser to avoid the somewhat misleading noun, and to fix our attention on the adjec-tive. If Bobby has a superego the size of a church steeple, he may not allow himself to be wildly angry with his parents. There may be moments in his life, though, where through a combination of circumstances, extreme rage against a parental figure may swell up in Bobby. At that juncture, Bobby may not allow himself to be aware of his anger. In fact, he may be the only one who doesn't notice how angry he looks—everybody else around him can't miss the cues to his condition. In short, Bobby's feelings of rage and anger may be "unconscious," in the sense that they are *repressed* from con-scious self-perception. But they influence behavior now, and are thus part of "the unconscious."

We sometimes use the term "repressed" and "suppressed" too loosely. According to psychoanalysts, Bobby may know how angry he is, and may successfully *suppress* his rage so as not to *do* or *say* anything about it. If he *represses* rage, it works the other way around: the rage *has* effect on behavior, but Bobby doesn't allow himself to become aware of it. It is incidentally, hard to know which of the two situations is better for Bobby, since this depends on what he would do with his rage if he experienced it. Repression that shoots rage "too deep down" for too long a time may be easier on Bobby now, but may extort a subsequent price in personality distortions. This is one of the assessments which complicates the challenge of giving advice to parents.

In the case of youngsters who have developed severe disturbances, it becomes as important to know what to tackle as it is to know what to leave alone for awhile. Both decisions belong in the realm of psychoanalytic counselling, which involves some skill in offering "interpretations" but more skill in learning when to keep one's mouth shut.

CHILD ANALYSIS, CHILD DEVELOPMENT, AND DELINQUENCY

Freud's daughter, Anna Freud, and her associates were instrumental in developing the concept of "Child Analysis" as a method of treating childhood and adolescent afflictions (A. Freud, 1964).

They also were very involved in conducting detailed studies of early phases of child development, focussing particularly on the development of emotions, libido, and character (A. Freud, 1946). Besides these officially recognized contributions to psychoanalysis, Freud and her colleagues were active in two directions that are less frequently mentioned, and less clearly marked in our awareness. These are:

1. The implications of what we know about child development for education and parenting, including the kind of additional training one must have to be more comfortable in handling developmental problems of childhood and adolescence and to "understand" developmentally conditioned deviant behavior so as to become less upset about it.

2. A focus on the special problems of delinquents, and a search for treatment methods which reach beyond the therapist's office into the home, or into special residential settings for institutional care of youngsters with a wide range of "delinquency-prone" problems, including youngsters from rougher layers of society who previously had not been targets of intensive helping efforts. A psychoanalyst we have mentioned elsewhere in this book, Aichhorn (1925), was especially knowledgeable about the habitat and societal customs of lower class children and opened the path of milieu treatment for delinquents. Some of Aichhorn's students and followers elaborated and modified his techniques for use in the United States and England, despite the dramatic social and other differences between today's slums and the Vienna of the early thirties (e.g., Redl & Wineman, 1952, 1962).

The stress on bringing educators into the orbit of psychoanalytical understanding of childhood problems was strong in the early days of psychoanalysis. The school also became closely tied with other fields of research into human behavior. Far from pretending to substitute analysis for such fields, psychoanalysts have been eager to find special aspects of larger problems that are faced in sociology, anthropology, social psychology, group psychology, and animal behavior, as well as history and the arts, to which psychoanalytic findings might add insights that otherwise might be missed.

It seems obvious, of course, that there are some places where psychoanalytic thinking does not belong, which are clearly the major domain of other sciences. One recognizes, for instance, that careful assessment of the sociocultural characteristics of a youngster's life space is an issue in its own right, and could never be supplanted by psychoanalytic speculations (Chapter 7). On the other hand, to ascertain what happens in the mind of the underprivileged delinquent before, during, and after he engages in his delinquent act, may sometimes profitably require the psychoanalytic microscope as well as other perspectives and tools. Our power of producing societal changes that affect the delinquent's fate during his lifetime may be limited. Our jurisdiction might be reduced to what we devise for Bobby so as to make his future less delinquency prone. This task includes a search for specific milieu attributes or psychological conditions to bring about internal changes. This is where the psychoanalyst might be asked to add his insights and inferences to the contributions of other sciences.

THE MEANING OF DELINQUENCY

There is confusion between the clearly *legal* issues of which behavior has what consequences under the law, and the meaning of delinquency for the delinquent. To reduce this confusion, let us start with the admission that psychoanalytic speculations are in no contradiction to the question of what, in a given society and according to a given value system, should be considered "right" or "wrong." The fact that a delinquent's behavior may be "understandable" on the basis of his case history does not mean it can be tolerated or excused or that others should have to suffer from its outrages. At the same time, there exists in its own right the question of what need be done besides incapacitating the delinquent—the issue of whether he can change or revamp his distorted impulse or value system. What we do to change a person, of course, depends very much on our insight into what produced his unique behavior and our understanding of what this behavior means to him. To define those factors is a matter for which the study of the human personality is of the utmost relevance.

Imagine yourself in a camp for delinquent youngsters who were borrowed from detention homes, reformatories, and social agencies for the duration of the summer. Danny, in cabin 5, is probably the toughest and most "street wise" of the youths, while his colleague Jimmy is two years younger, and has been detained (twice) for relatively "minor offenses." The group develops a good relationship with their counsellor, and things seem to be going fine. On a Wednesday morning, however, Danny is gone and Jimmy seems to be with him. Why should Jimmy have run away? And, from what we know about Danny—why would a street wise, tough, and experienced customer bother to load himself with a little kid, face all the risks of getting caught that this entails, and therefore endanger his delinquent venture—a thing only a raw beginner in "escapades" would do?

After we have the runaways back, this is what emerges: Danny would never make a purposive mistake, nor did he in fact like Jimmy enough to want him along. The whole expedition was really, in a sense, a jealousy episode. It was not (for either child) a delinquent act. On the contrary, it was a loyalty protest against a counsellor. In Jimmy's case, an unexpected, intensive, and open relationship to his counsellor stirred up old attachments and resentments which he apparently had not quite outgrown. Here he was, full of good feeling toward an adult in a semiparental role, who was an authority figure on top of it. How could he admit that he "fell for that stuff?" The counsellor, of course, had to accommodate the fact that the somewhat younger and much less "roughened" Jimmy needed a lot of extra affection and sometimes even protection from cruel kidding by older and tougher kids. To Danny that situation also revived old memories—the times when he thought his old man didn't care for him any more, because the whole family was enamoured with a brand new little brother's arrival. So Danny felt a deep rejection by his counsellor, and it all seemed as though history was going to repeat itself. How do you take revenge on somebody who prefers a younger kid to you? With ingenuity, you take the little "pet" away from him. At the same time, a runaway episode gives you the opportunity of sweet daydreams of revenge: the counsellor will miss that brat of his—serves him right. Added to this, there is the legitimate enjoyment of some feelings of being hurt. He wouldn't give a damn if just I myself had been gone; he probably wouldn't even have missed me! This is a frequent fantasy that youngsters develop in very early years, especially when they are caught loving an adult while they are supposed to be tough and mean to anyone in an official role. Only, Danny is too old for that. At his age, rage against a counsellor should more healthily have come out in open rebellion. So Danny has a double problem: there are the motives that occasioned his real delinquent troubles; in addition, he has a peculiar developmental phase hangup, which he also needs to resolve.

As far as our statement of the problem is concerned, it clearly is more complex than one justifying simple penalties for runaway episodes or special promises in case they stop. In fact, one of the lessons we learn from this incident is that we have to increase our ability to spot Danny's mood swings early, so he can tell us about his fantasies instead of having to translate them into "acting out" behavior. For it is important that we help the youth to disentangle himself from rejection fantasies of the past, and from the distorted idea that the counsellor's helpfulness is the same as his earlier abandonment experiences. Just how we do this is a complex story; we usually would combine individual interactions with Danny (or Danny and Jimmy) and good general programming. We also need intensive staff coverage at the camp, so that any incident which might plausibly lead to a repetition of Danny's unmanageable and distorted jealousy feelings could be tackled right away. For a while, somebody should always know where both youths are, especially at times when mood swings are frequently the order of the day—or night.

In summary: legally speaking, Danny seduced another boy to join him on a runaway episode. Psychologically, the episode was not a runaway, in that neither youth "wanted to be somewhere else." What Danny experienced was a fantasy repetition of old feelings of sibling rivalry, which he translated into symbolic action. What brought this on was not the youngster's revolt against authority. On the contrary, the episode was a healthy but sudden crisis of a very intensive dependency relationship to an adult, which, for a boy who thinks he has the job of being "anti-authority," is a rough discovery to face.

The actual behavior that occurred, and what it *really meant*, are not the same, and only if we know both can we begin to understand how we can help people change.

DELINQUENT INFLUENCE

So far, we have centered primarily on Danny's motives. But what of Danny's "seduction" of Jimmy? What of Jimmy's "seduceability"? What of the intersection of the two boys' motives, their "targeting" of the counsellor, the impact of their collusion? These are issues that relate to *group process*, *influence*, and *leadership*, areas that are of considerable concern to psychoanalysis as well as to social learning theory (Chapter 9) and to other perspectives (Chapter 7).

Freud combined the themes of group influence, and leadership in a 1921 monograph (*Group Psychology*) and he returned to these themes—separately and together—in two other books (*The Future of an Illusion* and *Civilization and Its Discontents*). Freud's thinking was heavily influenced by the work of two French sociologists (Tarde, 1890; LeBon, 1879), who saw group processes as facilitating emotional release and disinhibition through "contagion," "imitation," and other *irrational* links among group members. In modern parlance, Tarde and LeBon postulated that the unconscious of one group member could somehow communicate with—and influence—another, if propitiously regressive conditions existed. LeBon wrote prolifically about a temporary "group mind" which, he said, can cause respectable men and women to engage in disreputable, animalistic acts.

The French sociologists saw group processes as reciprocal and diffuse, and they did not worry about leadership, or about who influenced whom.

Freud felt that such a view was incomplete. Contagion, he wrote, implies libido (love) and/or aggression (hate). Such drives are evoked because *in the backdrop of crowds* lurks a "central figure" (or object) which inspires love and/or hate. We kill others, for example, in the name of collective libidinal objects such as country (patriotism), god (religion), or less consensual ego ideals (crime).

More recent psychoanalytic writers have amended and reformulated Freud's views. Bion (1961) subdivides irrational group process into fight/

flight (scapegoating), dependency (search for leadership), and pairing (sexually charged coalitions). Redl (1942) lists ten examples of *types* of group formation—each of which implies different "central figures," leadership and influence processes. One of these ten types features the "Seducer," who "seduces" delinquency among predelinquents who are "on the brink" by modelling disinhibition (Chapter 9). Another of the ten types is the "Bad Influence," who combines conflict-free self-indulgence with charismatic sophistication.

Psychoanalysis has returned to study contagion, to explain the onset of delinquency in group contexts (Redl, 1949). The study of contagion has allowed psychoanalysts to enter the group laboratory, where questions can be posed about *who* influences *whom* (and when) to be delinquent (Polansky, Lippitt, & Redl, 1950).

This cross-fertilization of group dynamics and psychoanalysis has provided views of gang delinquency which supplement the formalistic and procedure-oriented portraits that are sometimes yielded by sociological studies. The psychoanalytic emphasis in gang psychology is on nonrational processes such as seduction, group support for delinquent behavior, defenses against prosocial influences, the sources of peer love and loyalty, and so on (Redl, 1945).

It is interesting to note that the gang phenomena observed by psychoanalysts are available in all sorts of accounts that originate in other disciplines. The sociologist Wade (1967), for example, studied group vandalism, and precisely describes processes such as contagion, seduction, and emotional support for delinquency. Group-based behavior (gang delinquency) may well be a problem on which psychoanalysts, sociologists, anthropologists and social psychologists can converge.

WHEN AN OFFENDER IS A PSYCHOANALYTIC "CLIENT"

We have conceded the limits of the psychoanalytic perspective. What we assume, however, is that there are times when ignoring depth psychology can produce distortions in our view of delinquency or crime, and can spark inappropriate reactions to offenders.

Several features of psychoanalytic theory help us decide if and when the perspective should be applied. These features include: (1) the dominant role of irrational motives, pressures of which the individual may not be aware, which can manifest themselves in devious or indirect ways; (2) deficits that can occur in the ego's mediation of reality, or the ego's capacity to control affects or drives; (3) the presence of several layers of motivation (overdetermination), which complicate the question "why did he/she do it?"; (4) problems with "built in" norms or values which can be tenuous or tyrannical, or can be lopsidedly both; (5) the complexity that is produced by internal conflicts; and (6) cues that the person's past is "alive" in his reactions to his present circumstances.

Statistically, most human behavior (including criminal behavior) is probably fairly rational, goal-oriented, direct, contemporary, and uncomplicated. In such instances (as with professional thieves) the psychoanalytic perspective is not applicable—it is inapplicable to such acts not because it is invalid, but because it is unnecessary. A person's choice of fried eggs for breakfast is not illuminated by Freudian insights, unless the person agonized interminably in making his choice, or exploded at the chef's failure to obey instructions as to egg temperature and timing. Fledgling analysts are alerted by Freud to the temptation of "reading in" complexity where it does not exist. "A cigar," Freud commented (while chain smoking), "is mostly just a cigar."

An offender's illicit activity, as we have seen with Danny, is not *per se* data about his motives. Neither is a detailed case history which highlights (or lowlights) features of an offender's checkered past. In reading case studies of murderers, Freud himself commented that "now we know everything, except why the murder was actually committed" (Wertham, 1941, p. 193). Diagnostic workups in very skilled hands can provide pictures of offender motives, but such workups must obviously be reserved for occasions where they are needed and relevant. This need and relevance must be ascertained through prescreening, by interviews, or other means.

The criterion that is customarily used for invoking diagnosticians is offense seriousness or the public's degree of alarm. In extreme cases, as with bizarre multiple-killings, this criterion makes sense. In other instances—as with mandated workups for pyromaniacs—the chaff gets digested with the wheat. The psychoanalytic perspective adds little to what we know about businessmen who cut their losses by burning down stores. It may tell us much, on the other hand, about fires that are set in response to feelings of powerlessness, inadequacy, boredom, frustration, self-hate, and loneliness.

The other side of the coin describes what we *miss* when we center on criminal behavior. The issue is the motivation and the personality of persons who are, *among other things,* offenders. As a delinquent, our boy Danny was a "tough kid," who struck us as sophisticated and self-possessed. In other ways, Danny struggled with feelings and concerns that were anything but tough. Unless we viewed Danny *as a whole,* we might be fooled by his "rap sheet" and by the facade that furnished no cues as to its underpinnings.

This fact is especially salient when we consider *our responses to crime* (our social control measures). In limited ways, the offender can engineer how authorities react in response to what he does. This is particularly the case where offenses are committed in the presence of authorities and where they have a challenging, disruptive, or dramatic quality. In such situations, criminal behavior can lend itself to the display of motives that have attention-getting, self-advertising, authority-bating as an aim. If we (authorities) accept such messages at face value, we ignore dependency bids, love hunger, brittleness, fear, and bitterness-in-search-of-confirmation. A standard response to a "tough customer" can involve unseemly duels with a straw man, and can feed, cement, and reinforce a last-ditch bluff.

Does it, in fact, matter? If the offender "asks for it," why not simply oblige him? If a delinquent challenges one's authority, why not "show him who's boss"? Why not treat advertised toughness as toughness, self-conscious obnoxiousness as obnoxiousness? Why *particularly* worry about punishment where the offender seems to provoke it?

We may not worry, of course. In a labile group, an *agent provocateur* may require control for the sake of others, and his temporary expulsion may be indicated. Dispassionate and judicious sanctions are not psychoanalytic "taboos"; they may, on the contrary, be esteemed—as external props, for instance, where the offender's self-controls require buttressing. We always punish constructively, however, *on our terms*, and not on the offender's. Sanctions as part of programming can be "matched" to the offender's reality testing capabilities, and can be timed to maximize impact on future conduct. Offender-provoked punishment, on the other hand, reinforces future misbehavior, though it may curb current misconduct.

For one, offender-provoked punishment smells of vengeance, because it is frustration-induced in us, no matter how carefully it may be rationalized. As such, it "confirms" underlying *premises* of antisocial conduct, such as "the world is against me," "I'm harassed," "life is (predictably) unfair," "authorities are cruel," "adults hate people like me," "It's a dog-eat-dog world," "they get me or I get them," and so on.

The psychoanalytic perspective on resocialization requires the *disconfirmation* of delinquency-prone assumptions built up through early (and often cumulative) experiences with destructive personal encounters. The offender's self-fulfilling prophecies about predictable arbitrariness, hostility, cruelty, disinterest of the world must be *unfulfilled*, as must his self-characterizations (self-assigned victim attributes, felt impotence) and his interpersonal strategies (fight/flight, protest). Offender-provoked punishments are *precisely* the sort of responses of social control personnel and agencies that the offender has "keyed" in his "tests" as offense justifications.

At best, unprogrammed sanctions risk being out of phase with the offender's capacity to "learn his lesson," a capacity that develops fairly late in the ego's career. Where reality testing is deficient, punishment becomes a happenstance frustration, unrelated (no matter what the punisher says) to the offender's current (hence, future) conduct.

THE "DELINQUENT EGO"

There is a wrinkle to the concept of "ego," which we have spared the reader, but must now mention. This wrinkle consists of the discovery that ego development—like a poorly directed army—can be disharmonious, that the ego can advance on one flank, while remaining firmly entrenched, or retreating, on another. This condition is one that is particularly apt to face us among delinquents, and it has practical consequences.

In describing offenders, Aichhorn (1955) wrote that

it seems as though only part of the ego of the delinquent had succeeded in making the transition from the unconscious pleasure world of the small child to that of reality. Why have they remained immature in one part of their ego? Because another part of their ego has developed a maturity corresponding to or exceeding their chronological age. The delinquent often shows himself especially adept in conforming to reality in situations where the bare struggle for existence is involved" (p. 153).

At first blush, this discovery fills our hearts with joy, since it describes *strength* where we may not have expected it. There is, however, a catch: "weak" ego components are areas where the delinquent needs help, but "strength" *translates into being skillful at being delinquent and showing ingenuity in resisting resocializing influences* (Redl & Wineman, 1962).

The ego's deficits are primarily vested in its control system. This faces us with unchecked impulsivity, low boiling points, impatient, urgent hereness and nowness, anxiety, and helplessness. The "strong" ego, however, locates temptations, enlists delinquent allies, finds alibis and excuses, manipulates, bullies, cajoles. It is this "subcompartment"—the "delinquent ego"—which "tests" us, "cons" us, fights, defies, circumvents, and *attempts to sustain the "weak" ego's pattern of impulsivity*. In resocialization we must "reach" the offender's "weak" ego, we must buttress and cement his control system, without having the delinquent ego "reach" us by posing tasks for us which, *given our own ego deficits*, we sometimes fail. Given this fact, the criminal justice system (which relies on external controls) faces hard and delicate challenges. It is difficult to envisage how such challenges can be met without exquisite professional skills based on diagnostic acumen and interpersonal competence.

PSYCHOANALYTIC MYTHOLOGY AND PSYCHOANALYTIC PERSPECTIVE

Few views in the social sciences have evoked stronger feelings, and provoked as much controversy, as those of Freud. This is not unexpected, because common sense sees man as rational, and our self-images (the dictionary "ego") stress purity of motive and pragmatic purposefulness. To the extent to which we resonate to our irrationality, we also fear—hence, reject—its import. Anyone who describes disowned layers of ourselves is apt to be an "unwelcome messenger" whose insights may be caricatured to facilitate their rejection.

Our excursion has not allowed us to dispel the stereotypes that are held about psychoanalysis. It may therefore help if we list a few of these in concluding this chapter:

1. *Psychoanalysis tells us that our difficulties (including criminal propensities) must be blamed on our parents*. Psychoanalysis emphasizes the importance of early experiences in personality development and character formation. It does *not* attribute untoward childhood events to particular child-rearing practices that call for "blaming" individual parents. Psychoanalysts also do not directly trace a person's behavior to his early experiences

nor can they *exculpate* the person for what he does. Most important, psychoanalysis does not deny or undersell the importance of contemporary events and pressures, nor ignore intervening stages of development. Psychoanalysts have carefully attended to adolescence, which is described as a stormy and revolutionary period in personal development. The term "identity crisis" is a psychoanalytic concept (Erikson, 1956).

2. *"Treatment" means spending several years on a "couch" with an expensive practitioner—something most delinquents cannot do.* A classical analysis for psychoneurotics has usually consisted of individual sessions which were apt to continue over several years. This type of therapy is still practiced; the modern trend, however, favors other service delivery models. Psychoanalytic therapists were among the first to introduce play therapy, group therapy, family therapy, and the use of therapeutic milieus. The targets of many such experiments have been youthful delinquents because of the links that tie psychoanalysis to education. Freud himself divorced psychological services from medicine, and opened the way for "lay" therapists. This "de-escalation" of credentials set precedents for new professions and paraprofessions, such as social work and child care work, which deliver all sorts of human services. There is no reason, for instance, why a good bartender cannot offer psychoanalytic "treatment," if he responds to undercurrents or overtones of his clients' alcohol-suffused consultations.

3. *Psychoanalysis is a science and practice whose field is mental illness or emotional disorders. For psychoanalysis to be relevant, offenders must be sick.* We shall address the concern with sickness and nonsickness elsewhere in this book (Chapters 5 and 11). We have reviewed Freud's personality theory, which outlines universal features of human development and psychic structure, and highlights the role of unconscious motives and irrationality. This view—if it does anything—blurs the line between "normality" and "illness." Freud described mechanisms common to neurotics and normals in his books *The Psychopathology of Everyday Life, Wit and Its Relation to the Unconscious,* and *The Interpretation of Dreams.* He also engaged in considerable self analysis.[1]

4. *Psychoanalysis deals with individual personal dynamics and it has no bearing on persons who are products of social problems.* This statement is the equivalent of saying, "Internal medicine deals with human digestion, and has no bearing on people with flat feet and sunburns." People have stomachs and feet and skin. They also have personal dynamics and social origins. Ultimately, our aim must be to combine all information that helps us understand human problems. This includes data that *cut across* people as well as insights into unique problems of individuals (Allport, 1937, 1960). The word "product" is also deceptive. Correlations do not really *explain* behavior. The authors of this chapter were born in Vienna and smoke cigars. The former need not *necessarily* illuminate the latter.

5. *Sigmund Freud treated middle-class Europeans eighty years ago. His observations cannot help us to understand underprivileged Americans.* Psychoanalysts knew about class differences, and were interested in the effect of

subcultures on human development. Their stress on cultural relativism helps explain the influence exercised by psychoanalysis on anthropology. Moreover, no one *expects* problems of a Detroit delinquent to resemble those of a central European housewife. Nor do we expect the problems of one Detroit delinquent to duplicate another's. The clinical perspective views each individual as a new source of data. What we expect is help from concepts about human personality, and from therapeutic technology (interpersonal skills).

A CAVEAT ABOUT PSYCHOANALYTIC PAROCHIALISM

The apologia above applies to a view of psychoanalysis that makes us relatively happy, and it need not and should not be shared by everyone. Readers may encounter theorists and practitioners whose views diverge from ours—and to these persons the disclaimers we have advanced may not, in full measure, extend.

This is as it must be, given shifting roles in the historical game. Psychoanalysis is close to a hundred years old. Over time, as movements grow and secularize, their congeniality and compatibility with other ideas and beliefs increase (Toch, 1965). At its inception, psychoanalysis was a revolution, protesting against the neurological "establishment" of its day. Battle lines, and convictions were firm.

Today, psychoanalysis permeates much of our tradition. The core is still there, but our view is ecumenical. As we see it, fertilization of ideas is no longer a threat, but a necessity. This is a faith we share with most, if not all, psychoanalysts.

NOTE

1. Recent psychoanalytic investigators (e.g., Shapiro, 1965) have shown that the neuroses dealt with by Freud have their lower-order counterparts in personality or "character" traits of relatively normal persons. Relatively modest versions of psychotic states can also be represented among normal people.

REFERENCES

Aichhorn, A. *Verwahrloste jugend* (1925) (translation *Wayward youth*). New York: Meridian Books, 1955.

Alexander, F. G., and Selesnick, S. T. *The history of psychiatry.* New York: Harper & Row, 1966.

Allport, G. W. *Pattern and growth in personality.* New York: Holt, Rinehart and Winston, 1937.

Allport, G. W. *Personality and social encounter: Selected essays.* Boston: Beacon Press, 1960.

Bettelheim, B. *A home for the heart.* New York: Knopf, 1974.

Bion, W. R. *Experience in groups and other papers.* London: Tavistock, 1961.

Erikson, E. H. The problem of ego identity. *Journal of the American Psychoanalytic Association*, 1956, 4, 56–121.

Freud, A. (Ed.). *The psychoanalytic study of the child: An annual volume.* London: Imago Publishing Company, 1946, ff.

Freud, A. *The psychoanalytical treatment of children.* New York: Schocken Books, 1964.

Freud, S. *An outline of psycho-analysis* (1940). In J. Strachey (Ed.), *Standard edition of the complete psychological work of Sigmund Freud*, Vol. 23. London: Hogarth Press, 1953, 144–207.

Freud, S. Twenty seventh lecture: Transference. In *A general introduction to psychoanalysis.* London: Boni and Liveright, 1924.

LeBon, G. *The crowd: A study of the popular mind.* London: T. F. Unwin, 1879; New York: Viking, 1960.

Polansky, N., Lippitt, R., & Redl, F. An investigation of behavioral contagion in groups. *Human relations*, 1950, 3, 319–348.

Redl, F. Group emotion and leadership (1942). In F. Redl (Ed.), *When we deal with children: Selected writings.* New York: Free Press, 1966, pp. 155–196.

Redl, F. The psychology of gang formation and the treatment of juvenile delinquents (1945). In F. Redl (Ed.), *When we deal with children: selected writings.* New York: Free Press, 1966, pp. 224–235.

Redl, F. The phenomena of contagion and "shock effect" (1949). In F. Rehl (Ed.), *When we deal with children: selected writings.* New York: Free Press, 1966, 197–213.

Redl, F., & Wineman, D. *Controls from within: Techniques for the treatment of the aggressive child.* New York: Free Press, 1952.

Redl, F., & Wineman, D. *Children who hate: The disorganization and breakdown of behavior controls.* New York: Collier Books, 1962.

Shapiro, D. *Neurotic styles.* New York: Basic Books, 1965.

Sjöbäck, H. *The psychoanalytic theory of defensive processes.* New York: Wiley (Halsted), 1973.

Strachey, J. Sigmund Freud: A sketch of his life and ideas. In S. Freud, *On the history of the psycho-analytic movement.* New York: Norton, 1966.

Tarde, G. *Les lois de l'imitation* (1890) (translation, *The laws of imitation*). New York: Holt, 1903.

Toch, H. *The social psychology of social movements.* Indianapolis: Bobbs-Merrill, 1965.

Wade, A. L. Social processes in the act of juvenile vandalism. In M. B. Clinard & R. Quinney (Eds.), *Criminal behavior systems: A typology.* New York: Holt, Rinehart and Winston, 1967, 94–105.

Wertham, F. *Dark legend.* New York: Duell, Sloan and Pearce, 1941.

chapter 9

The Social Learning Perspective

Mechanisms of aggression

Albert Bandura

The usefulness of the social learning perspective can be best tested if we examine one form of behavior and try to understand it insocial learning terms. In this chapter, we apply social learning concepts to the area of human aggression. As we shall see when we view violent crime (Chapter 13), aggression is a multifaceted phenomenon that has many determinants and serves diverse purposes. A complete theory of aggression must be sufficiently broad in scope to encompass a large set of variables governing diverse facets of aggression, whether individual or collective, personal or institutionally sanctioned.

Social Labeling Processes

Aggression is generally defined as behavior that results in personal injury and physical destruction. Not all injurious and destructive acts are judged aggressive, however. Although injury is a major defining property, in fact, aggression refers to complex events that include not only injurious behavior, but judgmental factors that lead people to attach aggression labels to some forms of harmful conduct but not to others.

Whether injurious behavior will be perceived as aggressive or otherwise

The bulk of this chapter will also appear in a forthcoming book entitled *Human Ethology* under the joint imprint of the Maison des Sciences de l'Homme and the Syndics of the Cambridge University Press. Copyright © 1977 Albert Bandura. Reprinted by permission.

The research and writing of this chapter was facilitated by Public Health Research Grant M-5162 from N.I.M.H., and by the James McKeen Cattell Award.

depends heavily on subjective judgments of intentions and causality. The greater the attribution of personal responsibility and injurious intent to the harm-doer, the higher the likelihood that the behavior will be judged as aggressive (Bandura, 1973; Rule & Nesdale, 1976b). The same harmful act is perceived differently depending on the sex, age, attractiveness, status, socioeconomic level, and ethnic background of the harmdoer. As a general rule, people judge the harmful acts of favored individuals and groups as unintended and prompted by situational circumstances but perceive the harmful acts of the disfavored as intentional and personally initiated. Value orientations of the labelers also influence their judgments of activities that cause harmful effects.

There are few disagreements over the labeling of direct assaultive behavior that is performed with explicit intent to injure or destroy. But people ordinarily do not aggress in conspicuous direct ways that reveal causal responsibility and carry high risk of retaliation. Rather, they tend to harm and destroy in ways that diffuse or obscure responsibility for detrimental actions to reduce self-reproof and social reprisals. Most of the injurious consequences of major social concern are caused remotely, circuitously, and impersonally through social practices judged aggressive by the victims but not by those who benefit from them. Students of aggression examine direct assaultive behavior in minute detail, whereas remote circuitous acts, which produce widespread harm, receive comparatively little attention.

Disputes over the labeling of aggressive acts assume special significance in the case of collective behavior involving dissident and institutionally sanctioned aggression. Agencies of government are entrusted with considerable rewarding and coercive power. Either of these sources of power can be misused to produce detrimental social effects. Punitive and coercive means of control may be employed to maintain inequitable systems, to suppress legitimate dissent, and to victimize disadvantaged segments of society. People can similarly be harmed both physically and socially by arbitrary denial or discriminative administration of beneficial resources to which they are entitled.

Just as not all individual acts that produce injury are necessarily aggressive, nor are all institutional practices that cause harm expressions of aggression. Some social practices instituted with well-meaning intent create detrimental consequences that were unforeseen. Others are performed routinely and thoughtlessly through established custom. Judgments of institutional aggression are likely to be made in terms of indicants of injurious intent, deliberate negligence, and unwillingness to rectify detrimental conditions.

Dissident aggression is also judged in large part on the basis of factors external to the behavior. Some of these include the perceived legitimacy of the grievances, the appropriateness of coercive tactics, the professed aims and credibility of the dissenters, and the ideological allegiances of the observers (Bandura, 1973). People vary markedly in their perceptions of aggression for social control and for social change (Blumenthal, Kahn, Andrews, & Head, 1972). The more advantaged citizenry tend to view even extreme levels of violence for social control as lawful discharges of duty, whereas disadvantaged members regard such practices as expressions of institutional aggression. Conversely, aggression for social change, and even group protest without injury, is judged as violence by patriots of the system but not by dissidents. Thus, in conflicts of power, one person's violence is another person's benevolence. Whether a particular form of aggression is regarded as adaptive or destructive depends on who bears the consequences. As this brief review suggests, factors influencing the social labeling of different forms of injurious behavior merit systematic investigation to a greater degree than they have received to date.

A complete theory of aggression must explain how aggressive patterns are developed, what provokes people to behave aggressively, and what sustains such actions after they have been initiated. Figure 9–1 summarizes the determinants of these three aspects of aggression within the framework of social learning theory.

ACQUISITION MECHANISMS

People are not born with preformed repertoires of aggressive behavior. They must learn them. Some of the elementary forms of aggression can be perfected with minimal guidance, but most aggressive activities—whether they be dueling with switchblade knives, sparring with opponents, military combat, or vengeful ridicule—entail intricate skills that require extensive learning.

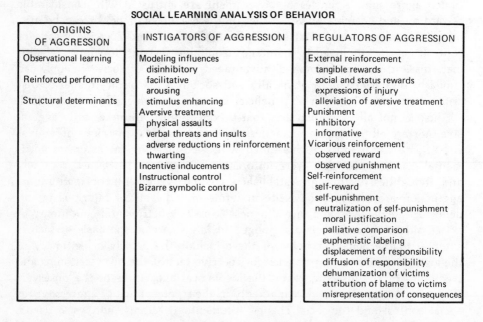

SOCIAL LEARNING ANALYSIS OF BEHAVIOR

ORIGINS OF AGGRESSION	INSTIGATORS OF AGGRESSION	REGULATORS OF AGGRESSION

Observational learning
 	
Reinforced performance
 	
Structural determinants
	Modeling influences
	  disinhibitory
	  facilitative
	  arousing
	  stimulus enhancing
	Aversive treatment
	  physical assaults
	  verbal threats and insults
	  adverse reductions in reinforcement
	  thwarting
	Incentive inducements
	Instructional control
	Bizarre symbolic control
		External reinforcement
		  tangible rewards
		  social and status rewards
		  expressions of injury
		  alleviation of aversive treatment
		Punishment
		  inhibitory
		  informative
		Vicarious reinforcement
		  observed reward
		  observed punishment
		Self-reinforcement
		  self-reward
		  self-punishment
		  neutralization of self-punishment
		    moral justification
		    palliative comparison
		    euphemistic labeling
		    displacement of responsibility
		    diffusion of responsibility
		    dehumanization of victims
		    attribution of blame to victims
		    misrepresentation of consequences

FIG. 9–1. *Schematic outline of the origins, instigators, and regulators of aggressive behavior in social learning theory.*

Biological Factors

New modes of behavior are not fashioned solely through experience. Biological factors, of course, set limits on the types of aggressive responses that can be developed, and influence the rate at which learning progresses. In addition to biological constraints on behavior, evolved biological systems predispose organisms to perceive and to learn critical features of their immediate environment.

The orchestration of aggressive actions, like other forms of visceral and motor responsiveness, depends on neurophysiological mechanisms. Research conducted with animals has identified subcortical structures, principally the hypothalamus and the limbic system, that mediate aggressive behavior (see Chapter 13). But these neural systems are selectively activated and controlled by central processing of environmental stimulation. Research by Delgado (1967) illustrates how social learning factors influence the types of responses that are likely to be activated by stimulating the same neural structure. Hypothalamic stimulation of a dominant monkey in a colony prompted him to attack subordinate males but not the females with whom he was on friendly terms. In contrast, hypothalamic stimulation elicited submissiveness in a monkey when she occupied a low hierarchical position, but increased aggressiveness toward subordinates as her social rank was elevated by changing the membership of the colony. Thus, electrical stimulation of the same anatomical site produced markedly different behavior under different social conditions.

It is valuable to know how neurophysiological systems operate internally, but from the standpoint of explaining aggression it is especially important to understand how they are socially activated for different courses of action. In everyday life, biological systems are roused in humans by provocative external events and by ideational activation. A remark interpreted as an insult will generate activity in the hypothalamus, whereas the same comment viewed innocuously will leave the hypothalamus unperturbed. Given a negative interpretation, social and cognitive factors are likely to determine the nature of the response.

In the social learning view, people are endowed with neurophysiological mechanisms that enable them to behave aggressively, but the activation of these mechanisms depends on appropriate stimulation and is subject to cognitive control. Therefore, the specific forms that aggressive behavior takes, the frequency with which it is expressed, the situation in which it is displayed, and the specific targets selected for attack are largely determined by social learning factors. As we shall see, these factors are varied and complex.

The role played by biological factors in aggression does vary across species, circumstances, and types of aggressive behavior. In infrahuman organisms, genetic and hormonal factors that affect neural organization and structural development figure prominently in aggressive responsiveness. Aggression in animals is largely determined by combat successes which depend on a robust physical build. The more powerfully developed members generally become belligerent fighters through victories; the physically less well-endowed become submissive through defeats. Because genetic and hormonal factors affect physical development, they are related to aggressiveness in animals.

People's capacity to devise and to use destructive weapons greatly reduces their dependence on biological structure to succeed in aggressive encounters. A puny person with a gun can easily triumph over powerfully built opponents who are unarmed. People's proclivity for social organization similarly reduces the importance of structural characteristics in aggressive attainments. At the social level, aggressive power derives from organized collective action. The chance of victory in aggressive confrontations is enhanced by the force of numbers acting in concert, and the physical stature of individual challengers does not much matter.

Structural characteristics related to aggressiveness also have different evolutionary and survival consequences for animals and humans. In many animal species, physical strength determines which males do the mating. Combat victors gain possession of females so that the most dominant males have the highest reproduction rates. In humans, mate selection is based more on such qualities as attractiveness, intelligence, parental arrangement, religious affiliation, and financial standing than on fighting prowess. Societal sanctions prohibit the brawny members of a social group from impregnating at will whomever they desire. Differential reproduction rates are primarily determined by religious beliefs, ideological commitments, socioeconomic factors, and birth control practices. For these reasons, one would not expect variations in human aggressiveness to be reflected in differential reproduction rates.

Observational Learning

Psychological theories have traditionally assumed that learning can occur only by performing responses and experiencing their consequences. In fact, virtually all learning phenomena resulting from direct experience can occur on a vicarious basis by observing the behavior of others and its consequences for them. The capacity to learn by observation enables individuals to acquire large, integrated patterns of behavior without having to form them gradually by tedious trial and error.

The abbreviation of the acquisition process through observational learning is vital for both development and survival. Because errors can produce costly, or even fatal outcomes, the prospects of survival would be slim indeed if the only way we could learn is by the consequences of our actions. The more costly and hazardous the possible mistakes, the heavier is the reliance on observational learning from competent models. This is particularly true of aggression, where the dangers of crippling or fatal consequences limit the value of learning through trial and error. By observing the aggressive conduct of others, one forms a conception of how the behavior is performed and on later occasions the symbolic representation can serve as a guide for action.

Learning by observation is governed by four interrelated subprocesses

(Bandura, 1977a). Attentional processes regulate exploration and perception of modeled activities. Organisms cannot be much influenced by observation of modeled behavior if they have no memory of it. Through coding into images, words, or other symbolic modes, transitory modeling influences are transformed for memory representation into enduring performance guides. The capacity for observational learning, whether assessed across species or over the course of development, increases with increasing capability to symbolize experience. Symbolic representations must eventually be transformed into appropriate actions. Motor reproduction processes, the third component of modeling, govern the integration of constituent acts into new response patterns.

Social learning theory distinguishes between acquisition of behaviors that have destructive and injurious potential and factors that determine whether individuals will perform what they have learned. This distinction is important because not all the things we learn are enacted. People can acquire, retain, and possess the capability to act aggressively, but the capacity may rarely be expressed if it has no functional value for them or is negatively sanctioned. Should appropriate inducements arise on later occasions, individuals put into practice what they have learned (Bandura, 1965; Madsen, 1968). Incentive and motivational processes regulate the performance of observationally learned responses.

Findings of numerous studies show that children can acquire entire repertoires of novel aggressive behavior from observing aggressive models, and retain such response patterns over extended periods (Bandura, 1973; Hicks, 1968). Factors that affect the four component processes influence the level of observational learning. In many instances the behavior being modeled is learned in essentially the same form. But models teach more general lessons as well. From observing the behavior of others, people can extract general tactics and strategies of behavior that enable them to go beyond what they have seen or heard. By synthesizing features of different modeled patterns into new amalgams, observers can evolve new forms of aggression.

In a modern society, aggressive styles of behavior can be adopted from three principal sources. One prominent origin is the aggression modeled and reinforced by family members. Studies of familial determinants of aggression show that parents who favor aggressive solutions to problems have children who tend to use similar aggressive tactics in dealing with others (Bandura & Walters, 1959; Hoffman, 1960). That familial violence breeds violent styles of conduct is further shown by similarities in child abuse practices across several generations (Silver, Dublin, & Lourie, 1969).

Although familial influences play a major role in setting the direction of social development, the family is embedded in a network of other social systems. The subculture in which people reside, and with which they have repeated contact, provides a second important source of aggression. Not surprisingly, the highest incidence of aggression is found in communities in which aggressive models abound and fighting prowess is regarded as a valued attribute (Short, 1968; Wolfgang, & Ferracuti, 1967).

The third source of aggressive conduct is the abundant symbolic modeling provided by the mass media. The advent of television has greatly expanded the range of models available to a growing child. Whereas their predecessors rarely, if ever, observed brutal aggression in their everyday life, both children and adults today have unlimited opportunities to learn the whole gamut of violent conduct from televised modeling within the comfort of their homes.

A considerable amount of research has been conducted in recent years on the effects of televised influences on social behavior. The findings show that exposure to televised violence can have at least four different effects on viewers: (1) It teaches aggressive styles of conduct; (2) it alters restraints over aggressive behavior; (3) it desensitizes and habituates people to violence; and (4) it shapes people's images of reality upon which they base many of their actions. Let us review briefly each of these effects.

Television is an effective tutor. Both laboratory and controlled field studies, in which young children and adolescents are repeatedly shown either violent or nonviolent fare, disclose that exposure to film violence shapes the form of aggression and typically increases interpersonal aggressiveness in everyday life (Bandura, 1973; Friedrich & Stein, 1973); Leyens, Camino, Parke, & Berkowitz, 1975; Liebert, Neale, & Davidson, 1973; Parke, Berkowitz, Leyens, West, & Sebastian, 1977; Steuer, Applefield, & Smith, 1971). Adults who pursue a life of crime improve their criminal skills by patterning their behavior after the ingenious styles portrayed in the mass media (Hendrick, 1977). Being an influential tutor, television can foster humanitarian qualities as well as injurious conduct. Programs that portray positive attitudes and social behavior foster cooperativeness, sharing, and reduce interpersonal aggression (Leiffer, Gordon, & Graves, 1974).

Another line of research has examined how inhibitions over aggression are affected by exposure to televised violence. There are several characteristics of televised presentations that tend to weaken people's restraints over behaving aggressively. Physical aggression is often shown to be the preferred solution to interpersonal conflicts. It is portrayed as acceptable, unsullied, and relatively successful. Superheroes do most of the killing. When good triumphs over evil by violent means, viewers are more strongly influenced than when aggressive conduct is not morally sanctioned by prestigeful figures. In experimental tests adults generally behave more punitively after they have seen others act aggressively than if they have not been exposed to aggressive modeling. This is especially true if the modeled aggressive conduct is legitimized by social justifications (Berkowitz, 1970).

Desensitization and habituation to violence are reflected in decreases in physiological reactions to repeated exposure to displays of violence. Heavy viewers of television respond with less emotion to violence than do light viewers (Cline, Croft, & Courrier, 1973). In addition to emotional desensitization, violence viewing can create behavioral indifference to human aggression. In studies demonstrating the habituation effect, children who have had prior exposure to interpersonal violence are less likely to intervene in escalating aggression between children they are overseeing (Drabman & Thomas, 1974; Thomas & Drabman, 1975; Thomas, Horton, Lippincott, & Drabman, 1977).

During the course of their daily lives, people have direct contact with only a small sector of the physical and social environment. In their daily routines they travel the same routes, visit the same places, see essentially the same group of friends and work associates. Consequently, people form impressions of the social realities with which they have little or no contact, partly from televised representations of society. Because the world of television is heavily populated with villainous and unscrupulous people, it can distort knowledge about the real world. Indeed, communications researchers have found that heavy viewers of television are less trustful of others and overestimate their chances of being criminally victimized than do light viewers (Gerbner & Gross, 1976). Heavy viewers see the society at large as more dangerous regardless of their educational level, sex, age, and amount of newspaper reading.

Many of the misconceptions that people develop about certain occupations, nationalities, ethnic groups, sex roles, social roles, and other aspects of life are cultivated through modeling of stereotypes by the media. Too often people's actions are based on such misconceptions.

Symbolic modeling plays an especially significant role in the shaping and rapid spread of collective aggression. Social diffusion of new styles and tactics of aggression conforms to the generalized pattern of most other contagious activities: New behavior is introduced by a salient example, it spreads rapidly in a contagious fashion, and it then either stabilizes or is discarded depending on its functional value.

Modeled solutions to problems that achieve some success are not only adopted by people facing similar difficulties, but they tend to spread as well to other troublesome areas. The civil rights struggle, which itself was modeled after Gandhi's crusades of nonviolent resistance, in turn, provided the example for other protest campaigns aimed at eliminating injustices and undesired social practices. The model of collective protest is now widely used as a means of forcing change.

Airline hijacking provides another recent example of the rapid diffusion and decline of aggressive tactics. Air piracy was unheard of in the United States until an airliner was hijacked to Havana in 1961. Prior to that incident, Cubans were hijacking planes to Miami. These incidents were followed by a wave of hijackings both in the United States and abroad, eventually involving seventy-one different countries (Figure 9–2). Just as aggressive strategies are widely modeled, so are the countermeasures that prove effective in controlling modeled aggression.

Learning by Direct Experience

People rarely teach social behaviors that are never exemplified by anyone in their environment. Therefore, in behavior acquired under natural condi-

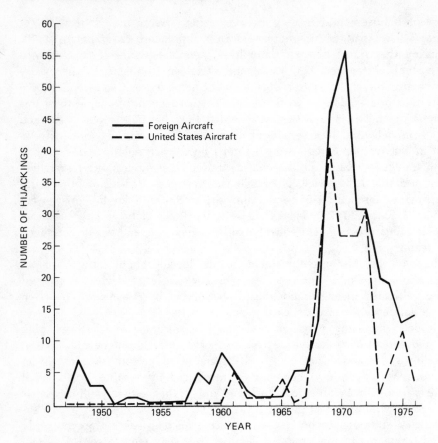

FIG. 9–2. *Incidence of hijackings over a span of thirty years. The rise in foreign hijackings during the 1948–1950 period occurred in Slavic countries during the Hungarian uprisings, and the second flare-up in 1958–1961 was comprised of almost entirely Cuban hijackings to Miami. A sudden widespread diffusion of hijackings occurred in 1969–1970, involving airliners from a total of seventy-one different countries.*

tions it is often difficult to determine whether reinforcing experiences create the new responses or activate what was already partly learned by observation. Although modeling influences are universally present, patterns of behavior can be shaped through a more rudimentary form of learning relying on the consequences of trial-and-error performance.

Until recently, learning by reinforcement was portrayed as a mechanistic process in which responses are shaped automatically by their immediate consequences. In more recent theoretical analyses, learning from response consequences is conceived of largely as a cognitive process, especially in humans. Consequences serve as an unarticulated way of informing performers what they must do to gain beneficial outcomes and to avoid punishing ones. By observing the differential effects of their actions, individuals discern which responses are appropriate in which settings, and behave accordingly. Although the empirical issue is not yet fully resolved, evidence that human behavior is not much affected by consequences until the point at which the contingencies are discerned, raises serious questions concerning the automaticity of reinforcement.

Viewed from the cognitive framework (Bandura, 1977a), learning from differential outcomes becomes a special case of observational learning. In this mode of conveying response information, the conception of the appropriate behavior is gradually constructed from observing the effects of one's actions rather than from the synthesized examples provided by others. A vast amount of evidence lends validity to the view that reinforcement serves principally as an informative and motivational operation rather than as a mechanical response shaper.

There have been few experimental attempts to fashion novel forms of aggression by differential reinforcement alone. It would be foolhardy to instruct novices how to use lethal weapons or to fight dangerous opponents by selectively reinforcing trial-and-error efforts. Where the consequences of mistakes can be dangerous or fatal, demonstration rather than unguided experience is the best tutor.

Learning through combat experience has been explored to a limited extent in training experiments with lower species designed to convert docile animals into ferocious fighters (Ginsburg & Allee, 1942; Scott & Marston, 1953). This is achieved by arranging a series of bouts with progressively more experienced fighters under conditions where trainees can win fights without being hurt. As fighting skills are developed and reinforced through repeated victories, formerly noncombative animals become more and more vicious in their aggressive behavior. While successful fighting produces brutal aggressors, severe defeats create enduring submissiveness (Kahn, 1951).

Patterson, Littman, and Bricker (1967) report a field study illustrating how passive children can be shaped into aggressors through a process of victimization and successful counteraggression. Passive children who were repeatedly victimized but occasionally succeeded in halting attacks by counteraggression, not only increased defensive fighting over time but began to initiate attacks of their own. Passive children who were seldom maltreated because they avoided others, and those whose counteraggression proved unsuccessful, remained submissive.

Modeling and reinforcement influences operate jointly in the social learning of aggression in everyday life. Styles of aggression are largely learned through observation, and refined through reinforced practice. The effects of these two determinants on the form and incidence of aggression are graphically revealed in ethnographic reports of societies that pursue a warlike way of life and those that follow a pacific style. In cultures lacking aggressive models and devaluing injurious conduct, people live peaceably (Alland, 1972; Dentan, 1968; Levy, 1969; Mead, 1935; Turnbull, 1961). In other societies that provide extensive training in aggression, attach prestige to it, and make its use functional, people spend a great deal of time threatening, fighting, maiming, and killing each other (Bateson, 1936; Chagnon, 1968; Gardner & Heider, 1969; Whiting, 1941).

INSTIGATION MECHANISMS

A theory must explain not only how aggressive patterns are acquired but also how they are activated and channeled. Social learning theory distinguishes between two broad classes of motivators of behavior. First, there are the biologically based motivators. These include internal aversive stimulation arising from tissue deficits and external sources of aversive stimulation that activate behavior through their painful effects. The second major source of response inducement involves cognitively based motivators. The capacity to represent future consequences in thought provides one cognitively based source of motivation. Through cognitive representation of future outcomes, individuals can generate current motivators of behavior. The outcome expectations may be material (e.g., consummatory, physically painful), sensory (e.g., novel, enjoyable, or unpleasant sensory stimulation), or social (e.g., positive and negative evaluative reactions). Another cognitively based source of motivation operates through the intervening influences of goal setting and self-evaluative reactions. Self-motivation involves standards against which to evaluate performances. By making positive self-evaluation conditional on attaining a certain level of behavior, individuals create self-inducements to persist in their efforts until their performances match self-prescribed standards.

As we shall show shortly, some aggressive acts are motivated by painful stimulation. However, most of the events that lead people to aggress, such as insults, verbal challenges, status threats, and unjust treatment, gain this activating capacity through learning experiences. People learn to dislike and to attack certain types of individuals either through direct unpleasant encounters with them, or on the basis of symbolic and vicarious experiences that conjure up hatreds. Because of regularities in environmental events, antecedent cues come to signify events to come and the outcomes particular actions are likely to produce. Such uniformities create expectations about what leads to what. When aggressive behavior produces different results depending on the times, places, or persons toward whom it is directed, people use cues predictive of probable consequences in regulating their behavior. They tend to aggress toward persons and in contexts where it is relatively safe and rewarding to do so, but they are disinclined to act aggressively when aggression carries high risk of punishment. The different forms that aggression elicitors take are discussed separately in the sections that follow.

Aversive Instigators

It has been traditionally assumed that aggressive behavior is activated by an aggressive drive. According to the instinct doctrine, organisms are innately endowed with an aggressive drive that automatically builds up and must be discharged periodically through some form of aggressive behavior. Despite intensive study, researchers have been unable to find an inborn autonomous drive of this type.

For years, aggression was viewed as a product of frustration. In this conception, frustration generates an aggressive drive which, in turn, motivates aggressive behavior. Frustration replaced instinct as the activating source, but the two theories are much alike in their social implications. Since frustration is ever present, in both approaches people are continuously burdened with aggressive energy that must be drained from time to time.

The frustration-aggression theory was widely accepted until its limited explanatory value became apparent from growing evidence. Frustration has varied effects on behavior; aggression does not require frustration. Frustration subsumes such a diverse set of conditions—physical assault, deprivation, insult, thwarting, harassment, and defeat—that it no longer has any specific meaning. As new instigators of aggression were identified, the definition of frustration was stretched to accommodate them. Not only is there great heterogeneity on the antecedent side of the relationship, but the consequence part of the formula, the aggressive behavior, also embraces a vast array of activities sifted through value judgments. One cannot expect a generalizable relationship to emerge from such a wide assortment of antecedents and behaviors.

The diverse events subsumed under the omnibus term frustration do have one feature in common—they are all aversive. In social learning theory, rather than frustration generating an aggressive drive that is reducible only by injurious behavior, aversive stimulation produces a general state of emotional arousal that can facilitate any number of responses (see Figure 9–3). The type of behavior elicited will depend on how the source of arousal is cognitively appraised, the modes of response learned for coping with stress, and their

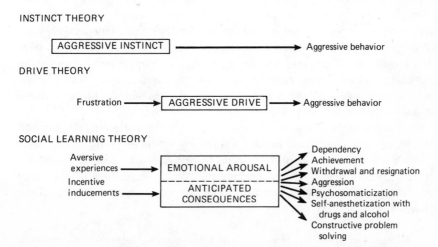

FIG. 9–3. *Schematization of alternative motivational analyses of aggression.*

relative effectiveness. When distressed, some people seek help and support; others increase achievement efforts; others display withdrawal and resignation; some aggress; others experience heightened somatic reactivity; still others anesthesize themselves against a miserable existence with drugs or alcohol; and most, intensify constructive efforts to overcome the source of distress.

Several lines of evidence, reviewed in detail elsewhere (Bandura, 1973), lend greater validity to the *arousal-prepotent response* formulation than to the *frustration-aggression* view. Different emotions appear to have a similar physiological state (Ax, 1953). The same physiological state can be experienced phenomenologically as different emotions, depending upon what people see as the incitements, and how they interpret them (Hunt, Cole, & Reis, 1958; Mandler, 1975). In individuals who are prone to behave aggressively, different sources of emotional arousal can heighten their aggresssion (Rule & Nesdale, 1976a; Tannenbaum, & Zillman, 1975).

In drive theories, the aroused aggressive drive presumably remains active until discharged by some form of aggression. Actually, anger arousal dissipates rapidly, but it can be easily regenerated on later occasions through rumination on anger-provoking incidents. By thinking about past insulting treatment, people can work themselves into a rage long after their emotional reactions have subsided. Persistence of elevated anger stems from thought-produced arousal, rather than from an undischarged reservoir of aggressive energy. Consider the example of a person who becomes angered by his apparent exclusion from an important meeting, only to receive the notice in the next day's mail. The person will show an immediate drop in anger arousal and aggressiveness without having to assault or denounce someone to drain a roused drive. Anger arousal decreased through cognitive means will reduce aggression as much, or even more, than will acting aggressively (Mallick & McCandless, 1966). By varying anticipated consequences, the same aggressive acts can raise or lower physiological arousal (Hokanson, Willers, & Koropsak, 1968).

Frustration or anger arousal is a facilitative, rather than a necessary, condition for aggression. Frustration tends to provoke aggression mainly in people who have learned to respond to aversive experiences with aggressive attitudes and conduct. Thus, after being frustrated, aggressively trained children behave more aggressively, whereas cooperatively trained children behave more cooperatively (Davitz, 1952).

There exists a large body of evidence that painful treatment, deprivation or delay of rewards, personal insults, failure experiences, and obstructions, all of which are aversive, do not have uniform behavioral effects (Bandura, 1969). Some of these aversive antecedents convey injurious intent more clearly than others and therefore have greater aggression-provoking potential.

PHYSICAL ASSAULTS   If one wished to provoke aggression, one way to do so would be simply to hit another person, who is likely to oblige with a counterattack. To the extent that counteraggression discourages further assaults it is reinforced by pain reduction and thereby assumes high functional value in social interactions. Although naturally occurring contingencies favor the development of pain-aggression relationships, there is some dispute over whether it is innate or acquired.

Azrin (1967) and Ulrich (1966) were major proponents of the nativistic view that pain-induced aggression is an unlearned reflexive behavior. As the determinants of pain-attack reactions were examined more closely, however, they began to lose their reflexive status. Young animals rarely, if ever, fight when shocked unless they have had some fighting experience, and in some studies shocks produce little or no fighting in 20 to 30 percent of mature animals (Hutchinson, Ulrich, & Azrin, 1965; Powell & Creer, 1969). If aggression is an unlearned dominant response to pain, then initial shocks should produce attack, which is not generally the case (Azrin, Hutchinson, & Hake, 1963). Contrary to the reflexive elicitation hypothesis, when combative responses are shocked, the pain reduces and eliminates rather than provokes fighting (Azrin, 1970; Baenninger & Grossman, 1969). The most striking evidence that pain-aggression reactions are determined more by situational factors than innate organization is the finding that in a small enclosure, approximately 90 percent of the shocks provoke fighting, whereas in a larger chamber, animals ignore each other and only 2 percent of the shocks elicit attack (Ulrich & Azrin, 1962). As environmental constraints to fight are removed, avoidance and flight responses to painful stimulation take priority over attack (Knutson, 1971; Logan & Boice, 1969; Sbordone, Garcia, & Carder, 1977). Physically painful experiences may be facilitative but clearly are not sufficient to provoke aggression in animals.

Pain stimulation is even a less consistent elicitor of aggression in humans than in animals. Nonsocial sources of pain rarely lead people to attack bystanders. Whether or not humans counteraggress in the fact of physical assaults depends upon their combat skill and the power of their assailant. Those who possess fighting prowess escalate counterattacks to subdue assailants (Edward, 1968; Peterson, 1971). Given other alternatives, low aggressors are easily dissuaded from counterattacks under retaliative threats.

VERBAL THREATS AND INSULTS   Social interchanges are typically escalated into physical aggression by verbal threats and insults. In analyzing dyadic interchanges of assault-prone individuals, Toch (1969) found that humiliating affronts and threats to reputation and manly status emerged as major precipitants of violence. High sensitivity to devaluation was usually combined with deficient verbal skills for resolving disputes and to restore self-esteem without having to dispose of antagonists physically. The counterattacks evoked by physical assaults are probably instigated more by humiliation than by physical pain. Indeed, it is not uncommon for individuals, groups, and even nations, to pay heavy injury costs in efforts to "save face" by combat victory.

Insult alone is less effective in provoking attack in those who eschew aggression, but it does heighten their aggressiveness, given hostile modeling and other disinhibitory influences (Hartmann, 1969; Wheeler & Caggiula, 1966). In subcultures in which social ranking is determined by fighting prowess, status threats from challengers within the group or rival outsiders are quick to provoke defensive aggression (Short, 1968).

The most plausible explanation of how insults acquire aggression-eliciting potential is in terms of foreseen consequences. Affronts that are not counteracted can have far-reaching effects for victims. Not only do they fear being targets for further victimization, but they are apt to forfeit the rewards and privileges that go with social standing. To the extent that punishment of insults reduces the likelihood of future maltreatment, the insult-aggression reaction becomes well established.

ADVERSE REDUCTIONS IN CONDITIONS OF LIFE   Aversive changes in the conditions of life can also provoke people to aggressive action. Explanations of collective aggression usually invoke impoverishment and discontent arising from privations as principal causal factors. However, since most impoverished people do not aggress, the view that discontent breeds violence requires qualification. This issue is well illustrated in interpretations of urban riots in ghetto areas. Despite condemnation of their degrading and exploitive conditions of life, comparatively few of the disadvantaged take active measures to force warranted changes. Even in cities that experienced civil disturbances, only a small percent of ghetto residents actively participated in the aggressive activities (Lieberson & Silverman, 1965; McCord & Howard, 1968; Sears & McConahay, 1969).

The critical question for social scientists to answer is not why some people who are subject to aversive conditions aggress, but rather why a sizable majority of them acquiesce to dismal living conditions in the midst of affluent styles of life. To invoke the frustration-aggression hypothesis, as is commonly done, is to disregard the more striking evidence that severe privation generally produces feelings of hopelessness and massive apathy. People give up trying when they lack a sense of personal efficacy and no longer expect their efforts to produce any beneficial results in an environment that is unresponsive or is consistently punishing (Bandura, 1977b; Maier & Seligman, 1976).

In accord with self-efficacy theory, comparative studies indicate that discontent produces aggression not in those who have lost hope, but in the more successful members whose assertive efforts at social and economic betterment have been periodically reinforced. Such persons, consequently, have some reason to expect that they can effect change by coercive action (Caplan, 1970; Crawford & Naditch, 1970).

More recent explanations of violent protest emphasize relative deprivation rather than the actual level of aversive conditions as the instigator of collective aggression. In an analysis of conditions preceding major revolutions, Davies (1969) reports that revolutions are most likely to occur when a period of social and economic advances that instills rising expectations is followed by a sharp reversal. People judge their present gains not only in relation to those they secured in the past; they also compare their lot in life with the benefits accruing to others (Bandura, 1977a). Inequities between observed and experienced outcomes tend to create discontent, whereas individuals may be satisfied with limited rewards so long as these are as good as those others are receiving.

Since most people who feel relatively deprived do not resort to violent action, aversive privation, like other forms of aversive treatment, is not in itself a sufficient cause of collective aggression. One must consider additional social learning factors that determine whether discontent will take an aggressive form or some other behavioral expression. Using such a multideterminant approach, Gurr (1970) examined the magnitude of civil disorder in Western nations as a function of three sets of factors. The first is the level of social discontent arising from economic decline, oppressive restrictions, and social inequities. The second factor is the traditional acceptance of force to achieve social change. Some societies disavow aggressive tactics, while others regard mass protests and coups d'etats as acceptable means of change. The third factor is the balance of coercive power between the system and its challengers as measured by amounts of military, police, industrial, labor, and foreign support the protagonists can marshall on their side. The analysis reveals that when aggressive tactics are considered acceptable and challengers possess coercive power, they will use less extreme forms of collective aggression and won't require much discontent. Revolutionary violence, however, requires widespread discontent and strong coercive power by challengers, while tactical traditions are of less importance.

Although aggression is more likely to be provoked by relative than by absolute privation, clarification of the role of relative deprivation requires greater consideration of the multifaceted bases of comparative evaluation. People judge their life circumstances in relation to their aspirations, to their past conditions, and to the life situations of others, whom they select for social comparison. Discontent created by raised aspirations, by reduction of rewards and privileges from accustomed levels, and by deceleration in the rate of improvement compared to others, undoubtedly has variant effects. Different sources of inequity (social, economic, political) may have differential aggression-activating potential. Response to inequitable deprivation is further influenced by mollifying social justifications and promise of social reforms. Considering the complex interplay of influences, it is hardly surprising that level of deprivation alone, whether defined in absolute or in relative terms, is a weak predictor of collective aggression (McPhail, 1971).

THWARTING OF GOAL-DIRECTED BEHAVIOR   Proponents of the frustration-aggression theory define frustrations in terms of interference or blocking of goal-seeking activities. In this view, people are provoked to aggression when obstructed, delayed, or otherwise thwarted from getting what they want. Research bearing on this issue shows that thwarting can lead people to intensify their efforts, which, if sufficiently vigorous, may be construed as aggressive. However, thwarting fails to provoke forceful action in people who have not experienced sufficient success to develop reward expectations, and in those who are blocked far enough from the goal that it appears unattainable (Bandura & Walters, 1963; Longstreth, 1966).

When thwarting provokes aggression it is probably attributable more to personal affront than to blocking of ongoing behavior. Consistent with this interpretation, people report more aggression to thwartings that appear unwarranted or suggest hostile intent than to those for which excusable reasons exist, even though both involve identical blocking of goal-directed behavior (Cohen, 1955; Pastore, 1952).

The overall evidence regarding the different forms of aversive instigators supports the conclusion that aversive antecedents, though they vary in their activating potential, are facilitative rather than necessary or sufficient conditions for aggression.

Incentive Instigators

The preceding discussion was concerned solely with aversive instigators of aggression, which traditionally occupied a central role in psychological theorizing, often to the neglect of more important determinants. The cognitive capacity of humans to represent future consequences enables them to guide their behavior by outcomes extended forward in time. A great deal of human aggression, in fact, is prompted by anticipated positive consequences. Here, the instigator is the pull of expected benefits, rather than the push of painful treatment. This positive source of motivation for aggression represents the second component in the motivational analysis depicted schematically in Figure 9–3.

The consequences that people anticipate for their actions are derived from, and therefore usually correspond to, prevailing conditions of reinforcement. The anticipatory activation and incentive regulation of aggression receive detailed consideration below. Expectation and actuality do not always coincide because anticipated consequences are also partly inferred from the observed outcomes of others, from what one reads or is told, and from other indicators of likely consequences. Because judgments are fallible, aggressive actions are sometimes prompted and temporarily sustained by erroneous anticipated consequences. Habitual offenders, for example, often err by overestimating the chances of success for transgressive behavior (Claster, 1967). In social interchanges and collective protest, coercive actions are partly sustained, even in the face of punishing consequences, by expectations that continued pressure may eventually produce desired results.

Modeling Instigators

Of the numerous antecedent cues that influence human behavior at any given moment, none is more common than the actions of others. Therefore, a reliable way to prompt people to aggress is to have others do it. Indeed, both children and adults are more likely to behave aggressively and with greater intensity if they have seen others act aggressively than if they have not been exposed to aggressive models (Bandura, 1973; Liebert, et al., 1973). The activation potential of modeling influences is enhanced if observers are angered (Berkowitz, 1965; Hartmann, 1969; Wheeler, 1966), the modeled aggression is socially justified (Berkowitz, 1965; Meyer, 1972), or is shown to be successful in securing rewards (Bandura, Ross, & Ross, 1963), and the victim invites attack through prior association with aggression (Berkowitz, 1970).

Social learning theory distinguishes four processes by which modeling influences can activate aggressive behavior. One mode of operation is in terms of the *directive function* of modeled actions. In many instances, behaving like others is advantageous because the prevalent modes have proven functional, whereas divergent courses of action may be less effective. After modeling cues acquire predictive value through correlated consequences they come to serve as informative prompts for others to behave in a similar fashion.

Aggressive behavior, especially when harsh and lacking justification, is socially censured if not self-condemned. Anticipated punishment exerts a restraining influence on injurious conduct. Seeing people respond approvingly or even indifferently toward aggressors conveys the impression that such behavior is an acceptable or normative mode of response. The same modeled aggression is much more effective in reducing restraints if it is socially legitimated than if it is portrayed as unjustified (Goranson, 1970). In aggressive conduct that is unencumbered by restraints because it is regarded as emulative, aggressive modeling is primarily instigational, whereas it serves a *disinhibitory function* in injurious behavior that is fear or guilt provoking. Since physical aggression usually incurs some negative effects, both instigational and disinhibitory processes are likely to be involved.

Seeing others aggressing generates *emotional arousal* in observers. For individuals who are prone to behave aggressively, emotional arousal can enhance their aggressive responding. Some of the instigative effects of modeling may well reflect the emotional facilitation of aggressive behavior.

Aggressive modeling can additionally increase the likelihood of aggressive behavior through its *stimulus enhancing effects*. Modeled activities inevitably direct observers' attention to the particular implements being used. This attentional focus may prompt observers to use the same instruments to a greater extent, though not necessarily in an imitative way. In one experiment (Bandura, 1962), for example, children who had observed a model pummel a plastic figure with a mallet spent more time pounding other objects with a mallet than those who did not see it used for assaultive purposes. In sum, the combined evidence reveals that modeling influences, depending on their form and content, can function as teachers, as elicitors, as disinhibitors, as stimulus enhancers, and as emotion arousers.

Instructional Instigators

During the process of socialization, people are trained to obey orders. By rewarding compliance and punishing disobedience, directives issued in the form of authoritative commands elicit obedient aggression. After this form of social control is established, legitimate authorities can secure obedient aggression from others, especially if the actions are presented as justified and necessary, and the issuers possess strong coercive power. As Snow (1961) has perceptively observed, "When you think of the long and gloomy history of man, you will find more hideous crimes have been committed in the name of obedience than in the name of rebellion" (p. 24).

In studies of obedient aggression, Milgram (1974) and others (Kilham & Mann, 1974; Mantell & Panzarella, 1976), have shown that well-meaning adults will administer increasingly severe shocks on command despite their victims' desperate pleas. Adults find it difficult to resist peer pressures calling for increasingly harmful actions, just as they are averse to defying legitimized authority. Seeing others carrying out punitive orders calmly likewise increases obedient aggression (Powers & Geen, 1972).

It is less difficult to hurt people on command when their suffering is not visible and when causal actions seem physically or temporally remote from their deleterious effects. Mechanized forms of warfare, where masses of people can be put to death by destructive forces released remotely, illustrate such depersonalized aggression. When the injurious consequences of one's actions are fully evident, vicariously aroused distress and self-censure serve as restraining influences over aggressive conduct that is otherwise authoritatively sanctioned. Obedience declines as the harmful consequences of destructive acts became increasingly more salient and personalized (Milgram, 1974). As the results of these and other studies to be cited later show, it requires conducive social conditions rather than monstrous people to produce heinous deeds.

Delusional Instigators

In addition to responding to external instigators, aggressive behavior can be prompted by bizarre beliefs. Every so often tragic episodes occur in which individuals are led by delusional belief to commit acts of violence. Some follow divine inner voices commanding them to murder. There are those who resort to self-protective attacks on paranoid suspicions that others are conspiring to harm them (Reich & Hepps, 1972). Others kill for deranged sacrificial purposes. And still others are prompted by grandiose convictions that it is their heroic responsibility to eliminate evil individuals in positions of influence.

A study of American Presidential assassins (Weisz & Taylor, 1970) shows that, almost without exception, the murderous assaults were delusionally instigated. Assassins tend to be loners who are troubled by severe personal failure. They acted either under divine mandate, through alarm that the President was in conspiracy with treacherous foreign agents to overthrow the government, or on the conviction that their own adversities resulted from Presidential persecution. Being unusually seclusive, the assassins barred themselves from the type of confiding relationships needed to correct erroneous beliefs and to check autistically generated resentments.

MAINTAINING MECHANISMS

So far we have discussed how aggressive behavior is learned and activated. The third major feature of the social learning formulation concerns the conditions that *sustain* aggressive responding. It is amply documented in psychological research that behavior is extensively regulated by its consequences. This principle applies equally to aggression. Injurious modes of response, like other forms of social behavior, can be increased, eliminated, and reinstated by altering the effects they produce.

People aggress for many different reasons. Similar aggressive actions may thus have markedly different functional value for different individuals and for the same individual on different occasions. Traditional behavior theories conceptualize reinforcement influences almost exclusively in terms of the effects of external outcomes impinging directly upon performers. But external consequences, as influential as they often are, are not the only kind of outcomes that regulate human behavior. People partly guide their actions on the basis of consequences they observe, and by consequences they create for themselves. These three forms of outcomes—external, vicarious, and self-produced —not only serve as separate sources of influence, but they interact in ways that weaken or enhance their effects on behavior (Bandura, 1977a).

External Reinforcement

As we have previously noted, consequences exert effects on behavior largely through their informative and incentive functions. For the most part, response consequences influence behavior antecedently by creating expectations of similar outcomes on future occasions. The likelihood of particular actions is increased by anticipated benefits and reduced by anticipated punishment.

Aggression is strongly influenced by its consequences. Extrinsic rewards assume special importance in interpersonal aggression because such behavior, by its very nature, usually produces some costs among its diverse effects. People who get into fights, for example, will suffer pain and injury even though they eventually triumph over their opponents. Under noncoercive conditions, positive incentives are needed to overcome inhibitions arising from the aversive concomitants of aggression. The positive incentives take a variety of forms.

TANGIBLE REWARDS   Aggression is often used by those lacking better alternatives because it is an effective means of securing desired tangible rewards. Ordinarily docile animals will fight when aggressive attacks produce food or drink (Azrin & Hutchinson, 1967; Ulrich, Johnston, Richardson, & Wolff, 1963). Observation of children's interactions reveals that most of the assaultive actions of aggressors produce rewarding outcomes for them (Patterson, et al., 1967). Given this high level of positive reinforcement of aggressive behavior, there is no need to invoke an aggressive drive to explain the prevalence of such actions. Aggressive behavior is especially persistent when it is reinforced only intermittently, which is usually the case under the variable conditions of everyday life (Walters & Brown, 1963).

There are other forms of aggression that are sustained by their material consequences though, for obvious reasons, they are not easily subject to systematic analysis. Delinquents and adult transgressors can support themselves on income derived from aggressive pursuits; protesters can secure, through forceful collective response, social reforms that affect their lives materially; governments that rule by force are rewarded in using punitive control by the personal gains it brings to those in power and to supporters who benefit from the existing social arrangements; and nations are sometimes able to gain control over prized territories by military force.

SOCIAL AND STATUS REWARDS   Aggressive styles of behavior are often adopted because they win approval and status rewards. When people are commended for behaving punitively they become progressively more aggressive, whereas they display a relatively low level of aggression when it is not treated as praiseworthy (Geen & Stonner, 1971; Staples & Walters, 1964). Approval not only increases the specific aggressive responses that are socially reinforced but it tends to enhance other forms of aggression as well (Geen & Pigg, 1970; Loew, 1967; Slaby, 1974).

Analyses of social reinforcement of aggressive behavior in natural settings are in general agreement with results of laboratory studies. Parents of assaultive children are generally nonpermissive for aggressive behavior in the home, but condone, actively encourage, and reinforce provocative and aggressive actions toward others in the community (Bandura, 1960; Bandura & Walters, 1959).

In aggressive gangs, members not only gain approval but achieve social status through their skills in fighting (Short, 1968). In status rewards, performance of valued behavior gains one a social rank that carries with it multiple benefits as long as the position is occupied. A rank-contingent system of reward is more powerful than one in which specific responses are socially rewarded. If failure to behave aggressively deprives one of a specific reward, the negative consequence is limited and of no great importance. A demotion in rank, however, results in forfeiture of all the social and material benefits that go with it. The pressure for aggressive accomplishments is especially strong when status positions are limited and there are many eager competitors for them.

During wartime, societies offer medals, promotions, and social commendations on the basis of skill in killing. When reinforcement practices are instituted that favor inhuman forms of behavior, otherwise socialized people can be led to behave brutally and to take pride in such actions.

REDUCTION OF AVERSIVE TREATMENT   People are often treated aversively by others, from which treatment they seek relief. Coercive action that is not unduly hazardous is the most direct and quickest means of alleviating maltreatment, if only temporarily. Defensive forms of aggression are frequently reinforced by their capacity to terminate humiliating and painful treatment. Reinforcement through pain reduction is well documented in studies cited earlier, which show that children who are victimized but can end the abuse by successful counteraggression eventually become highly aggressive in their behavior (Patterson, et al., 1967).

Patterson's (1978) analysis of familial interactions of hyperaggressive children further documents the role of negative reinforcement in promoting aggressive styles of behavior. In such families children are inadvertently trained to use coercive behavior as the means of commanding parental attention or terminating social demands. The children's antagonistic behavior rapidly accelerates parental counteraggression in an escalating power struggle. By escalating reciprocal aggression each member provides aversive instigation for the other, and each member is periodically reinforced for behaving coercively by overpowering the other through more painful counteractions. Mutual coercion is most likely to appear as a prominent factor in families that find their children's control techniques painful and therefore seek relief from clinics. However, intrafamilial coercion is not a significant factor in families of predelinquent children who are forced to consult clinics because of legal threats rather than mutual torment (Reid & Patterson, 1976).

A quite different view of aggression emerges if hyperaggressive children are selected from the population at large rather than from clinics. In one study (Bandura, 1960), the most hyperaggressive children in an entire community were identified in school settings and their social behavior was systematically observed. Despite the fact that these children were highly belligerent, assaultive, and destructive of property, few of their families had ever consulted a clinic. This was because their training in aggression did not produce torment in the home. The parents modeled aggressive attitudes and, while nonpermissive and punitive for aggression toward themselves, they actively encouraged and rewarded aggression directed at others outside the home. As a result of this differential training, the children were reasonably well behaved at home but readily assaultive toward others. If their youngsters misbehaved, it was because others were at fault. The parents of these hyperaggressive children not only saw little reason to consult clinics, but many of them considered aggression to be a valued attribute. In these families, the development of aggression is better explained in terms of a positive, than a negative, reinforcement model. Samples of hyperaggressive children drawn from different sources may thus yield different theories on the familial determinants of aggression.

In the social learning analysis, defensive aggression is sustained to a greater extent by anticipated consequences than by its instantaneous effects. People will endure the pain of reprisals on expectations that their aggressive efforts will eventually remove deleterious conditions. Aggressive actions may also be partly maintained in the face of painful counterattack by anticipated costs of timidity. In aggression-oriented circles, failure to fight back can arouse fear of future victimization and humiliation. A physical pummeling may, therefore, be far less distressing than repeated social derision or increased likelihood of future abuse. In other words, humans do not behave like unthinking servomechanisms directed solely by immediate response feedback. Under aversive conditions of life, people will persist, at least for a time, in aggressive behavior that produces immediate pain but prospective relief from misery.

EXPRESSIONS OF INJURY   In the view of drive theorists, the purpose of aggression is infliction of injury. Just as eating relieves hunger, hurting others presumably discharges the aggressive drive. It has therefore been widely assumed that aggressive behavior is reinforced by signs of suffering in the victim. According to Sears, Maccoby, and Levin (1957), pain cues become rewarded because the pain produced by aggressive acts is repeatedly associated with tension relief and removal of frustrations. Feshbach (1970) interprets the rewarding value of pain expression in terms of self-esteem processes. Perception of pain in one's tormentors is experienced as satisfying because it signifies successful retaliation and thus restores the aggressor's self-esteem.

A contrasting view is that signs of suffering ordinarily function as inhibitors rather than as positive reinforcers of aggressive behavior. Because of the dangers of intragroup violence, all societies established strong prohibitions against cruel and destructive acts, except under special circumstances. In the course of socialization most people adopt for self-evaluation standards that adjudge ruthless aggression as morally reprehensible. Consequently, aggression that produces evident suffering in others elicits both fear of punishment and self-censure which tend to inhibit injurious attacks.

Studies on how pain expressions affect assaults on suffering victims support the inhibitory effects. Aggressors behave less punitively when their victims express anguished cries than when they do not see or hear the victims suffer (Baron, 1971a, 1971b; Sanders & Baron, 1977). Contrary to drive theory, pain cues reduce aggression regardless of whether assailants are angered or not (Geen, 1970; Rule & Leger, 1976). People are even less inclined to behave cruelly when they see their suffering victims than when they merely hear the distress they have caused them (Milgram, 1974).

The scope of the experimental treatments and the populations studied are too limited to warrant the strong conclusion that pain expressions never enhance aggressive behavior. A gratuitous insult from a stranger in a laboratory may not create sufficient animosity for the victim to derive satisfaction from injurious retaliation. It is quite a different matter when an antagonist repeatedly tyrannizes others or wields power in ways that make life miserable for them. In such instances, news of the misfortune, serious illness, or death of an oppressor is joyfully received by people who ordinarily respond more compassionately to the adversities befalling others. However, when a victim injures an oppressor, the primary source of satisfaction may be the alleviation of aversive treatment rather than the causing of suffering. In experimental investigations, pain expressions occur without the other extraneous rewards accompanying victory over antagonists.

From the standpoint of social learning theory, suffering of one's enemies is most apt to augment aggression when hurting them lessens maltreatment or benefits aggressors in other ways. When aggressors suffer reprisals or self-contempt for harming others, signs of suffering function as negative reinforcers that deter injurious attacks.

Findings of studies with infrahuman subjects are sometimes cited as evidence that fighting is inherently rewarding. Animals will perform responses that produce an attackable target, especially if they have been trained for aggression and are subjected to aversive stimulation. However, because of inadequate controls, this line of experimentation failed to clarify whether the animals were seeking combat, escape, or social contact (Bandura, 1973). Studies including conditions in which animals perform responses to gain contact, without having opportunity to fight (Kelsey & Cassidy, 1976), demonstrate that social contact rather than combat is the source of reward.

There are certain conditions under which pain expressions may assume reward value. Examples can be cited of societal practices in which brutal acts are regarded as praiseworthy by those in positions of power. Inhumane reinforcement contingencies can breed people who take pleasure in inflicting pain and humiliation. Additionally, clinical studies of sexual perversion have disclosed cases in which pain cues acquire powerful reward value through repeated association with sexual gratification. As a result, erotic pleasure is derived from inflicting pain on others or on oneself.

There are no conceptual or empirical grounds for regarding aggression maintained by certain effects as more genuine or important than others. A comprehensive theory must account for all aggressive actions, whatever purpose they serve. To restrict analysis of aggression to behavior that is supposedly reinforced by expressions of injury is to exclude from consideration some of the most violent activities where injury is an unavoidable concomitant rather than the major function of the behavior.

One might also question the distinction traditionally drawn between "instrumental" aggression, which is supposedly aimed at securing extraneous rewards, and "hostile" aggression, the sole purpose of which is presumably to inflict suffering (Feshbach, 1970). Since in all instances, the behavior is instrumental in producing certain desired outcomes, be they pain, approval, status, or material gain, it is more meaningful to differentiate aggressive behaviors in terms of their functional value rather than whether or not they are instrumental.

Punishing Consequences

Restraints over injurious behavior arise from two different sources. *Social restraints* are rooted in threats of external punishment. *Personal restraints* operate through anticipatory self-condemning reactions toward one's own conduct. In developmental theories these two sources of restraint are traditionally characterized as fear control and guilt control, respectively. Punishing consequences that are observed or experienced directly convey information about the circumstances under which aggressive behavior is safe and when it is hazardous. Aggressive actions are therefore partly regulated on the basis of anticipated negative consequences. Since the behavior is under cognitive and situational control, restraints arising from external threats vary in durability and in how widely they generalize beyond the prohibitive situations.

The effectiveness of punishment in controlling behavior is determined by a number of factors (Bandura, 1969; Campbell & Church, 1969). Of special importance are the benefits derived through aggressive actions and the availability of alternative means of securing goals. Other determinants of the suppressive power of punishment include the likelihood that aggression will be punished, the nature, severity, timing, and duration of aversive consequences. In addition, the level of instigation to aggression and the characteristics of the prohibitive agents influence how aggressors will respond under threat of punishment.

When alternative means are available for people to get what they seek, aggressive modes of behavior that carry high risk of punishment are rapidly discarded. Aggression control through punishment becomes more problematic when aggressive actions are socially or tangibly rewarded, and alternative means of securing desired outcomes are either unavailable, less effective in producing results, or not within the capabilities of the aggressor. Here, punishment must be applied with considerable force and consistency to outweigh the benefits of aggression. Even then it achieves, at best, temporary selective control in the threatening situation. Functional aggression is reinstated when threats are removed, and readily performed in settings in which the chance of punishment is low (Bandura & Walters, 1959). Punishment is not only precarious as an external inhibitor of intermittently rewarded behavior, but its frequent use can inadvertently promote aggression by modeling punitive modes of control (Hoffman, 1960).

Punishment, whether direct or observed, is informative as well as inhibitory. People can profit from witnessing the failures of others or from their own mistakes. Given strong instigation to aggression and limited options, threats lead people to adopt safer forms of aggression or to refine the prohibited behavior to improve its chances of success. For this reason, antisocial aggression is best prevented by combining deterrents with the cultivation of more functional alternatives. Most law-abiding behavior relies more on deterrence through preferable prosocial options than on threats of legal sanctions.

There are certain conditions under which aggression is escalated through punishment, at least in the short run. Individuals who repeatedly engage in aggressive behavior have experienced some success in controlling others through force. In interpersonal encounters, they respond to counterattacks with progressively more punitive reactions to force acquiescence (Edwards, 1968; Patterson, 1977; Toch, 1969). The use of punishment as a control technique also carries risks of escalating collective aggression when grievances are justifiable and challengers possess substantial coercive power (Bandura, 1973; Gurr, 1970). Under these circumstances, continued aggressive behavior eventually succeeds in changing social practices that lack sufficient justification to withstand concerted protest.

Vicarious Reinforcement

In the course of everyday life there are numerous opportunities to observe the actions of others and the circumstances under which they are rewarded, ignored, or punished. Observed outcomes influence behavior in much the same way as directly experienced consequences. People can profit from the successes and mistakes of others as well as from their own experiences. As a general rule, seeing aggression rewarded in others increases, and seeing it punished decreases, the tendency to behave in similar ways (Bandura, 1965; Bandura, et al., 1963). The more consistent the observed response consequences, the greater are the facilitatory and inhibitory effects on viewers (Rosekrans & Hartup, 1967).

Vicarious reinforcement operates primarily through its informative function. Since observed outcomes convey different types of information, they can have diverse behavioral effects. Response consequences accruing to others convey contingency information about the types of actions likely to be rewarded or punished and the situations in which it is appropriate to perform them. A number of factors that enter into the process of social comparison can alter the customary effects of observed consequences. Models and observers often differ in distinguishable ways so that behavior considered approvable for one may be punishable for the other, depending on discrepancies in sex, age, and social status. When the same behavior produces unlike consequences for different members, observed reward may not enhance the level of imitative aggressiveness (Thelen & Soltz, 1969).

When observed outcomes are judged personally attainable, they create incentive motivation. Seeing others' successes can function as a motivator by arousing in observers expectations that they can gain similar rewards for analogous performances. Some of the changes in responsiveness may also reflect vicarious acquisition or extinction of fears through the affective consequences accruing to models. Indeed, the legal system of deterrence rests heavily on the restraining function of exemplary punishment (Packer, 1968; Zimring, 1973). But observed outcomes also reduce the deterrent efficacy of threatened legal consequences. The chance of being caught and punished for criminal conduct is relatively low. In locales in which transgressions are common, people have personal knowledge of countless crimes being committed without detection. Such exposure to unpunished transgressions tends to reduce the force of legal deterrents.

In addition to the aforementioned effects, valuation of people and activities can be significantly altered on the basis of observed consequences. Ordinarily, observed punishment tends to devalue the models and their behavior, whereas the same models became a source of emulation when their actions are admired. However, aggressors may gain, rather than lose, status in the eyes of their peers when they are punished for a style of behavior valued by the group, or when they aggress against institutional practices that violate the professed values of society. It is for this reason that authoritative agencies are usually careful not to discipline challengers in ways that might martyr them.

Observed consequences can change observers' valuation of those who exercise power as well as of the recipients. Restrained and principled use of coercive power elicits respect. When societal agents misuse their power to reward and punish, they undermine the legitimacy of their authority and arouse opposition. Such inequitable punishment, rather than securing compliance, may foster aggressive reprisals. Indeed, activists sometimes attempt to rally supporters to their cause by selecting aggressive tactics calculated to provoke authorities to excessive countermeasures.

The manner in which aggressors respond to the consequences of their behavior can also influence how observers later react when they themselves are rewarded for displaying similar responses. In one such study (Ditrichs, Simon, & Greene, 1967), children who observed models express progressively more hostility for social approval, later increased their own output of hostile responses that brought praise. However, when models appeared oppositional by reducing hostile responses that brought them praise, or reacted in a random fashion as though they were uninfluenced, observers did not increase their expression of hostility even though they were praised whenever they did so. Thus, susceptibility to direct reinforcement was increased by observed willing responsiveness, but reduced by observed resistance.

Observed outcomes introduce comparative processes into the operation of reinforcement influences. The observed consequences accruing to others provide a standard for judging whether the outcomes one customarily receives are equitable, beneficient, or unfair. The same external outcome can function as a reward or as a punishment depending upon the observed consequences used for comparison. Relational properties of reinforcement affect not only behavior, but the level of personal satisfaction or discontent as well. Equitable treatment tends to promote a sense of well-being, whereas inequitable reinforcement generates resentments and dissatisfactions. The effects of perceived inequity on aggression are those reviewed earlier in our discussion of relative deprivation.

SELF-REGULATORY MECHANISMS

The discussion thus far has analyzed how behavior is regulated by external consequences that are either observed or experienced firsthand. People are not simply reactors to external influences. Through self-generated inducements and self-produced consequences they can exercise some influence over their own behavior. In this self-regulatory process, people adopt through tuition and modeling certain standards of behavior and respond to their own actions

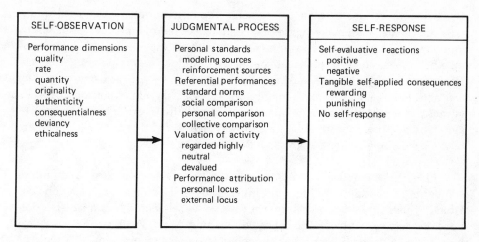

SELF-OBSERVATION	JUDGMENTAL PROCESS	SELF-RESPONSE

Performance dimensions
  quality
  rate
  quantity
  originality
  authenticity
  consequentialness
  deviancy
  ethicalness
	Personal standards
	  modeling sources
	  reinforcement sources
	Referential performances
	  standard norms
	  social comparison
	  personal comparison
	  collective comparison
	Valuation of activity
	  regarded highly
	  neutral
	  devalued
	Performance attribution
	  personal locus
	  external locus
		Self-evaluative reactions
		  positive
		  negative
		Tangible self-applied consequences
		  rewarding
		  punishing
		No self-response

FIG. 9–4. *Component processes in the self-regulation of behavior by self-produced consequences.*

in self-rewarding or self-punishing ways. An act therefore includes among its determinants self-produced influences.

A detailed account of self-regulatory processes, which is presented elsewhere (Bandura, 1976, 1978), falls beyond the scope of this chapter. In social learning theory, a self-system is not a psychic agent that controls behavior. Rather, it refers to cognitive structures that provide the referential standards against which behavior is judged, and a set of subfunctions for the perception, evaluation, and regulation of action. Figure 9–4 presents a diagrammatic representation of three main subfunctions in the self-regulation of behavior by self-produced incentives. The first component concerns the selective observation of one's own behavior in terms of a number of relevant dimensions. Behavior produces self-reactions through a judgmental function relying on several subsidiary processes which include referential comparisons of perceived conduct to internal standards, valuation of the activities in which one is engaged, and cognitive appraisal of the determinants of one's behavior. Performance appraisals set the occasion for self-produced consequences. Favorable judgments give rise to rewarding self-reactions, whereas unfavorable appraisals activate negative self-reactions.

Self-regulated incentives are conceptualized as motivational devices rather than as automatic strengtheners of preceding responses. By making self-reward and self-punishment contingent on designated performances, people motivate themselves to expend the effort needed to attain performances that give them self-satisfaction and they refrain from behaving in ways that result in self-censure. Because of self-reactive tendencies, aggressors must contend with themselves as well as with others when they behave in an injurious manner.

SELF-REWARD FOR AGGRESSION   One can distinguish several ways in which self-generated consequences enter into the self-regulation of aggressive behavior. At one extreme are persons who have adopted behavioral stand-ards and codes that make aggressive feats a source of personal pride. Such individuals readily engage in aggressive activities and derive enhanced feel-ings of self-worth from physical conquests (Bandura & Walters, 1959; Toch, 1969; Yablonsky, 1962). Lacking self-reprimands for hurtful conduct, they are deterred from cruel acts mainly by reprisal threats. Idiosyncratic self-systems of morality are not confined to individuals or fighting gangs. In aggressive cultures where prestige is closely tied to fighting prowess, members take considerable pride in aggressive exploits.

SELF-PUNISHMENT FOR AGGRESSION After ethical and moral standards of conduct are adopted, anticipatory self-condemning reactions for violating personal standards ordinarily serve as self-deterrents against repre-hensible acts. Results of the study by Bandura and Walters (1959) reveal how anticipatory self-reproach for repudiated aggression serves as a motiva-ing influence to keep behavior in line with adopted standards. Adolescents who were compassionate in their dealings with others responded with self-disapproval, remorse, and attempts at reparation even when their aggressive activities were minor in nature. In contrast, assaultive boys experienced rela-tively few negative self-reactions over serious aggressive activities. These differential self-reactive patterns are corroborated by Perry and Bussey (1977) in laboratory tests. Highly aggressive boys reward themselves generously for inflicting suffering on another child, whereas those who display low aggres-sive tendencies react with self-denial for behaving injuriously. In studies of aggressive modeling, the more reprehensible children judge aggressive actions to be, the less likely they are to adopt them when they are later exemplified by a peer model (Hicks, 1971).

DISENGAGEMENT OF INTERNAL CONTROL Theories of internal-ization generally portray incorporated entities in the form of a conscience, superego, and moral codes as continuous internal overseers of conduct. Such theories encounter difficulties in explaining the variable operation of internal control and the perpetration of gross inhumanities by otherwise humane, compassionate people. Such concepts as "superego lacunae," "islands of super-ego," and various "mental defense mechanisms" have been proposed as the explanatory factors.

In the social learning analysis, moral people perform culpable acts through processes that disengage evaluative self-reactions from such conduct rather than through defects in the development or the structure of their superegos (Bandura, 1973). Acquisition of self-regulatory capabilities does not create an invariant control mechanism within a person. Self-evaluative influences do not operate unless activated, and many situational dynamics influence their selective activation.

Self-deterring consequences are likely to be activated most strongly when the causal connection between conduct and the detrimental effects it pro-duces is unambiguous. There are various means, however, by which self-

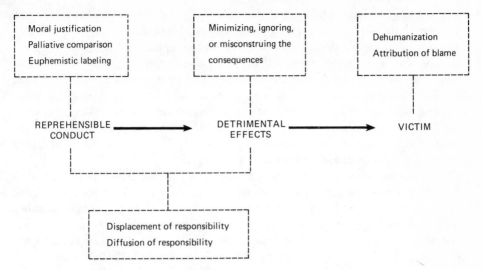

FIG. 9–5. *Mechanisms through which behavior is disengaged from self-evaluative consequences at different points in the behavior process.*

evaluative consequences can be dissociated from censurable behavior. Figure 9–5 shows the several points in the process at which the disengagement can occur.

One set of disengagement practices operates at the level of the behavior. People do not ordinarily engage in reprehensible conduct until they have justified to themselves the morality of their actions. What is culpable can be made honorable through cognitive restructuring. In this process, reprehensible conduct is made personally and socially acceptable by portraying it in the service of moral ends. Over the years, much destructive and reprehensible conduct has been perpetrated by decent, moral people in the name of religious principles and righteous ideologies. Acting on moral or ideological imperative reflects not an unconscious defense mechanism, but a conscious offense mechanism.

Self-deplored acts can also be made righteous by contrasting them with flagrant inhumanities. The more outrageous the comparison practices, the more likely are one's reprehensible acts to appear trifling or even benevolent. Euphemistic language provides an additional convenient device for disguising reprehensible activities and according them a respectable status. Through convoluted verbiage pernicious conduct is made benign and those who engage in it are relieved of a sense of personal agency (Gambino, 1973). Moral justifications and palliative characterizations are especially effective disinhibitors because they not only eliminate self-generated deterrents, but engage self-reward in the service of injurious behavior. What was morally unacceptable becomes a source of self-pride.

Another set of dissociative practices operates by obscuring or distorting the relationship between actions and the effects they cause. People will behave in highly punitive ways they normally repudiate if a legitimate authority acknowledges responsibility for the consequences of the conduct (Diener, Dineen, Endresen, Beaman, & Fraser, 1975; Milgram, 1974). By displacing responsibility people do not see themselves as personally accountable for their actions and are thus spared self-prohibiting reactions. Nor is self-censure activated when the link between conduct and its consequences is obscured by diffusing responsibility. Through division of labor, diffusion of decision making, and collective action people can behave injuriously without anyone feeling personally responsible for culpable behavior. They therefore act more aggressively when responsibility is obscured by a collective instrumentality (Bandura, Underwood, & Fromson, 1975).

Additional ways of weakening self-deterring reactions operate by disregarding or obscuring the consequences of actions. When people embark on a self-disapproved course of action for personal gain, or because of other inducements, they avoid facing the harm they cause. Self-censuring reactions are unlikely to be activated as long as the detrimental effects of conduct are disregarded, minimized, or misjudged (Brock & Buss, 1962, 1964).

The final set of disengagement practices operate at the level of the recipients of injurious effects. The strength of self-evaluative reactions partly depends on how the people toward whom actions are directed are viewed. Maltreatment of individuals who are regarded as subhuman or debased is less apt to arouse self-reproof than if they are seen as human beings with dignifying qualities (Bandura, et al., 1975; Zimbardo, 1969). Analysis of the cognitive concomitants of injurious behavior reveals that dehumanization fosters a variety of self-exonerating maneuvers (Bandura, et al., 1975). People strongly disapprove of cruel behavior and rarely excuse its use when they interact with humanized individuals. By contrast, people seldom condemn punitive conduct and generate self-disinhibiting justifications for it when they direct their behavior toward individuals divested of humanness.

Many conditions of contemporary life are conducive to dehumanization. Bureaucratization, automation, urbanization, and high social mobility lead people to relate to each other in anonymous, impersonal ways. In addition, social practices that divide people into in-group and out-group members produce human estrangement that fosters dehumanization. Strangers can be more easily cast as unfeeling beings than can personal acquaintances.

Psychological research tends to focus on the disinhibiting effects of social practices that divest people of human qualities. This emphasis is understandable considering the prevalence and the serious consequences of people's inhumanities toward each other. Of equal theoretical and social significance is the power of humanization to counteract injurious conduct. Studies examining this process reveal that, even under conditions that ordinarily weaken self-deterrents, it is difficult for people to behave cruelly towards others when others are characterized in ways that personalize and humanize them (Bandura, et al., 1975).

Attributing blame to one's victims is still another expedient that can serve self-exonerative purposes. Detrimental interactions usually involve a series of reciprocally escalative actions in which the victims are rarely faultless.

One can always select from the chain of events an instance of defensive behavior by the adversary and view it as the original instigation. Victims then get blamed for bringing suffering on themselves, or extraordinary circumstances are invoked to vindicate irresponsible conduct. By blaming others, one's own actions are excusable. People are socially aided in dehumanizing and blaming groups held in disfavor by pejorative stereotyping and indoctrination.

GRADUALISM AND DISINHIBITION   The aforementioned practices will not instantaneously transform a gentle person into a brutal aggressor. Rather, the change is usually achieved through a gradual desensitization process in which participants may not fully recognize the marked changes they are undergoing. Initially, individuals are prompted to perform aggressive acts they can tolerate without excessive self-censure. After their discomfort and self-reproof are diminished through repeated performance, the level of aggression is progressively increased in this manner until eventually gruesome deeds, originally regarded as abhorrent, can be performed without much distress.

As is evident from the preceding discussion, the development of self-regulatory functions does not create a mechanical servocontrol system wherein behavioral output is accurately monitored, compared against an internal standard and, if judged deviant, is promptly brought in line with the referent standard. Nor do situational influences exercise mechanical control. Personal judgments operating at each subfunction preclude the automaticity of the process. There is leeway in judging whether a given behavioral standard is applicable. Because of the complexity and inherent ambiguity of most events, there is even greater leeway in the judgment of behavior and its effects. To add further to the variability of the self-control process, most activities are performed under collective arrangements that obscure responsibility, thus permitting leeway in judging the degree of personal agency in the effects that are socially produced. In short, there exists considerable latitude for personal judgmental factors to affect whether or not self-regulatory influences will be engaged in any given activity.

Differing Perspectives on Disengagement of Internal Restraints

The preceding discussion analyzed reduction of internal control within the framework of social learning theory. Other researchers have addressed this issue from a different conceptual perspective. Zimbardo (1969) explains reduction of restraints over aggression in terms of deindividuation. Deindividuation is an internal state characterized by a loss of self-consciousness and self-evaluation, coupled with a diminished concern for negative evaluation from others. According to this view, the altered perception of self and others weakens cognitive control over behavior, thus facilitating intense impulsive actions.

People can be deindividuated by a variety of external conditions, including anonymity, immersion in a group, diffusion of responsibility, high emotional arousal, intense sensory stimulation, and physiological factors that alter states of consciousness. Many of the postulated determinants of deindividuation remain to be investigated. However, the conditions that have been examined empirically, such as group presence, anonymity, and emotional arousal, have variable effects on behavior depending on the presence of other personal and situational factors conducive to aggression (Bandura, 1973; Diener, 1977; Zimbardo, 1969). Unfortunately, there is little in the data of these studies bearing on the deindividuation link in the causal process. Deindividuating conditions are typically related to impulsive behavior without any independent assessment of the internal state. When the indicants of deindividuation are measured, they are often found to be unrelated either to the situational conditions or to the disinhibited behavior (Diener, 1977).

It should be recognized that this line of research presents especially difficult methodological problems. One cannot keep interrupting unrestrained aggressors for their perceptions of themselves and others without aborting the disinhibitory process. To measure the cognitive concomitants of external disinhibitory conditions prior to performance is to alter the very phenomenon being studied. Judgments of the promise of a theory in this field must therefore rest heavily on its success in identifying determinants of behavioral disinhibition and in bringing order among diverse findings. The inconclusive empirical results and neglect of the important role played by self-justification processes in disinhibition raise some question whether the theory of deindividuation is equal to the task of providing a full explanation of how aggression is freed from internal restraints.

Although deindividuation and social learning theory posit some overlapping determinants and processes of internal disinhibition, they differ in certain important respects. Deindividuation views intense aggression as resulting mainly from loss of cognitive control. Social learning encompasses a broader range of disinhibitory factors designed to provide a unified theory for explaining both impulsive and principled aggressive conduct. As indicated earlier, people frequently engage in violent activities not because of reduced self-control but because their cognitive skills and self-control are enlisted all too well through moral justifications and self-exonerative devices in the service of destructive causes. The massive threats to human welfare are generally brought about by deliberate acts of principle rather than by unrestrained acts of impulse. It is the principled resort to aggression that is of greatest social concern but is most ignored in psychological theorizing and research.

REFERENCES

Alland, A., Jr. *The human imperative.* New York: Columbia University Press, 1972.
Ax, A. F. The physiological differentiation between fear and anger in humans. *Psychosomatic Medicine,* 1953, *15,* 433–442.

Azrin, N. H. Pain and aggression. *Psychology Today*, 1967, *1*, 27–33.

Azrin, N. H. Punishment of elicited aggression. *Journal of the Experimental Analysis of Behavior*, 1970, *14*, 7–10.

Azrin, N. H., & Hutchinson, R. R. Conditioning of the aggressive behavior of pigeons by a fixed-interval schedule of reinforcement. *Journal of the Experimental Analysis of Behavior*, 1967, *10*, 395–402.

Azrin, N. H., Hutchinson, R. R., & Hake, D. F. Pain-induced fighting in the squirrel monkey. *Journal of the Experimental Analysis of Behavior*, 1963, *6*, 620.

Baenninger, R., & Grossman, J. C. Some effects of punishment on pain-elicited aggression. *Journal of the Experimental Analysis of Behavior*, 1969, *12*, 1017–1022.

Bandura, A. *Relationship of family patterns to child behavior disorders.* Progress Report, 1960, Stanford University Project No. M–1734, United States Public Health Service.

Bandura, A. Social learning through imitation. In M. R. Jones (Ed.), *Nebraska Symposium on Motivation, 1962.* Lincoln: University of Nebraska Press, 1962.

Bandura, A. Influence of models' reinforcement contingencies on the acquisition of imitative responses. *Journal of Personality and Social Psychology*, 1965, *1*, 589–595.

Bandura, A. *Principles of behavior modification.* New York: Holt, Rinehart and Winston, 1969.

Bandura, A. *Aggression: A social learning analysis.* Englewood Cliffs, N.J.: Prentice-Hall, 1973.

Bandura, A. Self-reinforcement: Theoretical and methodological considerations. *Behaviorism*, 1976, *4*, 135–155.

Bandura, A. *Social learning theory.* Englewood Cliffs, N.J.: Prentice-Hall, 1977a.

Bandura, A. Self-efficacy: Toward a unifying theory of behavioral change. *Psychological Review*, 1977b, *84*, 191–215.

Bandura, A. The self system in reciprocal determinism. *American Psychologist*, 1978, *33*, 344–358.

Bandura, A., Ross, D., & Ross, S. A. Vicarious reinforcement and imitative learning. *Journal of Abnormal and Social Psychology*, 1963, *67*, 601–607.

Bandura, A., Underwood, B., & Fromson, M. E. Disinhibition of aggression through diffusion of responsibility and dehumanization of victims. *Journal of Research in Personality*, 1975, *9*, 263–269.

Bandura, A., & Walters, R. H. *Adolescent aggression.* New York: Ronald, 1959.

Bandura, A., & Walters, R. H. *Social learning and personality development.* New York: Holt, Rinehart and Winston, 1963.

Baron, R. A. Magnitude of victim's pain cues and level of prior anger arousal as determinants of adult aggressive behavior. *Journal of Personality and Social Psychology*, 1971a, *17*, 236–243.

Baron, R. A. Aggression as a function of magnitude of victim's pain cues, level of prior anger arousal, and aggressor-victim similarity. *Journal of Personality and Social Psychology*, 1971b, *18*, 48–54.

Bateson, G. *The naven.* Stanford, Calif.: Stanford University Press, 1936.

Berkowitz, L. The concept of aggressive drive: Some additional considerations. In L. Berkowitz (Ed.), *Advances in experimental social psychology* (Vol. 2). New York: Academic Press, 1965.

Berkowitz, L. The contagion of violence: An S-R mediational analysis of some effects of observed aggression. In W. J. Arnold & M. M. Page (Eds.), *Nebraska Symposium on Motivation, 1970.* Lincoln: University of Nebraska Press, 1970.

Blumenthal, M., Kahn, R. L., Andrews, F. M., & Head, K. B. *Justifying violence: The attitudes of American men.* Ann Arbor, Mich.: Institute for Social Research, 1972.

Brock, T. C., & Buss, A. H. Dissonance, aggression, and evaluation of pain. *Journal of Abnormal and Social Psychology,* 1962, *65,* 197–202.

Brock T. C., & Buss, A. H. Effects of justification for aggression and communication with the victim on postaggression dissonance. *Journal of Abnormal and Social Psychology,* 1964, *68,* 403–412.

Campbell, B. A., & Church, R. M. *Punishment and aversive behavior.* New York: Appleton-Century-Crofts, 1969.

Caplan, N. The new ghetto man: A review of recent empirical studies. *Journal of Social Issues,* 1970, *26,* 59–73.

Chagnon, N. *Yanomamo: The fierce people.* New York: Holt, Rinehart and Winston, 1968.

Claster, D. S. Comparison of risk perception between delinquents and non-delinquents. *Journal of Criminal Law, Criminology, and Police Science,* 1967, *58,* 80–86.

Cline, V. B., Croft, R. G., & Courrier, S. Desensitization of children to television violence. *Journal of Personality and Social Psychology,* 1973, *27,* 360–365.

Cohen, A. R. Social norms, arbitrariness of frustrations, and status of the agent of frustration in the frustration-aggression hypothesis. *Journal of Abnormal and Social Psychology,* 1955, *51,* 222–226.

Crawford, T., & Naditch, M. Relative deprivation, powerlessness, and militancy: The psychology of social protest. *Psychiatry,* 1970, *33,* 208–223.

Davies, J. C. The J-curve of rising and declining satisfactions as a cause of some revolutions and a contained rebellion. In H. D. Graham & T. R. Gurr (Eds.), *Violence in America: Historical and Comparative perspectives* (Vol. 2). Washington, D.C.: U. S. Government Printing Office, 1969.

Davitz, J. R. The effects of previous training on postfrustration behavior. *Journal of Abnormal and Social Psychology,* 1952, *47,* 309–315.

Delgado, J. M. Social rank and radio-stimulated aggressiveness in monkeys. *Journal of Nervous & Mental Diseases,* 1967, *144,* 383–390.

Dentan, R. K. *The Semai: A nonviolent people of Malaya.* New York: Holt, Rinehart and Winston, 1968.

Diener, D., Dineen, J., Endresen, K., Beaman, A. L., & Fraser, S. C. Effects of altered responsibility, cognitive set, and modeling on physical aggression and deindividuation. *Journal of Personality and Social Psychology,* 1975, *31,* 328–337.

Diener, E. Deindividuation: Causes and characteristics. *Social Behavior and Personality,* 1977, *5,* 143–156.

Ditrichs, R., Simon, S., & Greene, B. Effect of vicarious scheduling on the verbal conditioning of hostility in children. *Journal of Personality and Social Psychology,* 1967, *6,* 71–78.

Drabman, R. S., & Thomas, M. H. Does media violence increase children's toleration of real-life aggression? *Developmental Psychology,* 1975, *10,* 418–421.

Edwards, N. L. Aggressive expression under threat of retaliation. *Dissertation Abstracts,* 1968, *28,* 3470B.

Feshbach, S. Aggression. In P. H. Mussen (Ed.), *Carmichael's manual of child psychology* (Vol. 2). New York: Wiley, 1970.

Friedrich, L. K., & Stein, A. H. Aggressive and prosocial television programs and the natural behavior of preschool children. *Monographs of the Society for Research in Child Development,* 1973, *38* (4) Serial No. 151.

Gambino, R. Watergate lingo: A language of non-responsibility. *Freedom at Issue,* 1973, No. 22.

Gardner, R., & Heider, K. G. *Gardens of war.* New York: Random House, 1969.

Geen, R. G. Perceived suffering of the victim as an inhibitor of attack-induced aggression. *Journal of Social Psychology,* 1970, *81,* 209–216.

Geen, R. G., & Pigg, R. Acquisition of an aggressive response and its generalization to verbal behavior. *Journal of Personality and Social Psychology,* 1970, *15,* 165–170.

Geen, R. G., & Stonner, D. Effects of aggressiveness habit strength on behavior in the presence of aggression-related stimuli. *Journal of Personality and Social Psychology,* 1971, *17,* 149–153.

Gerbner, G., & Gross, L. Living with television: The violence profile. *Journal of Communication,* 1976, *26,* 173–199.

Ginsburg, B., & Allee, W. C. Some effects of conditioning on social dominance and subordination in inbred strains of mice. *Physiological Zoology,* 1942, *15,* 485–506.

Goldstein, M. Brain research and violent behavior. *Archives of Neurology,* 1974, *30,* 1–34.

Goranson, R. E. Media violence and aggressive behavior: A review of experimental research. In L. Berkowitz (Ed.), *Advances in experimental social psychology* (Vol. 5). New York: Academic Press, 1970.

Gurr, T. R. Sources of rebellion in western societies: Some quantitative evidence. *Annals of American Academy of Political and Social Science,* 1970, *391,* 128–144.

Hartmann, D. P. Influence of symbolically modeled instrumental aggression and pain cues on aggressive behavior. *Journal of Personality and Social Psychology,* 1969, *11,* 280–288.

Hendrick, G. When television is a school for criminals. *TV Guide,* January 29, 1977, 4–10.

Hicks, D. J. Short- and long-term retention of affectively varied modeled behavior. *Psychonomic Science,* 1968, *11,* 369–370.

Hicks, D. J. Girls' attitudes toward modeled behaviors and the content of imitative private play. *Child Development,* 1971, *42,* 139–147.

Hoffman, M. L. Power assertion by the parent and its impact on the child. *Child Development,* 1960, *31,* 129–143.

Hokanson, J. E., Willers, K. R., & Koropsak, E. The modification of autonomic responses during aggressive interchange. *Journal of Personality,* 1968, *36,* 386–404.

Hunt, J. M., Cole, M. W., & Reis, E. E. S. Situational cues distinguishing anger, fear, and sorrow. *American Journal of Psychology,* 1958, *71,* 136–151.

Hutchinson, R. R., Ulrich, R. E., & Azrin, N. H. Effects of age and related factors on the pain-aggression reaction. *Journal of Comparative and Physiological Psychology,* 1965, *59,* 365–369.

Kahn, M. W. The effect of severe defeat at various age levels on the aggressive behavior of mice. *Journal of Genetic Psychology,* 1951, *79,* 117–130.

Kelsey, J. E., & Cassidy, D. The reinforcing properties of aggressive vs. nonaggressive social interactions in isolated male ICR mice (Mus Musculus). *Aggressive Behavior,* 1976, *2,* 275–284.

Kilham, W., & Mann, L. Level of destructive obedience as a function of transmitter and executant roles in the Milgram obedience paradigm. *Journal of Personality and Social Psychology*, 1974, *29*, 696–702.

Knutson, J. The effects of shocking one member of a pair of rats. *Psychonomic Science*, 1971, *22*, 265–266.

Leifer, A. D., Gordon, N. J., & Graves, S. B. Children's television: More than mere entertainment. *Harvard Educational Review*, 1974, *44*, 213–245.

Levy, R. I. On getting angry in the Society Islands. In W. Caudill & T. Y. Lin (Eds.), *Mental health research in Asia and the Pacific*. Honolulu: East-West Center Press, 1969.

Leyens, J. P., Camino, L., Parke, R. D., & Berkowitz, L. Effects of movie violence on aggression in a field setting as a function of group dominance and cohesion. *Journal of Personality and Social Psychology*, 1975, *32*, 346–360.

Lieberson, S., & Silverman, A. R. The precipitants and underlying conditions of race riots. *American Sociological Review*, 1965, *30*, 887–898.

Liebert, R. M., Neale, J. M., & Davidson, E. S. *The early window: Effects of television on children and youth*. New York: Pergamon, 1973.

Loew, C. A. Acquisition of a hostile attitude and its relationship to aggressive behavior. *Journal of Personality and Social Psychology*, 1967, *5*, 335–341.

Logan, F. A., & Boice, R. Aggressive behaviors of paired rodents in an avoidance context. *Behaviour*, 1969, *34*, 161–183

Longstreth, L. E. Distance to goal and reinforcement schedule as determinants of human instrumental behavior. *Proceedings of the 74th Annual Convention of the American Psychological Association*, 1966, 39–40.

Madsen, C., Jr. Nurturance and modeling in preschoolers. *Child Development*, 1968, *39*, 221–236.

Maier, S. F., & Seligman, M. E. Learned helplessness: Theory and evidence. *Journal of Experimental Psychology*, 1976, *105*, 3–46.

Mallick, S. K., & McCandless, B. R. A study of catharsis of aggression. *Journal of Personality and Social Psychology*, 1966, *4*, 591–596.

Mandler, G. *Mind and emotion*. New York: Wiley, 1975.

Mantell, D. M., & Panzarella, R. Obedience and responsibility. *The British Journal of Social and Clinical Psychology*, 1976, *15*, 239–246.

McCord, W., & Howard, J. Negro opinions in three riot cities. *American Behavioral Scientist*, 1968, *11*, 24–27.

McPhail, C. Civil disorder participation: A critical examination of recent research. *American Sociological Review*, 1971, *36*, 1058–1072.

Mead, M. *Sex and temperament in three savage tribes*. New York: Morrow, 1935.

Meyer, T. P. Effects of viewing justified and unjustified real film violence on aggressive behavior. *Journal of Personality and Social Psychology*, 1972, *23*, 21–29.

Milgram, S. *Obedience to authority: An experimental view*. New York: Harper & Row, 1974.

Packer, H. L. *The limits of the criminal sanction*. Stanford, Calif.: Stanford University Press, 1968.

Parke, R. D., Berkowitz, L., Leyens, J. P., West, S. G., & Sebastian, R. J. Some effects of violent and nonviolent movies on the behavior of juvenile delinquents. In L. Berkowitz (Ed.), *Advances in experimental social psychology* (Vol. 10). New York: Academic Press, 1977.

Pastore, N. The role of arbitrariness in the frustration-aggression hypothesis. *Journal of Abnormal and Social Psychology*, 1952, *47*, 728–731.

Patterson, G. R. A performance theory for coercive family interaction. In R. Cairns

(Ed.), *Social interaction: Methods, analysis, and illustration.* Monographs of the Society of Research in Child Development, 1978, in press.

Patterson, G. R., Littman, R. A., & Bricker, W. Assertive behavior in children: A step toward a theory of aggression. *Monographs of the Society for Research in Child Development*, 1967, *32*(5, Serial No. 113).

Perry, D. G., & Bussey, K. Self-reinforcement in high- and low-aggressive boys following acts of aggression. *Child Development*, 1977, *48*, 653–657.

Peterson, R. A. Aggression level as a function of expected retaliation and aggression level of target and aggressor. *Developmental Psychology*, 1971, *5*, 161–166.

Powell, D. A., & Creer, T. L. Interaction of developmental and environmental variables in shock-elicited aggression. *Journal of Comparative and Physiological Psychology*, 1969, *69*, 219–225.

Powers, P. C., & Geen, R. G. Effects of the behavior and the perceived arousal of a model on instrumental aggression. *Journal of Personality and Social Psychology*, 1972, *23*, 175–183.

Reich, P., & Hepps, R. B. Homicide during a psychosis induced by LSD. *Journal of the American Medical Association*, 1972, *219*, 869–871.

Reid, J. B., & Patterson, G. R. The modification of aggression and stealing behavior of boys in the home setting. In E. Ribes-Inesta & A. Bandura (Eds.), *Analysis of delinquency and aggression.* Hillsdale, N.J.: Erlbaum, 1976.

Rosekrans, M. A., & Hartup., W. W. Imitative influence of consistent and inconsistent response consequences to a model and aggressive behavior in children. *Journal of Personality and Social Psychology*, 1967, *7*, 429–434.

Rule, B. G., & Leger, G. L. Pain cues and differing functions of aggression. *Canadian Journal of Behavioural Science*, 1976, *8*, 213–233.

Rule, B. G., & Nesdale, A. R. Emotional arousal and aggressive behavior. *Psychological Bulletin*, 1976, *83*, 851–863a.

Rule, B. G., & Nesdale, A. R. Moral judgments of aggressive behavior. In R. G. Geen & E. O'Neal (Eds.), *Prospectives on aggression.* New York: Academic Press, 1976b.

Sanders, G. S., & Baron, R. S. Pain cues and uncertainty as determinants of aggression in a situation involving repeated instigation. *Journal of Personality and Social Psychology*, 1977, *32*, 495–502.

Sbordone, R., Garcia, J., & Carder, B. Shock-elicited aggression: Its displacement by a passive social orientation avoidance response. *The Bulletin of the Psychonomic Society*, 1977, *9*, 272–274.

Scott, J. P., & Marston, M. Nonadaptive behavior resulting from a series of defeats in fighting mice. *Journal of Abnormal and Social Psychology*, 1953, *48*, 417–428.

Sears, D. O., & McConahay, J. B. Participation in the Los Angeles riot. *Social Problems*, 1969, *17*, 3–20.

Sears, R. R., Maccoby, E. E., & Levin, H. *Patterns of child rearing.* Evanston, Ill.: Row, Peterson, 1957.

Short, J. F., Jr., (Ed.), *Gang delinquency and delinquent subcultures.* New York: Harper & Row, 1968.

Silver, L. B., Dublin, C. C., & Lourie, R. S. Does violence breed violence? Contributions from a study of the child abuse syndrome. *American Journal of Psychiatry*, 1969, *126*, 404–407.

Slaby, R. Verbal regulation of aggression and altruism. In J. De Wit & W. Hartup (Eds.), *Determinants and origins of aggressive behavior.* The Hague: Mouton Press, 1974.

Snow, C. P. Either—or. *Progressive*, 1961, *25*, 24–25.

Staples, F. R., & Walters, R. H. Influence of positive reinforcement of aggression on subjects differing in initial aggressive level. *Journal of Consulting Psychology*, 1964, *28*, 547–552.

Steuer, F. B., Applefield, J. M., & Smith, R. Televised aggression and the interpersonal aggression of preschool children. *Journal of Experimental Child Psychology*, 1971, *11*, 442–447.

Tannenbaum, P. H., & Zillman, D. Emotional arousal in the facilitation of aggression through communication. In L. Berkowitz (Ed.), *Advances in experimental social psychology* (Vol. 8). New York: Academic Press, 1975.

Thelen, M. H., & Soltz, W. The effect of vicarious reinforcement on imitation in two social racial groups. *Child Development*, 1969, *40*, 879–887.

Thomas, M. H., & Drabman, R. S. Toleration of real life aggression as a function of exposure to televised violence and age of subject. *Merrill-Palmer Quarterly of Behavior and Development*, 1975, *21*, 227–232.

Thomas, M. H., Horton, R. W., Lippincott, E. C., & Drabman, R. S. Desensitization to portrayals of real-life aggression as a function of exposure to television violence. *Journal of Personality and Social Psychology*, 1977, *35*, 450–458.

Toch, H. *Violent men*. Chicago: Aldine, 1969.

Turnbull, C. M. *The forest people*. New York: Simon & Schuster, 1961.

Ulrich, R. Pain as a cause of aggression. *American Zoologist*, 1966, *6*, 643–662.

Ulrich, R. E., & Azrin, N. H. Reflexive fighting in response to aversive stimulation. *Journal of the Experimental Analysis of Behavior*, 1962, *5*, 511–520.

Ulrich, R., Johnston, M., Richardson, J., & Wolff, P. The operant conditioning of fighting behavior in rats. *Psychological Record*, 1963, *13*, 465–470.

Walters, R. H., & Brown, M. Studies of reinforcement of aggression: III. Transfer of responses to an interpersonal situation. *Child Development*, 1963, *34*, 563–571.

Weisz, A. E., & Taylor, R. L. American presidential assassination. In D. N. Daniels, M. F. Gilula, & F. M. Ochberg (Eds.), *Violence and the struggle for existence*. Boston: Little, Brown, 1970.

Wheeler, L. Toward a theory of behavioral contagion. *Psychological Review*, 1966, *73*, 179–192.

Wheeler, L., & Caggiula, A. R. The contagion of aggression. *Journal of Experimental Social Psychology*, 1966, *2*, 1–10.

Whiting, J. W. M. *Becoming a Kwoma*. New Haven: Yale University Press, 1941.

Wolfgang, M. E., & Ferracuti, F. *The subculture of violence*. London: Tavistock, 1967.

Yablonsky, L. *The violent gang*. New York: Macmillan, 1962.

Zimbardo, P. G. The human choice: Individuation, reason, and order vs. deindividuation, impulse, and chaos. In W. J. Arnold & D. Levine (Eds.), *Nebraska Symposium on Motivation, 1969*. Lincoln: University of Nebraska Press, 1969.

Zimring, F. *Deterrence: The legal threat in crime control*. Chicago: Chicago University Press, 1973.

chapter *10*

The Gauging of Delinquency Potential

Charles Hanley

Look at the children on a school playground. Is there anything about these open-faced youngsters that will possibly affect the way they choose to live when they grow up? Next, be a judge, passing sentence on a convicted defendant. What shall it be: probation or prison? Finally, sit on a parole board and estimate a convict applicant's chances of becoming a model citizen. Could knowing enough about this offender improve your decision about his rehabilitation?

A willingness to answer these questions testifies to a belief in the existence of delinquency potential, a relatively enduring characteristic that channels particular individuals into criminal activity and acts to keep them there. Different social sciences have different biases. The bent of psychologists is to look within today's person for the causes of tomorrow's behavior. Asking a psychologist for ideas about prevention of delinquency most likely will produce recommendations about treatments that might alter personalities. Of course, in assuming that a subset of humanity is predisposed to criminal behavior, the psychologist does not deny that other factors, like socioeconomic or ethnic status, and temporary conditions, like bravado, intoxication, resentment, peer pressure, and plain opportunity, are powerful agents in bringing about crime. But the psychologist's assumption, with all its limitations, governs the subject matter of this chapter, which deals with the difficulties encountered when people try to measure delinquency potential.

Psychological measures of individual differences in personality and ability have now been around for more than a half century. Many have been applied in attempts to solve everyday problems. Part of the payoff from those attempts

237

is a set of concepts and principles concerning the hazards affecting any measuring activity. These principles and concepts illuminate difficulties that have prevented psychologists who are convinced of the reality of delinquency potential from discovering ways to measure such potential accurately enough to contribute to progress in eliminating crime.

In the present case, a good place to start is at the end, with routine application of an ideal measure of delinquency potential. Several different uses are apparent: (1) to locate predelinquents for preventive treatment; (2) to improve decisions about alternatives for rehabilitation of offenders; (3) to determine who should receive parole and to prescribe the type of supervision that is needed; (4) to provide an immediate measure of the effectiveness of a rehabilitation or prevention program. Other benefits are less direct. Success in any of these applications should increase insight into their nature and lead to improvement in their effectiveness.

To demonstrate the satisfactoriness of a psychological instrument, certain properties of the instrument and of the behavior it is to gauge must be estimated from actual data. Any index of delinquency potential is a possible *predictor* of behavior, and the behavior in turn constitutes a *criterion*. To the extent that scores on the predictor relate to scores on the criterion, *the predictor is valid.* When criterion scores clearly describe or represent the offense behavior *the criterion is valid.* A predictor is invalid, or useless, when it does not relate to the criterion, and that must occur whenever the criterion is invalid.

To be valid, both predictor and criterion must be *reliable.* A predictor is reliable if scores are relatively unchanged when people are measured a second time after a suitable lapse of time. Suppose, for example, that Sheldon and Eleanor Glueck (1950) are correct in believing Social Prediction Tables can detect future criminals by the time they enter elementary school. Children of that age do not qualify as criminal. It is therefore necessary to wait a decade or so to discover which youngsters are delinquent. This produces a ten-year lag between measurement on the predictor and measurement on the criterion. Scores on the measure of potential ought to be fairly stable over those ten years for the prediction to be any good. A test incapable of predicting what will happen when it is given again is unlikely to predict anything else. To serve as a test of validity, a criterion also must be reliable. The inability of social scientists to predict future behavior with a high degree of accuracy may be as much the result of poor criteria as it is the outcome of wrong theories or improper inferences from correct ones.

CRITERION PROBLEMS

Personnel psychologists have had modest success in forecasting job performance. The degree of precision they achieve results as much from attention to criteria as from any other feature of assessment. In contrast, investigators who wish to predict criminal behavior appear to give insufficient attention to criteria except, perhaps, after it is too late. Three aspects of criteria are crucial in prediction with humans: reliability, validity, and base rate.

Reliability

Distinguishing between validity and reliability in a criterion may seem difficult, but the difference exists. In predictions of delinquency, any error in recordkeeping contributes unreliability to criterion categories. And all inconsistencies in the criminal justice system—from apprehension to sentencing—make for unreliability in the delinquent-nondelinquent distinction.

Unreliability in a criterion is clearer in connection with behavior related to parole. Parole officers may apply different standards for revoking or continuing parole, or may change or inconsistently alter their standards, making the success-failure criterion unreliable (Takagi, 1969; Neithercutt, 1974). But even a reliable criterion—one that is consistent—may not be predictable by measures that ought to work, because it is invalid for the behavior it is supposed to represent.

Validity

Validity can be defined in various ways, only one of which, *predictive validity*, is essential for the concept of delinquency potential. A demonstration of predictive validity involves testing subjects at a particular time and measuring their criterion performance after a lapse of time.

If some subjects are already delinquent when they are first tested, their data must be discarded to avoid confounding predictive validity with what is termed *concurrent validity*. A measure of delinquency potential has concurrent validity when it can distinguish known criminals from normal persons.

Concurrent validity is a preliminary step in the construction of a predictive measure, but too often investigators stop after establishing concurrent validity. Evidence of concurrent validity is easy to obtain; however, information about predictive validity costs much time and money. A test with predictive validity probably will also possess concurrent validity, but the reverse is not typically the case. Concurrent validity misleads about delinquency potential for two reasons. First, many factors that lead to criminal behavior emerge only after the predelinquent has been originally tested. A twenty-year-old, for example, whose criminal behavior follows upon repeated frustrations in school, could not show the effects of these frustrations at age six. Thus, personality-scale items reporting scholastic unhappiness often have concurrent validity, but they cannot predict whether a young pupil will become an adult offender.

The second source of the discrepancy between concurrent and predictive validity is the outcome of criminal behavior itself. Social scientists who espouse some form of "labeling theory" (see Manning, 1975, for a critical review of their position) argue that the treatment received by someone who is caught in an offense sets off a process that converts an ordinary human into one with criminal attitudes.

Many scales with concurrent validity ask questions that might be tapping the end result of some such process rather than the personality characteristic responsible for starting it. Similarly, items expressing boredom or frustration in daily life, deviant sexual activity, or resentment toward society may only be indirect ways of asking whether or not a subject should be in prison. The more often a scale touches on postdelinquent life, the greater should be the gap between its concurrent validity and its predictive validity.

One more problem especially affects concurrent validity. Prisoners are not representative of the population of criminals. Not only do many criminals go unapprehended, but the majority of first-offenders are put on probation, not sent to prison. Studies of concurrent validity exclude probationers from the criminal sample. The comparison of prisoners to normals exaggerates differences between criminal and normal groups. With representation of all offenders, concurrent validity might not be as high. A prediction study, on the other hand, typically has convictions and arrests, not imprisonment, as its criterion; in it, the delinquent group includes the presumably less deviant offenders who receive probation. Thus the predictive validity of a measure of delinquency almost inevitably will be lower than its concurrent validity.

Return now to the distinction between criterion validity and criterion reliability! A criterion of delinquency is valid when it categorizes as criminal those who commit crimes and as normal those who do not. Reliability, by contrast, concerns only the consistency of the process that classifies people as criminal or noncriminal. Blind justice can be consistent and still make mistakes, such as by consistently convicting the innocent and acquitting the guilty. Add to this the impossibility of arresting everyone who commits an offense and of avoiding false arrests. The fallibility of the criterion arising from these various sources of error makes predictions of delinquency imperfect, regardless of the insight of the researcher and the precision of the measuring instrument.

Base Rate

Questions of reliability and validity aside, the base rate of the criterion categories is critical in the practical use of a predictor. The base rate of a behavior is its relative frequency in the population. If 40 percent of the twelve-year-old boys in Big City are convicted of at least one felony in their lifetimes, the base rate of such convictions is .40 for that particular population of boys.

There is an important general principle about base rate: the closer it is to .50 the more useful it will be as a measure that can predict the behavior. An example will make this clear. Suppose a test predicts with some accuracy which boys in Big City will become felons, and is equally accurate in Small Town, where the base rate is only .05. The hypothetical test can identify 70 percent of future felons and misclassify only 20 percent of ordinary future taxpayers. The table below shows the number of correct and erroneous predictions to expect for 10,000 Big City and 1,000 Small Town boys.

Predictions

	Future Felon		Future Taxpayer	
	Correct	Incorrect	Correct	Incorrect
Big City	2,800	1,200	4,800	1,200
Small Town	35	15	760	190

In Big City, the test identifies 2,800 of the 4,000 boys fated for felony and incorrectly predicts criminal behavior in 1,200 of the 6,000 ordinary boys—two hits for every false alarm. But with the same degree of accuracy, the test mislabels 190 ordinary Small Town boys as future felons in order to locate 35 real ones: false alarms outnumber hits by better than five to one.

The strong relationship between base rate and usefulness explains why it is hopeless to expect to identify ahead of time those rare individuals who will commit crimes that are lurid enough to make headlines throughout the world. Predicting who is likely to become a mass murderer will generate innumerable false predictions for the very few that are correct. How many misclassifications of this sort society will tolerate as the price for correct identifications depends upon what is done with the prediction once it is made. If remedial treatment is dangerous, the relative frequency of false alarms must be kept low for the predictor to be routinely applied. Risk-free treatments, on the other hand, make false alarms (which also are called false positives) less objectionable.

TREATMENT PROBLEMS

Predicting who will become an offender and who will continue to be a criminal has social utility only in prevention and rehabilitation. All such programs share the common aim of reducing a person's potential for criminal behavior in the future. Giving treatment to people who lack crime potential, however, is wasteful. The magnitude of the waste depends on cost and outcome of treatment. There may also be a misleading effect on evaluation of the treatment procedure; inclusion of normals in a treatment program makes testimony about its impact ambiguous.

Imagine a prevention program that might reduce delinquency potential to normal levels in half of the predelinquents it treats. For evidence of the program's effect, criterion behavior of a group of children finishing the program should be compared with that of an otherwise similar group of untreated children. With all children in the study predelinquent when it commences, half of the treated group will later become delinquent compared to 100 percent of the controls, a striking difference in outcome.

Assume, in contrast, that treated and control groups each contain only 20 percent predelinquents with the remaining children normal. Now the outcome will be 10 percent delinquency in the treated group and 20 percent in the controls. Although the delinquency rate is still cut in half by the prevention program, its benefits are not likely to be as apparent to nonexperts. At the same time, the second study, because of its large component of nondelinquents, must include many more subjects to assure the same degree of confidence that the favorable outcome was not merely a stroke of good luck. Finally, nearly everyone connected with the program wants it to succeed, believes it will succeed, and counts any improvement in the subjects as its justification. These payoffs are greatest when all subjects are predelinquents with personalities that need changing.

On several grounds, selecting the proper persons for treatment improves the accuracy of its evaluation. Tacit recognition of this principle occurs whenever experimental programs are placed in areas with high rates of delinquency. But even a high-delinquency area may not have a base rate close to .50. To get round this limitation, investigators tend to inflate the base rate in two ways. One of these becomes possible in the study of predictive validity, the second being feasible for concurrent validity.

For predictive validity, the researcher must draw a representative sample of individuals who will later show differences on the criterion. With most practical problems (including those involving criminal or delinquent behavior) the subjects will eventually be divided into two contrasting groups according to their scores on the criterion measure. Sometimes the dichotomy seems "natural," like success-failure on parole, where base rates are close to .50. But in other studies, an investigator chooses the cutting score on the criterion to separate nondelinquent sheep from delinquent goats. Naturally, the tendency is to pick a score that moves the base rate closer to .50. Growing up to be a criminal is not common in any group of children. To predict that outcome from earlier measurement requires that the researcher, among other responsibilities, define what being a criminal consists of. The definition usually is rather loose, with behaviors that most people would not ordinarily consider delinquent, like getting parking or traffic tickets, being classified as criminal.

Compared to males, females in this country have been so nondelinquent that behaviors like running away from home or sexual promiscuity must be counted for any showing at all of delinquent women in a study. Is sexual promiscuity still a cause for detention, or have our recent permissive standards made it even more difficult to locate bad girls? Will entry of women into previously masculine occupations generalize to criminal vocations and make female felons more available for research?

By defining almost any violation of a rule as a delinquency, the investigator consciously or unconsciously pushes the base rate nearer to the optimal .50. While such a definition makes it easier to detect a relation between personality and delinquency, the magnitude of that relation in real life is left unexplored. On the other hand, it is possible to go too far and limit subjects to hardened cases, as did the Gluecks (1959) when trying to predict future behavior of 500 tough delinquent boys. The prediction tables proved 93 percent correct, but the same percentage of all 500 boys were recidivists. The high base rate deprived the prediction tables of value, since predicting that all would fail would be correct 93 percent of the time.

In a true prediction study, the base rate in the sample will be close to the base rate in the population being sampled. If 10 percent of the subjects become criminals, so should 10 percent of the population they represent. Such is not true in a study of concurrent validity. There the researcher decides in advance on the number of delinquent and nondelinquent subjects. It should not surprise anyone that most studies of concurrent validity employ about equal numbers of delinquents and controls. Samples of these proportions are ideal for demonstrating that some relationship exists, but they lead to a woeful overestimation of the practical value of the measure, thanks to the unrealistic base rate.

For these statistical reasons and because of causal problems such as those we detailed earlier, concurrent validity studies give overly optimistic pictures of the feasibility of constructing predictive measures. Whatever value such studies will have relates to personality theory, an area far removed from the topic of this chapter.

Selection Ratio

With criterion problems solved, researchers can design and evaluate measures of delinquency potential, discovering in the process both their validities and base rate in the population of concern. At this point, most scholars publish their results.

How the application of such instruments affects crime rates, probation success, parole outcome, and reconvictions goes pretty much unreported. This silence is unfortunate. The chief reason for measuring delinquency potential is improvement of prevention and rehabilitation procedures, and there is no way of estimating the usefulness of the concept of delinquency potential without knowledge of what will be done about it. How that action fares—if there is any action—turns upon another psychometric concept—*selection ratio*.

A general principle in personnel selection is that tests will be more useful the fewer there are to be chosen out of a crowd of applicants. The principle holds for prevention and rehabilitation programs for criminals. Given a valid predictor, the more selective one is about which individuals to work with, the more certain one can be that they have a high potential for delinquency.

Consider an experimental prevention program for predelinquents. Can everyone for whom assessment predicts delinquency get into the program? Probably not! Recall the Big City example: a valid test diagnosed 4,000 of 10,000 boys as future delinquents. An experimental program could not handle that many boys.

The 10,000 boys are a pool from which to draw the actual number of children for the prevention program. Given a valid predictor, its highest scoring boys are wanted for the sample, if increasing the proportion of delinquents is the goal. How many to take depends upon the resources available for the prevention program. Suppose 500 are chosen. That decision sets the selection ratio at .05. A ratio this small is highly advantageous in personnel selection.

Whether a small selection ratio is as advantageous for treatment as it is for selection is another matter. Perhaps the treatment program theoretically should work equally well for any type of predelinquent; which predelinquents will become the worst criminals is not an issue. When this is the case, a low selection ratio is as beneficial as it is in personnel selection. Taking boys with the very highest scores—the top five percent in the example—drastically reduces the number of ordinary boys misdirected into treatment.

In contrast, a selection rate of .50, which places the high-scoring half of the 10,000 boys in the prevention program, markedly increases the number of normal children receiving unnecessary treatment.

But are all predelinquents equally malleable? Predictor scores may reflect how thoroughly criminal the child will become. Should that be true, a low selection ratio can damage an effective prevention program. Accepting only a small proportion of very high-scoring children into the program will confront the experimenters with the most severe problems. A low selection ratio makes the therapists work with the toughest customers in the group of predelinquents (Rose, 1967).

What kind of child should a prevention program aim at? The boy whose antisocial tendencies are relatively weak, or one in whom predisposition to crime is tenacious? Common sense imagines treatment to be more successful in mild cases: "Take predelinquents who are not hopelessly criminal, demonstrate that the program helps them, then try it with more difficult children!"[1]

Problems of reliability, validity, base rate, and selection ratio have to be overcome, if measurement of delinquency potential is to be of any use. For an idea of the degree of success investigators in this area have had during the last two decades, let us consider representative studies of two aspects of the topic: prediction of delinquency, and prediction of recidivism.

FORECASTING DELINQUENCY

A popular topic in research on delinquency potential is the prediction of future antisocial behavior among children and teenagers. The majority of efforts to measure delinquency potential have settled for concurrent validity, hence their instruments are impossible to evaluate as predictors. But several investigators have tracked subjects long enough to obtain meaningful estimates of predictive validity. Most projects of either kind, however, employed some kind of personality inventory, or questionnaire, as the basis for estimating delinquency potential.

Personality Questionnaires

Their validity aside, questionnaires in several ways are attractive devices for measuring personality differences. Questionnaires require minimum effort and skill to administer and score and are not difficult to construct. Analysis of results is relatively simple. A personality inventory is a collection of printed questions answered by the subject on a machine-scored sheet, typically using a true-false format. Most personality questionnaires contain more than one *scale*, or related set of questions, so that several different scores, each revealing something believed to be important about the subject, are harvested from a single testing session.

The best known and most widely used questionnaire today is the Minnesota Multiphasic Personality Inventory, or MMPI. It began life in the 1930s as an economical substitute for the expensive psychiatric diagnostic interview. By asking a large set of questions—550 in the standard form of the inventory—Hathaway and McKinley (1940) had the subject conduct a self-interview to duplicate what a psychiatrist might discover in a face-to-face session. Many items in the inventory were included in the hope that future research with the collection of items would facilitate construction of new diagnostic scales, a goal that has been met with a vengeance. Approximately three hundred scales having been added (Dahlstrom, Welsh, & Dahlstrom, 1972). Once Hathaway and McKinley had gathered answers from normal persons and various types of disturbed individuals—classified according to psychiatric nomenclature standard at the time—they constructed scales from questionnaire items that appeared to distinguish among psychiatric groups and normals. The goal was accurate diagnosis, making concurrent validity appropriate. For the inventory scales to make the same classifications as a competent psychiatrist was precisely what was wanted.

By 1950, the MMPI was in wide usage in the United States, despite the fact that the subjects used for construction of its scales were not representative of the general population in the country, a defect that may have contributed to the inability of many investigators to confirm the concurrent validity of the scales. Rather than restandardize the inventory with more representative groups of patients and controls and keep pace with changes in psychiatric classifications, MMPI devotees have chosen to freeze the inventory and to substitute the more esoteric method of *profile analysis* to interpret scores on the unsatisfactory scales. Profile analysis places great weight on differences in the magnitude of the scores a person obtains on the thirteen standard scales. The notion that each separate scale has a particular diagnostic validity has been dropped.

Unsatisfactory as the psychometric history of the MMPI has been, it could hardly be more popular as a research tool. Three decades after the inventory appeared, Buros (1975) could cite 3,840 scientific publications concerning it. During that period, the MMPI was routinely employed in counseling centers, and many prison systems administered it to all prisoners passing through classification centers. The presence in the files of thousands of prisoner MMPIs has facilitated many studies of its value in the prediction of prison adjustment and recidivism. But the inventory was rarely employed in schools. Thus its use in the prediction of delinquency requires that researchers administer it to youngsters prior to the time they become delinquent. Doing that is no minor task.

The most comprehensive study of the MMPI in the prediction of delinquency was undertaken by Hathaway in collaboration with Elio D. Monachesi (1953, 1963). Hathaway and Monachesi gathered MMPIs from thousands of ninth-graders in Minneapolis and outstate Minnesota. After a delay of several years, the research team searched court and police records to estimate the degree of delinquency in their subjects, securing information for a considerable number of them. Hathaway and Monachesi collected much additional data about their subjects, including teachers' ratings of delinquency potential in the children.

Valid teachers' ratings would be an inexpensive and convenient means of locating delinquency-prone pupils. Whether a teacher's contact with a child discloses any existing potential for later antisocial behavior—or, as some may argue, that contact enables the teacher to make a self-fulfilling prophecy—is not immediately relevant to the predictive power of the ratings. The question, of course, is highly related to prevention and rehabilitation of delinquency. But purely as predictions, teachers' ratings offer an alternative that psychological measures should improve upon to be the basis for locating pre-delinquents.

Supplied with this body of information, Hathaway and Monachesi (1963) used several types of analysis to estimate the predictive value of the inventory. The first analysis employed the standard MMPI scales. For each scale, scores of children who later became delinquent were contrasted with scores of children who did not. In the second analysis, frequencies of different types of MMPI profiles were compared for the two kinds of subjects. Finally, a question-by-question comparison of delinquent and nondelinquent responses in the Minneapolis sample turned up a number of items on which the two groups seemed substantially different. An analysis of this kind with as many items as the MMPI contains necessitates *cross-validation*, that is, replication on another sample to ensure that the differences were not due to chance. The outstate sample was used for the cross-validation.

The outcome of this effort was discouraging. Although the MMPI had some predictive validity, Hathaway and Monachesi (1963) were pessimistic about its usefulness: "The most accurate predictor of delinquency was teacher nomination . . ." (p. 99). "We have satisfied ourselves that we could not find a single dimension, measurable with available items, which could be effectively used as a delinquency proneness scale" (p. 90). One conclusion is particularly pertinent to the analysis of questionnaires: "To the degree to which we believe at all in the hypothesis of predictable outcomes, we have more faith in the discovery of some really new psychometric method than in further refinement of the general methods exemplified by the MMPI" (p. 33).

Those general methods, which dominate research on delinquency potential, include scrutinizing each item in a large, heterogeneous collection of material to discover, if luck holds, things that distinguish delinquents from nondelinquents. Discriminating items are then organized into a scale that is administered to new samples of subjects for cross-validation. This research procedure, called *criterion keying*, when employed for construction of psychological measures, requires no prior theoretical analysis of the behavior to be predicted. Anything may be included in the pool of information, and indeed, the more things that are assembled, the more certain are investigators and funding agencies that the study is well designed. Hathaway and Monachesi realized that the MMPI was not created expressly for the goal they had in mind, but nothing better was available when they began their study. However, many psychologists of that period had recommended the alternative of collecting only information critical for a single theory or point of view, so that if results did not fit the theory, it could be discarded once and for all. With criterion keying, no theory is tested. When the method fails to produce positive results, all theories continue to be preached by competing prophets and their disciples.

When criterion keying is successful, nothing is settled about the causes of the observed differences. Anyone designing a prevention program for predelinquents would have to rely upon intuition instead of logical deduction to interpret the import of the findings. Then, too, American culture is neither homogeneous nor unchanging. Criterion keying might yield a predictive scale valid in one locality and period and invalid in other places or times. Hathaway and Monachesi's discouraging conclusions have not dissuaded other investigators from using the MMPI to study delinquency potential, but none has pursued prediction on a large scale. Most other research employing the MMPI has achieved only concurrent validity.

Doubts about the usefulness of the MMPI in predicting delinquency hold as well for the K.D. Proneness Scale (Kvaraceus, 1950), which has occasionally shown concurrent validity. Feldhusen, Benning, and Thurston (1972) conducted a five-year follow-up of 1,500 pupils nominated by their teachers as especially socially approved or disapproved for behavior. The K. D. Proneness Scale had no predictive value, although the study, by contrasting extremely different youngsters, utilized a tactic that maximizes chances of demonstrating validity. The same outcome held three years later (Feldhusen, Thurston, & Benning, 1973).

British researchers have been less inclined than Americans to use criterion keying. When a questionnaire is employed, it is likely to be one of a set devised by the Eysencks to measure dimensions they consider fundamental in personality (see Chapter 9). According to H. J. Eysenck (1964), criminals should be more likely than others to be high both in Extroversion and Neuroticism. He predicted the connection between extroversion and delinquency via a deduction from earlier work indicating that extroversion interferes with the acquisition of conditioned responses. Such interference in early childhood, a period Eysenck accepts as critical for development of one's conscience—makes the extrovert grow up poorly socialized—a condition he implicitly assumes equivalent to being antisocial (Hoghughi & Forrest, 1970). Neuroticism, Eysenck believes, energizes behavior, so that a person high in neuroticism, or anxiety, should differ from others by being either delinquent or particularly law-abiding, depending upon the amount of extroversion present.

Evidence for or against Eysenck's hypothesis rests on concurrent validity of his two scales. While the Neuroticism Scale possesses concurrent validity, that validity still is in dispute for the extroversion measure (Hoghughi & Forrest, 1970). The Eysencks' (1970) have added a measure of Psychoticism they believe—from experience, not theory—distinguishes criminals from normals. An analysis of items from the three scales (1971) showed concurrent validity for psychoticism and neuroticism items. On the Extroversion Scale, Impulsivity items had concurrent validity, but Sociability items did not. Eysenck is alert to the double-barreled nature of the Extroversion Scale, but that has not saved it from severe criticism on theoretical grounds (Guilford, 1977).

The Eysencks' ideas have not progressed to the point where their theory of personality leads to successful prediction of future delinquency. And the theory does not seem likely to make that difficult leap with present instruments for measuring its three dimensions. Questions on the Extroversion, Neuroticism, and Psychoticism Scales (1971) resemble items on the MMPI. Typical are the following similarities:

Eysenck Item	MMPI Item
Do most things taste the same to you?	Everything tastes the same.
Was your father a good man?	My father was a good man.

Compared to the MMPI, the Eysencks' inventories are briefer, contain fewer scales, and have a relationship of sorts to psychological theory, but most of the content that is covered by their items duplicates material on the MMPI. No matter what rationale governs selection of items, those that did not predict in the classic Hathaway and Monachesi investigation should not work elsewhere, unless some fundamental cultural difference intervenes.

If delinquency potential exists in children, questionnaire scales are not satisfactory measures of it. At best, such scales can delineate attitudes that distinguish offenders from ordinary persons, and thereby improve procedures for rehabilitation. In addition, they might serve as temporary estimates of the impact of treatment (Cassel & Blum, 1969), on the assumption that a treatment which leaves scores unchanged on a delinquency potential scale is unlikely to produce much change in delinquent behavior.

Other Predictive Devices

Ability tests have often been given to delinquents and normals for comparison purposes. Many studies report average differences in intelligence favoring nondelinquents, but the overlap in scores is great, and differences are too small to be useful in prediction. One intelligence test, the *Porteus Maze*, also yields an estimate of impulsivity, a characteristic that plausibly predisposes to criminal behavior. For nearly fifty years, occasional publications have reported differences in the way delinquents and controls complete the test, which is a set of printed mazes on each of which the subject must draw the correct path to the goal. Impulsivity affects the Q score, a measure of neatness in execution of drawing. Riddle and Roberts (1977) reviewed fifteen different studies showing concurrent validity of the Q score going back to 1942, but none dealt with the prediction of delinquency. This is a pity, because Q score does not clearly depend upon events that occur following an individual's first arrest, and its concurrent validity may be closer to its predictive validity than is the case with questionnaire scales.

A standard technique for obtaining information about subjects is through nomination or rating by their associates. A number of studies of delinquency potential have collected teachers' ratings of children along with other types of information, and these ratings have had better predictive validity (Scarpitti, Murray, Dinitz, & Reckless, 1960; Werner & Gallistet, 1961; Kvaraceus, 1961; Hathaway & Monachesi, 1963; Feldhusen, Benning, & Thurston 1972). Khleif (1964) has shown that teacher's spontaneous written comments separate predelinquents from matched controls, and Stott (1960) used the *Bristol Social Adjustment Guides* to organize teachers' judgments for forecasting delinquency.

That teachers should be able to discern in their pupils qualities that might contribute to future delinquency should not surprise anyone who believes in delinqency potential. And, as we have noted, proponents of the labelling view of delinquency are delighted that the teachers show some insight into *their* part in creating delinquent attitudes in children. But from the standpoint of prediction, evaluations by a child's teachers offer a standard by which other methods of prediction can be appraised. To repeat a point made earlier, teachers' ratings are so convenient to obtain that no other technique for estimating delinquency potential is attractive unless it promises greater predictive accuracy.

Judgments of adults who have investigated the backgrounds of young children are the basis of several prediction tables devised by Sheldon and Eleanor Glueck (1950). Despite the enthusiasm of the two authors and early widespread endorsement of their scales by criminologists, doubts about their validity were expressed in the years following the first appearance of the scales, chiefly because of the usual confusion about concurrent and predictive validity, plus the common problem of unrealistic base rates. But Craig and Glick (1963, 1965) reported that a ten-year follow-up in New York City showed true predictive validity for a new Glueck scale based on evaluations of family cohesiveness and of the mother-son relationship. Trevvett (1965) obtained equally encouraging results with the same scale in Washington, D.C. Neither of these predictive studies, however, has escaped criticism (Weis,

1974). The Gluecks believed that delinquency potential has its roots in the family in early childhood. More accurate prediction might result from a combination of information about early family relations and school behavior.

Results from Hampton (1970) suggest that the mother's judgment of the son's personality has predictive value, and Kelley, Veldman, and McGuire (1964) found peer ratings to reflect potential delinquency. Judgmental methods may be less precise than standardized psychological measures, but their validity should not be ignored.

Having their associates nominate individuals with high potential for delinquency suffers from one limitation that is absent in other prediction methods. Tests and scales, for example, assign continuous scores to subjects, making it possible to establish a cut-off score that separates people into subgroups whose proportions fit the desired selection ratio. But nominations allow a judge to establish an idiosyncratic cut-off. One observer can designate many children as predelinquent, while another one could name very few of the same youngsters.

Teachers' nominations tend to "overpredict" delinquency. Teachers perceive too many children as predelinquent and too few as nondelinquent. This sort of mistake, which can also affect judgments by court officers, psychiatrists, and social scientists, very likely obeys principles that govern the quite different behavior realm illuminated by *signal detection theory*. In its language, (which we have used) correct identification of a child as predelinquent is a "hit." Calling a predelinquent normal is a "miss." Misclassifying a normal child as predelinquent is a "false alarm."

The relative frequencies of misses and false alarms vary both within and between observers and depend, in part, upon the cost of each kind of error. Observers supposedly adjust their criteria to minimize costs and maximize gains. Should overpredicting delinquency expose a child to expensive, lengthy, unpleasant, or hard-to-supply treatment, a false alarm may appear too costly in comparison to what society gains by successful treatment of a predelinquent. For this situation, observers can be expected to "underpredict" delinquency. They will pay for fewer false alarms by making fewer hits.

In overpredicting delinquency or any other behavior disorder, the observer acts as though the treatment nominees who do not need it will receive, is not as potentially harmful to them or to society as letting people who need help go untreated. False alarms are not seen as costly as misses. The result of a miss may also exact a personal cost, as in the case of a psychiatrist who misclassifies a homicidal patient as nonviolent. A mistake like that could cost someone's life and the psychiatrist his job and reputation.

The cure for overprediction is conversion of the nominating procedure into something that yields a more continuous scale. (The Bristol Guides are an attempt of that kind.) It is not really known, however, whether steps taken to eliminate overprediction leave validity untouched. Whether the validity of judgmental methods can be increased to make them the instrument of choice in measuring delinquency potential remains an open question.

PREDICTING RECIDIVISM

At national conferences, opponents of the criminal justice system denounce its ineffectiveness, citing in particular the high rates of recidivism, or continued criminal behavior. Other speakers angrily rebut the accusations, defend the system, and attack parents and schools for producing armies of young hoods. In the audience, however, one or two faces wear a quiet smile. What can they find pleasing in the debate on recidivism?

The cheerful ones are investigators who understand that a base rate near .50 is ideal for the application of a predictive device. Moreover, forecasting recidivism has additional desirable features that are absent in predicting other types of delinquency. The subjects can be assessed at the researcher's convenience. Imprisoned subjects are easier to keep track of; ordinary people move about so often that follow-ups are difficult. Particularly convenient is when recidivism is defined as revocation of parole rather than conviction on new charges. And a parole board may have considerable control over the selection ratio—in this case, the proportion of applicants who are paroled during any one time period. A drawback, to be sure, is the questionable reliability and validity of the criterion, success or failure on parole.

Experience Tables

A prisoner's record file is filled with material someone thought relevant to imprisonment, parole, and future criminal behavior. To be sure, it contains the dry and dusty information personnel departments collect about employees, things like age, sex, marital status, education, work history, and assorted falsehoods, but the prison file adds information on past arrests, convictions, sentences, and prison behavior. Some facts about family adjustment may be gleaned from various social agencies. *Experience tables*, sometimes called *base expectancy tables*, incorporate pertinent parts of this diverse information into indices that estimate probability of success or failure on probation or parole or of conviction for new offenses. The experience table was first championed by Hart (1923) as an improvement on the disorderly cognition of parole boards.

Particularly effective were tables developed by Mannheim and Wilkins (1955) to predict recidivism in graduates of the Borstal System in England. Past drunkenness was the most heavily weighted item in the index, which included additional material on work history—prior convictions, living away from home, and residence area, all chosen as convenient to obtain in a longer list of discriminating items. Many such tables have been drawn up by other investigators, the California Youth Authority Base Expectancy Index being a well-known example. Such tables usually put great weight on the age of first offense and on number of prior convictions, or to factors highly related to these two items. Mannheim and Wilkins were careful to note that causal relations were not suggested by their analysis and preferred to view their techniques as a tool for research rather than a basis for administrative action. A major problem they encountered was incomplete information in their subjects' record files.

An experience table is the product of criterion keying of the information in the record. For evaluating methods of forecasting recidivism, the experience table should play the same role that teachers' ratings fill in predicting delinquency. Both are inexpensive standards that other instruments ought to improve on to justify being used. Years ago, Ohlin and Duncan (1949) estimated that the employment of experience tables would improve accuracy of parole decisions on an average of 12 percent, but Dean and Duggan (1968) noted little increase over that figure by the newer tables. Members of parole boards also have access to the prisoner's file, and to varying extents, boards may be familiar with experience tables (Rogers, 1968). Introduction of an experience table into a process that it already silently affects may not result in a dramatic reduction in the proportions of parolees who fail.

The effectiveness of experience tables customarily is evaluated in comparison to the effectiveness of the parole board, as measured by the proportion of successful parolees. This comparison can bias results in favor of the tables. An example with hypothetical data on one board's performance may make this clear:

> Parole granted during one period to 50 percent (Selection Ratio)
> Success on parole for 60 percent of parolees (Base Rate)
> An experience table is accurate for 70 percent of the *parolees*.

The difference of 10 percent between table and board seems to favor the table. Dividing that difference by the board percentage of error—some 40 percent of parolees failed—represents a decrease in error of 25 percent. But is it? Notice that there is no estimate of the board's accuracy in denying parole, or any information on what the experience tables would recommend for unsuccessful applicants.

In ideal circumstances, parole board and experience table evaluations would be obtained for all parole applicants, and not just for parolees. A study of this kind probably requires considerable disguise of its features, but results should be decisive. The same design is needed with evaluation of any other measure of delinquency potential in the parole process.

Attractive as criterion keying has been to many applied social scientists, a scale built by criterion keying is difficult to justify to laypersons, despite evidence for its validity. Discussing experience tables in particular, Dean and Duggan (1968) noted two serious liabilities, both stemming from the use of criterion keying:

> First, the prevalent use of prison files as a data source limits the kind of research question which can be asked. Second, the non-theoretical nature of this research has prevented a systematic accumulation of knowledge relative to this problem (p. 450).

Dean and Duggan believed that an understanding of the source of recidivism can emerge only when theory guides research. This means that variables should not be selected for study merely because of their availability in prison files. Moreover, experts have expressed strong reservations about the reliability of much of the information that is found in files. Consider, for example, the comments of Vold (1949):

> The most discouraging thing about the whole field of prediction in criminology is the continued unreliability and general worthlessness of the so-called "information" in the original records (p. 452).

All of these points have been echoed more recently by Buikhuisen and Hoekstra (1974), who believed, like Arnold (1965), that postparole experiences have very decisive influence on recidivism. Gains from the construction of even the best experience tables are limited, for the discovery of empirically derived predictors lacks the impact of a comparable breakthrough for which a specific theory was responsible. A theory that leads to valid prediction of future offenses probably can also explain how persons become criminals, thereby guiding prevention programs, and it can probably infer what we should do with offenders once they are convicted, thereby guiding rehabilitation. Neither of these by-products arises in investigations limited to criterion keying of diverse material. Experience tables are even worse off in this respect than personality inventories, since a table cannot reflect changes that are brought about by rehabilitation. Few signs of improvement in a criminal's prospects alter an experience table; only ominous events like new convictions change it.

Personality Questionnaires

The complications involved in evaluating experience tables and parole tables and parole board decisions should not disguise the fact that both estimate delinquency potential in convicts. The prisoner's file often includes some kind of estimate of personality problems, possibly from the MMPI or other questionnaire that the prison personnel who are responsible for prisoner classification believe to have diagnostic value. Personality data can be analyzed by criterion keying, but scales that emerge are subject to the familiar limitations of criterion-keyed predictors. The frequency with which MMPI records have been available in prisoner files has encouraged the development of several scales for predicting recidivism. None appears successful outside the prison system in which it was originally created. Looking for gold in gravel that has been thoroughly panned by earlier miners is not the best way to start prospecting.

A more interesting approach was utilized by Gough, Wenk, and Rozynko (1965), who predicted parole outcome from various combinations of the California Youth Authority Base Expectancy Index, the MMPI, and the California

Psychological Inventory, a lineal descendant of the MMPI that is aimed at normal rather than pathological differences in personality. While the CPI is also a product of criterionkeying, its socialization scale possesses what is, for personality psychology, a theoretical basis (Gough & Peterson, 1952). The subjects Gough and his associates studied were 739 young male offenders paroled for two to three years. In the group, 56 percent were successful, but no information is given about the selection ratio in awarding or denying parole. The study, for this reason, illuminates the validity of the several instruments rather than their practical utility.

The base expectancy index was the most valid single predictor of parole outcome, but a combination of the index and several scales from the CPI, including its socialization measure, was better:

> To estimate how much better they could do, the investigators used predictor scores to divide their subjects into groups with either high or low probability of success, choosing cut-offs that put 56 percent into the high probability group. (Using the base rate to determine the proportion in each group avoids criticism that a cut-off capitalizes on chance differences between groups.)
>
> Given that base rate, predicting success for all parolees would be correct 56 percent of the time. The combination of base expectancy index and CPI scales did better, making 63 percent correct predictions. Actually, using the combination to make the final decision for applicants approved by the board would raise parole success to 67 percent, but the number of individuals paroled would be much smaller.

What cannot be determined in the Gough, Wenk, and Rozynko study—and in all other comparisons using parolees alone—is the extent to which the apparent superiority of a novel prediction instrument over the parole board recommendation is the outcome of a more favorable selection ratio rather than of its greater validity; asking the board to parole only 56 percent of their original selections might very well raise the proportion of parolees who are successful.

What such comparisons can show, however, is the degree to which delinquency potential can be measured. Unfortunately, as Dean and Duggan (1968) emphasized, investigations of prediction of parole outcome have used measures that are conveniently at hand. And that means, as far as psychological instruments are concerned, the MMPI. Panton (1962) constructed a twenty-six-item recidivism scale for the inventory by criterion keying, but Gough, Wenk, and Rozynko (1965) found this scale of no predictive value for their parolees. Mandel and Barron (1966) and Mack (1969) had no better luck with standard MMPI scales and profile analyses. Probation violation ought to reflect delinquency potential, but Smith (1968) found it unrelated either to the MMPI or to a base-expectancy index. More favorable outcomes for a twenty-two-item scale developed by Black (1967) were reported by Frank (1971) in an unpublished doctoral dissertation, but the past history of such MMPI measures arouses little optimism that the scale will have wide applicability. The pessimistic conclusions of Hathaway and Monachesi (1963) about the validity of the inventory for predicting future delinquency appear to hold as strongly for the prediction of recidivism.

Other Predictors of Recidivism

High Q scores are commoner among recidivists, according to Roberts, Erikson, Riddle, and Bacon (1974), confirming outcomes of earlier research on the concurrent validity of that score. Projective tests have figured in two predictive studies of recidivism. Jenkins and Blodgett (1960) reported that the *Sentence Completion Test* foretold parole outcome for 65 percent of a sample of delinquent boys whose rate of success was 52 percent. Wetzel, Shapiro, and Wagner (1967) found evidence for some predictive validity in the *Hand Test*, a less widely used instrument. Projective tests enjoy wide popularity among clinical psychologists, the sentence completion instruments being a favorite research tool. Yet such tests are not routinely involved in criminal justice decision making and are usually absent from prisoner files.

Predictive validity of *judgments* of personality has drawn somewhat more attention from researchers. Stott and Wilson (1967) continued Stott's earlier (1964) work on the Delinquency Prediction Scale of the Bristol Social Adjustment Guides, obtaining data for 395 juvenile delinquents reaching the age of twenty-one. Teachers using the guides had rated the boys when they were eight to fourteen years of age. Further offenses at eighteen to twenty years were predictable from these ratings. But Callard (1967) failed to uncover any differences between recidivists and nonrecidivists rated by teachers and by probation officers when the boys were in court for the first time. The officers also predicted which of the 158 eleven-to-fourteen-year-olds would or would not reappear in court. These forecasts were correct 64 percent of the time; base rate for not returning to court was 55 percent. Boys who were close to their mothers and whose parents were congenial were less likely to return, results that recall similar findings by Craig and Glick (1963) and Trevvett (1965) using a Glueck scale to predict delinquency. Finally, there is some predictive validity in judgments by clinicians about post release behavior of institutionalized delinquent boys (Cowden, 1966).

Opinions of people who know or have investigated an individual appear to be as valid as competing predictive devices. Judgments of this kind, however, less often illuminate the nature of delinquency potential. The probation officers Callard observed could predict recidivism, but this raises the question of how they achieved their degree of accuracy. To pursue the answer may require that the dedicated researcher follow paths far removed from the area of delinquency potential. Whether the detour will ever lead back is not at all certain.

Recidivism and Delinquency Potential

The success of various investigators in predicting parole outcome at better than chance levels supports the idea that delinquency potential exists and affects important behaviors. But the degree of influence does not appear large, at least at first sight. However, the opportunistic nature of most studies may have hidden real impact. A general principle in psychological measurement states that a strong relationship between two variables in a mixed population of people will look weak in a homogeneous population. All persons convicted of criminal offenses are not given the same treatment. Delinquents are not randomly distributed in the pigeon holes of the criminal justice establishment. Offenders on probation, for example, are probably more homogeneous in delinquency potential than offenders in general. Anyone taking a sample from a single subgroup of offenders may be fated to underestimate the effect of delinquency potential in causing crime.

The cure, of course, is the study of offenders who have been convicted but not yet sentenced. Only then is the full range of delinquency potential available for analysis. By *aggregating* information about different types of offenders, the true status of delinquency potential might be finally revealed. This recommendation, however, flies in the face of another remedy proposed for the problem.

IS DISAGGREGATION THE ANSWER?

Lumping together all offenders to search for qualities that distinguish them from the general population of taxpayers is called aggregating information. But even in a society with perfect justice, will the causes of every crime include a common personality element that merits the label of "delinquency potential"? Perhaps not. Crimes can change into recreations, and fun can be made illegal. Drinking beer was once criminal in the United States; now it supports the school system. The British made riding a motorcycle without a crash helmet a criminal offense. Both of these behaviors were prohibited for the offender's "own good." Quite different are "crimes such as murder, rape, robbery or burglary, which have been serious crimes in every civilized culture —and most uncivilized ones too—for many generations" (Walker, 1974, p. 61).

Disaggregation separates crimes and criminals into different types. By establishing homogeneous classes, it hopes to discover distinct causes for each type. Personality characteristics associated with one offense certainly may differ from those associated with another kind of crime. The jazz-age flapper drank bathtub gin for the same reason she wore a coonskin coat: both were all the rage. Conformity to a current fad neither then nor now diagnosed predispositions to rob banks, pass counterfeit money, or commit dozens of other felonies. Disaggregation attacks the crime problem by attempting predictions for specific types of crimes. Success of the disaggregation method might lead to one prediction procedure for violent crimes, another for drug offenses, and still other procedures, as analysis made clear the relationship between personality and other types of offense.

Another aspect of disaggregation is recognition that otherwise different personality characteristics may lie behind the same kind of crime (Chapter 9). Given this perspective, hunting for a single measure or single combination of measures to disclose high-risk persons before they get into trouble looks potentially less fruitful than seeking separate estimates of different types of delinquency potential.

So run arguments for disaggregation. What do they imply? For one, if specific crimes have specific associations with personality characteristics, then criminals ought to be psychologically consistent in their offenses from the beginning. Against the disaggregation strategy stands the assumption that the only important propensity is to delinquency in general. A model of this sort might postulate that the particular crime constituting a delinquent boy's first offense was unpredictable. Once he is a criminal, his offenses become less variable as he learns a criminal trade or falls into a convenient criminal rut.

Measurement of several delinquency potentials in place of a single predisposition makes severe demands on test-constructing ability and psychological insight. Creating instruments that can diagnose a person as a potential forger, rather than murderer, pickpocket, arsonist, burglar, or, for that matter, honest citizen, demands that the predicting instruments have *differential validity*. Instruments should be designed so that the typical criminal obtains high scores on only one of the predictors. Having many offenders score high on more than one scale would mean that delinquency potential is general rather than specific to particular crimes, making disaggregation useless.

The most successful differential assessment by psychological measures has been provided by Strong's original *Vocational Interest Blank* and its later revisions. The VIB is an inventory· mainly covering professional, managerial, technical, or white-collar occupations. Efforts to construct similar interest inventories related to blue-collar work have not shown the same degree of differential validity. Job satisfaction at lower levels of the occupational hierarchy is less dependent on personal liking for the work and more related to pay, working conditions, and social relations on the job (Anastasia, 1976). A factory worker, for example, has less intrinsic concern about what is being made in his factory than does a chemist working in a laboratory. Should this difference be paralleled in the criminal sphere, few delinquents will specialize in a particular crime because of its interesting features or their exceptional talent for it. Instead, typical felons should break the law for the same considerations of money, social relations, security, and opportunity that motivate work in their law-abiding peers.

If there are several delinquency potentials, the task of measuring them adds new problems to those that bedevil construction of a single scale. First, the measures must have higher reliability than usual to be able to discern whether differences between an individual's scores are diagnostic of predisposition to a particular type of offense. Second, the measures must not correlate much with each other. The validity of existing estimates of delinquency potential depends to a large extent on questions about family and school adjustment and resentment toward society. If items touching these areas appear on more than one predictor, subjects high on one scale tend to be high on others, and differential validity vanishes.

No one yet has set out to construct differential predictors of a variety of criminal types. Instead, individual investigations have sought to distinguish between dichotomies of offenders, usually by criterion keying of existing measures. One such dichotomy is the distinction between "person" and "property" offenders. Sometimes specification of a dichotomy goes a step further, as in the division of violent criminals into "overcontrolled" and "undercontrolled" categories (Chapter 13). Many such dichotomies are possible in disaggregating criminal offenses. A look at one such classification will illustrate the present status of the disaggregation approach to measurement of delinquency potential.

PREDICTING CRIMINAL VIOLENCE

Estimation of potential for violent crime suffers from all the handicaps that afflict measurement of general delinquency potential, with the additional burden of a severely reduced base rate. That base rate is far too small to offer much hope that present-day devices will be able to predict who will commit a violent crime for the first time. But potential for violence is more common in prison populations. For this reason, there have been numerous studies of the *diagnostic validity* of estimates of that potential.

Diagnostic validity is a form of concurrent validity. Its apparent concern is the present status of the individual with no thought of the future. Prison systems call diagnosis "classification." They classify offenders in various ways and act on the basis of these classifications in assigning inmates to different types of custody, such as minimum or maximum security. A measuring device that arrives at a classification similar to one of the prison procedures has diagnostic validity.

Following diagnosis, however, are treatment and its outcome. Placing someone in maximum security reveals an opinion about that person's potential in the future, just as diagnosing a tumor as a cancer rather than a wart carries an implicit prediction about developments to come. By asserting that a scale has diagnostic validity, its creator places the burden of predictive validity squarely on the criterion—perhaps *"shifts* the burden" would be a better way to put it. It is possible, for example, that a prison system might classify its customers in ways that have nothing to do with potential behavior, so that the classifications lack predictive value. Yet any scale that mirrors those classifications will have a high degree of diagnostic validity. Diagnostic validity is tied to the status quo.

Criterion problems have not dampened enthusiasm for studies employing diagnostic validity. Various schemes for disaggregating violent offenders challenge the usual belief that such people lack self-control and have vicious habits. As we shall see in Chapter 13, Megargee (1966) questioned this assumption when he classified some violent offenders as overcontrolled, others as undercontrolled.

> The prototype of overcontrol is the meek, middle-aged man who has never been able to express hostility toward his dissolute wife—or toward anyone else. Finally, her abuse provokes an explosion of rage in which he hacks her to pieces with the customary carving knife. Then he passes the remainder of his life peacefully as a model prisoner asssigned to the leathercrafting shop.

To test the hypothesis, Megargee, Cook and Mendelsohn (1967) categorized offenders from probation files as extremely assaultive, moderately assaultive, or nonassaultive, and added a control group of noncriminals. Criterion keying of the MMPI produced a twenty-one-item scale that was cross-validated on new samples of probation applicants. Because its items included many passive, nonaggressive statements, Megargee and his co-workers next examined prison files to sort inmates convicted of violent crimes into the two hypothetical types. The files gave little background on the prisoners, hence the decision categorizing them as over- or undercontrolled relied heavily upon the absence of information about prior acts of violence. The overcontrolled group had reliably higher scores on the O–H Scale, but the difference was modest. Sample size in each phase of the investigation was not large, and criterion keying demands a relatively large ratio of subjects to items for scale validity to stand up in new groups.

How much concurrent validity the Overcontrolled-Hostility Scale has is not currently clear. Deiker (1974) grouped prisoners according to offense and found small but reliable differences in the expected direction. But Fisher (1970) and Mallory and Walker (1972) did not. In studying women accused of crimes, Frederiksen (1976) concluded that the scale measured general assaultiveness rather than overcontrol in the women, unlike its presumed function in men. The idea that male violent offenders fall into the two types received support in an investigation by Blackburn (1968) but not in one by Warder (1969); however, neither investigator employed the O–H Scale nor the same measures of personality. Megargee and his collaborators have devoted their attention to establishing the personality correlates of the scale and not to improving methods for identifying each of the two violent types.

The concurrent validity of the O–H is much too low to arouse optimism about its predictive validity. And most of the investigators matched subjects on several experience table items, like age, race, education, and marital status. To make satisfactory matches of this sort, it is often necessary to discard a sizable number of subjects who may be splendid specimens of the types wanted for study. This procedure is acceptable, provided that the scores of the discarded subjects are like those retained for analysis. Investigations of the O–H Scale do not report this information. It may seem a contradiction, but it is possible to construct a measuring instrument that can test a theoretical proposition, yet be useless for other purposes.

In a different approach to violence and the MMPI, Sines (1966) turned standard delinquency research strategy upside down. Rather than grouping subjects by offenses, then looking for differences on scales, Sines first categorized individuals according to their MMPI profiles, then searched their records for differences via criterion-keying. The profile labeled "4'3" in his system appeared more often in inmates of prisons and mental hospitals, where it was associated with a past history of violence. Pursuing this lead. Davis and Sines (1971) confirmed the relation of the 4'3 profile to violent misbehavior, as did Persons and Marks (1971). Davis (1971) uncovered a similar association in institutionalized women. But Gynther, Altman, and Warbin (1973), examining correlates of a very similar MMPI profile in psychiatric hospital patients, found no association with violent behavior. Validity of the 4'3 profile for predicting violent behavior is unknown, but would have to be quite high to avoid frequent misclassification of nonviolent persons. Frequencies of the profile have varied from 4 to 20 percent in samples of male prisoners, and Davis could locate only thirty-two relevant profiles among 1,643 female MMPI records.

Low predictive validity for conventional estimates of violence potential was the outcome of several studies by Wenk and his associates. Representative of these is the report by Wenk and Emrich (1972), which showed that several combinations of predictors had little practical success in forecasting violent recidivism in youthful offenders. The investigators pointed to the need for better definition of criminal violence and for special techniques to assess it. The definition of criminal violence in terms of criminal convictions suffers from serious shortcomings. According to Toch (1969):

> a Violent Man is a person who has a propensity to take actions that culminate in harm to another. Such a person can be validly and reliably identified only on the basis of his record of violent acts. By "record," I don't mean his police "rap sheet," nor his list of accumulated convictions. Such documents are fragmentary and incomplete and are confined to unrepresentative acts that have come to the attention of authorities (p. 222).

Monahan has emphasized that the low base rate of criminal violence invariably creates a large number of false positives (or false alarms). In seven recent studies, 55 to 99 percent of those predicted to be "dangerous" were not. According to Monahan, violence "is vastly overpredicted, whether simple behavior indicators or sophisticated multivariate analyses are employed and whether psychological tests or thorough psychiatric examinations are performed" (Monahan, in press).

IS THERE AN ANSWER?

What other road is there to travel to locate valid estimates of delinquency potential? Perhaps it is the case study or "clinical" prediction. Toch (1969) came close to this procedure in seeking the causes of criminal violence.

The clinical method uses people on whom training, experience, or talent have conferred sufficient wisdom, to consider as much relevant information as possible about a given individual, then use their insight to make an estimate of delinquency potential. In a crude way, this is what teachers did when they were asked to predict which children might become delinquent. It is what judges supposedly do in passing sentence or granting probation, and what the public expects of parole boards. By careful scrutiny of a person from a variety of perspectives, highly valid estimates may be possible when the human observer is the yardstick. But the procedure does not seem "scientific," and it is expensive, for it must include extensive interviewing.

This viewpoint is not new. Two otherwise different schools of psychology agreed that standard scales have little merit for understanding the origins of individual differences. G. W. Allport (1937), a "self" theorist, advocated the case-study approach with minimal attention to standard personality measures. E. R. Guthrie (1944), the arch-behaviorist of his time, put little value on general personality traits. Both of these men recognized the uniqueness of each human's formative experiences and, one should add, for all but identical siblings, heredity. Endless combinations of these influences meant that standardized personality scales could not have more than a very approximate relation to behavior.

Despite much intervening research, measurement of delinquency potential has not improved since the appearance of an earlier version of this book. No other studies have approached the thoroughness of Hathaway and Monachesi's study of predelinquency. The ideas of the Gluecks still await adequate testing. Whether delinquency potential is a real function of personality is no better established now than then. Unsatisfactory criteria and unfavorable base rates and selection ratios remain major obstacles to progress. Unlike the cumulative effort seen in natural science, work in social science, of which that on delinquency potential is a good example, is noncumulative; new investigators rarely seem to build on what earlier workers found. If progress in reducing crime depends upon improvements in measuring delinqeucy potential, crime is going to continue in the future much as in the past. The silver lining in that cloud, perhaps, is that investigators in the future will find plenty of material to work on.

NOTE

1. In the past, unfortunately, the effectiveness of treatment programs for predelinquents has not been spectacular (Toby, 1965; Berleman & Steinburn, 1969).

REFERENCES

Allport, G. W. *Personality*. New York: Holt, Rinehart and Winston, 1937.
Anastasia, A. *Psychological testing* (4th ed.). New York: Macmillan, 1976.
Arnold, W. R. A functional explanation of recidivism. *Journal of Criminal Law, Criminology & Police Science*, 1965, *56*, 405–413.

Berleman, W. C., & Steinburn, T. W. The value and validity of delinquency prevention programs. *Crime & Delinquency,* 1969, *15,* 471–478.

Black, W. G. The description and prediction of recidivism and rehabilitation among youthful offenders by the use of the Minnesota Multiphasic Personality Inventory. *Dissertation Abstracts,* 1967, *28*(4–B), 1691.

Blackburn, R. Personality in relation to extreme aggression in psychiatric offenders. *British Journal of Psychiatry,* 1968, *114,* 821–828.

Buikhuisen, W., & Hoekstra, H. A. Factors related to recidivism. *British Journal of Criminology,* 1974, *14,* 63–69.

Buros, O. K. *Personality tests and reviews* (II). Highland Park, N.J.: Gryphon, 1975.

Callard, M. P. Significant differences between recidivists and nonrecidivists. *British Journal of Criminology,* 1967, *7,* 93–102.

Cassel, R. N., & Blum, L. P. Computer assist counseling (COASCON) for the prevention of delinquent behavior among teenagers and youth. *Sociology & Social Research,* 1969, *54,* 72–79.

Craig, M. M., & Glick, S. J. Ten years' experience with the Glueck Social Prediction Table. *Crime & Delinquency,* 1963, *9,* 249–261.

Craig, M. M., & Glick, S. J. Application of the Glueck Social Prediction Table on an ethnic basis. *Crime & Delinquency,* 1965, *11,* 175–178.

Cowden, J. E. Predicting institutional adjustment and recidivism in delinquent boys. *Journal of Criminal Law, Criminology & Police Science,* 1966, *57,* 39–44.

Dahlstrom, W. G., Welsh, G. S., & Dahlstrom, L. E. *An MMPI handbook.* Minneapolis: University of Minnesota Press, 1972.

Davis, K. R. The actuarial development of a 4'3 MMPI profile. *Dissertation Abstracts International,* 1971, *32*(2–B), 1207.

Davis, K. R., & Sines, J. O. An antisocial behavior pattern associated with a specific MMPI profile. *Journal of Consulting & Clinical Psychology,* 1971, *36,* 228–234.

Dean, C. W., & Duggan, T. J. Problems in parole prediction: A historical analysis. *Social Problems,* 1968, *15,* 450–459.

Deiker, T. E. A cross-validation of scales of aggression in male criterion groups. *Journal of Consulting & Clinical Psychology,* 1974, *42,* 196–202.

Eysenck, H. J. *Crime and personality.* Boston: Houghton Mifflin, 1964.

Eysenck, S. B. G., & Eysenck, H. J. Crime and personality: An empirical study of the three-factor theory. *British Journal of Criminology,* 1970, *10,* 225–239.

Eysenck, S. B. G., & Eysenck, H. J. Crime and personality: Item analysis of questionnaire responses. *British Journal of Criminology,* 1971, *11,* 49–62.

Feldhusen, J. F., Benning, J. J., & Thurston, J. R. Prediction of delinquency, adjustment, and academic achievement over a 5-year period with the Kvaraceus Delinquency Proneness Scale. *Journal of Educational Research,* 1972, *65,* 375–381.

Feldhusen, J. F., Thurston, J. R., & Benning, J. J. A longitudinal study of delinquency and other aspects of children's behaviour. *International Journal of Criminology & Penology,* 1973, *1,* 341–351.

Fisher, G. Discriminating violence emanating from over-controlled versus under-controlled aggressivity. *British Journal of Social & Clinical Psychology,* 1970, *9,* 54–59.

Frank, C. H. The prediction of recidivism among young adult offenders by the Recidivism-Rehabilitation scale and index. *Dissertation Abstracts International,* 1971, *32*(1–B), 557.

Frederiksen, S. J. A comparison of selected personality and history variables in highly violent, mildly violent, and non-violent female offenders. *Dissertation Abstracts International,* 1976, *36*(6–B), 3036.

Glueck, S., & Glueck, E. T. *Unraveling juvenile delinquency.* New York: Commonwealth Fund, 1950.

Glueck, S., & Glueck, E. T. *Predicting delinquency and crime.* Cambridge, Mass.: Harvard University Press, 1959.

Gough, H. G., & Peterson, D. R. The identification and measurement of predispositional factors in crime and delinquency. *Journal of Consulting Psychology,* 1952, *16,* 207–212.

Gough, H. G., Wenk, E. A., & Rozynko, V. V. Parole outcome as predicted from the CPI, the MMPI, and a base expectancy table. *Journal of Abnormal Psychology,* 1965, *70,* 432–441.

Guilford, J. P. Will the real factor of Extraversion-Introversion please stand up? A reply to Eysenck. *Psychological Bulletin,* 1977, *84,* 412–416.

Guthrie, E. R. Personality in terms of associative learning. In J. McV. Hunt (Ed.), *Personality and the behavior disorders.* New York: Ronald, 1944, 49–68.

Gynther, M. D., Altman, H., & Warbin, R. W. A new actuarial-empirical automated MMPI interpretive program: The 4–3/3–4 code type. *Journal of Clinical Psychology,* 1973, *29,* 229–231.

Hathaway, S. R., & McKinley, J. C. A multiphasic personality schedule (Minnesota): I. Construction of the schedule. *Journal of Psychology,* 1940, *10,* 249–254.

Hathaway, S. R., & Monachesi, E. D. *Analyzing and predicting juvenile delinquency and crime.* Minneapolis: University of Minnesota Press, 1953.

Hathaway, S. R., & Monachesi, E. D. *Adolescent personality and behavior.* Minneapolis: University of Minnesota Press, 1963.

Hampton, A. C. Longitudinal study of personality of children who became delinquent using the Personality Inventory for Children (PIC). *Dissertation Abstracts International.* 1970, *30*(10–B), 4792.

Hart, H. Predicting probation success. *Journal of Criminal Law & Criminology,* 1923, *14,* 405–413.

Hoghughi, M. S., & Forrest, A. R. Eysenck's theory of criminality. *British Journal of Criminology,* 1970, *10,* 240–254.

Jenkins, R. L., & Blodgett, E. Prediction of success or failure of delinquent boys from sentence completion. *American Journal of Orthopsychiatry,* 1960, *30,* 741–756.

Kelley, F. J., Veldman, D. J., & McGuire, C. Multiple discrimination prediction of delinquency and school dropouts. *Educational & Psychological Measurement,* 1964, *24,* 535–544.

Khleif, B. B. Teachers as predictors of juvenile delinquency and psychiatric disturbance. *Social Problems,* 1964, *11,* 270–282.

Kvaraceus, W. D. *KD Proneness Scale.* Yonkers, N.Y.: World Book, 1950.

Kvaraceus, W. D. Forecasting delinquency: A three-year experiment. *Exceptional Children,* 1961, *27,* 429–435.

Mack, J. L. The MMPI and recidivism. *Journal of Abnormal Psychology,* 1969, *74,* 612–614.

Mallory, C. H., & Walker, C. E. MMPI O–H scale responses of assaultive and nonassaultive prisoners and associated life history variables. *Educational & Psychological Measurement,* 1972, *32,* 1125–1128.

Mandel, M. G., & Barron, A. J. The MMPI and criminal recidivism. *Journal of Criminal Law, Criminology & Police Science,* 1966, *57,* 35–38.

Mannheim, H., & Wilkins, L. T. *Prediction methods in relation to borstal training.* London: Her Majesty's Stationery Office, 1955.

Manning, P. K. Deviance and dogma. *British Journal of Criminology,* 1975, *15,* 1–20.

Megargee, E. I. Undercontrolled and overcontrolled personality types in extreme anti-social aggression. *Psychological Monographs,* 1966, *80,* No. 611.

Megargee, E. I., Cook, P. E., & Mendelsohn, G. A. Development and validation of an MMPI scale of assaultiveness in overcontrolled individuals. *Journal of Abnormal Psychology,* 1967, *72,* 519–528.

Monahan, J. The prediction of violent criminal behavior: A methodological critique and prospectus. In National Research Council (Ed.), *Deterrence and incapacitation: Estimating the effects of criminal sanctions on crime rates.* Washington, D.C.: National Academy of Sciences, in press.

Neithercutt, M. G. Parole violation patterns and commitment offense. *Journal of Research in Crime & Delinquency,* 1972, *9,* 87–98.

Ohlin, L. E., & Duncan, O. D. The efficiency of prediction in criminology. *American Journal of Sociology,* 1949, *54,* 441–452.

Panton, J. E. Use of the MMPI as an index to successful parole. *Journal of Criminal Law, Criminology & Police Science,* 1962, *53,* 484–488.

Persons, R. W., & Marks, P. A. The violent 4–3 MMPI personality type. *Journal of Consulting & Clinical Psychology,* 1971, *36,* 189–196.

Riddle, M., & Roberts, A. H. Delinquency, delay of gratification, recidivism, and the Porteus Maze Tests. *Psychological Bulletin,* 1977, *84,* 417–425.

Roberts, A. H., Erikson, R. V., Riddle, Mary, & Bacon, Jane G. Demographic variables, base rates, and personality characteristics associated with recidivism in male delinquents. *Journal of Consulting & Clinical Pspchology,* 1974, *42,* 833–841.

Rogers, J. W. Parole prediction in three dimensions: Theory, prediction, and perception. *Sociology & Social Research,* 1968, *52,* 377–391.

Rose, G. Early identification of delinquents. *British Journal of Criminology,* 1967, *7,* 6–35.

Scarpitti, F. R., Murray, E., Dinitz, S., & Reckless, W. C. The "good" boy in a high delinquency area: Four years later. *American Sociological Review,* 1960, *25,* 555–558.

Sines, J. O. Actuarial methods in personality assessment. In B. H. Maher (Ed.), *Progress in experimental personality research* (III). New York: Academic Press, 1966, 133–193.

Smith, J., & Lanyon, R. I. Prediction of juvenile probation violators. *Journal of Consulting & Clinical Psychology,* 1968, *32,* 54–58.

Stott, D. H. A new delinquency prediction instrument using behavioural indications. *International Journal of Social Psychiatry,* 1960, *6,* 195–205.

Stott, D. H., & Wilson, D. M. The prediction of early-adult criminality from school-age behaviour. *International Journal of Social Psychiatry,* 1967–1968, *14,* 5–8.

Takagi, P. T. The effect of parole agents' judgments on recidivism rates. *Psychiatry,* 1969, *32,* 192–199.

Toby, J. An evaluation of early identification and intensive treatment programs for pre-delinquents. *Social Problems,* 1965, *13,* 160–175.

Toch, H. *Violent men.* Chicago: Aldine, 1969.

Trevvett, N. B. Identifying delinquency-prone children. *Crime & Delinquency,* 1965, *11,* 186–191.

Vold, G. B. Comments on "The efficiency of prediction in criminology." *American Journal of Sociology,* 1949, *54,* 451–452.

Walker, N. D. Lost causes in criminology. In R. Hood (Ed.), *Crime and public policy*. London: Heineman, 1974, 47–62.

Warder, J. Two studies of violent offenders. *British Journal of Criminology*, 1969, *9*, 389–393.

Weis, K. The Glueck Social Prediction Table: An unfulfilled promise. *Journal of Criminal Law, Criminology & Police Science*, 1974, *65*, 397–404.

Wenk, E. A., & Emrich, R. L. Assaultive youth: An exploratory study of the assaultive experience and assaultive potential of California Youth Authority wards. *Journal of Research in Crime & Delinquency*, 1972, *9*, 171–196.

Werner, E., & Gallistet, E. Prediction of outstanding performance, delinquency, and emotional disturbance from childhood evaluations. *Child Development*, 1961, *32*, 255–260.

Wetzel, H., Shapiro, R. J., & Wagner, E. E. Prediction of recidivism among juvenile delinquents with the Hand Test. *Journal of Projective Techniques & Personality Assessment*, 1967, *31*, 69–72.

PART THREE

Understanding and Treating the Offender

chapter 11

Perspectives on Treatment

Hans Toch

Some controversies about rehabilitative interventions are reminiscent of the theological debate which is reputed to have taken place (after hours) in a student dormitory at a seminary. According to the story, the extracurricular argument waxed heatedly until one participant turned to the other and said with chagrine, "I see it now: What you call 'devil' is what I call 'god,' and vice versa."

Examples of god-devil conflicts abound in the rehabilitation or treatment area.[1] The behavior modification movement, for instance (which in practice advocates rewarding offenders for behavior such as school attendance, neatness, and politeness), is equated by some critics with forcible brainwashing. Books that address issues of behavior modification or "behavior control" (such as London, 1969) talk about interventions such as lobotomy, electrical stimulation of the brain, psychotropic medication, and aversive conditioning featuring high voltage shocks. A prison expert, Tom Wicker of the *New York Times,* in a column dated February 8, 1974, told his readers that behavior modification "usually includes drug experimentation and in all too many cases, it is aimed more at producing docile prisoners than upright citizens." Such attacks are not merely semantic hairsplittings, but are strongly felt summaries of "devil" connotations attached by some persons to practices that are advanced and defended by other men on humanitarian grounds.

The word "helping"—as in "helping professions"—has acquired pejorative connotations in the minds of many persons. For research-oriented counseling theorists (Rogers, 1961; Truax & Carkhuff, 1967), a "helping relationship" was one in which an empathetic, warm, genuine, and insightful change agent (of almost any therapeutic persuasion) could demonstrably stimulate growth and self-governing behavior in a previously constrained and non-autonomous client. To antitherapy critics, however, the word "helping" connotes patronizing, dependency-inducing, quasi-blackmailing relationships in which status-seeking therapists cater to client immaturity and manipulate client vulnerabilities.

Discussions of treatment issues must occur against "loaded" backdrops, in part because interventions *do* pose ethical issues, which we ignore at our peril (Brodsky, 1977).[2] One issue, which we have mentioned before (Chapter 4) is that of the voluntariness of client participation. This issue is particularly germane to the criminal justice field, because convicted offenders are powerless clients, while criminal justice staff members have all sorts of incentives to "convince" the offender to "participate" in their programs.

This criminal justice issue becomes blatant in prison settings. It becomes particularly obtrusive where the inmates' chances for early release hinges on his "demonstrating a desire to improve himself." This occurs most clearly where the inmate is indeterminately sentenced and a parole board (with the advice of treatment staff) decides whether he is "ready" for freedom. The principle of indeterminacy has been historically linked to the idea of treatment, in that legislators assumed that rehabilitation has a specifiable end-point. This assumption is questionable. Moreover, useful therapeutic work can be done under time constraints. Freud himself set time limits for the termination of certain patients, and he reported increments in the productivity of his analytic sessions as deadlines approached (Freud, 1963a).

Except for clients who are masochistic or who are extremely involved in therapy, we can expect to encounter unconscious resentment where treatment can deprive the person of his freedom. Such resentment enters into "resistances" to therapy which—even if the client is not aware of them—make progress more problematic. Truly uncontaminated treatment relationships can only occur where staff do not "judge" clients or control their fate, or act as gatekeepers to the streets.

The role of the therapist himself, as well as that of the client, can be encumbered by "gatekeeping" functions. Therapy is prototypically collaborative change, in which client and therapist work together to free the client of problems (Freud, 1953). Collaborative change strategies are incompatible with conflict strategies, in which the theme of power is very much in the foreground. Where collaborative strategies demand honesty and openness, for example, conflict demands dissembling. A "gatekeeping" agent sits in judgment over his client, but he must withhold judgment in therapy, where one must be nonjudgmental. The roles are not only difficult to reconcile, but mutually incompatible.

Where therapists do opt out of "gatekeeping," they cannot prevent external gatekeepers from seeing treatment as a favorable indicator of client adjustment. Such external judgments, however, are present in any therapeutic

A youth comes into the consulting room. At first glance he seems to be the bully type. If we take a stern tone with him, he rejects us immediately and we can never get a transference established. If we are cordial and friendly, he becomes distrustful and rejects us or he takes this for weakness on our part and reacts with increased roughness. If we approach a boy who is intellectually superior with a severe air, he feels himself immediately on sure ground and master of the situation because he meets that attitude often in life. He looks with suspicion on people who are nice to him and is more than ever on his guard. The timid ones, who come in frightened, are easily reduced to tears by a stern demeanor and fall into a state which may be confused with sulkiness. . . .

I consider this first moment of our coming together of the utmost importance. It is more than a "feeling out" of the situation; it must have the appearance of certainty and sureness and must be put through as quickly as possible because in most cases it forms the foundation for our later relationship. The adolescent does the same thing when he comes into contact with me. He wants to know right away what kind of person he is dealing with. Children usually try to orient themselves quickly, but for the most part they are not clever about it. The adolescent, however, often develops an amazing ability at this. We can observe a momentary gleam in the eye, a hardly perceptible movement of the lips, an involuntary gesture, a "watchful waiting" attitude, although he may be in a state of conflict. The older he is, the harder it is to know whether he will prove stubborn, or openly scornful and resistant. It is especially difficult when he assumes an air of sincerity or unctuous submissiveness (Aichhorn, 1955, pp. 99–100).

Voluntariness can obviously not be induced by wading into personally sensitive areas, but is earned through the creation of a reassuring and safe climate. The worker wins over a client if he communicates genuinely friendly interest in the client's problems, and shows himself (if he can) to be very different from the threatening figures the involuntary client knows, fears, and expects. Communication is secured at whatever conditions the client sets, and at whatever level the client welcomes or can tolerate. In talking about his own techniques, Aichhorn writes:

I usually begin with a friendly look or attitude, sometimes I say, "How do you do," or I may only shake hands in silence. I say that there is nothing here to be afraid of, that this is neither a police station nor a court. Sometimes I tell a joke by way of introduction. This gives me an opportunity to size up the situation. We sit down opposite each other. . . .

In a natural fashion, I begin to speak of things which interest most boys but are in no way connected with their dissocial behavior. Eight out of ten are interested in football. One must know the teams, the best players, the last match, the scores, etc. Less often one finds a contact through books, mostly through adventure and detective stories. It is often easy to talk about movies and in this way make the child lose his caution.

With little girls I talk about fairy tales and games. Often one does not need to go far afield. A remark about the clothes or jewelry they wear may start the ball rolling. I let the half-grown girls tell me about styles in clothes, in haircuts, or the price of toilet articles. I ask the youngest children who are afraid to talk what they like to eat; we discuss desserts and candies. Thus I reach topics which the child carries on in the conversation (pp. 99, 101).

Voluntary participation must be worked for, and relationships must be painstakingly built. Treatment staff do not sell themselves through their credentials, but do so by showing that they deserve the trust of clients. They cannot do this if they play enforcement roles, or other inquisitorial games that criminal justice agents frequently play. The following vignette (a verbatim interview by Aichhorn) illustrates the contrast between a trust bid and a "cops and robbers" approach:

"Do you know where you are?"
"No."
"In the child-guidance clinic of the Juvenile Court."
"Oh yes. My father wants to put me in a reform school."
"Your father has told me what has happened and I'd like to help you."
"It's no use." He shrugged his shoulders and turned away.
"Certainly it's no use, if you don't want help."
"You can't help me."
"I know you don't have much confidence in me; we don't know each other yet."
"Not that, but anyway it's no use." He showed the same hopeless, uncooperative air.
"Are you willing to talk to me?"
"Why not?"
"I must ask you various questions and I'll make you a proposition."
"What?" The tone betrayed expectation.
"That you don't answer any questions you don't like."
"How do you mean?" He was astonished and incredulous.
"The questions you don't like you need not answer or you may tell me it's none of my business."
"Why do you say that?"
"Because I'm not a detective nor a policeman and I don't need to know everything. Anyway you wouldn't tell me the truth if I asked questions you didn't like."
"How do you know that?"
"Because that is what everybody does and you are no exception. I wouldn't tell everything either to someone whom I'd met for the first time."
"But if I talk and tell you lies, will you know that too?"
"No, but that would be too bad. And anyway it isn't necessary because I don't want to force you to answer me."
"At home they always said if I'd talk, nothing bad would happen to me, but when I did it was always much worse. So I quit talking."
"But here it's a little different. I'll be satisfied with what you are willing to tell. But I'd like to be sure you are telling me the truth."
"Good."
"You agree?" I offered him my hand which he took eagerly.
"Agreed." (Aichhorn, 1955, pp. 74–75).

These illustrations of Aichhorn's technique for reaching involuntary clients are paralleled in other settings in which treatment staff have worked with offenders. Street gang workers, for example, have had to build rapport with suspicious and hostile gang members, who were often strongly resistant. In one of his books Spergel (1967) notes that:

> in the early stages of contact the worker may be relegated to the status of undesirable alien. Covertly or overtly he is addressed as the "man" (policeman), "son of a bitch," "rat," "jerk," "faggot," "sucker," "creep," etc. Some of these names, and the roles they signify, may continue to be attributed to him for a very long time. Indeed, particularly with those groups which are highly criminal in orientation, the worker may remain a threat, at least in some aspects of his functioning, throughout his entire relationship with the members. At best, a relationship of this kind is characterized by considerable ambivalence of feelings on the part of the group (p. 88).

The worker deals with such resistances by hanging around, being helpful, showing interest in group activities, and participating where he is permitted. A New York gang worker writes in a report

> I was invited by Tony to sit and fill Pete's place since Pete had to leave. I told Tony that I would like to but I wasn't familiar with the game of pinochle. All of a sudden Tony took it upon himself to give me the rules and regulations of the game, which he did remarkably well. I made a couple of mistakes which Tony corrected. Probably for the first time now, they were talking to me for a full five or ten minutes, teaching me how to play pinochle. Tony was my partner and after about the fourth or fifth hand I got the gist of it fairly well. Every now and then Tony would help me with the count or Tommy, who was opposing me, and Blackie would help (New York City Youth Board, 1960, p. 128).

The hope of such moves is that limited acceptance (into activities such as pinochle games) can lead to more substantial involvements, and to the cementing of relationships.

Resistances to treatment are legitimate, and must be expected. The therapeutic agent is a change agent, and people are not obligated to change unless and until they want to. We are never ethically or legally entitled to force a client to reform (Morris, 1974). What we may be entitled to, however, is to make ourselves available to involuntary clients and to convince them (if we have the skill) to relate to us, to share their problems with us, and, ultimately, to consider options for change. Rapport is a first step in the transition from involuntariness to voluntariness. It is no more intrusive or coercive than other human contacts in social life. It is a necessary, *but not a sufficient* step to promote change, and cannot really impair or imperil human integrity. Street gang workers, for example, have gained skill in rapport-building to such an extent that tough gangs clamored for their services. The gangs with attached workers, however, frequently ended up engaging in *more* delinquency than comparable gangs with no workers (Klein, 1971).

LOVE IS NOT ENOUGH

There is a difference between preconditions for change, forces that induce change, actual change, and permanent change. One reason why we must match change clients and change strategies is because in treatment (as elsewhere) what helps the goose may be useless (or destructive) for the gander. Therapeutic communities (Chapter 20) and halfway houses (Chapter 15) are powerful change vehicles when they are used for relevant clients. Each, however, can prove fatal when the client-strategy "match" is inappropriate. A sociopath can easily destroy a halfway house, while resourceless men can be eaten alive in the intense confrontations of a therapeutic milieu (Whitely, Briggs, & Turner, 1973).

This fact about outcomes is crucial, because it relates to the contention that "nothing ever works." In reviewing treatment effectiveness, our crime-related experience is no different from other treatment-outcome research. Research conducted on kinds of therapy has shown that the "right" therapy helps people, and the "wrong" therapy harms them. If you *average* studies that sometiems assess the "right" and sometimes the "wrong" therapy, "good" and "bad" changes statistically cancel each other out, and we conclude that "nothing makes any difference" (Truax & Carkhuff, 1967).

Our current cynicism takes us one step beyond early disappointments relating to offender therapy, which stemmed from the discovery that *preconditions* for change (in the shape of client rapport with a friendly professional) are not effective vehicles for changing people—particularly for changing serious offenders, or offenders with serious problems. This insight principally came from the Cambridge-Sommerville Study (Powers & Witmer, 1951; McCord & McCord, 1959), which was the most ambitious therapy-oriented delinquency prevention program that has ever been undertaken.

The Cambridge-Somerville Study was inaugurated by Professor Richard Clark Cabot of Harvard, who also financed the project. Gordon Allport (1951) summarizes Cabot's views about how to reform delinquents.

> Granted that genuine reformation of criminals is a rare phenomenon, he had none the less observed that in all cases known to him, "there has been at least one necessary condition: *that someone should come to know and to understand the man in so intimate and friendly a way that he comes to a better understanding of himself and to a truer comprehension of the world he lives in.*" The personal factor is the indispensible factor. Friendly understanding—implying an ingredient of love—is the basis of all therapy (pp. 5–6).

The hypothesis that was generated by Cabot was that adult friendship would in itself be influential enough to produce law-abiding behavior among predelinquents. To test this hypothesis, Cabot sent an army of child-care workers into the field to offer warmth, contact, and support to 325 boys who had been rated as predelinquents. These boys were randomly selected out of a pool of 750 boys, the remainder of whom remained "untreated," and provided a control group. The study lasted close to ten years, after which its results were carefully assessed.

Cabot's workers—who came from a variety of backgrounds—mostly established good working relationships with boys, the boys' families, and (to a lesser extent) their schools. They provided "friendship" but they also sometimes offered supporting services, and often shared activities with the boys.

At the conclusion of the project period, delinquency statistics (police contacts, court appearances, imprisonment) were collated, and the boys were clinically rated for terminal "adjustment." On both counts, Cabot's beneficiaries proved no better off than the group of control boys, despite the astronomical investment of money and manpower. The project failed most dismally for boys who grew up in unfavorable home situations—who were reared (or nonreared) by unloving, rejecting, inconsistent parents, and who experienced seriously conflict-ridden homes (McCord & McCord, 1959). In Allport's words, these boys were "failures that could be traced to a wretched emotional situation in the home, so evil in its impact upon the boy that an outside friend could not offset its ravages" (Allport, 1951, p. xxiii). Traumatized boys, writes Allport, "generally develop unwholesome, often neurotic, defenses against their home situations . . . are unable to surmount their handicap, not even with the aid of counselors who would gladly serve them as parent-surrogates" (Allport, 1951, p. xxv).

Counselors could successfully supplement partially resourceless homes (particularly, in the area of tangible services) but they could not neutralize the impact of early influences. Such influences, write McCord and McCord, would have to be addressed in a therapeutic milieu (Chapter 20), because such an approach fills emotional vacuums and inculcates values, and "mobilize(s) the child's entire environment in an attempt to alter its behavior" (McCord & McCord, 1959, p. 181).

McCord and McCord argue for *differential* treatment, a concept which was not presupposed in Cabot's strategy. McCord and McCord write that "a treatment program tailored to the needs of each type of delinquent would, in all probabililty, meet with more success than a program which disregards the differences in causative background" (McCord & McCord, 1959, p. 185).

There is one dramatic feature to the differential treatment issue which is implicit in the Cambridge-Somerville study, and is extremely troublesome: offenders who are most amenable to treatment impact and most easily rehabilitated *may generally also be less serious, less recidivistic, and less disturbed.* In supplying treatment, we can thus select as our clients offenders who are almost guaranteed to respond to our warm, congenial ministrations. In such an approach, our "cure" rate would be high, and our impact on crime would be minimal or nonexistent. We can, by contrast, select offenders who are "bad risks," and if we do, we would sweat and toil in unfamiliar terrain, and we must expect client ingratitude and an excellent chance of failure. Programs for serious, disturbed, and recidivistic offenders also have to be intensive (thus, expensive) because the problems they address are relatively chronic.

This makes such programs unattractive for potential sponsors (such as legislatures and correctional managers) as well as for the treatment agents themselves. The idea is inviting—to supply psychologists, probation officers, counselors, and parole agents of the sort who work in the Cambridge-Somerville tradition. As far as rehabilitation is concerned, of course, this practice yields predictably unimpressive returns.

The "differential" model assumes that we can accommodate the amenable offender (with human contacts, supportive services, etc.) while we evolve more radical interventions that are designed to resocialize the patterned, disturbed, or hardened offender. This always involves meaningful classification, so that we can avoid wasting "big guns" where slingshots will do, while we helplessly observe the failure of short-term counseling to affect ingrained psychopathology or well-established patterns of life.

The following chapters are premised on the assumption that we can categorize or "type" offenders in ways that permit us to "match" them, as *change problems*, with interventions, *as change strategies*. In every case, this process entails a diagnostic effort, which defines the change problem that is represented by the client. Such diagnosis tells us whether a delinquent is a product of peer pressure or is emotionally disturbed (Chapter 12); whether a violent offender has a low boiling point or over-rigid controls (Chapter 13); or whether the offender has a deficient conscience or a character disorder (Chapter 14). It tells us whether an alcohol offender is addicted or not (Chapter 15), and defines the career stage of the drug offender (Chapter 16). It differentiates the disturbed sex offender from the sexually disturbed offender (Chapter 17). It tells us whether the white-collar offender is (or is not) a product of his setting (Chapter 18). Such distinctions are not merely of "academic" interest in helping us to understand the individual, but suggest what we must do, or not do, to make him law-abiding.

WHO SHOULD BE TREATED, WHERE?

Detached workers (including those of the Cambridge-Somerville project) raise the issue of treatment *outside* the criminal justice system for criminal justice purposes. Similar possibilities are raised where we talk about private therapists dealing with deviant patients, as in Chapter 17. And Thomas Szasz makes a plea (in Chapter 5) for a separation of Therapy and State, which implies that formal treatment should be conducted under nonagency auspices.

Several issues come to mind when we think about treatment "outside the system." One is the issue of prevention, which means dealing with *potential* clients of the "official" system in the hope of interrupting degenerating careers leading to arrest and conviction. Such programs are difficult to justify where a client has done nothing at all; after all (as we have seen in Chapter 10), the chances are excellent that he never will. But there are subthreshhold offenses, such as gang fights and classroom disruptions, which differ from formal crimes in degree only. We may legitimately approach nonarrested offenders, or refer them to formal programs, in response to *current* acts which may be stepping-stones to more serious *future* acts.

There is no real complexity about offenders who are self-referred to mental health settings because they feel themselves sliding into criminal careers. Similarly, exoffenders may be intent on self-help opportunities to prevent re-entry into criminal justice settings. Programs for exoffenders—in the shape of peer groups and residential therapeutic communities, are currently pro-liferating in number.

More indirectly, we can conceive of staff and therapeutic programs that are *nominally* located in criminal justice contexts, but are separated from decisions that affect the fate of clients. We have noted in Chapter 4 that prison work supervisors, who are noncustodial civilians, have impressive re-habilitative potential. The same point has been made about good prison chap-lains. Therapeutic communities are often physically quartered in prisons, but are administratively independent. Mental hygiene staff can operate in penal institutions under auspices that are entirely external. It is even con-ceptually possible for a person to be paid by the system, but to subserve "professional" goals. Such a person is not the tool of the system nor an instru-ment of the client; he provides skills to help solve human problems, in the way the prison surgeon removes appendixes or mends bones.

To the extent to which services are publicly supplied, we must make deci-sions about treatment emphases and allocations of resources. In this connec-tion, past dangerousness which is patterned is a criterion that *might* possibly give treatment priority, *provided* the offender also has a problem or a con-dition that we know how to address (Toch, 1977a). The dangerousness of nonpatterned offenders is irrelevant, because it cannot be predicted, and notoriousness or nuisance-value is nontreatment-relevant.

The logic of our concentrating on treating the youngest offenders is in-escapable. There is almost universal agreement by crime experts of every persuasion that the roots of criminal behavior are often embedded very early in life. If past experience piles up around the offender in cumulative fashion, early roots—fertilized by the slum, the prison, the frustrations of school, the unhappy home—can soon grow too large to unearth. The more promptly a remedial environment is brought to bear, the better the chance of prevent-ing adult criminality, and the less strenuous the task. Early diagnosis and treatment must thus be one of the prime objects in correction.

This does not mean, of course, that we must "treat" juveniles while we "punish" adults. Resources must be deployed strictly in relation to potential benefits, and age is not nearly so important as personality in defining the appropriateness of treatment and its potential payoffs. We have mentioned this fact before, but it must be deliberately underscored because the tragedy of the adult's wasted life is not nearly so obvious to the public as that of "the kid who needs help."

I am also not implying, as some do (e.g., Menninger, 1968), that it might be a good idea to routinely subject all offenders to clinical interviews and testing. Such activity is transparently wasteful where no real treatment opportunities exist. It also adds paper to folders and wastes resources. Moreover, given pressures to overpredict or overclassify (Chapter 10), clinical diagnosis can produce a proliferation of unflattering labels, such as Inadequate Personality (schnook), Dissociative Features (looks nutty), or Sociopath (crumb). These labels come in infinite pejorative varieties, such as Sociopathic Personality with Dissociative Features (nutty crumb), or Inadequate Personality with Sociopathic Features (crumby schnook).

Meaningful classification must yield well-rounded portraits of offenders as human beings and as social beings. To do so, it must consider *all* aspects of the person, including his strengths and weaknesses, liabilities and potentials, his destructive and constructive experiences. It must also not be sociologically nor clinically biased, which means that it must neither ignore the person nor shortchange his formative environment and culture. Classification must also be assignment-relevant. This means that all staff in the diagnosis business must know what treatment modalities (and other assignment options) we have available, and they must supply information that helps us to sensibly and humanely deploy our ecological resources (Toch, 1977b).

WHY AND WHEREFORE "TREATMENT"?

Are treatment programs for offenders (a) appropriate? (b) ethically defensible (do we have a right to treat)? One argument answering "no" to both questions relies on the definition of treatment as a response to illness. Van den Haag's syllogism, for instance, rests on the premises: "Only diseases can be cured by treatment. Few offenders are sick" (Van den Haag, 1975, p. 190).

The issue is compounded by the controversy (joined in this book between Chapters 5 and 17) about whether the term "illness" is an appropriate designation when paired with "mental." If we accept Szasz' argument (Szasz, 1961) that the nonphysical problems psychologists and psychiatrists treat are interpersonal difficulties, and are not "illness" in the sense that measles and cancer are "illness," we could not speak of offenders as being "more sick" or "less sick" than other persons. The controversy turns, rather, around the question, are offenders similar or dissimilar to persons to whom we offer rehabilitative services in the free world, who benefit from such services?[3]

This question relates to the shape of the human services industry rather than to the prevalence of pathology inside or outside the criminal justice system. The human services industry is changing, which complicates the issue. Our question necessarily relates differently to *traditional psychotherapy* as against *expanded* conceptions of treatment, such as community psychiatry, the use of new types of change agents in mental health roles, and so on.

From the *traditional* perspective, a number of offender groupings qualify neatly as therapy clients without change of criteria. For example, addicts in the free world are seen as in need of services, because these persons are helplessly constrained to behave in wasteful, silly, or self-destructive ways, which makes it difficult for them to lead normal and satisfying lives. In this respect there is no difference between obsessive-compulsiveness that involves constant handwashing, and addictive drug abuse or alcohol abuse (Chapters 15, 16), or compulsive deviant sexual behavior (Chapter 17). The fact that a man is in prison does not change the fact that he may be the captive of his sex drive, rather than a person who governs his sexual impulses and the way he expresses them.

There is also no difficulty about whether or not "neurotics" are entitled to treatment under traditional criteria. Psychoanalytic therapy was born to deal with the suffering (anxieties, psychosomatic symptoms, and dysfunctional behavior) of neurotics and borderline psychotics, who happen to be (and in the free world, still generally are) middle class persons who could afford therapy, and who could "buy" treatment services to "free" them of "symptoms."

We have seen (Chapters 7 and 9) and shall see again (Chapter 12) that the delinquent population contains its share of neurotic youths, though these youths are not usually middle class and unlikely—left to their devices—to seek therapeutic assistance. We have addressed the latter issue (voluntariness) already. What concerns us now is that these delinquents are *not* different —in their high anxiety level, for example—from conventional therapy clients. But does the delinquent's neurosis "produce" or "cause" his delinquency? If it does, are we entitled to treat the youth simply because he is captive? If not, isn't treatment wasteful?

The first question demands a yes/no answer which is probably nonsensical. Freud treated many women to free them of neurotic symptoms. Would this necessarily improve the marriages of these women, or ensure them careers in business? Is the Death of the "free world's" Salesman produced by *his* neurosis? Does Sammy's neurosis make him Run, at other people's expense? To answer "yes" or "no" means that we pretend to know what hypothetical alternate options or life-patterns a person has, and we would have to feel that we can "dissect" a person's neurotic feelings out of his or her attitudes, and traits, leaving a residual person (nonneurotic) about whom we can talk. It is *in principle* possible to make a nonneurotic delinquent out of a neurotic delinquent, and also, to make a nondelinquent neurotic out of a delinquent neurotic. In the criminal justice system, we cannot justify the former; in the free world, we cannot conceive of the latter.

Therapeutic practitioners generally assume that: (1) clients of therapy are partially limited or constrained by motives over which they have no control; (2) therapy (if successful) frees clients from internal constraints and makes them able to govern their conduct more fully. The hope is that *destructive* conduct would usually fall under the "constrained" heading rather than in the "freely elected" category. To the extent to which this is the case, traditional therapy could proceed to reduce the chances of a person's criminality, in that it would "free" him to behave in noncriminal ways. A person who is neither inhibited nor confused (a well-adjusted professional thief) would not be a candidate for treatment. A person who is personally constrained but autonomously criminal (a neurotic professional thief), might become a more effective offender after treatment.

The open-ended view of therapy is hard to defend in criminal justice settings, and it poses fine ethical issues in the free world. Such issues are neatly resolved only through the notion advocated by proponents of behavior modification (Bandura, 1968) and of allied approaches that we try to specify *goals* of treatment in terms of *directions of behavior change* that are mutually agreeable to client and therapist. This step removes our ethical dilemma where offenders and therapists agree that crime-free behavior must be the end result of correctional treatment. By the same token, we are left with questions about what we should do, if (1) the offender has problems which have nothing to do with a criminal career, (2) the offender wishes to be crime-free, but is well-adjusted, and (3) the offender has problems related to his criminality but tells us, "I'll pay my debt, but you won't get inside my head or otherwise monkey with me."

Non-crime-related problems are *least* troublesome. Criminal justice staff are custodians of offenders, and have social service obligations as well as criminal justice goals. Though staff can decide where—collectively and individually—to "draw the line," they must *minimally* ensure the health and welfare of clients.[4] An inmate is *entitled* to have his appendix removed and his cavities filled. He is similarly *entitled* to see a psychiatrist if he hallucinates, if he suffers from insomnia, contemplates suicide, or otherwise breaks down. The remaining issue is merely how far staff decide (on ethical and pragmatic grounds) to transcend minimal welfare responsibilities. *Optional* surgery and counseling services can be provided. We can do this on humanitarian grounds without assuming that we reduce the offender's recidivism because we serve his needs.

Criminal justice staff must clearly welcome any client efforts at resocialization, whether or not the client has a "problem" which requires traditional therapy. In this regard, treatment can and must be defined more broadly than it is defined by traditional therapies. The social learning approach (Chapter 9) opens up nontraditional strategies in which we can help the person change his behavior, without making assumptions that call for professional help. Treatment would be any approach that creates circumstances favorable to the development of desirable habits. The physical and social world of our clients would be designed or modified—with their consent—to affirm and support the behavior the client wishes to engage in, provided society approves of it. In actual treatment, the offender's "living environment" would be made prosocial (therapeutic), to counteract negative (antitherapeutic) influences of earlier environments.[5] The object in designing therapeutic environments would be to give the person a chance to rehearse new ways of behaving, new options that he can exercise *in addition* or in lieu of his past options. We would open up new life opportunities, because, according to Bandura, "when alternative means of obtaining benefits are lacking, people are slow to abandon behavior that operates against their long-term welfare, even in the face of negative consequences." Bandura points out that "psychology cannot tell people how they ought to live their lives. It can, however, provide them with the means for effecting personal and social change. And it can aid them in making value choices by assessing the consequences of alternative lifestyles and institutional arrangements" (Bandura, 1977, p. 213).

Where treatment means opening up new approaches to living, the difference between therapy and other change-inducing strategies—such as education—disappears (Chapter 20). We need not worry about whether offenders are "ill," because we are not "curing" them. And we need not worry about the credentials of change-agents, because anyone (guards, teachers, fellow-offenders) would qualify as "treaters" if they could promote new, desirable, behavior options. We would assume (Chapter 4) that "treatment is as treatment does," and the criterion of whether "treatment does" would be offender resocialization.

Resocialization in this sense is a different process from a haircut and/or an appendectomy, which have a short-term, tangible endpoint. A barber is hired to remove excess locks, not to cure hirsutism; to achieve the latter aim he would have to scalp his client, or more relevantly—must arrange to see him periodically for retrimming. Psychological predispositions to crime, like excess hair, are apt to be nourished again. To counter this possibility, one must attend to the posttreatment environment of offenders, particularly in the community. Treatment in the fullest sense of the word requires opportunities for intervening in the natural milieu of treatment clients, to modulate the pressures, temptations, challenges, and rewards it presents.[6] This idea is eloquently captured by Atthowe (1973), who writes

> When a person leaves a hospital, or a prison, or any type of treatment, he generally returns from whence he came. His family or "friends" more often than not will act in the same old ways that partially brought him to the institution or treatment in the first place. Perhaps the ex-patient or inmate may try to live alone. In this latter circumstance, society is more likely to respond to the interloper as an outsider or with fear; consequently, the returnee is more likely to become lonely, to drink to excess, and to isolate himself even more. In either situation we have failed to provide the returnee with expectations of what he would meet, the appropriate behaviors that he will need, and ways of maintaining these new behaviors; above all, we have failed to provide society with the necessary skills and the desire to prevent or to remediate human misery (p. 35).

Our third type of offender (who has crime-related problems, but steadfastly refuses treatment) poses the ethical issue. The problem, however, is ultimately the client's. If the person's crimes are serious enough (extreme violence, for instance), the man may have to choose between indefinite incarceration, on the one hand, and sacrificing his integrity (as he sees it), c : the other.[7] If the offender sacrifices his freedom to ensure his personal autonomy he makes a choice that must be available to all citizens of a society such as ours.

NOTES

1. Interdisciplinary dialogue about issues of treatment is becoming increasingly difficult as a result of emotionally vested polarized premises. Speakers at correctional conferences are apt to bemoan what they call the "tyranny of treatment." Among criminologists, it is fashionable to deride "the medical model," which can include concern with individual dynamics or personal suffering.

2. Another reason why treatment issues evoke strong feelings is because we unconsciously assume that therapy can tap private layers (through "head shrinking," etc.), which we would rather keep suppressed. Such threats of invasion are experienced at the interface between feelings and controls for feelings, and are therefore not rationally or consciously formulated.

3. Since sociological critics often equate the term "therapy" with the concepts "mental illness" and "medical model" this word usage deprives their attacks of relevance to the contemporary scene. Harper (1975), after reviewing current trends in psychotherapy, thus points out that "the whole idea of the psychotherapist's directing his attention to the 'healing' of a 'sick' mind has been wiped out of most of psychotherapy. . . . The whole medical model of a psychotherapist treating a sick patient is fading. . . . Few therapists seem to think any longer of patients as really ill persons who need 'treatment' in the medical sense of the word" (pp. 159–160).

4. Inmate entitlement to health-related services is always spelled out in statutes that establish and regulate correctional agencies. Such statements are also made in all available manuals of "standards" that regulate institutional care and the status of prisoners.

5. Aichhorn anticipated this prescription when he wrote that "the more the life of an institution conforms to an actual social community the more certain is the social rehabilitation of the child" (Aichhorn, 1955, p. 117). This syllogism must not be inverted by designating as "therapeutic," routine institutional practices and programs. An example used by Redl is the practice of talking about "music therapy" when referring to a room with piped music. Two connotations of "milieu therapy" cited by Redl are: "Don't put poison in their soup" and "you still have to feed them" (Redl, 1959).

6. On ethical grounds, follow-up interventions in the community must center on providing supports (where necessary) and opportunities for personal development (where the otherwise existing range is restricted). To think in terms of creating substitute environments or controlled antiseptic settings (1) creates make-believe change, in that coping competence is not created, nor tested, and (2) borders on coervice technology, which is literally "behavior control." Keniston (1968) makes this point with a tongue-in-cheek scenario of a hypothetical future:

> Congress—recognizing that prolonged reacculturative experience in a psychologically healthy community (antidotal therapy) was often necessary for the permanent recompensation of deep-rooted personality disorders—authorized the construction of 247 centers, largely in the Rocky Mountain Region, each with a capacity of 1000 patients. . . . On these salubrious sites, the network of Remote Treatment Centers has now been constructed. . . . the stringent security arrangements necessary in such centers have been criticized (p. 29).

7. The issue also relates to the limits of physical restraint. We can lead a horse to water, but if it refuses to drink, we may have to stand and watch it die. The Thirteenth Amendment authorizes "involuntary servitude" while the Fourteenth prohibits "cruel and unusual punishment." If a prisoner refuses to participate in programs, we can lock him in his cell. This act accomplishes the administrator's goal (noncruel punishment) and the inmate's goal (nonparticipation), and is facesaving. The limiting issue is posed where life is at stake. If the horse is a mental hospital patient, it might find itself force-fed through a plastic tube inserted in its larnyx.

REFERENCES

Ackerman, N. W. *The psychodynamics of family life: The diagnosis and treatment of family relationships.* New York: Basic Books, 1958.

Aichhorn, A. *Wayward youth: A psychoanalytic study of delinquent children, illustrated by actual case studies.* New York: Meridian Books, 1955.

Allport, G. W. Foreword. In E. Powers, and H. Witmer, *An experiment in the prevention of delinquency: The Cambridge-Somerville youth study.* New York: Columbia University Press, 1951.

Atthowe, J. M. Behavior innovation and persistence. *American Psychologist,* 1973, *28,* 34–41.

Bandura, A. *Principles of behavior modification.* New York: Holt, Rinehart and Winston, 1969.

Bandura, A. *Social learning theory.* Englewood Cliffs, N.J.: Prentice-Hall, 1977.

Brodsky, S. L. *Ethical Issues for Psychologists in Corrections.* Washington: American Psychological Association, Task Force on the Role in the Criminal Justice System (Mimeographed), 1977.

Freud, S. *A general introduction to psychoanalysis.* New York: Permabooks, 1953.

Freud, S. Analysis, terminable and interminable. In *Therapy and technique.* New York: Collier York (Collier Books), 1963a.

Freud, S. Further recommendations in the technique of psychoanalysis: On beginning the treatment. The operation of the first communications. The dynamics of the cure. In *Therapy and technique.* New York: Collier York (Collier Books), 1963b.

Harper, R. A. *The new psychotherapies.* Englewood Cliffs, N.J.: Prentice-Hall (Spectrum), 1975.

Keniston, K. How community mental health stamped out the riots (1968–1978). *Trans-Action,* 1968, *5,* 21–29.

Klein, M. W. *Street Gangs and Street Workers.* Englewood Cliffs, N.J.: Prentice-Hall, 1971.

London, P. *Behavior Control.* New York: Harper & Row, 1969.

McCord, W., & McCord, J. *Origins of crime: A new evaluation of the Cambridge-Somerville youth study.* New York: Columbia University Press, 1959; Reprinted, Montclair, N.J.: Patterson Smith, 1969.

Menninger, K. *The crime of punishment.* New York: Viking, 1968.

Morris, N. *The future of imprisonment.* Chicago: University of Chicago Press, 1974.

New York City Youth Board. *Reaching the fighting gang.* New York: New York City Youth Board, 1960.

Powers, E., & Witmer, H. *An experiment in the prevention of delinquency: The Cambridge-Somerville youth study.* New York: Columbia University Press, 1951.

Redl, F. The concept of "therapeutic milieu" (1959). In F. Redl, *When we deal with children: Selected writings*. New York: Free Press, 1966.

Rogers, C. R. *On becoming a person*. New York: Houghton Mifflin, 1961.

Spergel, I. *Street gang work: Theory and practice*. New York: Doubleday (Anchor), 1967.

Szasz, T. S. *The myth of mental illness: Foundations of a theory of personal conduct*. New York: Dell Publishing, 1961.

Toch, H. *Police, prisons and the problem of violence*. Washington, D.C. (National Institute for Mental Health): U.S. Government Printing Office, 1977a.

Toch, H. *Living in prison: The ecology of human survival*. New York: Free Press, 1977b.

Truax, C. B., & Carkhuff, R. B. *Toward effective counseling and psychotherapy*. Chicago: Aldine, 1967.

Van den Haag, E. *Punishing criminals: Concerning a very old and painful question*. New York: Basic Books, 1975.

Whiteley, S., Briggs, D., & Turner, M. *Dealing with delinquents: The treatment of antisocial behavior*. New York: Schocken, 1973.

chapter 12

The Juvenile Delinquent

William W. Wattenberg

In the mid 1950s, shortly after the conclusion of hostilities in Korea, the statistics collected by the Youth Bureau of the Detroit Police Department showed an abrupt increase in aggressive assaults; the rise was confined to black boys. An investigation was launched to find out what facts or events were associated with the one-year "explosion" (Wattenberg, 1957).

At the outset there appeared to be three tenable hypotheses:

1. The offenders had been the "door-key children" of World War II; had now reached the age at which serious fighting could be a symptom of the personality effects of neglect in childhood.
2. The restrictive covenants which had prevented racial movement of populations had been declared legally unenforceable by courts and there had been sufficient development of mixed neighborhoods to permit a rise in interracial clashes.
3. The spread of television sets into working class homes was occurring and more young people were witnessing violence through that medium.

Analysis of statistics revealed that the fighting was largely with other boys of the same race as the assailants. Interviewing of boys in detention for aggressive assaults and data gathered from their parents brought out that none had been "door-key children." Amusingly, it turned out that "I Love Lucy," and other family situation comedies were their favorite viewing fare. Eventually it was discovered that during the year in question there had been an abrupt rise in unemployment among youth; the rise in males out of school and out of work had primarily affected large numbers of black youth.

Analysis of specific incident reports showed that in several cases the fight that had led to a knifing had been instigated by older youths, apparently as exciting entertainment.

Assuming for the sake of discussion that it had all really been that simple in all instances, we are left with a series of questions which bear on the respective roles of different disciplines. To be sure, the rise in incidence of delinquent acts reflected economic, sociological, and institutional factors. But while experts may have recognized that these factors existed and could well be the subject of research and action, courts and their personnel, nevertheless, had to deal one way or another with the individual boys involved. Why was each boy especially vulnerable to instigation? Why did each during the fight lose control and resort to a weapon? What was the individual probability that if released, a boy would become a repeater? What program, addressed to each boy, would increase the probability he would have a clean record in the future?

Again, in somewhat oversimplified form, needs determine at what points the expertise of the clinicians and the disciplines they represent are brought to bear. Each is expected to throw light on the dynamics of offenders as individuals, to engage in individual diagnosis and prognosis, and to devise or choose programs which will rehabilitate and prevent. If the child-care worker is truly knowledgeable, he or she will understand that the individual offender is a casualty to social or psychological causal factors; he or she will also know the nature of the danger of an individual delinquent; that each may pose a very real threat to other people, to community welfare, and, indeed, to the worker as a person. It is in this context that a clinician brings his science and his art to bear, and, through consultation, makes both available to the other people in the youth's life space—be they parents, judges, probation officers, police, teachers, or whomsoever.

A PSYCHOLOGICAL TYPOLOGY OF DELINQUENCY

As a way of dealing with the how and why of these roles, it may be helpful to describe several "types" of delinquents. Each young person, of course, is unique. Yet, sufficient numbers share enough in the way of characteristics and behavior that we can describe some "types." One of the more interesting series of researches designed to locate such commonalities is the work extending now into its third decade by Richard Jenkins (Jenkins, 1969). In classifying populations served by clinics and training schools, Jenkins uses a basic technique. Trained readers go through the case records and note the presence or absence of specific behaviors, characteristics, and environmental items. Then, every item is correlated with every other. The correlation matrix is examined for clusters. If we were to use medical analogies, these could be called syndromes. Depending on the population used, there are variations in the lists and the specifics. For our purposes it will be useful to discuss the six fundamental reaction patterns as they were summarized in the second edition of the *Diagnostic and Statistical Manual of Mental Disorders* of the American Psychiatric Association. They are as follows:

The hyperkinetic reaction resembles the behavior seen in children with minimal brain damage.

The withdrawing reaction is prone to occur when real life offers too little satisfaction to the child, as may be the case for the child with inadequate parents who are detached, overly permissive in behavior, and yet punitive in attitude.

The overanxious reaction tends to occur particularly in middle-class, educationally ambitious families in which children are held to high standards of behavior and achievement and may come to feel that their acceptance in the family is dependent upon maintaining these standards.

The unsocialized aggressive reaction tends to occur as a reaction to parental rejection coupled with some parental over-protection.

The runaway reaction tends to occur as a reaction to simple undiluted parental rejection.

The group delinquent reaction tends to occur as a result of group rebellion in the adolescent years in the absence of parental, and particularly in the absence of paternal, supervision.

Before examining this particular list in detail, it should be pointed out that it is a composite of several independent investigations. Moreover, other workers using other methods, have developed different lists. Some such have even been used to classify adjudged delinquents and to determine which of a number of available facilities should be used for their treatment. There is enough congruency among the reports, however, to warrant using Jenkins' list as a model. Over time, it will undoubtedly be refined, modified, and made more definitive.

That said, let us now go back through the list, indicate how each reaction would be seen in a delinquent population, and what program possibilities should be weighed.

NEUROLOGICAL AND LEARNING DEFICITS

The first group delineated by Jenkins probably is represented in substantial numbers among delinquents. A series of studies by Pasamanick and his coworkers, using hospital records in Baltimore, indicate a strong correlation between neurological problems in children and the socioeconomic level of and race of the mother (Pasamanick, et al., 1956). Records pointed to malnutrition and toxemia during pregnancy as possible antecedent conditions of disease. Using data from the Longitudinal Studies of Child Health and Development, Valadian, Reed, and Acayan (1968), implicate low protein intake by the mother during her early adolescence as a cause of children's pathology.

In dealing with delinquents who have any significant degree of neurological deficit, there are two very obvious possibilities which ought to be explored either separately or in combination. First, although the subject of controversy is delinquency, the immediate problem is that of medical management. There is a plethora of reports by physicians who employed medication which had some success in modifying behavior. Second, many of the young people would be expected to have the type of specific learning disabilities which would compound their problems in school and which can be the subject of efforts aimed at educational remediation.

With respect to this group, the psychologist at the very minimum has two functions: (1) identification of contributing problems, and (2) participation in remedial planning. These two possibilities occur both in prevention and rehabilitation. At the level of prevention, school psychologists would play the key role. To the extent that school systems have programs for helping learning disabled children and for aiding parents in obtaining help for such children, it should be within the realm of possibility that steps to aid the children could be taken in the early grades, before behavior disorders broke out into the kind of actions which would call for police and court involvement.

However, once there has been an offense which brings law enforcement and court procedures into the picture, there may be problems not so much of responding to the need for assessment as of overlooking the relevance of many factors which may turn out to be crucial. This is especially true if the offender has a history of violence. Hertzig and Birch (1968) conducted a study in which they compared what had happened to one hundred male adolescents admitted to the in-patient psychiatry service of Bellevue Psychiatric Hospital, with the results of a similar study of girls. They concluded:

> The findings . . . are interpreted as suggesting that primary atypicality or abnormality of the nervous system may be a prerequisite for the development of serious behavioral disturbance in children and youth. The sex differences in the relationship of CNS abnormality to psychiatric diagnosis are considered as suggesting that the relation between CNS abnormality and behavior disturbance is indirect and involves an interaction between primary nervous system dysfunction and sociocultural as well as other aspects of the environment (Hertzig & Birsch, 1968, p. 536).

There is a factor further compounding the probability of assessment itself: the child's social class increases or decreases the likelihood that there will have been previous work-ups to suggest the need for careful study. The author had occasion to make a comparative study of material in the folders of children referred to special education classes. The folders of children from professional or middle class homes often bulged with reports from physicians and medical clinics to whom the parents had turned as soon as they realized there was something wrong with the child. The folders of inner-city youngsters were blank on that score. School personnel accepted the handy explanation that the learning problems were straightforwardly explicable on the grounds the poor student was the product of a poor environment and a bad home, or of unfortunate genes. If the child's medical care had been at crowded public clinics, he or she never had the benefit of becoming sufficiently known as an individual to a single physician. Accordingly, at the point when he or she got in trouble with the law, parents were not insistent on securing recognition of neurological conditions, and the previous records were barren of any such suggestion.

Even if the psychologist may find signs of organicity in his examination, the culture of the court and clinic may militate against insistence on going into the matter in depth, unless the offense is a publicized murder. If there is a glare of publicity, the professional dynamics undergo a revealing change. To satisfy public curiosity and their own desire for publicity, the professionals become avid for diagnosis. When those incentives are absent, it is easy, unfortunately for "everyone" to accept the belief that even if we know there are neurological complications we have no resources to alleviate them; the attempted assistance would make little difference in management in any event. If the clinician is more interested in applying behavior modification techniques, he may feel that the causes of behavior have little relevance.

Ironically, the greater the probable incidence of neurological complications, the greater is the probability they may be overlooked or ignored. In some instances there is a tacit understanding to that effect. A nasty muckraker in some instances could marshall evidence to prove conspiracy; recognition of that possibility is partially responsible for legislation mandating special education. As such reformist trends have a way of ultimately affecting courts, it may be only a matter of time before the issue is highlighted in law enforcement and court realms. That hopeful possibility is of no benefit to the thousands of young people now condemned to primarily punitive measures.

SOCIAL DEFICITS AND WITHDRAWAL

The second of Jenkins' categories, the withdrawing reaction, reads very much as though it were an oblique reference to schizophrenia or to schizoid processes. In times past it would have seemed only common sense to make a distinction between antisocial behavior and withdrawn behavior. Indeed, one of the earliest thrusts of the mental hygiene movement was that of sensitizing caretakers to the dangers of excessive shyness or withdrawal in children. It was implied, if not openly stated, that a juvenile thief was not likely to be as seriously troubled as a seclusive child. The import of the pioneering Wickman study (Wickman, 1928) was that teachers and clinicians were often at odds in their evaluations. However, in follow-up studies of child guidance clinic populatons, it was suggested that the distinction needs to be reexamined. For example, when Lee Robbins (1966) tracked down adults who thirty years earlier as children had been treated in child guidance clinics in St. Louis, it became evident that antisocial behavior presaged not only adult crime but also mental disorder, including schizophrenia.

In instances where the young person charged or found guilty of some offense engages in bizarre behavior or acts in a frankly psychotic manner,[1] that is, where the pathology is obvious, there is a good chance that clinicians are expected to help complete the documentation that will be used to make the necessary referral. They are expected to know local resources and to make both the formal and informal contacts that will transfer the afflicted child to agencies in the mental health establishment or into special education programs. Unfortunately if the prognosis is poor there is a tendency on the part of some programs to refuse to accept a child. If the young person's situation includes parents with whom it is difficult to work, placement may be close to impossible. In the interests of fiscal economy and cost effectiveness, there is a tendency to reduce or eliminate use of public residential facilities. Only a few saints or research people are willing to take responsibility for acting-out psychotics. Too often they are placed on a merry-go-round of incomplete referrals.

If we accept the young people at this bleak extreme, however, there is a better chance that clinical will bear fruit later. If the community has a well-functioning facility, especially if it has access to a research or training establishment, the young person may receive the best care available. The benefit he or she may derive will be in part a function of the time needed for his or her program.

However, if the pathology is masked, in the run-of-the-mill instances little effort will be made to ferret it out. Indeed, clinicians interested in completing referrals operate under some negative incentive—they may fear that if the record shows psychosis, the intake workers for many programs will turn thumbs down on the youngster. Again, exceptions must be made for the rare and dramatic offender who excites a publicized quest for the explanation of his behavior.

THE NEUROTIC DELINQUENT

The third category in Jenkins' nosology is the one which embraces the youths whose psychotherapy is the subject of the most intriguing contributions to child study literature. These are the young people whose delinquent acts are the symptoms of various neurotic processes, who may be involved in compulsive stealing, fire setting, aberrant sexual behavior, or in self-destructive activities. However, even if a child's behavior looks like mundane delinquency, inquiry may reveal that it is a manifestation of unconscious motivation. Usually, the inquiry that yields this judgment is set in motion either by the parents, or by workers who are puzzled by the fact that the family seems to be such a good one. Let the son or daughter of a clergyman, psychologist, policeman or youth-care worker turn up in the hands of the police, and there is an almost reflex reaction that the child in question needs "therapy"—by which is meant treatment by a psychiatrist, psychologist, or case worker interested in uncovering dynamics within the individual and the family. It is often hoped that processes utilizing insight, emotional reeducation, and planning will enable the family and the youngster to live more effectively in the future.

The same viewpoint prevails with respect to a wide range of social problems. In fact, in many middle class homes today, if a son or daughter seems to be headed for trouble, the family will use all sorts of ways to "get help." By this is meant resort to a range of resources which are often taken for granted. There are many clergy who will extend pastoral counseling to the members of their churches or synagogues. School systems employ social workers. There are the public and private agencies. With the advent of insurance covering mental health problems, there has been such an explosion in private out-patient clinics as to lead some to speak of a "mental health industry."

Utilization of these resources has a high degree of acceptability among middle class populations; with the advent of insurance coverage there has been some spread into regularly employed working class populations in industries where unions have successfully fought for coverage. This is one area in which we may be witnessing a major diversion trend.

The extent to which there has been substantial improvement may be impossible to document; the principal beneficiaries may be among youthful offenders who are being "warned and released." In some instances, the interview between either the arresting officer or a youth bureau officer on the one hand and the parents who have come to the station house to claim their child on the other, may involve a suggestion that "help" be sought. Or the parents may volunteer that idea as a token that if their son or daughter is released to them, they will "take care of things." If the notion of seeking "help" is not broached at that point, the parents may be urged to "do something" by a clergyman, a community volunteer, or, later, by court personnel. The fact that recourse to some form of psychotherapy or of family counseling occurs most frequently in the group which often eludes statistical recording prevents systematic study of both incidence and effectiveness. No one knows for sure in how many cases there was a deal in which the parents' promise to "get help" was exchanged for a police promise not to give the boy or girl a record. The present author has seen police log books containing three times as many contact records as figured in the official file cards. In one informal follow-up, 80 percent of the youthful offenders "warned and released" had no subsequent record. This is all to the good.

Mention should also be made at this point of the expanding role of private security forces, as a major and substantially uncontrolled branch of the law-enforcement establishment. Retail business, when it examines its balance sheets, is painfully aware that loss of merchandise cuts heavily into profits. Also, news of crime can reduce the attractiveness of shopping centers. Adolescents are drawn to the shopping centers, which have become the site of new social rites. To an as-yet-undocumented extent, the strolling, undifferentiated crowds seen today in the town-squares of Europe and Latin America and formerly peopling the main commercial streets of our big cities, have shifted their habitat. They now move in and through suburban shopping centers, where the lure of merchandise is more immediate. The combination of opportunity and temptation is overwhelming. Shoplifting is the inevitable consequence. The fact that the stores are built to encourage access and that many stores are frugal in their allotment of sales personnel, invites larceny.

When the security people do detect a youth in the act of shoplifting, the calculations used to make a disposition are complicated. If the shoplifter is outfitted in a fashion to indicate professionalism in crime, speedy transfer to the police and the preparation of formal charges occurs. However, if the boy or girl seems to come from a "good home" representative of potential customers, matters are handled discretely so as not to alienate the family. Frequently parents are called and informed. Especially if the youngster is a known repeater, the possibility of the family "getting help" is broached. Again, the family is sensitive to "giving my child a record." Data as to incidence, dispositions, and subsequent repeating are kept poorly if at all. At the present time, anything approaching careful study is unlikely.

THE "UNSOCIALIZED AGGRESSIVE" DELINQUENT

The "unsocialized aggressive" delinquents—Jenkins' fourth category—includes some of the most seriously disturbed youths. Mostly boys, these young people frequently have committed a wide range of offenses, often are involved in serious assaults, and frequently show little guilt. In the shorthand of labeling, they seem to have relatively weak ego structures (Chapter 7). The boys treated at Pioneer House seem to fit this pattern (Redl & Wineman, 1957). The Pioneer House was intended as a prototype of residential treatment based on psychoanalytic principles. In general, youths whose behavior and circumstances bear any similarity to the "unsocialized-aggressive" syndrome frequently pile up records so replete with offenses regarded as dangerous to the community, that some form of removal from the community is almost inevitable. The treatment these youths receive while in confinement is a matter of chance. In the United States, at least, there are few beds in the private residential facilities which offer any degree of therapy. Of the private facilities, some are under religious auspices, as for instance the Boys Home on the Range near Beach, North Dakota, where reliance is placed on various types of group interaction and where there is an orientation toward dairy farming and crafts. There also has been considerable work done with various forms of guided group interaction. More recently, as for instance in Achievement Place in Kansas, there has been experimentation with behavior modification techniques.[2] We have also had reports of use of token economies to calm down classroom situations.

There has been controversy, as might be expected, over use in public facilities of behavior modification techniques which rely on rigid rewards or contingencies. Some of the controversy has been triggered by professional disagreements; some by civil liberties considerations. The nature of the evidence provided by proponents is in and of itself cause for concern. Much follows a standard pattern: the baseline for an individual is established; the reinforcement schedule is activated and data gathered on the resultant new behavioral level; the contingencies are discontinued and the regression toward the baseline noted; and a final reinforcement schedule is used to produce a new level. The long-range effects of such programs rarely are investigated; the researchers are content to provide evidence that while the contingencies are in effect, the desired results can be demonstrated. By now, that much has been pretty clearly established. The question to be answered, therefore, is where do we go from there? If we were to accept this theoretical framework, the key concern from a long-range perspective would be the nature of the contingencies of reinforcement operative in the homes and communities to which the young people are returned after being ultimately released from the training school or residential home. The hope would be that the behavior shaped in the treatment facility would be such as to elicit reinforcement at work sites. How often this occurs in our real world has yet to be demonstrated.

Meanwhile, all we can say is that there are some places where there are exemplary programs, but variability is great. Sincere efforts are being made. There has been significant experimentation with after-care programs, some of them based on halfway houses. Unfortunately, young people closer to the norm are all caught up in the climate of "doing time easy." The experience, as evidenced by high recidivism rates, is that the young person has entered the revolving door which, time and again, will see him or her remanded to an institution. This facility produces so little basic change that after a short period of "freedom," during which offenses continue, the offender has further police contacts, which are followed by other court appearances, and new judicial decisions to commit.

THE DELINQUENT "RUNAWAY"

Something very similar seems to happen to those who conform to the fifth of Jenkins' categories, the "runaway" reaction. This category is a recent addition to the list, and may lead to some speculation. The behavior would appear to stem from almost unrelieved rejection at home. A telltale early symptom is that the child steals from his or her own home. The ties to the home are weak. The prognosis appears to be poor.

The young people in the descriptions seem to be juvenile versions of the classic "institutionalized" person. The males seem very much like the vagrants who once peopled the skid rows of our big cities or who wandered over the landscape. These are the pathetic losers. In their pitiable search for a home of some sort, they can and do adjust somewhat passively to any institutional setting. They attract little attention; this may be the reason for the paucity of relevant research or casework data. This, and the youths' low capacity for relating has kept most from having pursued any program of treatment long enough to provide data interesting and detailed enough to report. The exception seems to be those girls who, having drifted into prostitution, were successful enough as call girls to afford therapy.

On the current law-enforcement scene, we can wonder about the extent to which, except for petty thievery, the runaways' offenses fall within the category of "victimless crimes." If, as can be surmised, this proportion is large, part of the impact is clutter. The police, the courts, and the institutions see the youths as being in the way, so to speak. If we could just bring ourselves to exclude runaways from attention, we could all get on with the task of dealing better with more serious problems.

If we stop for a second reflection, wouldn't this be the ultimate degradation? Our law-enforcement establishment does nothing substantial for runaways when they reach adulthood, and probably will not do so in the future. To the probation officer or the custodial personnel in a training school, they may not seem important; they know how to get along without a hassle. To use Moynihan's classic phrase where it truly applies, their fate is "benevolent neglect."

THE DELINQUENT GANG MEMBER

Turning with a sad shrug from that aspect of the scene to Jenkins' sixth category, the group delinquent reaction, we come in contact with the gang members, the street corner society, and the denizens of "the street." For the sociologist, social psychologist, and psychologists this is very familiar territory. The boy or girl, coming from an easy-going, relatively unsupervised home, in early adolescence begins to obtain the bulk of his or her gratification in a peer group. In that group she or he takes on the value coloration of the setting. If depredations or combat are in the mores of the neighborhood, the gang may run up enough of a record so that its members are arrested, put on probation, or even sent away. Efforts may be made to divert the gang into some constructive activity. If their propensity is for combat and they reside in the core of a city, we may attempt to see what can be done if a street worker is assigned to them. Perhaps they can be induced to form a team or a club and enjoy themselves in socially acceptable ways.

Although court statistics based on adjudicated delinquents indicate the concentration of gangs is greatest near the core of our cities and, in a still-familiar gradient, diminishes as we move outward. the police in suburbia and the security people in shopping centers also have their hands full. The differences in official dispositions undoubtedly account for part if not all of the variation in rates. However, the social organization of the community does affect the likelihood that it can provide the facilities and adult leadership for the all-essential group settings to which this variety of delinquent is most likely to respond. These young people are not good candidates for any of the individual or one-to-one treatment modalities. If one attempts any of the individual insight therapies it is difficult for the therapist to mobilize anxiety for therapeutic purposes; if one attempts behavior modification, the contingencies of reinforcement that are available to the contemporaries in peer groups may far outweigh those available to the therapist.

If the gang or its members do not respond adequately to treatment in the community, and their string of offenses passes the tolerance level of the juvenile court, referral to a training school may ensue. Usually this occurs on an individual basis. Most of the boys and girls we are now discussing are sufficiently adept so that they quickly become embedded in any available peer group. This propensity makes them prime candidates for one or another form of group therapy. As for the degree of change to be expected, the problem is that long-range outcomes depend upon the nature of whatever groups the young person eventually joins. Hopefully, the individual may learn to be more selective, to avoid the settings which can lead to trouble, and to seek out those which are at least legal. Yet, in regard to employment, a very important matter in our work-oriented society, the problem may often be one of finding a job at all.

AFTER DELINQUENCY, WHAT?

With this last observation, we have come full circle; we focus again on the role of employment. While we are concerned, as we must be, with the juvenile segment of each delinquent's life span and with how his or her behavior impinges on the rest of us, we also must be worried about what happens when the boy becomes a man and the girl a woman. Will the delinquent become an adult criminal? Will she or he be in and out of courts and penal institutions the rest of her or his life? How long will be the list of victims? What will be the economic cost of the predations? What will that career produce in terms of drug traffic, violent crime, broken lives?

In our economically oriented society, the major event in the transition from juvenile to adult is the choice of life style attendant upon employment. In the consulting room of the therapist, in the shops and school rooms of institutions, in the program of the halfway house, we hope that the young offender will develop the attitudes and motivations and skills that will enable him or her to become a person capable of self-support through legal occupations. Whatever may be our strategy for preparing the person for that, its effectiveness depends upon the availability of jobs. If that fact is axiomatic, what does it imply?

As we deal with the particular young people whom we treat or guide or shape or counsel, to be sure we can use our influence to obtain favoritism in employment for each. However, if the total unemployment in the community remains stable, this is accomplished by "bumping" some other youth whom we may never see and never know, or by closing the door on some adult, whose children are thereby added to the ranks of the deprived.

This chapter has attempted to portray in some detail specific patterns which occur in significant numbers among delinquent youth. It has attempted to sketch some sample etiologies, and to indicate the range and practical availabilities of treatment and prevention strategies. To use a figure of speech, we have been lighting the arena in which we operate. At the start and now at the conclusion we must call attention to the fact that the arena has its surroundings, and these, too, are part of the scene. When, for each individual boy or girl, the time in the arena has run its course, that person melds into the surrounding community. The meaning of what may have happened in the arena will not be known until that merger has transpired.

NOTES

1. Jenkins did not identify the withdrawal category (or the neurotic type, which we shall discuss next) as delinquency-prone. We now know, however, that many such youths are found among apprehended offenders, and that they can be identified if delinquents are subjected to closer scrutiny.
2. Such techniques are successful in producing conformity for program participants while they are in the program. They are thus useful as management techniques for unsocialized aggressive youth; therapy that has long range effectiveness in building new behavior repertoires may require more intensive programming, such as therapeutic communities (see Chapter 20).

REFERENCES

Hertzig, M. E., and Birch, H. G. Neurologic organization in psychiatrically disturbed adolescents. *Archives of General Psychiatry*, 1968, *19*, 528–537.

Jenkins, R. Classification of behavior problems of children. *American Journal of Psychiatry*, 1969, *125*, 1032–1039.

Pasamanick, B., Rogers, E., & Lilienfeld, M. Pregnancy experience and the development of behavior disorders in children. *American Journal of Psychiatry*, 1956, *112*, 613–618.

Redl, F., and Wineman, D. *The aggressive child*. Glencoe, Ill.: Free Press, 1957.

Robbins, L. M. *Deviant children grow up*. Baltimore: Williams and Wilkins, 1966.

Valadian, C., Reed, B., & Acayan, L. Influence of preadolescent girls' health and development on future reproduction. Paper presented at the XII International Congress of Pediatrics, December 1968.

Wattenberg, W.W., & Moir, J. B. A phenomenon in search of a cause. *Journal of Criminal Law, Criminology & Police Science*, 1957, *48*, 54–58.

Wickman, E. K. *Children's behavior and teachers' attitudes*. New York: Commonwealth Fund, 1928.

chapter 13

The Violent Offender

David Lester

It has long been debated whether the violent offender represents a distinct type of criminal. Does the violent offender primarily commit violent crimes or does he also commit frequent, nonviolent crimes? To phrase this question in another way, we may ask, is' there such a phenomenon as the violent criminal career?

Several data are relevant to this debate. For one, it seems that a good proportion of violent offenders are first offenders, most of whom are never reconvicted (Hood & Sparks, 1970). Pittman and Handy (1964) reported that 37 percent of aggressive assaulters were first offenders and Gillin (1946) showed that 47 percent of murderers had no records. Clinard and Quinney (1967) argued that murderers, assaulters, and most rapists do not generally have criminal careers. They do not consider themselves to be real criminals and they seldom identify with crime. Crime does not play a significant part in their lives.

Of course, arrest and conviction do not follow every criminal act that a person commits. Our first offender may actually have committed other violent acts for which he was never arrested. However, leaving this aside, it seems foolish to talk of a violent criminal career for an individual who commits only one violent offense.

What about multiple offenders? Wolfgang and his associates (1972) found that knowledge of a delinquent's last offense did aid in the prediction of his next offense, though the association was not very strong. Knowledge of even earlier offenses helped little in the prediction of the next offense. This study, therefore, lends only weak support to the notion of a criminal career which is restricted to one type of crime. We must remember, though, that Wolfgang was studying young offenders whose careers may not yet have been crystallized.

Hood and Sparks (1970) reported data that indicated a stronger tendency toward criminal careers specializing in particular types of crime. They reported that, for those arrested for murder or manslaughter, the next arrest would tend to be for aggravated assault (for some 40 percent of the offenders); for men arrested for forcible rape, the next arrest would most likely be for aggravated assault (26 percent) or rape (15 percent). For men arrested for robbery, the next arrest would tend to be for robbery (35 percent) or burglary (35 percent).

Other investigators have provided data that suggest a very strong tendency for career criminals to specialize in particular types of crime. Peterson and associates (1962) thus found that only 9 percent of their offenders had committed both violent and property crimes, while the majority had committed only violent crimes or only property crimes. Wolfgang (1974) followed up all boys born in 1945 who resided in Philadelphia at least from ages ten to eighteen. Some 35 percent of these boys had one or more contacts with the police before the age of eighteen, and about 6 percent were chronic delinquents who had committed five or more offenses. These chronic delinquents were responsible for 52 percent of all the delinquencies committed by the sample, and they could be credited with a good proportion of the violent offenses. Of the 815 personal attacks (homicide, assault, and rape) on record, 53 percent were committed by the chronic delinquents, who also committed 62 percent of the property offenses.

The National Commission on the Causes and Prevention of Violence (1969a) summed up such conflicting reports and tried to make sense of them. They concluded that offenders arrested for major crimes of violence generally had long criminal histories, but usually mainly of nonviolent offenses. The Commission could find no answer to the question of why the nonviolent offender occasionally departs from his career to commit a violent offense. It uncovered no evidence that the seriousness of the violence increased with successive offenses and, indeed, suggested that the more serious the initial crime, the less likely it was to be repeated. Aggravated assault was the most likely violent crime to become a specialty. The Commission noted that a small number of hard-core offenders accounted for most crimes of violence. And finally, the Commission suggested that first offenders were very different from chronic offenders.

THE EPIDEMIOLOGY OF VIOLENT CRIME

Sociologists have spent a good deal of effort studying the occurrence and characteristics of violent crime. The major crimes of violence (homicide, rape, robbery, and assault) represent only about 13 percent of serious crime in the United States, some 600,000 crimes out of 4.5 million in 1968 (see Dinitz, et al., 1975). In the United States in 1976, the rate for murder was 9 (per 100,000 citizens); the rate for forcible rape was 26; and the rate for aggravated assault was 229. By contrast, the rate for burglary was 1439; the rate for larceny and theft was 2921; and the rate for motor vehicle theft was 446 (Uniform Crime Reports, 1977).

The National Commission on the Causes and Prevention of Violence (1976b; see Dinitz, et al., 1975) has summarized the salient features of statistical, descriptive studies. The Commission points out that violent crime occurs most frequently in large cities, and is primarily committed by males, especially those between the ages of fifteen and twenty-four. Offenders are mainly from the lower social classes, and black youths commit the highest proportion of violent crimes. The victims of violent crime resemble the violent offenders, in that murder and assault victims are primarily male and the rates of victimization are higher among the young, the poor, and blacks. Robbery victims are usually older whites, while rape victims tend to come from backgrounds similar to those of offenders. The violent crimes of homicide, assault, and rape tend to be acts of passion between persons who often are intimate or at least acquainted (again, unlike robbery). The greatest proportion of all serious violence is committed by repeat offenders.

Studies of sociological correlates of violent crime have shown that it occurs in areas characterized by low income, concentrations of racial and ethnic minorities, broken homes, working mothers, low levels of education and vocational skills, high unemployment, high proportions of single males, overcrowded and substandard housing, low rates of home ownership and single family dwellings, mixed land use, and high population density.

GENERAL THEORIES OF VIOLENCE

The Ethologists and our "Biological" Inheritance

The ethological position is that aggression is innate (Lorenz, 1966), and that it is instinctive behavior (which is a term that most psychologists dislike). This assumption has certain implications. Instinctive behavior has its own source of energy that is continually building up. This energy needs release. In animal species, there are usually environmental stimuli that allow for the release of aggression, such as when one animal encroaches on the territory of a neighboring member of the same species. There are also environmental stimuli that inhibit the expression of aggression, such as when two rats are fighting and the loser is finally pinned on his back. At this point, the victor will stop fighting, perhaps merely chewing on the fur of the vanquished. It is assumed that if aggressive energy is not released, it will continue to build up. Eventually, aggression must appear even though an appropriate stimulus is not present in the environment. (It is clear that a "steam releasing" or hydraulic analogy is most apt for the ethological position.)

The student of ethology asserts that men are biologically like other animals and therefore have an aggressive instinct. Since aggression must occasionally find release, the solution to the violence problem is to find legitimate and legal activities during which aggressive energy may be discharged, such as athletic sports or hostile humor. Aggression must be ritualized and displaced. Catharsis (emotional release) must be found. Humans do have stimuli that inhibit their aggression, such as an opponent pleading, wearing glasses, or lying on the floor. However, modern weapons (such as long-distance rifles) have made it possible for the aggressor not to perceive these or other inhibitory stimuli. Killings are less likely to occur by choking than by shooting, and even less likely to occur by shooting than by bombing.

Psychologists on the whole dislike this deterministic position. As Goldstein (1975) has said, humans *can* behave like animals but this does not mean that they *do*. Because we evolved from violent ancestors does not *necessarily* mean that we too are violent by nature.

Genetics

Attempts to identify a genetic basis for some criminal behavior have met with success in that studies of twins have shown that identical twins are more likely to be criminals than nonidentical twins. Since Lombroso's day (see Chapter 6), physiological differences have been sought between criminals and law-abiding citizens. Genetic research has focussed especially on violent crime, as a result of the identification of the XYY male. Normal males have a pair of sex chromosomes labelled as XY. (The female has sex chromosomes that are labelled as XX.) Some males have a third sex chromosome, and the XYY male was thought in the 1960s to be more prone to violent crime than normal males. In an interesting sequence from the simple to the complex, research has qualified this premature conclusion.

Hook (1973) summarized studies of the prevalence of XYY males, showing .01 percent in newborn males, with a range of 0 to 0.4 percent; two percent in mental-penal institutions (facilities for the criminally insane), with a range of 0 to 22 percent; 1 percent in penal institutions, with a range of 0 to 5 percent; and 1 percent in mental institutions, with a range of 0 to 2 percent. Hook concluded that only mental-penal institutions had been shown reliably to have more XYY males than the general population.

Owen (1972) reviewed XYY research, and concluded that XYY males were taller, had different types of fingerprints, and possibly had a higher incidence of abnormal electrical activity in their brains. XYY males were *not* shown to have any consistent personality or behavioral traits. The median intelligence quotient of those tested was in the 80s (with a range of 34 to 125).

As to criminal behavior, Hook (1973) concluded that XYY males in penal settings were not disproportionately dangerous, since their offenses were similar to those of the other inmates. Why then is there an increase in the incidence of XYY males in mental-penal settings? Hook felt it unlikely that XYY males were more prone to be born into environments which lead to deviant behavior. Physical features, such as increased height (which may make them seem more dangerous) and a high frequency of acne (which may make them less physically appealing) might account for such men being given longer and different kinds of sentences, but Hook felt that the evidence for this was poor. An explanation based upon neurological differences (such as an increased incidence of brain damage) was also without empirical support at the time, but remained a possibility.

Recently, a methodologically sound study of criminality in XYY males has been conducted in Denmark. Witkin, and associates (1976) located all males born in Copenhagen from 1944 to 1947. They traced 91 percent of those who were 184 centimeters tall or higher, and among these 4,139 men they found twelve XYY men and sixteen XXY men (Klinefelter's syndrome). Five of the XYY men (42 percent) and three of the XXY men (19 percent) had committed crimes, as compared to 9 percent of the normal men. Although the three groups differed in the incidence of crime, they did not differ in the incidence of violent crime, and only one of the XYY men had committed a violent crime.

Witkin found that the XYY and XXY men had significantly lower intelligence test scores than the normal men and felt that the low intellectual level was primarily responsible for their criminal behavior. (Among normal Danes, the criminals had lower intelligence test scores than the noncriminal men.) Although the XYY men and the XXY men were taller than normal Danes, the criminal members of these groups were actually *shorter* than the noncriminals.

Reduced intellectual capacity was not the sole explanation for the increased level of criminality, however, because holding intelligence test scores constant simply reduced the difference in criminality between the XYY men and the normal men, but did not eliminate it. Further research on the sample suggested that differences in electrical activity in the brain may also play some role. The brain waves of the XYY men were characteristic of very young people rather than of mature adults.

What are the treatment implications of this research? Witkin argued that since XYY and XXY men do not appear especially aggressive and since they are rare, attempts to identify such men would not serve to reduce violent crime. Furthermore, since we do not yet know what about the XYY male increases his likelihood of becoming a criminal, we do not know what treatment goals to establish for him.

Brain Damage and Aggression

It has long been known that particular forms of brain damage are associated with violent behavior. The critical area appears to be the limbic system (Mark & Ervin, 1970). The limbic system comprises the upper part of the brain stem called the thalamus, the hypothalamus, the cingulum, the hippocampus, the basal ganglia, the septal nuclei, the midbrain, and the amygdala.

If electrodes are sunk into parts of the brain and stimulated with mild electric current, this has been found to elicit aggressive behavior when areas such as the amygdala and the middle of the hypothalamus are involved. (Electrical stimulation usually produces the opposite effect to removal of the area.)

This kind of research has led to the speculation that in some violent humans either the limbic system has become hyperactive due to some damage or else the cortical inputs which inhibit and control aggression have become ineffective. These cortical inputs are heavily dependent upon learning and so the cortical inputs can be modified by experience. (This theory of violence is thus neither simply one of heredity nor one of experience, but rather a mix of these two components.)

Mark and Ervin (1970) have described cases of people in whom attacks of aggression and violence were triggered by seizures in the limbic system. They argue that trigger areas exist in the human brain that *can* initiate violence in *susceptible* individuals. This team has also suggested that many violent offenders may be suffering from brain dysfunction and can be helped by medical treatment.

Damage to the limbic system or cortex may be genetic or may be acquired by such physical experiences as a cutting off of oxygen, a head injury, a viral infection, or a tumor. Violent behavior could also occur as a result of a functional abnormality such as epilepsy. (Epilepsy is not itself a disease; it is a symptom of brain dysfunction and of electrical disorganization within the brain.) The kind of epilepsy most relevant for violent behavior is temporal lobe epilepsy. Episodes may start with distorted vision and auditory experiences, loss or lapse of consciousness, head turning, eye movements, and lip smacking and swallowing. There may be emotional changes such as depression or fear, and the individual may react to this fear with aggression.

Few people have clearly recognizable epileptic seizures, and the brain dysfunction is often difficult to observe in overt behavior. Mark and Ervin claim that violent people may in fact have brain dysfunctions of various kinds without having epileptic-like seizures. A brain dysfunction may even be deep enough in the brain so that recording electrical activity from the surface would not pick it up.

Most people who have brain damage that can lead to violence may be treated by drugs and supportive psychotherapy. The most common medications include tranquilizers, psychic energizers, and antiseizure preparations. If these do not work, surgery is another possibility. The traditional surgical treatment for severe temporal lobe epilepsy has been lobectomy, in which the front part of the malfunctioning temporal lobe is removed. Since this involves extensive removal of cortical tissue, it is not feasible for those with malfunctioning involving temporal lobes in both hemispheres. For these people, electrodes can be sunk into the temporal lobes and the precise cortical cells that are diseased can be destroyed by electrocoagulation. It has been found that removal or selective destruction of parts of the amygdala can reduce or eliminate violent behavior in some people. In addition, screening programs to detect persons with possible brain dysfunction could contribute to the prevention of violence.

Some serious ethical issues are raised by such treatments. Medical and surgical treatment can be severe and it is often not reversible. An amygdala that has been removed cannot be replaced. It has been debated whether violent persons who are imprisoned are able to make a free choice of surgical treatment. Furthermore, physicians often suspect brain damage even though they have no proof of its actual existence in a person. To base a surgical operation with drastic effects upon only a suspicion of brain damage is reckless. As a result, physicians favoring surgical treatment for violent behavior often find themselves in debate with psychologists opposed to such treatments and in court with lawyers representing the prisoners and patients who have been operated upon.

Psychoanalysis and Development Theories

In his early statements of psychoanalytic theory, Freud postulated the existence of only a life instinct (sexual energy or drive). He saw aggression as a response to frustration. In his view, the individual's natural spontaneous reaction to frustration was to aggress outwardly toward others. Later, Freud postulated the existence of a death instinct in addition to the life-oriented energy or drives, and, in this later theory, he saw aggression as often spontaneously directed toward the individual himself. The individual had to learn to displace this inward-directed aggression toward others.

Freud's later ideas have not gained general acceptance. Most psychoanalytic investigators have adopted the earlier formulation and see aggression as naturally outward-directed. The frustration-aggression theory of Dollard and associates (1939) assumed that aggression is an almost inevitable consequence of frustration (though frustration can lead to behaviors other than aggression, such as regression, sublimation, and aggressive fantasy). Aggressions are thus built into human existence, because everyone suffers frustration. The baby has to be weaned and the child toilet-trained. The adult has a need for intimacy with others—what Angyal (1965) has called the trend toward homonomy—and this conflicts with our own egocentric strivings (the trend toward autonomy). Thus, humans inevitably suffer frustration, and the aggression that results has to be released. Psychoanalytic theory describes a variety of defense mechanisms which permit the expression of aggressive urges in socially acceptable ways. The aggressive impulses can be displaced onto some acceptable object, for example. It may also be possible to vicariously satisfy our aggressive urges by observing violence in others (catharsis), a phenomenon whose existence is disputed by some psychologists (e.g., Goldstein, 1975).

Henry and Short (1954) have taken such basic ideas and asked what determines whether the child continues to aggress outwardly (his natural tendency) or whether he learns to suppress outward aggression and direct his aggression inwardly, thereby becoming depressed and suicidal.

Henry and Short identified a number of factors. At the social level, they saw the strength of external restraints as critical. When our behavior has to conform to the demands and expectations of others, they share in the responsibility for the consequences of our behavior, and this can make other-oriented aggression legitimate. When external restraints are weak, we ourselves have to bear the responsibility for the frustrations generated through violence, and other-oriented aggression fails to be legitimated.

At the psychological level, Henry and Short argued that child-rearing techniques are critical. If a child is punished by the same parent that supplies love and care, the child will not dare to express his anger toward his parent when he is punished. To express such anger threatens the supply of love. Thus, the child must learn to suppress the outward expression of aggression. The child who is punished by a different parent than the one who supplies love will not have to inhibit his anger after being punished, for to be angry at the punishing parent need not necessarily threaten the supply of love from the other parent.

Secondly, if a child is punished with love-oriented punishment, the consequent anger will be suppressed. If the parent punishes by threatening to withhold love, to express anger toward that parent threatens the supply of love still further. If, on the other hand, a child is punished with physical techniques, to express anger outwardly does not threaten the supply of love, and may merely cause another slap. In these ways, according to Henry and Short, people develop a style of expressing aggression outwardly or inwardly (Lester, 1972).

Palmer (1960) explored the link between frustration and aggression empirically. He found fifty-one murderers, and compared them with their brothers for the number of physical and psychological frustrations that they had suffered as children. According to Palmer, the murderers had experienced many more frustrations than their brothers. (The total frustration score was 9.2 for murderers as compared to 4.2 for siblings.) The murderers had experienced more difficult births, more forceps injuries, more serious illnesses, accidents, and operations in childhood (thirteen of the murderers and none of their brothers had been dropped on their head by their mothers), more beatings by people other than their parents, more deformities, more negative attitudes among mothers toward the forthcoming birth, more rigid treatment from their mothers, more severe toilet training, more negative experiences at school, more behavior disorders (such as bedwetting, nightmares, phobias), and more temper tantrums.

Palmer also found that the murderers had learned fewer acceptable outlets for anger (such as verbal attacks and sports) than their brothers and had learned more socially unacceptable outlets, such as fist fights and intoxication.

Palmer perceived a vicious cycle here. The murderers had experienced more frustration when growing up but they expressed their frustration in socially unacceptable ways that in turn led to punishment and further frustration. Incidentally, when they murdered, these men tended to kill people who resembled their early tormentors. One man who had been beaten by his father beat an old man to death, while a boy who had been frustrated by his mother killed a middle-aged woman.

Redl and Wineman (1951) worked with a small group of boys who were violently aggressive and uncontrollable. These delinquent boys had committed typical delinquent acts such as theft, lying, truancy, and so forth. But, in addition, their uncontrollable aggressiveness made them virtually unmanageable. Redl and Wineman argued that the root of the problem was not that the aggressive impulses (the id) of these children were too strong, and not that their consciences and moral controls (the superego) were too weak. Rather, Redl and Wineman conceptualized the problem of these children as one of ego-controls. The ego is that part of our psychological structure that keeps us in touch with reality, and perceives and judges the external environment; it also monitors what is going on in our mind, knows the demands of reality, and has the power to change our behavior in line with those demands. The problem with the uncontrollably aggressive delinquents, acccording to Redl and Wineman, was that their egos were both permeable and temptable (weak) and were expertly specialized in delinquency-prone ways (defective).

The source of such problems lay in the childhoods of the children. A child needs help in developing a strong ego. He has to be taught how to deal with frustration and with his emotions of anxiety, fear, and guilt. If he is abused, neglected, and hated, then learning these adaptations is made extremely difficult. Redl and Wineman noted that they had never met any children more traumatized by early experiences than their violent children.

A Sociopsychological Approach

Goldstein (1975) has argued that aggressive behavior is best viewed as a continuum and that all behaviors can be seen as containing some amount of aggressiveness. Thus, violent crime differs quantitatively (in degree) and not qualitatively from the aggression that all of us engage in on a lesser scale. Most parents use physical punishment; men imprisoned for crimes of violence are frequently first offenders; and assault and battery differs from homicide only in the availability of a weapon.

For aggression to occur, there must be an impetus to aggress, the inhibitions against aggressing must be overcome, and the situation must be perceived as appropriate. In any situation, there are tendencies in the individual both to aggress and not to aggress, and these tendencies can be categorized as long-term and short-term (or situational).

At the sociological level, the subculture to which the offender belongs affects the frequency of crimes of violence. Also, many youths belong to a subculture in which the use of violence is approved (Wolfgang, 1958) and in which a wide variety of stimuli (such as a jostle, a derogatory remark, etc.) are perceived as justification for an attack in order to demonstrate one's daring and courage or to defend one's status.[1]

Toch (1969) has argued that acts of aggression usually are quite consistent with a person's approach to life problems and his habitual patterns of behavior. In his study of assaults by civilians on police officers, for example, Toch found that both participants may be partly responsible for the assault, and the role that each plays is consistent with behavior in other situations.

Many precipitants of violence can be mentioned. Excessive drinking very frequently precedes violent acts. Long-term high doses of amphetamines produce panic and symptoms of paranoia, thereby facilitating the appearance of violent behavior: Ellinwood (1970) reported thirteen cases of homicide and assault in people intoxicated with amphetamines. Kinzel (1970) measured the area around the body into which a person does not like other people to intrude. He found that this area was greater for a sample of violent offenders than for nonviolent offenders. For the violent offenders, the area was also greater behind the body than in front of it, whereas for nonviolent offenders the reverse was true. Such studies suggest short-term factors that might trigger violence, and there are probably many other such factors that remain to be discovered.

Goldstein (1975) proposed a conflict model for the onset of violence. Given the simultaneous presence in a person of a number of opposing forces favoring and opposing aggressing in any situation, the more conflict there is, the longer it will take for the individual to act, the more intense his aggression will be, and the greater will be the cognitive consequences for the aggressor of the aggression, such as his need to re-evaluate the action and the victim.

A currently popular developmental approach to the study of violence and aggression (and to other behaviors) is social learning theory (Bandura, 1973). We have reviewed this theory—and its approach to aggression—in Chapter 8. In a long-term approach to learning less aggressive behavior, parents can be shown to teach their children not to be impulsive and violent by their use of less physical punishment or, in a positive way, by modeling forebearance in the face of provocation. Some experts endorse the common assumption that sports and the violence in the media make people more aggressive, other students see these stimuli as cathartic. Short-term measures for lessening aggression include reducing opportunities for alcoholic intoxication, controlling the availability of weapons (especially guns), and changing architectural plans for cities. For example, David and Scott (1973) have suggested that Toledo (Ohio) is laid out so as to facilitate property offenses, whereas Rosario (Argentina) is arranged so as to facilitate assault.

Goldstein, and Toch (1977) have also discussed those aspects of the criminal justice system that fail to reduce the incidence of violence and even increase it (such as "cops and robbers" games and prison subcultures). At the individual level, Bandura, Goldstein and Toch suggest identifying juveniles who have already acted delinquently and teaching them alternative strategies to violence, such as increasing their ability to verbalize rather than to act out aggressive desires, increasing their ability to predict the consequences of their actions, decreasing their egocentrism.

We have now reviewed some general theories of violence, and we will turn to the examination of specific crimes of violence.

MURDER

Only three major studies of murder have revealed useful psychological insights. We have reviewed two of these studies—the work of Henry and Short (1954) and that of Palmer (1960) in the section on psychoanalytic and developmental approaches. We shall now describe the remaining major study of murderous violence, which was conducted by Megargee (1966).

Megargee classified murderous behavior into two kinds: overcontrolled and undercontrolled.

1. The undercontrolled aggressive person is described as having low inhibitions against aggression. Whenever such a person is frustrated or provoked, he aggresses. He is not completely without control, however. He may refrain from attacking some people, such as his parents or the judge before whom he is brought, and he may displace his anger in these cases. But, typically, he aggresses against his frustrators. He tends not to aggress wildly, gouging eyes or wielding an ax. But he does aggress, and because he is constantly engaged in violent behavior he may occasionally kill his victim. He is often diagnosed as a psychopath or sociopath (Chapter 14) because of his minimal inhibitions against aggression and his chronic pattern of violence.

2. The overcontrolled person has abnormally rigid controls against aggression. No matter what the provocation, such a person will rarely aggress. His controls are so great that he rarely displaces his aggression or substitutes less drastic behavior, such as verbally reprimanding his frustrator. His aggression, therefore, builds up until his controls can no longer contain it. Then, some trivial frustration can bring about a release of all of the person's pent-up anger. The quiet, mousy citizen becomes a murderer, and the murder is often a violent one. The victim may be shot thirty times, or the body knifed repeatedly and dismembered. After such aggression has been released, customary controls can be reinstated, and the murderer becomes once again a model citizen.

Megargee's research supports these ideas. For example, extremely assaultive juvenile delinquents were found to be somewhat less aggressive and more controlled on psychological tests and in behavioral observations than moderately aggressive juvenile delinquents.

The treatment implications of such findings are clear. Psychotherapy must work on the control of aggression, and the undercontrolled murderer must be taught to control his aggression or to release it in socially acceptable ways. He must be taught to recognize his anger and to foresee the consequences of his aggressive behavior. He must be taught alternative strategies to use when he is angry. On the other hand, the overcontrolled murderer must be taught how to release some of his aggression and anger in small amounts and in socially acceptable ways, so that it never builds up to the point where it can overcome his controls.

THOSE WHO THREATEN MURDER

A fair number of people make homicidal threats, and such threats of violence are not to be taken lightly. Macdonald (1963) studied a hundred people who had been hospitalized in psychiatric institutions for making violent threats. Some had threatened their potential victim directly, and some had told their intentions to others. Some had made one threat; others had made many over a number of years. Some had made their threats seriously; others as a joke.

Macdonald considered the patients as having problems with the expression of their anger. Some aggressed in an impulsive fashion whenever they were criticized or annoyed. Some were overtly sadistic, and boastful of it. (They often kept large private armories or vicious dogs.) Other patients were generally unaggressive and seemed to have trouble expressing anger. The two groups neatly correspond to Megargee's undercontrolled and overcontrolled personality types.

About one third of the patients had experienced parental brutality or seduction, and about one half were judged to be psychotic. The majority of their threats were made to family members; often the family member helped precipitate the threat, as is often found in cases of murder among intimates.

Macdonald followed up his patients over time, and during the next five years, three of them had murdered someone and four had killed themselves. This proportion of murderers is extremely high (among paroled murderers, only one in every two hundred kills again in the next twenty years), which made this group seem to be very prone to violence.

RAPE AND SEXUAL ASSAULT

Sexual deviations in general will be treated in Chapter 17, but some features of rape merit attention here.

Although psychological research has been conducted into rapists, not much has been learned that is of use (Lester, 1975).

Psychological tests have shown that rapists tend to be well adjusted, at least as well adjusted as nonsexual offenders, and better adjusted than child molesters. Kercher and Walker (1973) found rapists giving high galvanic skin responses to heterosexual stimuli, and they concluded that heterosexual stimuli were unpleasant for rapists. This, if it is a valid conclusion, raises interesting questions as to the source of this reaction to heterosexual stimuli, and has obvious treatment implications.

More useful research on rape has been conducted by Cohen and associates (1971), who have described a fourfold classification of rapists that ties together the motives for rape, the modus operandi of the rapist, and his early history.

Type I—Displaced Aggression

This type of rapist is angry at some female—his mother, spouse or lover. However, he is unable to aggress against the particular female who is frustrating him. He displaces the anger onto some randomly chosen, unknown female. The assault may be brutal, especially on the sexual areas. The rape usually takes place in a car or in the victim's home into which the rapist has entered by a ruse—for example, as a deliveryman. He feels anger during his act, and erection and orgasm are difficult for him. His personal, social, and marital adjustment may be good. He is the most well adjusted of all rapists and has the best prognosis. Psychotherapy for such a person would focus on his recognizing the true source of his anger, and in teaching him how to express resentment in socially acceptable ways.

Type II—Compensatory

This rapist is an inadequate man trying to find a girlfriend. He is shy and socially inept. His fantasy is that the victim will submit and ask him to stay. He usually backs off if the victim struggles, and he is often charged with intent to commit rape rather than actual rape. Such a man's victim must fit his taste in women, and the attack usually occurs in open spaces such as parks and deserted streets. He may approach the victim from behind and touch her breasts or genitals. His aim is sexual, and he often ejaculates prematurely. Apart from his rapes, such a man will be law-abiding. He will be an underachiever, with a stable career in menial jobs. Typically, he will be unmarried. Psychotherapy for this type of rapist would focus on social and personal adjustment. He needs to be educated in social skills and helped with career advancement, and he needs much support during these changes.

Type III—Sex-Aggression Fusion

This type of rapist has somehow associated sex with aggression and has to fight for sex in order to enjoy it. If the victim struggles, he gets more excited, and the rape may be indiscriminately brutal. However, the man's felt emotion is sexual arousal and not anger. Typically, such a rapist will have dated and married, but all of his relationships are tinged with violence. His marriage may be unstable, his work record may include firings, and he may have a criminal record for assaults. As a child, he will have shown behaviors such as cruelty to animals, truancy, and running away. Treatment of such a man is very difficult, and must aim toward complete reorganization of a personality that began to form in very early childhood.

Type IV—Impulse

The fourth type of rapist may be a psychopath or sociopath who rapes at whim, whenever the momentary urge strikes him. The act of rape may be incidental to a crime, and the victim may be assaulted because she is available. This sort of rapist will tend to have the typical repertoire of psychopathic traits (see Chapter 14) and will have a criminal record that includes all kinds of crimes.

An analogous classification has been proposed for child molesters by Cohen and associates (1969), with corresponding treatment implications.

PARENTS WHO ABUSE CHILDREN

Parents who willfully inflict physical injury on their own children have been consistently reported to have particular characteristics (Spinetta & Rigler, 1972; Gelles, 1973).

1. Demographic characteristics. Child-abusing parents have a high incidence of divorce, separation, and unstable marriage, and a history of minor criminal offenses. There is often much social and economic stress, an absence of family roots in the community, lack of support from an extended family, social isolation, high mobility, and unemployment. The abused child is often the result of an unwanted pregnancy, and the most dangerous period for the child is during the first three years of its life.

Economic and social distress, of course, are neither necessary nor sufficient causes for child abuse, and many middle class and upper class parents exist who abuse their children.

2. Parental history. Abusing parents are generally found to have been abused themselves or to have been physically and emotionally neglected when they were children. The histories of such parents often include lack of protection, lack of love, rejection, indifference, and hostility, and feature parents who were often absent or so unwholesome as to offer little opportunity for identification. Emotional loss of a parent is common.

3. Parental attitudes toward child-rearing. Abusing parents look to the child to satisfy their own needs. They thus make great demands on their children, and they do so before the children can meet these demands. They look to their children as sources of reassurance, comfort, and love. They have frustrated dependency needs and cannot empathize with their own children. They disregard their child's needs, its limited abilities, and helplessness.

4. Psychiatric disturbance. In the 1950s, most authors felt that child-abusing parents were psychiatrically disturbed and that they were very often psychotic. By the end of the 1960s, psychosis was considered to be infrequent in child-abusing parents. The psychiatric disturbance is now felt to be a milder personality disorder in the majority of cases.

The major disagreement among students of child-abusing parents lies in explaining the control, or lack of control, of aggression. Everyone agrees

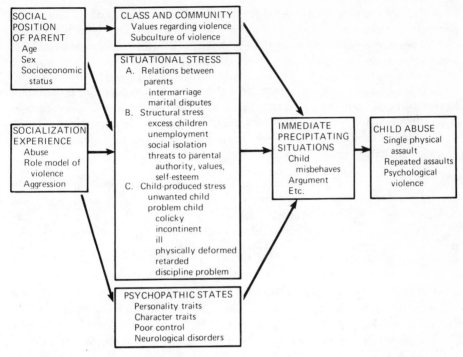

FIG. 13–1.   *Gelles' model of child abuse.*

that the parent's aggressive impulses are expressed too freely. But what is the source of these aggressive impulses? Various assumptions are made about the parents' inability to face life's daily stresses, their deep feelings of inadequacy in the parent role, low intelligence, and an immature impulsive personality structure.

5. The role of the child. Recent investigators have begun to focus on characteristics of the child that make it more likely that a parent will abuse it—characteristics such as a premature birth, mental retardation, physical handicaps, and innate differences in personality (such as whether the baby is "easy" or "difficult," or whether it is a "cuddler" or a "noncuddler"). The victim of child abuse may well help to precipitate violence (Friedrich & Boriskin, 1976), as is the case with other crimes of violence (Wolfgang, 1958), although, of course, the role of the victim in child abuse is not usually intentional or within the child's control.

Other investigators (such as Lynch, 1976) have explored the interaction between the child and the abusing parent in order to discover which kinds of crises, parent characteristics, and child characteristics lead to a disruption in the bond between the parent and the child, thereby facilitating the occurrence of child abuse.

Gelles (1973) has incorporated the personal inputs with the social stress inputs to produce a model that shows how these various causes of child abuse can combine.

Other investigators have tried to describe different types of child-abusing parents. The first major typology that gained acceptance was Merrill's (1962), and more recent typologies parallel his. Merrill described four types of child-abusing parents.

TYPE I. This type of parent is beset with a pervasive and continual aggressiveness, sometimes focussed and sometimes unfocussed. The anger is not controlled, and it needs only minor irritants to stimulate its release. These parents (both mothers and fathers) have become undercontrolled as a result of their own early childhood experiences.

TYPE II. These parents are rigid, compulsive, and cold people who defend their right to treat their children in the way that they do. They reject their children, and are concerned with their own pleasure. They are unbending in their demands on their children—often insisting on excessive cleanliness, for example—and tend to blame their children for any troubles that they experience as parents.

TYPE III. These parents are passive and dependent persons. They are unassuming and reticent people who are reluctant to express their feelings and desires. They appear very unaggressive. They often compete with their children for their spouse's attention, and they are generally depressed, moody, and immature.

TYPE IV. These parents are frustrated persons, usually fathers who are young, intelligent men with acquired skills, who have some physical disability or impediment that prevents them from supporting their families. They stay home and care for the children while the wife works to support the family. Their frustration leads to swift and severe punishment for their children.

The treatment implications of the research into child abuse are many and varied. If we focus upon the psychopathology of parents, we urge them to seek counseling and psychotherapy of various kinds. If we focus upon immediate precipitating situations, we urge the establishment of crisis intervention centers for the parent who is about to physically abuse a child. If we focus upon situational stresses, we urge the implementation of social programs to deal with these stresses, such as programs to reduce unemployment, to prevent unwanted pregnancies, to teach parents useful child-rearing techniques, and so forth.

Zalba (1966) has discussed the immediate problems that confront the caseworker when child abuse is discovered. Should the child be removed from the home? How should one weigh the safety of the child against depriving him of the only security he knows his home, parents, and siblings? Will another sibling be victimized if the first child is removed? And does the abused child need counseling and help?

Child-abusing parents are often difficult patients to work with. They may be demanding, hostile, and indifferent. They may deny their problems, have difficulties with authority figures, and have problems in impulse control. For this reason, group psychotherapy often has advantages, because other patients in the group can often induce change where a psychotherapist cannot.

Zalba argued that long-term, consistent, relationship-oriented psychotherapy is the preferred method of treatment. The treatment objectives are: to work closely with the parents, and to perform certain ego functions for them, such as setting limits, making realistic judgments, and pointing out distorted perceptions and the consequences of actions. The hope is that eventually the parent will incorporate some of the counselor's "ego strengths."

Helfer (1975) has stated several possible goals for the long-term treatment of the child-abusing parent:

1. The abusing parents often have unrealistic expectations about their child, and they demand role reversals and compliance from the child. Abusing parents must therefore be taught how the normal child develops, how to react to normal child behavior, what to expect of children, how to play with children, and in general, about rearing and parenting skills. This can be done in courses, group meetings, and school cooperatives.

2. The abusing parent has a lack of trust and a poor self-image, and does not know how to help others and be helped by them. This asocial orientation can be modified by providing a parent-aide (a nonprofessional who establishes a friendship), supplying a mutually supportive lay group such as Parents Anonymous, finding parents babysitters and getting them a telephone and transportation, and by getting parents involved in group psychotherapy.

3. Abusing parents often end up with unsuitable mates and friends. They need to be taught skills in selecting friends and mates, and they need marriage counseling once mates are selected. Furthermore, parents must be conjointly involved in treatment plans and their implementation.

4. Finally, the abused child will very likely become a parent who abuses his children. Therefore, the child must be helped to experience a fulfilling childhood.

To deal with immediate crises that occur when the parent feels that an impulse to abuse a child is growing, a number of communities have set up hotlines. These services provide a place to call which is immediate whenever the impulse to abuse arises (National Center on Child Abuse and Neglect, 1975). The techniques used for hotline counseling include listening, calming the caller, clarifying feelings and opinions, and making referrals; in general they are much the same as in any crisis intervention service (Lester & Brockopp, 1973). Other interventions which have been developed to aid in treatment include foster grandparents to help the battered child; visiting nurses for home visits and advice on health care; homemaker services to assist the mother who cannot cope with the demands of her children; crisis nurseries where a mother can leave her child for a few hours when she is in great distress. Finally, there is Mothers Anonymous—a group for abusing mothers which functions much as Alcoholics Anonymous does for alcoholics—whose members are fellow parents, and help in trying to change a mother's life course and who can also give immediate assistance in times of distress (Kempe & Helfer, 1972). Parenthetically, crisis intervention is increasingly being used to intervene in all sorts of family violence, as in Bard's (1969) experiments involving a special family crisis unit in the New York City police (Chapter 2).

What is the prognosis for treatment of child abusers? Delsordo (1963) felt that in the classical battered child syndrome (Type I) prognosis is extremely poor, while in cases of disciplinary abuse and misplaced abuse (Type II) prognosis is good. In the case of parents who are mentally ill, prognosis is always poor, and such parents should be separated from their children until their psychiatric disturbance has been dealt with.

ARMED ROBBERY

Armed robbery offenders usually commit other types of theft, such as burglary, rather than other violent crimes. Most armed robberies do not involve any actual violence and few victims suffer any injury (Dinitz, et al., 1975). Primarily, armed robbers are thieves who wield guns to intimidate victims, and who occasionally use force to achieve their goals. Carol Spencer followed up a group of men who carried a weapon during their crimes or who used intimidation to carry out some criminal act, and found that about 80 percent of the men had never been convicted for actual violence (see Dinitz, et al., 1975). Spencer argued that such offenders rarely manifest assaultive behavior. However, little is known about the psychological factors that determine whether a thief will use the weapon. Conklin (1972) has noted that the armed robber tends to be an older, white, professional offender who uses his gun as a means for avoiding violence. The unarmed robbers, by contrast, tend to be young and black, often work in groups, and commit low-yield impulsive property offenses. Such youths are responsible for a fair amount of nonlethal physical damage (as in a typical "mugging").

THE EMERGENCY TREATMENT OF THE PATHOLOGICALLY VIOLENT OFFENDER

Lion (1972) has offered advice on how to handle the more pathologically violent person in an emergency situation. Lion's basic proposition is that the violent patient is frightened of his own aggressive urges and wants help in preventing loss of control. His aggressive behavior is often a defense against feelings of helplessness and fragility. Thus, the more people try to restrain him, the more violent he may become. The first step a counselor must take is to endeavor to get the violent person away from bystanders and onlookers.

To calm the person, typical crisis intervention techniques seem to work. The person should not be asked to explain why he is angry, for that may merely re-arouse the traumatic event that led to his fear and hostility. The counselor should merely acknowledge the person's anger with a statement such as, "You sure are angry as hell." If the counselor has power, such as that which is conferred on a physician, the patient may be assured that he will not be permitted to act upon his violent urges.

A patient's dangerousness is not related to his noisiness, or the disruptiveness of his behavior, or the nature of his complaint. His psychomotor agitation is a result of his anxiety, and is good. The quiet patient lacks anxiety, and may not even seek help. His violent actions may be explosive and extreme.

If the presenting complaint is a diffuse fear of killing someone, the patient is probably a borderline individual who seeks help when his tenuous hold on reality begins to break down. Often his childhood has been emotionally deprived, and his parents may have abandoned him or been brutal to him. Yet he was dependent on his parents for love and protection, and these conflicting urges were difficult to reconcile. He often showed love toward his parents then, but when a spouse or employer stresses him now the suppressed anger breaks through. The person may be dangerous because his anger is poorly channeled and improperly sublimated. He may drive his car dangerously, go on a rampage, or get into tavern brawls. A psychotherapeutic goal is to get such a person to see at whom he is actually angry and to get him to express his anger verbally.

If the patient mentions a specific target, an equivalent childhood history may be found, but the person has found a substitute focus for his resentment, and has adopted a tough and independent image. His anger is usually toward the same-sex parent. Such an individual is more dangerous the less anxiety he shows. If he is a man, he often becomes murderous when intoxicated, and may show great anxiety in male company in taverns (which psychiatrists call homosexual panic), to which he may react with aggression rather than flight. He may have amnesia after a brawl.

In taking a case history from a violent patient, it is important to explore all the manifestations of aggression in the history, although this often makes the counselor himself anxious. A patient's cruelty and sadism is important for an evaluation of his dangerousness. His fantasies are also important, Pyromania, cruelty to animals, and temper tantrums in the patients' early history may relate to his current problems. The case history should also cover possible indirect expressions of anger (such as psychosomatic illnesses, tics, stuttering, enuresis), child abuse, maternal seductiveness, job and military record, ownership of weapons, and use of drugs. An organic evaluation can exclude or identify brain dysfunctions.

A psychiatric diagnosis can be an important clue. The paranoid schizophrenic may attack an unforeseen object, and a withdrawn schizophrenic may commit an act such as planting a bomb on a plane merely to kill one hated relative. The obsessive-compulsive or schizoid personality may be prone to episodic dyscontrol (Menninger & Mayman, 1956), during which all controls break down and there ensues a brief psychotic episode.

Menninger and Modlin (1971) have suggested clues that the counselor can look for in evaluating the clinical potential for violence:

1. fear of or concerns about losing control;
2. evidence that the person has been looking for help, however indirect his presenting complaints, and from whatever helping source (minister, doctor, lawyer,
   neighbor);
3. reports of suggestive actions such as dangerous driving, cleaning a gun, and
   so on;
4. episodes of altered states of consciousness;
5. previous homicides, assaults, or suicide attempts;
6. evidence in the person's case history of severe emotional deprivation or overt
   rejection, parental seduction, exposure to brutality and extreme violence, childhood fire setting, or cruelty to animals or other children.

Hellman and Blackman (1966) have found that a triad of bed wetting, fire
setting, and cruelty to animals marked the childhoods of 75 percent of a group
of patients who had committed violent crimes as compared to only 25 percent
of a group who had not committed violent acts.[2]

Violent patients often evoke strong emotions in the psychotherapist. The
therapist may fear that the patient will kill him, and Lion recommends using
cotherapists if necessary to reduce the therapist's anxiety during the therapy
sessions. The therapist may also fear that the patient will kill someone else
and that he, the therapist, will be blamed. The violent patient can also evoke
aggressive urges in a therapist, and the therapist must beware of unconsciously sanctioning a patient's violence.

The goals of violence-related psychotherapy include:

1. Training the patient to seek help when he feels himself losing control. In this
   connection, the patient must have immediate twenty-four-hour-a-day access to
   his therapist, because such patients often cannot tolerate delay. Lion recommends
   that for patients who are from lower social classes, a medical facade is useful to
   reassure them—including a white coat with a stethoscope in the pocket for the
   therapist to wear, and a medical setting.
2. Teaching the patient to express anger verbally, and getting him to see that his
   violent behavior is self-destructive.
3. Teaching the patient to predict the outcome of his violent actions prior to carrying them out.
4. Teaching the patient to recognize his emotions, especially his anger, to label his
   emotions and to deal with them rather than merely to experience them, possibly
   making them worse by drinking alcohol.
5. Recognizing that potential victims often play a part in provoking violent behavior, and dealing with their role too.

Treatment can lead to depression in the violent patient, and this depression must not be allowed to get too intense. The therapist must lead the patient
to healthier ways of dealing with anger, but he must not block the patient's
previous ways of coping before new, alternative ways are developed.

NOTES

1. The subculture of violence phenomenon is well illustrated by gangs. Miller (1975) has estimated that the number of gangs in the United States reaches well into the hundreds, and that thousands of gang members contribute about one third of violent crimes and terrorize neighborhoods and schools with their violence. Gang members are predominantly male, ranging in age from ten to twenty-one. Most gangs are in low income neighborhoods and most have black or Hispanic members. Recently there has been an increase in the victimization of others by gangs, but most gang violence is still aimed at members of rival gangs. Miller feels that the increase in the availability and use of firearms has facilitated the increase in violence and gang-related killings.

2. As we have seen in Chapter 10, there has been little research supporting the potential of quantitative scales to predict homicide, in contrast to the field of suicide prevention, where much effort has been put into attempts to predict suicide (Lester, 1972). This difference has been due primarily to the pessimism of authorities in the field (Monahan, 1975; Toch, 1977) and to the poor success of early attempts at predicting violence.

Some early attempts did improve the accuracy of predicting violence over chance levels. Wenk and Emrich (1972) used psychological test data and life history data and were able to predict violence in previously violent youths three times better than chance. Kozol and associates (1972) used clinical judgments with adjudged dangerous sex offenders who had been indeterminately confined, and reported that 8 percent of those whom they considered to be safe for release committed serious violent crimes after release, whereas 35 percent of those they judged to be unsafe committed such offenses. However, this level of accuracy is far from being satisfactory as a basis for making decisions about people's lives. Furthermore (as noted in Chapter 10), the base rate of violent behavior in our society is so low that any predictor tends to classify large numbers of nonviolent people as potentially violent.

REFERENCES

Amir, M. *Patterns in forcible rape.* Chicago: University of Chicago Press, 1971.

Angyal, A. *Neurosis and treatment.* New York: Wiley, 1965.

Bandura, A. *Aggression: A social learning analysis.* Englewood Cliffs: Prentice-Hall, 1973.

Bard, M. Family intervention police teams as a community mental health resource. *Journal of Criminal Law, Criminology, and Political Science,* 1969, 60, 247–250.

Clinard, M., & Quinney, R. *Criminal behavior systems.* New York: Holt, Rinehart and Winston, 1967.

Cohen, M., Garofalo, R., Boucher, R., & Seghorn, T. The psychology of rapists. *Seminars in Psychiatry,* 1971, 3, 307–327.

Cohen, M., Seghorn, T., & Calmas, W. Sociometric study of the sex offender. *Journal of Abnormal Psychology,* 1969, 74, 249–255.

Conklin, J. E. *Robbery and the criminal justice system.* Philadelphia: Lippincott, 1972.

David, P., & Scott, J. A cross-cultural comparison of juvenile offenders, offenses, due process and societies. *Criminology,* 1973, 11, 183–205.

Delsordo, J. Protective casework for abused children. *Children,* 1963, 10, 213–218.

Dinitz, S., Dynes, R., & Clarke, A. *Deviance.* New York: Oxford University Press, 1975.

Dollard, J., Doob, L., Miller, N., Mowrer, O., & Sears, R. *Frustration and aggression.* New Haven: Yale University Press, 1939.

Ellinwood, E. Assault and homicide associated with amphetamine abuse. *American Journal of Psychiatry,* 1970, *127,* 1170–1175.

Friedrich, W., & Boriskin, J. The role of the child in abuse. *American Journal of Orthopsychiatry,* 1976, *46,* 580–590.

Gelles, R. Child abuse as psychopathology. *American Journal of Orthopsychiatry,* 1973, *43,* 611–621.

Gillin, J. *The Wisconsin prisoner.* Madison: University of Wisconsin Press, 1946.

Goldstein, J. *Aggression and crimes of violence.* New York: Oxford University Press, 1975.

Helfer, R. *Child abuse and neglect: The diagnostic process and treatment programs.* Washington, D.C.: U.S. Government Printing Office, 1975. DHEW Pub. No. OHD 75–69.

Hellman, D., & Blackman, N. Enuresis, firesetting and cruelty to animals. *American Journal of Psychiatry,* 1966, *122,* 1431–1435.

Henry, A., & Short, J. *Suicide and homicide.* Glencoe: Free Press, 1954.

Hood, R., & Sparks, R. *Key issues in criminology.* New York: McGraw-Hill, 1970.

Hook, E. Behavioral implications of the human XYY genotype. *Science,* 1973, *179,* 139–150.

Kempe, C., & Helfer, R. *Helping the battered child and his family.* Philadelphia: Lippincott, 1972.

Kercher, G., & Walker, C. Reactions of convicted rapists to sexually explicit stimuli. *Journal of Abnormal Psychology,* 1973, *81,* 46–50.

Kinzel, A. Body-buffer zone in violent prisoners. *American Journal of Psychiatry,* 1970, *127,* 59–64.

Kinzel, A. Violent behavior in prisoners. In J. Fawcett (Ed.), *Dynamics of violence.* Chicago: American Medical Association, 1971, 157–164.

Kozol, H., Boucher, R., & Garofalo, R. The diagnosis and treatment of dangerousness. *Crime and Delinquency,* 1972, *18,* 371–392.

Lester, D. *Why people kill themselves.* Springfield, Ill.: Charles C Thomas, 1972.

Lester, D. Murder. *Correctional Society of Psychiatry,* 1973, *19*(4), 40–50.

Lester, D. *Unusual sexual behavior.* Springfield, Ill.: Charles C Thomas, 1975.

Lester, D., & Brockopp, G. (Eds.), *Crisis intervention and counseling by telephone.* Springfield, Ill.: Charles C Thomas, 1973.

Lester, D., & Lester, G. *Crime of passion.* Chicago: Nelson-Hall, 1975.

Lion, J. *Evaluation and management of the violent patient.* Springfield, Ill.: Charles C Thomas, 1972.

Lorenz, K. *On aggression.* New York: Harcourt Brace Jovanovich, 1966.

Lynch, M. Risk factors in the child. In H. Martin (Ed.), *The abused child.* Cambridge, Mass.: Ballinger, 1976, 43–56.

Macdonald, J. The threat to kill. *American Journal of Psychiatry,* 1963, *120,* 125–130.

Macdonald, J. Homicidal threats. *American Journal of Psychiatry,* 1967, *124,* 475–482.

Mark, V., & Ervin, F. *Violence and the brain.* New York: Harper & Row, 1970.

Megargee, E. Undercontrolled and overcontrolled personality types in extreme antisocial aggression. *Psychological Monographs,* 1966, *80,* Whole no. 611.

Menninger, K., & Mayman, M. Episodic dyscontrol. *Bulletin of the Menninger Clinic*, 1956, *20*, 153–165.

Menninger, R., & Modlin, H. Individual violence. In J. Fawcett (Ed.), *Dynamics of Violence*. Chicago: American Medical Association, 1971, 71–78.

Merrill, E. Physical abuse of children. In V. Francis (Ed.), *Protecting the battered child*. Denver: American Humane Association, 1962.

Miller, W. *Violence by youth gangs and youth groups as a crime problem in major American cities*. Washington, D.C.: LEAA, 1975.

Monahan, J. The prediction of violence. In D. Chappell & J. Monahan (Eds.), *Violence and criminal justice*. Lexington: Heath, 1975, 15–31.

Monroe, R. *Behavioral disorders*. Cambridge, Mass.: Harvard University Press, 1970.

National Center on Child Abuse and Neglect. *Child abuse and neglect: The problem and its management*. Washington, D.C.: U.S. Government Printing Office, 1975. DHEW Pub. No. OHD 75–30073.

National Commission on the Causes and Prevention of Violence. *Crimes of Violence*, (vol. 12). Washington, D.C.: U.S. Government Printing Office, 1969a.

National Commission on the Causes and Prevention of Violence. *To establish justice, to ensure domestic tranquility*. Washington, D.C.: U.S. Government Printing Office, 1969b.

Normandreau, A. Violence and robbery. *Acta Criminologica*, 1972, *5*(1), 11–106.

Owen, D. The 47, XYY male. *Psychological Bulletin*, 1972, *78*, 209–233.

Palmer, S. *A study of murder*. New York: Crowell, 1960.

Peterson, R., Pittman, D., & O'Neal, P. Stabilities in deviance. *Journal of Criminal Law, Criminology, and Political Science*, 1962, *53*, 44–48.

Pittman, D., & Handy, W. Patterns in criminal aggravated assault. *Journal of Criminal Law, Criminology, and Political Science*, 1964, *55*, 462–470.

Pokorny, A. Human violence. *Journal of Criminal Law, Criminology, and Political Science*, 1965, *56*, 488–497.

Redl, F., & Wineman, D. *Children who hate*. New York: Free Press, 1951.

Spinetta, J., & Rigler, D. The child-abusing parent. *Psychological Bulletin*, 1972, *77*, 296–304.

Toch, H. *Violent men*. Chicago: Aldine, 1969.

Toch, H. *Police, prisons and the problem of violence*. Washington, D.C.: Department of Health, Education and Welfare, 1977, Pub. no. (ADM) 76–364.

Uniform Crime Reports. *Crime in the United States, 1975*. Washington, D.C.: FBI, 1977.

Wenk, E., & Emrich, R. Assaultive youth. *Journal of Research in Crime & Delinquency*, 1972, *9*, 171–196.

Witkin, H., Mednick, S., Schulsinger, F., Bakkestrom, E., Christiansen, K., Goodenough, D., Hirschhorn, K., Lundsteen, C., Owen, D., Philip, J., Rubin, D., & Stocking, M. Criminality in XYY and XXY men. *Science*, 1976, *193*, 547–555.

Wolfgang, M. *Patterns in criminal homicide*. Philadelphia: University of Pennsylvania Press, 1958.

Wolfgang, M. Violent behavior. In A. Blumberg (Ed.), *Current perspectives on criminal behavior*. New York: Knopf, 1974, 240–261.

Wolfgang, M., Figlio, R., & Sellin, T. *Delinquency in a birth cohort*. Chicago: University of Chicago Press, 1972.

Zalba, S. Treatment of child abuse. *Social Work*, 1966, *11*, 8–16.

chapter 14

The Antisocial Personality— Psychopathy and Sociopathy

Albert I. Rabin

Nearly two hundred years ago, the French physician and pioneer in the field of mental disorders, Pinel, encountered a rather unusual case. The person involved did not fit the usual categories of mental disturbance employed at that time. Pinel described the case briefly as *Manie sans delire*—"madness without confusion." Subsequent generations of doctors who have concerned themselves with psychiatric nosology have emerged with similar observations and classificatory formulations. Thus, the English alienist J. C. Pritchard devised the term "moral insanity" in 1835. He and his successors applied the term in those instances where abnormality or "insanity" expressed itself in the circumscribed field of morality. It was in 1888 that Koch substituted the presumably less odious term "psychopathic inferiority" for Pritchard's moral insanity. However, implied in the new term was the notion of constitutional predisposition for the disorder (McCord & McCord, 1964).

It is interesting to note Pritchard's (1835) description of the condition, which later came to be known as psychopathic inferiority or psychopathic personality. He states that:

> there is a form of mental derangement in which the intellectual functions appear to have sustained little or no injury, while the disorder is manifested principally or alone in the state of the feelings, temper or habits. In cases of this nature the moral or active principles of the mind are strangely perverted or depraved, the power of self-government is lost or greatly impaired, and the individual is found to be incapable, not of talking or reasoning . . . but conducting himself with decency and propriety in the business of life (p. 15).

Subsequently, during the first half of the twentieth century, the concept of "psychopathic personality," without the implications of constitutional inferiority, has emerged. The term has become quite popular as a psychiatric category though there have been criticisms that it has become a "wastebasket" classification into which were placed all the cases that did not fit into the traditional time-hallowed rubrics of psychosis and neurosis. Nevertheless, the psychopathic personality or psychopathy has remained a part of the psychiatric and clinical language, although it no longer is considered an official diagnostic category of the American Psychiatric Association.

The Diagnostic and Statistical Manual of Mental Disorders (1952 ed.) replaced the term psychopathic personality with *sociopathic personality*. According to this manual, "Individuals to be placed in this category are ill primarily in terms of society and of conformity with the prevailing cultural milieu, and not only in terms of personal discomfort and relations with other individuals." The term sociopathic personality in this manual is a broad category that includes a variety of disturbances, including sexual deviation, alcoholism, and drug addiction in addition to the "antisocial" and "dyssocial" reactions, which are more akin to the traditional concept of psychopathic personality. The antisocial reaction is described as characteristic of those "individuals who are always in trouble, profiting neither from experience nor punishment and maintaining no loyalties to any person, group, or code. They are frequently callous and hedonistic, showing marked emotional immaturity with lack of sense of responsibility, lack of judgement, and an ability to rationalize their behavior so that it appears warranted, reasonable, and justified" (p. 38).

A subsequent edition (the second) of the same diagnostic manual (1968), which is the most recent at this writing, has dropped the term sociopathic personality as well as the older one of psychopathy. These terms are replaced by the term "antisocial personality," which is one of a number of personality disorders listed. The general category of personality disorder "is characterized by deeply ingrained maladaptive patterns of behavior that are perceptibly different in quality from psychotic and neurotic symptoms. Generally, these are life-long patterns, often recognizable by the time of adolescence or earlier" (DSM II, 1968, p. 41).

One of the subtypes of personality disorder which has replaced sociopathy and psychopathy as a diagnostic entity in the 1968 diagnostic manual is the "antisocial personality." The most essential features of this disorder are embodied in the following description: "The term is reserved for individuals who are basically unsocialized and whose behavior pattern brings them repeatedly into conflicts with society. They are incapable of significant loyalty to individuals, groups, or social values. They are grossly selfish, callous, irresponsible, impulsive, and unable to feel guilt or to learn from experience and punishment. Frustration tolerance is low. They tend to blame others or offer plausible rationalization for their behavior" (DSM II, 1968, p. 43).

It depends on the vintage of the literature one examines which term or diagnostic label is employed. Throughout this chapter, the terms psychopathic personality, sociopathic personality and antisocial personality will be used interchangeably.

THE CLINICAL PICTURE

In the preceding paragraphs we have detailed rather briefly the historical antecedents and the modern definitional sequence of a concept—from psychopathic personality to sociopathic personality, to the present antisocial personality. It may be noted that the trend has been in the direction of greater specificity and greater restriction of the range of behavioral phenomena and characteristics which may be encompassed by the concept. There has also been a tendency toward greater concreteness and operationalization in the definition. We shall now go somewhat beyond the naming of traits which is permitted by the limited space of the diagnostic manuals and attempt a more comprehensive view which reflects the literature as well as clinical experience.

One of the classics of the clinical literature on the psychopathic personality is Cleckley's *The Mask of Sanity* (1976) which was published in five editions since 1941. In addition to the presentation of a series of fascinating case studies and discussions of etiology and treatment, the author lists a series of characteristics which are some of the most essential features of the psychopath. The characteristics are as follows:

1. Superficial charm and good "intelligence."
2. Absence of delusions and other irrational thinking.
3. Absence of "nervousness" or psychoneurotic manifestations.
4. Unreliability.
5. Untruthfulness and insincerity.
6. Lack of remorse and shame.
7. Inadequately motivated antisocial behavior.
8. Poor judgment and failure to learn from experience.
9. Pathological egocentricity and incapacity for love.
10. General poverty in major affective reactions.
11. Specific loss of insight.
12. Unresponsiveness in general interpersonal relations.
13. Fantastic and uninviting behavior with drink and sometimes without.
14. Suicide rarely carried out.
15. Sex life impersonal, trivial, and poorly integrated.
16. Failure to follow any life plan (Cleckley, 1976, pp. 337–338).

It may be readily noted that several of the characteristics on the list do not actually describe what a psychopath *is*, but what *he is not*. The characteristics indicate that such a person is *not psychotic* (no delusions or irrational thinking) and *not neurotic* (absence of nervousness or psychoneurotic manifestation). Furthermore, by implication he is not mentally retarded for he has "good intelligence." The other characteristics of the psychopaths are interrelated and cluster into several major patterns.

Other authors have stressed fewer common characteristics of psychopaths and derivatives of the more fundamental ones. Thus, for example, a British source (Craft, 1966) delineates two basic or "primary features" that are a necessary ingredient of the diagnosis of psychopathic personality. First is the "affectionlessness" or "lovelessness" of the psychopath—a lack of feeling for other human beings. Second is the impulsivity of behavior, without any prior reflection or deliberation. Craft also lists several secondary features of the psychopath which are often a consequence of the primary ones he mentioned.

Craft sees *aggression* as the outcome of a combination of his two primary features. If you have no feelings for others and act on impulse, it can be readily understood that there is no bar to the expression of antisocial and hostile behavior toward others. Other "secondary" features do not evolve so clearly from primary ones. Cleckley's "lack of shame or remorse," the "inability to profit from experience or punishment," and the "lack of drive or ambition" are more remotely a consequence of the affectionlessness and impulsivity mentioned before. One may suppose, of course, that a person who has no feelings for others would not be concerned about shame, which is an essentially social emotion. Similarly, not profiting from experience, which refers to society's reaction to one's behavior, is another form of ignoring others. Finally, the lack of motivation, presumably in the area of achievement, may be interpreted as being concerned very little with gaining the approval and meeting the standards of people in one's environment; it may also signify an inability or lack of desire to contribute one's share to the general social welfare.

A somewhat similar picture is drawn by McCord and McCord in their volume entitled *The Psychopath* (1964). They see the psychopath as "asocial," "highly impulsive," "aggressive"; also as "driven by uncontrolled desires," as feeling little guilt, and having a "warped capacity for love." These authors concentrate primarily on positive characteristics (those that are present) of the psychopathic syndrome, and do not concern themselves so much with what it is not, in their definition of the disorder. To be sure, all of the writers on the topic are very concerned with the issue of differential diagnosis, which will be allotted space in the latter part of this chapter.

Further extension of our survey of attempts to define the psychopath would not be very productive, for, as we have noted, there is considerable common ground among the several lists of characteristics presented. They may differ in degree of specificity as well as in the extent of centrality of the features to the diagnosis. In the following paragraphs, some of the most central of these features, as we see them, will be highlighted and discussed in greater detail.

The Inadequate Conscience or Superego

We have pointed out that Pritchard, early in the nineteenth century, described psychopathic personality as a form of "mental derangement." He also called it a form of "moral insanity" or "moral imbecility." The reference here is to the relative weakness or absence of moral judgment as a guide to behavior. This deficit in morality as the important censorship of socially acceptable behavior is still one of the major criteria of the diagnosis of psychopathy. Some of the more specific characteristics that appear in Cleckley's (1976) list (see p. 324) can be subsumed under the present subtitle concerning the inadequate superego. For example, the "lack of shame and remorse," the "unreliability," the "untruthfulness" and "insincerity," and even the "unpredictability" and "inadequately motivated, antisocial behavior" are part of the same syndrome of an insufficiently developed, if at all acquired, conscience or superego.

The notion of the defective superego has two major aspects. The first is represented in the psychopath's inability to apply the moral standards of society to his behavior: he cheats, lies, steals, does not keep promises—the "unreliability," "untruthfulness" and various kinds of antisocial behavior mentioned above. Somehow he has not absorbed the "thou shalts" and the "thou shalt nots" of his society and the broader cultural milieu. The second, and dynamically closely related aspect is the absence of guilt. Guilt is an important quality of any well-developed conscience. When a normal person violates the moral code, he feels guilty; he feels unhappy and blames himself for the transgression. In addition to this *post facto* emotional and painful experience, guilt also performs a warning or preventive function. People ordinarily try not to transgress the moral code, for if they do they will feel guilty, unworthy, and unhappy—a painful experience to be avoided. Thus, the anticipated transgression is avoided as well. The psychopath, with a defective or inadequate superego, is not subject to the experience of guilt; there is a "lack of shame or remorse." There is none of this automatic self-punishment that goes along with the contemplation or commission of immoral and unethical acts. The psychopath continues to behave irresponsibly, untruthfully, insincerely, and antisocially without a shred of shame, remorse, or guilt. He may at times express regret for the antisocial acts and crimes he may have perpetrated; however, these are often words spoken for their effect, for they do not express any genuine and sincerely felt emotion.

The absence of guilt and remorse permits the psychopath to continue his antisocial behavior indefinitely unless the authorities or people in the immediate environment decide to exercise some control. When confronted with his lies and dishonesties the psychopath will often try to explain them away and rationalize by giving some plausible reason for his behavior. However, for the most part, as in all rationalizations, *good* and often persuasive reasons are not the real or *true* ones.

A related issue comes from the list of the psychopath's characteristics quoted above. The reference here is to the statement, "Suicide rarely carried out." Suicide is frequently threatened, especially by some incarcerated psychopaths. They even go so far as to make suicidal "attempts." However, these are a sham. They may scratch the wrist with glass and shortly afterwards call attention to their bleeding; or, prepare a noose for their hanging and be found by the guard "in the nick of time." They really do not experience the profundity of guilt and the depth of despair that lead the very depressed individual to a genuine suicidal attempt; they "act" the part and utilize the behavior as a method of manipulation. Hence suicide is "rarely carried out," although some feigned "attempts" may accidentally be successful.

Emotional Immaturity—Egocentricity and Impulsivity

In the earliest years of life, the young infant or small child is almost entirely concerned with himself, with his wants and needs. He is *egocentric*—in the center of his own world. All that counts is the satisfaction and gratification of his desires. He may become angry and lash out even at his mother or mother surrogate for failure to grant his immediate wishes. As the child grows up, he gradually becomes more "socialized" and learns to adapt himself in a world full of people who also have their rights and privileges. He becomes aware of the needs of others, which sometimes may be in conflict with his own, and learns to delay and postpone gratification. Inevitably, he must learn to make compromises and realize that he cannot forever remain in the center of the world. He learns to consider the rights, needs, and feelings of others and obey the rules which evolved in his society for the purpose of its smooth and efficient functioning. There is ultimately the realization of what the consequences may be if everyone were to remain egocentric—constantly pulling in his own direction. Thus, the mature person relinquishes his egocentricity and, in the process of growing up and assuming the adult role, acquires a more *sociocentric* orientation.

Such an advanced development is somehow never reached by the psychopathic or antisocial personality. The psychopath grows up physically and is often well developed and attractive in appearance (as Cleckley pointed out). He also matures as far as formal intellectual functions are concerned; he acquires many of the perceptual, motor, and cognitive skills necessary for the manipulation of the environment. However, he remains immature emotionally. He continues to be egocentric and impulsive, being solely concerned with the immediate fulfillment of his needs. Since he can suffer no delay or postponement and cannot tolerate frustration when thwarted by the environment, he remains rather childish in this respect. As a rule he proceeds "to get what he wants when he wants it," without consideration for others.

Among the several "neurotic styles" described by Shapiro (1965) is the *impulsive style*. He suggests, "The distinctive quality of this subjective experience revolves around an impairment of normal feelings of deliberateness and intention. It is manifested in the nature of the experience for these people of 'impulse' or 'irresistible impulse,' and of the significance of 'whim' in their mental lives" (pp. 134–135). He goes on further to describe the experience "as a virtually reflexive response to an external provocation or opportunity." The typical phrase: "I didn't mean to do it, but then I saw the money lying there on the table, and somehow I just took it" illustrates the lack of deliberateness and intentionality in the impulsive behavior of the psychopath.

As a result of the socialization process, the ordinary person develops, in varying degrees, a capacity for self-control—for censoring action before it actually takes place. In the instances where he transgresses the special code, social sanctions are applied and he is punished. This experience of what behaviorists call "negative reinforcement" usually alerts the person in similar instances, so that transgression and the consequent punishment are avoided. Not so with the psychopath, however. He does not usually learn or profit from past experience, for the capacity for self-control has never fully developed and the ability to inhibit behavior is very weak. He may go on committing the very acts or crimes for which he was punished before. Past experience does not seem to affect his future behavior. The immediate and infantile needs are strong and the control apparatus is weak; the result is that behavior remains governed by the former and unguided by the latter.

In a previous presentation on the psychopathic (sociopathic) personalities (Rabin, 1961), I discussed the "absence of life plan" as one of the major characteristics of psychopathic personality. From the present discussion of impulsivity, however, it becomes obvious that what Cleckley (1976) listed as "failure to follow any life plan" is a direct consequence of the dominance of immediate expression and gratification of needs. The psychopath lives in the present—in the "here and now"; he is unable to postpone gratification for the future or to anticipate. He is not capable of visualizing the future or planning for it, since he lives primarily in the present and is preoccupied with it. There is little evidence of long-range planning, let alone a "life-plan," for the future. An earlier comment concerning "impairment of sense of intention" comes to mind. Furthermore, the impulsive individuals (Shapiro, 1965) are "remarkably lacking in active interests, aims, values, or goals much beyond the immediate concern of their own lives (p. 143)."

Life, for the psychopath, is a hit-or-miss affair. It consists of a series of impulsive acts which are not instrumental in long-range planning for a career, in the achievement of socially desirable goals, or in the attainment of stability of social, economic, and emotional status. Although the psychopath may at times resolve to follow a certain plan for his future, he fails in the actual realization of such a program. Too many immediate and temporary lures dissuade him. In a sense, he remains self-defeating and can be described as a drifter—a boat without moorings on a turbulent sea.

The psychopath moves often from one job to another. His sudden outbursts at fellow workers, managers, customers; his flagrant lying and dishonesty as well as unreliability and lack of a sense of responsibility—all contribute to the instability of the work history which is a further demonstration of the inability to select, maintain, and follow a consistent and stable life plan.

Finally, "loss of insight" is very much a characteristic related to impulsivity and egocentricity. It is the incapacity to maintain a reasonable degree of objectivity in viewing and evaluating oneself—the inability to see oneself as others do. The egocentric individual, by definition, is unable to "step out of his own boots" and have a look at himself from an outsider's perspective.

It is this lack that permits the psychopath to contribute so much to the misery of others with relative impunity and absence of self-blame.

Stunted Capacity for Love and Emotional Involvement

This brings us to the last broad area of deficit in functioning which characterizes the psychopathic or antisocial personality. As was noted in the previous paragraph, the egocentricity not only involves a lack of consideration for others, but also a lack of understanding of other people and an inability to identify with the way they look at things. Hence, the lack of "insight" refers to "looking in" upon oneself, reflecting and evaluating from the viewpoint of others for which the psychopath has little capacity. He is also directed outward, not inward. Some authors attribute this difficulty to the genuine lack of capacity for empathy, for "feeling into" other people.

Since egocentricity is a major trait, there is the inability to maintain genuine affectional ties and meaningful interpersonal relationships. The psychopath is concerned with his own needs and their gratification and has little concern for those of others. He is in the center of his own universe and is not ready to put himself out for someone else. Other people are important only to the extent that they can be used to his own end—self-gratification. Altruism is not one of his strong points.

True friendship is not part of the psychopath's experience. He may be the recipient of love and affection from others who may tolerate many of his vagaries, but he hardly reciprocates with similar consideration for them. He may betray them and even exploit their trust in him for his own purposes. Sacrificing for a friend is out of the question. There is callousness and insensitivity in relation to other people.

A logical corollary of the above is the lack of capacity for a genuine love relationship, for true involvement with another person. This is not to say that he does not get involved in sex and sexual relationships. On the contrary, such affairs are quite frequent and stormy. But there is little depth and genuineness, there is little stability and permanence—promiscuity is the rule. The psychopath may profess true and undying love, but it is all a sham, for he readily abandons his beloved with few qualms and little remorse. There often may be protestations of love and friendship accompanied by a convincing display of emotion and affection. However, it is not the real thing; it is superficial, contrived, and manipulative—used as a device for gaining selfish ends such as trust, support, or sexual gratification.

The psychopath's sexual activities are primarily characterized by physical discharges and are casual in nature, without much emotional or psychological involvement. As Cleckley once commented, their "amativeness is little more than a simple itch and even that the itch is seldom, if ever, particularly intense" (Cleckley, 1976, p. 362).

Finally, regarding the emotional poverty of the psychopath, Cleckley (1976) makes the interesting comment that the psychopath lacks a sense of tragedy or tragic feelings. Perhaps the lack of empathy and involvement with others as well as the reduced emotional range, generally, are at the basis of this serious emotional deficit. It may also be questioned whether there really is the capacity for experiencing genuine depression as well, for the important ingredients are lacking—the concern for objects (and their loss) as well as the capacity for insight and self-evaluation.

Composite Picture—Longitudinal Data

Based on statistical data of an extensive thirty-year follow-up study of children who were originally seen in a child guidance clinic, Robins (1966) offers a detailed description of the median subject who subsequently received the diagnosis of psychopathic (sociopathic) personality. The "median" case is a "male unskilled worker who has been out of work about one and a half years in the last ten years, who has changed jobs on the average of once every 15 months; and who has never held any job for as much as 5 years . . . lives in central city rather than in the suburbs . . . moves every 12 to 14 months . . . (p. 131)." In addition, according to Robins, this "median" case costs the community much money as a recipient of public aid, charity, or support by being an inmate in prison: he has had many arrests, at least one of which was for committing a major crime, and served some time in jails. He is married, living with his wife, but was divorced at least once. Desertion, unfaithfulness, and failure to support the present as well as the previous wife, are part of the picture. His excessive drinking has caused him loss of jobs and arrests. Despite a history of "sexual exploits," he is without friends and does not participate in the activities of any organization. Contacts with the family of origin are slight.

The Antisocial Personality and Criminality

When we review some of the descriptions of the psychopathic or antisocial personality, we can readily see that many such persons, sooner or later, find themselves in conflict with the law. The impulsivity and aggression, the selfishness in achieving one's own immediate needs, and the disregard for society's rules and laws bring these people to the attention of the criminal justice system. Among the most recent criteria proposed for a diagnosis of antisocial personality (Spitzer, et al., 1975) are: three or more serious arrests, physical fights, defaulting on debts, and so on.

There is little wonder that many persons diagnosed as antisocial personalities reside for varying lengths of time in penal institutions. Various estimates run as high as 30 percent, but a conservative estimate is that 10 percent of all those incarcerated in prisons are antisocial personalities (McCord & McCord, 1964). Furthermore, it is also estimated that about 5 percent of the residents in American mental institutions are so diagnosed.

Thus, we see that psychopathic or antisocial personality and criminality are not synonymous terms. Some criminals are psychopaths, but as we noted above, the majority of the criminal population is not. There are, of course, many antisocial personalities who manage to stay out of the clutches of the law. They may be sufficiently ingenious in avoiding the attention of the authorities and maintain themselves with varying degrees of precariousness in normal society. Among these there may be persons who for long periods of time may hide behind a cloak of affluence or professional respectability (Cleckley, 1976).

DIFFERENTIAL DIAGNOSIS

It is worth reiterating that the antisocial personality and criminality are not the same thing, and even that people break the law for a variety of reasons, not only because of their particular constellation of personality characteristics. Thus, breaking the law or criminality is certainly to be differentiated from and is not synonymous with psychopathy or antisocial personality.

There are also several psychopathological disorders that may on occasion or in some respect show some similarity to that of the antisocial personality. It is important to distinguish between these fairly common abnormal conditions and the kind of personality we have been describing.

Although psychopathy was once described as a condition of "moral imbecility" it does not refer to a general "imbecility" or mental retardation. The retardation or the deficit is in superego development and moral behavior but not in general mental functioning. On the contrary, many authors point out that intellectually the psychopath is quite normal, has an average or better IQ, and does not demonstrate any particular deficit in that area. Although the psychopath "fails to learn from experience" it is not on the basis of mental retardation. It is because of his defective emotional controls and his high degree of impulsivity that he is unable to benefit from past experience, not from the forgetting of that experience.

Different psychotic reactions such as schizophrenia or manic states may occasionally manifest some antisocial behavior similar to that noted in psychopathy. Hence, some comments regarding differential diagnosis are in order. The two conditions mentioned (schizophrenia and mania) are labeled as psychotic, referring to the loss of contact with reality. Various thought and perceptual disturbances are characteristic of these conditions. However, as we noticed from the long list of criteria defining psychopathic personalities, the presence of hallucinations and delusions as well as cognitive deficits are "negative signs" or counterindicators of the diagnosis. Moreover, although the schizophrenic patient may demonstrate an outburst of negativism and aggression, and the manic patient some blatant characteristics of irresponsibility, these are merely brief and infrequent events. They are not characteristic of the lifelong behavior of these individuals, as would be the case with the psychopath or antisocial personality.

Finally, the distinction between the psychological disturbance of neurosis and that of antisocial personality is usually fairly clearcut. The neurotic individual is characterized by the frequent experience of anxiety and guilt and exhibits self-punishing symptoms—physical disorders, automatic system equivalents of anxiety, restriction of activities, and a general state of dissatisfaction and unhappiness. All these symptoms do not ordinarily describe the person diagnosed as an antisocial personality—who lashes out against others, against the environment rather than against himself. As we mentioned earlier, since he is not subject to feelings of guilt and anxiety, his conflicts are not internal. Only in some instances are neurotics said to "act out"—to express their internal unconscious conflicts. "The neurotic delinquent whose behavior springs from anxiety created by unresolved unconscious conflicts" is mentioned by McCord and McCord (1964) as one of several types of delinquency and criminality. The presence of anxiety is perhaps the most important distinguishing feature between the antisocial personality and the "acting out" neurotic.

Implied in the foregoing discussion—the description of the antisocial personality and its differences from other syndromes of mental deviation—is the so-called "medical model," which has been rightly subjected to considerable criticism in recent years. Lest the reader gain the notion that the antisocial personality is always easy to diagnose, I wish to disabuse him of this notion. There is a good deal of overlap among the diagnostic categories provided by traditional psychiatry and misdiagnosis is not too rare. Consequently, diagnoses attaching the label of "psychopath," "sociopath," or antisocial personality should not be undertaken too lightly. All too often some bit of impulsive, egotistic, annoying behavior may generate the use of the pejorative diagnostic label. Such a trend is as unjustified on clinical as it is on ethical grounds.

THEORIES OF CAUSATION

Upon reading the description of the antisocial personality—its characteristics and behavior patterns—the curious reader may ask, "How does he get that way?" or, "What are the reasons and causes for the development of such a deviant character structure?" Unfortunately, the answer is not very simple. There are a number of theories that attempt to offer an explanation of the etiology of this disorder. Some are supported by relevant research data. But we have not arrived at *the* answer yet. Hence, we shall discuss the several theories and the related research in some detail.

The Notion of Heredity

That heredity is the cause of all kinds of abnormalities in behavior and mental functioning has been a dominant hypothesis since the beginning of the nineteenth century. Psychopathic personality, too, was considered to have a strong hereditary basis. However, the influence of parents and the environment has been a relatively neglected factor. Disorders may "run in families," but this is not necessarily proof of "bad seed" or of the importance of genetic factors; it may support an environmental or learned behavior hypothesis as well.

After a critical review of the literature on the subject, McCord and McCord (1964) have concluded that "heredity cannot yet be excluded as a causal factor. With more adequate delineation, with more rigidly controlled experiments, and with more sensitive measurement, an hereditary link may possibly be established. Given our current knowledge, however, the extravagant claims of the geneticists must be questioned (p. 61)."

It seems that the "wait and see" attitude with respect to the heredity hypothesis is the most reasonable one. Whatever evidence exists is contradictory and far from conclusive.

The "Abnormal Brain" Hypothesis

Clinical observations of children and adults following brain disease or injury indicate certain changes in their behavior as well as other psychological consequences. Such persons often become more aggressive, overactive, emotionally labile, irritable, and frequently, antisocial. The resemblance of many of these symptoms to those of the antisocial personality led to the advancement of the hypothesis that some brain injury or abnormality is responsible for this condition. Despite the fact that gross neurological symptoms are ordinarily absent in the antisocial personality, the belief still persisted in some quarters that brain abnormality was present, although the areas affected might not involve the usual reflexes tested in neurological examination. The underlying hypothesis is that the parts of the brain concerned with emotional control and the "higher mental processes" are responsible for the subtle effects resulting in the antisocial personality.

Before we proceed with a discussion of brain-behavior relationships, it is important to heed the caution expressed in the notion that a relationship does not establish cause and effect. It was succinctly pointed out by one investigator (Hare, 1970) that "it is possible that a cortical disturbance produces some form of abnormal behavior, but it is also possible that the behavior is directly or indirectly responsible for the disturbance" (p. 27). Thus, at best, only a relationship or concomitance can be established, especially in humans.

One of the fairly popular trends in research involves a method of diagnosis and detection of brain damage and abnormality that was introduced several decades ago. This method is known as electroencephalography; the records obtained by the procedure are called electroencephalograms, or in the abbreviated forms—EEG's. These tracings of the electrical activity of the outer part of the brain or the cortex are popularly known as "brain waves."

The usual procedure in obtaining an encephalogram, or brain-wave tracing, is to attach electrodes at different points on the scalp and connect them with an amplifier. The electrical activity of the cortex is transmitted via the electrodes to the amplifier and the connected recording apparatus which, in turn, registers the fluctuations in the electrical potential. The resulting brain waves vary in amplitude (height) and quantity (number) per units of time (per second).

Several types of brain waves (electroencephalograms) are considered important diagnostically. The *alpha* waves, which appear at the rate of eight to thirteen per second, are ordinarily found in normal adults. Faster *beta* and *gamma* waves are also found often in normal individuals. But the very slow *delta* waves (less than eight per second) are especially observed in young children and in adults with brain pathology.

Overall, the picture regarding EEG findings in sociopathic or antisocial personalities has not changed markedly during the past two decades. Seventeen years ago (Rabin, 1961), I referred to Ellington's review (1954) which presented a summary of the research concerning the relationship between psychopathy and the electrocortical activity represented by brain wave tracings. The survey indicated that EEG abnormality among psychopaths has been found with remarkable regularity "in 47 to 58 percent of the cases." Ellington further points out, however, that this fact does not help in distinguishing psychopathy from other mental disorders in which the incidence of abnormal EEG's is fairly high. His conclusion is that "beyond differentiating the few organic cases which will be found, the EEG is of no value in the differential diagnosis of mental disorders or in personality assessment at the present time" (Ellington, 1954, p. 272).

There is no question that there is some electroencephalographic evidence of abnormal cortical activity in many psychopaths, but such an abnormality prevails in many other disorders as well. On the other hand, many psychopaths show "normal" electrocortical activity, while a sizeable percentage of normals yield abnormal brain wave patterns. Although statistically a differentiation between groups (e.g., normal and psychopathic) may be possible, no valid conclusion of cortical abnormality as a causative factor in psychopathy can be reached. The EEG is still too imperfect a diagnostic instrument for the purposes of fine discrimination and differential individual diagnosis. Furthermore, the underlying basis for the EEG abnormalities that are obtained has not been fully determined. Are those abnormalities due to developmental retardation as some investigators tend to believe (Hare, 1970; Bay-Rakal, 1965), to cortical damage, or to a combination of psychological, structural, or physiological influences?

Some interesting speculations are offered by Hare (1970) who suggests, "We might hypothesize that the temporal slow wave activity frequently observed in the EEG records of psychopaths reflects a malfunction of some limbic inhibitory mechanisms and that this malfunction makes it difficult to learn to inhibit behavior that is likely to lead to punishment." Further, in his opinion, the "malfunction could result from hereditary or experiential factors or, more likely, from injury, disease, or biochemical or vascular changes that temporarily dampen the inhibitory activity of important mechanisms" (p. 34).

Although there is apparent "consistency" in EEG findings in psychopathy (Hare, 1970), some studies (e.g., Syndulko, et al., 1975) are not in agreement.

Yet, there is also some evidence that a "greater proportion of psychopaths exhibit signs of neurological disorders (tremors, exaggerated reflexes, tics)" and that "compared with normal people a greater proportion of psychopaths have a history of early diseases which damage the brain" (McCord & McCord, 1964). Thus, although not definitely a causal or *the* causal factor in all psychopaths, brain abnormality and immaturity may be involved in many instances. However, the final conclusion we can draw is consonant with Robins' statement: "Despite numerous electroencephalographic studies indicating varying but high rates of abnormality in adult criminals, there is no proof that brain damage or abnormality as reflected in the EEG is a necessary precondition for the development of antisocial reaction (Robins, 1967, pp. 955–956)."

Other Physiological Variables

What we have so far discussed is the possible relationship between central nervous system (brain) abnormalities and the development of the antisocial personality. Over the years investigators have also examined and studied other possible physiological components that may partly cause psychopathy.

One of the areas of investigation in psychopathy is the autonomic nervous system, which is closely involved with affect and emotional experience and expression. This nervous system is relatively autonomous or independent of the brain and of the central nervous system which governs and directs the peripheral nervous network of the sensory and motor nerve fibers. These, in turn, control the sense organs and muscles respectively. The autonomic nervous system activates the visceral ("gut") organs such as stomach, heart, lungs, intestines, glands, and others. This system is subdivided into the sympathetic nervous system and the parasympathetic nervous system. The former functions especially in "fight or flight" situations and accelerates the function of the heart, the adrenal and sweat glands, and respiration, while it inhibits peristaltic activity of the stomach and intestines and constricts the blood vessels in the peripheral parts of the body (arms, legs, etc.). The parasympathetic system has a somewhat opposite effect by reducing the heart rate, constricting the lungs, and facilitating peristalsis in the gastro-intestinal tract.

Generally, the autonomic nervous system is quite responsive to individually or personally felt emotion. There is a concomitant reaction, especially of the sympathetic system, to the experience of anxiety, for example. The question arises as to what are the differences in the activation of the autonomic nervous system between psychopaths, who are described as experiencing little or no anxiety, and neurotics and others, who do experience anxiety in varying amounts.

A number of studies that concern themselves with autonomic responsivity to simple stimuli when a person is at rest, and in reaction to stress, have been reviewed in some detail (Hare, 1970). The studies show that the differences in autonomic activity between psychopaths and others are not very impressive. Hare concludes that there is evidence of some hypoactivity on several autonomic measures during states of quiescence and that these correspond to the "clinical statements about the psychopath's lack of anxiety, guilt . . ." A recent experimental study (Fenz, et al., 1974) is consonant with this conclusion. When psychopaths were compared with normal controls with respect to autonomic, and particularly heart rate, activity in the anticipation of a stressful situation, they showed considerably less responsiveness.

Another aspect of psychophysiological theorizing regarding the etiology of psychopathy involves the concept of *arousal*. The term implies, broadly speaking, the psychological and physiological state of the organism. Arousal may be viewed as a dimension, ranging from a low or minimal level to a very high and maximal level. Very low arousal involves sleep or drowsiness, large and slow EEG brain waves, and low electrocortical activity. At the other extreme there is great emotional excitement (rage, anxiety), fast and uneven EEG tracings, and diffusion of attention, as well as confusion. The middle ground is a state of relaxed attention, accompanied by alpha waves, and relatively controlled, but not rigid, attention. According to some theorists (c.f., summary by Hare, 1970) psychopathy is constitutionally characterized by a low state of arousal which is experienced as unpleasant, and, consequently, there is a seeking of excitement in order to increase arousal to a more comfortable (i.e., higher, but moderate) level. The experimental evidence in support of this notion is not overwhelming. And, even if psychopaths are prone to be "pathological stimulation seekers" (Emmons & Webb, 1974), the evidence is insufficient to consider this as a major cause in producing such a complex syndrome as the psychopathic or antisocial personality. Yet, such a notion is quite consonant with a constitutional hypothesis for which some developmental evidence has been accruing in recent years (Thomas, Chess, & Birch, 1968). In their monograph on *Temperament and Behavior Disorders in Children*, these investigators have shown that even at birth, children differ in their temperamental profiles, and that behavior disorders evolve from the interaction of certain temperamental patterns with inhospitable environmental circumstances. We shall return to this issue in our next section, where environmental and psychological factors that are possible causes of psychopathy will be surveyed.

Psychological Hypotheses

So far, we have been concerned primarily with what might be called the *somatogenic hypothesis* concerning psychopathy. This hypothesis refers to bodily (somatic) processes—physiological, neurological, and genetic—that may be involved in the causation of psychopathy. The present section will deal with what may be broadly termed the *psychogenic hypothesis*. Here the reference is to the psychological and experiential events that take place in the environments in which the psychopaths grow up and which have lasting influence on the patterns of their deviant personality development.

Several psychological hypotheses have been postulated in an attempt to explain the roots of psychopathic behavior. Some of the authors have been concerned with the investigation of the environmental conditions and circumstances that are apparently influential in the production of the psychopath or antisocial personality. These are concentrated on surveys of objective, reported or observed, external factors. Other workers have taken these environmental factors into account, but are not satisfied with "counting noses" and wish to develop theory regarding the genesis and development of psychopathy. They focus upon the dynamics of personality formation and on how the experiences of the individual in particular settings have led to the resulting character development. There is an attempt to deal with the motivational underpinnings that may underlie the development of psychopathy.

The former approach is more sociological or psychosocial rather than psychological. In the follow-up study mentioned earlier in this chapter (Robins, 1966), a search for "childhood factors characteristic of the presociopathic personality" was made. The ". . . most likely candidate for later diagnosis of sociopathic personality from among children appearing in a child guidance clinic, . . . appears to be the boy referred for theft or aggression who has shown a diversity of antisocial behavior in many episodes . . . (which) involves him with strangers and organizations as well as with teachers and parents (p. 157)." More than half of the boys who had these characteristics were later, as adults, diagnosed as sociopathic personalities. Generally they had "a history of truancy, theft, staying out late, and refusing to obey parents." Moreover, they lied without guilt, were irresponsible in money matters, tried homosexual relationships and, according to parents, were bed wetters and poorly groomed. Finally, as far as familial background and influence is concerned, it seemed to be the antisocial behavior of the father that was very much related to later sociopathic behavior on the part of the diagnosed offspring, whether male or female. Compared with other diagnostic groups, the sociopath's antisocial behavior involved him with the law and other agencies (e.g., clinics, hospitals) at a much earlier age (Robins, 1966; Humphrey, 1974).

The preceding summary stressed factual information obtained with sizable samples of individuals who had been diagnosed as sociopathic personalities. Psychiatrists and psychologists who have been working with individual cases and groups, however, have developed certain notions about the possible psychological processes that underlie the genesis of sociopathic personality and go beyond description, counting of symptoms, and environmental circumstances and events.

The major psychological hypothesis concerning the causation of psychopathy is basically a genetic-developmental one. It proposes that certain experiences in childhood, especially in infancy, affect the course of character formation which results subsequently in what is called the psychopathic adult. The questions that come to mind are: What are the processes involved in the effects of early childhood experiences on later personality development?

What, specifically, are those experiences that are alleged to make the difference in the development of the normal and psychopathic personality? In the following sections we shall explore these fundamental questions in the hope of clarifying and elucidating the dynamic psychological hypothesis.

The human neonate, unlike the newborn of other species, remains relatively helpless for a long time following birth. In order to thrive and survive the infant requires constant care and attention. There is no question as to the infant's need for food, physical comfort, and for protection against disease. In recent years, however, the need for and the importance of "mothering," by the biological mother or a surrogate, has been stressed by a number of clinicians and investigators. The term mothering does not refer only to the care for the physical needs of the child, but also to the psychological security ordinarily provided by a mother figure; to the close and constant physical contact; to the readiness of the mother to minimize the child's frustrations; to oral and auditory responses which are reassuring, pacifying, and soothing to the infant; as well as, generally, to a consistent and continuous relationship with a loving adult. According to a number of theoreticians, this early relationship between mother and child is most important for the child's future development for it serves as a prototype for interpersonal relationships in adulthood. It is the source from which the capacity to receive and express affection, to experience genuine love, empathy, and consideration for others, evolves.

The concept of identification is another important issue in the process of early personality development. Under ordinary circumstances the growing child imitates the behavior of his parents and generally adheres to the demands they make upon him. This is sometimes described as "modeling" behavior. The parents are viewed as all-powerful by the infant or young child and by acting like them he somehow becomes like them and acquires the feeling of power and security. Later in the development of the child, he faces a number of demands and expectancies, a number of "dos" and "don'ts," obligations and prohibitions, which further direct and fashion his behavior. The behavioral expectancies of the parents are usually the transmitted standards and codes of behavior of the community, society, and culture.

Obedience on the part of the child is generally rewarded and the expected behavior is reinforced. On the other hand, punishment is forthcoming where parental demands and prohibitions are not obeyed. In instances of noncompliance the child often faces withdrawal of love as a major sign of their disapproval. According to some theorists, the withdrawal of love is a devastating experience for the child, which he tries to avoid at all cost. He learns what he *must* do, or how he must behave—he becomes *socialized* by imitation and in order to avoid the threat of parental punishment and disapproval.

Later, as time passes, the child not only continues to identify with his parents and imitate their overt behavior, but also begins to accept their verbal messages—the demands and prohibitions—as his own. It is said that the child "internalizes" parental standards via his experiences at home and through the process of identification. Parental demands are no longer experienced as coming from outside himself, but have become part of himself, his own—his conscience. What had been previously experienced as "I must" has now become "I ought" (or "I must not" is replaced by "I ought not").

Along with the parental demands for certain kinds of behavior and control, or inhibition of other kinds of behavior, the threat of punishment is also incorporated as part of the process of conscience formation. Now, if an infraction of the internalized code occurs, "pangs of conscience" follow—an uneasy and anxious feeling which one would rather avoid (as painful and devastating as the loss of support and approval of the parent).

The description of the development of conscience presented above holds true if there is a positive relationship between parent and child.

> It is obvious that if the threat of withdrawal of love is to operate as an effective restraint, there must have been some love between parent and child present in the first place. A child cannot respond to something he has never had. It is not surprising, therefore, . . . that a high proportion of psychopaths are the product of broken homes, loveless homes, or impersonal institutions (Storr, 1972).

What we have sketched here is the course of childhood development with respect to earlier experiences via mothering, socialization, and identification. Some of the probable origins of early interpersonal relationships and the sources of moral judgement, conscience, and guilt, can thus be traced. The favorable conditions under which such developments take place have been pointed out in the last quotation (Storr, 1972) and the possible obstacles to such trends have been hinted at. We shall now proceed with a more detailed exposition of the "psychological hypothesis" as to what goes wrong in the orderly process of normal child development to produce the deviant course that results in psychopathy.

Bowlby's (1951) comprehensive review of a large number of retrospective studies reported in the literature (mainly in the 1930s and 1940s) presents fairly consistent evidence concerning the effects of early maternal deprivation upon the child's later personality development. He lists a number of pathogenic conditions:

1. "Lack of any opportunity for forming an attachment to a mother figure during the first three years."
2. A three-to-six-months deprivation (sudden separation from mother) during the first few years of life.
3. Changes of mother figures during the first three years of life.

Any one of the conditions, according to Bowlby, "can produce the affectionless and psychopathic character." It may be useful now to return to our previous description of the mothering process and see how the absence of this experience, its interruption during the crucial years of infancy, or the lack of consistency in the mother figure, may bring about the abnormal development which results in the psychopathic personality. We shall attempt to reconstruct the infantile experience, à la Bowlby, from the data he summarized.

In Bowlby's description of the impersonal institutions (such as orphanages) in particular, and of many family interactions as well, various conditions of maternal deprivation are noted, and mothering, as it exists under the usual "normal" conditions does not take place at all or at least, not consistently. The infant is thus deprived of the opportunity to develop a close reciprocal relationship with another human being. He grows up without an early model after which he can pattern his subsequent interpersonal interaction and relationships. It is at this point that some of the psychopath's symptoms begin to flourish. The "pathologic egocentricity and incapacity for love," "unresponsiveness in . . . interpersonal relationships," impersonal sex life, and so on (Cleckley, 1976) are directly traceable to the lack of an adequate model and lack of intimate experience with it in infancy and early childhood.

Furthermore, the presence of maternal deprivation is an important obstacle to normal identification and to conscience or superego formation. As we pointed out earlier (Storr, 1972), the absence of a positive affectional relationship with an adult leaves the child with little motivation to imitate him, to please him, or to be like him. Parental disapproval has little emotional meaning to the child in such a situation. He is not threatened by loss of love, for he never had it. Thus, the socialization process and the internalization of parental standards, which are the foundations of the conscience, are hampered and distorted. The child may have "nothing to lose" by being disobedient. He may often obey for reasons of physical punishment and other threats, but he does not make the required standards his own. Generally, he learns to watch out for himself and tries to avoid punishment; but he is not concerned with pleasing his parents, nor using them as a model for himself and his behavior. Thus he does not develop pangs of conscience or guilt about infraction of rules or disobedience.

The "lack of remorse and shame," "failure to follow a life plan," "antisocial behavior," and "untruthfulness and insecurity"—some of the major characteristics of the psychopath (Cleckley, 1976)—can also be seen as consequences of inadequate superego formation, stemming from the childhood condition referred to above. Thus, the psychological hypothesis, has evolved, which provides a detailed theoretical explanation as to how "psychopaths are made." It addresses itself to the genesis of the basic psychopathic traits that we have described at length at the beginning of this chapter.

Much criticism followed the original publication of Bowlby's monograph (1951). The problems of definition of such central concepts as mothering, deprivation, mutuality, and so on are very crucial. Also, the criticism extended to the types of studies, mainly retrospective, upon which the maternal deprivation hypothesis is based. It is also important to note that these studies have neglected other significant figures in the family, especially the father, whose pathology turns out to be of great moment in the data reported by Robins (1966).

In a World Health Organization monograph (Ainsworth et al., 1962), which contains much of the criticism, Ainsworth presents a comprehensive review of the arguments and a systematic statement concerning the maternal deprivation hypothesis. According to her,

> maternal deprivation has a differential effect on different processes; most vulnerable seem certain intellectual processes, especially language and abstraction, and certain aspects of personality, most especially the ability to establish and maintain deep and meaningful interpersonal relations, but also the ability to control impulse in the interest of long-range goals (p. 149).

She also pointed out the importance of the age variable, parental loss (Greer, 1964) or separation, and the extent of continuity and discontinuity in parent-child relationships. These and other claims need longitudinal research in order to sort out more precisely their relationship to the formation of the psychopathic personality.

The formulation by Bowlby does not represent the only psychological hypothesis regarding the etiology of psychopathy, though it is perhaps the dominant one. Some social learning theorists, for example, have proposed a "sociopsychological formulation of antisocial (psychopathic) personality" (Ullman & Krasner, 1969). They blame the absence of opportunity to learn certain patterns of behavior in the milieu in which they grow up for the fact that persons develop the particular deficits of the psychopath. They stress, for example, the psychopath's deficiencies in *role playing*, which is closely related to the processes of identification we discussed above. Actually, identification does not focus on learning, but assumes it. The relationship between lack of opportunity for role playing and identification is at the basis of the rather poor moral development of psychopathic children (Campagna & Harter, 1975).

The McCords' "Neurosocial Theory of Causation"

In the preceding pages we detailed several theoretical notions and some research findings concerning the etiology or causation of the antisocial personality. One gets the impression that a comparison with the blind men describing an elephant, in the famed fable, is again appropriate in this situation. Actually, there is no reason why one should select or adhere to an exclusively hereditarian, neurologic, or even psychological hypothesis or theory. A combination may in many instances, if not in most, be quite defensible. Thus, a person with a certain hereditary predisposition and temperament, one aspect of which *may* be a certain type of nervous system, when interacting with or confronting a malevolent environment (maternal deprivation, rejecting parents, or sudden loss and separation in infancy) *may* develop a personality pattern described as antisocial.

In their "neurosocial theory of causation," McCord and McCord have, in fact, proposed such a synthesis and integration. They state that "each causal theory, alone, has fundamental defects which invalidate its claims. . . . The last 20 years of research indicate that a combination of neurological and social insights can produce a plausible, if not definitive, explanation of the disorder" (McCord & McCord, 1964, p. 84). Consonant with this conclusion, these authors propose three major causal patterns of psychopathy:

1. *Severe rejection* as the sole cause of psychopathy.
2. *Mild rejection* combined with brain damage—especially affecting the area concerned with inhibition of behavior.
3. *Mild rejection*, without neurological disorder, but in combination with certain pathogenic influences.

As we can readily see, the first pattern is essentially what we termed the "psychological hypothesis." The second pattern is the only genuine "neuro-social" causal pattern of the triad, wherein some environmental conditions ("mild rejection" actually refers to the psychological consequences) are combined with varying degrees of brain damage responsible for insufficient impulse control. The third pattern involves the aspect of modeling after a psychopathic parent as a major factor in the causation of the disorder. It is in agreement with one of Robins' conclusions about her findings "that for children who were only mildly antisocial, having an antisocial father greatly increases the subject's antisocial behavior as an adult" (Robins, 1970, p. 227). The "mildly antisocial behavior" in childhood may be related to the "mild rejection" suggested above, and when this is combined with a deviant role model (antisocial father), the antisocial personality development is the ultimate outcome.

The "state of the art" as far as the antisocial personality is concerned is that of a diffusely defined concept with many hypothesized causal factors. Perhaps future research will yet identify more specific relationships between cause and effect. But we cannot escape the complexity of multiple determination in human existence.

TREATMENT OF THE ANTISOCIAL PERSONALITY

Now that we have reviewed the possible genesis of the antisocial personality, have explored the hypotheses, and have examined some of the research designed to test them, the question as to what can be done about the problem looms large in front of us. What can be done to prevent this sort of disorder to begin with, and what can be done to modify and change its course and continued path of destructiveness? Can the condition be "cured"? Generally the answers to these questions have been rather pessimistic. The history of treatment of antisocial personalities has recorded many failures. Yet, some successes have also been reported, thus holding out some hope for the future. However, as we noted, the search for the "ounce of prevention" might be the path to follow, although the hope for the "pound of cure" should also be maintained.

As we may have gleaned from the discussion of theories, environmental-psychological causes appear to be paramount in shaping the antisocial personality. Efforts at prevention may best be directed at this area. Providing young infants and children with healthy home environments and cutting psychological deprivation to a minimum may be a tall order. However, various programmatic efforts, including institutional alternatives and parental surrogates, are under way and should be encouraged. More systematic studies, especially longitudinal studies of home environments and their effects upon deviant personality development should be undertaken in order to place the environmental-psychological hypothesis on a sounder footing (Ainsworth, 1962). In the meantime, policy based on partial and, admittedly, incomplete information is the best that can be recommended.

The last paragraph hints at possibilities of what may be called "primary prevention," but what about the modification of personality and behavior of those adolescents and adults who have "earned" the diagnosis of antisocial personality? Imprisonment of the psychopathic criminal has not aided much in his rehabilitation. Violation of parole and recidivism are the rule rather than the exception, according to the evidence we have. Modes of temporary segregation from the community other than imprisonment have been similarly unsuccessful in the long range. Hospitalization in psychiatric institutions is usually of brief duration, frequently on an emergency basis. Quite often, psychopaths shuttle back and forth from penal to psychiatric institutions until paroled or discharged, to resume the antisocial behavior for which they were originally incarcerated. Quite often, prison authorities feel that these prisoners have psychological problems which should be treated in a hospital setting, but psychiatric institutions return the men to prison, for past experience has shown that the ordinary hospital regime, including individual counseling or group therapy as well as various other ancillary methods of treatment, is of little value in attempting to change the psychopath.

As far as individual psychotherapy is concerned, little success with the psychopathic individual is reported. Generally, he has little motivation for change and for forming a relationship with the therapist. McCord and McCord (1964) have summarized the situation as follows: ". . . the typical psychopathic personality seems singularly resistant to change. He lacks a desire for change and the anxiety . . . which most therapists believe is a prerequisite for treatment. Most psychopaths see nothing wrong with themselves and, therefore, no reason to change" (p. 118). This is readily understandable, for our description of the psychopath includes lack of insight, absence of guilt and anxiety, unconcern with the future—a lack of some of the basic motivational features which bring a person to the therapist for help. In an earlier version of this chapter (Rabin, 1961), I pointed out that "a major obstacle to psychotherapy with the psychopath is lack of cooperation. Although the psychopath may go through the motions of 'cooperating' with the therapist, they are for the most part mere sham and deception. Often he does not even pretend; he resists the therapist . . . 'You can bring a horse to water but you cannot make him drink it' " (p. 291).

After several decades of clinical contacts with psychopaths and following a review of reported results of intervention, Cleckley (1976) has not grown any more optimistic about outcomes. A modified therapeutic approach proposed by Thorne (1959) has received considerable attention from several writers on the subject. Thorne outlined a number of requirements, or conditions, under which therapy with the psychopath may succeed. The therapist must have control of the patient's finances; relatives and others must not bail the psychopath out of his troubles, for he should face the consequences of his behavior (and the therapist is not to do that either). Also, the therapist must constantly point out to the patient his self-defeating behavior, encourage him to limit it, and provide him with incentives to engage in more prosocial, rather than antisocial behavior. Furthermore, Thorne points out that it would be a long and protracted process (ten years) as well as a very costly one ($15,000 annually at the 1959 rate!). Considering all this effort and expense, "it is not surprising," says Hare (1970), "that no controlled research using Thorne's methods has been carried out . . ."

For more than two decades the trend of treatment of psychopathy has been away from the individual therapeutic approach to group therapy, milieu therapy, and the "therapeutic community" (Jones, et al., 1953). Jones' pioneering effort included different hospital units which were set up to treat a variety of chronic conditions, including antisocial personalities. In these autonomous "communities" consisting of staff and patients, the inmates work in shops and other enterprises, participate in discussion groups, are given vocational guidance, and are absorbed in the Unit community which, over time, develops a "culture of its own." Under these conditions, according to Jones (Chapter 20) patients are resocialized and are effectively prepared for rehabilitation in the "normal" society. Although precise figures are difficult to come by, a modest measure of optimism seems to be justified by the results. A number of variations on the therapeutic community theme have sprung up in Holland (Van der Hooven Clinic in Utrecht), at the Balderton psychopathic unit in England (Craft, 1966), in Denmark as well as in the United States.

In a review of some of these efforts, one psychiatrist (Rappeport, 1974) concludes that for the best results in the treatment of psychopaths "one needs a secure institution, long (indeterminate) sentences, a devoted and well trained staff, and varying mixtures of group and individual therapy . . . job training and social reeducation . . ." (p. 265). Like Thorne, Rappeport stresses the great expenses involved in what may be called the "total push" program.

The same author (Rappeport) also quotes from a 1973 Progress Report of the Patuxent Institution at Jessup, Maryland, which shows recidivism inversely related to the extent and amount of treatment offered the residents of the institution. According to this report, 81 percent of untreated cases were recidivists, 46 percent of those "minimally treated," 39 percent of those who received "more treatment," and only 7 percent of the "fully treated" group.

The average time for successful treatment was estimated between three to five years.

It should be added that the effectiveness of the Patuxent Institution is not universally accepted. In addition to the question of the constitutionality of the indeterminate sentence, which has been raised in recent years and has served as a center of controversy, the validity of the conclusions drawn from the reported statistics on recidivism is also under attack. Although Patuxent claims 37 percent recidivism as compared with 60 percent statewide (Maryland), critics feel that such factors as age of inmates upon release, length of stay in prison, tightness of parole supervision, and so on, are not controlled in such comparisons and render the value of the findings questionable (Holden, 1978).

There appears to be some cause for hope and a degree of optimism. What is needed is a careful statement of the operations that are involved, and of treatment theory and methodology, so that any alleged successful efforts may be critically examined, and, hopefully, replicated.

REFERENCES

Ainsworth, M. D., et al. *Deprivation of maternal care: A reassessment of its effects.* Geneva: World Health Organization, 1962 (Public Health Papers, 14).

Bay-Rakal, S. The significance of EEG abnormality in behavior problem children. *Canadian Psychiatric Association Journal,* 1965, *10,* 387–391.

Bowlby, J. *Maternal care and mental health.* Geneva: World Health Organization, 1951.

Campagna, A. F., & Harter, S. Moral judgment in sociopathic and normal children. *Journal of Personality and Social Psychology,* 1975, *31*(2), 199–205.

Cleckley, H. *The mask of sanity.* St. Louis: The C. V. Mosby Company, 1976.

Craft, M. *Psychopathic disorders.* Oxford: Pergamon Press, 1966.

Diagnostic and Statistical Manual—Mental Disorders. Washington, D.C.: American Psychiatric Association, 1952.

DSM–II: *Diagnostic and Statistical Manual of Mental Disorders* (2d ed.). Washington, D.C.: American Psychiatric Association, 1968.

Ellington, R. I. The incidence of EEG abnormality among patients with mental disorders of apparently nonorganic origin: A critical review. *American Journal of Psychiatry,* 1954, *111,* 263–275.

Emmons, T. D., & Webb, W. W. Subjective correlates of emotional responsivity and stimulation seeking in psychopaths, normals, and acting out neurotics. *Journal of Consulting and Clinical Psychology,* 1974, *42*(4), 620.

Fenz, W. D., Young, M. J., & Fenz, H. G. Differences in the modulation of cardiac activity between psychopaths and normal controls. *Psychosomatic Medicine,* 1974, *36*(6), 488–502.

Greer, S. Study of parental loss in neurotics and sociopaths. *Archives of General Psychiatry,* 1964, *11,* 177–180.

Hare, R. D. *Psychopathy: Theory and research.* New York: Wiley, 1970.

Hare, R. D. Psychopathy, autonomic functioning, and the orienting response. *Journal of Abnormal Psychology,* Monograph Supplement, 1968, *73*(3), Part 2, 1–24.

Holden, C. Patuxent: Controversial prison clings to belief in rehabilitation. *Science* (February 1978), *199*, 665–668.

Humphrey, J. A. A study of the etiology of sociopathic behavior. *Diseases of the Nervous System*, 1974, *35*(9), 432–435.

Jones, M., et al. *The therapeutic community: A new treatment method in psychiatry.* New York: Basic Books, 1953.

Maas, J. P. Cathexes towards significant others by sociopathic women. *Archives of General Psychiatry*, 1966, *15*, 516–522.

Mark, I. *Patterns of meaning in psychiatric patients: Semantic differential responses in obsessives and psychopaths.* Maudsley Monograph No. 13. London: University of Oxford Press, 1966.

McCord, W., & McCord, J. *The psychopath: An essay on the criminal mind.* Princeton, N.J.: D. Van Nostrand Company, 1964.

Pritchard, J. C. *A treatise on insanity and other disorders affecting the mind.* London: Gilbert & Piper, 1835.

Rabin, A. I. Psychopathic (sociopathic) personalities. In H. Toch (Ed.), *Legal and criminal psychology.* New York: Holt, Rinehart and Winston, 1961.

Rappeport, J. R. Antisocial behavior (Ch. 12). In S. Arieti (Ed.), *American Handbook of Psychiatry* (2d ed., Vol. III). New York: Basic Books, 1974.

Robins, L. N. *Deviant children grown up: A psychiatric and sociological study of sociopathic personality.* Baltimore: Williams & Wilkins, 1966.

Robins, E. Antisocial and dyssocial personality disorders. In A. M. Freedmand and H. I. Kaplan (Eds.), *Comprehensive textbook of psychiatry.* Baltimore: Williams & Wilkins, 1967.

Robins, L. N. Antecedents of character disorders. In M. Roff & D. F. Ricks (Eds.), *Life history research in psychopathology.* Minneapolis: University of Minnesota Press, 1970.

Shapiro, D. *Neurotic styles.* New York: Basic Books, 1965.

Spitzer, R. L., et al. Research diagnostic criteria for a selected group of functional disorders. New York Psychiatric Institute, 1975.

Storr, A. *Human destructiveness.* London: Sussex University Press, 1972.

Syndulko, K., et al. Psychophysiology of sociopathy: Electrocortical measures. *Biological Psychology*, 1975, *3*(3), 185–200.

Thomas, A., Chess, S., & Birch, H. G. *Temperament and behavior disorders in children.* New York: New York University Press, 1968.

Thorne, F. C. The etiology of sociopathic reactions. *American Journal of Psychotherapy*, 1959, *13*, 319–330.

Ullman, L. P., & Krasner, L. *A psychological approach to abnormal behavior.* Englewood Cliffs, N.J.: Prentice-Hall, 1969.

chapter 15

The Alcohol Offender

Charles Winick

The alcohol offender represents the extreme of the "drinking problem" in America, which has been a concern of moralists, legislators, and citizen groups for many generations. Some people regard the widespread availability of alcohol, and the many and attractive formats and even names of drinks (e.g., Rob Roy, Pink Lady, Bullshot) under which it can be consumed, to be undesirable. Others feel that alcohol helps to trigger a wide range of criminal activity, traffic accidents, other antisocial or unhealthy behavior, and many disease processes.

Proponents of permitting adults reasonable access to alcohol can cite many and often contradictory functions drinking serves, as a social facilitator and aid to adaptation ("It cools me in the summer and warms me in the winter"; "It calms me down and peps me up"; "It enables me to be by myself more comfortably and it makes it easier for me to walk into a room full of strange people"; "It makes social contact with the opposite sex easier and helps me to get along without the opposite sex"; "It raises my level of functioning to where I can work and it enables me to pass the time when I am not working"). Proponents of a "hands off drinkers" policy also note that there are enormous individual differences in responses to and uses made of alcohol. They remind us of persons who drink regularly, yet can function effectively; Winston Churchill presumably put away a fifth of Scotch whiskey daily while directing Britain's part in World War II. They point to history and argue that alcohol is so necessary in this country that Prohibition, from 1920 through 1933, was a dismal failure, and that only one out of fifteen social drinkers becomes an alcoholic. Another argument in favor of permitting people to drink as they wish is that even in Communist countries like Russia, where there is extensive control over the individual citizen, there appears to be considerable alcoholism.

In this chapter, our approach to the psychology of the alcohol offender is through an examination of alcohol control patterns, of various degrees of alcohol consumption, types of epidemiology of alcohol use, theories of the genesis of alcoholism, effects of alcohol use, law enforcement, treatment, social costs, policy development, and the future.

ALCOHOL CONTROL PATTERNS

Every state has an Alcoholic Beverage Control agency which establishes and enforces rules for the sale of alcoholic beverages by bars, restaurants, package stores, and other vendors.

Adoption of the twenty-first Amendment to the United States Constitution in 1933 ended Prohibition, but gave the states the duty of controlling the traffic in alcoholic beverages. State regulations generally place restraints on hours of sale, mandate that the premises be visible from the outside, discourage sales on credit and to drunk persons, circumscribe advertising, and set standards for the kind of persons able to obtain liquor licenses. All states have some regulations on the sale of alcoholic beverages to minors, although there are differences in determination of the age below which a person is a minor. There is a wide range of penalties for violation of these laws, and in who may be prosecuted for doing so.

TERMS EMPLOYED TO DESCRIBE DEGREES OF ALCOHOL CONSUMPTION

Alcohol is a drug, more correctly known as ethyl alcohol or ethanol, and is one of a group of sedatives or soporifics, which include solid drugs like barbiturates, gases like ether, and liquids like paraldehyde. These sedatives are not like narcotics, which take away pain but do not necessarily put a person to sleep. On the contrary, the sedative group that includes alcohol doesn't have any effect against pain but does put a person to sleep.

Alcohol receives attention and has a disease named after it because it has been accessible for so long, is freely available without a prescription, and is such a widely acceptable social lubricant. A person may be a social drinker, a heavy drinker, a problem drinker, or an alcoholic, in ascending order of gravity of possible consequences.

The *social* drinker imbibes as part of larger social, familial, or ceremonial activities, in a manner that poses no significant problems for his general ability to function. In a national interview study, however, 21 percent of adult males and 5 percent of females proved to be *heavy* drinkers, defined as persons averaging five drinks per occasion, at least once a week (Cahalan, et al., 1969). *Problem* drinking has been defined as a repetitive use of alcohol which causes physical, psychological, or social harm to the drinker or to others (Cooperative Commission, 1967). Some 15 percent of adult males and 4 percent of females, or 9,000,000 persons, have such problems with alcohol (Cahalan, 1970). It is usually estimated that about half of the problem drinkers are *alcoholics* or experience symptoms of alcoholism.

That alcoholism is a disease is generally accepted in many quarters, although the nature of the condition is not precisely understood (Jellinek, 1960). The American Medical Association declared alcoholism to be a disease in 1956 and physicians usually agree with this view, though they have not been providing leadership in efforts to clarify the dimensions of alcoholism. Physiologists, social scientists, and reformed alcoholics have been the leading proponents of the disease concept.

One reason for the lack of clarity surrounding the nature of alcoholism is that it has been defined in terms of five different dimensions: loss of control over drinking, frequency and amount of alcohol consumed, addiction, interference with life functions, and being more concerned with how other activities interrupt drinking than with drinking interrupting other activities. We can define alcoholism as a chronic disease involving drinking in excess of ordinary dietary use or community social habits, which interferes with social, health, or economic functioning, and includes loss of control once drinking has begun.

Viewing alcoholism as a disease has helped to legitimate community and physicians' interest in the condition and facilitated the establishment of treatment facilities. There is general agreement that alcoholism may in turn reflect many different conditions, of which it could be a symptom (Scott, 1968). Identifying it as a disease could make a medical problem out of what may be a social or family situation. The disease concept nonetheless has helped to blunt the older view that drinking is a vice which results from moral weakness. At the same time, it may convey a misleading sense of the inevitability of a disease process and give the drinker an alibi for not changing his behavior.

TYPES AND EPIDEMIOLOGY OF ALCOHOL USE

The manufacture and sale of alcoholic beverages in America is a big business, with $22.5 billion spent on them in 1977. This represents about 3 percent of personal income, with per capita consumption averaging 2.7 gallons of absolute alcohol annually. Beer, wine, aperitifs, gin, vodka, whiskey, and liqueurs are among the many alcoholic beverages consumed.

Popular culture references to alcoholic beverages are frequent in movies, fiction, and television, and beverages are extensively advertised, with about $600 million spent each year to promote their sale. Hard liquor is not advertised on television, and there are restrictions on how beer and wine may be advertised in the medium. For example, the effects of the beverage cannot be mentioned, and women are not shown doing serious drinking. Advertising is indirect and deals with status, sex, and situational themes, such as a group of attractive people in a hunting or ski lodge.

Drinking of alcoholic beverages is a statistically normal behavior in America, with 77 percent of the men and 60 percent of the women drinking at least once a year (Cahalan, et al., 1969). In the years since the women's liberation movement began, women seem to be drinking more. Most males in each age group from twenty-five to sixty-five drink at least once a month.

The proportion of young people aged fourteen to eighteen who drink increases with age, but there is not a sharp increase after age eighteen. By the age of seventeen, most of the young people who will be drinking have started to do so. There appears to be little correlation between drinking behavior of teenagers and statute differences between the states in terms of the age at which drinking is permitted. Over half the states permit persons aged eighteen to purchase and consume alcohol.

From 70 percent to 93 percent of high school students drink. There are more boy than girl drinkers in the early teen years but the sexes become approximately equal in use by their late teens. There is a decline in alcohol consumption after the age of fifty.

In terms of ordinary social drinking, there are broad patterns of social class preferences. Lower-lower class drinkers tend to drink sherry and other inexpensive dessert wines. Blue collar workers or lower-upper class members have traditionally been beer drinkers. Mixed drinks, like the Manhattan or daiquiri, are most popular with the middle class, and brand name Scotch has long been the preferred beverage of the upper-middle class executive. At the very top of the socioeconomic status escalator, the upper class, the favorite is likely to be sherry, although not the inexpensive kind, which is found at the bottom of the social-class ladder! People seem to model their beverage preferences on the drinking behavior of the socioeconomic class into which they are moving.

Society is especially concerned about the heavy drinker, irrespective of his class membership. The highest proportion of heavy drinkers is in the Middle Atlantic, East North Central, Pacific, and New England states, notably in urban areas (Cahalan, et al., 1969). The South, perhaps because of having so many conservative Protestants who dislike alcohol, has a small proportion of heavy drinkers.

Heavy drinkers are likely to be women twenty-one to twenty-four years old, men thirty to thirty-four years, and both women and men forty-five to forty-nine years, of lower socioeconomic status; service workers; single, divorced, or separated men or women; big city residents; Catholics; Protestants; persons without religious affiliations; and those whose fathers were Italian, Irish, British, Caribbean, or Latin American.

About five percent of teenagers are problem drinkers, which is defined as getting "tight" at least once a week. But using the criterion of intoxication four times a year or more, 23 percent of youths pose problems. Usually, problem drinking in youths is one dimension of a larger pattern of misbehavior (Jessor & Jessor, 1973).

Differing rates of alcoholism appear to characterize various ethnic groups and have been the subject of considerable investigation. Jews and Italian-Americans, for example, have relatively low alcoholism rates and Irish-Americans relatively high rates of alcoholism (Snyder, 1958; Bales, 1946). Groups with low prevalence of alcoholism are exposed to alcohol early on, within the family, and in small quantities. The beverages are served in diluted form and tend to be taken with meals. Parents offer a model of moderate drinking and drinking is not interpreted as a sign of manhood. Intoxication is not culturally acceptable and there is general agreement on the ground rules of drinking (National Institute of Mental Health, 1969). The relatively high rates of alcoholism among the Irish have been attributed to their being raised in a situation of permissiveness toward drinking, including identification with older role models and the importance of taverns. Among the Irish, alcohol's functions are more convivial than religious.

Of all the ethnic groups in America, the Indians most risk becoming alcoholics. Among Indians, infant mortality, accidents, and pneumonia are significantly related to the use of alcohol, which may be responsible, directly or indirectly, for the majority of Indian deaths (Littman, 1970). Almost three times the national average of Indians are arrested for alcohol-related crimes and homicides, usually stemming from drinking-generated fights (National Institute of Mental Health, 1973).

White traders introduced alcohol to Indians early in the nineteenth century as a barter device. When the Indian Prohibition Act (1832) forbade the provision of liquor to Indians, many acquired the habit of drinking very quickly, to avoid detection (Andrist, 1971). Although the Act was repealed in 1953, many of the early drinking patterns still continue. Continual reductions in reservation land, usually accomplished with little sensitivity to Indian cultural processes, led to disjunction and poverty, for which drinking offered some relief. The Indian who leaves the reservation may face prejudice and discrimination, which can be eased by alcohol.

Recent treatment programs have attempted to be responsive to unique aspects of Indian cultural life (Dailey, 1966). Most of the new programs are organized and implemented by Indians, like the Alaskan minigrants to native villages to develop alternatives to spree drinking. Alcoholics Anonymous (AA) and disulfiram (antabuse) programs have been modified to incorporate special aspects of Indian life.

Skid Row

Many large cities have a Skid Row, an older area where homeless or uprooted men, who are frequently alcoholics, live. The area usually has deteriorated housing, sleazy bars and restaurants, and a generally blighted appearance. The indigent drinking man on Skid Row is often serviced by a variety of public institutions, going to which may be called "making the loop" or "making the circle" (Wiseman, 1970).

Skid Row alcoholics are 5 to 25 percent of the population of alcoholics in most cities, but represent from 40 to 50 percent of the cities' arrests for public drunkenness. Small fights, begging, and minor thefts are relatively common in Skid Row but may be ignored by the police, who tend to use limited resources for handling problems in the area, but know how to employ various forms of informal coercion which optimize their ability to control the situation (Bittner, 1967).

The great majority, perhaps as many as 95 percent, of Skid Row men who might be arrested for public drunkenness, are not actually arrested. The police are sensitized to contingencies which lead to trouble and make arrests selectively to deal with such situations. Since Skid Row men are likely to be guilty of various minor offenses at any given time, their arrests are seldom challenged, whether or not the specific current arrest is valid.

The level of police arrest activity of Skid Row and other alcoholics may reflect the degree to which space is available in local jails. Booking officers on duty at the local precinct and judges at arraignment may similarly consider the realities of the community's jail situation.

Sometimes, police may engage in preventive arrest of a Skid Row man, because such an arrest could prevent subsequent serious trouble or protect the man. Some officers think that arresting such men is doing them a favor or even perhaps saving their lives. The man who is arrested may, of course, not take the same view of what is happening to him. In recent years, with decriminalization of public drunkenness in many states, a variety of religious and treatment organizations have established facilities on Skid Row, which may be functional equivalents to jail.

THEORIES OF THE GENESIS OF ALCOHOLISM

A variety of theories has been proposed to explain the genesis of alcoholism. No one theory enjoys full acceptance, although many have some support.

The *psychoanalyst* views the alcoholic as a person dominated by a permissive mother in childhood, who has not learned self-control. This pattern may occur in combination with an inconsistent father who sometimes forbids and sometimes gratifies the child's needs for dependency. For such persons, alcohol provides a way of recapturing early feelings of omnipotence, unhampered by the need to accept external reality or self-criticism (Knight, 1937).

Other psychoanalytic writers see the person in the grip of some unresolved conflict which began in childhood and still influences the behavior of the adult, and in which ingestion and extreme dependency are crucial symptoms. Yet another psychoanalytic view stresses the survival into adulthood of a need for the experience, normal in infancy, of unitary pleasure of body and mind.

Personality theory offers some characteristics which are found fairly frequently in a substantial number of alcoholics, and postulates that some combination of these characteristics could contribute to the origins of a person's alcoholism (Catanzaro, 1967). Such personality traits include a high level of anxiety, which is eased by drinking; emotional immaturity; ambivalence toward authority or conflict between dependence and assertion; grandiosity, which may be present both in sobriety and drinking; feeling of isolation; compulsiveness and perfectionism, which arise from guilt; confusion over sex roles, which is temporarily alleviated by the alcohol, inability to express anger adequately. These personality characteristics may be present before alcoholism begins or may be exacerbated by drinking.

Family factors are said to contribute heavily to the beginnings of alcoholism. In a group of severe alcoholics, it is likely that half of their first degree male relatives—brothers, sons, fathers, will become or are alcoholics (Winokur, 1970). This relationship may reflect hereditary considerations, role-modeling, or exposure to the same emotional, cultural, and social environment. Another possibility is that alcoholics are often the last-born children in their families. Because these children grow up in an overprotected environment, they may become very dependent and express this dependence by heavy drinking. The dependency may become angry overdependency because it cannot be satisfied by normal interpersonal relationships.

The person's *self-concept* has been implicated in the causation of alcoholism. A drinker may have a self-concept which is not fully integrated, and can be using alcohol in order to discharge aspects of his personality which are not congruent with his image of himself. By continuing to drink, such a person avoids confronting the dissonances of his self-concept. Alcoholic beverages may also enable the drinker to have higher levels of self-esteem than are otherwise possible (McCord, 1972). Alcohol may contribute to shaping the person's self-concept (Reichman, 1978). A young person who is unwilling or unable to handle the frustrations and anxiety involved in establishing a self-concept may be attracted to alcohol, which relieves him of identity conflicts and permits the development of an image of the self that is satisfying and seems to fulfill his needs.

McClelland and associates (1972) argue, on the basis of a ten-year study, that men drink alcoholic beverages in order to feel stronger. Men who have a special concern for personalized power drink more heavily than other men. Diffuse sensations of increased strength stemming from distilled liquor are easily elaborated into fantasies of increased power. If a man has an extreme need for personalized power and chooses drinking rather than other possibilities as its outlet, he may drink excessively.

Physiological predisposition theorists argue that many people are heavy drinkers, but only those who have some bodily readiness will become alcoholics. Jellinek (1960) implies that only those persons who have an allergic reaction, or a special metabolic or physiological vulnerability to alcohol will become addicted to it. This abnormal predisposition will only be found in certain people. A related view is that in some people heavy drinking leads to cerebral damage, which destroys brain areas concerned with judgment and will power so that the alcoholic cannot stop drinking.

A *learning theory* approach to alcoholism deals with the reward or reinforcement which is provided by drinking behavior (Roebuck & Kessler, 1972). Desirable changes in mood, alleviation of discomfort, and other pleasant experiences may contribute to the reward, along with improved relationships with others, and the enhancement of self-esteem. According to some views of learning theory, the heavy drinker experiences much internal tension, which creates a drive which is reduced by alcohol, which represents a reinforcement for the drinking response.

An *operant conditioning* view relates stress and learning to the origin of alcoholism (Lipscomb & Holden, 1974). A person who experiences stress may find the consumption of alcohol to be an effective way of responding to the stress, especially if alternative coping behaviors are not available or are perceived as less effective. Each time the person drinks in a stress situation and has his perceptions confirmed, the habit strength of the response increases. When any response is closely followed by a desirable or reinforcing state of affairs (e.g., reduction of stress), the probability of recurrence of the coping response is enhanced. Each time there is reinforcement, there is more likelihood that the response will become habitual.

Jessor and Jessor (1973) have conducted a longitudinal study from a *social learning* viewpoint of young persons who become alcoholics. They see young people's becoming alcoholic as an adaptive activity, which is the end product of an interaction among a "behavior system," a "personality system," and a "perceived environment system."

Alcoholism is sometimes described as part of a larger pattern of antisocial behavior (Schuckit, 1973). In these cases, objective measures such as the existence of a police record and running away from home are used to identify antisocial behavior. Alcoholism becomes just one more reflection of an underlying syndrome.

Most alcoholic drinking is learned, in the sense that one identifies certain beverages with specific social institutions and kinds of people. The drinker learns how to ask for a drink, how long its consumption ought to take, and what brand name to request. Since most alcoholic beverages are not sweet, the initial taste may be unpleasant and the drinker must learn to perceive a sour, sharp, bitter, or peaty taste as pleasant, by repeated exposure in a social learning context to members of his reference group. The importance of such reference group learning is seen when Scotch drinkers ask for their favorite brand by name in a bar, are served the inexpensive "house" brand, and extol the virtues of the taste of what they think is their favorite. Expecting certain kinds of taste sensations, they ignore the evidence of their own senses (Winick, 1968).

A variety of *sociological* theories of alcoholism has been proposed. We have seen in Chapter 7 that Robert K. Merton (1957) notes that although most people subscribe to the American goal of materialistic success, how such a goal is to be achieved is not clear, and some persons do not have easy access to the goal. A condition of anomie, or a nonparticipation in norms, may result. One response to anomie is retreatism via alcohol.

Indirect measures of the role of anomie in the origins of alcoholism can be obtained in studies of Jews and Indians. Jews represent a group with a high degree of solidarity, little anomie, and a low rate of alcoholism (Synder, 1964). In contrast, Indians represent a group with a low degree of solidarity, high anomie, and a high rate of alcoholism.

Downward social mobility has also been implicated in alcoholism (Jones & Borland, 1975). Such mobility can lead to bitterness and anxiety, for which drinking can serve as a self-prescribed remedy.

SOME EFFECTS OF ALCOHOL USE

The extended controversies over policies toward drinking have frequently dealt with various presumed or actual effects of alcohol, and over the years, considerable information about effects of alcohol has been developed.

One dimension consists of alcohol's impact on various organ systems. Evidence of enlarged cerebral ventricles has been reported (Tumarkin, et al., 1955). Repeated intoxication may injure the cerebral cortex and cause cumulative destruction of nerve tissue. Cirrhosis of the liver is a serious disease which is approximately eight times more frequent in excessive drinkers than in abstainers or moderate drinkers. It is so closely linked with inebriety that the death rate from cirrhosis of the liver has been used to determine the total number of alcoholics in a given area (Jolliffe & Jellinek, 1941).

In addition to organ damage, excessive alcohol use has a variety of negative effects on family functioning, job performance, and ability to pursue other goals. It may lead the drinker to constrict his life space and withdraw from social and interpersonal functioning. Decreased self-esteem, low frustration tolerance, mood swings, and difficulties in coping with tension or anxiety are other possible effects.

How alcoholic beverages affect the drinker is a function of the amount of pure alcohol consumed over a specific period of time, the amount entering the bloodstream and the speed of its metabolization. The less concentrated the beverage and the more slowly it is consumed, the less impact it will have. Six ounces of wine have as much alcohol as a jigger (1½ ounces) of 80-proof liquor. (The proof is double the amount of alcohol, so that 80-proof means 40 percent alcohol.) Six ounces of dessert wine, like port, sherry, or vermouth, have twice the alcohol of a jigger of 80-proof liquor.

Some 20 percent of the alcohol is absorbed directly from the stomach to the blood, which carries it to the brain. The alcohol will affect the brain until it is metabolized. It takes an average adult from sixty to ninety minutes to metabolize the alcohol in a jigger of hard liquor, a medium glass of wine, or twelve ounces of beer, depending on his body size and weight.

The more concentrated the amount of alcohol in a beverage, the more rapidly is it absorbed; the higher the concentration of nonalcoholic components, the slower is the absorption of alcohol. The concentration is generally around 3 to 6 percent by volume in beers, 12 to 14 percent in table wines, 20 percent in fortified cocktail or dessert wines, 22 to 50 percent in liqueurs, and 40 to 50 percent in distilled spirits such as whiskey, gin, and vodka.

Although alcohol is a sedative, it may function like a stimulant if taken in small quantities. It is a depressant when consumed in large quantities. A person who ingests some alcohol may seem to be garrulous and stimulated, because one of its effects is the lowering of inhibitions through depression of the brain centers which usually inhibit such behavior.

Jellinek (1966), who felt that alcoholism was a genus with many species, has suggested that alcohol ought to be regarded as a drug that lies somewhere between a habit-forming and an addiction-producing substance. The latter, such as opiates, lead to addiction in most of their regular users, require relatively small amounts in order to achieve this result, and feature a process of addiction that may develop in several weeks. In contrast, alcohol leads to addiction in less than one tenth of its users, requires large amounts, and takes some years to do so: In fact, the average clinical alcoholic is forty-two years old. Addiction to alcohol is most likely if it is consumed daily in large quantities, especially in the morning. As in the case of any addiction, there are predictable withdrawal symptoms, which include convulsions, delirium, and tremors (see Chapter 16).

Typologies of Drinking States

One typology posits the social, weekend, spree, neurotic/psychotic, and plateau drinker (Kennedy, 1962). The social drinker may become a weekend drinker, who uses alcohol excessively from Friday evening through Sunday. In contrast, the spree drinker is drunk for a number of days, becomes sober on his own, and then returns to normal life. A drinking problem in the case of a neurotic or psychotic is often very likely to advance to true alcoholism. A plateau drinker, who is often "tight" but seldom drunk, may be on Skid Row, and is more interested in the duration of his drinking than its intensity.

The classical disease concept promulgated by Jellinek (1960) presents a predictable and progressive course, with each step evolving from the one preceding it. In the first or prealcoholic or symptomatic stage, the prospective alcoholic experiences marked relief by drinking, with almost daily ingestion. After this phase, which can last up to two years, there is the second or prodromal period, lasting from six months to five years, and it is characterized by blackouts, surreptitious drinking, preoccupation with alcohol, and heavy but not conspicuous consumption. The crucial third phase reflects loss of control, rationalization, aggression, and the beginning of alcohol-centered behavior. The fourth and chronic phase reflects prolonged intoxications, loss of alcohol tolerance, and ethical and thinking impairment.

LAW ENFORCEMENT AND THE ALCOHOL OFFENDER

Some impression of the extent to which alcohol-related offenses have contributed to the criminal justice system may be obtained from United States arrest figures for 1976. Out of a total of 9,600,000 arrests for all offenses, there were 1,297,000 arrests for drunkenness, 1,029,300 for driving under the influence, and 369,700 for violation of the liquor laws—which adds up to 2,696,800, or 28 percent of the total number of arrests. Not included are the 657,500 arrests for disorderly conduct or the 39,400 for vagrancy, many of which involve alcoholism (Kelley, 1977). Overall, 1976 arrests for drunkenness are down 45.5 percent from ten years ago, undoubtedly reflecting a sharp decline in the number of states in which public drunkenness represents a violation of law rather than any large drop in the number of drinkers.

A drinker may be arrested under a public intoxication statute, a disorderly conduct statute, or, if he is involved in aggressive behavior, under an assault charge. Arrests for drunken driving are also common. Many persons who appear to be drunk, however, are taken into custody by the police and held overnight without any specific charges being filed.

In samples of chronic inebriate offenders, only about one third appear to have criminal histories which include serious crime (Lindelius & Salum, 1973). Most alcoholics have not engaged in such crime and most criminals are not alcoholics, although there are more drinking problems among criminals than are to be found in the general population. Also, there are more criminals among heavy drinkers than are to be found in the general population. On the whole, criminal activity usually precedes heavy drinking in the life cycle, perhaps as part of the same processes which lead many criminals to "mature out" of drug use and of serious antisocial activity by their thirties (Winick, 1964).

Exactly how many persons arrested for a crime are alcohol-involved is difficult to determine with any certainty, because such persons are not required to take a blood alcohol test, with the exception of traffic offenders. In general, drinking may improve the likelihood of a person being a crime victim, or the likelihood that an offender will commit the crime, or may contribute to events leading to a crime.

Alcohol intoxication's release of inhibitions may, of course, contribute to criminal activity. A drinker may also experience decreases in perceptual and cognitive alertness which affect his appraisal of a potentially violent or threatening situation. One kind of crime in which there appears to be a clear relationship between the offense and drinking is homicide. The proportion of homicide victims who have been drinking has consistently been in the 40 to 60 percent range. Homicides are also likely to take place in the locale where the drinking occurs, which, most frequently, is the home. And homicides where alcohol is present are often victim-precipitated.

Although a person of lower socioeconomic status is more likely than others to be arrested for offenses related to alcohol use, higher status persons and celebrities may also find themselves in difficulties. In a study of ninety-seven physicians who were alcoholics, 48 percent had been arrested, 37 percent jailed, and 20 percent had lost their drivers' licenses (Bissell, 1978). These figures are surprising in view of the enormous prestige and high income of American physicians.

The Alcoholic in Court

Several courts handling alcohol cases during the 1960s seemed to be moving in the direction established by the United States Supreme Court (*Robinson* v. *California*, 1962), when it said that narcotic addiction was a "status offense," a disease which the person could not control, and for which a penalty would represent "cruel and unusual" punishment. Thus, an appeals court in the District of Columbia decided that a man convicted of public intoxication was not guilty because his chronic alcoholism was a disease, and that reflecting his disease publicly was not a crime (*Easter* v. *District of Columbia*, 1966). However, the United States Supreme Court in a subsequent public drunkenness case did not accept this logic (*Powell* v. *Texas*, 1968). In a 5 to 4 decision, the court found that some ambiguity surrounded the definition of alcoholism, that the penal sanction should not be dropped in the absence of viable alternatives, and that the crime was the public aspect of the intoxication rather than the intoxication itself. As a result of this Supreme Court decision, local courts have been reluctant to liberalize the treatment of alcoholics, although legislatures have been doing so during the last decade.

Many cities have a separate drunk court, which usually has few visitors and few lawyers representing the defense. Even prosecuting attorneys and arresting officers are scarce. Over nine tenths of drunkenness defendants are convicted, compared with about one third of those charged with other crimes. In some courts, the charge is not even read, or the defendants may be put in a large group to which the same charge is read. Very few defendants have an opportunity to make the kind of statement in their own behalf which is routinely possible in other kinds of trials (Goldfarb, 1976).

The majority of persons charged with drunkenness plead guilty and are given a short sentence in jail. Although the judge may fine the defendant, the latter's indigence usually makes a fine unrealistic and detention is the likely outcome of conviction in those states with effective drunkenness statutes.

In cases involving drunkenness the defendant generally pleads guilty, so that the judge's primary decision involves the nature of the sentence or other disposition of the case. He can warn the defendant and let him go with a suspended sentence, or send him to a hospital or to a prison. Some judges require a defendant to take appropriate instruction in an alcoholism course. Judges use considerable discretion in analysis of the defendant's background, appearance, previous record, roots in the community, age, and other symptoms.

Many of the persons who are in jail for drunkenness, who are usually called chronic drunkenness offenders, may not become intoxicated very often even if they drink a lot (Spradley, 1970). However, they are usually called "drunks" by the criminal justice personnel with whom they are in contact.

The Alcoholic Prisoner

It is generally believed that from one third to one half of the inmates of America's jails are there for violation of laws regulating public intoxication. Most of these inmates are serving relatively brief terms, probably from two to four weeks. The same persons tend to be arrested repeatedly, with one fourth of the total of those arrested for drunkenness representing three fourths of all such arrests. Most of these men have not been arrested for any offense that is not linked to drinking.

A portrait of the chronic drunkenness offender was sketched by Pittman and Gordon (1958). The representative man serving a sentence of thirty days or longer in Rochester, New York for public intoxication was aged forty-eight and not married; he had a grammar school education, considerable residential instability, and a lower socioeconomic class background. Blacks were overrepresented in the sample. The average person in this group, which had been convicted two or more times for public intoxication, had been arrested seventeen times, with the number of arrests increasing progressively with age.

Public intoxication accounted for 78 percent of the recorded arrests, with an average of four arrests per man on other charges. In general, there was no significant increase in the number of arrests for charges other than public intoxication after age thirty-five. Inebriates engaged in more serious crimes seem to abandon such activity at around age thirty-five, after which many adapt to life by drinking.

Over one third of the prisoners had been convicted of relatively serious nondrink-related crimes. It is likely that such convictions had occurred before the age of forty, after which the offender dropped out of active crime for reasons of age, ineptness, and adaptation to the norms of drinking and life on Skid Row.

The alcoholic prisoner may arrive in jail with various health problems resulting from malnutrition, fights, unhygienic living conditions, and abuses of his digestive system. He typically is not a source of problem behavior and is likely to be a docile inmate, who often is the lowest status person in terms of activities available to inmates.

One justification for incarceration of drunks was that prison provided a place to stay, medical care, regular food, reasonably hygienic living, and that it often saved the life of the drunk prisoner, who might have had no other alternative. With greater legislative acceptance of the notion that the community has a responsibility to provide treatment for alcoholics, such a justification is less relevant.

Treatment in Prisons and Jails

Some short- and long-term penal institutions have self-help programs for alcoholics, sponsored by groups like AA or the Salvation Army. The generally good attendance at such meetings could reflect the break they provide from institution routine, a chance to get together with friends and have a snack and a smoke, rather than a strong motivation to shake the drinking habit (Chapter 4). Such groups may be more successful in a prison which has a fairly long-term population, than in a jail with a relatively high inmate turnover. Some jail or prison groups regularly try to refer inmates approaching release to AA chapters in their home communities.

Less than one tenth of the country's jails, however, have a program for treatment of the alcoholic prisoner. Not only may treatment be nonexistent, but participation in a drunk jail may be an uncomfortable experience. Delousing of body and clothes, abuse from other inmates and staff, and various other indignities are not uncommon.

In some jails, the older alcoholics are highly prized by the administrators. These inmates can be pleasant, reliable, and effective in a variety of institutional tasks, and are familar with jail procedures. They represent a convenient source of labor.

The United States Penitentiary at Leavenworth, Kansas has demonstrated that a completely self-contained alcoholism treatment program, with group therapy, individual counseling and educational and other support services, can be established in a large prison. The Alcohol Treatment Unit at Leavenworth can provide treatment for fifty men in a multidisciplinary setting. At the Federal Correctional Institution at Forth Worth, Texas, Steps Toward Alcoholism Rehabilitation (STAR) was begun in 1972 in order to provide treatment for the convicted felon whose crime was related to his abuse of alcohol. The program, which is based on reality therapy, tries to enhance feelings of personal responsibility, and includes a twelve-hour "marathon" group therapy session.

Driving "Under the Influence"

In most states and many European countries a person with a blood-alcohol level of 0.05 percent or less is regarded as sober and able to drive an automobile. Someone with a level of 0.15 percent or more is legally intoxicated or "under the influence." If there is a concentration of 0.10 percent, which can be reached by having approximately six drinks in a short time span, blurred vision and slurred speech result from dulling of the lower motor functions.

A person who is convicted of driving under the influence of alcohol may receive a fine, suspension of driver's license, mandatory participation in an education program, a prison sentence, or some combination of these penalties. There are great differences among the states and among communities within a state as to which such penalties are meted out to offenders, depending on the availability of facilities, community priorities, and the attitudes of judges (see Chapter 3). Prosecutions for driving under the influence are most likely in areas like the South, where drinking outside the home is relatively frequent.

There are very high odds, perhaps one in one thousand, of being arrested for driving while intoxicated (Nichols & Reis, 1974). Around one-third of those persons who are arrested already have a conviction for driving when intoxicated, and approximately one fifth will be convicted again within the next two years for a similar offense (Pollack, 1973).

Whether or not a drunken driver is arrested reflects the degree of police priority on such matters, the number of police, and their detection procedures (Borkenstein, 1975). Whether or not the driver will be convicted reflects priorities of the prosecutor, the nature of the indictment, arraignment, and court procedures, and the ability of the driver to mount an effective defense (Blumenthal & Ross, 1973). A driver represented by a lawyer usually receives better consideration by administrative agencies, prosecutors, and court, is more likely to have his case delayed or charges reduced or dismissed, and less likely to be assigned to rehabilitation programs, than is a defendant not represented by an attorney.

How many persons who drive under the influence of alcohol are problem drinkers or alcoholics? The range of estimates is very large, from 20 percent to 78 percent, because of variations in definitions of alcohol problems and in criteria for selecting cases (Zylman, 1975). Police and court approaches also vary widely.

There has been a recent turning away from law as a central modality for solving problems that involve alcoholism and automobiles. Courts tend to be unable or unwilling to impose heavy fines, license suspensions, and prison sentences on drunken drivers and police have not apprehended such drivers very diligently (Gusfield, 1975). Drunken drivers have high recidivism rates and the general trend toward decriminalization of alcoholism has contributed to relative inactivity on the part of police and courts. Imposition of a national 55-mile-per-hour speed limit, making safer cars, improvements in public transportation, fuel shortages, and the decreasing use of cars for pleasure driving have probably exerted more influence on the decline in highway accidents than has the criminal justice system.

TREATMENT

The acceptance of alcoholism as a disease which can and should be treated was substantially enhanced by establishment in 1970 of the National Institute of Alcohol Abuse and Alcoholism (NIAAA), largely as a result of its championing by ex-Senator Harold Hughes of Iowa, a recovered alcoholic. The Institute, which had a budget of $168 million for the 1977–1978 fiscal year, supports treatment, research, and demonstration projects in each of the states.

NIAAA financial support for treatment is important because some communities are reluctant to initiate treatment activities for the alcoholic, which usually cost four to seven times as much as jailing. Often, a lingering disapproval of the alcoholic and a feeling that taxpayers' money should be used for conditions that are not morally implicated combine to lead communities to implement a punitive approach to alcoholics and to provide only minimal treatment.

The Institute has also established a national clearinghouse which identifies, codes, and indexes new findings and information on alcoholism in a computer-based retrieval system. As a result, any community or any scientist interested in current information on treatment or other aspects of alcoholism can obtain such material at no cost and in a matter of days.

There is no specific medical specialty that is devoted to the treatment of alcoholism, although psychiatrists play an important role in counseling, and internists frequently handle a drinker's general medical problems. Occupational and recreational therapists may contribute to the drinker's efforts to reorganize his expenditures of time, and family therapists often work with the whole family of the alcoholic. Alcohol education is also part of most centers which provide treatment for alcoholics.

Antabuse

Antabuse is the trade name for disulfiram, a drug which produces a violent and very unpleasant reaction when combined with alcohol. The reaction includes vomiting, nausea, headache, vision problems, and palpitations. Once a patient has taken disulfiram, he knows that taking alcohol in the next few days will make him feel sick. Thus, the decision to take the antabuse is, in effect, a decision not to drink during the period that the antabuse is effective.

Antabuse acts as a kind of chemical conscience by protecting the patient against his uncontrollable urge to drink and giving him a sense of security. He knows that if he drinks he will become quite ill and, in fact, may even die if he drinks enough alcohol. Antabuse is supervised by a physician and can be an adjunct to many different kinds of treatment. In some European countries, the use of antabuse can be a condition attached to prison furloughs or parole.

Alcoholics Anonymous

A unique American contribution to treatment is Alcoholics Anonymous (AA), which was started in 1935 by two laymen (a physician and a stockbroker) who were recovered alcoholics (Gellman, 1964). Although AA is a national movement with a branch in almost every community of any size, it is a minimally structured institution. Each member tries to keep sober and help to keep others sober via the peer fellowship of self-help (Toch, 1965).

The "Anonymous" is attractive to many drinkers who value the open and accepting nature of the group, which is free and democratically ignores class and status. AA has received enormous favorable publicity, which can facilitate the members' expectations of assistance. There are Twelve Steps to sobriety, and some of these steps provide a quasi-religious framework for the organization. Auxiliaries for wives (Al-Anon) and children (Al-Ateen) exist to reinforce changes occurring in the AA group member.

The roughly ten thousand AA groups service around 320,000 members, who meet in many different settings such as hotels, churches, hospitals, prisons, and YMCAs. In the New York City area, approximately 750 groups average 1,300 meetings weekly. AA groups usually have a twenty-four-hour telephone service, so that help is available around the clock.

Members of an AA group are accepting of the alcoholic, in comparison with other people who reject him. Other group members who are no longer drinking provide role models of what is possible. The groups themselves are loosely organized.

Bill Wilson, a stockbroker who was cofounder of AA, had previously been helped by the Oxford Movement, a religious movement based on the self-transforming impact of confession (Thomsen, 1975). Six of the Twelve Steps refer to God (e.g., "Humbly ask Him to remove our shortcomings").

Abstinence is believed by AA to be the only way in which alcoholism can be treated successfully. For an alcoholic, social drinking is believed to be impossible. The AA member is encouraged to achieve abstinence one day at a time; each day in which alcohol is not consumed represents progress. Approximately two fifths of active AA members appear to sustain sobriety. AA has established branches in various settings in cooperation with many different institutions. Since it does not have a required physical setting or paid staff, its costs are minimal.

Diversion and Civil Commitment Programs for Alcoholic Offenders

Diversion programs for alcoholics have not assumed the importance of similar efforts for drug abusers (Chapter 16). Such efforts, however, have been under way since the 1940s, and may involve referral to AA, a halfway house, a lecture series on alcohol, or individual or group psychotherapy. An alcoholic driver may be forced to attend sessions of a special school devoted to exploring drinking problems. Candidates for diversion programs are chosen by the perceived likelihood of their responding favorably to such treatment and are usually persons without a heavy record of drunkenness offenses.

Civil commitment programs for alcoholics exist in twenty-one states, and in these states persons may be sent involuntarily to residential treatment facilities. Such programs tend to have a low success rate. The opponents of this approach argue that more favorable outcomes are unlikely until medicine develops better methods of treating alcoholism.

Occupational Alcoholism Programs

One current approach to dealing with the alcoholic is based on reaching him while he is still working, through a labor-management sponsored program. Under the pressure of the possibility of losing his job, the worker may be encouraged to seek help for his alcoholism. Some large companies have their own programs; local unions may set up programs for their members, and others are cooperatively sponsored by both labor and management.

In all these cases a worker's alcoholism is interpreted, for purposes of health insurance and personnel procedures, as an illness or condition that shoud be viewed nonjudgmentally but supportively. As union contracts are renegotiated, there is a growing tendency for alcoholism to be included among the conditions that are covered by health insurance. In 1977, the federal government also declared the recovered alcoholic to be entitled to the same employment and reemployment rights as other handicapped persons.

The larger the company, the more enlightened its policy toward alcoholic workers is likely to be. In some companies, the worker is encouraged to return to his job after appropriate treatment, which often involves one or two weeks of detoxification and subsequent referral to an outpatient program. A major thrust of such efforts is early identification of the alcoholic, before his work is substantially impaired.

In the treatment of alcoholism, perhaps the highest rates of success have been found in labor-management programs. An alcoholic worker may be advised by his supervisor, in cooperation with the union shop steward, that his job performance is suffering and that some kind of treatment would be constructive. Assured that his job will be waiting for him and doubly spurred by labor and management, the employee may have a strong motivation to remain in treatment until his situaton improves. Recovery rates in occupational alcoholism programs have been running as high as 65 to 70 percent. One reason for such high rates of success is that the anchorage provided by the union and work situation can facilitate long-term follow-up of the patient, with appropriate assistance for coping with personal and social problems. Fairly long-term help is necessary for many alcoholics, whose needs for assistance do not cease with discharge from the hospital.

Religious-Sponsored Outreach Treatment

The Salvation Army and other religious groups provide a range of services to alcoholics, who may be walk-ins and self-referrals, or who may be referred by courts or hospitals, agencies, or outreach workers. These services are often available without charge, and the alcoholic is accepted at whatever level he is willing or able to enter the situation. Services may include shelters for homeless men, regular meals, counseling, religious activities, alcohol education, modest kinds of work at the facility, medical assistance, the support of group living and a structured daily schedule. The turnover in alcoholic residents of such religious-oriented facilities is generally high. The therapy's focus is to return men to society as productive citizens.

In the established American tradition of "rescue" work, many religious organizations not only have contact, service, and treatment facilities in the area of Skid Row, but may have staff members who visit jails to talk to persons incarcerated for drunkenness and appear in court in order to reassure the judge that the organization will accept the defendant for appropriate treatment.

Religious groups have long been identified with assistance to the alcoholic because so many other social institutions did not want to provide services to these clients. The religious groups, particularly various Protestant

denominations, accepted responsibility for alcoholics, who were seen as out-
casts by much of the rest of society.

Halfway Houses

Many communities have found that a halfway house, where an alcoholic
may live after release from prison or hospital, is a useful way of resocializing
the exinmate into a new way of life. Such facilities attempt to provide a transitional residence, with a supportive staff and assistance in coping with problems of daily living, in which the resident can explore an alcohol-free way of
life. The staff often includes some recovered alcoholics, who can sympathize
with the resident's situation, who represent a positive role model, and who
are experienced in dealing with rationalizations and other defense mechanisms.

The halfway house offers a protected situation where the former alcoholic can experiment with new techniques for facing problems and make mistakes in a nonpunitive environment, rather than in the workaday world
where a mistake might have serious consequences. Halfway houses provide
aid in developing skills of daily living in preparation for the resident's return
to the community, without recourse to the use of alcohol. A number of halfway houses require that the resident take antabuse while in residence. Most
halfway houses have a day room where the residents can relax together. Visits
to cultural activities and other leisure-oriented uses of time provide success
experiences and alternatives to alcohol.

Outcome of Treatment

Although there is no agreement on the exact nature of the disease of alcoholism, there is agreement that it is a chronic condition. Any chronic illness
may be expected to involve relapsing and to prove relatively difficult in terms
of long-term symptom remission.

Because so much of alcoholism's symptoms involve social-familial behavior, it is especially difficult to evaluate the effects of alcoholism treatment
services in terms of conventional criteria. A man may continue drinking after
treatment, but the time between "benders" may lengthen (Vera Institute of
Justice, 1970). He might make more effective use of health and social service
resources, learn to handle stress by tranquilizers and other nonalcoholic
means, and move toward a more favorable work situation. Even though he
may still be drinking, such changes in his life space would have to be considered as evidences of therapeutic movement. A person might also become a
"positive dropout" from treatment and discontinue contact with the treatment
agency, but his social behavior might significantly improve. Because most
treatment of alcoholism occurs on a voluntary basis, there is no easy way of
tracing treatment outcomes on a large-scale basis.

There is controversy over the goal of treatment for alcoholism. One approach tries to treat the drinking behavior itself, while another view is that
the person's social and interpersonal behavior must be attended to. The most

heated controversy surrounds the goal of abstinence, which is believed by AA and many other groups to be absolutely essential. An analysis by the RAND Corporation concluded that treated alcoholics who drank moderately were not more likely than abstaining treated alcoholics to relapse into alcoholism (Armor, et al., 1976). This analysis has been disputed by those who hold that an alcoholic is an alcoholic for his whole life, and that to resume any drinking after sobriety has been achieved implies a return to the active phase of the disease. Others feel that alcoholism is not a condition that is life-long and that it leaves few neurological or chemical traces, so that a recovered alcoholic can engage in social drinking if he wishes to do so.

SOCIAL COSTS

The social costs of alcoholism have been estimated to exceed $15 billion (U.S. Dept. of Health, Education, and Welfare, 1971). Of this amount, two billion goes for community treatment and other services; traffic accidents account for $1.8 billion; $3 billion goes for private treatment and property damage, and $10 billion is represented by lost work time. Somewhere between 20 percent and 60 percent of American hospital beds are occupied by patients with alcohol-related conditions.

Approximately 50,000 persons are killed each year in automobile accidents. A significant amount of alcohol is found in either the victim or driver in approximately half of these incidents. Of the 1 to 2 million persons seriously injured in automobiles, a significant amount of alcohol can be found in from 25 to 40 percent.

The costs of emotional distress, disrupted families, withdrawal, functioning below potential, suicide, increases in anxiety and acting-out and hostility, and shortened life span are difficult to assess in dollars and cents, but also contribute to the national balance sheet on alcoholism (Aarens, et al., 1977).

POLICY DEVELOPMENT

During the last few years, policy toward alcohol has been developing in several directions. One approach to policy change is to attempt to enforce laws dealing with instruction on alcohol. All the states mandate instruction about alcohol in schools, usually at the high school level, but such instruction has usually been minimal, moralistic, inadequate, or nonexistent. The drug abuse epidemic of the 1960s made both teachers and students more interested in mood modifying substances of all kinds, including alcohol.

In order to counter the substantial volume of advertising for alcoholic beverages, there is a movement toward anti-alcoholism messages in mass media. Such commercial messages, especially on television, try to present health hazards of alcohol and lessen the stigma connected with its treatment. Some states, like California, have groups that are attempting to eliminate local advertising by beer and wine distributors on radio and television and have been successful in keeping such advertising out of some print media (Winick, 1974, 1976).

Another path to policy change is to engage in emotional re-education, encouraging people to examine how they handle stress. One approach to curbing alcoholism is to encourage people to widen their repertory of techniques for coping with stress. The use of alcohol for self-medication would obviously diminish if people develop better methods of coping with stress.

Education and prevention efforts concerned with alcoholism appear to have much in common with similar efforts dealing with other kinds of drug abuse. But these two fields have, in general, represented different approaches and constituencies and have avoided commingling their programs of prevention and treatment into joint activity. But alcoholism and drug abuse do have much in common and there are a number of efforts under way to encourage cooperative prevention efforts, especially as more young people move from alcohol to drug abuse, or from drug abuse to alcohol. Therapeutic communities which were originally established to treat heroin addicts, like Daytop Village in New York City, now find that over one third of their residents have an alcoholism problem, and are modifying treatment procedures to deal with the commonalities in both opiate and alcohol abuse.

Similarly, personnel running prevention programs find that they can present the notion of a "chemical cop-out" as applicable to both alcohol and other drugs, and can call attention to alternatives which make heavy use of alcohol and other drugs less important. The very notion of positioning alcohol as simply another mood-modifying drug has proven useful in prevention programs that represent hopes for the future.

Policy toward driving while under the influence of alcohol is also changing. One approach to decreasing driving problems related to drinking is to require that all bars be accessible by public transportation. Using mass media to educate people to the hazards of driving while intoxicated is another direction of change.

Policy toward alcoholism may also be affected by the substantial numbers of famous people who have publicly identified themselves as recovered alcoholics, in efforts to destigmatize alcoholism, encourage persons to seek treatment, and show that alcoholism can be treated successfully. In May 1976, for example, the National Council on Alcoholism, the leading voluntary agency concerned with the subject, assembled twenty-five famous persons, including actor Dick Van Dyke, astronaut Buzz Aldrin, and an army general, who said that they had been alcoholics. The impact of such disclosures, and of similar reports by people like Senators Harold Hughes (Iowa) and Harrison Williams (New Jersey) can be substantial.

Decriminalization

In recent years, there has been a major trend toward decriminalization of public drunkenness, as part of a change in attitudes toward crimes without victims, concern about the strain on the criminal justice system of processing so many cases, and a growing acceptance of the disease concept of alcoholism. Decriminalization removes public drunkenness from behaviors which are of concern to police, courts, and correctional institutions.

Decriminalization laws generally specify that public intoxication is not a criminal offense but a public health concern. Police usually have the power to take anyone who is drunk in public to a sobering-up center, a detoxification facility, a hospital, or to his home. Such laws typically establish a routinized procedure for servicing the alcoholic via medical and social service channels.

In New York State, where decriminalization occurred in 1976, each large city has a wide range of treatment programs. New York City, for example, has 114 facilities including halfway houses, detoxification and auxiliary services. The detoxification period averages six days, and is followed by appropriate referral. The New York City facilities service around sixteen thousand persons each year, most of whom would previously have been arrested, convicted, and spent time in jail.

After the New York State bill was passed, sobering-up stations were established in key locales. These temporary shelters are usually open twenty-four hours a day. They are crisis intervention centers which provide protective services to persons incapacitated by alcohol, and also offer referral opportunities. A typical station has a twenty-bed dormitory, a laundry, and a dining hall. The maximum stay is usually three days, because the goal of these centers is provision of an opportunity to "sleep it off" and to establish minimal hygiene and bodily functioning levels.

If a community decides to decriminalize public drunkenness, it can do so even if the law does not change. Police may reduce their encounters with inebriates, or ignore them when encountered (Chapter 2). Similarly, prosecutors may not seek indictments or convictions, and judges may dismiss charges.

Availability of Alcohol

Some epidemiologists believe that there is a relationship between alcoholism and the availability of alcohol. Social scientists at the Ontario Addiction Research Foundation have argued that there is increased use of alcohol, leading to more illness and crime, as alcohol becomes more widely available and relatively cheaper in terms of disposable income. They recommend that a society wishing to cut down on destructive drinking increase the relative price of alcohol, raise beverage taxes, increase the legal drinking age, and regulate the number and type of places at which liquor is sold. This approach has the common sense appeal of giving governments some action they can take, but critics have pointed out that price increases may exert disproportionately more pressure on the poor and deprive them of the alcohol which is the only coping mechanism which many of them have (Korcok, 1977).

Another approach to reducing the availability of alcohol is through a policy of decreasing the number of outlets for its sale. In eighteen states, sale of alcoholic beverages is a government monopoly, which excludes the private sector and ensures minimal advertising and no price cutting. Efforts are under way in a number of other states to transfer their distribution machinery to the public from the private sector.

THE FUTURE

The alcoholic offender will continue to provide problems for society, although the criminal justice system will be less concerned with him as the concept of decriminalization of the public drunkenness offender spreads. Just what services we should be providing for criminal justice clients who have histories of alcoholism is not clear, but will surely become a more salient question than it has been.

Over the last decade, there has been a tendency for the age of onset of alcoholism to decline, so that younger persons are coming into contact with institutions of social control and treatment which were originally established for a much older population. Procedures that relied on the motivations of middle-aged persons may become irrelevant for the younger alcoholics of the future.

Alcoholism treatment is unique because so much of it, as represented by AA, has developed outside of the established traditions of medical and social welfare service and research. As a result, there has been little of the kind of interaction which has nourished other fields. As alcoholism becomes more visible and engages more resources, it must become more organically related to ongoing work in collateral scientific and service areas. Now that the federal government, with NIAAA, has assumed some leadership in alcoholism, it is in a position to establish achievable goals and standards.

The future will surely see a clarification of the role of the recovered alcoholic in prevention and treatment. There is a considerable body of opinion which holds that only a recovered alcoholic can truly understand and deal with the problems of alcoholics, but this belief is also being questioned. Giving credentials to those who work with alcoholics will be an issue of increasing concern to state agencies, community groups, courts, and other agencies of the criminal justice system.

The movement toward decriminalization of public drunkenness offenders, that has been successful in so many parts of the country, is likely to continue and will represent a pressure for change on those states that have resisted decriminalization. This legislative activity could also have an impact on the thinking of the United States Supreme Court, which has been somewhat resistant to full clarification of the legal status of the inebriate.

Another contributor to change is the increase in the number of young people who are drinking colorless "white goods" like gin, vodka, and light rum, rather than the established whiskeys, which have more taste and color. Vodka has had the most rapid sales growth rate of any alcoholic beverage in American history over the last quarter century. Perhaps because of concern about health and diet, more young people are also beginning to drink wine, and they seem to be staying with it longer than was customary for older Americans. Because of lack of experience with these phenomena, we do not know what proportion of young wine drinkers will transfer their interests to hard liquor, how many will become alcoholics, how many will stop drinking, and how many will become harmless social drinkers.

Answers to these and similar questions should be clarified as the result of research, such as that projected in five Alcohol Research Centers for long-term interdisciplinary research on alcoholism established by the federal government in 1977. At the current stage in the development of policy and attitudes toward alcoholism, perhaps only well-documented research data will permit full acceptance of any significant change in policy. Research should also clarify whether a separate discipline of "alcohology" will emerge or if the current disciplinary and interdisciplinary approach will continue to serve our needs.

REFERENCES

Aarens, M., et al. *Alcohol casualties and crime*. Berkeley: School of Public Health Social Research Group, 1977.

Andrist, R. K. *The long death*. New York: Collier, 1971.

Armor, D. J., et al. *Alcoholism and treatment*. Santa Monica: RAND Corporation, 1976.

Bales, R. F. *Cultural differences in rates of alcoholism. Quarterly. Journal of Studies of Alcohol*, 1946, 6, 480–499.

Bissell, L. *The alcoholic physician and nurse*. Presentation to Columbia University seminar on substance abuse, January 23, 1978.

Bittner, E. The Police in Skid-Row: A study of peace keeping. *American Sociological Review*, 1967, 32, 701–706.

Blumenthal, M., & Ross, H. L. *Two experimental studies of traffic Law*. Washington: Department of Transportation, 1973.

Borkenstein, R. F. Problems of enforcement, adjudication, and sanctioning. In S. Israelstam & S. Lambert (Eds.), *Alcohol, drugs and traffic safety*. Toronto: Addiction Research Foundation, 1975.

Cahalan, D. *Problem drinkers*. San Francisco: Jossey-Bass, 1970.

Cahalan, et al. *American drinking practices*. New Brunswick, N.J.: Rutgers Center of Alcohol Studies, 1969, 22, 189.

Catanzaro, R. J. Psychiatric aspects of alcoholism. In D. J. Pittman (Ed.), *Alcoholism*. New York: Harper & Row, 1967, 31–44.

Cooperative Commission on the Study of Alcoholism. *Alcohol problems: A report to the nation*. New York: Oxford University Press, 1967, 37–38.

Dailey, R. C. *Alcohol and the North American Indian*. Paper at the seventeenth annual meeting, North American Association of Alcoholism Programs, 1966.

Easter v. *District of Columbia*, 361 F. 2d 50, 1966.

Gellman, I. *The sober alcoholic*. New Haven, Conn.: College and University Press, 1964.

Goldfarb, R. *Jails*. Garden City, N.Y.: Doubleday, 1976, 207–306.

Gusfield, J. R. Categories of ownership and responsibility in social issues. *Journal of Drug Issues*, 1975, *5*, 285–303.

Jellinek, E. M. *The disease concept of alcoholism*. New Brunswick, N. J.: Center for Alcoholic Studies, 1960.

Jellinek, E. M. *The alcoholism complex*. New York: Christopher D. Smithers Foundation, 1966.

Jessor, R., & Jessor, S. L. *Problem drinking in youth*. Boulder, Col.: Institute of Behavior Science, 1973.

Jolliffe, N., & Jellinek, E. M. Vitamin deficiencies and liver cirrhosis in alcoholics. *Quarterly Journal for Studies of Alcohol*, 1941, *2*, 544–583.

Jones M. B., & Borland, B. L. Social mobility and alcoholism. *Journal of Studies of Alcohol*, 1975, *86*, 62–68.

Kelley, C. M. *FBI Uniform Crime Reports 1976*. Washington, D. C.: Government Printing Office, 1977, 173.

Kennedy, R. J. H. The forms of drinking. In W. C. Bier (Ed.), *Problems in addiction*. New York: Fordham University Press, 1962, 15–28.

Knight, R. P. The psychodynamics of chronic alcoholism. *Journal of Nervous and Mental Diseases*, 1937, *86*, 538–547.

Korcok, M. Consumption data challenged. *U.S. Journal of Drug and Alcohol Dependence*, November 1977, *1* (10), 3.

Lindelius, R., & Salum, I. Alcoholism and criminality. *Acta Psychiatrica Scandinavica*, 1973, *49*, 306–314.

Lipscomb, W. R., & Holden, J. Risk of being "alcoholic." In C. Winick (Ed.), *Sociological aspects of drug dependence*. Cleveland: CRC Press, 1974, 15–34.

Littman, G. Alcoholism, illness, and social pathology among American Indians in transition. *American Journal of Public Health*, 1970, *60*, 1769–1787.

McClelland, D. C., et al. *The Drinking man*. New York: The Free Press, 1972.

McCord, J. Etiological factors in alcoholism. *Quarterly Journal of Studies of Alcohol*, 1972, *33*, 1020–1027.

Merton, R. K. *Social theory and social structure*. Glencoe, Ill.: Free Press, 1957.

National Institute of Mental Health. *Alcohol and alcoholism*. Washington: Government Printing Office, 1969, 27–28.

National Institute of Mental Health. *Suicide, homicide, and alcoholism among American Indians*. Washington, D.C.: National Institute of Mental Health, 1973.

Nichols, J. L., & Reis, R. J. *One model for evaluation of ASAP rehabilitation effort*. Washington, D.C.: Department of Transportation, 1974.

Pittman, D. J., & Gordon, W. C. *Revolving door*. Glencoe, Ill.: Free Press, 1958.

Pollack, S. *Drinking driver and traffic safety*. Los Angeles: USC Public Systems Research Institute, 1973.

Powell v. Texas, 392 U.S. 514, 1968.

Reichman, W. *Alcoholism and career development*. New York: Baruch College, CUNY, 1978.

Robinson v. California, 370 U.S. 600, 1962.

Roebuck, J. B., & Kessler, R. G. *The etiology of alcoholism*. Springfield: Charles C Thomas, 1972.

Schuckit, M. A. Alcoholism and sociopathy. *Quarterly Journal of Studies of Alcohol*, 1973, *34*, 157–164.

Scott, P. D. Offenders, drunkenness, and murder. *British Journal of Addiction*, 1968, *63*, 221–226.

Snyder, C. R. *Alcohol and the Jews*. Glencoe, Ill.: Free Press, 1958.

Snyder, C. R. Inebrity, alcoholism, and anomie. In M. B. Clinard (Ed.), *Anomie and deviant behavior*. New York: Free Press, 1964, 189–212.

Spradley, J. *You owe yourself a drunk*. Boston: Little Brown, 1970.

Thomsen, R. *Bill W*. New York: Harper & Row, 1975.

Toch, H. *The social psychology of social movements*. Indianapolis: Bobbs-Merrill, 1965.

Tumarkin, B., et al., General atrophy due to alcoholism in young adults. *U.S. Armed Forces Medical Journal*, 1955, *6*, 67–74.

U.S. Department of Health, Education, and Welfare. *First Special Report on Alcohol and Health*, 1971, viii.

Vera Institute of Justice. *First annual report of the Manhattan Bowery project*. New York: The Institute, 1970.

Winick, C. The life cycle of the narcotic addict and of addiction. *U. N. Bulletin of Narcotics*, 1964, *16*, 22–32.

Winick, C. *The new people*. New York: Bobbs-Merrill, 1968, 147.

Winick, C. Mass communications and drug dependence. In C. Winick (Ed.), *Sociological aspects of drug dependence*. Cleveland: CRC Press, 1974, 77–99.

Winick, C., & Winick, M. Drug education and the content of mass media dealing with "dangerous drugs" and alcohol. In R. E. Ostman (Ed.), *Communication research and drug education*. Beverly Hills: Sage, 1976, 15–38.

Winokur, G., et al. Alcoholism (III). Diagnosis and familial psychiatric illness in 259 alcoholic probands. *Archives of General Psychiatry*, 1970, *23*, 104–111.

Wiseman, J. P. *Stations of the lost*. Englewood Cliffs, N.J.: Prentice-Hall, 1970.

Zylman, R. DWI enforcement program. *Accident Analysis and Prevention*, 1975, *7*, 179–190.

chapter 16

The Drug Offender

Charles Winick

The drug offender is one aspect of America's drug problem, a problem which has thwarted decades of government and private efforts at solution. "The" answer to "the" drug problem has been proposed time and again, only to be found wanting.

There are various definitions of the problem. Some people believe that the approximately 235 million prescriptions written each year for mood-modifying drugs—more than one for every person in America—constitute a significant source of concern. These drugs are providing a cushion for their users' adaptation to reality via chemical means, so that the users have less motivation to face their problems (Lennard, et al., 1971). Others regard our drug laws as a problem, because they feel that drug dependence should be viewed as a victimless crime (Schur, 1965).

Still others are concerned that drug use is disproportionately high among the poor and minority groups, who may be docile and undemanding because they have access to a chemical copout, thus not seeking the jobs and education to which they should be entitled. Some writers point to the identification of Chinese with opium, blacks with heroin, and Mexicans with marihuana, and argue that crack downs on drug use reflect Americans' fear of competition from new entrants to the work force (Helmer, 1975).

In addition, there are critics who see drug use as a scourge which helps to finance organized crime and requires more militant domestic and international action than it has been receiving. Some people see drug use as a problem that emerges before elections and is then forgotten (Epstein, 1977).

TERMS USED TO DESCRIBE DEGREES OF DRUG USE

A number of different terms are used to communicate about dimensions of compulsive drug use. Psychological or physical dependence, or both, on a drug is a condition that arises in a person after administration of the drug on a periodic or continuous basis (Eddy, 1965). The characteristics of dependence are functions of the drug involved, so that one refers to "drug dependence of the _____ type." Drug abuse is the use of a substance in a manner or amount sufficient to create a hazard to the individual and/or community, or outside of medical supervision, or illicitly obtained. In sum, drug abuse is the nonmedical use of a drug in a way which adversely affects the user's life.

Addiction, which is sometimes generally defined as being under the influence of a drug more often than one is not, is associated with the continued use of barbiturates and opiates. It is characterized by three separate phenomena: tolerance, habituation, and physical dependence. Tolerance is the diminishing effect of the same dose of a drug, or the need to increase the dose in order to get an effect similar to the initial one. Habituation is the emotional or psychological need which is met by the drug. Dependence is the body's need to get the drug, without which it responds with the abstinence syndrome (Himmelsbach & Small, 1937).

The abstinence syndrome is a characteristic series of involuntary responses found in regular drug users deprived of drugs. In a mild form it includes watering of the eyes, perspiration, running nose, sneezing, and yawning. A moderate response includes pupil dilation, tremors, gooseflesh, and loss of appetite. In its more marked form fever, deep breathing, insomnia, blood-pressure increase, and restlessness are found. Severe symptoms include vomiting, diarrhea, and weight loss. A typical heroin addict will find the effect of his last "shot" beginning to wear off in about six hours, and typical morphine addicts, in perhaps twelve hours. The abstinence syndrome manifests itself when the effect of the shot wears off.

Some very prominent Americans have been medical addicts, or persons whose illnesses were so painful that their physicians regularly gave them addicting drugs. President Ulysses S. Grant had cancer of the throat and became addicted during the final stages of his painful illness. He even wrote a paper praising the pain-killing properties of cocaine. But there are relatively few medical addicts compared with the large number of persons who have become addicted for other reasons. A few medical addicts, like sportscaster Bill Stern and boxer Barney Ross, were addicted in the course of medical treatment and subsequently obtained opiates illegally.

Terms that relate to addiction are not used with much precision. In recent years drug abuse seems to have become the most popular term, especially after the establishment of the National Institute of Drug Abuse in 1974. Some scholars feel uncomfortable with the phrase because it implies a moral evaluation and a medical judgment. In fact, such phrases are employed descriptively and are not used in indictments. It is no longer a crime to be an addict or a drug abuser, although it used to be. In the *Robinson* v. *California* (1962) case, the Supreme Court ruled that imprisonment constituted cruel and unusual punishment for being an addict, because addiction was an illness. The crime is now defined as possession or sale of substances rather than a condition of the body.

TYPES OF SUBSTANCES AND THEIR EPIDEMIOLOGY

There are four kinds of drugs which account for most of our current offenses: depressants, stimulants, hallucinogens, and solvents/inhalants. It is possible to approximate the incidence and prevalence of use of these substances in various ways: sample surveys of the general population; surveys of special populations; comparing the quantity of licit drugs distributed with the number of prescriptions written for the drugs each year; extrapolating from the incidence of drug-related conditions like hepatitis (from infected needles) and overdose; extrapolation from hospital emergency room admissions; projections of arrests and seizures of illegal drugs; and obtaining drug-use histories from persons seeking help for other situations.

Although such data are less than ideal, they provide information which has proven very useful in planning treatment, court, and prison facilities for the person using drugs illegally. They also provide information toward understanding the effects of current policies and planning changes in them.

Depressants

Opiates are depressants and derive from opium. The opium poppy is not grown in the United States, and its legal growth and distribution is controlled by international agreement, via the International Narcotics Control Board.

Opium itself is generally smoked with a pipe. Although it was popular in the 1920s and 1930s in this country, opium smoking is now relatively rare, both because the price of opium is extremely high and because it is relatively difficult to prepare for use without an expert "chef." Morphine, an opium derivative, has great medicinal value because of its pain-relieving qualities. Codeine and dilaudid are also opium derivatives which are often prescribed by physicians for their analgesic qualities. Other widely used synthetic opiates include demerol and methadone. Heroin is about twice as potent as morphine and is the drug of choice of most of today's opiate addicts. It is completely illegal in this country, so that anyone possessing heroin is violating at least one law.

During the 1930s, heroin users usually administered the drug with a hypodermic needle directly into the flesh of the arm or leg. An ounce of "pure" heroin (about 87 percent pure) used to cost $25 to $40, and the typical addict would mix one part heroin with two parts sugar and milk. With World War II, "pure" heroin became scarcer and the average purity of heroin dwindled to 1 percent. The addicts then began to inject the heavily diluted heroin directly into a vein ("main line") in order to maximize its effect. This procedure, which is comparatively complicated because of difficulties in "hitting" a vein, has remained in use up to the present day.

Epidemiologists and statisticians have argued that heroin use, like other kinds of drug dependence, is spread among friends and associates in a manner similar to that in which communicable diseases are spread (De Alarcon, 1969). New users tend to occur in "generations" of about a year (Hunt, 1973).

The staff of the Illinois Drug Abuse Program, working with informants in Chicago, investigated when they began heroin use, and reported eleven macroepidemics between 1967 and 1971 (Hughes & Crawford, 1976). A macroepidemic is defined as involving more than fifty new addicts in a few years. There were twenty-eight microepidemics, each involving fewer than fifty new addicts. An epidemic may start quickly, spread rapidly to a peak, and then decline, leaving substantial numbers of heroin-dependent persons. The drug-using friendship group is the major vehicle for the spread of heroin use. Macroepidemics tend to occur in areas experiencing major population change, where there has been a breakdown in stability and social control.

Because of the great impact of social and cultural factors, the epidemiological model is not completely predictive of the spread of drug dependence. Relevant factors include drug availability, the existence of a drug subculture, law-enforcement activity, and the relative presence of opportunities for education and jobs as well as other conventional means of upward mobility. The presence of such means is inversely correlated with drug dependence, especially of the heroin type.

Another problem in application of the communicable disease model is that in drug dependence the host seeks out the disease agent. This is the reverse of what is found in the large-scale communicable disorders that represent the basis of the public health approach.

Although it is not possible to cite exact figures, a reasonable estimate of the number of persons dependent on heroin is around 700,000. Of these, perhaps 110,000 are in prison and 170,000 in treatment—half in drug-free and half in methadone maintenance programs. About 420,000 users are neither in prison nor in treatment. Between 1967 and 1974, heroin use increased by 1000 percent. Starting in metropolitan areas, it spread to suburban areas and smaller cities. Illicit methadone has been used by around 3 percent of eighteen- to twenty-five-year-olds.

Although daily use of an opiate for around a month will probably lead to addiction, it is possible to use opiates like heroin on a more episodic basis and not become addicted. Some users may "joy-pop" on weekends, or use heroin every few days but alternate it with other substances.

Barbiturates are used medically to calm people and to facilitate sleep. They are addicting and have, in the last decade, come to be used by more young people, although they had previously been preferred by older persons. Barbiturates are used widely, both legally and illegally.

Barbiturates, tranquilizers, and amphetamines used nonmedically are often referred to as "dangerous drugs." They are more frequently abused than either heroin or cocaine. In 1976, barbiturates claimed over 1,700 lives in the United States, through suicides and accidental poisoning. In 1975, 11,000 persons whose primary drug of dependence was barbiturates were admitted to federally funded treatment programs. There are about 280,000 nonmedical barbiturate users who are "in trouble" (Nightingale, 1977). From 2 to 3 percent of American adults have used barbiturates illegally.

Since the mid-1950s, there has been a huge increase in both legal and illegal use of tranquilizers, which are also classified as depressants. They range from relatively mild drugs such as meprobomates to stronger drugs such as thorazine and reserpine. The permanent medical value of these drugs for non-psychotics still remains to be confirmed, although they have been very effective in facilitating the release of psychotic patients from state mental hospitals. Ever since the tranquilizers were introduced, there are more people leaving than entering the hospital each year. But about 490,000 nonmedical users of tranquilizers are "in trouble" as a result of their use (Nightingale, 1977).

Polydrug or multiple substance dependence is probably the most prevalent drug problem in American cities. An individual might prefer to use one substance, like heroin, but it may not be available; its price could be too high, or a seller might be temporarily out of stock. As a result, the typical user takes what his circumstances and access make possible at any given time. Nationally, about three tenths of the regular heroin users also regularly take barbiturates and sedatives, or other downers that might be available.

Barbiturates and alcohol, which are often taken by the same person, are cross-tolerant. Unfortunately, they are also synergistic, so that the toxic effects of the two drugs taken together are greater than the addition of their individual effects.

Stimulants

A number of stimulant drugs are used by drug offenders: marihuana, cocaine, and amphetamine. Marihuana, which is both a stimulant and a depressant, is obtained from the cannabis or hemp plant, which can be grown almost everywhere successfully. Marihuana creates a lightness and a humorous feeling, and a distortion of the sense of time, and usually releases inhibitions. If he takes a large enough dose, the marihuana user becomes sluggish and may go to sleep. In some form, marihuana is used by perhaps a quarter of a billion people throughout the world as an intoxicant. In America, it is usually smoked in the form of a cigarette ("joint").

Amphetamine or "speed" is a stimulant which is sometimes used by students to stay awake while studying and helps long-haul truck drivers keep alert. Medically, its major use has been as a prescription appetite suppressant in the treatment of obesity. Its side effects and toxicity have led Canada, England, and Japan to ban it. It was an important drug of dependence in the 1960s, but has declined in popularity in recent years (Winick, 1972). There was considerable dissemination of the slogan "speed kills" and wide publicity was given to amphetamine-related bizarre behavior and serious organ damage. Many amphetamine users, after an extended high, took heroin or barbiturates to calm down, found such downers to be more attractive, and stayed with them. Some seven million Americans have used amphetamines illegally.

Cocaine, which is derived from the coca leaf, the anesthetic qualities of which were partially discovered by Freud, has medical use as a local anesthetic. Addicts sometimes mix heroin and cocaine into a "speedball," which supplies the immediate "kick" of cocaine with the extended afterglow of heroin. Cocaine's popularity for illegal use has zoomed since 1968.

About four million Americans have illegally used cocaine. In recent years, cocaine has been taken, usually by sniffing, by increasing numbers of middle class persons. Around 4 percent of high school students and 10 percent of college students have tried cocaine, which costs around $1,800 per ounce on the illegal market, as compared with $100 for its use as an anesthetic in a medical setting. Cocaine is typically used several times a month or less, usually in the company of others, and often in combination with alcohol, marihuana, heroin, or other drugs.

A street unit of cocaine costs about the same ($10) as a unit of heroin, but there is an overwhelming desire to take it at frequent intervals, such as every twenty to thirty minutes, in contrast to the several hours between shots of heroin. As a result, the cost of a cocaine habit is relatively high. Because of its high cost per minute ratio, the number of persons using enough to get into trouble through illness and crime is small. But it is among the most powerfully reinforcing of all dependence-producing substances.

Hallucinogens

Hallucinogens, which lead to the perception of apparent sights, sounds, and other stimuli which are not actually present, have become less popular since the late 1960s, when there was great interest in many psychedelic drugs.

Peyote derives from a spineless cactus with buttonlike growths that is widely grown in Mexico and the Southwest. Peyote in its pure form (mescaline) has been used as a psychotomimetic drug to induce a temporary psychosis for experimental purposes. In addition to hallucinations, peyote can also lead to extreme anxiety and great gastric distress.

Lysergic acid diethylamide, known as LSD–25, LSD, or "acid," is the best known psychedelic substance. It became a subject of national concern in the 1960s after some widely publicized experiments with Harvard students, conducted by psychologist Timothy Leary, led to the latter's dismissal by the university. It had been developed as a psychotomimetic drug used experimentally to study psychoses.

LSD's diversion to illicit use began in the 1960s and, soon after, illegal manufacture of the substance spread from California to the rest of the country. (Most of the post-World War II innovations in alcoholic beverages, like vodka mixtures and tequila, as well as most of the new illegal drugs, like LSD, STP, and psilocybin, started in California and moved East.)

The most recently popular hallucinogen is phencyclidine, known as "angel dust" or PCP. It is a nonaddictive depressant which comes in the form of a white powder, that is smoked or sprinkled on vegetables. PCP may lead to a distortion of the user's body image and has led to episodes of paranoia and violence. The average age of use is around fourteen, with many youngsters contributing fifty cents or seventy-five cents toward the $5 needed for one dose of the synthetic.

Hallucinogens cause such intense reactions that they are seldom used on an intensive basis. They may cause a number of side effects, including panic and psychotic reactions.

Solvents and Inhalants

Solvents, like household cleaning chemicals, and inhalants, like toluene-containing model kit glue, are mostly used by preadolescents. About 7 percent of junior and senior high school students have used these products for a "high," at least once. In many communities, they are not sold to minors without the presence of an adult.

Typically the user saturates a cloth with these products or places them inside a paper bag, and then inhales them. Because they are so relatively inexpensive and available, inhalants tend to be attractive to relatively young people (Winick & Goldstein, 1970).

Adolescents are the persons in our society who are most at risk in terms of drug dependence. Drugs represent an important option that may meet many different adolescent needs. They provide an opportunity for coping with stress, a form of relief from different kinds of pain, a method for sidestepping difficult situations, an equivalent to the rites of passage which are so lacking in modern life (Winick, 1968).

Popular literature often refers to "hard" drugs, such as heroin, and "soft" drugs, such as marihuana. In reality, there are no such drugs; there is, however, hard and soft use. Any psychoactive drug may be taken without harm if the dose is small enough and the period between doses large enough (Seevers, 1972).

Marihuana

Marihuana is such an emotionally freighted subject that it has become a paradigm of society's attitudes toward many other mood-modifying substances. Its use was legal until 1937, when the Marihuana Tax Act made it a contraband product. It subsequently became, in federal and state laws, erroneously classified as a narcotic. In the late 1930s, there was widespread confusion about its effects. Marihuana was believed to cause criminal behavior and to be a steppingstone to the subsequent use of heroin (Winick, 1965).

During the 1930s and 1940s, marihuana use was associated with marginal groups like jazz musicians and artists (Winick, 1960, 1961b) and became a focus of the lyrics of many jazz compositions (Winick, 1962b). Marihuana also was likely to be found in ghetto areas, smoked by blacks, Chicanos, and other minorities. Penalties for its possession were strict, with most state laws echoing the federal statute, which provided from two to ten years imprisonment for a first offense.

In the 1950s and 1960s, marihuana use became more broad-based, moving to suburbs and penetrating high schools and colleges in all areas of the country. Many young people observed their friends trying marihuana and not experiencing significant consequences or going on to heroin. By the mid-1960s, marihuana had become a symbol of the culture of rock music, figuring in songs by such culture icons as the Beatles, Bob Dylan, and the Rolling Stones (Winick, 1974b). It was a centerpiece of attitudes of anti-authoritarianism, negative views of government, sexual freedom, and opposition to America's involvement in Southeast Asia (Winick, 1973).

In the 1970s, the children of many important officials and legislators were "busted" for possession of marihuana, and as the criminal justice system began bulging with a growing number of marihuana arrests—500,000 a year, costing around $600 million to prosecute—there was growing pressure to decriminalize the substance. Our other drug problems were almost being overshadowed by marihuana, which figured in seven out of ten drug arrests in the mid-1970s.

Further impetus to ease marihuana penalties came from legal studies, which concluded that the substance had been erroneously classified as a dangerous narcotic (Kaplan, 1971). But most importantly, change came from the National Commission on Marihuana and Drug Abuse (1972, 1973), which recommended what might be called a liberal hard line approach to marihuana, in the form of the elimination of penalties for possession of the substance for personal use, although cultivation, sale, or distribution would remain felonies. These recommendations carried great weight because the Commission membership, which had been appointed by President Nixon, was relatively conservative. The Commission's call for decriminalization of marihuana has been implemented in a number of states, like Oregon, New York, California, Ohio, Mississippi, Colorado, Maine, Minnesota and Alaska where costs of handling marihuana arrests have dropped to practically nothing. Even in these states penalties for trafficking and sale remain harsh, and full legalization, like that enjoyed by alcohol, seems remote. States with decriminalization laws have witnessed more open use of marihuana but not any significant increase in prevalence of use.

Decriminalization of marihuana, as it has been accomplished in these states, makes possession of small amounts of the substance a violation, which is like a traffic ticket, punishable by a nominal fine and not treated legally as a crime. Those persons calling for decriminalization often make it clear that they do not necessarily favor marihuana use but that they are opposed to antimarihuana laws. Italy, Columbia, and the Netherlands have also decriminalized simple possession and use of marihuana. Decriminalization does not violate the 1961 Single Convention on Narcotic Drugs, since the Convention only requires that possession be illegal but leaves penalties to the discretion of each signatory nation.

During the Vietnam war, the use of marihuana was heavily politicalized, but its use today is decreasingly related to radical causes and it no longer generates much emotionalism. It now tends to be seen as a mild recreational drug regularly "toked" in public and privately by millions of Americans. There are about 3,000,000 daily users and 13,000,000 current users, with some 35,000,000 who have smoked it at least once. The bulk of these persons began using marihuana since the 1960s, after the drug lost many of its rebellious drug-culture connotations. Marihuana use is now highest among the better educated and younger members of the population.

THEORIES OF ADDICTION AND DEPENDENCE

A valid and confirmed theory of how and why addicts and other drug dependents develop their relationship to the substance could have great predictive value and impact on policy. There is one set of theories for the traditional drug problem of addiction and another, more broadbased, group of theories for drug dependence in general. No one theory enjoys full acceptance, because no single theory seems able to explain the illegal use of drugs by such a heterogeneous group of people. Another problem is that illegal drug use may be of varying degrees of salience to their users; for some, the drugs may be quite central but for others, they could be relatively unimportant.

How do addicts develop, if not for medical reasons? One explanation is *sociological* and emphasizes the social conditions which give rise to addiction. War and economic depression seem to be related to the onset of upsurges in the cycle of addiction. This cycle is almost a generation long. Thus, addiction reached a peak in the early 1920s, declined until the late 1930s, and assumed importance again in the 1950s and 1970s. Drug use is taught by peers of the new drug user, but, contrary to popular belief, the experienced user is often reluctant to "turn on" a nonuser. The first shot is seldom pleasurable; most people who take one or two shots do not go on to become addicts.

Studies of teenagers in Chicago suggest that there is a special addict subculture which has its own values and is well developed (Finestone, 1957). The "cat," or juvenile drug user in Chicago tries to develop a "hustle," or any nonviolent method of making money that does not require work. The user's hustle has been defined as an activity that uses guile or deceit to get money— the most likely one is selling drugs (Waldorf, 1973). The cat cultivates his "kick" or any taboo activity which intensifies living, such as drug use.

Similar studies in New York have reported that drug users tend to cluster in cliques on the periphery of gangs (Chein, 1965). The addict subculture is likely to exist in those areas of the city which: are the most deprived economically; have considerable family disorganization and high mobility; have populations that have recently arrived in the area; lack effective adult controls. Being born in a particular delinquent area in certain big cities would therefore seem to make a young minority group member such as a black, Chicano, or Puerto Rican, especially likely to be exposed to drug addiction.

The sociological theories of drug addiction stress the social rather than the individual personality components of the addict. They assume that people learn to be addicts, rather than being predisposed to addiction by early childhood experiences. Lindesmith (1947) has suggested that a drug user becomes an addict only after he has undergone withdrawal and realizes that the drug removes withdrawal distress. He argues that the heroin user, after daily ingestion for several weeks, becomes physically dependent on the drug and undergoes withdrawal if heroin is not taken. Once the user has gone through withdrawal, he or she continues to use the drug in order to avoid the pain of withdrawal rather than to experience the original euphoria. However, McAuliffe and Gordon (1974) disagree and believe that long-term heroin users often achieve euphoria and seek it. Euphoria is said to consist of the initial "rush" and the continuing effect. Heroin provides a "flash," a sense of exceptional well-being, an ascendancy to a "high." Those users who are able to achieve euphoria enjoy more prestige than others who barely are able to stave off withdrawal.

An argument against the euphoria thesis is that the amount of actual heroin ingested by street users is so heavily diluted that the likelihood of euphoria is relatively slight. However, the excitement of the hustle may be very compelling. At the same time, the user can get some kind of revenge on society for the deprivations he has undergone through the vehicle of his drug use.

One sociologist argued that young people remain marihuana users because they have gone through a specific series of procedures, which they come to associate with the pleasure of smoking marihuana (Becker, 1953). The sociological explanations of addiction and dependence stress that psychiatrists, who assume that users have a special personality make-up, usually study users only *after* they have become dependent; hence they cannot really know, but can only speculate on, what the premorbid personality may have been like.

The attractions of personal involvement with the subculture of heroin figure in one *social psychological* typology of the onset of drug use (Chein, 1965). According to this theory, addicts are either:

1. strongly influenced by craving for the drug but with relatively little personal involvement with the subculture;
2. strongly influenced by personal involvement but with relatively little craving;
3. strongly influenced by both craving and personal involvement;
4. neither strongly craving nor personally involved, but with histories of personal dependency.

In another social-psychological explanation of the reasons for a relatively high rate of drug dependence in a particular subgroup, the author notes that three conditions always exist in such a group (Winick, 1974d):

1. relative availability of the substance;
2. disengagement from normative proscriptions against use of the substance;
3. "Role strain" (Chapter 7) and/or deprivation.

The presence of these three conditions enables us to predict which subgroups will have a high prevalence of drug dependence. Within each subgroup, we can also predict which individuals will be drug dependent.

A related *life-cycle theory* of drug dependence argues that these three conditions are very likely to be present among adolescents, who represent the group most likely to begin drug use (Winick, 1962a, 1964b). There are comparatively few older drug users because they have "matured out" of their dependence, typically by their thirties. For perhaps the majority of the drug dependent, their condition is self-limited by age.

Some theories call attention to the *career* dimensions of the drug-dependent person. "Taking care of business," the title of a report by Preble and Casey (1969), has come to be associated with the web of activity, the "ripping and running" which constitute a daily series of challenging and interesting activities that keep the heroin user involved and busy. Chein (1965) argues that this range of activities, the hustle, which is so demanding in terms of time involved and skills acquired, is one of the attractions of drug addiction and dependency.

Most addicts are so busy seeking and selling drugs, and stealing, or supporting their habit by prostitution if they are women, that they have neither time nor opportunity to learn a vocation. The drug replaces the vocational decision, just as it replaces other decisions.

The *psychoanalytic* view suggests that the typical young addict comes from a family in which there is a very weak and ineffectual father and a relatively strong mother. The mother is likely to be seductive as well as destructive, and to be rejecting in an overprotective way. Such a mother may actually have an unconscious need to keep her son on drugs, while protesting that she is eager for him to get off drugs. With a weak and ineffectual father and a strong mother, the addict would have difficulties in identifying with an appropriate adult figure of masculinity.

This difficulty in identification is used to explain why addicts generally have such disturbed sexual functioning. The young male adolescent does not have any model of a successfully functioning adult male with whom he can identify, whereas his model of a female is that of a special kind of aggressive temptress. Perhaps as a partial reflection of the difficulties in sexual identification related to this kind of family constellation, the young addict usually uses an opiate instead of sex, and his descriptions of the effects of heroin often include statements about its being a kind of orgastic sensation, especially in the stomach. It seems to be easier for the addict to buy drugs and thus have a sex substitute than to develop any relationship with a member of the opposite sex. Rorschach studies confirm addicts' emotional constriction, sex difficulties, and orality.

In psychoanalytic terms, a representative addict would be described as narcissistic, oral-dependent, and masochistic. This means that the addict relates to the world primarily through his mouth, and is unable to assume adult responsibilities. An oral person wants others to take care of him. Psychoanalysts have noted that the typical addict seems to take narcotics for the first time at around age sixteen, the age at which adolescents are traditionally confronted by the challenge of sex, and begin to think about their choice of a vocation. For some adolescents, the use of a narcotic drug represents one way of evading the responsibility of relationships with the opposite sex as well as the responsibility of selecting a career.

Psychoanalytic theories generally describe drug dependent persons as if they constitute a homogeneous group. In the last decade, there has been a growing sensitivity to the wide range of personality types found among drug dependents and caution about attributing any simple group of traits or characteristics to them.

Some *psychiatric* theories, which are not psychoanalytic (Wikler, 1953), suggest that addiction is a psychiatric disability, but one that can be adopted by a number of different kinds of disturbed persons. These theorists observe that the ingestion of opiates leads to a state in which such needs as pain, hunger, and sexual urges are substantially diminished, and that different kinds of people are able to respond to this method of coping with their primary urges. These students note that once a person becomes addicted, he can no longer be described in terms of his pre-addiction personality, because the use of the drug creates a new and unique response pattern.

One *learning theory* view interprets addiction as an acquired drive which becomes a basic drive (Bejerot, 1972; Lovett, 1974). Adherents of this approach see drug use as learned behavior which derives from the drug's euphoric effects, physiological effects, or the social situation of drug taking. The user modifies his way of life in order to fit the drug, and regards sexual urges and hunger as less important than the drug-related learned behavior (Tozman & Kramer, 1973).

There is a *social learning* theory which conceptualizes drug use as a problem behavior that elicits negative sanctions from established agents of social control (Jessor, Jessor, & Finney, 1973). Drug use is considered to be functional and adaptive, like other socially learned behavior. The network employed in this approach includes perceived environment, behavior, and personality. Building on the theoretical framework of social learning (Rotter, Chance, & Phares, 1972), this theory documents how both personality and environmental factors play a significant role in variations of social behavior like drug use.

The more psychologically oriented explanations of addiction recognize

the increase in the number of current addicts who seem to be associated with various other antisocial activities, as compared with the addicts of the past.

The older heroin addict of the 1950s was a very busy person, "taking care of business" in order to get money for the drug. Today's methadone patient who does not have to hustle may get bored and engage in outbursts of violence or almost random crime.

One occupational group has remained fairly consistent in its illegal use of opiates—physicians. From 1 to 4 percent of our 365,000 practicing physicians are opiate (usually demerol) users, and it can be speculated that the same proportion were taking opiates twenty and thirty years ago. Physicians who take drugs may be the busiest and most successful practitioners. They clearly do not take drugs because they are unsuccessful but in order to meet various needs; many may have some organic ailment. It is possible that one kind of person who becomes a physician—compulsive and very responsive to status and goal needs—is likely, under some circumstances, to be especially aware of possible discrepancies between his self-concept and his actual achievement, and to take drugs in order to face such discrepancies or other feelings of personal inadequacy. Although physician addicts usually take drugs to which they have access because of their vocation, their access is not the primary reason for drug use (Winick, 1961a); pharmacists have greater access to drugs and there are practically no pharmacist addicts, probably because the kind of person who becomes a pharmacist is likely to be quite different from the kind of person who becomes a physician.

Nurses also appear to be substantially overrepresented among opioid users (Winick, 1974a). Nurses are, of course, in direct contact with drugs and their duties may routinely involve their handling and administering various analgesics and sedatives. Among the reasons for nurses' illegal drug use are fatigue, physical ailments, termination of family relationships, quarrels, and ambivalence about nursing, magical thinking or feeling that the drug use could be controlled, problems of incipient retirement, misinformation about drugs, and problems with drinking. Because of the shortage of nurses, it seem relatively easy for the addicted nurse to get another job after her condition has been discovered at one place of employment.

Another occupational group long associated with the use of drugs consists of jazz musicians (Winick, 1960). Their irregular working hours, performances in night clubs before semi-intoxicated audiences, association with the occasionally criminal elements of the booking and entertainment worlds, the unfinished nature of every jazz performance, the frequent recurrence of themes of masochism and sex in jazz music, and the heavily publicized drug use of some famous jazz musicians—all combine to create an atmosphere in which drug use may be accepted as part of the environment. Jazz has traditionally been a protest music and a vehicle of expression for musicians who have a dissident statement to make. Since one conspicuous symbol of deviant behavior in our culture is the use of drugs, the jazz musician is thus in a deviant field and is italicizing his dissidence in taking drugs.

When rock music became the dominant type of popular music in America, beginning in 1954 and reaching a crescendo by the 1960s, its heavy drug content reflected the personal drug habits of many rock superstars (Winick, 1974b). Famous performers like Jimi Hendrix and Janis Joplin died of overdoses within a few months of each other in 1970 and it was widely believed that drug use contributed to the death (1977) of Elvis Presley, the "King of Rock." Many fans believed that a "high" represented the best way to enjoy the music, and identified with the presumably heavy drug use of many rock stars.

Musicians and drug users contribute to and draw from each others' verbal subculture and shared jargon. The user's language may reflect his ambivalence toward the drugs, which both attract and repel him. Thus "shit" is one popular term for heroin. When on drugs, the user is "stoned."

There are a number of distinguished artists who have taken drugs: Coleridge, De Quincey, Elizabeth Barrett Browning, Poe, Baudelaire, and Hans Fallada. The physician-author of the Sherlock Holmes novels (Dr. A. Conan Doyle) reported that Holmes averaged three "shots" a day of morphine or cocaine, after each of which he "sank back into the velvet-lined armchair with a long sigh of satisfaction." These creative persons functioned quite successfully in their chosen fields.

In general, opioid use has remained restricted to the groups noted above. It has not become a drug widely used for recreational purposes, like marihuana or cocaine.

Details of Heroin Sales

The opium which is the source of heroin is grown in one of three areas: Turkey, the Golden Triangle in Southeast Asia (Laos, Burma, Thailand), or Mexico. The opium from the former two areas is likely to be processed into heroin base, after smuggling, in Marseilles or Genoa.

A kilo of heroin which cost $5,000 in Marseilles or Genoa will ultimately be sold in American cities for around $1 million, in $5 glassine containers ("nickel bag") containing ninety milligrams. Between one and ten milligrams in each bag are heroin. The heroin sold in Europe is around 80 percent pure, but after passing through several American levels of distribution, it becomes heavily adulterated, probably at least twenty-four times by the time it is sold on the street.

Street heroin is typically mixed with quinine, lactose, dextrose, and a milk sugar called bonita, by the wholesaler. The mixing of heroin with other substances is usually done with ten kilos of heroin at a time. The ten kilos are purchased by the importer for around $150,000 and sold within twenty-four hours to intermediary dealers, after initial dilution, for about $630,000. The dealer who arranges for the dilution, which typically is done overnight, thus clears $460,000 in profit, all cash, after expenses.

The individual addict usually buys a glassine packet or a small gelatin capsule (no. 5 size), which holds the heavily adulterated heroin, from a pusher or connection (peddler). The peddler will usually ask for the money first ("up front") and will then go to his cache and get the drugs. In order to avoid the risk of handling the narcotics himself he may conceal the drugs enroute and tell the purchaser where to pick them up. All the circumstances surrounding the sale of illegal drugs are designed to make the task of law-enforcement officers difficult—so difficult that it is remarkable that they are as successful as they are in making arrests, especially since they rapidly become known to the drug salesmen. The narcotics police officers' increasing skill at their job as they get more and more experience is cancelled, to a great degree, by the extent to which they become known to pushers.

Field studies of the movement of heroin have concluded that there are seven levels in the illegal distribution system, from importer to ultimate addict-user. At each level, there is dilution of the drug to a lower level of potency and repackaging into smaller quantities for transactions at the next level. The levels, in descending order to the ultimate consumer, are: importer, kilo connection, connection, weight dealer, street dealer, juggler, and addict. At the street level, where small quantities of heroin are involved, differences in price in an area vary by a factor of about two, but price differences are minimal at the higher levels of the distribution system, where large quantities are handled.

Changes in the street price of heroin are correlated with the incidence of various crimes (Brown & Silverman, 1974). If the price increases, the incidence of crime goes up because addicts need more money. For example, in New York City, a 50 percent increase in the retail price of heroin is related to a 17 percent increase in robberies and an 8 percent increase in burglaries and petty larceny. A 10 percent increase in the heroin price is correspondingly related to increases in the incidence of various crimes: 4 percent more robberies, 2 percent increase in burglaries and larcenies under $50, and a 3 percent rise in auto theft.

Many heroin users can function in the community without detection or having to engage in criminal activities or becoming involved in an addict subculture. A crucial determinant of how the user will identify with the drug world is whether or not he will become a dealer; once he gets involved in dealing, the likelihood of drug use becoming more salient in his life increases sharply.

LAW ENFORCEMENT AND THE DRUG OFFENDER

From World War I to the 1960s, drug dependence was seen as primarily a task for law enforcement. It was believed that laws against possession and sales of controlled substances would deter users and sellers. In prison, no special program was provided for the drug dependent, who served his time and then usually returned to the community from which he had come.

In the 1960s, drug dependence was reconceptualized as a problem with both law enforecment and health dimensions. Although there has been substantial change in how drug dependence is treated there has been little change in its relationship to the criminal justice system, except that it continues to consume more and more resources of the system.

The Federal Food, Drug and Cosmetic Act of 1938, modified in 1962, 1965, and 1970, is the basic drug regulatory law. The 1914 Harrison Act has previously been amended frequently, usually to increase penalties for violation or to add to the list of controlled drugs. The Comprehensive Drug Abuse Prevention and Control Act of 1970 is the operative federal law regulating drugs that may cause dependence. Substances are placed in one of five categories on the basis of their potential for dependence and abuse. The most hazardous substances are in Schedule I and the least hazardous in Schedule IV, as follows:

I. Drugs with no established medical use and with high abuse potential such as heroin.
II. Drugs with high potential for abuse, used in medical practice, like morphine, codeine, amphetamines, cocaine, and short-acting barbiturates, such as pentobarbital, seconal, tuinal.
III. Narcotic drugs in combination with other substances, such as codeine with empirin; used in medical practice; abuse may lead to severe dependence.
IV. Long acting barbiturates; tranquilizers.
V. Formerly exempt narcotics used in cold medications, like turpenhydrate with codeine; may lead to limited dependence.

In order to prescribe any of the substances listed in Schedule II through V, a physician must have a special license issued by the Drug Enforcement Administration. The lower the drug's schedule number, the more severe are the penalties for illegal possession.

The United States, in 1967, ratified the 1961 Single Convention on Narcotic Drugs, which requires each signatory country to provide internal controls on specific substances, including marihuana. It has not yet ratified the 1971 Convention of Psychotropic Substances, which established multinational control of synthetic dangerous drugs whose primary effect is mood altering, such as hallucinogens, amphetamines, barbiturates, and tranquilizers. The United Nations felt that these newer dangerous drugs were sufficiently threatening to require regulation.

From a third to a half of arrests for drug offenses result from police investigation of other crimes. A drug user may be arrested for robbery, burglary, or larceny and, if found to have a controlled substance in his possession, will be charged with a drug violation. Other arrests result from informers, who may cooperate with police either to get drugs or to obtain a lesser charge if already involved with the police. The plainclothesmen on a drug squad also cruise high risk areas, usually urban ghettos, and sometimes pose as users, looking for evidence of illegal drug sales.

There has been continued debate about the effect of "tough" drug laws. An opportunity to test the impact of a really stringent antidrug law emerged in 1973, when New York State passed the country's harshest penalties for illegal possession of controlled substances. The law limited plea bargaining, required a life sentence for anyone selling more than an ouce of narcotics, had a predicate felony provision mandating a minimum sentence for a second felony offense, increased all sentences, and offered a $1,000 reward for turning in a drug pusher. Forty-eight new court parts were created to deal with the expected influx of new cases. (A judge and his associated retinue in a court part cost approximately $625,000 per year.) An evaluation of the law concluded that the law had no impact on the number of cases of drug abuse; arrests declined; drug-related crime increased; and drug sales and prevalence of heroin use increased (Winick, 1975). Fewer drug cases were processed by the courts, because defendants fought their cases harder and each case took longer.

In general, a drug user who is arrested once stands a good chance of being rearrested. In one large-scale study in seven communities, the average user in treatment had been arrested 5.5 times (U.S. Office of Economic Opportunity, 1971). In these communities, there was great variation in sentencing patterns, so that the average longest uninterrupted time served in prison in months ranged from 7.9 in Tacoma to 30.3 in Los Angeles (Winick, 1974c).

Comparative information on arrest rates of drug dependent persons is difficult to interpret, because whether or not arrests will take place is a function of many factors, which vary from community to community. Such factors include the number of police available for antidrug duties, quantity and kind of drugs being sold, sophistication of the sellers, community priorities, the number of young people, and general economic conditions.

The federal agents of the Justice Department's Drug Enforcement Administration concentrate on attempting to arrest high level importers and smugglers; state and local police try to apprehend other sellers. In recent years, there has been a trend toward "quality" arrests, directed at sellers rather than ordinary users.

TREATMENT

Since there are several kinds of relationships to drugs of dependence, and their users may be at different stages of their life cycle, various approaches to treatment have evolved. If there is one word which characterizes current approaches to treatment, it would be "multimodality," or the provision of a broad and comprehensive range of services for a recognizably diverse group of clients, who are at different stages of need and readiness for treatment. The multimodalities include emergency services, detoxification, residential treatment, drop-in centers, methadone maintenance, therapeutic communities, counseling, casework, and vocational training.

At any given time, some 240,000 people are in treatment for all types of drug dependence (Nightingale, 1977). Since the average length of time that a person remains in treatment is seven months, the treatment system can service almost 450,000 drug dependents in a year.

The most frequently found type of treatment for the drug dependent is drug-free out-patient therapy, which involves 100,000 persons in some kind of counseling. The second most widespread approach is represented by methadone maintenance, which is servicing approximately 90,000 heroin addicts.

Conventional approaches to psychotherapy have had to be modified in order to treat the drug dependent. This person may have problems in handling insight, could be dealing with frequent life crises and the need to engage in criminal activity in order to get money for drugs, and might face court appearances and medical problems. Recognition of drug dependence as a chronic relapsing condition required changes in the therapist's expectations. Today, we understand that there are many different types of drug dependence, requiring a variety of kinds of programs (Brill, 1977).

Treatment programs generally have very guarded expectations of what constitutes success. "Cure" is a relatively inappropriate term to describe the expected outcome of treatment of the drug dependent. Therapists now tend to work toward limited goals and recognize the relapsing nature of the syndrome, as well as the unlikelihood of achieving abstinence from what is a chronic relapsing condition. If a drug dependent person used to take a drug daily and now does so every other day, or has returned to work, such movement represents progress. The modern approach attempts to provide easy entry to treatment at a variety of points. It also offers treatment on the community level, where the person lives, keeping institutional stays as brief as possible.

A person needs more than insight into his or her problems in order to achieve success in the workaday world; many, if not most, of the persons enrolled in treatment programs have inadequate educational and work skills. The programs try to provide educational skills, at least sufficient for achievement of a high school equivalency level, and to lead into appropriate vocational training. Job development and placement are also important components of many large programs.

Employers are often asked to provide entry-level jobs for graduates of treatment programs, or patients in methadone maintenance, as a reflection of their community obligations, just as they may make special efforts to hire members of minority groups. Without such assistance, the patient's chances for success in the "re-entry" phase of treatment will be severely undercut. ("Re-entry" refers to the patient's efforts to establish himself in the conventional world of work and achievement.)

Community-based treatment programs proliferated in the 1960s, at the time that many paraprofessionals, students, and young professionals who had participated in the drug culture were helping to create such programs. One example of community-based treatment is provided by over two hundred "free clinics," set up to provide young people with a full range of medical and social services via a kind of "one-stop shopping." The first such center, the Haight-Ashbury Free Clinic, was opened in the late 1960s to provide emergency service for the large number of hippie youths in San Francisco who were experiencing drug-related problems and who were unable or unwilling to go to a conventional facility. Since then, a national network of such clinics has sprung up, and now provides a wide range of services, many of which are geared to the drug user. Because such non-Establishment clinics may be open at unusual hours, have a dedicated and young staff, and provide nonjudgmental services at no cost, they are especially attractive to young persons with drug-related problems.

The "Rational Authority" Approach

"Rational authority" is not a treatment method but has been used to strengthen various modalities. It involves the use of any available means to engage recalcitrant drug offenders in treatment. These means include coercion by the courts and structuring treatment with the threat of imprisonment (Brill & Lieberman, 1969).

The first use of rational authority in order to mandate some kind of treatment for the drug dependent consisted of intensive parole supervision in California and New York. During the 1950s each state established a group of parole officers with a very light case load (twenty to twenty-five) of drug offenders. Since each officer had only a small number of parolees to supervise, it was thought that intensive services could be provided. The treatment was backed by the threat of return to prison if the offender did not respond to the kind of case work in an authoritarian setting represented by parole. The early reports from intensive parole services were favorable (Diskind & Klonsky, 1964).

Beginning in 1961, California pioneered in the use of civil commitment for the drug dependent; the federal government followed suit with the Narcotic Addict Rehabilitation Act of 1966; and New York State acted next (1966). Other states soon started similar plans. Typically, a defendant charged with a drug offense would appear in court, where the judge would sentence him to a six-month period of residential treatment, to be followed by two and a half years of parole supervision. If the defendant did not revert to drug use, his record would be expunged but if he were rearrested for drug use, he would start the whole process again, starting with incarceration for treatment.

Under most civil commitment laws, a drug dependent person need not be arrested, but may be brought to court by a neighbor or parent. A hearing is held and if the judge concludes that the subject is drug dependent, the latter may be committed for treatment for a fixed period of time, to be followed by another period on parole. After successful completion of the regimen, the record is expunged.

The first evaluations of the California civil commitment program showed discouraging results (Kramer, 1968). But as with many other innovations in treatment of drug offenders, the negative results did not deter other jurisdictions from pursuing civil commitment plans. A number of states spent huge sums in order to build and staff centers for the treatment of the civilly committed. By the early 1970s, however, there was a general feeling of disillusionment with civil commitment. Not the least reason for the lack of success was that many drug offenders did not want to be under the jurisdiction of a court for at least three years and preferred to serve a shorter prison term. However, thirty-four states and the federal government still provide for civil commitment.

Building on the lessons learned by the experience with civil commitment the federal government in 1972 began funding Treatment Alternatives to Street Crime (TASC) programs, which operate in fifty-five cities, for persons who are drug dependent and have committed a criminal act.

TASC is an attempt to break the cycle of drug dependence-crime-arrest-prison-drug dependence. Treatment is often introduced as soon after arrest as possible because of the assumption that rehabilitation is most effective when the drug dependent person is most susceptible. If the treatment is successful, the charges will be dropped. If there is a trial, the user may then be sentenced into treatment, received a suspended sentence, or go on probation, with the stipulation that he submit to treatment. The treatment is sometimes also a condition of parole. In terms of recidivism rates, TASC has been relatively successful; by 1977, only 12 percent of the 29,000 offenders in the program had been rearrested on a new charge.

Some cities have argued that treatment programs which are extensions of the court are really agents of social control (Smith, 1975). As a result, treatment programs may alter their goals to satisfy their correctional sponsors, and therapists' relationships to clients may be adversely modified. Despite this argument, so long as drug dependent persons continue to get arrested and so long as they are reluctant to volunteer for treatment programs, the use of rational authority will probably increase.

Therapeutic Communities

Therapeutic communities for the treatment of drug dependent persons have achieved enormous publicity ever since Synanon began in 1959 in Santa Monica. Synanon, founded by exalcoholic Chuck Dederich, pioneered the combination of approaches often called "The Concept." This includes a nonprofessional exaddict staff which provides role models for residents, insistence on abstinence and severe penalties for backsliding, graded work activities, success experiences by upward mobility within the organization, an ideology of what life should be, regular encounter group therapy, and perception of the drug dependent person as an emotionally immature individual who must concentrate considerable personal growth into a relatively short time (Yablonsky, 1965). At a therapeutic community like New York City's Phoenix House, which is the largest in America, a residential period of around eighteen months is customary.

TCs often exercise a significant influence on the community because they tend to be very visible symbols of achievement, frequently visited by "squares." They produce graduates who have impressed legislators and other officials and were often more verbal than representatives of other treatment

modalities. Their rationale that a corrective social learning experience is necessary in order to replace the drug user's previous and defective or pathological
social learning experience is in line with many theories of modern psychology.

There are now approximately 425 therapeutic communities in the United
States with 28,000 patients. They receive 16 percent of the federal support
for treatment. Per residential patient, the cost is approximately $5,000 per
year. In 1974 there were over one thousand TCs in existence. Their number
has declined because of consolidations, difficulties of neighborhood-oriented
TCs in adapting to new administrative requirements which emerged as funding became more centralized, and the movement of some of their charismatic
leaders into the larger bureaucracy.

The encounter technique was a powerful tool in therapeutic communities
in the early and mid-1960s, when many residents had difficulties in identifying and expressing their problems. Today, as a result of the social activism
of the last decade, drug dependent residents are more likely to verbalize problems, and the encounter procedure could be less important.

Some therapeutic communities, like New York's Addict Rehabilitation
Center, have cut their residential requirement to six months. Other centers
are relaxing the severe penalties imposed for violation of the rules of the
"house." In some TCs, a resident may spend some months working in the
facility and then be assisted in getting a job in the community, while continuing to live in the facility.

The original expectations—that therapeutic communities represented the
best treatment for most drug dependents—may have been over-optimistic.
The kind of change these programs demand may be very difficult for many
persons, especially since it involves total immersion in a new situation twenty-
four hours a day. For those who are appropriately motivated, however, the
type of experience provided by a TC may be very effective (Winick, 1974b).
Even persons who do not complete the full program at a TC show sharp
reductions in criminal activity during and after leaving the program (De Leon,
Holland, & Rosenthal, 1972), suggesting that it represents a significant socialization experience. Therapeutic communities have shown great adaptability
in responding to changes in the types of problems they have to meet, such as
polydrug-dependence, mixed dependencies which include alcohol, the aggressiveness and youth of their clients, and the growing sophistication of the
street drug user.

Methadone Maintenance

Until the 1960s, abstinence was the only acceptable treatment goal for drug
dependent persons in America, although England had had some success with
opiate maintenance programs. This goal was modified when methadone maintenance became an important modality, as a result of pilot studies conducted
at Rockefeller University by Dole and Nyswander (1965). In methadone
maintenance, the patient usually comes to a clinic for a daily stabilization
dosage of methadone, an addicting synthetic opiate that presumably will not

provide a high, that will help the patient to function at home, at school, or in a job, and that will block the craving for heroin.

Methadone was believed to be a "good" opiate, as opposed to heroin, which was a "bad" opiate. A patient could get through the day with only one ingestion, whereas he might need heroin every few hours.

A high dose is considered to be 80 mg. per day or more and a low dose would be less than 80 mg. Dole and Nyswander originally recommended a daily maintenance dose of 80 to 120 mg., although doses as low as 50 mg. have been found to be as effective (Garbutt & Goldstein, 1972).

A methadone patient who appears to be functioning reasonably in the community is permitted take-home medication. Frequently, such a person comes into the clinic Monday and Wednesday, drinks one dose and is given another to take home and use the next day. On Fridays, he drinks one dose and gets two bottles for the weekend.

Methadone patients' urine is checked as one way of confirming their abstention from heroin. "Clean" urine indicates that the patient has abstained, while "dirty" urine reflects proscribed drug use. In response to this strategy, various hustles have been developed by patients in order to attempt to "beat" the test.

The original data on the effects of methadone maintenance were enthusiastically hailed because they seemed to promise a dramatic reduction in crime on the part of program participants (Gearing, 1971). The patients increased their noncriminal activities (job, school, homemaker) from 50 to 85 percent. There was also a lesser but substantial (from 50 percent down to 14 percent) decline in the proportion of methadone patients who were on welfare.

Most methadone maintenance programs dispense the medication but provide minimal counseling, vocational training, job placement, or educational services. The more such social rehabilitation services are available, the more successful the program is likely to be.

Even in those clinics with minimal supporting rehabilitation services, daily visits with staff members can provide the patient with some kind of corrective family experience. This surrogate family situation, plus the methadone, seems to help a number of the patients to turn their lives around. Just how many patients are so helped is a subject of controversy.

The Gearing (1971) findings on thousands of New York City methadone patients had shown great increases in their social and personal productivity, but more recent field and interview data call such optimism into question (Preble, 1977; Lukoff, 1974). There could be several reasons for the discrepancies between the earlier, positive findings and the more recent and less encouraging data. One reason is that the earlier data derive from treatment agencies, which obtained information by asking their patients, with no independent check from Social Security work records or police files. The agencies are less probing than street investigators or outside evaluators who do not accept patients' self-reports, but examine other records.

Recent follow-ups of methadone patients have uncovered many kinds of socially undesirable behavior. Some 69 percent of the 32,000 patients on methadone maintenance in New York City are receiving Medicaid, which is an indirect indicator of enrollment in welfare or Social Security benefit programs. One pattern of adaptation is for a person to enroll in a methadone program, then apply for welfare benefits and use some welfare money to buy cheap wine (40 proof costs less than $1 per pint), which is alternated with the methadone. Panhandling may supplement the person's income (Preble, 1977).

Another pattern is to add illegally acquired tranquilizers or barbiturates to the methadone and wine, with the patient selling about one third of his methadone to finance the purchase of the pills and wine. A third combination involves wine and pills during the week, with methadone and cocaine on weekends. This approach is relatively expensive because of the high price of cocaine, and is financed by sale of part of one's methadone and participation in stealing and robbery. All of these patterns of adaptation are, of course, contrary to the expectations of the sponsors of the program.

How could methadone maintenance programs have expanded so rapidly when so much ambiguity surrounds their effectiveness? A substantial proportion of American servicemen in Vietnam had become heroin users in the late 1960s, and the increase in street crime had become linked with the growth of heroin use in America. During the Vietnam heroin panic of the early 1970s, concern about the need to provide treatment for returning veterans and fear of street crime facilitated the spread of methadone programs. Coincidentally, at around the same time, Lukoff (1974) and others began raising serious questions about the validity of their high success rates. Methadone maintenance patients may seem to be engaging in fewer crimes since they are arrested less frequently. This is because the type of crime in which they participate after joining the program is less likely to come to police attention, such as numbers running, con games, fencing, shoplifting, and stealing automobile parts.

Ideological questions also began to be raised about some possible unanticipated consequences of methadone maintenance. Minority group spokespersons expressed discomfort about the prospect of large numbers of their constituents remaining on methadone for years or indefinitely, depending for their drug on funds controlled by politicians. Other critics were uneasy about the large number of methadone patients who took alcohol and other substances. It was also argued that many methadone patients might have "matured out" of heroin use (Winick, 1962a), if left to their own devices. Instead of leaving drug use, they may be "hooked" for many years, getting drugs free and with implied community approval.

It is plausible that methadone patients could be ready to mature out because such persons tend to be older and to have experienced more previous treatment than those seeking assistance in therapeutic communities (Cohen, 1975). The methadone patients also tend to have used addicting drugs for a longer period of time.

In many communities, illegally obtained methadone is relatively easily available on the street. Some is stolen en route to legitimate programs, some is sold by patients from weekend take-home doses, some may be diverted by people on the staff of a methadone clinic. The availability of illegal methadone has had a considerable number of unanticipated consequences that have serious reverberations on society's ability to control drug use.

One consequence of methadone maintenance is that heroin use is seen as a less frightening activity than it used to be, because even if heroin is not available for a while, the user is still able to cope with the situation by taking illegally acquired methadone. Another outcome is the considerable proportion —as much as a third in some communities—of young opiate dependents who have started on drug careers via street methadone.

Methadone maintenance programs may be run for profit by a private individual. They may be sponsored by a community or health service group. Some are operated by a government agency, like a municipality health department. Others are addressed to fairly specific kinds of clients, such as Chicanos or adolescents. Universities, hospitals, and mental hygiene facilities may have methadone programs as part of their service and training activities. Some programs are committed to research and demonstration goals, others to returning a profit to their sponsors, still others to providing service to a large number of clients.

The government ultimately pays for most methadone programs, whether public or private. It assumes the cost of the government-run programs and, through Medicaid, pays the cost, usually around $1,200 per year, of each patient in a private program. Many patients prefer to enroll in a private program because of reluctance to be involved with an official agency and because they feel that it will be supervised less rigorously than a government clinic.

An ultimate goal of many programs is not to maintain the patient on methadone for life but to enable him to stop using it and ultimately to lead a drug-free existence. But this goal has proved very difficult to achieve. Patients attempting to detoxify from methadone seem to experience greatest difficulty at a dosage of around 20 mg.

A small number of patients are being maintained on L-acetyl methadol (LAAM), a long-acting methadone-like drug which can be administered every third day, thus obviating the need for take-home medication and frequent visits to the clinic which might interfere with other activities.

Intensive efforts to develop narcotic antagonists—nonaddicting substances that cause the user to have a rejecting, nauseous, or other unpleasant reaction to opiates—have not succeeded in producing an effective drug that lacks side effects. Cyclazocine, the most widely used antagonist, has side effects for many users. Naloxone is another antagonist with fewer side effects but short duration of action. Naltrexone is also being tested. However, no antagonist has been adopted widely.

For some years, there has been considerable agitation for introduction of heroin maintenance programs. A major argument for such programs is that while most heroin users do not enroll in methadone maintenance programs, they presumably would enroll in heroin maintenance. In England, where heroin maintenance clinics were established during the 1960s, it was found that some addicts could be maintained and function effectively. But the results were inconclusive and most of the clinics have switched to methadone. Major arguments against such experimental clinics are: most patients would become soporific and unable to function; some heroin would be diverted and sold illegally; and patients might have to visit a clinic three or four times daily for a fix and thus be unable to function on a job. It is also argued that to treat heroin addiction by heroin maintenance is to admit the community's total inability to deal with the problem.

SOCIAL COSTS OF DRUG DEPENDENCE

An analysis of the social costs of the various kinds of drug dependence would include expenses for law enforcement, courts, prison, treatment, crime, and property losses, and the cost of illnesses, shortened life span, and taxes not paid because of nonwork and loss of life.

Economists have not computed the total expense resulting from all drug dependence but they have given some attention to outlays resulting from heroin. Heroin dependence, although it involves a relatively small number of people compared to other health disorders (heart disease, 14 million; alcoholism, 9 million; hearing disorders, 6 million; mental retardation, 4 million; stroke, 2 million; diabetes, 1.5 million), accounts for a social expenditure far out of proportion to its actual prevalence.

The heroin dependent usually begins committing thefts and other criminal activities in his immediate neighborhood. He then typically moves into other areas where he is less well known, which offer new opportunities for crime. One clue to the amount of crime related to heroin use may be inferred from the fact that 62 percent of all New York State prison inmates have committed some crimes that are related to illegal drug activities.

Heroin users tend to commit crimes that involve financial gain. One analysis identified a variety of users' criminal activities: those of the burglar (23 percent), "flat footed hustler," who will commit any available crime (12 percent), shoplifter (12 percent), robber (9 percent) (Preble & Casey, 1969). Retail stores in slum neighborhoods have an exceptionally high rate of shoplifting by heroin dependent persons.

Preble and Casey (1969) have attempted to estimate the cost to the community of heroin dependence. Dealing with 1966–1967 data, they conclude that the 80,000 heroin users at that time accounted for $1.1 billion in crime, $15 million for law enforcement, $30 million for prison expenses, $3 million in parole and probation, $96 million for police, $465 million in preventive services, and $59 million in insurance. Where a range of expense is possible, they take the most conservative figure, concluding that heroin dependence costs the country a total of $1,572,000,000 per year. If we assume that there are now approximately 700,000 heroin-dependent persons, it is reasonable to multiply the $1,572,000,000 figure by 8.75, for a total of $13,775,000,00 Even if this figure were to be reduced by 50 percent, it would still represen substantial outlay. An official federal White Paper on Drug Abuse estima the cost of drug abuse to the nation to be from $10 to $17 billion annu (Domestic Council, 1976).

There is a Marxist view of the relationship between heroin use and crime which challenges conventional thinking on the subject (Karmen, 1974). In this view, periodic drug seizures by police provide pretexts for supply crises that lead to price increases, so that crime syndicates indirectly manipulate state power in order to further their interests. A large number of pushers and other distributors participate in the criminal aspect of the system, while narcotic police and court officials, social workers, psychiatrists, and other technicians work in the criminal justice and treatment systems. Poor people are able to buy merchandise stolen by heroin users and sold at very low prices, while the victims of the theft buy replacement products because of theft-enforced obsolescence. Young people who might have engaged in revolutionary activities have their energies blunted by heroin, which also makes tolerable the unpleasant work they do.

There is general agreement that the highest social costs are associated with the compulsive use of drugs which possess the greatest dependence liability. In addition to heroin, other substances in this category are barbiturates, especially when mixed with other drugs, and amphetamines, particularly when administered intravenously.

POLICY DEVELOPMENT

For many years society stereotyped its drug problem by assuming that there was one "bad" drug—heroin. Heroin addicts were believed to have relatively homogeneous personalities and backgrounds. Drug use was thought to be dysfunctional. Arrest, trial, and conviction leading to a prison term were regarded as deterrents to future use and as procedures which represented the best way of achieving abstinence, which was a central goal of public policy. Education and prevention activities were discouraged because it was felt that they might make drugs attractive to many persons who would otherwise be unaware of their gratifications.

In the 1930s, the Public Health Service established hospitals in Lexington, Kentucky, and Fort Worth, Texas, to provide treatment for narcotic addicts. During this period, outpatient treatment, which had been opposed by the American Medical Association in an influential 1924 policy statement, was discouraged and there was a stress on keeping narcotic drugs out of the country, except for the relatively small amount needed for legitimate medical use. These policies continued into the 1950s, when drug problems assumed more salience because more people were involved in them. Crime was also rising and was believed to be significantly related to illegal drug use.

The 1960s witnessed growing use of many drugs not previously available and the involvement of middle and upper class youths in the drug scene, providing a crucial occasion for generational conflict of values. A number of new programs and substantial financial support were introduced into treatment and prevention programs. President Richard Nixon, concerned about the number of American soldiers who were introduced to and used heroin while serving in Vietnam, declared an all-out "war on drugs" and millions of dollars were made available, mostly for treatment and law enforcement. Mr. Nixon also appointed the National Commission on Marihuana and Drug Abuse to advise on policy and in 1971 set up a White House Special Action Office for Drug Abuse to underscore the problem's priority. During this period of the early 1970s, many national polls reported that drug abuse, as it was increasingly called, was believed by Americans to be the nation's most important problem.

In 1972, Congress passed the Drug Abuse Office and Treatment Act, which established the National Institute of Drug Abuse to coordinate drug prevention and treatment programs. Creation of the Institute helped legitimate the problem of drug dependence. It established a permanent professional staff to monitor developments and encourage research, train personnel, fund service programs, and maintain a clearinghouse for information. Creation of the Institute also positioned drug dependence as a sociomedical problem, although it had previously been viewed as a concern of the criminal justice system. For the 1977–1978 fiscal year, the Institute's budget for research, training, and community and other programs came to $262 million.

Government strategy in dealing with drugs of dependence currently involves three parallel activities: limiting supply, discouraging use by prevention, and treating users. The limitation of supply is the mission of the Drug Enforcement Agency, a division of the Department of Justice. Prevention programs fall to the Office of Education and treatment is the responsibility of the National Institute of Drug Abuse. Drug abuse is no longer seen as our premier problem but as one of many serious problems which will not yield to an easy solution.

THE FUTURE

There will probably be a considerable number of Americans using controlled substances illegally, at least for the immediate future. We are viewing the problem less simplistically than we did in the 1960s. However, it is difficult for legislatures to see the desirability of prevention activities, which probably represent our only opportunity to cut down the size of the drug problem in any appreciable way. The policy directions of the last several years appear likely to be those that will be followed, unless laboratory research produces a major breakthrough.

We are reluctantly recognizing that drug dependence cannot be eliminated from society. Supply reduction, which now costs the federal government over $350 million annually, can never really be effective in a country with such sprawling borders. Demand reduction through prevention is politically unattractive; moreover we do not really know how to achieve it effectively. Treatment is expensive and poses ideological problems.

Policy makers are learning that not all drug use is equally destructive, so they are trying to give greatest weight to drugs with the highest social costs, particularly those taken intravenously. With this awareness is likely to come a realization that success in minimizing drug dependence will be less likely to reflect specific drug programs than to reflect larger social changes, such as expanding education, training, job opportunities, and other improvements in the quality of life. If alternatives to drugs were genuinely attractive, drug use would decline.

REFERENCES

Becker, H. S. Becoming a marijuana user. *American Journal of Sociology*, 1953, *59*, 235–242.

Bejerot, N. *Addiction—an artificially induced drive.* Springfield, Ill.: Charles C Thomas, 1972.

Brill, L. The treatment of drug abuse. *American Journal of Psychiatry*, 1977, *134*, 157–160.

Brill, L., & Lieberman, L. *Authority and addiction.* Boston: Little, Brown, 1969.

Brotman, R., & Freedman, A. M. *A community mental health approach to addiction.* Washington: Government Printing Office, 1969.

Brown, G. F., & Silverman, L. P. Retail price of heroin. *Journal of American Statistical Association*, 1974, *69*, 595–606.

Casey, J. J., & Preble, E. Narcotic addiction and crime: social costs and forced transfers. In C. Winick (Ed.), *Sociological aspects of drug dependence.* Cleveland: CRC Press, 1974, 283–308.

Chambers, C. D. Speculations on a behavioral progression typology of pleasure-seeking drug use. In C. Winick (Ed.), *Sociological aspects of drug dependence.* Cleveland: CRC Press, 1974, 127–132.

Chein, I. *The road to H.* New York: Basic Books, 1965.

Cohen, R. Treatment seeking behavior. In E. Senay and V. Shorty (Eds.), *Developments in the field of drug abuse.* Cambridge, Mass.: Schenkman, 1975, 347–355.

Commission on Marihuana and Drug Abuse. *Marihuana: A signal of misunderstanding.* Washington: Government Printing Office, 1972.

Commission on Marihuana and Drug Abuse. *Drug use in America: Problem in perspective.* Washington: Government Printing Office, 1973.

Craig, S. R., & Brown, B. S. Comparison of youthful heroin users and nonusers from one urban community. *International Journal of Addictions*, 1975, *10*, 53–64.

Davis, F., & Munoz, L. Heads and freaks. *Journal of Health and Social Behavior*, 1968, *9*, 156–164.

De Alarcon, R. The spread of heroin in a community. *U.N. Bulletin of Narcotics*, 1969, *21*, 17–22.

De Leon, G., Holland, S., & Rosenthal, M. S. Phoenix House: criminal activity of dropouts. *Journal of the American Medical Association*, 1972, *222*, 686–689.

Diskind, M. H., & Klonsky, G. *Recent developments in the treatment of paroled offenders addicted to narcotic drugs.* Albany: New York State Division of Parole, 1964.

Dole, V., & Nyswander, M. A medical treatment for diacetylmorphine (heroin) addiction. *Journal of the American Medical Association*, 1965, *193*, 646–650.

Domestic Council Task Force. *White paper on drug abuse.* Washington: Government Printing Office, 1976.

Eddy, N. B., et al. Drug dependence: Its significance and characteristics. *Bulletin of the World Health Organization*, 1965, *32*, 721–733.

Epstein, E. J. *Agency for fear.* New York: Putnam, 1977.

Feldman, H. W. Ideological supports to becoming and remaining a heroin addict. *Journal of Health and Social Behavior*, 1968, *9*, 131–139.

Finestone, H. Cats, kicks, and color. *Social Problems*, 1957, *5*, 3–13.

Garbutt, G. D., & Goldstein, A. Blind comparison of three maintenance dosages in 180 patients. Proceedings of the Fourth National Conference on Methadone Treatment, 1972, 487–488.

Gay, G. R., Newmeyer, J. A., & Winkler, J. J. The Haight-Ashbury free medical clinic. In D. E. Smith & G. R. Gay (Eds.), *It's so good, don't even try it once*. Englewood Cliffs: Prentice-Hall, 1972.

Gearing, F. R. *MMTP: Progress report through March 31, 1971—a five-year overview*. New York: Columbia University School of Public Health and Administrative Medicine, 1971.

Gearing, F. R. Myth versus fact in long-term methadone maintenance treatment. Proceedings of the Fifth National Conference on Methadone Treatment, 1973, 452–455.

Helmer, J. *Drugs and minority oppression*. New York: Seabury, 1975.

Himmelsbach, C. H., & Small, L. F. *Rossium treatment of drug addiction* (supplement no. 125 to the Public Health Reports). Washington: Government Printing Office, 1937.

Hughes, P. H., & Crawford, G. A. Epidemiology of heroin addiction in the 1970s. In E. Josephson & E. E. Carroll (Eds.), *Drug use; epidemiological and sociological approaches*. New York: Wiley/Halsted, 1974, 89–104.

Hunt, L. G. *Heroin epidemics: A quantitative study of current empirical data*. Washington: Drug Abuse Council, 1973.

Jessor, R., Jessor, S. L., & Finney, J. A social psychology of marihuana use. *Journal of Personality and Social Psychology*, 1973, *26*, 1–15.

Kaplan, J. H. Marihuana: the new prohibition. New York: Pocket Books, 1971.

Karmen, A. The drug abuse-crime syndrome: a radical critique. In C. Winick (Ed.), *Sociological aspects of drug dependence*. Cleveland: CRC Press, 1974, 309–319.

Kramer, J., et al. Civil commitment for addicts: The California program. *American Journal of Psychiatry*, 1968, *125*, 816–818.

Lennard, H. L., et al. *Mystification and drug misuse*. San Francisco: Jossey-Bass, 1971.

Lindesmith, A. R. *Opiate addiction*. Bloomington, Ill.: Principia Press, 1947.

Lovett, J. W. A metabolic basis for drug dependence. *Canadian Psychiatric Association Journal*, 1974, *19*, 487–494.

Lukoff, I. F. Issues in the evaluation of heroin treatment. In E. Josephson & E. E. Carroll (Eds.), *Drug use: Epidemiological and sociological approaches*. New York: Wiley/Halsted, 1974, 129–158.

McAuliffe, W. E., & Gordon, R. A. A test of Lindesmith's theory of addiction. *American Journal of Sociology*, 1974, *79*, 795–840.

Nash, G. Sociology of Phoenix House: a therapeutic community for the resocialization of narcotic addicts: In C. Winick (Ed.), *Sociological aspects of drug dependence*. Cleveland: CRC Press, 1974, 199–216.

Nightingale, S. L. Treatment for drug abusers in the United States. *Addictive Diseases*, 1977, *3*, 11–20.

Preble, E. Methadone, wine, and welfare. In R. S. Weppner (Ed.), *Street ethnography*. Beverly Hills: Sage, 1977, 229–248.

Preble, E., & Casey, J. J. Taking care of business—the heroin user's life on the street. *International Journal of Addictions*, 1969, *4*, 1–24.

Robinson v. California, 370. U.S. 660, 1962.

Rotter, J. B., Chance, J. E., & Phares, E. J. *Applications of a social learning theory of personality*. New York: Holt, Rinehart and Winston, 1972.

Schur, E. M. *Crimes without victims*. Englewood Cliffs: Prentice-Hall, 1965.

Seevers, M. H. Characteristics of dependence and abuse of psychoactive drugs. In S. J. Mule & H. Brill (Eds.), *Chemical and biological aspects of drug dependence*. Cleveland: CRC Press, 1972, 13–21.

Smith, R. C. Addiction, coercion, and treatment: reflections on the debate. In E. Senay & V. Shorty (Eds.), *Developments in the field of drug abuse*. Cambridge, Mass.: Schenkman, 1975, 853–862.

Tozman, S., & Kramer, S. The intensity of the addiction drive or what price pleasure. *British Journal of Addictions*, 1973, *68*, 303–307.

U.S. Office of Economic Opportunity. *Uniform evaluation of programs to combat narcotic addition*. Washington: Government Printing Office, 1971.

Waldorf, D. *Careers in dope*. Englewood Cliffs: Prentice-Hall, 1973, 50.

Wikler, A. *Opiate addiction*. Springfield, Ill.: Charles C Thomas, 1963.

Winick, C. Use of drugs by jazz musicians. *Social Problems*, 1960, *7*, 240–253.

Winick, C. Physician narcotic addicts. *Social Problems*, 1961a, *9*, 174–186.

Winick, C. How high the moon: Jazz and drugs. *Antioch Review*, 1961b, *21*, 53–68.

Winick, C. Maturing out of narcotic addiction. *U.N. Bulletin of Narcotics*, 1962a, *14*, 1–7.

Winick, C. The taste of music: Alcohol, drugs, and jazz. *Jazz Monthly*, 1962b, *8*, 8–12.

Winick, C. Atonic, the psychology of the unemployed and marginal worker. In G. Fisk (Ed.), *Frontiers of management psychology*. New York: Harper & Row, 1964a, 269–286.

Winick, C. The life cycle of the narcotic addict and of addiction. *U.N. Bulletin of Narcotics*, 1964b, *16*, 22–32.

Winick, C. Marihuana use by young people. In E. Harms (Ed.), *Drug addiction in youth*. New York: Pergamon, 1965, 19–35.

Winick, C. *The new people*. New York: Bobbs-Merrill, 1968.

Winick, C. *The amphetamine abuse problem*. New York: American Social Health Association, 1972.

Winick, C. Some reasons for the increase in drug dependence among middle-class youths. In H. Silverstein (Ed.), *Sociology of youth*. New York: Macmillan, 1973, 433–441.

Winick, C. Drug dependence among nurses. In C. Winick (Ed.), *Sociological aspects of drug dependence*. Cleveland: CRC Press; 1974a, 155–168.

Winick, C. Mass communications and drug dependence. In C. Winick (Ed.), *Sociological aspects of drug dependence*. Cleveland: CRC Press, 1974b, 77–102.

Winick, C. Some aspects of careers of chronic heroin users. In E. Josephson & E. E. Carroll (Eds.), *Drug use: Epidemiological and sociological approaches*. New York: Wiley/Halsted, 1974c, 105–128.

Winick, C. A sociological theory of the genesis of drug dependence. In C. Winick (Ed.) *Sociological aspects of drug dependence*. Cleveland: C-R-C-Press 1974d, 3–14.

Winick, C. Some aspects of the "tough" New York State drug law. *Journal of Drug Issues*, 1975, *5*, 400–411.

Winick, C. *An evaluation of 24 therapeutic communities*. New York: Addiction Services Agency, 1976.

Winick, C., & Goldstein, J. *The glue sniffing problem*. New York: American Social Health Association, 1970.

Yablonsky, L. *The tunnel back: Synanon*. New York: Macmillan, 1965.

chapter 17

The Sex
Offender

Albert Ellis

An enormous amount of water has passed over the dam since the publication of a chapter on "The Sex Offender and His Treatment" in the first edition of this book (Ellis, 1961). Although quite a bit was known about sex offenses twenty years ago, and a few monographs and weighty tomes on the subject had already been published, there has been a great surge of interest in this area during the last two decades, and many of the "findings" reported in our earlier review had better be revised. The present chapter will attempt to update our knowledge about sex offenders and to lay out some important trends for the future in regard to the study and the treatment of such offenders.

DEFINITION OF SEX OFFENSES

Gebhard, Gagnon, Pomeroy, and Christenson (1965) conducted a massive study of sex offenders, in the course of which they analyzed the responses of over 1,500 men interviewed by Alfred C. Kinsey's Institute for Sex Research. Gebhard and his colleagues point out that all legal, cultural, and psychiatric definitions of sex offenses leave much to be desired. They propose their own definition, which shares salient features with my earlier formal definition (Ellis, 1961), and is also very comprehensive. According to this definition, "a sex offense is an overt act committed by a person for his own immediate sexual gratification which (1) is contrary to the prevailing sexual mores of the society in which he lives, and/or is legally punishable, and (2) results in his being legally convicted" (Gebhard, Gagnon, Pomeroy & Christenson, 1965, p. 8). Although this definition has its limitations, I suspect it is as good as any that has yet been devised, and we shall accept it for the purposes of the present chapter. I shall also assume—since research continually bears out this point—that with the exception of prostitutes, who do not even fall into the technical definition of sex offender (since they perform illicit sex acts mainly for money and not for their own immediate sexual gratification), the vast majority of offenders in modern society are males; and therefore almost all the main points made in the following pages will apply to male rather than female sex offenders.

CLASSIFICATION OF SEX OFFENSES

As I have pointed out previously (Ellis, 1961, 1967), it is not always easy to classify sex offenses accurately, since they not only differ from one legal jurisdiction to another but are frequently described in the statutes in almost undefinable terms, such as "carnal abuse," "open lewdness," and "unnatural practices." If we stop to unravel some of the semantic confusion created by the use of such vague terms, we find the following acts commonly prohibited and penalized:

1. Forcible sexual assault
2. Forcible rape
3. Statutory rape
4. Incest
5. Noncoital sex relations with a minor
6. Exhibitory sex acts
7. Obscenity
8. Homosexuality
9. Transvestism
10. Voyeurism or peeping
11. Sex murder
12. Sodomy
13. Adultery
14. Fornication
15. Prostitution
16. Pimping or pandering
17. Brothel-keeping

During the last two decades there has been a tendency in American courts and in the media to take forcible sexual assault and rape very seriously and to heavily penalize an adult's taking sexual advantage of a minor; but most of the other offenses in our list tend to have become more legally and publically acceptable; they lead to fewer prosecutions and to considerably lesser penalties. In large cities like New York and San Francisco, for example, even though laws against homosexual behavior between consenting adults still exist on the statute books, there are very few arrests for such behaviors unless they are accompanied by other illegal acts. And several states, following the pioneering lead of the State of Illinois, have removed acts such as homosexuality between consenting adults from the sex offender list. Many old laws against fornication, habituation, or cohabitation between unmarried males and females still are on some statute books, but these laws are widely ignored and rarely used as a basis for criminal prosecution.

Gebhard and his associates suggest a rough dichotomy between (a) sex offenses that represent common behavior and are only mildly taboo; and (b) offenses that represent uncommon behavior and are usually strongly taboo. In the former category they place sexual relationships between consenting individuals sixteen years old or older, and occasional peeping. In the latter category they place sexual relationships with minors and children, incest, forced relationships, exhibitionism, and frequent peeping.

MacNamara and Sagarin (1977) propose a more elaborate typology for sex offenses:

1. Conduct beyond the level of tolerance and requiring legal prohibition, both for the protection of potential victims and for the purpose of expressing through codified law the moral outrage of the members of society.
2. Conduct that, by agreement of large numbers of people, is best seen as psychopathological but that nevertheless requires legal prohibition in order to protect members of society from being victimized.
3. Conduct that dominant forces in the society, but by no means in numbers approaching a value consensus, believe should be discouraged, but by other means than criminal sanction.
4. Conduct that is best seen as a proper area for private decision by the individuals personally involved.

The first three of these categories would merit legal sanctions, though of a decreasing nature; and the last category would include sex behavior that could be mistaken or foolish for the individual participating in it, but would not be subject to social sanction.

PSYCHOLOGICAL CLASSIFICATION OF SEX OFFENDERS

It has been a common practice to separate sex offenders into relatively "normal" or "healthy" individuals who happen to commit a sex crime and "deviant" or "disturbed" individuals who have a basic psychological problem and who commit and are convicted of a sex offense largely because of this underlying problem (Group for the Advancement of Psychiatry, 1950; Ellis, 1961, 1967; Ellis, 1976a). It has also been found useful to distinguish offenders who have a general criminal record, and who have participated in a number of nonsexual as well as sexual offenses, from those who only get into difficulties for sex acts and otherwise have a record of good citizenship and "normal" behavior (Abrahamsen, 1950; East, 1955; Ellis & Brancale, 1956; Glueck, 1956; Guttmacher, 1951; Karpman, 1954; Kopp, 1962; Pacht, Halleck, & Ehrmann, 1962; Pollens, 1938; Radzinowicz 1957; Tappan, 1950).

Both the above distinctions probably have their value, but they also have their limitations. In spite of the caveats of "antipsychiatrists" such as Thomas Szasz (1961, 1977) and Ronald Laing (1967), clinicians observe conditions we can legitimately call "mental illness" or severe psychological disturbance; and it is most probable, from the present state of research in psychology and psychiatry, that mental illness has profound biological and sociological roots (Ellis, 1962, 1976b, 1977a, 1978a). Moreover, in the course of dealing with sex offenders legally, and especially in trying to treat them so that they will not repeat their illegal acts, it is very valuable for the processing agencies (not to mention the legislative bodies that establish laws relating to sex offenses) to know whether certain offenders seem to have (1) a general emotional problem, (2) a specific sex problem that may be connected with a general emotional difficulty, or (3) no real psychological disturbance but only episodic sex difficulties that erupt under unusual conditions, such as when the offender is under the temporary influence of drugs or alcohol, or when his regular sex partner is somehow not available. It is also important to know whether a given offender, such as an individual convicted of rape, is a generally hostile person who tends to commit a good number of crimes against society, or whether he is a sexually impulsive or compulsive person who tends to be much more of an unethical seducer than a forcible assaulter (Gebhard, Gagnon, Pomeroy, & Christenson, 1965; MacNamara & Sagarin, 1977).

At the same time that we recognize the important distinction between an emotionally disturbed and a relatively "healthy" sex offender, it is of dubious value to use terms like sex *deviant* or *pervert* for individuals who consistently commit banned acts and who sometimes get into trouble with the law for doing so. I have noted elsewhere that

> although the use of the term *sex deviation* may have once served some purpose, I doubt whether it does today. It means different things to different people— including to different authorities. It tends to cover, quite vaguely, a multiplicity of sex behaviors—by no means all of which we can agree produce bad results. It applies, often, to enjoyable and harmless idiosyncracies, rather than to truly self-harming or people-harming conduct. Even when it seems clearly descriptive of behavior that is harmful—as when an individual obsessively-compulsively engages in voyeurism and thereby sabotages a large segment of his life—it often constitutes much more of a vice than a crime—like addiction to alcohol or to cigarettes (Ellis, 1976a, p. 285).

In other words, although it may well be useful for us to distinguish between emotionally disturbed and nondisturbed sex offenders, labeling the former in a pejorative manner as *deviates, perverts,* or *abnormals* does little good and much potential harm. Such terms strongly imply that the labeled individual is an intrinsically rotten person; that his state is rather hopeless, that he is practically doomed to commit highly disturbed and/or criminal acts in the future; and that the only kind of effective "treatment" for him would be perennial incarceration. If, moreover, sexually disturbed individuals who commit offenses are seen as *deviants* or *perverts,* a biased attitude tends to spread over the entire realm of sexual disturbance, and many acts that otherwise would be considered as the individual's personal problem tend to be made the subject of legal restrictions and to be defined as public offenses.

If a man has an extreme fear of being turned down in a job interview and consequently stays home all the time and forces his family or the welfare department to support him, we may view him as emotionally ill and try to help him with his problem. But if this same man also has an extreme fear of being rejected by women and consequently becomes a transvestite, tries to convince other men that he is really a woman, and publically flirts with such men, we frequently invoke laws against his cross-dressing activities and we may put him in jail if he is caught in female attire. In both instances—the nonsexual and the sexual—the individual has what might be called a serious emotional problem or a vice; but if we label him a *sex deviant* he may be in line for legal prosecution, while if we only label him *an emotionally disturbed person* we may have a much better chance of helping him to tackle his problem and cure himself.

THE BASIC CAUSES OF SEX OFFENSES

No one has yet come up with a viable hypothesis about *the* cause of sex offenses, and it is quite probable that no one ever will. A careful reading of much of the clinical and research material on sex offenders will show that there are many different types of sex offenders and that the very same person may commit a sex crime on one occasion for one fairly clearcut reason and on another occasion for quite a different reason. On one occasion an offender may be refused sex favors by several women, may feel exceptionally bitter and hostile about this, and may deliberately go out and rape a strange woman on the street. At another time, this same offender may set out to rob an apartment, may accidentally find an attractive woman in bed, and may rape her because she seems easily available. On still another occasion, the same man may meet a woman at a bar, go off to her apartment in order to talk with her, and get so aroused by the conversation and the alcohol he ingested that he may wrongly think that his hostess wants to have sex with him when she keeps saying that she does not, and may end up raping her. Usually, we would say that an individual like this is overimpulsive and has low frustration tolerance, and that therefore he is at least moderately disturbed emotionally (Chapter 13). But the man's disturbance would be the main reason for his assaultiveness in only the first of the three instances we have mentioned, and would be only incidentally involved in the last two.

There are many different causes of sex offenses, including biological, cultural, individual, and accidental causes. On the biological side, some individuals are more highly sexed than others; or they may have innately stronger rebellious or hostile tendencies; or they are brain injured or senile; or they are mentally defective and not clearly able to see the difference between a suitable sexual overture (e.g., kissing a woman when one has been out on a satisfactory date with her) and an unsuitable overture (e.g., kissing a strange woman one encounters on the street). On the cultural side, a good many males are raised in what Wolfgang and Ferracuti (1967) call "the subculture of violence," and are encouraged by their peer group to act in a super-"masculine" way that may invite a higher percentage of violent sex crimes, such as rape and sexual assault, than the same persons might commit if they were reared in another kind of subculture (Ellis & Gullo, 1971; Toch, 1969).

In regard to individual values and preferences, people for a variety of reasons acquire goals, purposes, and moral views that can encourage them (as in the case of overcontrolled devout religionists) to engage in acts that their society generally proscribes; while other individuals (some of them equally devout) would be exceptionally nonprone to engage in almost any kind of publicly offensive sexuality. In terms of accidental factors, we have the consistent observation that people who normally would not resort to almost any kind of public sex or antisocial behavior will frequently do so only when they are under the influence of alcohol or drugs (Ellis & Brancale, 1956; Gebhard, Gagnon, Pomeroy, & Christenson, 1965).

Granted, that many factors may contribute to different people committing sex offenses, or even to the same person committing them at different times, the question still arises, are there some statistically prevalent causes that particularly motivate a person to perform a commitable offense and to then get caught and convicted for committing it? The answer is: Yes, there probably are.

Important in this connection is the observation by Ellis and Brancale (1956) derived from one of the pioneer studies of sex offenders, that there are at least three kinds of sex "offenses" and that individuals who perpetrate them may be of quite different psychological makeup. The first kind of "offense" is one like voyeurism or peeping that is kept within legal limits, even though the peeper has a pronounced desire to engage in this kind of activity and engages in it on several occasions. A peeper of this sort may draw the blinds in his own home and peep at people in nearby houses who happened to leave their shades partially up when they are in their bedrooms or bathrooms; or he may frequent topless bars or other public places where he can legally peep at unclothed or semiclothed women; or he may amass a large collection of pornographic photos. In such pursuits, this kind of peeper would take minimal or no legal risk.

The second kind of sex offense is one like strictly illegal voyeurism, in the course of which the voyeur makes pretty sure that he will not be caught. Thus, a voyeur may haunt lovers' lanes where people make love to each other in secluded areas or in parked cars, or where homosexuals make love to each other in open areas. He may do such things on innumerable occasions and virtually never get caught, since the people on whom he is spying are themselves engaged in public sex acts that they would not want brought to the attention of the authorities. Therefore, chances are that even if the peeper's victims catch him in the act, they will not do anything more than chase him away.

The third kind of sex offense is one like peeping done in a disorganized, compulsive, and uncautious manner, so that it frequently leads to the apprehension and conviction of the peeper. A voyeur may thus prowl around apartment houses late at night, and look in the window of individuals or of couples who are unclothed. Taking greater risks, he may even enter the apartments of sleeping women and look at them while they are asleep. Such an individual is not only committing a clearcut sex offense, but is doing so in a manner that almost ensures his sooner or later getting caught and convicted.

As we might well expect, if we take a sample of sex offenders who are apprehended and convicted for their behavior it tends to have a large percentage of individuals who perpetrate the third kind of sex offense we have mentioned. Such men not only are doing things that are technically against the law—as perhaps 95 percent of American males do at one time or other during their lives according to Kinsey, Pomeroy, and Martin (1948)—but they do these things in a rather peculiar, overly dangerous self-defeating manner that leads to their arrest and conviction. That is why almost all studies of *convicted* sex offenders tend to show that they include a fairly high percentage of seriously disturbed individuals ranging from about 15 to 50 percent of the samples studied, depending on the kinds of diagnostic criteria used by the investigators (Abrahamsen, 1950; Ellis & Brancale, 1956; Karpman, 1954; Pacht, Halleck, and Ehrmann, 1962).

If we look only at those sex offenders who appear to have a high degree of emotional disturbance, and ask why and how they became disturbed, we come up with two basic theories, which happen to be almost diametrically opposed. The orthodox psychoanalytic theory largely upholds the view, originally propounded by Freud, that people become disturbed, particularly during early years of family training, largely because of their psychosexual drives and the distortions of these drives that are induced by their parents and their culture (Freud, 1965; Karpman, 1954; Stekel, 1930). This theory holds that general emotional disturbances are mainly the result of early sexual disturbances, and that once the individual's libidinal drives are frustrated and distorted by environmental influences, he or she has little choice but to be emotionally disturbed—and therefore to get into all kinds of difficulties later, including the perpetrating of sex crimes. According to this theory, virtually all the sex disturbances that accompany sex offenses result from fixations upon or regressions to early sex-related problems.

The opposing theory, whose early modern proponent was the psychotherapist Alfred Adler (1968), hypothesizes that general human disturbances are produced first, and that sexual disturbance is almost always a derivative of general malfunctioning. Almost all non-Freudians tend to hold this theory today, including many well-known psychotherapists and sex therapists. Those who hold this view include Ellis (1962, 1973a, 1976a, 1977a), Fromm

(1963), Horney (1972), Hartman and Fithian (1972), and Masters and Johnson (1970). Clinical and research data seem to support the Adlerian hypothesis over Freudian assumptions, and it seems to have a good deal of validity.

Cognitive-behavior therapy in particular, which has been inspired by the work of Beck (1976), Ellis (1962, 1973a, Ellis & Grieger, 1977), Kelly (1955), Mahoney (1974), and Meichenbaum (1977), has produced a great deal of experimental data that substantiate the theory that humans can behave irrationally because of irrational and anti-empirical cognitions, and that by changing some of their basic ideas and philosophies they can help themselves to make a significant change in their dysfunctional traits and behaviors. More specifically, Ellis (1976a, 1977a, 1978a, 1978b) has hypothesized that people generally disturb themselves by creating and rigidly holding onto three major kinds of *musts*, *demands*, or *whinings*, and that when they do so, they become disturbed sexually and in other ways. These three basic kinds of demandingness include personal demandingness, demandingness of others, and demandingness of the world.

1. *Personal demandingness:* Sexually disturbed individuals can make inordinate personal demands on themselves, and may insist that they *must* or *should* do well and win others' approval for doing so. This type of perfectionism often results in feelings of anxiety, depression, and inadequacy, and in consequent withdrawal, inhibition, phobias, and compulsions in the sexual area.

2. *Demandingness of others:* In addition to demanding great performances of themselves, people may place unrealistic demands on others, and may insist that these others *must* treat them kindly and lovingly and help them sexually in any way they want, or else be rated as horrible individuals. This type of demandingness results in feelings of hostility, unlovingness, and self-pity, in withdrawal from certain forms of sex, and in obsessive-compulsive and often violent behavior focussing on sex acts such as rape or exhibitionism.

3. *Demandingness of the world:* Like most sexually disturbed individuals, the sexually malfunctioning person may make inordinate demands on the world that it treat him kindly and make things easy for him. He may devoutly believe that he must find sex easily and immediately enjoyable, and that the world *has* to provide him quick and easy gratifications. He may end up with low frustration tolerance, with trying to get away with doing things the easy way, and with lack of discipline. And because of these traits he may more easily become a sex offender, such as a peeper or an exhibitionist.

If we look at the three main types of demandingness that we have listed, we can see that they distinctly apply to many sex offenders who know perfectly well that they had better not commit the crimes that they commit, and who risk apprehension and penalization. These offenders, because they demand perfect performance of themselves, require others to cater to them, and want life to make things easy for them, wind up becoming compulsive, angry, and self-pitying—and therefore they commit antisocial acts that lead to their arrest and conviction. Almost all sex offenders that I have personally examined have, in one way or another, been exceptionally childish and whining—

as, of course, are many nonsexual offenders, too. While they maintain their puerile, self-indulgent philosophies, they stand a good chance of becoming and remaining offenders.

INCIDENCE OF SEX OFFENSES

No highly reliable reports of the incidence of sex offenses have yet been published because of the difficulties inherent in gathering such statistics. Most technical offenders—that is, most individuals who actually commit an act that an official statute has labeled as an offense—are never arrested. Of those who are arrested, a large percentage are not convicted in spite of the fact that they have clearly committed a statutory offense. Many of those who are convicted are allowed to plead guilty to a lesser charge (such as loitering, assault and battery, or disorderly conduct), and are therefore never charged or convicted of a specific sex offense. Consequently, individuals who are finally convicted represent only a relatively small percentage of those who commit a sex act that is legally banned in the jurisdiction where they reside (Drummond, 1953; Ellis, 1961, 1967; Ellis & Brancale, 1956; Gebhard, Gagnon, Pomeroy, & Christenson, 1965; MacNamara & Sagarin, 1977; Wolfenden Report, 1957).

The Uniform Crime Reports issued by the United States Department of Justice, Federal Bureau of Investigation, graphically show the situation. For example, for the year 1973 the FBI had records of 51,000 rapes reported in the United States. Of these, only 26,000 resulted in arrests and 19,750 resulted in prosecutions. Finally, only 10,470 convictions occurred. The FBI estimates that during 1973 some 255,000 rapes actually were perpetrated—which means that of this estimated total only one out of five were reported to the police and only one out of twenty-five resulted in convictions. There is every reason to believe that a similar discrepancy exists between the number of offenses perpetrated and the number reported and successfully convicted, for such offenses as exhibitionism, peeping, sex with minors, nonassaultive sexual abuse, and so on. In the case of certain other statutory sex offenses, such as homosexuality and prostitution, even greater discrepancies probably exist, because (as we noted earlier) in most jurisdictions in recent years these infractions have been almost entirely ignored by police.

Perhaps the best and most detailed statistical study of sex offenses to date, has been done by Radzinowicz and his associates (1957), who made a thoroughgoing inventory of offenses known to the police in England and Wales, and estimated that in 1954 about 16,000 such offenses occurred. Of the known sexual offenses, the distribution of indictable cases was found to be as follows: indecent assault on females, 50 percent; attempts to commit unnatural offenses and indecent assaults on males, 21 percent; indecency with males, 13 percent; defilement of girls between the ages of thirteen and sixteen, 9 percent; unnatural offenses, 7 percent; rape and the like, 2 percent; incest, 2 percent; and defilement of girls under the age of twelve, 1 percent.

In the United States, there tend to be about 40,000 arrests a year for major sex offenses, and several times that number for minor offenses. But as we have mentioned, these figures are somewhat meaningless since they represent only a small fraction—perhaps less than 5 percent—of the statutory sex offenses that are actually committed every year.

CHARACTERISTICS OF SEX OFFENDERS

Most modern authorities on sex offenders have stressed that there exist many myths, particularly in the eyes of the public, about the over-impulsivity, aggressiveness, and recidivism of sex offenders (McCary, 1973; Mohr, Turner, & Jerry, 1964). Some of the truths in this connection would appear to be as follows:

1. The majority of convicted offenders are found to be rather harmless, minor transgressors rather than dangerous "sex fiends."
2. Only a relatively small proportion (about 20 percent) of sex offenders use force or duress upon their victims.
3. When they are not psychologically treated, convicted offenders are found to be repeaters of both sexual and nonsexual offenses, even though their rates of recidivism may be lower than those of nonsexual criminals.
4. Few offenders may truly be designated "psychopaths," in the sense that this term is used for nonsexual offenders (Chapter 14). On the other hand, many sex offenders, when intensively examined, are found to be severely neurotic, borderline psychotic, psychotic, or organically brain-impaired. A large percentage, perhaps the majority, of convicted sex offenders suffer from some type of mental or emotional disorder, but this is not usually so pronounced as to meet the legal definition of mental illness.
5. Aside from those convicted of rape and incest, most offenders tend to be sexually inhibited and constricted rather than overimpulsive and oversexed. The distinct majority of offenders have some measure of emotional immaturity.
6. Convicted sex offenders tend to show subnormal intelligence in a higher percentage of cases, and bright normal or superior intelligence in a smaller percentage of cases, than do members of the general population. Subnormal intelligence is particularly likely to be found among offenders convicted of statutory rape, incestuous relations, and bestiality and least frequently found in those convicted of forcible rape, exhibitory acts, and the dissemination of "obscene" material.
7. The majority of offenders are quite young, mostly in their teens or early twenties; from 50 to 60 percent are unmarried. Most of the offenders come from relatively poor educational and socioeconomic backgrounds.

THE TREATMENT OF SEX OFFENDERS

For a variety of reasons, sex offenders are difficult to treat psychologically (Gebhard, Gagnon, Pomeroy, & Christenson, 1965; Gagnon & Simon, 1967; Bell & Hall, 1971), and tend, like nonsexual offenders, to be somewhat rebellious and to resist treatment. They derive considerable immediate gratification from their behavior and often do not want to work at becoming long-range hedonists and at surrendering their gratification. We have noted that such men are frequently severely disturbed, organically impaired, or mentally deficient. They are often treated in jails, prisons, and mental institutions where they have an incentive to pretend to work at therapy in order to effect quick release from incarceration (Chapter 4). They usually have at their disposal either semitrained therapists or well-trained professionals who can give them only a very limited amount of time.

Nonetheless, a defeatist attitude toward the treatment of sex offenders is far from warranted. Several investigators, including the present writer, have found that individual sex offenders can be successfully treated both in institutions and in the community. According to these investigators, unusually good results can often be obtained if the therapist employs a highly directive technique—such as the rational-emotive therapy (RET), which shows the offender what his disturbance-creating philosophies are, how he created and is sustaining them, how he can question and challenge them so that he can give them up, and how he can use activity-oriented affective and behavioral measures to decondition himself from the kinds of self-defeating conduct he is pursuing (Ellis, 1956, 1962, 1971, 1973a, 1977a; Ellis & Harper, 1961, 1975).

Unusual advances in the psychological treatment of sex offenders and other individuals with serious sexual disturbances have been made during the last fifteen years, sparked by the pioneer efforts in behavior therapy of Wolpe (1958, 1969; Wolpe & Lazarus, 1966), and in cognitive-behavior therapy by Ellis (1954, 1956, 1962), Masters and Johnson (1970), and others. Although the use of behavior therapy methods with convicted sex offenders has its distinct ethical dangers, it has been amply demonstrated, in literally scores of clinical presentations and experimental studies, that sexually disturbed individuals who are eager to change their self-defeating behaviors and are willing to cooperate with a cognitive-behavior therapist and to follow his or her direction can frequently make remarkable personality and sexual changes, and can often do so in a relatively brief period of time (Bancroft, 1969, 1970; Barlow, 1973; Barlow, Leitenberg, & Agras, 1969; Bebbington, 1977; Birk, Huddleston, Miller, & Cohler, 1971; Bond & Evans, 1967; Card, 1977; Colson, 1972; Cooper, 1963; Davison, 1968; DiScipio, 1968; Evans, 1968; Feldman & MacCulloch, 1971; Gray, 1970; Harbison, Quinn, & McAllister, 1970; Herman, 1971; Jackson, 1969; James, 1962; Kraft, 1967a, 1967b, 1969a, 1969b; Larson 1970; Levin, Hirsch, Shugar, & Kapche, 1968; LoPiccolo, 1971; Marks & Gelder, 1965; McConaghy, 1969, 1970; McGuire, Carlisle, & Young, 1965; Moan & Heath, 1972; Ramsey & Van Velzen, 1968; Rekers, 1977; Thorpe, Schmidt, & Castell, (1963); Wagner, 1968; Wickramasekera, 1968, 1972, 1976).

Not only have cognitive-behavior methods of treatment of sex offenders seen notable advances during the past twenty years, but more conventional treatments, including psychoanalytic and psychoanalytically oriented procedures, have also advanced considerably. Even twenty years ago (Ellis, 1961), a number of therapists using these methods had reported successful treatment of sexually disturbed individuals. Reports of successful treatment outcome included those of Allen (1949), Fink (1954), A. Freud (1951), Gurvitz (1957), Hadfield (1958), Karpman (1954), Lewinsky (1952), London & Caprio (1950), Poe (1952), Robertiello (1959), Rubinstein (1958), and Shentoub (1957). More recently, substantial successes in therapy with sex offenders and/or disturbed persons engaging in somewhat bizarre sex behavior has been reported by a great many analytically oriented therapists, including Allen (1969), Bell and Hall (1971), Bergler (1966), Bieber et al. (1962), Hatterer (1970), Ovesey (1969), and Socarides (1968).

As an example of the use of cognitive-affective-behavioral treatment of a sex offender, let me outline the rational-emotive therapy approach taken with a twenty-eight-year-old social worker who several times a year had compulsively engaged in "flashing" or exhibitionism, had been arrested twice, and was on the verge of ruining his professional career if he continued his behavior. The man had been married for eight years, had two young children, and functioned well at his job, including his work with a number of sexually disturbed individuals. He came to therapy under some duress, since after his last conviction the judge had given him his choice of undertaking treatment or serving a jail term.

This client was treated cognitively, by my demonstrating to him, within the first few sessions of therapy, that he had all of the major demands or musts that frequently drive people into disturbed behavior: (1) He strongly believed that "I *must* do well in my sexual and general life, I *have to* win the approval of significant others, and particularly, since I am a professional, I *absolutely should not* do anything stupid or aberrated." He consequently downed himself mightily for failing to please his wife sexually and for not having extramarital affairs, in the course of which he could at least show other women how impressive he could be in bed. And when he engaged in what he full well knew was foolish, compulsive sex activity, he flagellated himself even more, thought of himself as a "stupid lunatic," and felt that, as such, he was unable to help himself and to change his ways. (2) He fervidly believed that his wife "*must* not treat him so critically and deprive him sexually, and that she was a *horrible person* for being so mean and frustrating." And he obtained real satisfaction in rebelling against his wife's ultraconventional ways by engaging in the kinds of public sex acts that he knew she would most deplore and upset herself about. He also thought that other attractive women "*should* give in to me easily and let me satisfy them sexually," and was hostile toward most women for the sexual barriers that they put up against him and other males. (3) He dogmatically held that "life *must* not be that much of a hassle, especially to someone like me who spends a large part of his days doing good things and helping others." He took the position that "I *can't stand* the difficulties which life needlessly throws in my way." He therefore had abysmally low frustration tolerance, and felt self-pity and depression whenever he was sexually or otherwise balked.

With all three of these forms of intense *mus*turbation, this client suffered from guilt and anxiety, from hostility, from depression, and from low frustration tolerance. I quite actively and directively, as is common in rational-emotive therapy, disputed his *mus*turbatory thinking, and taught him how to use logico-empirical, scientific methods of self-analysis. To this end, I supervised his filling out Self-Help Forms published by the Institute for Advanced Study in Rational Psychotherapy (Ellis, 1977b), his using the technique of Disputing Irrational Beliefs (DIBS) (Ellis, 1974), doing referenting to concrete experience (Danysh, 1974; Ellis, 1975; Ellis & Harper, 1975), and employing various other cognitive methods frequently used in RET (Ellis, 1962, 1971, 1973a, 1977a; Ellis & Grieger, 1977; Ellis & Knaus, 1977).

Within several weeks of starting this kind of rational analysis and the disputing of his basic irrational beliefs, this exhibitionist began to transform dire needs and compulsions into preferences and desires, and to work to achieve some of these desires. Thus, he still *wanted* to do well sexually and obtain more approval from his wife; but he felt that he didn't *have to*. He still *desired* his wife to change some of her ultraconventional and antisexual ways; but he didn't *need* her to do so. He still *wished* to have life treat him better and to reap more rewards and fewer disappointments from his activities; but he stopped *demanding* that he get his wants immediately and fully gratified. As he kept surrendering *shoulds, oughts*, and *musts*, and substituting preferences, wishes, and desires, he lost his compulsivity, and felt better able to control his antisocial sex behavior.

Emotively, I used a number of methods commonly employed in RET to help this client change his feelings of anxiety, depression, hostility, and low frustration tolerance. I fully accepted him with all his disturbances, and showed him that although I thought that he was engaging in foolish, self-defeating behavior, and that I didn't approve of *it* (this behavior) I didn't in any way despise or denigrate *him* for performing it. I used a technique called rational-emotive imagery (Maultsby, 1975; Maultsby & Ellis, 1974), to help the man get in touch with, and fully acknowledge, some of his hostile and depressed feelings—and to change these feelings to those of annoyance and sorrow instead of anger and self-pity. I helped him to employ realistic, forceful, emotive self-statements—such as, "I *don't* need what I want!" and "So my wife frustrates me. Tough! There's no damned reason why she *shouldn't*!" —until he started to believe and feel them (Ellis, 1977a). I gave this client, on several occasions, some shame-attacking exercises (Ellis, 1973b, 1977a), to help him see that he could well perform "shameful" and "asinine" acts and not denigrate himself for them, even if others thought that he was an idiot for performing as he did.

Behaviorally, I employed a variety of activity-oriented methods of a desensitizing and reconditioning nature, as is usually done in RET (Ellis, 1973a, 1977a; Ellis & Grieger, 1977; Ellis & Knaus, 1977; Wolfe & Brand, 1977). I gave him *in vivo* homework assignments of approaching women in a non-exhibitionistic way and risking rejection. I had him use operant conditioning or self-management methods, in the course of which he reinforced or rewarded himself when he did not engage in compulsive behavior, and penalized himself when he did engage in it. I supervised him in some of the elements of assertion training, so that he could not only ask for sexual favors but also ask his wife and associates for nonsexual things, and refrain from building up hostile feelings against them when he refused to be assertive (Ellis, 1977a). At times I showed him how to use Jacobsen's (1958) relaxation technique and other methods of diverting himself, at least temporarily from his compulsive ideas and feelings, when he felt that he was about to overwhelm himself with them.

By experiencing this combination of cognitive, emotive, and behavioral RET methods, the client was able, within a period of seven months, to stop condemning himself and accept himself fully, in spite of his wife's criticisms and his own failings, including his compulsive sexuality. He still felt distinctly displeased at his wife's behavior, and he seriously contemplated leaving her, especially when the children had grown a little older. But he almost completely lost his anger at his wife; and by being able to express his displeasure unangrily, he was even able to effect some sexual and other compromises with her and to improve their relationship somewhat. Finally, he worked on his self-pity and low frustration tolerance, decided that he could accept the adversities of life without viewing them as holy horrors, and began to be less and less compulsive about sexual and nonsexual activities. As the client remarked during one of our closing sessions,

> I see more and more now that not only have I been a perfectionist, and demanded that I do quite well in all things and that others appreciate me for doing well, but I see that I have had an overweening demand for certainty: that all the things in life fit into their proper slots, and that with the perfect order that would then ensue, I would not have to be inconvenienced, or at least seriously inconvenienced, in almost any way. Now I see that this kind of order and certainty is somewhat desirable, but decidedly not necessary. And when things go awry with my wife or with others, I accept them the way they are. Not that I don't try to change them. I do. But I often see that they are unchangeable—and then I *still* accept them, instead of, as you would put it, endlessly whining about them and rebelliously leaning over backward to get my way—even at my own great expense. What crap! What childishness! I can see it easily in my own clients; but now I also see it in myself. And I intend to give up that childish demandingness, that Jehovian command on the universe, if it's the last thing I do! Then I won't have to compulsively screw myself!

Almost four years have passed since I last saw this client professionally, and I still see him occasionally when he attends workshops at our Institute in New York. From my talks with the client, I find that he no longer engages in exhibitionism; he is engaging instead in extramarital affairs that he was afraid to try to consummate in the past, and has arranged with his wife to probably get a divorce within the next few years. Meanwhile, he is doing better than ever at his social work activities.

A final word on the treatment of sex offenders: Much has yet to be learned about this subject; it is likely that new psychological and physiological ways of helping individuals who want to change sexual disturbances that lead them to commit offenses will continue to be discovered (Money et al, 1975). Research in this area is particularly important. We already know, though, that treatment does not necessarily mean incarceration, nor even treatment that is court-imposed. Incarcerating and punishing sexual and non-sexual offenders may certainly, in some cases, help both the offenders and the society in which they live; but there are also great risks involved in this kind of forced "treatment." As Gagnon and Simon note in this connection: "The punitive treatment given sex offenders is ineffective in the case of the compulsive offender, and excessive for those whose behavior is linked to processes only indirectly sexual in nature. Furthermore, punitive and anxiety-ridden responses of society reduce the amount of research activity needed to determine the most successful forms of treatment and prevention" (1970, pp. 11–12). And as a good many authors have pointed out, imprisonment has its own risks to the physical and mental health of offenders, and contributes to sex offenses, such as homosexual rape, which often originate in and are encouraged by prison conditions (Gerassi, 1967; Jones, 1976).

SOCIAL PROPHYLAXIS

As with all antisocial offenses, the main problems with regard to sex offenders is prevention rather than cure. Both the offenders and the social groups to which they belong would obviously be better off if individuals did not commit criminal acts in the first place, rather than if they first committed them and were later cured of their propensities to do so.

As usual, there are at least two opposed schools of thought on the subject of prevention. The conservative or punitive school tends to assume that a more rigorous application of sex offender laws and stricter punishment for those who are convicted under these laws would help cut down the crime rate; the more liberal or rehabilitation-oriented school tends to claim that fewer antisexual laws and a much greater emphasis on treatment rather than punishment would go a long way toward ultimately cutting down on sex offenses.

Both schools of thought tend to hold somewhat extreme views, and they perhaps unrealistically ignore the good points made by the opposing school. Neither school too seriously considers the possibility that perhaps in regard to some offenses more rigor might be a good order of the day, while in regard to other offenses less rigor might profitably prevail. Yet there are some recent indications that this kind of discrimination between one kind of sex offense and its treatment and another kind and *its* treatment is becoming more relevant today than perhaps it ever was in the past.

The value of a differential view has been particularly evident in regard to recommendations concerning the legal and treatment procedures to be instituted in the case of rape. In the old days, rape was seen as an exceptionally serious crime, and the penalties for it, especially in certain American states, were enormous—for example, up to thirty years in jail or the death penalty for some convicted rapists (Sherwin, 1949, 1967; Grigeroff, 1968; McDonald, 1971; Ploscowe, 1951; Slovenko, 1967). As time went by, however, partially because of the severity of these early rape laws, an almost incredible amount of laxity in regard to the implementation of laws began to become something of a general rule, and males who were almost certainly guilty of violent rape and of statutory rape were frequently not arrested, were allowed to cop a minor plea, cavalierly acquitted, or convicted and given ridiculously easy sentences.

Alarmed by this state of affairs, as well as by the fact that women who accused males of having raped them were often subjected to brutal examinations, to all kinds of legal harrassment, and to indignities that were sometimes much worse than that inflicted by the males who had criminally assaulted them, many people, especially those allied with the women's movement, began to protest strongly against prevailing practices. As a result of these protests, rape is now considered in a much more serious manner than it was, say, twenty years ago; and much more effective steps are likely to be taken to bring rapists to trial and to conviction, as well as to make suitable provisions to encourage women to bring rape charges. In this particular instance, then, a certain kind of sex offense that has presumably been taken too lightly in the past, is now, with excellent reason, being taken much more seriously (Amir, 1977; Brownmiller, 1975; Gager & Schurr, 1976; McDonald, 1971).

At the same time, some other kinds of sex offenses that once were taken quite seriously are now being regarded in a much lighter vein. As we mentioned above, certain crimes, such as homosexuality and oral-genital relations, which are still listed on many statute books as crimes "against nature," are in many jurisdictions rarely prosecuted. The police do not look for such offenses, as they often did a couple of decades ago; and even when such acts are brought to public attention they are dealt with rather lightly, and only slight penalties are handed out in the case of convictions. If, however, the victims of such offenses are below age, and especially if they are very young, a much greater fuss is made and penalties for convictions are often severe.

The same differential attitude has been suggested in regard to the commission of certain other sex offenses, such as prostitution and the dissemination of pornography, which are not only widespread in our society, but which have literally millions of patrons each year who themselves can hardly be placed in a seriously disturbed or "abnormal" category. Enlightened observers frequently note that these sorts of "crimes" had best be decriminalized or ignored when the perpetrators and the "victims" are adults; but when either or both happen to be minors a much stricter kind of consideration had better be taken by the guardians of public morality (Benjamin & Masters, 1964; Gibbens, 1977; Polsky, 1967; MacNamara & Sagarin, 1977). I would tend to argue that this kind of differentiation between sex offenses that involve minors and those that do not, and between offenses that involve physical assault and those that include no element of physical violence or coercion is an appropriate way of viewing acts that are in rather different categories; and that offenses involving minors and/or assaultiveness should preferably be considered far more seriously than the ones that do not.

In general, I would endorse or advance the following recommendations for the prevention of and treatment for sex offenses:

1. It would be preferable if we legally proscribed only those sex acts that involve the use of force or duress, entail an adult's taking sexual advantage of a minor, or are public acts distasteful to the majority of those in whose presence they are committed. Sex acts other than these, which are engaged in in private between two competent adults, need not be subject to legal processes or penalties.

2. All sex offense laws might well be rewritten so that offenses are specifically and scientifically designated and are defined in meaningful, consistent, nonoverlapping terms.

3. When individuals commit any sex offense that would be legislated under the two preceding rules, they can, preferably after conviction but before being sentenced, be given a thorough psychological examination to determine whether they are psychologically disturbed and whether their sex offense largely stems from a general psychological disturbance.

4. Sex offenders who are diagnosed as being psychologically disturbed should preferably receive psychotherapeutic treatment either in their own community or in some special facility that specializes in the care of disturbed offenders. If institutionalization is required, convicted offenders could be required to remain in protective custody as long as they are regarded as being sufficiently disturbed to constitute a menace to the rights and safety of their fellow citizens.

5. Sex offenders had better not be viewed as horrible, villainous criminals who have to be harshly punished as an atonement for their sins. They can, rather, be diagnosed either as relatively healthy individuals who are rash enough to get into occasional difficulty, or as more seriously disturbed persons who are sufficiently disorganized to keep getting into legal difficulties because of their sexual behavior. In either case, education and treatment, rather than excoriation and punishment, is the most appropriate measure for these already sufficiently unfortunate individuals.

6. It is most desirable, for the prevention and treatment of sex offenders, that every community favor increasing and improving the quality of sex education and emotional education, so that children are provided at an early age with scientific, objectively presented sex information and so that they are encouraged, when young and when older, to engage in forms of sexuality that are likely to prove healthy and harmless.

REFERENCES

Abrahamsen, D. *Report on study of 102 sex offenders at Sing Sing Prison.* Utica, N.Y.: State Hospitals Press, 1950.

Adler, A. *Understanding human nature.* Greenwich, Conn.: Fawcett, 1968.

Allen, C. *The sexual perversions and abnormalities.* New York: Oxford, 1949.

Allen, C. *A textbook of psychosexual disorders.* London: Oxford, 1969.

Amir, M. *Patterns in forcible rape.* Chicago: University of Chicago Press, 1977.

Bancroft, J. Aversion therapy of homosexuality. *British Journal of Psychiatry,* 1969, *115,* 1417–1431.

Bancroft, J. A comparative study of aversion and desensitization in the treatment of homosexuality. In L. E. Burns and J. L. Worsley (Eds.), *Behaviour therapy in the 1970's.* Bristol, England: Wright, 1970.

Barlow, D. H. Increasing heterosexual responsiveness in the treatment of sexual deviation. *Behavior Therapy,* 1973, *4,* 655–671.

Barlow, D. H., Leitenberg, H., & Agras, W. S. The experimental control of sexual deviation through manipulation of the noxious scene in covert sensitization. *Journal of Abnormal Psychology,* 1969, *74,* 596–601.

Beck, A. T. *Cognitive therapy and the emotional disorders.* New York: International Universities Press, 1976.

Bebbington, P. E. Treatment of male sexual deviation by use of a vibrator: case report. *Archives of Sexual Behavior,* 1977, *6,* 21–24.

Beech, H. R., Watts, F., & Poole, A. D. Classical conditioning of sexual deviation. *Behavior Therapy,* 1971, *2,* 400–402.

Bell, A., & Hall, C. S. *The personality of a child molester,* Chicago: Aldine, 1971.

Benjamin, H., & Masters, R. E. L. *Prostitution and morality.* New York: Julian Press, 1964.

Bergler, E. *Homosexuality: disease or way of life?* New York: Collier, 1966.

Bieber, I., & others. *Homosexuality.* New York: Basic Books, 1963.

Birk, L., Huddleston, W., Miller, E., & Cohler, B. Avoidance conditioning for homosexuality. *Archives of General Psychiatry,* 1971, *25,* 314–323.

Bond, I., & Evans, D. Avoidance therapy, Its use in two cases of underwear fetishism. *Canadian Medical Association Journal,* 1967, *96,* 1160–1162.

Brownmiller, S. *Against our will.* New York: Simon and Schuster, 1975.

Card, R. D. A preliminary report of a treatment program for working with various forms of sexual deviancy. *Journal of Sex Education Therapy,* 1977, *3(1),* 5–7.

Colson, C. E. Olfactory aversion therapy for homosexual behavior. *Journal of Behavior Therapy and Experimental Psychiatry,* 1972, *3,* 185–187.

Cooper, A. A. A case of fetishism and impotence treated by behavior therapy. *British Journal of Psychiatry,* 1963, *109,* 649–652.

Danysh, J. *Stop without quitting.* San Francisco: International Society for General Semantics, 1974.

Davison, G. C. Elimination of a sadistic fantasy by a client-controlled counterconditioning technique. *Journal of Abnormal Psychology,* 1968, *73,* 84–90.

DiScipio, W. Modified progressive desensitization and homosexuality. *British Journal of Medical Psychology,* 1968, *41,* 267–272.

Drummond, I. *The sex paradox.* New York: Putnam, 1953.

East, N. *Sexual offenders.* London: Delisle, 1955.

Ellis, A. *The American sexual tragedy* (rev. ed.). New York: Twayne, 1954. New York: Grove Press and Lyle Stuart, 1962.

Ellis, A. The effectiveness of psychotherapy with individuals who have severe homosexual problems. *Journal of Consulting Psychology,* 1956, *20,* 58–60.

Ellis, A. The sex offender and his treatment. In H. Toch (Ed.), *Legal and criminal psychology.* New York: Holt, Rinehart and Winston, 1961.

Ellis, A. *Reason and emotion in psychotherapy.* New York: Lyle Stuart, 1962.

Ellis, A. The psychology of sex offenders. In A. Ellis and A. Abarbanel, *The encyclopedia of sexual behavior.* New York: Hawthorn Books, 1967.

Ellis, A. *Growth through reason.* Palo Alto, Calif.: Science and Behavior Books and Hollywood: Wilshire Books, 1971.

Ellis, A. *Humanistic psychotherapy: the rational-emotive approach.* New York: Julian Press and McGraw-Hill Paperbacks, 1973a.

Ellis, A. *How to stubbornly refuse to feel ashamed of anything.* Cassette recording. New York: Institute for Rational Living, 1973b.

Ellis, A. *Technique of disputing irrational beliefs (DIBS).* New York: Institute for Rational Living, 1974.

Ellis, A. *How to live with a "neurotic."* New York: Crown Publishers, 1975.

Ellis, A. *Sex and the liberated man.* New York: Lyle Stuart, 1976a.

Ellis, A. The biological basis of human irrationality. *Journal of Individual Psychology,* 1976b, *32,* 145–168.

Ellis, A. *How to live with—and without—anger.* New York: Reader's Digest Press, 1977a.

Ellis, A. *Rational self-help form.* New York: Institute for Rational Living, 1977b.

Ellis, A. Toward a theory of personality. In R. Corsini (Ed.), *A sourcebook of personality theory.* Itasca, Ill.: Peacock, 1978a.

Ellis, A. Rational-emotive therapy. In R. Corsini (Ed.), *Current psychotherapies.* (rev. ed.). Itasca, Ill.: Peacock, 1978b.

Ellis, A., & Brancale, R. *Psychology of sex offenders.* Springfield, Ill.: Charles C Thomas, 1956.

Ellis, A., & Grieger, R. *Handbook of rational-emotive therapy.* New York: Springer, 1977.

Ellis, A., & Gullo, J. *Murder and assassination.* New York: Lyle Stuart, 1971.

Ellis, A., & Harper, R. A. *A guide to successful marriage.* New York: Lyle Stuart and Hollywood: Wilshire Books, 1961.

Ellis, A., & Harper, R. A. *A new guide to rational living.* Englewood Cliffs, N.J.: Prentice-Hall and Hollywood: Wilshire Books, 1975.

Ellis, A., & Knaus, W. *Overcoming procrastination.* New York: Institute for Rational Living, 1977.

Evans, D. R. Masturbatory fantasy and sexual deviation. *Behavior Research and Therapy,* 1968, *6,* 17–19.

Feldman, M. P., & MacCulloch, M. J. *Homosexual behaviour: theory and assessment.* Oxford: Pergamon Press, 1971.

Fink, H. K. *Long journey.* New York: Julian Press, 1954.

Freud, A. Clinical observations on the treatment of manifest male homosexuality. *Psychoanalytic Quarterly,* 1951, *20,* 237–238.

Freud, S. *Standard edition of the complete psychological works of Sigmund Freud.* London: Hogarth, 1965.

Fromm, E. *The art of loving.* New York: Bantam, 1963.

Gager, N., & Schun, C. *Sexual assault: Confronting rape in America.* New York: Grosset and Dunlap, 1976.

Gagnon, J., & Simon, W. *Sexual encounters between adults and children.* New York: Sex Information and Education Council of the U.S., 1970.

Gagnon, J., & Simon, W. *Sexual deviance.* New York: Harper & Row, 1967.

Gebhard, P. H., Gagnon, J. H., Pomeroy, W. B., & Christenson, C. F. *Sex offenders: an analysis of types.* New York: Harper & Row, 1965.

Gerassi, J. *The boys of Boise.* New York: Macmillan, 1967.

Gibbens, T. Behavioural types of rape. *British Journal of Psychiatry,* 1977, *130,* 32–42.

Glueck, B. C. Psychodynamic patterns in the homosexual sex offender. *American Journal of Psychiatry,* 1956, *11,* 584–590.

Gray, J. J. Case conference: Behavior therapy in a patient with homosexual fantasies and heterosexual anxiety. *Journal of Behavior Therapy and Experimental Psychiatry,* 1970, *1,* 225–322.

Grigeroff, A. K. *Sexual deviations in the criminal law.* Toronto: University of Toronto Press, 1968.

Group for the Advancement of Psychiatry. *Psychiatrically deviated sex offender.* Topeka, Kansas: Group for the Advancement of Psychiatry, 1950.

Gurvitz, M. Sex offenders in private practice: treatment and outcome. Paper delivered at the American Psychological Association Annual Convention, September 3, 1957.

Guttmacher, M. S. *Sex offenses.* New York: Norton, 1951.

Hadfield, J. A. The cure of homosexuality. *British Medical Journal,* 1958, *1,* 1323–1326.

Harbison, J., Quinn, J., & McAllister, H. The positive conditioning of heterosexual behavior. Paper delivered to Conference on Behavior Modification, Dublin, 1970.

Hartman, W., & Fithian, M. A. *Treatment of sexual dysfunction.* Long Beach, Calif.: Center for Marital and Sexual Studies, 1972.

Hatterer, L. J. *Changing homosexuality in the male.* New York: McGraw-Hill, 1970.

Herman, S. H. *An experimental analysis of two methods of increasing heterosexual arousal in homosexuals.* Ph.D. thesis, University of Mississippi, 1971.

Horney, K. *Collected writings.* New York: Norton, 1972.

Jackson, B. A case of voyeurism treated by counter-conditioning. *Behaviour Research and Therapy,* 1969, *7,* 133–134.

Jacobsen, E. *You must relax.* New York: Pocket Books, 1958.

James B. Case of homosexuality treated by aversion therapy. *British Medical Journal,* 1962, *1,* 768–770.

Jones, D. A. *The health risks of imprisonment.* Lexington, Mass.: Lexington Books (Heath), 1976.

Karpman, B. *The sexual offender and his offenses.* New York: Julian, 1954.

Kelly, G. *The psychology of personal constructs.* New York: Norton, 1955.

Kinsey, A. C., Pomeroy, W. B., & Martin, C. H. *Sexual behavior in the human male.* Philadelphia: Saunders, 1948.

Kopp, S. B. The character structure of sex offenders. *American Journal of Psychotherapy,* 1962, *15,* 15–20.

Kraft, T. A case of homosexuality treated by systematic desensitization. *American Journal of Psychotherapy,* 1967a, *21,* 815–821.

Kraft, T. Behavior therapy and the treatment of sexual perversions. *Psychotherapy and Psychosomatics,* 1967b, *15,* 351–357.

Kraft, T. Desensitization and the treatment of sexual disorders. *Journal of Sex Research,* 1969a, *5,* 130–134.

Kraft, T. Treatment of sexual perversions. *Behaviour Research and Therapy,* 1969b, *7,* 215.

Laing, R. *The politics of experience.* New York: Pantheon, 1967.

Larson, D. An adaptation of the Feldman and MacCulloch approach to treatment of homosexuality by the application of anticipatory avoidance learning. *Behaviour Research and Therapy,* 1970, *8,* 209–210.

Levin, S., Hirsch, I., Shugar, G., & Kapche, R. Treatment of homosexuality and heterosexual anxiety with avoidance conditioning and systematic desensitization. *Psychotherapy,* 1968, *5,* 160–168.

Lewinsky, H. Features from a case of homosexuality. *Psychoanalytic Quarterly,* 1952, *21,* 344–354.

London, L. S., & Caprio, F. S. *Sexual deviation.* Washington, D. C.: Linacre Press, 1950.

LoPiccolo, J. Case study: Systematic desensitization of homosexuality. *Behavior Therapy,* 1971, *2,* 394–399.

MacNamara, D. E. J., & Sagarin, E. *Sex, crime, and the law.* New York: Free Press, 1977.

Mahoney, M. *Cognition and behavior modification.* Cambridge, Mass.: Ballinger, 1974.

Marks, I. M., & Gelder, M. G. Transvestism and fetishism: clinical and psychological changes during faradic aversion. *British Journal of Psychiatry,* 1965, *111,* 573–578.

Masters, W. H., & Johnson, V. E. *Human sexual inadequacy.* Boston: Little, Brown, 1970.

Maultsby, M. C., Jr. *Help yourself to happiness.* New York: Institute for Rational Living, 1975.

Maultsby, M. C., Jr., & Ellis, A. *Technique for using rational emotive imagery (REI).* New York: Institute for Rational Living, 1974.

McCary, J. L. *Human sexuality.* New York: Van Nostrand, 1973.

McConaghy, N. Subjective and penile plethysmograph responses following aversion relief and apomorphine aversion therapy for homosexual impulses. *British Journal of Psychiatry,* 1969, *115,* 723–730.

McConaghy, N. Penile response conditioning and its relationship to aversion therapy in homosexuals. *Behavior Therapy,* 1970, *1,* 213–221.

McDonald, J. M. *Rape offenders and their victims,* Springfield, Ill.: Charles C Thomas, 1971.

McGuire, R. J., Carlisle, J. M., & Young, B. G. Sexual deviations as conditioned behavior. *Behaviour Research and Therapy,* 1965, *2,* 185–190

Meichenbaum, D. *Cognitive-behavior modification.* New York: Plenum, 1977.

Moan, C. E., & Heath, R. G. Septal stimulation for the initiation of heterosexual behavior in a homosexual male. *Journal of Behavior Therapy and Experimental Psychiatry,* 1972, *3,* 23–30.

Mohr, J., Turner, R. E., & Jerry, M. B. *Pedophilia and exhibitionism.* Toronto: University of Toronto Press, 1964.

Money, J., et al. 47,XYY and 46,XY males with antisocial and/or sex-offending behavior: Antiadrogen therapy plus counseling. *Psychoneurendocrinology,* 1975, *12,* 165–178.

Ovesey, L. *Homosexuality and pseudohomosexuality.* New York: Science House, 1969.

Pacht, A. R., Halleck, S. L., & Ehrmann, J. C. Diagnosis and treatment of the sexual offender: a nine year study. *American Journal of Psychiatry,* 1962, *118,* 802–808.

Ploscowe, M. *Sex and the law.* New York: Prentice-Hall, 1951.

Poe, J. S. Successful treatment of a forty-year-old passive homosexual. *Psychoanalytic Review,* 1952, *29,* 23–36.

Pollens, B. *The sexual criminal.* New York: Macaulay, 1938.

Polsky, N. *Hustlers, beats, and others.* Chicago: Aldine, 1967.

Radzinowicz, L. *Sexual offenses.* London: Macmillan, 1949.

Ramsey, R. W., & Van Velzen, V. Behaviour therapy for sexual perversions. *Behaviour Research and Therapy,* 1968, *6,* 17–19.

Rekers, G. A. Self-monitoring and self-reinforcement processes in a pretransexual boy. *Behaviour Research and Therapy,* 1977, *15,* 177–180.

Robertielo, C. *Voyage from Lesbos.* New York: Citadel Press, 1959.

Rubinstein, J. Psychotherapeutic aspects of male homosexuality. *British Journal of Medical Psychology,* 1958, *31,* 74–78.

Shentoub, S. A. De quelques problems dans l'homosexualité masculine active. *Revue Français Psychanalyze,* 1957, *51,* 485–534.

Sherwin, R. V. *Sex and the statutory law.* New York: Oceana Publications, 1949.

Sherwin, R. V. Laws and sex crimes. In A. Ellis and A. Abarbanel (Eds.), *Encyclopedia of sexual behavior.* New York: Hawthorn Books, 1967.

Slovenko, R. (Ed.). *Sex and the law.* Springfield, Ill.: Charles C Thomas, 1967.

Socarides, C. W. *The overt homosexual.* New York: Grune and Stratton, 1968.

Stekel, W. *Sexual aberrations.* New York: Liveright, 1930.

Szasz, T. *The myth of mental illness.* New York: Harper, 1961.

Szasz, *Psychiatric slavery.* New York: Free Press, 1977.

Tappan, P. W. *The habitual sex offender.* Trenton: State of New Jersey, 1950.

Thorpe, J., Schmidt, E., & Castell, D. A comparison of positive and negative (aversive) conditioning in the treatment of homosexuality. *Behaviour Research and Therapy,* 1963, *1,* 357–362.

Toch, H. *Violent men: an inquiry into the psychology of violence.* Chicago: Aldine, 1969.

Wagner, M. K. A case of public masturbation treated by operant conditioning. *Journal of Child Psychology,* 1968, *9,* 61–65.

Wickramasekera, I. Aversive behavior rehearsal for sexual exhibitionism. In I. Wickramasekera (Ed.), *Biofeedback, behavior therapy and hypnosis.* Chicago: Nelson-Hall, 1976.

Wickramasekera, I. Technique for controlling a certain type of sexual exhibitionism. *Psychotherapy,* 1972, *9,* 207–210.

Wickramasekera, I. The application of learning theory to the treatment of a case of sexual exhibitionism. *Psychotherapy,* 1968, *5,* 108–112.

Wolfe, J. L., & Brand, E. *Twenty years of rational therapy.* New York: Institute for Rational Living, 1977.

Wolfenden, J. *Report of the Committee on Homosexual Offences and Prostitution.* London: Her Majesty's Stationery Office, 1957.

Wolfgang, M., & Ferracuti, F. *The subculture of violence.* London: Tavistock, 1967.

Wolpe, J. *Psychotherapy of reciprocal inhibition.* Stanford: Stanford University Press, 1958.

Wolpe, *The practice of behavior therapy.* New York: Pergamon, 1969.

Wolpe, J., & Lazarus, A. A. *Behavior therapy techniques.* New York: Pergamon, 1966.

chapter 18

The White-Collar Offender

Gilbert Geis
Robert F. Meier

- In 1941, two thirds of the nation's industrial assets were held by the country's one thousand largest corporations; by 1971, this same proportion was held by two hundred corporations.

- Between 1969 and 1971, sales by the nation's largest corporations increased 12.5 percent, but employment in these companies dropped by 5.2 percent.

- In 1969, the corporate share of the federal income tax was about 35 percent; it fell to about 26 percent in 1972 (Cressey, 1976, p. 211).

Such results might have occurred as the consequence of perfectly normal, and legal, business practices. But the foregoing facts document the enormous concentration of wealth and power in our society today. That power offers opportunities for abuse by persons who make decisions in the corporate world. It is the criminality of such persons—as well as the criminal behavior of other affluent and successful people—that constitutes the subject-matter of this chapter.

There are two noteworthy characteristics of literature on white-collar crime. First, in line with the interests of Ralph Nader and other consumer advocates, the aim is to identify and to control acts, not to analyze and understand their dynamics. Second, there has been a conspicuous absence of sociological and social-psychological theory to guide and orient questions for white-collar crime research.

The chapter will first examine the correctional approach and offer suggestions for escape from its pitfalls. Subsequently, we will review the work of

Edwin H. Sutherland on white-collar crime. We will conclude by setting forth some social psychological constructs for the examination of white-collar crime.

"CORRECTING" WHITE-COLLAR CRIME

The correctional expert is informed and motivated by the purpose of ridding society of deviance. In his discussion of correctionalism, David Matza (1969, pp. 15–17) observes: "The correctional perspective is reasonable enough, perhaps even commendable, except that it makes empathy and understanding difficult and sometimes impossible."

Modern correctionalism permeates the work of Ralph Nader. The most explicit example occurs in his foreword to the papers presented at the Conference on Corporate Responsibility in Washington, D.C. in 1971:

> We have long been familiar with the often adverse ways corporations affect people, but specific structural remedies to correct corporate abuses have not been forthcoming. The aim of the conference and therefore this book is to push beyond diagnosis to prescription, to emphasize not merely what is wrong, but ways to right it (Nader, 1973, p. vii).

An associate of Nader, Mark Green (1971), addressed the same theme when he asked, "How does government enforcement actually work—or not? And, if not, why not?" (p. xviii).

These issues have become identified as *the* issues with respect to white-collar crime today. And it was precisely the same kinds of issues that initially were identified and articulated by the pioneers in criminology who began looking at white-collar crime a quarter of a century ago.

Although Edwin H. Sutherland, the originator of the term "white-collar crime," is not generally thought to be a muckraker in his approach to the subject, his work on closer scrutiny fits into the genre in certain respects. Karl Schuessler (1973, p. x), one of Sutherland's former graduate students, has noted that ". . . Sutherland was concerned with a scientific criminology that might, because of its capacity for prediction, have some practical value for purposes of social engineering." For Sutherland, any potential conflict between these values was resolved by regarding them as compatible means to the same end: the advancement of scientific criminology was seen as advancing the control of crime.

While Sutherland's interest in white-collar crime can be traced back to about 1925, his published work on the subject did not appear until the 1940s, culminating in *White Collar Crime*, which appeared in 1949. Sutherland was willing to merge scientific and correctional issues, but he was aware that others did not share his viewpoint. He therefore took utmost pains to disclaim anything other than a scientific approach to his subject. In the first sentences of the preface to his monograph he says:

> This book is a study in the theory of criminal behavior. It is an attempt to reform the theory of criminal behavior, not to reform anything else. Although it might have implications for social reforms, social reforms are not the objective of the book (Sutherland, 1949, p. v).

Sutherland's (1937) major research contribution on professional theft was more sympathetic to the offender than his view of white-collar crime. While not condoning theft, Sutherland clearly was intrigued by it. Jon Snodgrass (1972, p. 8) has observed, "Sutherland seemed to have a quiet admiration and genuine respect for professional thieves. He tended to ennoble their occupation." Sutherland's appreciation for professional thieves, however, does not extend to his attitudes regarding white-collar and corporate offenders.

Over time, Sutherland came to regard white-collar criminals as the upperworld counterparts of professional thieves. In both groups, Sutherland maintained, illegal activity was an integral part of occupational effort, and for both groups there was no loss of prestige among colleagues because of criminal involvement. Both sets of activities also required considerable training, tutelage, and specialized skill. There was, however, a significant difference between professional theft and white-collar criminality, a difference that shifts Sutherland's perspective. This difference lies in the self-concept of offenders. "Professional thieves, when they speak honestly, admit that they are thieves," Sutherland observed, while white-collar criminals "think of themselves as honest men" (Sutherland, 1973, pp. 95–96). This alleged hypocrisy and false virtue of white-collar criminals drew Sutherland's severe reprobation. It is evident that Sutherland came to admire and glamorize the professional thief, and to loathe the white-collar criminal, a loathing that translated into his claim that businessmen were the most subversive force in America (Sutherland, 1973, p. 92), and his equating of the advertising tactics of the power and light utility companies to the propaganda of German Nazis (Sutherland, 1949, p. 210). Not only must white-collar behavior be controlled, Sutherland insisted, but the public must come to appreciate what criminologists had understood for some time—that white-collar and corporate offenses are serious criminal depredations.

Correcting Correctionalism

In studies of white-collar crime, attention usually has been concentrated on persons of prestige, but logic suggests that the designation embrace all individuals who violate laws regulating their occupational activities, such as grocers who shortweight and factory workers who knowingly are negligent in the construction of products whose faults might cause consumer injuries or deaths (Bensman & Gerver, 1963). Violators of antitrust laws (Geis, 1967), pharmacists who break criminal laws dealing with the writing of prescriptions (Quinney, 1963), and politicians who accept bribes (Alexander, 1977) are also among those criminal offenders who appear on the white-collar crime roster (Geis & Meier, 1977).

The social and psychological factors that might govern so diverse a range of human behaviors would, if enunciated, prove too amorphous to be useful for scientific or policy purposes. Analytically, the offenses must be broken down into homogeneous categories so that productive ideas can be generated regarding underlying mechanisms. The categories that might be employed would depend, of course, on the ends being sought. The researcher may group by occupation, task, offender status, the legal definition of the violation, or in terms of any other approach that might likely serve his purposes.

Sutherland himself, contrary to this view, chose to regard white-collar offenses as part of general criminal activity, *all* of which (from arson to illegal zymurgy) was to be explicable by a single theory, which he labeled "differential association" (Sutherland & Cressey, 1957). The theory consists of a set of postulates which describe rather simplistically the manner in which people introject ideas and values and then behave in terms of what they have absorbed. The most powerful influence on human behavior, Sutherland suggested, is the primary group, those individuals who share most intimately in a person's life. From such sources, the person acquire views of what is right and what is wrong, permissible and impermissible, legal and illegal. The slum youngster of the Depression period may learn that it is admirable to foray for coal in railroad yards or to swipe milk bottles from stoops in the wealthier neighborhoods, and he may argue that the most important characteristic of both acts is their contribution to the survival or well-being of his family.

The individual also develops a set of rationalizations or neutralization techniques (Sykes & Matza, 1955); these allow him to regard as reasonable behavior that others might find unacceptable. Fee-splitting by a medical doctor becomes in this manner a legitimate process of reward for services rendered, a system that has been outlawed only because of wrong-headed "socialistic" sentiments or legislative ignorance about the necessary nature of actual medical practice. Antitrust violations are defined as imperative in order to stabilize an errant market situation and/or as compassionate acts aimed at keeping on the job employees who otherwise might have been laid off. At worst, such crimes are regarded as "technical" violations of obfuscatory regulations.

Lest these modes of thought appear unusual, readers might well examine their own feelings about running through a stop sign near their house at two o'clock on a traffic-free morning, helping themselves to supplies where they work, using the office telephone for personal business, or showing someone else's identification card to obtain an alcoholic beverage defined as illegal for such as themselves. All these acts, like white-collar (as well as traditional) offenses, can be seen by some "sensible" persons as acceptable actions. So do con men regard the fleecing of "greedy" marks (Maurer, 1940), and so do shoplifters regard theft from large department stores, which are seen as having plenty to spare from their ill-gotten gains (Smigel, 1956).

Sutherland's social psychological postulates are particularly compelling as signposts warning us away from rote dependence upon shibboleths about the causation of criminal activity, ideas which suggest that poverty, broken homes, Oedipal complexes, and similar things cause crime. What we learn combines with what we are (Sutherland rather neglects this second item) to determine what we do—this is the essence of differential association. This formula may prove useful for predicting that we speak with a Southern accent if we are born in Biloxi and spend our life there and that, as Americans, we are apt to find snakes unpalatable. But it does not carry us very far toward understanding why some persons with deep indoctrination favoring lawbreaking avoid doing so, while others, with contrary experiences, violate the law. It is obvious enough that human beings can be inventive, or to suppose that contradictory currents have sifted into what misleadingly appeared to be impermeable social or personal systems. Such hypotheses caution us to keep our predictions suitably general, so that we say, "All things being equal, it is likely that a person who entertains a keen desire for financial gain, who perceives that he will not be caught, and who has not adequately learned inhibitions about criminal behavior, will cheat when a suitable opportunity arises." The last item in the equation offers proof enough of the pitfalls of prediction on an individual basis, for the chance to commit a specific crime often depends on luck and circumstance.

In the first edition of his criminology textbook, published more than half a century ago, Sutherland (1924, p. 86) concluded a review of crime causation with the observation that "the most important thing to know about crime is the mechanisms by which it is produced, and . . . such knowledge can be secured best by the individual case studies." Later criminologists suggest that such a formulation addresses but part of the major issues. It is essential also to understand why certain behaviors are singled out for attention by the criminal law, while others, though they seemingly produce as much or more harm, are neglected (Pearce, 1976). Criminologists also want to investigate patterns of law enforcement—who, among the universe of perpetrators, is caught, tried, and convicted? And how do sentences differ? (Quinney, 1977).

These are requisite ingredients of a cosmopolitan criminology. Sometimes, however, the currently popular approach camouflages a reductionist concept: Without the law, it suggests, there would be no crime; therefore the cause of crime is the criminal law. The suggestion that the fundamental cause of crime is capitalism suffers when confronted with the existence of criminal activities in all precapitalistic societies of any complexity and the appearance of such activity in contemporary noncapitalistic systems, such as the Soviet Union, Cuba, and China. In the Soviet Union, for instance, a fiddling taxi driver sounds very much like his American counterparts:

> The cheating's wrong, I know that . . . I cheat because everyone else does. The Party high-ups live like kings—on the people's money. Factory directors take a share of their plant's profits. Foremen take wage "kickbacks," workers smuggle out what raw materials they can under their coats, shop assistants water the wine. . . . Why should I be a martyr? I would if it would help, but it wouldn't change a single thing (Connor, 1972, p. 255–256).

Types and quantities of crime may vary in terms of dominant economic arrangements within social systems, but laws and law-breaking apparently are endemic to human organizations. It seems reasonable, therefore, to follow Sutherland's suggestions, and using case studies, to concentrate some continuing attention on the attributes of criminal behavior itself.

WHITE-COLLAR OFFENDERS

In Finance

The most extensive clinical analysis of a single white-collar offender is that of Richard Whitney by Walter Bromberg (1965, pp. 384–389). Whitney's obituary notice (Krebs, 1974) observed that he "seemed to be one of those privileged patricians upon whom Providence could only smile." He had purchased a seat on the New York Stock Exchange at the age of twenty-three, and soon became a principal broker for J. P. Morgan and Co. But Whitney fell deeply into debt through speculation, and turned to thievery to cover himself, embezzling funds entrusted to him by the Exchange and by the New York Yacht Club, of which he was treasurer. After being found out, he was sentenced to five to ten years imprisonment for grand larceny. In prison, both guards and fellow convicts always deferentially referred to him as "Mr. Whitney."

For Bromberg, Whitney's behavior is understood in terms of a "fantasy of omnipotence." He notes that the psychological examination of Whitney found him scoring 174 on the Army Alpha intelligence test, a result placing him above the ninety-ninth percentile. Whitney reacted to the psychiatric probes, Bromberg notes, "in an urbane and sportsmanlike manner. The picture emerging . . . was sharp and definitive, with no smudges of neurotic inferiority, depressive reactions, or other defenses against inner conflicts" (p. 388). The examiners found Whitney to be markedly egocentric, and they were surprised by his statement that he never imagined he would run afoul of the law, despite his long administrative experience on the Stock Exchange. Bromberg (1965) summarizes this case and others like it in the following terms:

> [O]ffenders display little guilt; their consciences have become identified with the common business ideal of success at any price. Beguiled by the need for success, their fantasies of omnipotence and wealth, indistinguishable from the reality of their financial world, outrun their judgment. On the base of a narcissistic character structure, a dichotomy develops insidiously between practical judgment and daydreams of conquest. Self-advancement through fraud easily enters the hiatus thus created; the transition from successful manipulation to larceny occurs unobtrusively (p. 389).

Some of the foregoing is platitudinous, however fancily dressed in the verbal costume of its discipline. Some is tautological, not useful for prediction. At the same time, though, Bromberg tells us, in a very rare report based on actual contact with white-collar criminals, that their environment is crimino-genic and that its values subtly corrupt. He offers a framework for more precise and detailed social psychological investigation.

Some further insights may be gleaned from parts of the very considerable literature on white-collar crime which caters to public interest in large-scale frauds. Note, for instance, Shaplen's (1960) observation about Ivar Kreuger, one of the most sensational high-finance swindlers of our time: "The more he tempted, the more contemptuous he became of those who gave, and it was this human frailty of his, as much as anything, that ultimately defeated and destroyed him" (Shaplen, 1960, p. 10). In his recent presidential address to the Society for the Psychological Study of Social Issues, Ezra Stotland (1977) stressed the same matter as a particularly promising line of inquiry for psychologists seeking to comprehend white-collar crime and criminals. The offender often makes a fool of his victims, Stotland notes, and the offender's feeling of satisfaction may be increased if victims do not know that they have been swindled. Stotland (1977) also points to laudatory words used to describe some white-collar crime and criminals. We talk of con *artists* and the *sharp* trader; or the *smart* thing to do. We also speak of the *skill* of the defrauder, of his imagination, rather than of his sneakiness.

In Business

The only book-length work by a convicted white-collar criminal who fits into the genre of criminal-authors is that by W. E. Laite, Jr., (1972), a three-time member of the Georgia State Assembly who was sent to prison for failing to pay proper overtime wages to his workers, not fulfilling the terms of a government contract, and stealing or misusing federal property. Laite's response to the situation is self-pitying:

> I felt wronged, mistreated—here I was going into custody several years after the offense had *allegedly* occurred. The punishment seemed unrealistic and severe. I felt I had been punished enough already—by the publicity and harassment, by the financial drubbing that had my family economically drained (p. 23) (italics added).

The remainder of the prison inmates are described by Laite as "foul-mouthed, sadistic riff-raff." He found them "different from me in a very basic and dangerous way." Later, with a note of pride, much like that of a society columnist with a good catch, Laite presents the credentials of other white-collar criminals at the facility to which he was transferred: "Five bank presidents, the president of a life insurance company, and a sheriff from Tennessee. There was also a Catholic priest from Miami" (p. 191).

Willard Gaylin's (1970) fine study of conscientious objectors, made while they were incarcerated, offers a prototype of the kind of study that ought to be conducted with white-collar offenders. Such offenders are accessible, since they generally are placed in special institutions, those that are the most likely to be described in the media as "country clubs." Gaylin observed the poignant difficulties of the war objectors as they sought to reconcile their intense moral convictions with the yawning indifference to such matters within the prisons. Should they continue to protest, rather pointlessly, and lose "good time," or should they capitulate and finish out their sentence as graciously and as quickly as possible? Researchers working with white-collar criminals might locate other kinds of themes that mark the nontraditional offender as he (perhaps) struggles to bring into alignment what he has done, the society's response to it, and his past and present condition and future prospects.

In Politics

The Watergate crimes and the concurrent investigation of Vice President Agnew for accepting bribes spawned considerable public soul-searching among participants in the scandals (cf. Dean, 1976; Magruder, 1974). A report from the Agnew case, documents the transformed psychological set necessary for most of us to perceive white-collar offenders as "real" criminals. Two newspaper reporters note the tactics that federal prosecutors used for this purpose. The nuances within the reporters' own story, which is reproduced below, indicate how skittish they themselves are about confronting directly, as they would for a regular offender, the clear implication that Agnew and his cronies were run-of-the-mill thieves:

> Men under investigation were called "bad men." . . . In a way, the prosecutors employed terms like these to condition themselves for the job at hand—mean, nasty work that often entailed sending a man to jail. It was one thing to dispose of a mugger in that fashion, but quite another when it came to men much like themselves—college-educated, middle class, articulate. These were not street people, but men with roots in the community. The humiliation of jail was total and absolute. It destroyed families, careers, and the men themselves (Cohen & Witcover, 1974, p. 71).

Very little social-psychological research has been devoted to the Watergate and Agnew cases, perhaps because so much has been written in the media that behaviorial scientists believe their observations likely to be redundant, second hand, and/or trite. But these cases provide a voluminous data base that can be reinterpreted with social-psychological constructs. The work of Herbert C. Kelman (1976) offers an excellent example of how such a task might be handled. Kelman seeks "conceptual handles" for understanding "the conditions under which systematic abuses of power become possible and probable" (p. 303). He locates an answer that strikingly resembles that proferred by Bromberg (1965), following his analysis of the case of Richard Whitney:

> Through processes of authorization, the situation becomes so defined that standard moral principles do not apply and the individual is absolved of responsibility to make personal moral choices. Through processes of routinization, the

action becomes so organized that there is no opportunity for raising moral questions and making moral decisions. Through processes of dehumanization, the actor's attitudes toward the target and toward himself become so structured that it is neither necessary nor possible for him to view the relationship in moral terms (Kelman, 1973, p. 38).

The triumvirate of key terms in the analysis receive further elaboration. *Authorization* refers to the idea that "when immoral, criminal, or corrupt acts are explicitly ordered, implicitly encouraged, tacitly approved, or at least permitted by legitimate authorities, people's readiness to commit or condone them is considerably enhanced" (p. 306). Kelman notes that many witnesses before the Senate Watergate committee expressed an orientation to authority based on unquestioning obedience to superior orders. *Routinization* is seen to have two levels, one individual, the second organizational. At the individual level, the job is broken down into discrete steps, most of them carried out in automatic, regularized fashion. At the organizational level, the task is divided among different offices, each of which has responsibility for only a small portion. This arrangement limits the scope of decision-making and diffuses responsibility. Finally, *dehumanization* (as we have seen in Chapter 8), refers to the idea that "targets of action are deprived of their human status so that the principles of morality no longer apply to them" (p. 311). Opponents are defined as "foreign, subversive, and dangerous," not entitled to the protection of sympathy expressed to other human beings. These considerations, taken together, vitiated the capacity of the Watergate conspirators to behave as moral beings, according to Kelman.

What should society do in the face of behavior such as the Watergate crimes and white-collar offenses in general? Kelman pits his scruples opposing punishment against a deeper consideration—"that failure to take action in the face of a great evil—allowing the evil to stand unchallenged and unrighted—is tantamount to acceptance of the evil and thus inherently dehumanizing" (p. 316). On this basis, he opts for some kind of meaningful social retaliation against the offenders, though he is willing to settle for acts of restitution on their part, acts which might "existentially affirm . . . the very principles that the original crime had violated" (p. 316).

WHITE-COLLAR CRIME IN CONTEXT

It is a moot point whether doctors are more or less honest than the average person—or the average professional person—in the United States. What is not arguable is that medical practitioners have been caught in innumerable kinds of white-collar crime, and that their social and vocational positions (Atkinson, et al., 1977) are related to their law-breaking.

Systematic study of medical white-collar crime with a social-psychological focus is nonexistent. One excellent journalistic article (Whitman, 1953) describes widespread law-breaking by doctors, and there is a considerable literature on medical quackery (Young, 1967). Newspapers document relentlessly, almost monotonously, criminal charges against doctors. Medical offenses involve not only financial predation, but also crimes against the person, such as unwarranted surgery, which reasonably might be defined as a form of assault. In addition, as Stotland (1977) has observed, trepidation in government circles about medical fiscal venery undoubtedly has inhibited establishment of a national health service, to the detriment of large segments of the population. It should be noted, in this regard, that the United States lags far behind more than a dozen countries in terms of life expectancy and infant mortality, two sensitive indices of national health (Gross, 1967).

The litany of medical crime need only briefly be sampled to establish its pervasiveness. The American College of Surgeons, for instance, has charged that about half of the operations performed in American hospitals are performed by unqualified doctors, largely because of fee-splitting, under which referring doctors receive an illegal kickback from the doctor performing the surgery (New York Times, October 4, 1961). A 1966 Government lawsuit charged that the 4,500 doctors who own medical laboratories overcharge the public for tests and conspire illegally to keep everyone but themselves out of the medical laboratory business (New York Times, July 7, 1966). In 1970, the Internal Revenue Service said that about half of the 3,000 doctors who received $25,000 or more in Medicare or Medicaid payment failed to report a substantial amount of their income (Wall Street Journal, September 22, 1970). A 1976 study by Cornell University investigators maintained that from 11 to 13 percent of all surgery in the United States is unnecessary, a function of diagnostic incompetence or of greed stemming from the lure of high fees for surgery. There are about 20 million operations performed in the United States annually: the Cornell researchers believed that at least two million or more were unwarranted (New York Times, May 3, 1976). A later survey (New York Times, September 1, 1977) found that the rate of surgery on the poor and near-poor—financed by Medicaid—is twice that for the general population. It was estimated in this survey that the cost of unnecessary surgery in the United States is $3.92 billion.

Three factors offer grounds upon which it might be predicted that medical practitioners would *not* commit illegal acts:

1. Physicians, by reasonable standards, are able to fulfill their personal needs legally. On the basis of the evidence of their white-collar criminality, we can more readily appreciate that greed is not a class-specific trait, but a relative concept emerging from the standards of a person's reference group. We know that upper class individuals jumped from windows during the Depression, though their remaining assets exceeded by far the wherewithal of lower class persons who faced continued existence with equanimity. Cressey's (1953) classic study of embezzlers similarly tells of the "nonsharable problem"—the demand that the person puts upon himself and for which, twist as he may, he cannot find a resolution other than through violation of the criminal law.

2. Physicians, by reasonable standards, appear to have a "proper" up-bringing: good schools, friends, and social advantages. The pleasure of clinical analysis, of course, is that it can retroactively take any life and find within it indications of maladjustment, a father either "too stern" or "too easy going," or even "too normal" in the face of other family conditions. The evidence from physician law violation only further assures us that there is no single set of child-rearing principles that guarantees subsequent conformity to changing social and legal norms.

3. Physicians in training are exposed to professional socialization, a process that emphasizes the interests of others, such as patients, above their own interests. The patent violation of such standards indicated by the roster of criminal acts committed by medical doctors suggests that professional socialization refers, at best, to an ambiguous and oftentimes contradictory collection of attitudes and values (Merton, 1976). Indeed, such attitudes and values, when they mesh with other factors, may be conducive to deviance rather than conformity.

It seems evident that there are very considerable pressures generated in medical practice toward acquisition of wealth. It is because they are such powerful incentives that economic rewards are entrenched in capitalist—and many socialist—countries (Clark & Hollinger, 1977). Firms offer vacations, prizes, and cash bonuses with the reasonable expectation that people will work harder to achieve these carrots.

But such kinds of incentives are not *supposed* to operate as reinforcements for the professional person. Self-aggrandizement is incompatible with the professional orientation. Physicians are not expected to be concerned with their patients' ability to pay bills—what should matter is the nature of their illness and how it best may be cured. This is what is supposed to be taught, along with proper skills to reach the goals. Why, in many cases, doesn't the training produce the results desired?

Socializing Doctors

There have been a number of studies of the process by which young men and women are molded into a professional cadre that shares to a high degree a body of attitudes and values, in regard both to professional matters and toward larger social issues. Studies indicate that medical school provides an encompassing environment in which the subculture of the profession is intensively stressed (Becker, et al., 1961). There is heavy emphasis on the "right way of doing things." In school and in the teaching hospital, faculty and supervisors monitor both professional and personal behavior closely. Technical skills are evaluated; so is the degree to which students have assimilated the professional *role* of physician.

The self-image of the medical student alters as he or she proceeds through training. A study comparing students in each of the four years in the medical school sequence found that 31 percent of the first-year group thought of themselves primarily as physicians, as did 30 percent of the second-year class, and 59 percent of the third-year class. By the fourth year, 83 percent of the graduating cadre had internalized the role model (Huntington, 1957). Particularly interesting were the 17 percent of the seniors who still did not view themselves as "real" physicians. These people had not, as had their fellows, taken on the mantle so assiduously woven for them. With graduation, however, the period of supervision, critique, and control for most medical students is over.

Two of the major settings in which doctors practice their calling can be examined to indicate how pressures toward law-violation swamp the socialization process—the individual or solo practice of medicine, and the autonomous professional organization (R. Hall, 1975, pp. 84–98). In the latter setting, supervision from older physicians may prevail, though hardly to the extent that it existed during the period of the student's education. Whitman's (1953) investigation indicates that, as in the corporate world, group medical practice may impose strong pressures toward law-breaking, since senior personnel already may have established illegal practices, and the newcomer is in a weak position to resist on ethical or other grounds. The ethos of medical work, in addition, even in group practice, tends to inhibit close scrutiny of one's colleagues. Thus, a study by Freidson and Rhea (1965) found that many medical clinic physicians were unable to rate their colleague's level of competence, on the ground that they felt unable or unwilling to judge "good" medical practice in areas of specialty other than their own.

In solo practice, the doctor finds himself virtually without formal supervision and accountability, having been thrust into a business role that only peripherally (if at all) was examined in medical school. Here, to succeed, the doctor must attract and retain patients. Since the attraction of patients takes place in a competitive environment, "enterprise may be more important than medical knowledge and skill" (O. Hall, 1948, p. 329). Carlin (1962), studying lawyers, thought he located the forces pushing the attorney in solo practice into law-breaking, in conditions which offered little freedom of choice of clients, type of work, or conditions of practice. It is not unlikely that some similar combination of factors operate in the same manner for entrepreneurial doctors.

STIGMA AND STATUS

There are, in addition, two particular problems regarding white-collar crime that may be illuminated by insights from the social-psychological literature. These concern (1) how the white-collar offender fails to perceive the seriousness of his act; and (2) how others around the white-collar offender fail to appreciate the acts' seriousness.

1. White-collar offenders usually deny, distort, defuse, or deflect the reasonable interpretations of their criminal behavior. Businessmen, for example, claim that there is a "very fine line" between law violations and acceptable

business practice. Physicians claim that the border between incompetence resulting in an unfavorable malpractice verdict or a criminal charge and reasonable professional judgment is similarly gray. One of the most consistent findings is the essentially noncriminal self-concept of the white-collar offender, regardless of the occupational context in which his behavior takes place (Clinard & Quinney, 1973, pp. 191–192).

There are at least two major reasons for this failure of the offender to think of himself as a criminal, or, in sociological terms, to be "labelled." First, the legal process, with its usual inattention to white-collar crime, reinforces the idea that this is not serious behavior (Dershowitz, 1961). In addition, the offender must undergo a process of dissonance reduction based on the fact that his social roles are valued and "respectable"—community leader, member of the PTA, an Elk, good family provider, respected citizen, on the board of directors of the local hospital, active in the political arena, and so on. Obviously, roles such as these are not consistent with the appellation "criminal." Festinger (1957) suggests that the need to reduce dissonance pushes toward denial of the less-acceptable label; in this instance the offender denies that he or she is indeed a criminal.

2. White-collar crimes do not generate substantial public outrage and concern (Rossi, et al., 1974). Nor are the careers of white-collar offenders much changed if they are prosecuted for law-breaking. Of the fifteen persons who were fired from General Electric in the wake of heavy equipment antitrust prosecutions, twelve were reemployed at higher levels elsewhere (Heilbroner, 1972, p. 36). Within several months after his release from jail, one former G.E. employee was named president of a large corporation (Geis, 1967, p. 115). Some of these persons may have been fearful about their lives after release from incarceration, but their apprehensions were unfounded. Similarly, a study of fifty-eight physicians losing malpractice suits found that none reported negative effects on their practice, and five actually reported an expanded practice. The heaviest financial loser also had the largest gain in practice. He thought that other physicians felt sorry for him and had increased their rate of referrals (Schwartz & Skolnick, 1962).

The unwillingness to stigmatize white-collar offenders is consistent with Heider's (1958) balance theory. Heider posits relationships between two persons and an impersonal entity—an object, idea, or event. If we view criminality as the event, the white-collar offender as one person, and another individual as the third member of the triad, we see the need to balance or reconcile criminality (which would receive a negative evaluation) with the interpersonal bond between the individuals. The offender may be liked by the other, but he has committed a criminal act. Denying the illegality of the act makes the behavior more consistent with previous valuations of the offender. In this manner, a state of congruity can be achieved by the individuals (Osgood & Tannenbaum, 1955).

Another useful perspective is that of social exchange theory (Blau, 1964; Homans, 1974). Interpersonal relations, this theory posits, are a function of the relative costs and rewards that accrue to the participants in a relationship.

Unless certain expectations remain unfulfilled, the rewards persons give one another in the course of social interaction will serve to maintain mutual attraction and continued association (Lott & Lott, 1974). An upper class individual, by virtue of his position, power, and wealth, could be expected to be able to offer more rewards to others, such as gifts, employment, or other tangible things. His status thus insulates him from bearing the full burden of his illegal behavior.

CONCLUDING OBSERVATIONS

There is a parochialism about much behavioral science research. Violence is defined by popular opinion in the United States as street crime, such as mugging, raping, and forms of assault. Psychologists uncritically accept definitions such as this, though it is obvious that some forms of death-dealing violence also involve white-collar criminals—knowingly cutting corners on required safety devices, failing to deliver medical care (Geis & Monahan, 1976). The time seems overdue for social psychology to break some of its ties to the laboratory, to unloose the bonds of parochialism, and to turn more of its professional talents to the investigation of socially significant matters.

A fundamental part of our thesis is that the phenomenon of white-collar crime represents just such a matter.

What sparse research currently exists offers only fragmentary clues about control mechanisms for white-collar crime, while those materials advocating particular preventive tactics, such as the works of the Nader group, tend to be built on unexamined premises. We need to reconcile, for instance, the strong movement for decarceration of many traditional kinds of offenders with the regular calls for imprisonment of white-collar criminals. We do not know whether adequate philosophical or empirical grounds exist to support such a distinction, or whether the distinction is based largely on common anti-business feelings within the academic community, and a general malaise about professionals such as doctors on the part of their patients, based in some measure on public perception of them as "money-hungry" (Haar, et al., 1977).

Paradoxically, social psychological research suggests that if white-collar crime is to be reduced it is essential that it be defined in heavily invidious terms by the public at large and by members of the reference group with whom the offender identifies. It also seems necessary that the rationalizations of the offender be penetrated and that offenders be made to confront less palatable interpretations of what they have done.

Nonetheless, the leverage of tactics concentrating on individual offenders, either for purposes of specific or general deterrence, should not be over-rated. Gurr's (1977) comprehensive survey of crime in four cities—London, Stockholm, Calcutta, and Sydney—over several centuries led him to conclude that it was not matters susceptible to criminological manipulation, such as legislation or penal policy, that bore most directly upon criminal activity, but items of a more abstract and fundamental nature, such as the economic condition of a jurisdiction and its general ethos. This is not to say that short-term and limited improvements cannot be realized in regard to white-collar crime, particularly in regard to its identification and condemnation. It does suggest however, that much criminal activity is responsive to the kinds of things for which we stand. Individualism, hedonism, materialism—these are crimino-genic social values: they may have utility for the production of many social and individual boons; and they may be preferable on some grounds to dif-ferent social emphases. But they have their price, and part of that price clearly appears to be the phenomenon of white-collar crime.

REFERENCES

Alexander, H. E. (Ed.). *Campaign money: Reform and reality in the states.* New York: Free Press, 1977.

Atkinson, P., Reid, M., & Sheldrake, P. Medical mystique. *Sociology of Work & Occupations,* 1977, *4,* 243–280.

Becker, H. S., Geer, B., Hughes, E. C., & Strauss, A. L. *Boys in white: Student cul-ture in medical school.* Chicago: University of Chicago Press, 1961.

Bensman, J., & Gerver, I. Crime and punishment in the factory: The function of deviancy in maintaining the social system. *American Sociological Review,* 1963, *28,* 588–598.

Blau, P. *Exchange and power in social life.* New York: Wiley, 1964.

Bromberg, W. *Crime and the mind.* New York: Macmillan, 1965.

Carlin, J. *Lawyers on their own.* New Brunswick, N.J.: Rutgers University Press, 1962.

Clark, J., & Hollinger, R. On the feasibility of empirical studies of white-collar crime. In R. Meier (Ed.), *Theory in criminology: Contemporary views.* Beverly Hills, Calif.: Sage, 1977.

Clinard, M. B., & Quinney, R. *Criminal behavior systems: A typology* (2d ed.). New York: Holt, Rinehart and Winston, 1973.

Cohen, R. M., & Witcover, J. *A heartbeat away: The investigation and resignation of Spiro T. Agnew.* New York: Viking Press, 1974.

Connor, W. D. *Deviance in Soviet society: Crime, delinquency, and alcoholism.* New York: Columbia University Press, 1972.

Cressey, D. R. *Other people's money.* New York: Free Press, 1953.

Cressey, D. R. Restraint of trade, recidivism, and delinquent neighborhoods. In J. F. Short, Jr. (Ed.), *Delinquency, crime, and society.* Chicago: University of Chicago Press, 1976.

Dean, J. *Blind ambition.* New York: Simon and Schuster, 1976.

Dershowitz, A. M. Increasing community control over corporate crime: A problem in the law of sanction. *Yale Law Journal,* 1961, *71,* 289–306.

Festinger, L. *A theory of cognitive dissonance.* Stanford, Calif.: Stanford University Press, 1957.

Freidson, E., & Rhea, B. Knowledge and judgment in professional evaluation. *Ad-ministrative Science Quarterly,* 1965, *10,* 107–124.

Gaylin, W. *In the service of their country: War resisters in prison.* New York: Gros-sett & Dunlop, 1970.

Geis, G. The heavy electrical equipment antitrust cases of 1961. In M. Clinard & R.

Quinney (Eds.), *Criminal behavior systems*. New York: Holt, Rinehart and Winston, 1967.

Geis, G., & Meier, R. F. (Eds.). *White-collar crime: Offenses in business, politics, and the professions* (rev. ed.). New York: Free Press, 1977.

Geis, G., & Monahan, J. Social ecology of violence. In T. Lickona (Ed.), *Moral development and behavior*. New York: Holt, Rinehart and Winston, 1976.

Green, M. J. *The closed enterprise system*. New York: Grossman, 1971.

Gross, M. L. *The doctors*. New York: Dell, 1967.

Gurr, T. R., Grabosky, P. N., & Hula, R. C. *The politics of crime and conflict*. Beverly Hills, Calif.: Sage, 1977.

Haar, E., Halitsky, V., & Stricker, G. Patients' attitudes toward gynecologic examination and to gynecologists. *Medical Care*, 1977, *15*, 787–795.

Hall, O. Stages of a medical career. *American Journal of Sociology*, 1948, *53*, 327–336.

Hall, R. *Occupations and social structure* (2nd ed.). Englewood Cliffs, N.J.: Prentice-Hall, 1975.

Heider, F. *The psychology of interpersonal relations*. New York: Wiley, 1958.

Heilbroner, R. *In the name of profit*. Garden City, N.Y.: Doubleday, 1972.

Homans, G. *Social behavior: Its elementary forms* (rev. ed.). New York: Harcourt Brace Jovanovich, 1974.

Huntington, M. The development of a professional self-image. In R. Merton, L. Reader, & P. Kendall (Eds.), *The student-physician*. Cambridge: Harvard University Press, 1957.

Kelman, H. C. Violence without moral restraint: Reflections on the dehumanization of victims and victimizers. *Journal of Social Issues*, 1973, *29*, 25–61.

Kelman, H. C. Some reflections on authority, corruption, and punishment: The social-psychological context of Watergate. *Psychiatry*, 1976, *39*, 303–317.

Krebs, A. Richard Whitney, 86, dies; headed stock exchange. *New York Times*, December 6, 1974.

Laite, W. E., Jr. *The United States* vs. *William Laite*. Washington, D.C.: Acropolis Books, 1972.

Lott, A., & Lott, B. The role of reward in the formation of positive interpersonal attitudes. In T. L. Huston (Ed.), *Foundations of interpersonal attraction*. New York: Academic Press, 1974.

Magruder, J. Watergate reflections. *New York Times Magazine*, May 19, 1974, *31*, 103–112.

Maurer, D. W. *The big con*. Indianapolis: Bobbs-Merrill, 1940

Matza, D. *Becoming deviant*. Englewood Cliffs, N.J.: Prentice-Hall, 1969.

Merton, R. *Sociological ambivalence and other essays*. New York: Free Press, 1976.

Nader, R. Preface. In R. Nader & M. Green (Eds.), *Corporate power in America*. New York: Grossman, 1973.

Osgood, C. E., & Tannenbaum, P. H. The principle of congruity in the prediction of attitude change. *Psychological Review*, 1955, *62*, 42–55.

Pearce, F. *Crimes of the powerful*. London: Pluto Press, 1976.

Quinney, R. Occupational structure and criminal behavior: Prescription violations by retail pharmacists. *Social Problems*, 1963, *11*, 179–185.

Quinney, R. *Class, state and crime: On the theory and practice of criminal justice*. New York: McKay, 1977.

Rossi, P., Waite, E., Bose, C., & Berk, R. The seriousness of crimes: Normative structure and individual differences. *American Sociological Review*, 1974, *39*, 224–237.

Schuessler, K. Introduction. In E. H. Sutherland. *On analyzing crime.* Chicago: University of Chicago Press, 1973.

Schwartz, R. D., & Skolnick, J. H. Two studies of legal stigma. *Social Problems,* 1962, *10,* 133–142.

Shaplen, R. *Kreuger: Genius and swindler.* New York: Knopf, 1960.

Smigel, E. O. Public attitudes toward stealing as related to the size of the victim organization. *American Sociological Review,* 1956, *21,* 320–327.

Snodgrass, J. The American criminological tradition: Portraits of the men and ideology in a discipline. Unpublished Ph.D. dissertation, University of Pennsylvania, 1972.

Stotland, E. White-collar crime. Presidential address, Society for the Psychological Study of Social Issues, San Francisco, 1977.

Sutherland, E. H. *Criminology.* Philadelphia; Lippincott, 1924.

Sutherland, E. H. *The professional thief.* Chicago: University of Chicago Press, 1937.

Sutherland, E. H. *White collar crime.* New York: Dryden, 1949.

Sutherland, E. H. *On analyzing crime.* Chicago: University of Chicago Press, 1973.

Sutherland, E. H., & Cressey, D. R. *Principles of criminology* (4th ed.). Philadelphia: Lippincott, 1947.

Sykes, G. M., & Matza, D. Techniques of neutralization: A theory of delinquency. *American Sociological Review,* 1957, *22,* 664–670.

Walker, N. *Behaviour and misbehaviour.* Oxford: Blackwell, 1977.

Whitman, H. Why some doctors should be in jail. *Collier's,* Oct. 30, 1953, *132,* 23–27.

Young, J. H. *The medical messiahs.* Princeton: Princeton University Press, 1967.

chapter 19

The Female Offender

Marguerite Q. Warren

Today it is not at all surprising to pick up a recent journal in the area of crime and delinquency and find an article, or even a series of articles, on female criminality. Research is being conducted, conferences are being held, and books written on the subject. These developments are quite new. As recently as 1967, an extensive study of corrections in the United States was published by the President's Commission on Law Enforcement and the Administration of Justice (a 222-page report) and did not include any reference to the woman offender.

Why this history of past neglect? The reasons most frequently given cite the low official rates of female crime and the fact that female crime is seen as less threatening to society. At least two factors have contributed significantly to the recent arousal of interest in this area: (1) a focus on women's issues arising from the efforts of the women's movement, and more concretely and specifically (2) the increase in female crime.

Before we address the topics of understanding and treating the woman offender, it is important to ask a few questions about that increase in female crime. Is it real? Is it general across crime categories? How does it compare with increases in crime rates for men? Is the phenomenon different for juveniles and adults? A second preliminary topic we must address concerns the manner in which women offenders are now being dealt with by the criminal justice system. A third preliminary question to be addressed involves identifying the characteristics of women offenders and comparing them where appropriate with male offenders. These three preliminary foci cannot be extensive, because the data on women offenders are sparse indeed.

SOME FACTS ON FEMALE CRIME AND THE CRIMINAL JUSTICE SYSTEM[1]

Two types of crime data can be presented here: official data on arrests, convictions, and incarcerations for women; and self-report delinquency data by adolescent girls. In both cases, we can review comparison data for males.

Official Data on Arrests

As reported by the FBI's Uniform Crime Reports, total arrests for adult women increased by 102 percent during the fifteen-year period, 1960–1975 (UCR 1976). For females under age eighteen, the increase was 254 percent. Overall, the increase for property crime (+433 percent) was much greater than for violent crime (+156 percent). For the females under age eighteen, the increase in violent crime (+504 percent) was greater than for property crime (+420 percent). The largest increases during those fifteen years were for larceny/theft (+465 percent, fraud (+488 percent), and narcotics violations (+1,012 percent for total females and +5,378 percent for those under age eighteen). Since the larceny/theft category includes shoplifting, and since the fraud category includes such activities as writing checks on insufficient funds, it has been suggested that these are crimes that women particularly have an opportunity to commit as they engage in their homemaker activities.

Some have argued that the increase in female crime has been considerably exaggerated. Assuming accuracy in the above data, how can this be so? Two points are made in this argument. The first is that, although the female crime rate has increased, it has not increased proportionately any more than the male crime rate in a number of crucial instances. For example, the percentage increase is no higher for women than for men with respect to violent offenses generally (homicide and aggravated assault specifically) and with respect to narcotic violations.

The second point is that the actual numbers and percentages of crimes committed by women are small, compared to men (UCR 1975). For example, of the total 1975 arrests (6,751,545 for men and 1,268,100 for women), women's crime represents less than 16 percent. Only two in ten property crimes are committed by women and only one in ten violent crimes. Only 7 percent of robberies and only 5 percent of burglaries are committed by females. Of the major offense groups, women's crime contributes most to the larceny/theft category (31 percent). This low contribution to the crime rate of a part of the population constituting more than 50 percent of the total remains the most consistent, significant, and unexplained fact in criminology. We shall return to this point later when we talk about theories of causation for women's crime.

Official Data in Court Convictions

Only minimal information is available on the proportion of males and females charged with offenses, who are convicted by the courts. Between 1963 and 1971 the proportion of women we find among individuals convicted in the U.S. District Courts increased gradually from 7 percent to 9 percent, an increase of 30 percent (Hindelang, et al., 1975). Data from the California Bureau of Criminal Statistics show the percentage of females among convictions in California Superior Court between 1966 and 1972 increasing slightly for total crimes (9 percent to 11 percent) and for violent crimes, but property crimes showed a small decrease in proportion of female convictions (from 7 percent to 5 percent) over the time period (Simon, 1975). During the period 1957–1973, there was a steady increase in the proportion of girls (19 percent to 26 percent) among Juvenile Court delinquency dispositions (Hindelang, et al., 1976). The conviction data do not present as clear a picture as the arrest data. However, evidence from both sources suggests the same two conclusions, namely, that women's contribution to the total crime picture has increased somewhat, and women's contribution to the total crime picture is still very low in relation to their proportion in the population. We now ask about women's representation in the incarcerated population.

Official Data on Incarceration Rates

According to a 1972 National Jail Census, only about 6 percent of jail inmates are women, and even these women are held for less serious offenses than men. In the jail setting, women are incarcerated primarily for larceny, drug violations, and a category called "other" (e.g., receiving stolen property, resisting arrest, arson, malicious mischief, gambling) (Goldkamp, 1977).

In 1971, girls represented 30 percent of the juvenile detention population. Of all adjudicated delinquents in custody (in detention and training schools) in 1971, 13 percent were female. Of 6,410 girls in custody, about 70 percent were there for "status" offenses (e.g., incorrigibility, runaway, truancy) (Hindelang, et al., 1975).

At the end of 1976, there were 9,983 women in state and federal prisons, compared with 253,308 men (NPS, 1977), and women represented less than 4 percent of the imprisoned population. This proportion has remained relatively stable for many years. However, the number of women in prisons increased by 15 percent in the year between the ends of 1975 and 1976, while the increase for men was 9 percent. The increase holds for both state and federal institutions, and for all regions of the country.

Self-Report Delinquency Data

Are the lower rates of crime and delinquency among women a reflection of lower levels of delinquent behavior or do they reflect a lower risk of apprehension and/or arrest for illegal conduct? Some answers to this question are available from self-report studies in which adolescents are asked to indicate (usually on an anonymous questionnaire) which of a list of delinquent behaviors they have engaged in within a year's period. The youths may also be asked to indicate the numbers of times they have been involved in each offense category. Studies by Hindelang (1971) and by Williams and Gold (1972) suggest that the higher arrest rate for boys may reflect in part an additional risk of apprehension. Williams and Gold found that, while boys in their study accounted for 70 percent of the self-reported offenses, they accounted for 85 percent of police contacts.

In a more recent study, Feyerherm (1977) reports a picture that is complicated by differences among offense types. Testing a sample of 562 males and 537 female high school students, Feyerherm found:

1. Boys, compared with girls, reported being involved in almost three times the number of thefts.
2. The proportion of thefts committed by boys was even greater when larger theft amounts were reported.
3. Girls confessed to only 20 percent of the car thefts.
4. Less than 9 percent of malicious behavior (property destruction) was reported by girls.
5. Girls reported 15 percent of fights and 19 percent of carrying weapons offenses.
6. More girls than boys reported using heroin and using pills to get high.
7. About the same number of girls as boys said they had used marijuana and psychedelic drugs.

With respect to the relationships between self-reported offenses and risk of apprehension, Feyerherm presents the following information:

1. Ninety-two percent of the males and 78 percent of the female high school students admitted to some delinquent behavior during the previous year.
2. Males who reported delinquencies indicated a greater frequency of delinquencies as well.
3. Thirty-two percent of males and 21 percent of females reported police contacts.
4. Nine percent of males and 4 percent of females reported having been arrested.

Feyerherm did not find clear evidence of a greater risk of apprehension for males. Rather, the risk varied for the sex groups by type of offense.

Self-report data are not available on adults. Also, little of this type of data is available over time so that it is difficult to explore the question of increasing crime by women from the self-report source. However, the evidence from self-report studies supports the evidence from official data that the female contribution to the delinquency picture is low in relation to their proportion in the population. Before discussing hypotheses concerning the meaning of the low female crime rate, some of the (again sparse) information on the characteristics of female offenders must be presented.

CHARACTERISTICS OF THE FEMALE OFFENDER

Most of our information on female offenders comes from descriptions of institutionalized populations. The most extensive study, conducted by Glick and Neto (1976), is based on the female populations of sixteen state prisons, forty-six county jails, and thirty-six community correctional centers. In all, 6,466 women from fourteen states were studied.[2]

According to this study incarcerated women are young; two thirds of the female inmates were under thirty years of age. The median age of misdemeanants was twenty-four and the median age of felons was twenty-seven years. While blacks comprised only 10 percent of the adult female population in the study states, 50 percent of the incarcerated women were black. Indians were also overrepresented, but other minority groups were not. Incarcerated women tended to be less educated than women as a whole; four out of ten women had a high school education or better. At the time of their incarceration, 27 percent of the women were single; 19 percent were nonmarried but had been living with a man, and 20 percent were married, 28 percent were separated or divorced, and 7 percent widowed. Only 56 percent of the women had dependent children living at home prior to incarceration, although 73 percent had actually borne children. The average number of children per inmate mother was 2.48. In 85 percent of the cases, the woman's parents or other relatives took care of the children while the mothers were incarcerated. Husbands provided only 10 percent of all child-care arrangements. Only half of the women came from two-parent homes. Over half of the women had received welfare support during their adult lives and one third had been supported by welfare during childhood. Almost all of the women had worked at some time in their lives; 40 percent had worked in the two months prior to incarceration. Whether or not a woman was working had no bearing on the type of crime she committed.

On twenty-six attitudinal items, women scored higher than expected on self-esteem; for example, 73 percent agreed with the statement: "Compared to other women I haven't done too badly with my life"; 69 percent agreed that "Most people listen to what I have to say." The inmates expressed a desire to work and felt that working was an appropriate female role. However, they supported traditional sex roles, feeling that it is important for women to have children and for men to be the primary support of the family.

Misdemeanants serving one year or less had been convicted in the following proportions: 41 percent for property crimes, 20 percent for drug offenses, and 11 percent for violent crimes. Of convicted felons serving one year or more, 43 percent had been sentenced for violent crimes, 29 percent for property crimes, and 22 percent for drug offenses. Nearly one third of the women had been arrested for the first time at age seventeen or younger. Another half were first arrested between ages eighteen and twenty-four. Almost one third had spent time in juvenile institutions. The women with the most extensive involvement with the criminal justice system were the habitual offenders—prostitutes, drug offenders, and petty thieves.

The most extensive study of juvenile women comes from the California Youth Authority, which has in its custody females from age thirteen to twenty-one. The profile description of the female committed to the CYA is based on 180 individuals committed during 1975. The 1975 population is lowest since before 1960; the commitment rate has been dropping steadily since 1965, when 980 girls were admitted. The commitment rate has also been dropping for males, from more than 5,000 in 1965 to half that number in 1972–1973. Slightly more than 3,000 males were committed in 1975. In the profile that follows, the figures in parentheses represent proportions of males, comparable to those for females (California Youth Authority, 1975).

Of females, 45 percent (for males 43 percent) came from neighborhoods which were below average economically. Only 7 percent (6 percent) lived in neighborhoods considered nondelinquent. At least part of the family income for 37 percent (37 percent) came from public assistance. Only 23 percent (30 percent) came from unbroken homes. Over one half (one half) had at least one parent or sibling who had a delinquent or criminal record. Eight percent (3 percent) were married and 19 percent (6 percent) had children. Slightly over half (68 percent) had five or more delinquent contacts prior to commitment, and 43 percent (57 percent) had previously been incarcerated. The most frequently listed problem for girls was mental or emotional disturbances, which were recorded for 40 percent; the most frequent problem attributed to boys was undesirable peer influences,[3] recorded for 43 percent. Of those in the labor force, 6 percent (13 percent) were employed full time while 85 percent (67 percent) were unemployed. Six percent (10 percent) had graduated from high school, 52 percent (53 percent) had reached the eleventh grade, and 21 percent (20 percent) were last enrolled in the ninth grade or below.

Compared to the male youths, females came from backgrounds which were more disadvantaged. Proportionately more girls had been seriously enough disturbed emotionally to have been subject to psychiatric evaluation or treatment. More of the females had been members of more than one household, and more had lived in five or more different houses since they were born. More of the girls had a record of persistent truancy, and more were reported to have disliked school markedly.

With respect to changes in the female population over time, a 1977 report of the California Youth Authority (CYA) shows yearly changes in the population from 1970 to 1976 (A Comparison of Admission Characteristics of YA Wards, 1970–1976). The proportion of females committed for violent offenses has risen from 14 percent to 43 percent, those committed for property offenses, from 14 percent to 31 percent. Drops have occurred in status offenses and narcotics violations. The proportion using weapons in their offenses increased from 9 percent to 27 percent. These data give the clear impression that the average severity represented by a 1976 case is much greater than for a 1970 case. The same picture holds for males. These changes are obviously related to the drop in populations that are committed. The less serious cases are now being handled in county probation departments using state funds provided as probation subsidies. Since a change in policy and procedure, rather than a change in characteristics of the offender population, is involved here, we cannot say that records of the female population have increased in severity over time. The present cases may be as serious as the most serious cases of a decade ago. We can say, however, that records of the current CYA female population are as serious as those of the current CYA male population (comparable proportions of violent offenses, and only slightly fewer prior offenses and weapons used by females).

In summary of the factual picture of female crime and criminals, several points can be made: (1) female crime is increasing, especially in the larceny/theft category; (2) the increase in crime by females under age eighteen is greater than for adult women, especially for the most serious crimes (homicide, aggravated assault, robbery, burglary); (3) in spite of the increase in numbers of crimes committed by females, these crimes continue to represent a very low proportion of the total crime picture; (4) women represent an even smaller proportion of the incarcerated population than their proportion among arrests would suggest; (5) many female juvenile offenders (compared with males) come from unstable family situations and are described as having emotional problems.

Now, we turn to a number of theories of crime causation to see how these theories fit the data on female crime.

CAUSAL THEORIES OF FEMALE CRIME

As we review a number of crime causation theories, we will note that some theories have been presented as though they apply generally (i.e., to both males and females), but they appear to have been applied only to males. Other theories have been developed specifically to explain male offense behavior, or specifically to explain female offense behavior. Still others have focussed on males but, as an afterthought, seem equally applicable to females. We will also ask as we look at the theories whether each tries to account for the differences in male and female crime rates or speaks to the increasing female crime rate.

Comments on the differences between patterns and manifestations of male and female deviance began early in the history of criminology. Quetelet (1842) noted that in France between 1826 and 1830, there were twenty-three female to every one hundred male criminals, and said:

> Now, the reason why females have less propensity to crime than males, is accounted for by their being more under the influence of sentiments of shame and modesty, as far as morals are concerned; their dependent state, and retired habits, as far as occasion or opportunity is concerned; and their physical weakness, so far as the facility of acting is concerned. I think we may attribute the differences

observed in the degree of criminality to these three principal causes. Sometimes the whole three concur at the same time: we ought, on such occasions, to expect to find their influence very marked, as in rapes and seductions; thus, we have only one woman to 100 men in crimes of this nature. In poisoning, on the contrary, the number of accusations for either sex is nearly equal. . . . If we attempt to analyze facts, it seems to me that the difference of morality in man and woman is not so great as it is generally supposed . . . (1812 translation, p. 91).

Biological and Psychological Theories

The first book specifically concerned with the etiology of female crime was written by Lombroso in 1903 (Chapter 6). As with his theories of male crime, Lombroso saw some female crime as based on inborn tendencies; however, Lombroso's "born criminal" who was female was limited to prostitution, with "most female criminals only criminals from accident or passion" (1911, p. 406). Thus, although Lombroso is best known for his belief that inborn tendencies cause crime, he suggested that other factors were predominant. He saw susceptibility to male suggestions as particularly important in infanticide and abortion, eroticism as important in poisoning and homicide, excessive temptation in shoplifting, parental neglect and desertion in early thieving and prostitution. In explaining the lower crime rate for women, Lombroso agreed with Quetelet that women's life style and lower strength limited crime opportunities. In addition, he suggested that prostitution largely takes the place of crime for women, thus explaining why women seem less criminal than men (1911, p. 192).

In books entitled *Sex and Society* (1907) and *The Unadjusted Girl* (1923), W. I. Thomas continued the biological theme, but also added psychological and social factors to explanations of female crime. His idea that female physiology results in "natural female roles" (passive and nurturing) continues in some current work. Freud is given credit for the development of the anatomy-is-destiny theme. He suggested that deviant women of any kind are rebelling against their sex role, being aggressively rebellious, driving, and ultimately neurotic (Jones, 1961). Thomas, applying this idea specifically to female crime, believed that criminal behavior resulted from a perversion of or rebellion against natural feminine roles. The middle class woman, according to Thomas, commits little crime because she is socialized to sublimate her natural desires. The lower class woman, however, is amoral, behaving criminally through the desire for excitement and new experiences (1923, p. 98).

The Criminality of Women by Otto Pollak, published in 1950, is one of the few major works on female criminality. Pollak used and expanded on the "iceberg" theory of Lombroso. Little female crimes show, the theory goes, because most of it is "hidden." According to Pollak, women are both biologically equipped to dissemble and are socialized into doing so (such as by concealing menstruation or pretending orgasm in the sex act). Thus, their part in crime often remains undiscovered and goes unrecorded. Women act as instigators rather than perpetrators of criminal activity.

Recent work along these themes has continued. Konopka (1966) and Vedder and Somerville (1970) comment on the instigatory role girls play in boys' activities (e.g., gang fights). Konopka suggests that girls are emotionally different from boys, and that emotional problems (loneliness and dependency) drive girls to delinquency. Vedder and Somerville, as well as Konopka, view female delinquency as a result of blocked access or maladjustment to the normal feminine role.[4]

Of the works described above, Quetelet and Lombroso were very data-oriented. As such, they tried to explain one of the most obvious facts they found in their data, the difference in crime rates for the two sexes. Their explanations involved both biological and social determinism. Pollak also tried to interpret crime rate differences. He saw an artifact at work in which much crime committed by females went unreported or unpunished by a chivalrous criminal justice system (1950, p. 151). Thomas, Konopka, and Vedder and Somerville were more interested in making theoretical statements concerning the nature and meaning of female crime than in accounting for crime rates.

Sociological Theories

During the period 1920–1970, sociologists were conducting major research projects on male adolescent delinquents. During this time, what were they thinking about female crime? The answer is "not much." The sociological crime causal theories, called Strain theories (described in Chapter 7), suggest that crime results from the discrepancies between an acceptance of the goals of a materialistic society and an inability to achieve those goals through legitimate means. The subjects of research in this group of theories have been primarily male adolescents. One study by Datesman, Scarpitti, and Stephenson (1975) assessed *perceived* opportunity, using samples of female as well as male delinquents and nondelinquents. Delinquent girls perceived their opportunities in life as relatively circumscribed compared to nondelinquent girls, and compared to both delinquent and nondelinquent boys.

Strain theories were not created to explain male/female differences in crime rates. Nor was there a specific claim that the theories explained female crime. However, we can ask whether the theory is consistent with the facts. Since females in our society can be expected to be as highly oriented toward materialistic goals as males, and since women appear to have less in the way of legitimate opportunities for achieving those goals, the "strain" should be greater for women than for men. Thus the female crime rate should be higher than the male crime rate. Clearly, this inference is at odds with the facts.

Subcultural deviance theories (see Chapter 7) suggest that cultures are deviant and that individual offenders simply behave in ways which their subculture prescribes. For example, Walter Miller's (1958) theory interprets lower class delinquency as arising from a direct expression of several focal concerns (values) of lower class or working class individuals and groups. The focal concerns include trouble, smartness, excitement, fate, toughness, and autonomy. Miller specifically mentions that the first four of these concerns apply to both lower class males and females. Females are not mentioned in connection with the focal concerns of toughness and autonomy. In a recent monograph on gang violence (1975), Miller indicates that 90 percent or more of youth gang activity is a male enterprise. Females participate primarily as "auxiliaries." Female gangs are rare and commit less serious crime, according to Miller. There is no suggestion in Miller's work that lower class females belong to a different subculture than lower class males or that there is any reason to expect different focal concerns. Thus, no explanation for the lower female crime rate is presented by Miller.

Social Psychological Theories

Control theory, as represented by Hirschi (1969) (see Chapter 7), is a social psychological perspective that is built around the idea that individuals are deterred from crime by their bonds to society; by their attachments to parents and friends, commitments to conventional organizations and behaviors, involvements in legitimate activities, and beliefs in a law-abiding society. In order for this theory to help us understand the facts on female crime, one would have to argue that females are more strongly bonded to society in terms of some or all of these components. Is there any evidence for such an argument? Fortunately, Hirschi included both sexes in his studies of juvenile delinquents and nondelinquents in a California school system. Based on questionnaire data, Hirschi found, for example, that, compared with boys, girls report more often that their mother and father know where they are and who they are with when they are away from home; girls like school better, care more what their teachers think of them; girls spend more time sitting around talking with friends and parents, work more around the house; girls more often say they are willing to report crime, have more respect for the police (Wilson, Hirschi, & Elder, 1965). All of these items would suggest a stronger bonding for females, and thus, a lower female crime rate would be predicted. With respect to the issue of the increasing female crime rate, no data are available to indicate a change in bonding strength or prevalence since Hirschi's study (1969).

A number of both sociological and psychological theories have considered self-image to be a useful concept in thinking about delinquency causation. Several questions have been raised: What is the relationship between self esteem and delinquency? Does a difference in self-esteem exist for males and females and, if so, how does it relate to the difference in crime rates? Does a person's self-description have some relevance for our understanding of delinquency?

In a statement of containment theory, Reckless and Dinitz (1967) suggested that individuals are protected against being deviant by both outer and inner controls. Outer constraints are the social pressures to obey the norms of one's group. As for inner controls, "components of self-strength, such as favorable concept of self, act as an inner buffer or inner containment against deviancy" (1967, p. 515). Dinitz, Dynes, and Clarks (1969, p. 187) also maintain that "there is a tendency for deviants to develop negative conceptions of themselves." Jensen (1972) has provided support to this position, finding self-reported delinquency and self-esteem persistently negatively related. Jensen, however, also points to the wide variation in the magnitude of the relationship; for example, for black males, the higher the social status, the greater the tendency for delinquency to be negatively related to self-esteem.

The previously mentioned Datesman, Scarpitti, and Stephenson study (1975) measured self-concept in large samples of male and female delinquents and nondelinquents, using Osgood's semantic differential scales. They found that delinquents of both sexes exhibited a somewhat more negative evaluation of self than their respective nondelinquent counterparts (p. 111). However, when looking at sex and racial groups separately, the researchers found different results for black and white females; black female delinquents had significantly lower self-esteem than black nondelinquents, while there was no difference for white delinquent and nondelinquent females. The authors suggest as a possible interpretation of these racial differences the fact that the present and past delinquency records of the black females were more severe than those of the white females.

There seems, then, to be some evidence that self-esteem and delinquency are negatively related, although the size of the relationships may vary for sex, race, and social class groups. What is less clear is whether a negative self-concept contributes to delinquency, or whether delinquency contributes to a negative self-concept, or both.

Do males and females have different levels of self-esteem in a direction which would help explain crime rate differences? The data here are inconsistent. Jensen (1972) used two items from the Richmond Youth Project Questionnaire (Wilson, et al., 1965) as a measure of self-esteem; these items are, "At times I think I am no good at all," and "I certainly feel worthless at times." To these can be added an additional items from the same study: "On the whole, I am satisfied with myself." These items show no significant sex differences and, even the small differences which appear, are not in a consistent direction.

Johnson (1973), using the Tennessee Self-Concept Scale, showed delinquent boys to have more self-esteem than delinquent girls. The Datesman, et al. data (1975) show both delinquent and nondelinquent female groups to have higher self-esteem than the comparable male groups, with the findings applying equally to black and white subjects. If an association generally exists between high self-esteem and nondelinquency, we should expect to find females having a lower crime rate, an expectation consistent with the data.

One can raise a number of issues concerning the content of the person's self-definition and its relationship to delinquency. One of these issues involves whether or not the person defines himself/herself as a person likely to get into trouble. In an early statement of containment theory, Reckless, Dinitz, and Murray (1956) suggested that individuals who are socialized into a perception of self as a person not likely to get into trouble would be protected from delinquency, even in a high delinquency neighborhood. One can further ask whether males and females define themselves differentially in terms of delinquency potential. The questionnaire used in the Richmond Youth Project (Wilson, et al., 1965) included three items relevant to this question: (a) Do you ever think of yourself as a "delinquent"? (b) Does anyone else ever think of you as a "delinquent"? (c) Being sent to juvenile court would bother me a lot (agree/disagree). All three of these items showed large differences in favor of nondelinquency self-definitions for female subjects.

To ask where self-images come from is too big a question for us to consider here. However, it is worth mentioning that Schwartz and Baden (1973) applied containment theory to females to determine the relative influence of peers versus adults on self-concepts of adolescents. For girls identified as potentially deviant, the significant influence was peers, while mother and teacher were the significant influences for girls not identified as potentially deviant. If peers represent the reference group for self-definition of potentially delinquent girls, then another study is worth mentioning. Morris (1965) found that delinquent behavior is relatively more accepted by peers for males than for females, and that female delinquency is generally regarded more critically than male delinquency by delinquents and nondelinquents of both sexes. One could conclude that potentially nondeviant girls have reference figures (mother and teacher) that will discourage delinquency; and that potentially deviant girls may well have their delinquency reduced by the disapproval of their reference figures (peers). And this, of course, is consistent with our low female crime rate.

In considering the content of self-definitions, one other study is worth describing. Bertrand (1969), in an extensive study in four countries, found that the "normal" role pattern for males includes permission to engage in a certain amount of illegal behavior and that the "normal" role pattern for females does not permit such behavior. The assumption follows that the male who commits an offense will not necessarily see himself as deviant while "society requires that women do" (p. 74). Bertrand's study was a creative attempt to measure George Herbert Mead's theory of self-development (1934). Mead thought of the process of socialization involving an inner dialogue between the I and the Me. The I enables us to take the attitudes of others. By doing so, the orientations of these others are internalized in the form of a Me. This enables us to see ourself as an object and thus to evaluate ourselves. Bertrand suggests that, because of the cultural emphasis on passivity in women, it is the Me dimension of the self, or the self as object, which characterizes self-concepts of females and the I dimension, or the self as agent, which characterizes male self-concepts. In support of this hypothesis, Bertrand found that both delinquent and nondelinquent males saw themselves as agent more than did delinquent or nondelinquent females. She also hypothesized that the female delinquent would be the person most likely to perceive herself as acted upon and as victim. Although Bertrand did not find sex differences in all of her comparison samples, when significant differ- .

ences did appear for the two sexes, they were in the predicted direction; for example, 75 percent of Anglo-Canadian female delinquents and only 45 percent of male delinquents viewed themselves as object. It is unclear how these findings translate into predictions of differential crime rates. One could argue that males, with higher perceptions of self as agent, may actively look for crime opportunities, and that females, not looking for these opportunities, are still from time to time pushed into delinquency.

How well do the various crime causal perspectives stand up vis-à-vis the data on female crime? Of contemporary perspectives, only control theory leads to direct predictions of lower female crime rates. In addition, there are some aspects of self-concept and socialization theory that seem relevant to differential crime rates. If there is a high social expectation that females will not get into trouble with the law, self-perceptions of females should certainly reflect this view. Assuming that self-perception is related to behavior, we are led to an accurate prediction of crime rate differences.

Writing from a socialization perspective, Hoffman-Bustamante (1973) made an admirable attempt to integrate this perspective with the data on female crime. She suggests that the lower female crime rate is an outcome of five major factors:

1. From an early age males and females face different role expectations. Girls are expected to be conforming and boys are often rewarded for flaunting controls.

2. There are sex differences in the applications of social control, with girls more closely supervised and more strictly disciplined.

3. There are structurally determined differences in opportunities to commit particular offenses. Males are more likely to be familiar with weapons through childhood toys, hunting activities, experience in the military, and so on. Males are also more likely, through their ordinary activities, to have knowledge of appropriate places to rob.

4. There is differential access or pressures toward criminally oriented subcultures and careers. Time spent on the street by males brings knowledge of delinquent activity. Skills learned in street settings bring potential membership in subcultural groups.

5. Sex differences are built into crime categories. For example robbery is defined as theft which takes place in the presence of the victim and involves the taking of property by force or threat. These offense characteristics mean that males are better prepared to accomplish the proscribed act.

According to Hoffman-Bustamante, all of these five factors illustrate the close relationship between crime and learned sex roles, and contribute to the lower crime rate for women.

With respect to the increasing crime rate for women, none of the theoretical perspectives we have described attempt to account for the phenomenon. In the writings which express the current and increasing interest in female crime (e.g., Simon, 1975; Adler, 1975), one frequently hears the two themes: As opportunities become more equal between men and women, crime will become more equal also; as women become subject to the same stresses and strains to which men are subjected, they will respond in a comparable way. These themes suggest that women are not basically more virtuous than men (a suspicion Quetelet had back in the 1830s), and that current and future changes in the status of women may mean a decreasing discrepancy between the crime rates of the two sexes. Although the logic of these themes is appealing, it is important to remind ourselves that, although the female crime rate is increasing, so is the male crime rate. The decreasing discrepancy between the male and female rates is a fact which may in part be explained by the changing status of women; however, it is clear that other explanations are needed to explain the crime increase for both sexes.

UNDERSTANDING AND TREATING THE FEMALE OFFENDER

It is the nature of most causal theories that they tend to propose a single or very small number of invariable conditions which lead to crime. This characterization fits most of the theoretical perspectives we have discussed. An exception to this is the first theorist we mentioned, Cesare Lombroso (1911). Having noted a variety of causes of female crime, Lombroso suggested a variety of remedies. For crimes that he thought were committed at the suggestion of men (e.g., abortion, infanticide), Lombroso's proposed remedy consisted of separating men and women. For minor offenses, Lombroso thought a reprimand would suffice. For serious crimes (e.g., poisoning, swindling, homicide), Lombroso suggested that women be "confined in a convent where, on account of their great susceptibility to suggestion, religion could be substituted for the eroticism that is the most frequent cause of their crimes" (p. 406). Lombroso had one other suggestion. Since women are so vain, he noted, their hair could be cut off as a penalty.

Although we might not agree with Lombroso's suggested causes nor with his treatments, the idea of differential causes and therefore differential remedies seems a sensible one. In Chapter 7, we tried to show the differential appropriateness of various causal theories for various offenders. We did not suggest that one needs a different theory for each offender in order to understand the meaning of the individual's offense behavior, but that a classification of individuals according to the causal dimensions of greatest relevance to them would be a way of recognizing that offender populations are heterogeneous with respect, not only to the crimes they commit, but also the reasons for those crimes.

The concepts of differential appropriateness of causal theories and of the need to classify offenders for purposes of matching offender characteristics with type of treatment, are as relevant for a female as a male population. Women, like men, commit crimes for a variety of reasons. We can assume that personal differences in the meaning of the offense will be relevant to understanding the offender, predicting future behavior, and intervening in the offender's life in a useful way. Although there is considerable research evidence regarding the importance of viewing crime causation and intervention programs differentially,[5] very little of this research has been done with female offender populations. The research reported in earlier sections of this chapter was useful in telling us about crime rates and characterizations of female offenders as reflected in their life situations. But it provided little information about the varieties of motivational and behavioral patterns to be found in a population of serious offenders, and it is these factors which are crucial to understanding and treating individual women.

For information on the varieties of motivational patterns in female offenders, we will use the sources of data to be found in a treatment project conducted in the California Youth Authority from 1961–1969 (Palmer, 1974). Almost 250 female offenders (and more than eight hundred male offenders) were studied in this project for a minimum of two years each. More than half of the females (and males) were in intensive treatment in a community-based program (experimental cases). Randomly assigned comparison cases went through the agency's training schools. Both the experimental and comparison subjects were seen regularly by researchers, who followed their progress. All of the youths were classified in such a way as to identify the reasons for their delinquency. From this causal pattern, goals of treatment for experimental subjects were specified and an intervention strategy was prescribed.

The girls in the project (called the Community Treatment Project or CTP) ranged in age from thirteen to eighteen at intake, averaging about sixteen and a half. Almost all the girls stayed in the program until they were eighteen, some until they were twenty-one. The delinquent histories of the girls, and their personal and family backgrounds, were much like those of the total female California Youth Authority population described early in this chapter (p. 449).

The classification system used in CTP subdivided the youths into three categories of social maturity based primarily on an assessment of the complexity of each individual's perceived world. Following this classification step, the youths were further subdivided within Maturity Levels into subtypes, totaling nine categories in all (Warren, et al., 1966).

Early in the Community Treatment Project, staff wondered whether the same typology could be applied to both males and females. As it turned out, the classification system, like other specifications of stages of social growth and development,[6] proved equally applicable to both sexes. Girls as well as boys were classified in each of the nine categories. However, the proportion of the two sexes placed in each category and at the three Maturity Levels differed. The lowest Maturity Level included 4 percent of the males and only 1 percent of the females; the middle Maturity Level comprised 32 percent of the males and only 21 percent of the females; and the highest Maturity Level, 64 percent of the males and 79 percent of the females. It seemed that the average female delinquent perceives a more complex world than the average male delinquent.[7]

When the subtypes within each Maturity Level are considered, several differences prove striking. The first of these involves two subtypes of youths who are highly peer group- or gang-oriented. The subtype called Cultural Conformist (at the middle Maturity Level) and the subtype called Cultural Identifier (at the higher Maturity Level) includes a moderate percentage of boys and almost no girls (only 3 percent for both subtypes combined). The absence of the Cultural delinquents among the girls is consistent with the picture painted by subcultural theorists like Miller (1958); compared with males, females are less aligned with delinquent peers, less comfortable with a delinquent identity, and less committed to delinquent values and perspectives. The finding is also compatible with Morris' conclusion that the adolescent peer group is more disapproving of female than of male delinquency (1965).

An additional striking difference between the subtype proportions for males and females involves two of the subtypes at the highest Maturity Level. The Conflicted (or neurotic) subtypes include a much higher proportion of the girls' population than of the boys'. We will begin with a view of this group as we consider the most frequently occurring subtypes among female delinquents. The three subtypes that are found most often among female delinquents are entitled Conflicted, Power-Oriented, and Passive Conformist. We shall describe each of these groups, noting its motivational and behavioral patterns. Because Hirschi's control theory held up well in handling the crime rate data, each subtype can be considered in terms of bonds to society. In addition, since self-concept appears to be a useful construct in understanding female delinquency, each of the three subtypes must be explored along these dimensions. We shall also present brief descriptions of the treatment programs that were developed for each type of delinquent in CTP. Although we make no claim that these treatment plans are the only possible ones, or even those that would prove most successful, the plans are worth describing because the success rates for girls in CTP were very high, absolutely, and in comparison with the randomly assigned girls who went through the traditional Youth Authority program (as well as in comparison with both experimental and comparison boys). For example, within sixty months of program entry, 91 percent of experimental girls had received a favorable discharge from the agency (as opposed to 78 percent of comparison girls) and no experimental girl had received an unfavorable discharge (as opposed to 17 percent of comparison girls).

The Conflicted Female Offender

Almost three fourths of the CTP girls were classified as Conflicted. Other studies have also found a high proportion of neurotic female delinquents (e.g., Chwast, 1971; Cloninger and Guze, 1970; D'Orban, 1972; Hammer and Ross, 1977; Johnson, 1973). In some classification systems, this group is usually called "neurotic" for reasons we will shortly describe.

Females who are classified in the Conflicted category have reached a stage of social maturity where they operate from an internalized value system which they use to judge themselves and others, to model themselves after persons they respect, to understand cause and effect relationships, to perceive needs and motives in others, to accept the concept of accountability for one's own behavior, and so on. But in addition, as the label Conflicted suggests, individuals so classified have a good deal of internal wear-and-tear involving anxiety, guilt, a "bad me" self-image, "negative life script," distorted perceptions, and dysfunctional behavior. Delinquency has some private meaning and does not represent simply a material gain or a response to cultural pressure. It may involve the acting out of a family problem, an identity crisis, or a long-standing internal conflict.

It is important to distinguish two subgroups of the Conflicted category because of some major treatment-relevant differences. The "anxious" subtype (44 percent of CTP girls) shows a number of symptoms of emotional disturbance such as chronic or intense depression or anxiety, or psychosomatic complaints. The tensions and fears of these girls usually result from conflicts produced by feelings of failure, inadequacy, or underlying guilt. The "acting-out" subtype (29 percent of CTP girls) has little tolerance for conscious anxiety and often attempts to deny (to herself and others) feelings of inadequacy, rejection, or self-condemnation. They may do this by verbally attacking others, by using boisterous distractions, by playing a variety of "games," and so on.

Girls in this category are often openly hostile to their mothers and sometimes explain their delinquency as an attempt to give their mothers a bad time. One Conflicted girl says that she prostitutes because that is the thing which will give her mother the most trouble. A fourteen-year-old Conflicted girl, whose baby had been taken away from her at her mother's insistence, now reports having sex with every available man; she says, "I just lie there saying, 'I hope I get pregnant, I hope I get pregnant.'" A girl who has a record of credit card forgeries, only shops at the best stores and buys the most elegant clothes because her mother is so "dowdy."

Anger and resentment at the mother seem less conscious in other cases. For some teenage girls, a role-reversal has been going on with the mother for many years; that is, the daughter has been taking care of mother and her emotional problems since the daughter has been quite young. This caretaker role sometimes begins when the father leaves the home; the daughter attempts to play the responsible-father role, cannot handle the assignment, gives up, and becomes delinquent.

Conflicted youth are typically from neurotic families in which at least one of the parents also carries a great deal of guilt and a "bad me" self-image. Family life is characterized by poor communication, "skeletons in the closets," and a feeling on everyone's part that other family members are not meeting (unspoken) expectations. Often, the delinquent youth seems to be bearing the family burden or making a rescue attempt. The primary feeling which permeates the family is one of ambivalence—members care about each other but also feel that they are not cherished and have somehow been hurt. Thus, the bonds to society which grow out of attachments to parents are weakened or take on a now-and-then quality.

With respect to other bonds to society—commitments to conventional organizations, involvements in legitimate activities and law-abiding beliefs— the Conflicted girl is typically prosocial. She can usually do well in school and seems to prefer conventional activities. When she behaves delinquently, she violates her own beliefs, thus having a continuing basis for her guilt and "bad me" image. This picture of bonds to society is complicated, but one can at least say that some of the bonds are weak or operating only intermittently.

The self-concept of the Conflicted girl seems to have two major parts. Although she does not think of herself as delinquent, she often thinks of herself as crippled, hurt, inferior, or inadequate. On the other hand, she also presents a compensatory image of actual or potential worthiness or accomplishment. The combination does not provide, in any stable way, "an inner buffer against deviancy," such as Reckless and Dinitz (1967) propose as a protective control.

The most important treatment element for the Conflicted offender seems to be a well-matched treater. Ideal treater characteristics include an ability to accept and not be frightened by the neurotic process, an ability to see through the defensive process, an ability to recognize the often-concealed real strengths and accomplishments of the offender, and the willingness to serve as an observable model (i.e., to have a degree of openness about self, and true self-respect). In addition to these general characteristics, the treater who has greatest success with the openly anxious subtype emphasizes introspection rather than action, and focusses treatment and discussion on feelings of anxiety, guilt, anger, aggression, sex, fantasies, and so on. The relationship between the treater and the girl is personalized but somewhat formal, especially in the early stages of treatment. The treaters believe that increased self-respect and feelings of gratification will come from honestly struggling with the presenting problems.

A number of differences exist between the successful treater of the Conflicted-anxious and the Conflicted-acting-out offender. Because girls in the acting-out subgroup prefer to reveal very little of themselves and because attempts to outrun the anxiety are common, therapy is often conducted on-the-run. Treaters are careful not to threaten the individual's need for feelings of autonomy. The treaters offer frequent opportunities for communication while not challenging the individual's stance of being in little need of help. When the girl finally accepts the treater as an "unusual" authority figure who does not want to control her totally, the offender may finally turn to the treater as a resource. At this point, the most effective stance for the treater to take is not to concentrate on the girl's behavior (which is often aimed at being distracting) but rather on the meaning of her behavior. What is the offender trying to communicate with her behavior? Opportunities for greatest progress in treatment occur around crises, which the acting-out subtype often encounters. In these situations the treater can demonstrate for the offender the treater's noncontrolling strength, openness, and concern.

With respect to the treatment modalities which seem most appropriate for Conflicted offenders, we have already implied a great deal when we talked about treater characteristics. Early in the relationship with the anxious subtype, and later in the relationship with the acting-out subtype, either individual or group psychotherapy can be used successfully. Treatment groups, including both the anxious and acting-out subtypes, had some success in CTP. Both the groups and the individual sessions had the conventional psychotherapeutic intent of increasing the girl's insight into her own dynamics and developing her coping skills. Family group therapy was used with some success in a few cases where the family was available and was willing to participate. The minimum goal here was to allow the family problem to be removed from the shoulders of the girl.

Typically, Conflicted girls were not able to live with either of their parents. In the community-based program, they were placed in foster homes and group homes. These homes did not try to provide substitute parents—rather, the adults in the homes were chosen because they were good listeners, an activity in which they often engaged far into the night.

At an earlier point in this book (Chapter 11), we have discussed the treatment of the neurotic offender, noting that the result might be the substituting of a neurotic nondelinquent for a neurotic delinquent. The Community Treatment Project, as one branch of a state correctional agency, was certainly committed to reducing or eliminating delinquency among the individuals assigned to it. But, in the case of the Conflicted offender, it was held that the neurosis was the heart of the behavior problem, and treatment goals listed for the Conflicted subtypes included: " . . . reduction or resolution of internal conflicts; reduction of fear of own needs and impulses, and of use of defense mechanisms in harmful ways (to self or others); changed self-image in direction of capacity for enjoyment and happiness . . . , sense of personal worth and of potential worth (as a mature person) to others. . . ." For the high proportion of Conflicted girls who did well in and following the CTP program, important factors seemed to be a disengagement from family problems, the availability of a strong and caring female identification figure (the treater), and improved self-esteem.

The Power-Oriented Female Offender

The second most frequently occurring subtype in the female delinquent population (14 percent) is called Power-oriented or Counteractive. In other classification systems, this kind of offender is sometimes called psychopathic or sociopathic (Chapter 14).

Delinquents who are classified in the Power-oriented category have reached a stage of social maturity in which they underestimate the differences among others and between themselves and others, underestimate the complexity of others, do not operate from an internalized value system but rather seek external structure in terms of rules and formulas for operation, perceive the world and their role in it along a power dimension. In addition, as the terms power-oriented and counteractive suggest, the person classified in this category is often aggressively counteractive to power, attempting to undermine or circumvent the intent of authority figures. Typically, such persons do not wish to conform to standards set by anyone else and often attempt to take on a power role for themselves. Persons in this subtype do not have close or trusting relationships with others. They usually try to create an image of emotional indifference, imperturbability, and invulnerability. Sometimes, especially under stress, they appear openly angry and threatening. They are often described by correctional staff, who try to control them, as resentful, persistently annoying due to crude efforts at being the center of attention, verbally and/or physically explosive, suspicious, and/or grandiose in their thinking.

Girls in this group seem to pride themselves on their ability to successfully manipulate or outsmart others. One Power-oriented girl married at age nineteen a man of a race other than her own because her father "will hate that." She reported that she bugs her husband until he slaps her and then she calls the police. In fact, her husband has been in jail a number of times for this reason. On her most recent visit to the jail to see her husband, the guards told her that he tried to commit suicide. She couldn't help smiling as she talked about how much power she had over her husband.

Other girls in this category may not be quite so emotionally damaged as the girl described above. Yet most of them come from homes with a cold, brutal, and rejecting father, and a weak, helpless, and superficial mother. The front of invincibility and toughness which this type of girl uses frequently turns out to be a cover-up (of which she is rarely conscious) for long-standing and extremely intense fears of and primitive dependence on the abusive parent.

The protective attachments to family are missing; the girl is contemptuous of the mother and hates and fears the father. The extent of the distrust of others means that peer attachments are also not available. The manipulativeness and unwillingness to conform leads to rejection for this type of girl in school and in youth agencies. And there is no belief system which disallows delinquency. The absence of bonds to society is most clear-cut in this type of offender. The Power-oriented girl defines herself as cynical, "cool," smooth, delinquent, powerful, invulnerable—a definition which is in no way at odds with offense behavior.

Treatment goals for this type of girl include a reduction in fear of control by responsible adults; a reduction in fear of close, nonsuperficial relationships; a change in self-definition in the direction of real (vs. imagined) competence; and an increase in social perceptiveness. A well-matched treater is important in trying to achieve these goals. Treaters who work well with the Power-oriented girl understand the dependency needs that underlie the compensatory "I am cool" facade. But the focus of the treatment is external. The treater exerts friendly but firm parental control, implying that the girl is worth controlling. The treater acts promptly to deal with manipulation attempts, makes definitive decisions, and acts upon them with high self-confidence. The treater listens for signs of honest communication and rewards these immediately, as well as rewarding any movement in the direction of treatment goals. The treater's initial stance is formal and impersonal; only late in the treatment can the treater, without threat to the youth, offer open emotional support and affection.

In CTP, treatment groups which emphasized the interpersonal interactions within the group in a here-and-now fashion were used with Power-oriented girls. In some instances coed groups, with a male and female therapist, were utilized. Group meetings were frequent and mandatory early in the treatment. At a later stage, individual sessions were planned to work on various external problems, such as school progress, jobs, marriage plans, and so forth. Family group therapy did not appear to be appropriate because of the destructiveness and inaccessibility of underlying feelings in the family. The preferred placement for the Power-oriented girl was a foster home or a group home in which the control system was very clear and the girl was not rejected because of her manipulative attempts.

Treatment with the Power-oriented youth is long and goals are very difficult—sometimes impossible—to reach. Law-violation behavior among these girls in CTP was reduced. However, the interpersonal destructiveness, such as that illustrated in the case of the girl who kept sending her husband to jail, was not always eliminated. This type of problem represents one of the most serious in the whole criminal justice area, for this Power-oriented girl, and others like her, have children—who then learn at their mother's knee what their mother learned before them. This intergenerational phenomenon is a frightening prospect because we cannot at this stage guarantee successful treatment.

The Passive Conformist Female Offender

Only one other category of delinquent girl occurs often enough for us to describe it here. The Passive Conformist category includes only 7 percent of the CTP female population, but appears to represent a somewhat larger proportion of girls in other delinquent populations.[8] Individuals classified in this category have reached the same stage of social maturity as that described for the Power-oriented group. However, they differ in their orientation toward the power dimension. The Passive Conformist type views others as powerful and herself as weak. As the label suggests, individuals so classified are dominated by the need for social approval, responding with almost-automatic compliance to whoever they think has the power at the moment; they overestimate the power and adequacy of others, seeing themselves as helpless and childlike. They consider themselves to be lacking in social know-how and usually expect to be rejected by others, no matter how hard they try to please.

Although such persons long to be accepted by their peer group, they usually rate no more than fringe membership.

Offense behavior most often results from an attempt to gain peer approval. One Passive Conformist girl threw a rock through a picture window after what she perceived as pressure from others. She was very pleased with herself before the group was caught because she thought that she had finally proved to the other youths that she was an acceptable member of the group. In some instances, the offense behavior is a result of flight to avoid anticipated disapproval of others. A girl in this category was committed to the correctional agency for stealing a car. According to her story, she was late for school and therefore couldn't go to school because she would be "yelled at." Then she couldn't go home to her foster home because they would disapprove of her cutting school. The only alternative she saw was to run away, and for that she needed a car.

The family situation for girls classified as Passive Conformist seems to present a picture of instability and inconsistency. There appears to be some concern for the youth by a parent who, however, is unable to provide a stable structure for growth. In many cases, there is also a rejecting parent, whose approval the youth cannot win. In growing up, the youth has not seen love and strength combined in either parent. The attachment bonds to parents are thus uncertain.

Attachments to friends are superficial at best. Although the Passive Conformist girl would prefer to engage in conventional activities, she is vulnerable to peers who prescribe otherwise. And, in the absence of outer controls, she has no inner belief system that will protect her from deviance.

Although the Passive Conformist girl presents herself as sincere, cooperative, and well-intentioned, she also admits that she has no capacity to be responsible for control of herself or her environment. She feels that she is dependent on the rules of others for keeping out of trouble. She wants to be a "good person" and hopes that others will be helpful and understanding. With this self-definition, it is clearly a matter of chance whether the "helpful" others will encourage delinquency or law-abiding behavior.

Treatment goals for the Passive Conformist youth follow rather obviously from the state of the youth's problem. They especially include a change in self-definition in the direction of security in decision-making, ability to meet the demands of others, ability to assert herself with others, capacity for growth, and feelings of personal worth. An additional goal involves maturing to the point where an internal evaluation guides the youth's behavior.

A well-matched treater initially provides a high structure/low threat environment in order to reduce fear of external demands which the youth feels unable to meet. Reflecting a stance of concern plus strength, the treater communicates in calm, concrete, and predictable ways. In addition, the treater is a reward-focussed person who gives generous positive feedback for even slight signs of achievement. The treater is an enabler, a way-and-means person who can teach the Passive Conformist the ways to adulthood.

In addition to individual contacts between the treater and the Passive

Conformist youth, activity-oriented therapy groups and problem-discussion groups proved useful in treating this type of girl in CTP. Role-playing and role-training were both used to improve social perceptiveness and to teach interpersonal skills.

Under some conditions, girls in this category were placed in their own homes. The conditions included the girl's preference for that setting and the parents' willingness to receive some educational help in providing a more consistent and supportive environment for the girl. Because of the flight response to crisis, easily available alternative placements were planned ahead; the girl thus had an acceptable place to which she could run.

Most of the girls in the Passive Conformist category thrived during treatment. They found a place in which they could be dependent in an acceptable way. Their social perceptiveness increased so that they were better able to predict the reactions of others to them and were thus better able to control their immediate world. Beyond this, some of the girls grew up and took charge of their own lives. Not all made this last step and some remained vulnerable to demands from their external world. Even in the latter cases, the delinquency often did not continue, since most of the young women found for themselves roles as wives and mothers in which expectations and conformity patterns are well defined.

NOTES

1. Crime data are not totally stable, of course. For example, both amounts and rates of crime, as well as characteristics of offenders, may change over time. In order to minimize the difficulty caused by this lack of stability, we report only trends which have been observable over several years' time or data which show some consistency over various studies.

2. Data on adult males in state prisons (NPS, 1974) are available on many of the items reported for women. Incarcerated males are very similar to females on age, educational level, proportion of blacks, and proportion single. Thirty percent of males were married, 60 percent had dependents. A somewhat higher proportion of men than women were working just prior to incarceration (65 percent full time). Conviction offenses for the male felons were 54 percent for violent crimes, 32 percent property crimes, and 9 percent for drug offenses.

3. The designation of problems was made by a social worker who saw each youth for one or more interviews during a Reception Center process.

4. A number of contemporary women writers have suggested that this idealized female role was neither desirable nor possible, especially for minority and lower class women. The linking of criminality with the rejection of the idealized feminine role assumes that crime is primarily masculine and that criminal women want to be more like men. There are, of course, other alternatives to the idealized role.

5. See, for example, Adams, 1970; Cavior and Schmidt, 1974; Glaser, 1974; Hunt, 1977; Jenkins, 1964; Jesness, 1971; Jesness, DeRisi, McCormick, and Wedge, 1972; Kelly and Baer, 1971; Palmer, 1965, 1970, 1974, 1976; Quay and Parsons, 1971; Warren, 1969, 1971, 1976.

6. Using Conceptual Level theory, Hunt and Dopyera (1966) assessed developmental stages in male and female junior high school students. Loevinger (1976) has measured stage of ego development in numerous male and female populations.

7. Hunt and Dopyera (1966) also found more girls than boys at the higher Conceptual Level stage.

8. A sample of the Schenectady, New York juvenile court population showed the Passive Conformist group to represent 18 percent of the female population (Paquin, 1976).

REFERENCES

Adams, S. N. The PICO Project. In N. Johnston, L. Savitz, & M. E. Wolfgang (Eds.), *The sociology of punishment and correction* (2d ed.). New York: Wiley, 1970, 548–561.

Adler, F. *Sisters in crime.* New York: McGraw-Hill, 1975.

Bertrand, M. A. Self image and delinquency: A contribution to the study of female criminality and woman's image. *Acta Criminologica*, 1969, 2, 71–144.

California Youth Authority. A comparison of admission characteristics of Youth Authority wards, 1970–1976. Sacramento, Calif., 1977.

California Youth Authority. Annual report of the California Youth Authority. Sacramento, Calif., 1975.

Cavior, H. E., & Schmidt, A. A test of the effectiveness of a differential treatment strategy at the Robert F. Kennedy Youth Center. Federal Bureau of Prisons research report, 1974.

Chwast, J. Socio-psychological aspects. *International Journal of Offender Therapy*, 1971, 15 (1), 24–27.

Cloninger, C. R., & Guze, S. B. Female criminals: Their personal, familial, and social backgrounds. *Archives of General Psychiatry*, 1970, 23 (6), 554–558.

Datesman, S. K., Scarpitti, F. R., & Stephenson, R. M. Female delinquency: An application of self and opportunity theories. *Journal of Research in Crime and Delinquency*, July 1975, 107–123.

Dinitz, S., Dynes, R. R., & Clarke, A. C. *Deviance: Studies in the process of stigmatization and societal reaction.* New York: Oxford University Press, 1969.

D'Orban, P. T. Female crime. *Criminologist* (London), 1972, 7 (23) 29–51.

Feyerherm, W. H. The interrelationships of various indicators. Ph.D. Dissertation, School of Criminal Justice, State University of New York, Albany, 1977.

Glaser, D. Remedies for the key deficiency in criminal evaluation research. *Journal of Research in Crime and Delinquency*, 1974, 11, 144–154.

Glick, R. M., & Neto, V. V. National study of women's correctional programs. California Youth Authority Publication, Sacramento, Calif., 1976.

Goldkamp, J. S. Bail decision-making and the role of pre-trial detention in American justice. Ph.D. Dissertation, School of Criminal Justice, State University of New York, Albany, 1977.

Hammer, M., & Ross, M. B. Psychological needs of imprisoned adult females with high and low conscience development. *Corrective and Social Psychiatry*, 1977, 23 (3), 73–78.

Hindelang, M. J. Age, sex, and versatility of delinquent involvements. *Social Problems*, (Spring 1971), 18, 522–535.

Hindelang, M. J., Dunn, C., Sutton, L. P., & Aumick, A. Sourcebook of criminal justice statistics—1974, 1975, LEAA, NCJISS.

Hindelang, M. J. Dunn, C., Aumick, A., & Sutton, L. P. Sourcebook of criminal justice statistics—1975, 1976, LEAA, NCJISS.

Hirschi, T. *Causes of delinquency.* Berkeley: University of California Press, 1969.

Hoffman-Bustamante, D. The nature of female criminality. *Issues in Criminology,* 1973, *8* (2), 117–136.

Hunt, D. A paradigm for developing and analyzing differential treatment programs. In C. S. Davis, & M. R. Schmidt (Eds.), *Differential treatment of drug and alcohol abusers.* Palm Springs: ETC Publications, 1977.

Hunt, D. E., & Dopyera, J. Personality variation in lower-class children. *Journal of Psychology,* 1966, *62,* 47–54.

Jenkins, R. L. Diagnoses, dynamics and treatment in child psychiatry. Psychiatric Research Report 18, American Psychiatric Association, 1964.

Jensen, G. J. Delinquency and adolescent self conceptions: A study of the personal relevance of infraction. *Social Problems,* 1972, *20,* 84–103.

Jensen, G. J., & Eve, R. Sex differences in delinquency. *Criminology,* 1976, *13* (4), 427–448.

Jesness, C. F. The Preston Typology Study: An experiment with differential treatment in an institution. *Journal of Research in Crime and Delinquency,* 1971, *8,* 38–52.

Jesness, C. F., DeRisi, W., McCormick, P., & Wedge, R. The Youth Center research project: Final report. Sacramento: California Youth Authority and American Justice Institute, 1972.

Johnson, A. A. A comparison of neuroticism in delinquent girls and boys and subsequent implications for treatment of girls. *Dissertation Abstracts International.* Ann Arbor, Mich.: University Microfilms, 1973, No. 73-5409.

Jones, E. *The life and works of Sigmund Freud.* New York: Basic Books, 1961.

Kelly, F. J., & Baer, D. J. Psychical challenge as a treatment for delinquency. *Crime and Delinquency,* 1971, *17,* 437–445.

Konopka, G. *The adolescent girl in conflict.* Englewood Cliffs, N.J.: Prentice-Hall, 1966.

Loevinger, J. *Ego development.* San Francisco: Jossey-Bass, 1976.

Lombroso, C. *Crime and its causes and remedies.* Copyright 1911, Little, Brown. Reprinted 1968, Montclair, N.J.: Patterson, Smith.

Mead, G. H. *Mind, self and society.* Chicago: University of Chicago Press, 1934.

Miller, W. B. Lower class culture as a generating milieu of gang delinquency. *The Journal of Social Issues,* 1958, *14* (3), 5–19.

Miller, W. B. Violence by youth gangs and youth gangs as a crime problem in major American cities. Washington: U.S. Government Printing Office, 1975, NIJJDP, LEAA.

Morris, R. Attitudes toward delinquency by delinquents, non-delinquents, and their friends. *British Journal of Criminology,* 1965, *5* (July), 249–265.

National Prisoner Statistics Bulletin, Bureau of the Census, Prisoners in state and federal institutions on December 31, 1976. February, 1978, LEAA, NCJISS.

National Prisoner Statistics, Bureau of the Census, Computer tape of the Survey of Inmates of State Correctional Facilities, 1974. Data collected for LEAA.

Palmer, T. B. Final report of the Community Treatment Project, phases 1, 2 and 3. Sacramento: California Youth Authority and National Institute of Mental Health, 1976.

Palmer, T. B. The Youth Authority Community Treatment Project. *Federal Probation,* 1974, *38,* 3–14.

Palmer, T. B. California's Community Treatment Projects the phase I, II and III experiments: Developments and progress. Research Report #10, 1970.

Palmer, T. B. Types of treaters and types of juvenile offenders. *California Youth Authority Quarterly*, 1965, 18, 3, –4–23.

Paquin, H. Characteristics of youngsters referred to Family Court intake and factors related to their processing. NSF Report, School of Criminal Justice, SUNY, Albany, 1976.

Pollak, O. *The criminality of women*. Philadelphia: University of Pennsylvania Press, 1950.

President's Commission on Law Enforcement and Administration of Justice. *The challenge of crime in a free society*. Washington: U.S. Government Printing Office, 1967.

Quay, H., & Parsons, L. The differential classification of the juvenile offender. Morgan, W.Va.: Robert F. Kennedy Youth Center, 1971.

Quetelet, L. A. J. *A treatise on man and the development of his faculties*. A facsimile reproduction of the English translation of 1842. S. Diamond, Gainesville, Fla.: Scholars' Facsimiles and Reprints, 1969.

Reckless, W., & Dinitz, S. Pioneering with self-concept as a vulnerability factor in delinquency. *Journal of Criminal Law, Criminology & Police Science*, 1967, 58 (December), 515–523.

Reckless, W., Dinitz, S., & Murray, E. Self concept as an insulator against delinquency. *American Sociological Review*, 1956, 21, 744–746.

Simon, R. J. *Women and crime*. Lexington Books. Lexington, Mass.: D. C. Heath, 1975.

Schwartz, M., & Baden, M. A. Female adolescent self concept: An examination of the relative influence of peers and adults. *Youth and Society*, 1973, 5 (1), 115–28.

Thomas, W. I. *The unadjusted girl*. New York: Harper & Row, 1923.

Thomas, W. I. *Sex and society: Studies in social psychology of sex*. Copyright, 1907, Little, Brown. Reprinted 1974, New York: Arno Press.

Uniform Crime Reports for the United States, 1975. U. S. Department of Justice, FBI, 1976.

Vedder, C. B., & Somerville, D. B. *The delinquent girl*. Springfield, Ill.: Charles C Thomas, 1970.

Warren, M. Q. Intervention with juvenile delinquents. In M. Rosenheim (Ed.), *Pursuing justice for the child*. Chicago: University of Chicago Press, 1976.

Warren, M. Q. Classification of offenders as an aid to efficient management and effective treatment. *Journal of Criminal Law, Criminology & Police Science*, 1971, 62, 239–258.

Warren, M. Q. The case for differential treatment of delinquents. *Annals of the American Academy of Political and Social Sciences*, 1969, 381, 47–60.

Warren, M. Q., & the Staff of the Community Treatment Project. *Community Treatment Project research report 7*. Sacramento: California Youth Authority and National Institute of Mental Health, 1966.

Williams, J. R., & Gold, M. From delinquent behavior to official delinquency. *Social Problems*, 1972, 20 (Fall), 209–229.

Wilson, A. B., Hirschi, T., & Elder, G. Richmond Youth Project, technical report no. 1. Mimeo. Survey Research Center, University of California, Berkeley, 1965.

chapter 20

Learning as Treatment

Maxwell Jones

In Chapter 4 we asked ourselves, "Can education be treatment?" which in turn poses the questions "What is education?" and "Education for *what?*"; these questions must also be applied to the concept of "treatment."

It could be argued that in a sane world (which could be a relatively conflict free world, and/or a world where individuals' coping mechanisms are relatively adequate to meet everyday stresses) people would grow up to understand the fundamentals of coping and growing as a social process. Even in elementary school, children have the *capacity* to understand the dynamics of behavior, but their teachers do not impart such knowledge, and in most cases they may lack the necessary skill themselves. Take an eight-year-old boy who is aggressively demanding towards his peers, but ingratiates himself to the teachers. He may be given favored status by the teachers because he knows how to please them, and can be trusted not to overlook shortcomings in his classmates; in other words, he helps the teacher to keep other children in line. Here we have the ingredients of a predatory entrepreneur. Does the teacher really want to reinforce these essentially success-oriented values? We hope not. But can the teacher see in this situation a possible reflection of the frightened child of an overbearing father, whose wife's only ability to cope is by submission? Even if the parents were known to the teacher and the impact of their behavior on their child was obvious, would the teacher be in any position to help his pupil? Nearer to the teacher's area of influence, would he ever learn the contradiction between the boy's helpful ingratiating behavior towards *him*, and his overbearing attitude towards his peers?

This vignette typifies the problem of socialization in relation to education. It raises our first basic question: What are schools supposed to accomplish? We can reasonably ask the same question about prison or "reform" schools, as we shall do below.

ASOCIAL LEARNING

Is preparation for a satisfying and fruitful life the primary responsibility of parents, or teachers, or is it best left to the uncertain pressures and prejudices of the child's own peer group? The social structure surrounding most elementary school children is haphazard at best. Information sharing—that is, communication of facts and feelings—seldom flows with any freedom between the interfaces of home, classroom, and playground. In this context the child may identify with any one of these areas and "grow" in relation to the aims and expectations of one or more of these social organizations.

But this "growth" may be more imitation and conformity to the mores of one particular group than the outcome of a systematic social learning process. The need for a social organization where the communication of thoughts and feelings (and interactions) among people of all ages can be a daily occurrence is seldom conceptualized, far less practiced. Indeed the opposite trend is more in evidence. Part of the function of a school is to free some parents to "do their own thing" without interference from their offspring. Clearly some degree of insulation between the age groups is called for, particularly in a competitive society. But even the opportunity for shared social intercourse in the evenings can now be largely taken over by the emergence of endless television programs, which can highlight and inculcate violence or other questionable social values.

These trends are understandable and they can easily be rationalized, but can we escape altogether from an uneasy feeling that modern living frees many of us from responsible social roles? The ultimate outcome of this trend is part of the plight of the deviant, the underprivileged, the mentally ill, and the aged, where in extreme cases a supportive social structure is virtually nonexistent.

The corollary of this argument is that unless society starts by assuming responsibility for the social environment in which young people grow up, many adult individuals must find themselves in a jungle where they feel isolated and vulnerable. If winning at football is one of the most treasured values at school, what boy is going to express concern about the negative effects of physical violence on many of those involved, whether they be players, parents, or merely spectators? The price for having such humane reservations can be painful, but one thing is almost certain—few people will want to listen to the questioning voice. From an early age one learns that the best and safest course to follow is conformity to one's peer group.

And yet the potential for change and "growth" is always there. The coach who is a humanist and shows as much concern for his players' well-being, both physical and emotional, as he does for winning, can instill a value system which may have lasting effects on the players' moral values. This trend is reinforced if social interaction and discussion is extended beyond football to what winning in life does really mean.

This may sound foolish when one considers the conventional model presented by college and professional football, where the value of brutalizing an opponent may be heavily reinforced by wildly cheering spectators. It may even be argued that the outlet for aggression legitimized in the American football scene serves a useful purpose in releasing the tensions of everyday life. But the scenario also serves as an illustration of the transparency of many of our moral values. Rough play resulting in injury may delight one section of the spectators and infuriate the other. However, no one labels such violence as "criminal." The same process can operate in reverse. In retrospect it could be said that anticommunist witch hunts in the United States did not indicate deviant behavior on the parts of the "victims" of the hunt but rather the reaction of a group in society who were able to treat another group as deviant. This phenomenon has come to be known as labelling (Schur, 1969), since it identifies the ability of powerful elements in our society to establish the norms of behavior, and to fatefully label those who deviate from them.

Szasz (1970) develops the theme of deviancy as it relates to psychiatry and crime in a most illuminating way: ". . . Institutional psychiatry is largely medical ceremony and magic. This explains why the labeling of persons— as mentally healthy or diseased—is so crucial a part of psychiatric practice. It constitutes the initial act of social validation and invalidation, pronounced by the high priest of modern, scientific religion, the psychiatrist; it justifies the expulsion of the sacrificial scapegoat, the mental patient, from the community" (p. 267). Szasz (1970) compares the fate of a person committed to a mental hospital with that of a criminal: ". . . to support their ideology and to justify their powers and privileges, institutional psychiatrists combined the notions of mental illness and criminality and resist efforts to separate them. They do this by claiming that mental illness and crime are one and the same thing and that mentally ill persons are dangerous in ways that mentally healthy persons are not" (p. 17). The implications of this view are traced out in Chapter 5, and we shall return to them later.

THE NATURE OF SOCIAL LEARNING

So far we have been examining some of the social factors associated with a casual processing of learning, and with the determinants of acceptable or deviant behavior. This brings us to a consideration of what we mean by social learning. Arthur Koestler (1968) tells us that "man cannot inherit the past; he has to recreate it." For Koestler the essence of education is discovery *for oneself*—a process of reliving a problem and resolving it largely by one's own efforts. Starting with the basic assumption that though there is nothing new under the sun, the reliving of problems which are new to the individual, even if they have previously been solved by others, imbues the experience with a quality of creativity—that is, a positive emotional experience which has the personal stamp of a *living learning* situation. The opportunity for such experiences is greatly enhanced by the intervention of a catalyst who helps the student to proceed along the road to discovery, but leaves the actual process of problem solving to the student. I have used the term "social learning" for this process, and called the catalyst a "facilitator" (Jones, 1976).

By the *process* of social learning I mean two-way communication in a group, motivated by some inner need or stress, leading to overt or covert expression of feeling, and involving cognitive processes and change. The term implies a change in the individual's attitude and/or beliefs as a result of the experience. These changes are incorporated, and modify his personality and self-image.

The nature or direction of the change cannot be predicted, but in the final analysis is determined by the quality of the various individual inputs, the capacity of each group member to listen to his peers, and to compare his own attitudes or beliefs with those of the other members. Such a process is largely foreign to the sort of culture where competitiveness, one-upmanship, inattentiveness, selective listening, or passive memorizing are characteristic of our experience and our education. Nor does the presence of a facilitator insure that the group will address itself to learning as a social process. Although in theory, his function is to help the group help itself to problem-solve, learn, and grow, his own attitudes, beliefs, and values inevitably show through, no matter how "objective" he attempts to be.

In brief, our concept of social learning is both broader and more limited than that used in Chapter 9, but it is supported by some of the same evidence. The value of the concept is that it affords a clear alternative to the stereotype of the learner as a passive listener, for whom the excitement of discovery as a social process is all too rare.

The physical structure of a lecture theatre or classroom epitomizes the dilemma we face when we attempt to introduce social learning. The lecturer or teacher literally occupies the center of the stage, being the only person that everyone can see without craning or turning around. Clearly the expectation is for communication channels to flow to or from the central person rather than randomly between any two people in the room. Eye contact and other forms of nonverbal communication, even if thought to be significant, cannot occur between most people in the room, other than between teacher and pupils.

To change this physical organization, to replace it with something like a Greek theatre, or saucer-shaped auditorium, where everyone is visible to everyone else, is to alter the group's awareness of its members and to increase enormously the possible varieties and quality of communication.

When a teacher abandons his podium, the pupils their desks, and everyone sits in a circle, we create a new social structure in the physical sense, and it is a relatively short step to informal interaction between any two people in the group. Established patterns die hard, of course, and for a time the communication may still tend to flow from teacher to pupil and back again. But here we have at least created the basic element of free communication, at first in the sphere of information sharing and later, if confidence grows, in the relationships of individuals to the group at a feeling level. We are introducing a comparatively new element in the interactional situation, in that the class need no longer passively follow the leader (teacher) along the formalized lines of subject matter, but can begin to explore the world of spontaneous interaction. Such a transition is not easy. Anyone who has attempted to promote openness and intimacy knows the enormous built-in resistances to the lowering of personality barriers or defenses, based on the universal need to hide much of one's identity from the world at large, or even from a specific group.

In our culture only the idea of "illness" sanctions intimate disclosures, usually between the medical profession and the subject and/or his family. And this intimacy requires a vow of secrecy between doctor and patient, the so called Hippocratic oath which, taken too seriously, may be a hindrance to later social learning. But trust based on such a flimsy pretext as the realization of a certificate to practice medicine lacks the evolution of trust as a learning process which concerns us here.

REDUCING THE IMPACT OF INSTITUTIONS

How can the principles of social learning and personal education be applied to the prison system? We anticipate problems, both in terms of what we know about prisons and about our society.

In this context we look for parallels between developments in the mental health field and in prisons. The dangers inherent in incarcerating patients in large mental hospitals have been studied extensively. In a sense the cure has been recognized as being worse than the disease. The term *institutionalization* denotes the negative effects of the hospital environment on long-term patients. The passive-dependent relationship between patients and staff, the relative loss of identity of staff, the relative loss of identity of individual patients, along with their having little or no responsibility for themselves or others, the stereotyped nature of their existence with little interest or variety, where each day seems like its predecessor and nothing tangible is accomplished—all contribute to the phenomenon called institutionalization. The role of the patient was to be "sick," which became synonymous with "helpless." The helpers (staff) were in the business of unwittingly reinforcing this self-image of hopeless helplessness. Such a social organization as a whole might be diagnosed as "sick."

For reasons that are none too clear—part economical, part political, part an attempt to behave as though the problem had disappeared—the prevailing "solution" has been to try to empty the mental hospitals as far as possible, and to transfer the patients to live in the community outside. Not surprisingly, many, if not most of the formerly institutionalized patients lacked the resources to live independently as ordinary citizens, and being largely unemployable, drifted into boarding homes run by private enterprise. Their "keep" now came to be the financial responsibility of welfare instead of the mental health system. Admittedly the federal government had also launched a community mental health program,[1] which had as one of its functions the care of ex-mental hospital patients in the community, but little success has accompanied the plan. Of two thousand community mental health centers originally planned for the United States, about 25 percent were created, and many have been abolished or reconverted.

In brief, what had started as an awakening of public conscience in relation to the tragic fate of state hospital patients resulted in a relatively hurried and unplanned reorganization of community mental health programs with little significant change for the better in the lives of many, if not most, of the ex-patients.

In Chapter 4, we have drawn a picture of the conditions which obtain in most prisons, and of their institutional consequences. Can planned social action hope for real change here, when relatively little was accomplished in the case of the state hospitals? The question is academic, because prison populations are increasing rather than decreasing. And if it is impracticable to partly empty the prisons at this point in history, the focus for social change must be within the prisons themselves. Can a prison sentence benefit at least some inmates? If the answer is to be affirmative, some change must occur in the inmate's self-image or his attitude towards others.

If the social organization of a prison is intended to implement change in the direction of a positive attitude toward society, it must afford opportunities for social learning within the prison. This implies a social structure where two way communication of thoughts and feelings, social interaction, listening and learning can occur. In addition, social roles of a responsible nature are needed, along with shared decision making and limit setting assumed by the inmates themselves, or in conjunction with the prison staff. We have already pointed out the enormous resistances to such change in schools, mental hospitals, and other institutions. Is it realistic to even consider such a social system for change in a prison? The author's experience in a special unit for "psychopaths" in London (1947 to 1959) and four years as consultant and observer with the Department of Corrections in California (1959 to 1963) suggests that high priority may in fact be given in prisons to the development of a more open system, or, as it came to be called, a therapeutic community (Jones, 1953, 1962).

CHANGING THE PRISON SOCIAL STRUCTURE

Let us start with the social organization of prisons and make an assumption which at present is incapable of proof, namely, that the social structure of the environment where inmates and staff live together in close contact can be seen on a continuum from destructive to constructive. Different individuals react differently to such a structure depending on variables such as personality types, roles, role relationships, the rules, and the culture (attitudes, values, and beliefs) that exists in both the populations of inmates and staff.

In Chapter 4 we discussed the social structure of prisons, in which prisoners and staff live with each other in circumstances which engender feelings of hopelessness in almost everyone. Such a structure would be largely unplanned, but would evolve from necessity. What we must consider are the prerequisites which might allow for the implementation of a different social structure, which would promote learning and personality growth in *both* inmates and staff.

Size can be of paramount importance. Although hard data are lacking, an upper limit of four hundred prisoners might satisfy needs for economy and security. Smaller size would undoubtedly improve opportunities for communication throughout the entire prison, with better information sharing and a more visible leadership. The more the warden of the prison and his chief executives are known to prisoners and staff, the better the prospects of administrators being seen as human beings and as potentially trustworthy, rather than as distorted fantasy figures associated with the abuse of authority, cruelty, unfairness, and of generally not caring. Of course "visibility" brings its own dangers, and if negative fantasies are largely true, a bad image of authority can be made worse!

CHANGE AND THE PRISON LEADERSHIP

Middle management, placed at the interface between prisoner's cells and top management, may be caught in a dilemma—wanting to be seen as efficient managers in their areas of responsibility, a necessary prerequisite for promotion to higher management, and afraid to take risks, such as in following humanitarian feelings towards prisoners which might be misinterpreted as "weakness."

Absurdities of poor communication between the prisoners themselves, through the staff to middle management and finally to top management can be perpetuated. In the event of a serious incident such as violence, a hunger strike, or a riot, an example of such absurdity is enacted in the attempt to find a "cause"—which is doomed to failure from the start. Without accurate information nothing can be learned, and indeed such negative influences as punishment (usually the wrong people) or stricter discipline (which may already be a root cause of unrest) are imposed, to reassure the legislature or the general public.

It goes without saying that changes in the direction of an open system at top administrative levels meets with difficulties. The unrest and anxiety which inevitably accompany organizational change may create incidents. The press and mass media, hungry for news, can make public accounts of "what happened," which are usually grossly inaccurate because of the absence of open communication we have already described. As long as the primary concern of the prison officials is to avoid incidents, which usually means firmer controls, tightening of discipline, punishment, and so on, it is difficult to institute learning as a social process.

Perhaps the only way out of this dilemma is to endow certain prison authority figures with a degree of trust (by the legislature, public bodies, etc.) so that experimentation with the social organization of the prison becomes permissible, even if risky. Indeed, if change is to occur in the social structure of any setting, sanctions from the highest levels of authority would appear to be essential.

Even if such sanctions are present, is leadership competent to respond to the challenge? The prison is a closed system with a poor reputation, little or no sharing of information or decision making, and no real concern. Such a climate, charged with fear and distrust, is the exact antithesis of a climate conducive to change. Spontaneity and creativity are stifled and unquestioning conformity to rigid authority brings approval and promotion. The tragic fact is that this form of institutionalism is a poor breeding ground for leadership, in many different institutions. But one could argue that leadership potential is present in all social systems, and is merely stifled unless a flexible system nourishes such potential.

The proof of the pudding is that important models for change in the direction of open systems have evolved in prisons over the past three decades. Henderson Hospital and Grendon Underwood in England, the special unit at Barlinnie in Scotland, Van der Hoven Clinic in Utrecht, Holland, Herstedvester in Denmark, and Penetang in Canada are cases in point. In the United States, California, starting with the election of late Earl Warren as Governor, had a notable record of prison reform. Much of the record has to do with the leadership of Richard A. McGee, who headed the Department of Corrections. The California leadership survived several changes in government, and over more than two decades effected sweeping changes in the penal system (Briggs, 1975). It was a prime example of leaders who operated a relatively open system which allowed many outstanding change agents to emerge.

In the final analysis however, prison reform must run parallel with changes in public attitudes; and as in the educational system, so in the prison system, the forces of reaction seem to predominate at the present time.

INTRODUCING SOCIAL LEARNING INTO A PRISON

We have argued that no significant change in the direction of a more open system can occur unless there is positive support from higher authority. Ideally members of the upper echelons of a social system must have had the training and experience so that they can operate as skilled facilitators. This implies permitting regular (at least weekly) meetings of the relevant personnel, free communication of content and feelings, interaction without fear of reprisals, and an increasing level of trust.

Usually a department of corrections will have, at most, one or two staff members with relevant training and experience. This may suggest the establishment of an inservice program with, if possible, a facilitator (trainer) from an outside agency or university department. Further training, of the kind run by the National Training Laboratory at Bethel, Maine is helpful. It seems logical to assume that unless the higher-echelon members of an administrative structure can deal with their own interpersonal conflicts, share information, and solve problems by a process of interaction and social learning, they will be unable to understand and endorse a social learning process for their staff, and ultimately at the inmate level (Jones, 1976). Given positive sanctions from above, an experimental unit feels safety and understanding which enhances the effectiveness of its operation.

It might be expedient to start with a physical unit housing twenty to thirty inmates. To initiate such a pilot project on the lines of a therapeutic community, special motivation to change is needed in both inmates and staff. Social learning is a painful process and personal growth becomes uninviting once individual defenses are threatened. Can I trust my peer group? Will confidences be respected, or am I risking my job security? And so on.

It may be preferable to start with a volunteer staff who by virtue of their personality makeup and/or training are in tune with the implications of working with inmates in a nonauthoritarian way. Such volunteers can be freed from their normal duties to attend training seminars based on group interaction, problem solving, and social learning principles (Jones, 1976). If possible, the leader or leaders should have had experience in an open group—if not in prison, then in the mental health field. At the very least, staff should have some group work training and familiarity with group dynamics.

When the staff have enough confidence to deal with their own interpersonal difficulties, to listen to each other and to trust each other, they can spend a week together in the facility where they will work. This week can further test their capacity for communication, for shared decision making, for identifying roles and role relationships, and so on.

The aim at first must be to avoid preconceptions, or at least to examine critically the attitudes held by staff and see what validity they have. This examination of staff attitudes and beliefs is a necessary prelude to any attempt to observe objectively what occurs in the interactional field involving both inmates and staff. Later, by sharing relevant observations with inmates and inviting them to do likewise, it should be possible to open up communications and enhance the status of inmates. This process is aided by shared tasks in a work situation, by frequent informal contacts, and by a living demonstration of an open and inquiring outlook that is not based exclusively on a desire to effect change to a "better" way of life.

The establishment of a community which seeks to share its problems by verbalizing them implies that "talking is a good thing." This often appears to create the very kind of situation we are anxious to avoid. For many prisoners, talking is bad and a highly dangerous procedure, and informal contact and shared work situations may be necessary prior to discussing anything approaching a personal topic. It is here that the inmate peer group can often do much by its own informal observation and discussion of "here and now" phenomena.

The staff must be given sufficient freedom of action within the social structure of the prison to be able to identify with their inmates and their inmates' problems rather than operating with any preconceptions of staff-inmate relationships held by the prison authorities. Thus, the idea that the content of the group discussions may be used by staff to influence the authorities and possibly extend the inmate's term of imprisonment will not only lead t) a block in communication, but also create anxieties in the staff which limit their usefulness in their role. However, the observation by a staff member that this factor is operating and is blocking communication would, if perceptive, offer a common ground for discussion of the significance of the phenomenon as it is affecting both inmate and staff groups. It is the creation of a set of circumstances which encourages social interaction, accurate observation, and free discussion which must be seen as the primary purpose of the unit. The formal goal of such a unit would be to aid the individual's return to society and the prevention of further incarceration. In the first instance, however, moral implications should be avoided—concepts like the establishment of a "better" way of life, or even a greater sense of social responsibility imply a conversion to the staff's value system. In a society where moral values and cultural concepts are as varied, not to say confused, as in our civilization, it is difficult to defend a stance of this kind.

I would anticipate that any therapeutic community would, in time, develop its own increasingly characteristic culture based on the discussion of frequently recurring problems and the conscious attempt to reconcile its various divergent viewpoints. The community, both inmates and staff, would tend gradually to establish more clearly understood roles and role-relationships. The inmates' collective perception of their role would inevitably affect the new inmate. And it is possible to conceive of a culture which had certain specific merits for the rehabilitation task in hand—a state of affairs very different to the familiar custodial prison environment.

In prison, anomalies of personal growth overlap with profound problems of differing and often competing cultures. A multidisciplinary approach would seem to be indicated, as this allows for the dispassionate observation of such phenomena. What happens in this living situation might be compared to what happens when staff meet daily to discuss "their" problems. The culture becomes more defined, emotional problems can often be resolved, and personnel are being trained to observe, listen, and interact. Also, individuals come to have a feeling of identification with both the staff and inmate groups, which increases their feeling of security and their anxiety tolerance. One is tempted to say that maturation, social learning, and training can all be identified in this process.

A fluid structure would favor the slow development of a culture well suited to the more explicit task of observation, training, education, and rehabilitation. It would also, ultimately, favor the emergence of a methodology of social learning suited to the personality problems of prisoners.

AN ILLUSTRATIVE INCIDENT

Let me give an example of social learning in a prison setting at the staff level. I was acting as facilitator to a staff training group, and just before the third meeting of the weekly group was scheduled to start, the leader excused himself on the grounds of illness and departed for home. The group started talking, but no one mentioned the leader. I commented on this, and was told by his deputy that an injury received from an inmate some weeks previously had become so painful that the leader decided to go and seek medical advice As this information appeared to come as a surprise to most of the staff, I asked how they felt about the situation. This touched off a flow of interaction, and a discussion about the leader's personality. People saw the leader as something of a "loner" who had a tendency to make unilateral decisions, and to exploit this deputy, who was often used as a scapegoat. I commented that this information would have been more useful if the leader had been present. The response was that group members were angry at the suddenness of their leader's departure, and at his failure to communicate the reason for it to anyone but his deputy, who almost without warning had to take on the responsibility and authority of the leadership role. The deputy received much sympathy and support, and expressed new confidence in his competence as a leader. This led to a new awareness of the formal leader's tendency to be authoritarian, and to make decisions on behalf of, rather than with, the group. He was seen as an efficient manager who protected his team from problems (especially those outside the unit), so that almost without realizing it, the staff had condoned his tendency to operate unilaterally so as to protect themselves from anxiety. They saw that they had a responsibility for such a state of affairs, and that every group tends to get the leadership that it deserves. Also, it became clear that they were afraid to confront their leader directly, and had to wait for his absence to express their feelings. At this point people began to feel guilty and to wish that the leader *was* present. I pointed out that feelings respect no time schedule, and that open discussion means social learning, whereas "gossiping" with a buddy over coffee only reinforces negative attitudes. The group began to realize that they would be helping their leader, provided they shared their experience with him immediately on his return. The deputy who had previously avoided confronting the leader about his tendency to devalue people, now felt ready to do so in a group situation, confident of the group's support. Finally we learned for the first time that the deputy had been contemplating resigning because of the frustrating relationship with his leader.

This incident, which led to a rich learning situation when shared with the leader on his return, illustrates social learning in a staff group that was constituted for this purpose. It usuallly takes several months of weekly group meetings, ideally with eight or ten staff members and a facilitator, before a significant level of trust can be established. At first, confidentiality is seen as important, which reflects the relatively low trust level of the group. As more people get involved and share their feelings with the group, a group identity tends to be superimposed on each individual identity. This leads to a feeling of confidence, competence, and security which enhances the individual's performance at work and in his social relationships generally.

INMATE STAFF GROUPS

A somewhat similar interaction, on a larger scale, is possible when inmates and staff meet in a large group of twenty to thirty people. If such meetings are held daily they can provide an invaluable living-learning situation for everyone present.

At first, as in group meetings generally, the inmates expect to be told what to do, a by-product of their conformist experience. But an explanation by a staff leader of the injunction to talk about any difficulties they are experiencing either between themselves or with staff soon initiates interaction. At first inmates tend to limit discussion to material grievances associated with food, privileges, noise, rules, and so on. Inevitably there has to be a testing out of the integrity and good will of staff which may take weeks or months. After all, the culture of a prison is based on a deep distrust of everyone: the outside society, law enforcement officers, and even one's peer group. For inmates this distrust is the pattern of a lifetime, and the group meeting is seen as highly dangerous, especially as staff invite inmates to "snitch." Progress towards more open communication will depend in part on the skill and integrity of staff (heavily influenced by the sensitivity and quality of everyday interactions with the inmates), and by the presence of some inmates who lack the quality of despair that is characteristic of many prisoners or "losers." Somehow a change in the defensive hostility between the prisoners and the staff has to emerge. The staff's sensitivity to the needs of at least some of the inmates may lead to a tentative belief that staff, or perhaps one member, really cares. It may start with a relatively trivial matter to do with smoking or mail, but the fact that something gets *done* may spark a change of attitude in some of the inmates. Evidence that the confidentiality of the group is respected by staff can only grow through the test of time. This experience is linked with a growing sense of group identity, which for lonely "losers" has an almost fairytale improbability, but might be watched circumspectly if one or two less despairing peers test out the possibility of change. (How this transition may be hastened by the formation of an all-inmate group without staff will be discussed later.)

In time, "risk takers" who are prepared to share some of their private worlds with the group will emerge, if the group justifies their trust by its skill, sensitivity, and caring. This evolutionary process can be compared with a new life span, where situations which have ended in disaster in the past can be re-examined in the present, in the relatively safe, make-believe world of the group. This is the essence of social learning which has already been discussed, which has much in common with group analytic techniques, transactional analysis, Gestalt therapy, and so on.

PROCESS REVIEW

Obviously no group can be any better than the sum of attributes of the individuals forming it. In this sense every group is unique and will evolve its own distinctive methodology. This process of interacting, listening, and learning can be enormously enhanced if immediately following the daily inmate-staff group, a staff process review is held.

A review is an attempt to "relive" the group and examine the group process from the beginning to end. Did the group start on time? Who sat beside whom? Did staff form clusters? Who spoke first? And so on. Verbal and nonverbal communication are recycled with a view to examining staff performance. Did staff miss a cue, for example, an interaction which lent itself to interpretation? Was staff defensive, blocking inmate criticism of its behavior, of its apparent lack of concern, or its lack of consistency in fulfilling an obligation to honor an agreement made in a previous group, or an apparent "leak" of confidential material to a higher authority? And so on.

More subtle and demanding is willingness on the part of the staff to listen to criticism from their own peers and to see this criticism as part of a process of social learning and not as a "put down." An outside facilitator who is chosen by the staff for his or her group dynamic and social system skills can add significantly to the willingness of staff to listen and learn from their peers. The facilitator has a degree of objectivity which helps to avoid such things as staff splitting into subgroups. He can also help as a role-model in demonstrating the use of confrontation as a technique for social learning.

A daily review of this sort is a very effective training device. The various personalities and training backgrounds of staff offer differing perspectives and reactions to the same inmate-staff group. The day-in, day-out examination of performance may be painful at times, but social learning is often a painful process. To examine in retrospect what one did and why one did it in group interactions heightens everyone's sensitivity and skill. Not only can one focus on such things as the timing, sensitivity, and aptness of one's inputs, but the complementarity of staff group members in reinforcing another's inputs can be discussed. For instance, a well-timed interpretation of some defensive inmate behavior, such as the inmate's unwillingness to talk about a problem of stealing, may result in an opening up of an issue, and if this is handled sensitively by the staff as a whole, the trust level rises and more sharing of potentially dangerous issues may ensue.

Some people like to hold a review of this kind in the presence of the inmates as silent listeners. With a fairly experienced group this can further enhance the level of trust between inmates and staff, and can help blur the distinction between treatment and training.

THE ASKLEPIEION EXPERIENCE

A significant development in penal institutions in recent years is associated with the name of Martin Groder, a psychiatrist. He was working at the maximum security Federal Prison at Marion, Illinois from 1968 to 1974, and developed a form of therapeutic community which was named Asklepieion after the temple of the Greek god of healing. Groder had been influenced by his contacts in California with Synanon and Eric Berne's transactional analysis (Berne, 1964), and managed to convince the authorities to sanction an inmate group of some twenty-five volunteers who would evolve their own treatment program. The prison officers were not involved in forming the group, which was attended by Groder and two mental health staff members. To start with, the inmates, who lived in a separate unit that was quartered in the prison hospital, were given lectures on T.A. and began to use Synanon confrontration groups. These special "games" could be invoked at any time of day or night by any member of the group. The focus of the interactions was always on one member, whose behavior and performance in the group was heavily confronted by his peers. Twice a week, regularly scheduled games were held, which concerned everyone in the group. Jobs around the unit were allocated according to merit—the unsavory chores (toilet cleaning, etc.) amounted to punishment, except in the case of the newcomer, who always started at the lowest level of job. The basic rules prohibiting physical violence or threats of violence, gambling, drugs, or homosexual behavior, were rigidly enforced, and an offender was automatically extruded from the group.

The prison itself housed approximately seven hundred felons who were thought to represent the most dangerous element in the United States prison system. Fighting, gambling, drug trafficking, and so on, were a common occurrence in the prison as a whole, but Asklepieion was a group of inmates who without interference by law enforcement officers were establishing and maintaining their own rules and their therapeutic culture. The principles of the peer group therapeutic culture, established twenty years earlier in London by the original therapeutic community, were rediscovered.[2] Therapeutic responsibility and discipline at Marion were shared by the community as a whole. The peer group was deemed all important and confidentiality was strictly adhered to. Inputs from any treatment modality were discussed by the group and adopted in accordance with their relevance to the group. Gestalt, Primal Therapy, Behavior Modification, and so on, made their contributions to the overall therapeutic culture. With such an open system, the propensity to learn was reinforced. Thus the Synanon game was modified at Marion and became less "violent" than at Synanon, because Marion inmates believed that confrontation without caring was unproductive. In this context a "violent" verbal attack on a peer was immediately reacted to by the group and the angry peer was confronted.

Despite the apparent success of Asklepieion (a recidivism rate of 13 percent among inmates exposed to this program for six months or more)[3] the experiment was discontinued in June, 1976. One reason for its closure was failure to win over people in power at the Marion penitentiary and in the Federal Correctional System as a whole. Linked with this failure was a false feeling of security within the therapeutic community itself. For a group of long-term prisoners, who have survived the rigors of many years in prison with all its associated dangers and frustrations, the sudden escape to a social system which inmates control, can be intoxicating. The transition from a lifetime of vulnerability to a state of relative independence within a supportive group, may lead to feelings of grandiosity, egocentricity, and machismo.

The same phenomenon is discernable in members of Synanon and other peer treatment programs. Ingroup solidarity is misleading and it blurs the true state of affairs at the interface between the therapeutic community and the outside world. This dilemma is met by some members of Synanon by remaining permanently in their closed world. But Asklepieion was a subgroup in a larger federal prison system, and could not enjoy the independence available to Synanon (see p. 394).

Monte McKenzie, an inmate, carried the Asklepieion model with him when he was transferred to the Arizona State Prison at Fort Grant. On leaving prison McKenzie started an organization in Phoenix called "OK Community," which applies the same group support to exinmates that the prisoners use in their prison group. McKenzie has also started a therapeutic community like Asklepieion in the Pheonix prison, Durango. Seven or eight other therapeutic communities in prisons are scattered around the United States, notably in Arkansas, Minnesota and in the Oxford Federal Prison.

The prison therapeutic communities under discussion treat character disorders of the kind we have dealt with in Chapter 14. These are persons who are described as having the following characteristics: good intelligence; defective conscience; relative absence of anxiety; few, if any, psychosomatic symptoms; inability to form lasting relationships; disregard for the truth (the disposition to "con" peers and manipulate people to gain one's objectives); lack of foresight; irresponsible behavior; rejection of authority; argumentativeness; and an apparent inability to learn from experience.

The original group at Marion was made up of felons with long sentences and usually with a long history of repeated offenses. The approximately thirty prisoners who made up this original group remained with their group for many months or years. (At Fort Grant some seventy inmates spend an average of a year in the group, and at Durango sixteen to twenty inmates spend usually four to six months in the group.) Selection of members is by the prisoners themselves, who are concerned primarily with evidence of motivation to change behavior. No prison personnel participate in these groups, and the facilitator/trainer may have learned his skills while serving his sentence as a member of a therapeutic community.

The group lives in a separate unit twenty-fours hours a day, and the focus of treatment (social learning) is aimed at the despair and the feelings of abandonment which members see as the core of problems that face men with character disorders. This assumption seems to fit the early traumatic developmental histories of most group members, who try to deny their feelings of hopelessness by defenses described as "Do me something—you owe it to me," or "Fuck off—it don't matter," or "Making fools of." According to the treatment philosophy of these therapeutic communities, when the person with a character disorder decides to give up in despair, he also plans to "get even" with society, whom he sees as responsible for his despair, and by his deviant behavior he hides from hopelessness. "Do me something—you owe me" implies that the individual himself is not responsible for his plight. Inmates view psychotherapy by a therapist as a mistake, because it plays into the already existing dependency and defensive mechanisms. By the same token, "Fuck off—it don't matter," is a discounting mechanism, and allows the individual to rationalize a return to his destructive behavior. The "making fools of" defense is also an attempt to avoid the truth by making someone else look ridiculous to prove that others have the same feelings and failures as oneself. Thus, group members argue, the character-disordered person tries to avoid the real issue—his own despair, and his feelings of powerlessness to do anything about it.

With these principles in mind one can better conceptualize the twenty-four-hour-a-day total commitment of the inmate peer group to its task. After all, the rules protect inmates from their familiar prison risks: they guarantee no violence, no drugs, no gambling, no homosexuality, since automatic extrusion from the group follows. In this "safe" environment, inmates can call a group anytime of day or night they feel it appropriate to deal with an interpersonal or other problem. Thus, when someone fails to keep his commitment to leave an upset individual alone, the whole group can confront him immediately and his behavior can be examined. The inmate may recognize a familiar tendency to get even by displacing his own problem of helplessness onto someone who is vulnerable. The group reinforces his awareness of the need to change his behavior. The excitement of the "game" (no risk of violence, etc.) makes for intensive interaction, and facilitates the learning of more acceptable patterns of behavior. The very intensity of the interaction, which has no time limits or cramping schedules (group times, etc.), denotes "caring." This is a distinct departure from the Synanon type games where punishments—shaving head, and so on—may be dehumanizing. Moreover in Synanon we see the scapegoating mechanism in reverse—it is society as well as the drug addict who is "sick" (deviant). This premise may explain some of the "violence" shown by Synanists to members who deviate from the Synanon culture.

It is probable that the small percentage of drug addicts who can survive in Synanon are the same type of "tough" character disorders which the Asklepieion type therapeutic communities are treating. Such men come from a culture where "toughness" is highly regarded and may even be essential for survival. The "foul" language, the intensity and high-anxiety level of Synanon groups, the shouting, the direct confrontation of *anyone*, the disregard of authority, the confidentiality, all contribute to a therapeutic culture relevant to this type of individual (Yablonsky, 1967).

When I look back at twelve years (1947 to 1959) of trying to help persons with character disorders in London, I'm stuck by a familiar emphasis on the power of the peer group of "patients or inmates," a common struggle for a group identity to overcome feelings of isolation and helplessness.[4] For us in London, daily community meetings with approximately ninety patients of both sexes featuring confrontation for behavior incompatible with the therapeutic culture, had the same quality of interaction in a "safe" environment leading to social learning and behavior change as that of the Asklepieion groups (Jones, 1953).

The striking difference between Asklepieion and the original therapeutic community lies in the almost total absence at Marion of the "professional," be he psychiatrist, psychologist, or other trained individual. For character disorders in prison, where the inmates are surrounded by guards, etc., the trust level between prison personnel and prisoners must be low.[5] For this reason, an inmate group like Asklepieion makes much sense. The "We're all in it together" factor also accounts for the extreme exclusiveness of peer group movements, such as Synanon and to a lesser extent the AA movement for alcoholics.

But training is by no means absent in these movements. The use of peer "professionals" has advantages mainly associated with the inside knowledge of the individual who has himself experienced addiction to drugs, or alcohol, or has been in prison. The therapeutic communities stemming from the Asklepieion model feature intensive self education by reading and through lectures; they will use recognized treatment modalities if they are deemed relevant. In some prisons, like Fort Grant in Arizona, a teaching membership requires six years of continuous involvement in a therapeutic community, and to become a "clinical teacher," requires two years involvement. Many ex-prisoners are getting paid to do therapeutic work in prisons; some are now free to do therapeutic community work, including in programs which they have pioneered.

Inmate groups attempt to break through extreme and hardened defenses. It is difficult to fool your peer group when you are living in close proximity twenty-four hours a day without prison personnel present.[6] In essence, confrontation by peers wears away any remaining pretenses, and it forces inmates to face reality and to forego infantile positions of abandonment and despair.

Whatever opinion one holds, exposure to a therapeutic community in prisons, hospitals, and other helping institutions must be recognized as having an intensity and a dedication which is potent and impressive. But the evidence of "caring" transcends other features, and must raise doubts about the flatness, lack of enthusiasm, and the dehumanizing beliefs so common in the office-hour world of mental health professionals and their clients, not to mention the scapegoat of them all—the mental hospital!

NOTES

1. The enabling legislation for these centers is the Community Mental Health Act of 1963.
2. It is possible that the therapeutic community at the Social Rehabilitation Unit, Belmont Hospital (now renamed Henderson Hospital), which started in 1947, affected in varying ways social organizations in both Europe and the United States, but such influences would be virtually impossible to identify.
3. A similar recidivism rate is claimed by the maximum security ward at Utah State Hospital in Provo, run as a therapeutic community (*Newsweek*, February 14, 1977).
4. When I visited the group at Durango, one inmate who had spent thirteen years in prison, and had been convicted of two rapes and an assault with a deadly weapon, told me that he was an outcast in the "adult world," and that his only recourse was to be caught committing a crime to be sent to prison where he could be with people who accepted him.
5. Even so, this can be largely overcome, as was done at the prison at Chino. See Whitely, Briggs, & Turner, 1973, Chapters 5 and 6.
6. At Durango the men could opt for work which earns $25 a week, but prefer to remain confined to their own area.

REFERENCES

Berne, E. *Games people play: The psychology of human relationships.* New York: Grove Press, 1964.

Briggs, D. *In place of prison.* London: Temple Smith, 1975.

Jones, M. *The therapeutic community.* New York: Basic Books, 1953.

Jones, M. *Social psychiatry in the community, in hospitals, and in prisons.* Springfield, Ill.: Charles C Thomas, 1962.

Jones, M. *Maturation of the therapeutic community.* New York: Behavioral Science Publications, 1976.

Koestler, A. "Rebellion in a vacuum." In A. Tiselius & S. Nilsson (Eds.), *Nobel Symposium 14, The place of value in a world of facts.* Stockholm: Almqvist and Wiksell, 1968.

Schur, E. M. "Reactions to deviance: A critical assessment." *American Journal of Sociology,* 75: 309, 1969.

Szasz, T. S. *The manufacture of madness.* New York: Harper & Row, 1970.

Whiteley, S., Briggs, D., & Turner, M. *Dealing with deviants.* New York: Schocken Books, 1973.

Yablonsky, I. *Synanon. The tunnel back.* Baltimore: Penguin Books, 1967.

Name Index

Subject Index